American Civil Wars

☙

American Civil Wars

cs

A CONTINENTAL HISTORY,

1850–1873

ALAN TAYLOR

W. W. NORTON & COMPANY
Independent Publishers Since 1923

FRONTISPIECE: *"Reading the Emancipation Proclamation," 1864, engraving by James W. Watts after a drawing by Henry Walker Herrick. Inspired by the liberation of enslaved people, the artist depicted them with dignity and pride, avoiding the racist stereotypes that prevailed during the nineteenth century to dehumanize them. The race of the soldier is unclear, but the artist shows a close physical familiarity that suggests a common bond between the family and the soldier.*

For information about permission to reproduce selections from this book, write to Permissions, W. W. Norton & Company, Inc., 500 Fifth Avenue, New York, NY 10110

For information about special discounts for bulk purchases, please contact W. W. Norton Special Sales at specialsales@wwnorton.com or 800-233-4830

Manufacturing by Lakeside Book Company
Book design by Chris Welch
Production manager: Anna Oler

ISBN 978-1-324-03528-2

W. W. Norton & Company, Inc., 500 Fifth Avenue, New York, N.Y. 10110
www.wwnorton.com

W. W. Norton & Company Ltd., 15 Carlisle Street, London W1D 3BS

1 2 3 4 5 6 7 8 9 0

For Gary Gallagher, Joan Waugh,
Louise Nocas, and Roy Ritchie

and in memory of Roland Grillon

I was on a vast plain, dark and lonely, with the black clouds low over it, and the rain falling in a heavy, sullen downpour, and, as I stood with clasped hands, but without the power to pray, a great white arch grew out of the darkness. It seemed high as heaven, and wide as the horizon, and I wondered at its beauty and majesty. But, as I looked, I saw a black line down the center of it grow to a visible break, and this break grow wider and wider, until one-half of the arch fell to the ground, amid groans and cries, far off, but terrible. At the same moment I saw a *Presence* of great height, dim and shadowy, standing beside the ruined arch, and he cried for the *birds of prey* in a voice that filled all space. Turning north, and south, and east, and west, he cried, "*Come! And I will give you flesh to eat!*"

—AMELIA BARR, *1859. An English woman who lived in Austin, Texas, Barr had this vivid dream after a day spent discussing with friends the crisis in the American Union. At dawn she woke up her husband to describe the vision. He replied, "It is war, then, Milly, and may God help us!"*

CONTENTS

Maps   xiii

Preface   xix

INTRODUCTION UNSETTLED   I

ONE LIVES   16

TWO FUGITIVES   47

THREE DESTINIES   69

FOUR THUNDER   103

FIVE DISUNION   130

SIX MISERIES   161

SEVEN REVOLUTIONS   193

EIGHT WEST   228

NINE INVASIONS   263

TEN ELECTIONS   299

ELEVEN BORDERS   336

TWELVE RECONSTRUCTIONS   375

EPILOGUE SLEEPING GIANTS   410

Acknowledgments   417

Notes   419

Bibliography   489

Illustrations and Credits   515

Index   517

Maps

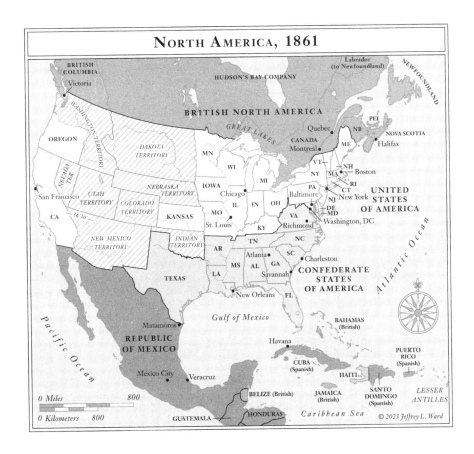

NORTH AMERICA, 1861

BRITISH COLUMBIA
Victoria

HUDSON'S BAY COMPANY

Labrador
(to Newfoundland)

NEWFOUNDLAND

BRITISH NORTH AMERICA

GREAT LAKES

WASHINGTON TERRITORY

OREGON

DAKOTA TERRITORY

MN

Quebec

CANADA
Montreal

PEI

NB

NOVA SCOTIA

Halifax

ME

NEVADA TER.

UTAH TERRITORY

COLORADO TERRITORY

NEBRASKA TERRITORY

WI

IOWA

Chicago

MI

VT

NY

NH

MA

Boston

RI

CT

New York

PA

Baltimore

UNITED
STATES
OF AMERICA

San Francisco

CA

36° 30'

KANSAS

IL

IN

OH

MO

St. Louis

KY

NJ

DE

MD

Washington, DC

VA

Richmond

NEW MEXICO TERRITORY

INDIAN TERRITORY

AR

TN

NC

Atlanta

SC

Charleston

Atlantic Ocean

TEXAS

MS

AL

GA

Savannah

LA

CONFEDERATE
STATES
OF AMERICA

New Orleans

FL

Gulf of Mexico

Pacific Ocean

Matamoros

REPUBLIC
OF MEXICO

Mexico City

Veracruz

BAHAMAS
(British)

Havana

CUBA
(Spanish)

HAITI

PUERTO
RICO
(Spanish)

0 Miles   800

0 Kilometers   800

BELIZE (British)

GUATEMALA

HONDURAS

JAMAICA
(British)

SANTO
DOMINGO
(Spanish)

Caribbean Sea

LESSER
ANTILLES

© 2023 Jeffrey L. Ward

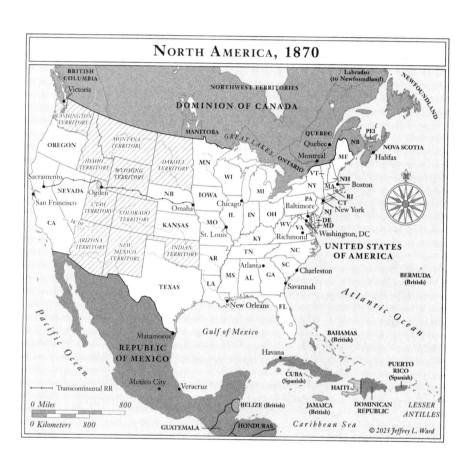

NORTH AMERICA, 1870

BRITISH COLUMBIA
Victoria

NORTHWEST TERRITORIES

DOMINION OF CANADA

Labrador
(to Newfoundland)

NEWFOUNDLAND

WASHINGTON TERRITORY

MANITOBA

GREAT LAKES

ONTARIO

QUEBEC
Quebec

PEI

NB

NOVA SCOTIA
Halifax

OREGON

MONTANA TERRITORY

IDAHO TERRITORY

WYOMING TERRITORY

DAKOTA TERRITORY

MN

WI

MI

Montreal

ME

VT

NY

NH

MA

Boston

Sacramento

NEVADA

Ogden

NB

IOWA

Chicago

IL

IN

OH

PA

RI
CT
New York

San Francisco

UTAH TERRITORY

COLORADO TERRITORY

Omaha

MO

Baltimore

NJ
DE
MD

CA

36 30

KANSAS

St. Louis

KY

WV

VA

Richmond

Washington, DC

ARIZONA TERRITORY

NEW MEXICO TERRITORY

INDIAN TERRITORY

AR

TN

NC

UNITED STATES
OF AMERICA

BERMUDA
(British)

TEXAS

LA

MS

AL

GA

SC

Atlanta

Charleston

Savannah

New Orleans

FL

Atlantic Ocean

Matamoros

Gulf of Mexico

BAHAMAS
(British)

Pacific Ocean

REPUBLIC
OF MEXICO

Havana

PUERTO RICO
(Spanish)

Transcontinental RR

Mexico City

Veracruz

CUBA
(Spanish)

HAITI

LESSER ANTILLES

0 Miles   800

0 Kilometers   800

BELIZE (British)

GUATEMALA

HONDURAS

JAMAICA
(British)

DOMINICAN REPUBLIC

Caribbean Sea

© 2023 Jeffrey L. Ward

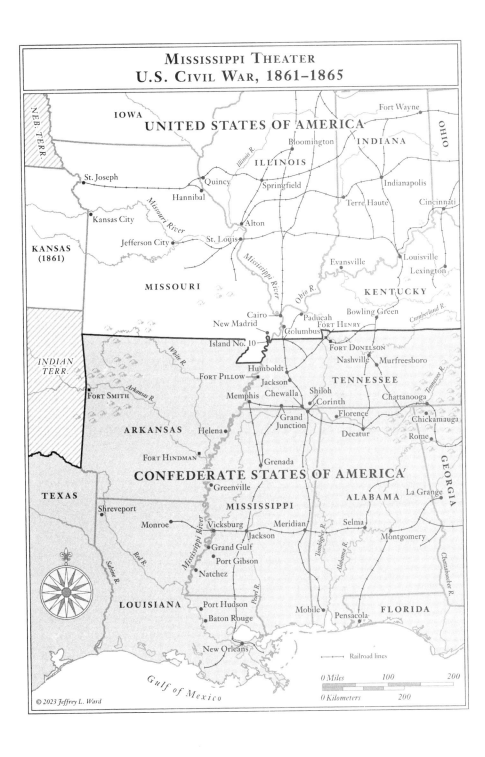

MISSISSIPPI THEATER
U.S. CIVIL WAR, 1861–1865

NEB. TERR.

IOWA

UNITED STATES OF AMERICA

Fort Wayne

OHIO

Bloomington   INDIANA

ILLINOIS

St. Joseph

Quincy   Springfield   Indianapolis

Hannibal   Illinois R.   Terre Haute   Cincinnati

Kansas City

Alton   Louisville

Jefferson City   St. Louis   Evansville   Lexington

KANSAS
(1861)

MISSOURI   KENTUCKY

Mississippi River

Ohio R.

Bowling Green

Cumberland R.

Cairo   Paducah
New Madrid   FORT HENRY
Columbus

INDIAN
TERR.   Island No. 10   FORT DONELSON

Nashville   Murfreesboro

White R.

FORT PILLOW   Humboldt
Jackson   TENNESSEE

Arkansas R.   Chewalla   Shiloh   Tennessee R.

FORT SMITH   Memphis   Corinth   Chattanooga

Florence

ARKANSAS   Helena   Grand   Decatur   Chickamauga
Junction   Rome

FORT HINDMAN   Grenada   GEORGIA

CONFEDERATE STATES OF AMERICA

Greenville   ALABAMA   La Grange

TEXAS   MISSISSIPPI

Shreveport   Selma

Monroe   Vicksburg   Meridian   Montgomery

Mississippi River   Jackson

Red R.   Grand Gulf   Alabama R.
Port Gibson

Sabine R.   Natchez   Pearl R.

LOUISIANA   Port Hudson   Mobile   FLORIDA
Baton Rouge   Pensacola   Chattahoochee R.

New Orleans   Railroad lines

Gulf of Mexico   0 Miles   100   200

© 2023 Jeffrey L. Ward   0 Kilometers   200

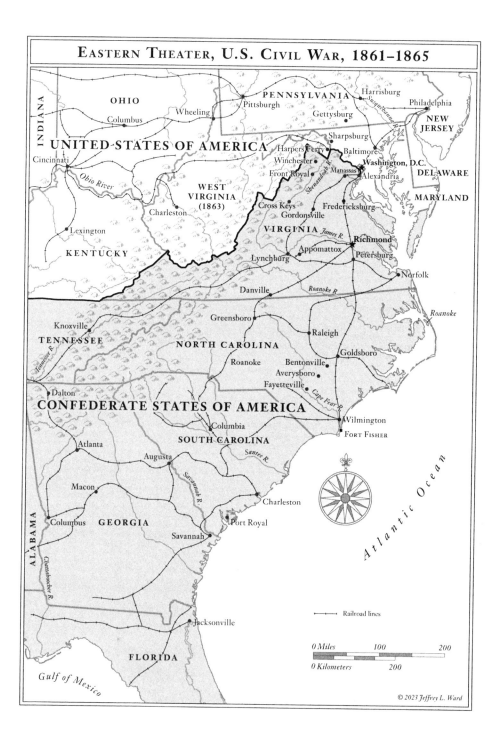

Eastern Theater, U.S. Civil War, 1861–1865

INDIANA

OHIO

UNITED STATES OF AMERICA

Columbus

Wheeling

Cincinnati

Ohio River

Lexington

KENTUCKY

WEST VIRGINIA (1863)

Charleston

PENNSYLVANIA

Pittsburgh

Harrisburg

Susquehanna R.

Philadelphia

Gettysburg

NEW JERSEY

Sharpsburg

Harpers Ferry

Winchester

Front Royal

Baltimore

Washington, D.C.

DELAWARE

Manassas

Alexandria

MARYLAND

Shenandoah R.

Cross Keys

Gordonsville

Fredericksburg

VIRGINIA

James R.

Richmond

Lynchburg

Appomattox

Petersburg

Danville

Roanoke R.

Norfolk

Roanoke

Knoxville

TENNESSEE

Tennessee R.

Dalton

Greensboro

NORTH CAROLINA

Roanoke

Raleigh

Goldsboro

Bentonville

Averysboro

Fayetteville

Cape Fear R.

Wilmington

CONFEDERATE STATES OF AMERICA

Atlanta

Columbia

SOUTH CAROLINA

Fort Fisher

Augusta

Santee R.

Macon

Savannah R.

Charleston

ALABAMA

Columbus

GEORGIA

Port Royal

Savannah

Atlantic Ocean

Chattahoochee R.

Jacksonville

FLORIDA

Gulf of Mexico

Railroad lines

0 Miles   100   200

0 Kilometers   200

© 2023 Jeffrey L. Ward

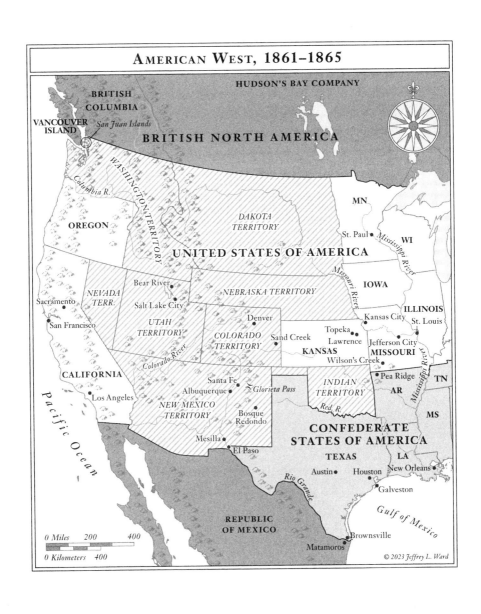

AMERICAN WEST, 1861–1865

HUDSON'S BAY COMPANY

BRITISH COLUMBIA

VANCOUVER ISLAND

San Juan Islands

BRITISH NORTH AMERICA

Columbia R.

WASHINGTON TERRITORY

OREGON

DAKOTA TERRITORY

MN

St. Paul

Mississippi River

WI

UNITED STATES OF AMERICA

Bear River

Missouri River

IOWA

NEVADA TERR.

Sacramento

Salt Lake City

NEBRASKA TERRITORY

Denver

ILLINOIS

Kansas City

St. Louis

San Francisco

UTAH TERRITORY

COLORADO TERRITORY

Sand Creek

Topeka

Lawrence

Jefferson City

MISSOURI

Colorado River

KANSAS

Wilson's Creek

CALIFORNIA

Los Angeles

Santa Fe

Albuquerque

Glorieta Pass

INDIAN TERRITORY

Pea Ridge

TN

Mississippi River

AR

NEW MEXICO TERRITORY

Bosque Redondo

Red R.

MS

Mesilla

El Paso

CONFEDERATE STATES OF AMERICA

TEXAS

LA

Austin

Houston

New Orleans

Pacific Ocean

Rio Grande

Galveston

Gulf of Mexico

REPUBLIC OF MEXICO

0 Miles   200   400

0 Kilometers   400

Brownsville

Matamoros

© 2023 Jeffrey L. Ward

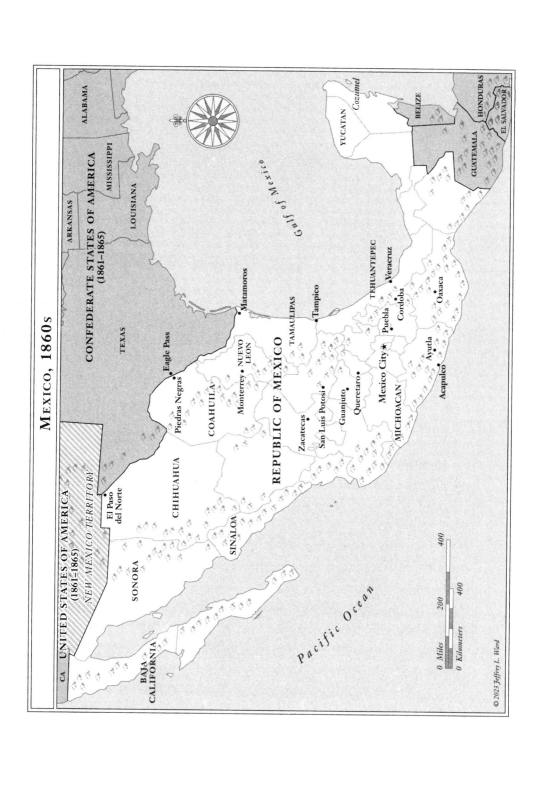

Mexico, 1860s

PREFACE

American Civil Wars presents a history of the United States from 1850 to 1873 but does so in a continental context that includes Mexico, British North America (primarily Canada), and Native peoples of the West. *American Civil Wars* continues a series launched with *American Colonies* (2001) and extended by *American Revolutions* (2016) and *American Republics* (2021). In all four books, the plural titles convey a core attempt to see our history as continental rather than simply the isolated story of one nation. The books do present the United States as becoming the most powerful nation on the continent—yet one riven by internal divisions that complicated relations with adjoining empires and nations, both settler and Native.

Meant to introduce a vast subject, *American Civil Wars* offers basic coverage of political and military events in the United States (and Confederacy). It does so, however, more concisely than usual, freeing up more attention for the rest of the continent.

From 1861 to 1865, most Americans fought to save their federal Union by suppressing a southern rebellion meant to create a new nation, the Confederate States of America. But that was not the only civil war in North America. In 1862, the American struggle invited a French invasion of Mexico that triggered a renewed and enlarged civil war between that nation's Conservatives and Liberals. Both American Unionists and Mexican Liberals felt engaged in a common contest to vindicate republics. They saw shared enemies in southern slaveholders, Mexican elitists, and European monarchs striving to suppress free government defined by majority rule. Both Unionists and Liberals invested their causes with epic, indeed global stakes for the liberation—or suppression—of human rights around the world.

Still tied to the British Empire, Canada and the Maritime provinces uneasily watched the Mexican and American civil wars, seeing both as linked to their own existential crisis. Could Canadians find a way to prevent their own violent division between Francophones and Anglophones? Could they do so by creating their own dominion to avert the threat of an American invasion meant to force them all into the federal Union? In the end, the only American invasion of Canada came from Irish radicals demobilized from the Union army. At the same time, Native peoples in the West faced a more overwhelming invasion by the United States. By telling all of those stories, *American Civil Wars* emphasizes the interaction and interdependency of North America's peoples.

American Civil Wars

ः

INTRODUCTION ⊗ UNSETTLED

Nothing on earth is settled under this Constitution, but the
principle that everything is unsettled. —HENRY CLAY[1]

P rior to the Civil War, Americans did not have a nation. Instead,
they lived in a union of states, each a republic that retained
almost all domestic sovereignty. Americans revered their Union,
but that was not the same thing as sharing a sense of national identity.
Indeed, union enabled citizens to avoid fully bonding as Americans by

protecting every state from the others. Americans considered a union essential to preserve the liberty of free men. Republics were rare and embattled in a world dominated by empires run by monarchs and aristocrats. In 1848 Europe's lords and kings crushed widespread republican revolutions that had begun with great promise. After those defeats, republican radicals fled to the United States, enhancing Americans' conviction that they alone could sustain free government.[2]

But to keep that rare and cherished freedom, Americans needed to preserve their Union, designed to keep peace between their states. They sought to avoid the wars that bloodied a divided Europe—and that promoted rule by monarchs. In 1839, Senator Henry Clay of Kentucky warned Americans that a rupture in the Union would produce a civil war's "desolated fields, conflagrated cities, murdered inhabitants, and the overthrow of the fairest fabric of human government that ever rose to animate the hopes of civilized man." Such destruction would invite dictators to seize power in the states. In 1850, an Illinois senator told a colleague: "Sir, where *compromise* ends, *force* begins, and when *force* begins, *war* begins, and the tocsin of civil war is the death knell of Republicanism."[3]

Union preoccupied Americans because it was so precious and uncertain. In 1851, Senator Daniel Webster (Massachusetts) noted: "The Union of these States is the all-absorbing topic of the day; on it all men write, speak, think, and dilate, from the rising of the sun to the going down thereof." But they could not agree on what that Union should be. Many northerners favored building a unifying nationalism that could sustain a stronger and perpetual Union ruled by the majority. But many Americans, especially in the South, feared national consolidation as a tyrannical vehicle for oppressing minority regions. Advocating "states' rights," they preferred a loose and consensual confederation of equal, sovereign states, each retaining a right to secede. Noting deep and intense conflict over what the Union should be, John Quincy Adams lamented, "It is the odious nature of the question, that it can be settled

PREVIOUS PAGE: *"Underground Railroad March, Dedicated to the North Star," c. 1860, lithograph by unknown.*

only at the cannon's mouth." Here was the tragic paradox: Americans needed a Union to keep their peace, but by clashing over the meaning of Union, they invited a bloody division.[4]

Between 1800 and 1850, Americans pushed territorial expansion to increase their distance from a potential enemy that could exploit weaknesses within the Union. Aggressive expansion especially appealed to slaveholders, who sought to stem the outflow of fugitives. By joining the Union, southerners gained legal rights to retrieve runaway slaves from northern states, but slaves could find safe havens by fleeing across borders to Canada, Mexico, or Native nations. A Texas planter complained that "all frontier[s] bordering on the United States" tended "to admit not only slaves but every class of depridators and refugees." Slaveholders meant not simply to add plantations but also to subtract places where enslaved people could find haven. Otherwise, masters would lose more slaves to flight and might lose their own lives to revolts meant to facilitate mass escapes across any nearby border.[5]

At the same time, Americans also worried that an expanding Union would grow too big, breeding an imbalance of power that favored one region at the expense of another. Then a minority region might secede, provoking a civil war that would drench the continent in American blood, dooming free government. After many decades of managing sectional tensions in Congress, Senator Clay sighed, "Nothing on earth is settled under this Constitution, but the principle that everything is unsettled."[6]

Systems

Americans boasted of their rapid territorial and population growth. Endowed with fertile land, abundant timber, navigable rivers, and a temperate climate, the United States was (compared to Europe) thinly populated but growing fast. Beginning along the Atlantic seaboard in 1776, the United States had burst westward across the Mississippi by 1810. Forty years later, Americans had colonized the Pacific coast, although much of the intervening Rocky Mountains, Great Basin, and Great Plains remained in Indian possession. Abundant land and plenty of food attracted millions of immigrants: 600,000 during the 1830s, 1,700,000 during the 1840s, and 2,300,000 during the 1850s. The relative abundance also encouraged early marriages and large families, so the population grew by 35 percent during the 1840s and 1850s: four times greater than Europe's rate. The population reached 30 million by 1855, surpassing Great Britain—which thrilled Americans and alarmed Britons. Economic growth increased per capita wealth by 1.7 percent annually between 1820 and 1860.[7]

The early nineteenth century brought a transportation revolution through new technologies. Steamboats, canals, turnpikes, and railroads dramatically lowered the costs of shipment and increased the pace of movement. During the 1850s, the railroad became king, as Americans laid 21,000 miles of rail, increasing their total to 30,000, more than in the rest of the world. A trip between New York and Chicago shrank from three weeks to two days. Towns along the rails boomed. As the terminus for fifteen rail lines, Chicago grew by 375 percent during the 1850s. Technology also transformed communication, as the telegraph conveyed news almost instantaneously across the country.[8]

Improved transportation and communication promoted a more integrated national market as goods moved more quickly and cheaply over long distances. That integration fed regional specialization as people developed their comparative advantages in local resources. So, the fertile Midwest shipped bumper crops of grain, pork, and beef eastward to feed the growing populations of coastal cities. Unable to compete with those midwestern farms, the farmers of New England began to specialize in garden crops and dairy production to serve the nearby cities. An abundant supply of cheap food enabled town and city folk to make their living in workshops and factories. Most Americans now procured their tools, clothing, and consumer goods via retailers from manufacturers— rather than relying on themselves and local artisans. Americans were creating a society of mass production and mass consumption.[9]

Most Americans still lived in the countryside on farms and plantations, but the urban, manufacturing sector grew faster after 1820. By 1860, when a fifth of Americans lived in cities and worked in factories, the United States ranked second in the world in industrial output and was closing fast on the leader, Great Britain. Immigrants prevailed in the working class while native-born whites dominated the emerging middle class of clerks and managers.[10]

For their growth and prosperity, Americans credited their republican Union framed during the American Revolution in reaction against British monarchy and aristocracy. Compared to Europeans, free Americans enjoyed political rights and a higher standard of living. For all their blessings, they expected praise from visitors. The French traveler Alexis de Tocqueville rather liked Americans but found them boastful and needy. Calling themselves "the only religious, enlightened, and free people," they were "not very remote from believing themselves to be a distinct species of mankind." While praising their republic, Americans denigrated European countries, especially Britain. An irritated Briton retorted by asking in what European country "is every sixth man a slave whom his fellow-creatures may buy and sell and torture?"[11]

Committed to slavery, southerners felt locked in a hemispheric struggle against the British Empire as "the center and source of anti-slavery fanaticism." During the 1830s, the British had freed the 800,000 slaves in their West Indian colonies, and that empire encouraged other nations to abolish the slave trade and emancipate enslaved people. A South Carolina congressman declared, "Our systems are at issue and the contest will be for mastery of the world. One or the other must go down or yield."[12]

To protect and promote slavery in the Americas, southerners sought control of the Union's foreign and military policy. Prior to the Civil War, two-thirds of the presidents and secretaries of state and four-fifths of the secretaries of war and the navy came from the South. Although American law barred importing slaves from overseas, federal leaders refused to cooperate with the British naval efforts to suppress that trade. While waging a diplomatic struggle against British antislavery, southerners hoped to avoid a shooting war. They wanted no disruption in trade with Britain, the primary market for their cotton.[13]

Considering republics natural and inevitable in North America, Americans dismissed the British colonies to their north in Canada as temporary anomalies destined eventually to join the Union. Americans saw Canadians as cursed by a colonial system that tethered them to Britain, ruled by a monarch and aristocrats. But most Canadians disdained the republican Union as corrupt, chaotic, and demagogic. Celebrating British rule for offering the proper balance of order and liberty, they derided Americans as bombastic hypocrites who boasted of freedom while keeping millions of Blacks in slavery. A New Brunswick newspaper declared, "Ere we annex ourselves to a slave-holding Republic, we'll go down with the British flag—the *true* emblem of *true* liberty—flying at the mast-head."[14]

Canada was a culturally divided society, with a majority of French-speaking Catholics living in Canada East (now Quebec) along the lower St. Lawrence, including the leading towns of Montreal and Quebec. English-speaking settlers prevailed upstream in Canada West (now Ontario) along the Great Lakes. In 1841, British leaders imposed a union on the two Canadian colonies in a bid to control the French Canadians by yoking them to the Anglophones, whose population grew faster owing to immigration from Britain. The Canadian union did not include the Atlantic provinces of New Brunswick, Nova Scotia, Prince Edward Island, and Newfoundland, which remained distinct British colonies.[15]

The Canadian union included 1.1 million people and stretched for 1,800 miles from the mouth of the St. Lawrence River, on the east, to the head of Lake Superior, on the west. More rural than the United States, Canada had only a few small cities. The largest, Montreal, had just 40,000 inhabitants.[16]

A land of immense forests and many dispersed farms, Canada lacked the American urban extremes of wealth and poverty. Nor did Canada sustain slavery. The hinterland offered modest opportunity for immigrants who labored hard to clear the forest to make farms. Because land sold more cheaply than in the United States, most immigrants could afford farms after a few years of work for wages. Limited by a shorter growing season, Canadian farmers could raise enough to feed their families but too little to get rich. But the immigrants could own land, a source of pride as well as sustenance—and a prospect impossible for most people in crowded and class-ridden Great Britain.[17]

Because Canadian roads were few and wretched, goods and people moved along the waterways: the St. Lawrence and its major tributaries, the Richelieu River to the south and the Ottawa River to the west, as well as the immense web of Great Lakes reaching westward into the heart of the continent. If the waterways pulled Canada across half a continent, the nearby American border to the south and the proximate subarctic to the north pinched the temperate, arable land for settlement. The settled part of Canada was long but thin, making it vulnerable to invasion from their nearby, numerous, and aggressive American neighbors. In 1850, the 1.8 million people of Canada were roughly a twelfth of the 23 million in the United States.[18]

During the late 1840s, the British allowed greater autonomy to Canada in the form of "responsible government." Britain retained control over foreign and military affairs and appointed the judges and executive officers (led by a governor general), but they now had to answer to an elected Canadian parliament. By offering a more liberal administration, the home government sought to counteract American influence. In 1848, the colonial secretary, Earl Grey, explained to Canada's governor general:

> The more I see and hear of the state of affairs in the United States, the more convinced I am of the extreme importance of consolidating in British America a system of government really popular and at the same time not so ultra-democratic in principle as that of the great republic. As the effect of the institutions of the United States becomes more and more developed, the more dangerous I think them to the peace of the world.

The imperial government provided Canadians with "a constitution in which they might maintain their own independence instead of being absorbed in the [American] Union." In 1854, Lord Palmerston boasted: "We have our N[orth] American Provinces now united & loyal, and dissatisfied with the United States."[19]

During periodic border disputes, American congressmen and journalists blasted British rule over Canada and called for annexation. But both Union and Empire had too much to lose from war, for each was the other's leading trading partner. American corporations and states relied on investment capital from Britain to develop canals and railroads. The slaveholders who dominated American foreign policy also balked at adding Canada to the northern states lest that weaken southern power within the Union. By casting British rule as unnatural, Americans settled for inaction, for they counted on nature to deliver Canada up to the United States in due time.[20]

In 1846 the Democratic president James K. Polk, from Tennessee, provoked a war with Mexico to consolidate American control over Texas and conquer New Mexico and California. It was a one-sided war. Richer, larger, and industrializing, the Union could raise more troops and supply them better. The 23 million Americans far outnumbered the 7.5 million Mexicans. Most of Mexico's land was too arid or mountainous for commercial agriculture, and Mexicans lacked navigable rivers to move their crops to market or their men to the front. Most Mexicans lived in small villages dispersed across 3 million square miles and often separated by broad deserts or tall mountain ranges. By contrast, the United States possessed many booming cities, vast tracts of fertile land, and many navigable rivers that reached superior ports. Americans enjoyed a per capita income three times that of Mexicans. Economic superiority endowed American troops with greater firepower, particularly in artillery. Naval supremacy enabled Americans to move troops and supplies over long distances to strike at Mexico's ports. That navy also could blockade those ports to intercept supplies and prevent the collection of the customs duties that the Mexican government relied on for revenue.[21]

Deep social divisions worked against Mexican national cohesion. A small elite of wealthy and white families dominated the country, but two-thirds of Mexicans were poor and illiterate Indians and most of the rest were mixed-race people called *mestizos*. Trapped by debt peonage, the poor usually worked as peasants, known as *campesinos*, on landed estates called *haciendas*. Mexico had relatively few middle-class farmers—the class that predominated in the United States. A Mexican bishop declared that Mexico was divided between "those who have nothing and those who have everything. . . . There are no gradations or mean."[22]

Unstable government also hampered Mexico as ambitious generals overthrew the federal government in frequent coups. The flamboyant general Antonio López de Santa Anna became president eleven times. Ideological divisions pitted liberal federalists against conservative centralizers. Deeply in debt to foreign creditors, primarily British, and unable to collect most taxes, the Mexican government had to devote 87 percent of its revenue to paying interest, leaving precious little to fight the United States. Mexico struggled to feed, clothe, arm, and pay its troops, so many deserted to go home. An American journalist, Jane Swisshelm, denounced the conflict as a "giant whipping a cripple." In 1846, American troops conquered the northern tier of Mexico including California. A year later, they seized the capital, Mexico City. In the peace treaty of February 1848, the Mexican government conceded 525,000 square miles of territory, including Texas, New Mexico, Arizona, and California.[23]

Divisions

Highly participatory, American politics generated powerful identities and loyalties. Both parties, Whigs and Democrats, organized festive parades that attracted hundreds, culminating with free food and drink at barbecues. Elections were masculine, competitive, and drunken. With partisans plying supporters with alcohol, reason faltered and emotions surged, leading to clashes with fists, sticks, knives, and even guns to control polling places. Ambitious young men rose by serving on campaign committees that organized parades, turned out the vote, and battled with the rival party. The friends of a winning candidate reaped government patronage jobs and contracts, both deeply coveted in the hypercompetitive American society.[24]

Relatively elitist, the Whigs appealed to propertied men, usually Protestants, by promoting an activist government that invested in economic development and pushed moral reforms, especially temperance. Democrats, however, distrusted government activism for favoring the special interests of wealthy corporations, especially banks. Democrats wanted the federal government only to deliver the mail, provide cheap land, help recover runaway slaves, and fight Indians, Britons, and Mexicans.[25]

As the more populist (and racist) of the parties, the Democrats won more elections in an electorate restricted to men, and usually just white men. Between 1829 and 1860, Democrats captured two-thirds of the seats in the House of Representatives and three-fifths in the Senate. Democrats controlled the House for twenty-four years and the Senate for twenty-eight. They also won six of the eight presidential contests.[26]

In 1850, most Americans were Protestants who regarded their faith as intertwined with republicanism, for both preached individual choice, self-improvement, and voluntary association. American Protestants divided into many competing denominations, primarily Baptists, Methodists, and Presbyterians. That competition increased popular participation in religious life, as did the populist and evangelical style of American preachers.[27]

Most immigrants were Catholics, who confronted cultural dominance by American Protestants. Only 30,000 in 1790, the number of American Catholics surged to 1.6 million by 1855. The newcomers clashed with American-born workers, who resented immigrants as unwanted competition. Nativists also charged that Catholics would subvert republican government out of an alleged slavish loyalty to their monarch, the Pope. Protestant mobs sometimes rampaged through immigrant neighborhoods to burn Catholic chapels and convents.[28]

During the 1840s, Whigs and Democrats divided over the culture war raised by immigration. In the North (where most immigrants settled), middle-class Protestants favored the Whigs, who promoted moral reforms that included restricting access to alcohol (a movement known as temperance) and expanding public schools to teach Protestant values. Most immigrants voted for Democrats, who championed an egalitarian individualism that opposed temperance and Protestant lessons in public schools. By promoting a confrontational foreign policy toward Britain, Democrats especially appealed to Irish immigrants who hated British rule over their homeland.[29]

Competing with free Blacks for housing and jobs, poor immigrants usually adopted the white supremacy championed by most Democrats. Defending southern slavery as the price of preserving the Union, Democrats regarded racial inequality as a national bond of unity. Irish immigrants sought to refute nativist taunts that likened them to Blacks, including cartoons depicting "Paddy" as a swarthy ape. Asserting their whiteness, Irish Americans often rampaged through Black neighborhoods, burning houses and churches and lynching those who resisted. Immigrants learned that rising in American class began by embracing white supremacy.[30]

During the early 1850s, the Whig party began to collapse, divided by internal tensions over slavery. Exploiting the new political vacuum, nativists created the "American Party," but critics called them the "Know-Nothings." Nativists sought to deny political office to Catholics and disenfranchise immigrants by prolonging the period of naturalization to twenty-one years. During the mid-1850s, the new American Party suddenly captured several state legislatures and 120 seats in Congress. In 1856, their presidential candidate won 22 percent of the popular vote. But the American Party flamed out as quickly as it had arisen, as politics became preoccupied with an even greater controversy: whether slavery should expand westward into federal territories.[31]

Political leaders insisted that the Federal Constitution left issues of slavery within states entirely to each state to decide. After the American Revolution, emancipating slaves was possible in the North, where Blacks and masters were relatively few. But racism and segregation intensified as Blacks became free in the North—where they comprised only about 2 percent of the region's population. Denied access to public education and good jobs, most northern African Americans worked as stevedores, sailors, barbers, bootblacks, domestic servants, and laundresses. After escaping from slavery, Frederick Douglass, struggled to find work in a northern city: "I was indeed free—free from slavery, but free from food and shelter as well." Discrimination forced Blacks to cluster together in undesirable neighborhoods and to avoid crowds of white people as sources of violence. Free blacks also remained vulnerable to kidnappers who hauled them south for sale as slaves.[32]

Some northerners were abolitionists who wanted southerners immediately to emancipate their slaves without any compensation. Abolitionists highlighted the suffering of Blacks from whipping, hunger, sexual predation, and the rupture of their families by forced sales and migration. Favoring equal rights for all, abolitionists also challenged the North's racist laws that enforced segregation and discrimination. But abolitionists remained a small minority in the North, where most people despised them as dangerous radicals who threatened social order as well as the Union. Mobs led by prominent men attacked abolitionists and destroyed their meeting halls.[33]

By the 1840s, most southerners claimed that slavery was good for Blacks, making them contented, docile, and grateful to their masters: "the happiest laboring class in the world." Considering African Americans unfit for liberty, racists exaggerated the supposed misery, insanity, indolence, and criminality of free Blacks in the North.[34]

Despite casting slaves as content, masters warned that they would become murderous if agitated by outsiders. Southerners regarded abolitionists as reckless fanatics spreading insidious lies to disturb the happy relationship of masters and slaves. Southerners insisted that a Black revolt would massacre white people if, as Jefferson Davis asserted, slaves' "weak minds should be instigated to arson, murder, and rapine." So southern leaders repressed criticism of slavery, shutting down antislavery societies and abolitionist publications. And they expected northern help in that repression.[35]

Ninety percent of American Blacks lived in the South as slaves. From 698,000 in 1790, the enslaved population soared to 4 million by 1860, when slaves comprised a third of the South's population. Because slave labor was so profitable, the price of a male field hand doubled from $600 in 1800 to $1,200 in 1850. By refusing to legalize slave marriages or protect families from disruptive sales, southerners kept their human property liquid for sale, movement, and inheritance. In 1860, the monetary value of enslaved people exceeded that of all the nation's banks, factories, and railroads combined. Masters would never part with so much valuable human property without a fight. James H. Hammond of South Carolina said southerners could not be "persuaded by arguments, human or divine, to surrender, voluntarily two billion dollars."[36]

Cotton cultivation drove the soaring value of slaves. Planters benefited from a booming export market as textile factories multiplied in Britain, France, and the American northeast. Cotton exports surged from 178,000 bales in 1810 to 4 million by 1860 (a bale weighed about 400 pounds). By 1840 cotton accounted for over half of the value of all American exports, and the United States produced more cotton than the rest of the world. No backwater, the South was the powerful half of a nation committed to Black slavery as well as white freedom.[37]

Requiring a growing season of at least 200 frostless days, cotton thrived in the Lower South but not in the Upper South (Kentucky, Maryland, Missouri, and Virginia). As cotton planters expanded their fields and crops, they bought more slaves from the Upper South, where there was a "surplus." Between 1790 and 1860, in one of the largest forced migrations in world history, slave traders and moving masters herded over a million slaves to the Lower South. That migration disrupted slave families and communities, as those removed had to leave behind wives, husbands, parents, and children.[38]

Cotton cultivation demanded long hours of hard work through a prolonged growing season. Planting in the spring led to weeding under the hot summer sun and culminated in the fall harvest. Picking cotton bloodied hands from the sharp edges of husks around the fibers. If a slave met a work quota today, the master would expect more tomorrow—with failure punished by the whip. A Louisiana planter advised that whipping should "be repeated at proper intervals, until the most entire submission is obtained."[39]

To maximize profits by limiting costs, masters provided the mini-mal diet, clothing, and shelter needed to keep slaves alive and work-ing. A former slave, Frederick Douglass, remembered "the close-fisted stinginess that fed the poor slave on coarse cornmeal and tainted meat, [and] that clothed him in trashy tow-linen and hurried him on to toil through the field in all weathers, with wind and rain beating through his tattered garments."[40]

Slavery defined southern society. Alabama planters noted, "Our con-dition is quite different from that of the non-slaveholding section of the United States. . . . Their laborers are merely hirelings, while with us our laborers are our property." Southerners insisted that slavery pro-moted economic growth by enabling masters to compel concerted labor to improve farms and plantations. An Alabama congressmen praised "the immense superiority of a system of associated slave labor over free individual labor."[41]

Cotton endowed southerners with political and international clout. Britain and France and the northeastern United States needed southern cotton. Without it, factories would close, leaving unemployed workers to starve. A critic of slavery noted the "unhallowed alliance between the lords of the lash and the lords of the loom." In 1858, Hammond boasted, "The slaveholding South is now the controlling power of the world. . . . Cotton is king."[42]

Slavery made the United States distinctive within continental North America. Although Mexico sustained a coercive labor system of indebted peons, they could not be bought and sold as commodities, for Mexicans banned slavery as incompatible with republican government. Canadians rejected slavery as at odds with the rights of Britons to "rational liberty." Mexicans and Canadians claimed moral superiority over Americans who boasted of their freedom while keeping 4 million Blacks enslaved. In 1857, a Mexican leader mocked the U.S. Constitution: "In that liberal Constitution which is so cried up, do we not see the most atrocious principle embedded, the most cruel, the most degrading for mankind—that of slavery?" He marveled that "a people that proclaims itself liberal and democratic to the point of hyperbole rivets into its Constitution an article that dishonors civilization and mankind." Mexico and Canada attracted fugitives from American slavery. Those runaways generated tensions across the thin borders of the continent, for American slave-holders insisted that their security depended on closing every escape from their labor system.[43]

ONE ∝ LIVES

I know that the rich and powerful neither feel nor, far less,
try to cure the calamities of the poor. . . . This is, and has
always been, the world. Those who will not recognize it merely
deceive themselves. —BENITO JUÁREZ, 1865[1]

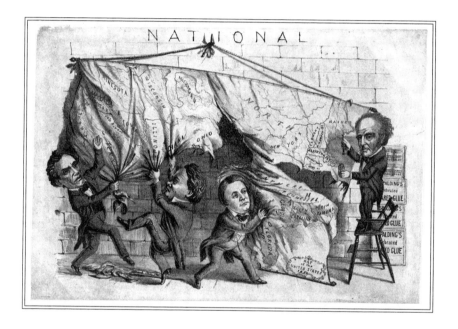

Born in 1807 in upstate New York, Jane Maria Eliza McManus
lived in a society committed to distinct gender roles and male
superiority. American laws denied political rights to women,
deeming them dependents on fathers or husbands, who alone could
vote and hold office. Bold and assertive men allegedly contrasted with
women, cast as pious, benevolent, retiring, and chaste. A patient and
nurturing wife was supposed to sustain the household, raise children,
and support and regenerate her husband involved in public competition
and strife.[2]

While marginalized in politics, women were essential to economic life. A farm or shop needed the skilled labor of wives and unpaid work of children. Women tended gardens, milked cows, and made butter, cheese, candles, cloth, and soap—all while cooking meals, cleaning the house, and tending children. In towns and cities, adolescent daughters went to work in the new textile and shoe factories, sending a share of their earnings home to their parents. Urban working families needed wives to find some work, often making garments. Only urbanized middle-class and elite families (with the help of servants) could afford the fantasy of "separate spheres" in which women remained cosseted in a domestic life, nurturing their husbands coming home at night from the world of work and politics.[3]

Jane's father was a prosperous lawyer who sent his daughter to the state's leading academy for girls. Run by the pioneering educator and writer Emma Willard, the Troy Female Seminary prepared students to marry prestigious men by offering courses on manners, morals, baking, algebra, geometry, philosophy, history, French, Italian, Spanish, German, and painting. Willard believed that well-educated mothers and wives could contribute to the American republic by nurturing the characters of their sons.[4]

In 1825, at age eighteen, Jane married Allen B. Storm, who was studying law with her father. They had a son a year later. The unhappy marriage ruptured in 1832, when she resumed her maiden name, McManus. She later described Storm as "a bad, improvident husband," who drank more than he worked before absconding. In the third person, Jane described her plight: "She works all the harder to make up [for] his deficiencies . . . works day and night" and "smiles when her heart is breaking."[5]

Moving to New York City, McManus worked as a broker for a land-speculating company that acquired vast tracts in Tejas (Texas), then a part of Mexico. To recruit settlers, McManus sought help from an old

OPPOSITE: *"Dividing the National Map," 1860, cartoon by unknown, showing the division of the Union by the four presidential candidates—from left to right: Lincoln, Douglas, Breckenridge, and Bell.*

friend of her family, Aaron Burr, a former vice-president. After killing
Alexander Hamilton in a duel in 1805 and flirting with treason in the
West in 1807, Burr was controversial but clever and charming. Gossips
cast McManus as his latest mistress, which seemed plausible given his
reputation and despite his age: seventy-six in 1832. Burr's new wife, the
wealthy widow Eliza Jumel, sought divorce to stop him from plundering
her fortune for his land speculations. To stick the knife deeper, Jumel
employed Alexander Hamilton, Jr., as her attorney. Jumel's divorce suit
named McManus as the other woman, citing salacious testimony from
her maid. Respectable families froze McManus out of society balls and
dinners. That ostracism pushed her further into her preferred orbit in
the masculine realm of business and politics. In a letter of recommen-
dation, Burr praised McManus as courageous, insightful, and persistent:
"a woman of business" superior to "any man."[6]

Starting in 1839, McManus supported herself by writing for newspapers and magazines, delighting readers with a concise and accessible
style. Because women were supposed to avoid publicizing their views,
she hid behind pen names, but politicians soon identified her as adept
at shaping public opinion. A New York governor praised McManus as
"a prodigiously smart and keen writer."[7]

During the 1840s, McManus wrote as a Democrat for the influential
United States Magazine and Democratic Review, edited by John L. O'Sullivan. The *Democratic Review* insisted that expansion alone could hold
together a United States increasingly divided over slavery. The editors
urged expansion both into Canada where slavery was unsustainable and
into southern climes that favored plantations. McManus and O'Sullivan
promoted the popular fantasy that slavery would fade in temperate zones
and become concentrated in tropical climes.[8]

During the summer of 1845, the *Democratic Review* coined and pop-
ularized the celebrated concept of an American "manifest destiny"
to expand into continental domination. O'Sullivan got credit for the
phrase, but McManus probably wrote the relevant (unsigned) essay that
justified annexing Texas and Oregon as "the fulfillment of our manifest
destiny to overspread the continent" and thereby accommodate "our
yearly multiplying millions." Although "manifest destiny" suggested

confidence in American might, the author felt embattled by British power "thwarting our policy and hampering our power, limiting our greatness and checking the fulfillment of our manifest destiny." Expansion alone, she argued, could protect a vulnerable republic from British meddling and containment.[9]

Jane McManus visited Mexico as a war correspondent. Although an expansionist, McManus disliked Polk's war, for she naïvely thought that Americans could acquire all North America through diplomacy and purchase: "I would not see our eagle [act] merely as a bird of prey!" She mourned as American generals bombarded civilians in Mexican towns and some troops raped women and looted and burned their churches. McManus warned: "There is danger of a strong military ascendancy in the United States and it will expand to control the destiny of the republic." But then she regretted the peace treaty for taking too little land from Mexico, which she saw as a potential land of settler opportunity for working-class Americans.[10]

In the fall of 1849, McManus married William Leslie Cazneau. Both were forty-two years old and committed expansionists. In 1850 they settled at Eagle Pass, on the Texan side of the Rio Grande, the new boundary with Mexico. The Cazneaus developed a ranch and speculated in lands, hoping to profit by attracting American settlers.[11]

In 1852, Jane Cazneau published *Eagle Pass* to defend slavery "for what it is—a political necessity and a constitutional existence" rather than "an abstract question of right and wrong." She thought that slavery had converted "stupid and ferocious blacks" into civilized Christians "even in the worst of our slave States." Cazneau feared that emancipation would lead to "the most perfect equality for the blacks in marriage relations, social influence and political rights." Like most Democrats, Cazneau fixated on racial mixing as inevitable and disastrous if Blacks and whites coexisted in freedom. She thought it "highly absurd to insist on breaking up the Union for the sake of helping such pretty [white] girls to black husbands." By letting every state decide the future of slavery, Cazneau would "leave emancipation to the progress of light and God's Providence." In the meantime, she demanded, "Who can be so weak as to fear the addition of one, two, or three Slave states?"[12]

By setting aside sectional squabbles, Americans could grab even more of Mexico, to make ten more states. That would "leave the matchless Union victor of undisputed sway—mistress of this continent—guardian of the Atlantic—arbitress of the Pacific—protectress of the Gulf and its cluster of island gems!" Conquered tropical lands could solve the racial conflict by whitening America, as slaveholders would shift enslaved people southward and "leave room behind them for free labor to step in and reign. Slavery may roll away more and more to the South and prepare the way for white industry." Cazneau dismissed Yankees' fears that expansion would strengthen slavery: "Wherever our bird of power flies, wherever our stars shine, there is increase of light and liberty." Her lyrical hopes soared far beyond the grimmer realities of an uneasy Union.[13]

Swisshelm

Born in 1815, Jane Grey Cannon grew up in a strict Presbyterian family in Pittsburgh, Pennsylvania. When she was twelve, her father died of tuberculosis and left more debts than assets to his widow. Jane went to work painting velvet, making lace, and teaching school. While breaking with her church's rigid elders, she devoted her life to eradicating sin in American society.[14]

In 1836, Cannon married a handsome but pigheaded farmer, James Swisshelm. They clashed when James refused to live near her family and demanded that Jane convert to his Methodist faith and stop reading so many books. Separations alternated with tense cohabitation. They had one child, a daughter named Mary Henrietta but called Zo. Jane later championed divorce as better than living "in a mockery of marriage with an unloved, hated object," which she considered "legal prostitution." She urged wives to kill husbands who attacked them in a "drunken fury" but called it "a crime for a woman to become the mother of a drunkard's child"—as she had done.[15]

Spending 1838 in Louisville, Kentucky, Swisshelm saw the horrors of slavery, including a master who sold his mixed-race children and whipped the enslaved mother when she protested. Swisshelm started a school for Black children but gave it up when neighbors threatened to burn her out. A young neighbor later recalled Swisshelm as "an enthusiast in everything, and she seemed to set her whole soul in freeing slaves." But in Kentucky "An Abolitionist was regarded much as we would regard a man who made it his business to spread a deadly disease." One day, while walking home, Swisshelm patted a neighbor's son, "a curly-headed darling," on the head. Looking up, the boy screamed and ran away, calling Swisshelm a "nigger lover." Decades later, the witness could still recall, "The great eyes of the sad-faced woman filled with tears."[16]

Leaving her husband, Swisshelm moved back to Pittsburgh and, in 1847, with a bequest from her mother, began publishing a newspaper, *The Pittsburgh Saturday Visiter.* Championing a "woman's right, under God, to choose her own sphere of action," Swisshelm sought to help women "wipe off the brand of inferiority which has been arbitrarily stamped on them."[17]

Combining the Calvinist self-assurance of her upbringing with a new feminism, Swisshelm developed a fiery style that exposed and eviscerated the misdeeds of powerful men. She wrote for common women who lived "in the immediate vicinity of the laundry, the bedchamber, and the kitchen." When a southern editor derided Swisshelm as "a man[in] all but the pantaloons," she replied:

Perhaps you have been busy
Horse-whipping Sal or Lizzie,
Stealing some poor man's baby,
Selling its mother, may be.
. . . .
But you lack manliness,
A body clean and new,
A soul within it, too.
Nature must change her plan
Ere you can be a man.

A Pittsburgh newspaper editor understated when he described Swisshelm as "one of the strong-minded women of the country." Her fierce style contrasted with her appearance of "slight figure, of less than medium height, with pleasant face, eyes beaming with kindliness, soft voice, and winning manners."[18]

In 1857, Swisshelm moved to Minnesota, then a free territory, where she launched another newspaper, the *Saint Cloud Visiter*, with the creed that "the Bible, and the Constitution of the United States are antislavery." She clashed with southerners who moved to Minnesota bringing slaves contrary to territorial law. They included Sylvanus B. Lowry of Kentucky, who became the Democratic mayor and political boss of Saint Cloud. When Lowry demanded that her newspaper support the Democratic president, Swisshelm seemed to submit. On February 18, 1858, she published a front-page editorial endorsing the Democrats because they championed "a Southern gentleman's right to whip women, rob mothers of their children, and sell [them] upon the auction block." She assured common white people that the Democrats soon would reduce "all the poor and friendless of this country to a state of slavery."[19]

Feeling double-crossed, Lowry had his lawyer denounce Swisshelm as "utterly depraved." She retorted by insulting the lawyer's wife. In March, Lowry, the lawyer, and a friend broke into her office to destroy the press and cast the type into the nearby Mississippi River. They left a note likening Swisshelm to a prostitute and threatening her life. With money from local businessmen, she obtained a new press and reopened her paper to blast Lowry, Democrats, slavery, and domineering men. To dodge a libel suit brought by the lawyer, Swisshelm agreed to publish a recantation in the *St. Cloud Visiter*. Instead, she renamed the paper the *St. Cloud Democrat* and resumed her attacks.[20]

Swisshelm felt driven by the great Calvinist anxiety: although God could and would never forgive her, she must strive to help others. That contradiction served another core belief of Calvinists: that God made a special covenant with a favored nation. While unmoved by any individual case for salvation, He would reward nations that embraced morality, justice, and faith. So even if her zeal and exertions could not secure

Swisshelm a place in heaven, they could help Americans earn divine favor in this world.[21]

A male journalist recalled Swisshelm's "courage, and self-reliance," praising her as "the most widely read and popular female writer in this country." Although "one of the sharpest politicians among American women," Swisshelm was also "a good housekeeper, I know, for I have eaten her biscuits." He reverted to phrenology to explain her: "She has a very large head, high over firmness and self-esteem, wide at combativeness, massive in the intellectual-moral regions" with "an inquisitive nose, sharp almost to fierceness and eyes four times as sharp as her nose." He cited her family tradition of Protestant militancy: "I am certain she would make an admirable martyr—for she would risk the stake any time for the privilege of the last word." If shipwrecked with others on a deserted island in the Pacific, "Mrs. Swisshelm would be elected Queen in fifteen minutes, and have a provisional government organized before dinner."[22]

Strong of mind and will, Jane McManus Cazneau and Jane Grey Swisshelm escaped from unhappy marriages to break into the male-dominated realm of political journalism. But they had many more differences. Cazneau championed the Democrats, converted to Catholicism, and pushed for a territorial expansion that prolonged slavery. Cazneau personally defied some gender norms but, unlike Swisshelm, did not crusade against them publicly. Between them, Cazneau and Swisshelm revealed polarities that divided Americans and clouded the prospects for the Union during the 1850s.

Railsplitter

Americans delighted in rags-to-riches stories, and few told them better than Abraham Lincoln, who claimed descent from "undistinguished families" documented only by the "short and simple annals of the poor." By highlighting his original obscurity, Lincoln emphasized his later prominence and prosperity as the rewards of hard work. In 1860, Lincoln assured an audience, "I am not ashamed to confess that twenty-five years ago I was a hired laborer, mauling rails, at work on a flat-boat—just what might happen to any poor man's son."[23]

Claims of rising from the poor had become political capital for an ambitious man appealing to American voters who dreaded inherited wealth as "aristocratic." Lincoln insisted that social mobility through merit defined America: "The man who labored for another last year, this year labors for himself, and next year he will hire others to labor for him." The cult of the self-made man blamed persistent poverty on bad choices by the poor. If a man remained a "hired laborer, it is not the fault of the system, but because of . . . improvidence, folly, or singular misfortune." No snob, Lincoln sought to help common men get ahead by promoting their access to land, education, and capital. He revered the American Union as the last, best hope on earth for common men to realize their potential. He worried, however, that slavery was corroding republican government by imperiling the dignity of free labor.[24]

Lincoln was born in February 1809 in a log cabin and a slave state, Kentucky. His family lived in a county where the population of 7,500 included over 1,000 slaves, who worked as farm hands and boatmen. Possessing no slaves, Lincoln's father, Thomas Lincoln, failed to prosper, and he blamed a legal and political system that favored wealthy planters. Lincoln moved his family across the Ohio River to Indiana, and later to Illinois, two states that banned slavery.[25]

Thousands of other common Kentuckians moved across the Ohio to escape the slave regime that devalued free labor while widening inequalities of wealth and power among white folk. Often, however, the migrants disliked Blacks even more than their masters, so Indiana and Illinois denied civil rights and public education to African Americans. In a referendum of 1848, a ban on free Blacks entering Illinois passed with 70 percent of the vote.[26]

On the Indiana and Illinois frontier, Abraham Lincoln grew up on new farms carved from a forest recently taken from Indians. Lincoln recalled that "the panther's scream filled the night with fear, and bears preyed on the swine." He worked long days with a hoe to turn the soil, a gun to kill animals, an axe for trees, and (most famously) a maul to split logs into fence rails. Lincoln educated himself with borrowed books.

He memorized long passages that imprinted his later speeches with the folksy wisdom of *Aesop's Fables*; the cadences of the King James Bible; the moral quest of John Bunyan's *Pilgrim's Progress*; the human dilemmas in William Shakespeare's plays; the self-improvement championed by Benjamin Franklin; and the patriotism of Mason Locke Weems's *Life of George Washington*.[27]

His barely literate father and other local men worried that reading was ruining young Lincoln. A neighbor remembered him as "awful lazy" and another as "no hand to pitch in at work like killing snakes." Angered to find his son reading instead of working, Lincoln's father burned some of his books. The boy came to despise his father as brutish and ignorant and later, as an adult, refused to see him.[28]

Lincoln felt drawn to the strong and sensitive women of the family, especially his older sister Sarah and their mother, Nancy Hanks. He later recalled, "All that I am or hope ever to be, I get from my mother," esteemed as more intellectual and caring than his father. A relative recalled that when Lincoln's sister died while giving birth, he "sat down on a log and hid his face in his hands while the tears rolled down through his long bony fingers." Thereafter, a neighbor recalled, "he was alone in the world you might say." Nor did he have a God to console him, for Lincoln could not believe in one or an afterlife. "It isn't a pleasant thing to think that when we die it is the last of us," he told a neighbor. "I never saw a sadder face," his best friend remembered.[29]

Humor helped Lincoln cope with depression, and his jokes and stories won him many friends. That popularity soothed insecurity over his tall, gangly body and homely face. Leaving home, he settled in New Salem, a small commercial village in Illinois, where he worked as a clerk in a store. In 1832, when twenty-three, he ran for a seat in the state legislature. A friend recalled, "Lincoln *had nothing only plenty of friends*." Lincoln boosted his electoral prospects by volunteering to fight Indians, who were hated on the frontier. The New Salem volunteers elected Lincoln as their captain: his first political victory. The war proved brief, so he returned home without seeing combat and in time for the August election.[30]

As a Whig, Lincoln supported government measures to promote

commercial development, a position that won him a majority in New Salem but not in the surrounding countryside, where farmers voted Democrat from suspicion of commercial men. Although he lost that first race, Lincoln prevailed in his second bid, in 1834, after helping farmers harvest their crops.

To boost his statewide political prospects and earn more money, Lincoln studied law and, in 1837, opened a practice in Springfield, the state capital. Despite his limited formal education, Lincoln thrived as a lawyer, thanks to his keen mind, hard work, and folksy, funny style that delighted clients and jurors. Self-disciplined, he avoided the tobacco and alcohol that consumed so many other men in his time. His law partner recalled Lincoln as "the most ambitious man in the world."[31]

To boost his career, Lincoln sought a wife of high status and found her in Mary Todd, the daughter of a banker from Lexington, Kentucky. Twenty-two years old, she dazzled high society with her beauty, wit, and vivacious grace, although one of Lincoln's friends considered her "sarcastic—haughty—aristocratic." Eager to marry a powerful man, Mary Todd often said that she expected her husband to become president of the United States. In Springfield she flirted with the rising Democratic leader in Illinois, Stephen A. Douglas, but he did not return the favor. So she turned to his rival, Lincoln, who shared her Whig politics. They married in November 1842. Despite frequent squabbles, they remained devoted opposites in temperament, he moody and she talkative. To please her, Lincoln dressed better and moved them into a nicer house.[32]

In 1846, Lincoln won a seat in Congress, where he caused an uproar by denouncing the Democratic president, James K. Polk, for attacking Mexico. Accusing Polk of "foul, villainous, and bloody falsehood," Lincoln insisted that "the blood of this war, like the blood of Abel, is crying to Heaven against him." Back home, Democrats denounced Lincoln as "this Benedict Arnold of our district" guilty of a "base, dastardly, and treasonable assault upon President Polk." Many Whigs felt uneasy with Lincoln because territorial expansion was so popular in Illinois. He declined to run for reelection.[33]

Regrouping rather than retiring, Lincoln adapted to a shifting political landscape created by the rise of antislavery sentiment in northern Illinois, settled by New Englanders. Lincoln favored the moderation of his political hero: Kentucky's Henry Clay, who owned slaves but criticized slavery. "I can express all my views on the slavery question by quotations from Henry Clay," Lincoln declared. Rejecting abolition as unconstitutional and dangerous, Clay and Lincoln favored "African colonization," a push for gradual and voluntary emancipation by masters coupled with the overseas deportation of freed Blacks. That implausible program appealed to politicians who wanted to disavow slavery without challenging the racial prejudice of voters, who insisted that white people could not coexist with millions of freed Blacks. Most African Americans, however, rejected colonization as a cruel fraud, for they demanded freedom and equality in the nation of their birth.[34]

In private, Lincoln despised slavery as unjust and cruel. A sensitive man, he hated to see any people suffering from oppression. Traveling on a steamboat along the Ohio River in 1841, Lincoln saw a dozen enslaved people chained together "precisely like so many fish upon a trot-line. In this condition, they were being separated forever from the scenes of their childhood, their friends, their fathers and mothers, and brothers and sisters, and many of them, from their wives and children." He later added, "That sight was a continual torment to me." Lincoln also saw slavery as a threat to the consciences of white people in the North: "The great body of the Northern people do crucify their feelings in order to maintain their loyalty to the constitution and the Union."[35]

Lincoln insisted that the Founders of the Union had declared that all men were created equal and deserved the full fruits of their own labor. "No man has the right to keep his fellow man in bondage, be he black or white," Lincoln declared, "and the time will come, and must come, when there will not be a single slave within the borders of this country." But he did not expect that time to come soon because the federal government lacked the constitutional power to abolish slavery in the southern states. He concluded, "I hold it to be a paramount duty of us in the free states, due to the Union of the states, and perhaps to liberty itself (paradox though it may seem) to let the slavery of the other states alone." He concluded, "Our duty is to wait." Of course, waiting was easier for free whites than enslaved people. His congressional colleague Alexander H. Stephens of Georgia noted that the Union "rose to the sublimity of a religious mysticism" for Lincoln.[36]

Lincoln did believe that Congress had the constitutional power to block slavery's expansion westward into federal territories. By reserving the West for development by common white farmers, he defended the "free labor system" that "opens the way for all—gives hope to all, and energy, and progress, and improvement of condition to all." Lincoln worried that southern planters meant to preempt the West, blocking the free labor essential to social mobility and true democracy. Lincoln also hoped that slavery would succumb to a "natural death" if that system could not expand.[37]

Planter

Most southern whites insisted that they all benefited from slavery— although only a minority owned slaves. Ambitious young farmers aspired to obtain a plantation and the enslaved people to work it. "A man's merit in this country is estimated according to the number of Negroes he works in the field," a planter explained. "The non-slaveholder knows," a southern journalist wrote, "that as soon as his savings will admit, he can become a slaveholder, and thus relieve his wife from the necessities of the kitchen and the laundry and his children from the labors of the field."[38]

Southern whites claimed that slavery guaranteed their liberty and dignity. A Virginian said of the common white man: "However poor, or ignorant or miserable he may be, he has yet the consoling consciousness that there is a still lower condition to which he can never be reduced." A southern newspaper concluded, "Freedom is not possible without slavery." Southerners insisted that slavery resolved class conflict among whites by substituting a racial caste system. Senator James Hammond of South Carolina declared:

> In all social systems there must be a class to do the menial duties, to perform the drudgery of life. That is, a class requiring but a low order of intellect and but little skill. Its requisites are vigor, docility,

[and] fidelity. Such a class you must have, or you would not have the class which leads progress, civilization, and refinement. It's the very mud-sill of society. . . . Fortunately for the South, she found a race adapted to that purpose to her hand.

In effect, slavery kept Blacks as a permanent underclass, rendering all whites fundamentally superior—and thereby relatively equal with one another. Voters elected congressmen and governors who vowed to protect the South against meddling abolitionists, northern politicians, and British imperialists.[39]

Belief trumped reality in the South, for slavery, in fact, limited overall economic development and increased inequality among whites. While large plantations with white-columned mansions claimed the fertile lands beside rivers, many small farms prevailed on the region's pine-covered hills. Southern capital flowed into the plantations, leaving little to develop industries. In 1860, the South had only a tenth of the nation's manufacturing capacity. Seeking industrial work, most immigrants bypassed the South to settle in the North, increasing the population and political weight of that region. For want of towns and cities, the South also lacked the transportation infrastructure and cultural capital of the North: fewer schools, libraries, cities, canals, and good roads. In 1860, the $103 per capita income of white southerners compared poorly to $141 in the North. An unequal society, the South became more so over time, as slaveholding became concentrated in fewer hands: 36 percent of white families owned slaves in 1830, but only 26 percent did so in 1860.[40]

Like Lincoln, Jefferson Davis was born in a log cabin in Kentucky, but his father saw slavery as a boon to ambitious white men. In 1810, Samuel Davis moved his family farther south and west to acquire a 400-acre plantation in Mississippi, which offered plenty of cheap and fertile land recently taken from the Choctaw Indians. Davis thrived by compelling a dozen slaves to raise cotton. Dispersing to cultivate large farms, the settlers developed few towns in Mississippi, which a traveler characterized as "one vast cotton field." They sought, a visitor explained, "to sell cotton in order to buy negroes—to make more cotton to buy more negroes, *ad infinitum*." As the enslaved population grew to half of the new state's total, planters worried about a murderous revolt. A master warned, "We will one day have our throats cut in this country."[41]

Thriving as a planter, Samuel Davis could afford to send his son Jefferson to private boarding schools. When he ran away from school to return home, his father put him to work beside slaves in the cotton fields for two days. Reconciled to education, young Davis returned to school, studying French and ancient Latin and Greek—a classical education far beyond the means of young Lincoln. In 1823, at age fourteen, Davis matriculated at Transylvania University, the leading college in Kentucky. Davis thrived academically and socially, meeting two classmates who became federal senators.[42]

In 1824 Davis transferred to the United States Military Academy at West Point, where he trained for the army's officer corps. Violating many rules, he incurred 137 demerits in his senior year, a stark contrast to the record of West Point's ideal student, Robert E. Lee of Virginia, who never got a demerit in four years. Disliking Davis as insubordinate, the academy's Yankee superintendent, Sylvanus Thayer, wished him good riddance when he graduated in 1828.[43]

As the privileged son of a planter, Davis disliked most of his Yankee peers as penny-pinching and mercenary. "You cannot know *how pitiful they generally are*," Jefferson told his brother. Tall, slim, and handsome with erect posture and polished manners, Davis impressed colleagues as a gentleman and horseman: another pointed contrast with the awkward, gangling, and homely Lincoln. Davis's arrogance was also at odds with Lincoln's self-deprecating style.[44]

As a junior officer, Davis joined an underfunded army of only 6,000 men scattered across hundreds of miles in many small frontier posts of ramshackle construction. Their primary assignment was to chase and fight Indians, but Davis saw little combat. After serving in the army for six years, Davis resigned in 1835 so that he could marry the eighteen-year-old daughter of his commander, Col. Zachary Taylor, who had opposed her marriage to an officer. Davis returned with her to live in Mississippi. The marriage proved brief, just three months, as Sarah Knox Taylor succumbed to the malaria endemic to the lower Mississippi valley. Planter families often paid dearly for living where mosquitoes thrived.[45]

Davis developed a 1,200-acre plantation, Brierfield, a gift from his older brother and mentor, Joseph, who kept a larger, adjoining plantation named "Hurricane." To work the land, Jefferson acquired seventy-two slaves by 1849. During the 1850s, Davis made about $30,000 annually, far beyond the $124 average for free white men in Mississippi. Despite his new wealth, Jefferson paid only $16 a year in state tax on his slaves. Slaveholders ran the state of Mississippi in their own interest, keeping their own taxes down by spending little on public improvements and education.[46]

In 1835 in Mississippi, whites had butchered scores of Blacks suspected of plotting a revolt. But Davis insisted that the "kindness" of masters made slaves "happy and contented." Citing the supposed "natural inferiority" of Blacks as perpetual children, he had "no more dread of our slaves than I have of our cattle." Slavery, Davis claimed, was divinely ordained "for the benefit of both races," as Africans allegedly "entered the temple of civilization" through "the portal of slavery alone."[47]

The Davis brothers conducted a social experiment on their adjoining plantations. To promote hard work and reduce escapes, the Davis brothers provided better cabins, an ample diet, sufficient clothing, and medical care to the slaves, who also could make a little money by raising chickens to sell for meat and eggs. In a designated "Hall of Justice," Joseph Davis presided over juries of the enslaved to try peers accused of violating the plantation rules. In theory, only these juries could impose whipping or other punishments. But white overseers often ignored the Hall of Justice. Indeed, the Davis Bend plantations had a dark side of intense work enforced by severe discipline. Sick slaves received odious medicines when suspected of malingering, and Jefferson Davis built a log dungeon to hold offending slaves in isolation on a starvation diet.[48]

Jefferson Davis courted Varina Banks Howell, the seventeen-year-old daughter of the best friend of his brother. Educated by tutors, Varina had a lively mind and Whig views. At first, she disliked the cocksure Jefferson, who took "for granted that everybody agrees with him when he expresses an opinion, which offends me." Having grown up in towns, Varina did not relish living on a rural plantation surrounded by enslaved people. But Davis was genteel, handsome, rich, and "rode with more grace than any man I have ever seen." She warmed to him, and they married in February 1845.[49]

Later that year, Davis ran for Congress as a Democrat. A visitor described him as "a young man of handsome person and inflammable temperament, who talks violently for 'Southern rights.'" Davis cherished the Union so long as it protected southern interests: "May our Union ever be preserved by justice, conciliation, and brotherhood . . . without a stain of blood that flowed in civil war." Insisting on the equal sovereignty of every state in the Union, Davis declared, "We of the South are now a minority, we must continue to be the minority, [so] our only reliance is on the constitution as a barrier against [northern] encroachment."[50]

Winning his congressional seat, Davis sought to enhance the South's relative power by annexing Texas and conquering Mexico. In 1846, he left Congress to take command of a regiment of volunteers sent to invade Mexico. His departure angered Varina, who delighted in the social whirl of the capital and dreaded losing her husband. Davis served ably and bravely in Mexico, but he irritated his superior officer, General John Quitman, by claiming too much credit for victories. Quitman denounced Davis as "a selfish and fiercely ambitious man." But most Mississippians regarded Davis as a war hero, so the legislature rewarded him with a seat in the U.S. Senate. He was thirty-nine years old.[51]

Proviso

Davis returned to a Congress bitterly divided over the Wilmot Proviso introduced in 1846 by a renegade Democrat from Pennsylvania, David Wilmot. It sought to outlaw slavery in all territories conquered from Mexico. By claiming the West, Wilmot and his supporters, known as Free Soilers, meant to shape the American future that developed as settlers created new properties and towns. Wilmot expressed the antislavery version of white supremacy that prevailed in the North. Having no "sympathy for the slave," Wilmot sought to reserve "a fair country, a rich inheritance, where the sons of toil, of my own race and own color, can live without the disgrace which association with negro slavery brings upon free labor." Free Soilers claimed that they would save the nation from an alleged "Slave Power" conspiracy by wealthy planters out to dominate the country. A Free Soiler declared, "The question is not, whether black men are to be made free, but whether we white men are to remain free."[52]

Southerners insisted that slavery had to grow to survive, so they denounced Wilmot's Proviso as a threat to their way of life. They claimed a right to take slaves into any federal territory as essential to their equality within the Union. So they raged against an attempt to exclude them from a vast new territory that they had helped to conquer. Davis felt insulted "that the South should be restricted from further growth—that around her should be drawn, as it were, a sanitary cordon to prevent the extension of a moral leprosy." Southerners dreaded confinement with a growing enslaved population in one corner of the nation. In their nightmare scenario, if confined, slavery would become explosive, leading to a massive and genocidal revolt. Davis considered slavery "an institution so interwoven with [the South's] interests, its domestic peace, and all its social relations, that it cannot be disturbed without causing their overthrow."[53]

Demanding parity between the regions, southerners interpreted the Proviso as a raw power grab by Yankees, who would create more free states until they could impose emancipation on the South. Davis declared that Southerners would never "consent to be a marked caste, doomed, in the progress of national growth, to be dwarfed into helplessness and political dependence." He warned that northerners' "lust of power, and an irrational hostility to your brethren of the South" would culminate in "staining the battle-fields of the Revolution with the blood of civil war."[54]

In 1846, the Wilmot Proviso passed the House of Representatives, 83 to 64, but the measure lost in the Senate, where the South had more support from northern Democrats. For the next fifteen years, the proviso persisted in American politics, bitterly dividing the nation.[55]

In 1849, Davis's former commander, General Zachary Taylor, became the new president. Although a southern slaveholder, Taylor was a Whig nationalist. In 1850, he faced a crisis when the great prize of the Mexican conquest, California, applied for admission to the Union as a free state.

In the preceding two years, a gold rush had drawn more than 200,000 settlers, most of them Yankees opposed to enslaved labor as an unfair advantage for masters in culling gold flakes from streams and hillsides. To break the stalemate over the Wilmot Proviso, Taylor endorsed admitting California immediately without a territorial stage.[56]

Outraged southerners felt cheated out of their fair share in the conquest. Having already decisively lost the House of Representatives, thanks to faster northern population growth, southerners dreaded that a new free state would tip the balance in the Senate against them. They wanted New Mexico as a slave territory and to split California, with the southern half reserved for slavery.[57]

In the spring of 1850, civil war seemed imminent as Congress deadlocked, Texas prepared troops to seize half of New Mexico, while Taylor mobilized federal troops to fight them. Then at a July 4 picnic, the president ate too many cherries and iced milk. Falling ill, he died of gastroenteritis five days later. The new president, Millard Fillmore of New York, was a flexible politician who cooperated with Senator Stephen A. Douglas to finalize several bills that formed the "Compromise of 1850."[58]

That compromise admitted California as a free state and organized New Mexico as a territory without a congressional ban on slavery. Congress also paid Texas $10 million to abandon its claims to eastern New Mexico. A new law barred slave trading in the District of Columbia while allowing slaveholding to persist there. Finally, Congress stiffened the federal Fugitive Slave Law to compel northern officials to cooperate with slave hunters and prevent northern juries from obstructing them. South Carolina senator John C. Calhoun doubted that the compromise could hold: "Indeed, it is difficult to see how two peoples so different and hostile can exist together in one common Union."[59]

Cabinet Maker

Like Lincoln, John A. Macdonald celebrated his own social mobility, although his home was Canada rather than the United States. Social and geographic mobility had more than one country in North America. Born in Glasgow, Scotland, in January 1815, Macdonald immigrated at the age of five across the Atlantic with his parents. His father was gregarious but feckless, failing at a succession of small businesses before fleeing from Scotland for a new life in Canada, where his wife had relatives.[60]

In 1820, the Macdonalds settled in Kingston, a small commercial port at the northeastern corner of Lake Ontario, near its outlet into the St. Lawrence River that flowed northeastward to Montreal, Quebec City, and the Atlantic (at the Gulf of St. Lawrence). With the nearby Americans as a potential enemy, a garrison of British redcoats protected the town and represented the colony's dependence on the empire. Commerce endowed Kingston with extra prosperity, enabling merchants and lawyers to build substantial limestone homes. They had the political clout to erect a hospital, prison, lunatic asylum, and courthouse—all of stone worked by masons from Scotland.[61]

Macdonald got a conventional middle-class education: six years of grammar school, but no college thereafter. Like Lincoln, Macdonald loved to read, educating himself in literature, history, politics, and mathematics. As young men, both felt pulled by rationality to question conventional religion. Also like Lincoln, Macdonald lost respect for his genial but often inebriated and ever-failing father while cherishing his better-read and more ambitious mother, Helen Shaw Macdonald. From her, he learned how to charm women.[62]

Also like Lincoln, Macdonald pursued a legal career as the best route upward for a clever and ambitious young man. On both sides of the border, lawyers became essential to commercial societies with plenty of disputes over property and assaults. They also emerged as leaders in societies that valued argument and oratory in politics—and needed legal expertise in writing legislation, which became more abundant and complex to keep up with economic development. A contemporary noted, "I know of no money-making business in Canada except the law, store-keeping, tavern-keeping and . . . horse-trading." Those last three businesses generated the disputes that paid the lawyers.[63]

Macdonald considered himself a self-made man, but he benefited from Scottish patrons and partners in a land where Scots abounded and helped one another. They owned and ran Canada's banks, railway syndicate, and the leading newspapers, especially the influential Toronto

Globe of George Brown. Scots founded and directed the first three universities in British North America: McGill in Montreal, Dalhousie in Halifax, and the University of Toronto. In education, law, and business, it helped to be a Scot.[64]

In 1835, at age twenty, Macdonald opened his own law firm in Kingston, attracting attention and business by forcefully defending apparently guilty men. In one case he secured acquittal for a young man accused of leaving a dead horse in a Methodist church; it helped the defense that Macdonald had inside knowledge, having covertly participated in the prank. He later joked that the case "taught me the weakness of circumstantial evidence." After a few years, Macdonald shifted into more lucrative legal work representing banks in civil suits. He invested his income in real estate speculation, buying up Kingston town lots and larger tracts in the forests to the west. Macdonald also helped lead companies that pushed new technologies to improve Kingston and enrich shareholders: hospital, water works, gas lights, insurance, and railways.[65]

In 1842 Macdonald traveled to Britain, where he met and married his second cousin, Isabella Clark Macdonald. He was also smitten with British culture, industrial progress, and imperial power after visiting the megalopolis of London, the Scottish capital of Edinburgh, and the university towns of Cambridge and Oxford. Macdonald admired British leaders, the aristocrats whom Americans professed to despise. He returned home convinced that Canada should cling to British rule in order to avoid falling under American control: "Under the broad folds of the Union Jack we enjoy the most ample liberty to govern ourselves as we please and at the same time we participate in the advantages which flow from association with the mightiest empire the world has ever seen."[66]

In 1844 he won a seat in the Canadian parliament. Although cursed with a big nose, weak chin, and mop of unruly hair, Macdonald exuded self-confidence and commanded attention with dapper clothes, theatrical gestures, keen humor, and a remarkable memory for names and faces. A newspaper editor recalled, "Because women know men better than they know themselves and better than men ever suspect, there was among women a passionate devotion to . . . John A. Macdonald such as no other political leader in Canada has inspired." Women could not vote, but they influenced many men who did.[67]

Practical rather than ideological, Macdonald cut deals and made compromises. Proud of playing a "long game," he had great patience: "If I don't carry a thing this year, I will next." He added, "Only make a beginning, and you will get through some way or other." Taking setbacks in stride, Macdonald looked for the next opportunity: "When fortune empties her chamberpot on your head—Smile and say, 'We are going to have a summer shower.'" Although no great orator, he was a deft and tireless organizer of elections and legislative majorities. When asked his occupation, he wryly replied "cabinet maker."[68]

Macdonald considered politics an exquisite game. Playing deftly, he recruited, advised, and funded candidates—and expected loyalty in return. Useful politicians reaped patronage appointments for key friends and supporters. One legislator promised to support Macdonald "whenever I think you are right." Macdonald retorted, "Anyone will support me when they think I am right. What I want is a man that will support me when I am *wrong!*" He later joked that his ideal cabinet would be "all highly respectable parties whom I could send to the penitentiary if I wished." Although usually genial, Macdonald became ruthless when crossed. A contemporary noted, "Macdonald indeed kills off all he can, but whom he cannot kill with kicks, he kills with kindness. Die somehow, they must."[69]

Most politicians liked Macdonald as he plied them with champagne, jokes, and ribald stories. An old friend recalled, "There wasn't much fun that John A. wasn't up to." Opposition members often enjoyed his company but feared his guile. A popular anecdote insisted that Macdonald and an opposition member were happily drinking together when the latter declared, "Ah, John A., how I love you. How I wish I could trust you."[70]

Affairs were less jolly at home. After two years of marriage, Isabella became a bedridden invalid, apparently afflicted with neuralgia and tuberculosis, compounded by depression, which worsened during her husband's many absences from home. To deal with the pain, she became addicted to ever-larger doses of opium, which withdrew her from reality and her husband. Despite her illness, she bore a son in August 1847, and a second in 1850. The first suddenly died a year later. Isabella's sister recalled "the little white-robed figure lying so still and quiet in its tiny cot in a darkened room." The second, Hugh John, lived to become an adult. Isabella died in December 1857. Overwhelmed by the responsibilities of single parenthood, John A. entrusted his son to his sister and her husband to raise. Macdonald coped with family pain by drinking more.[71]

Politics was Macdonald's chief opiate, for he delighted in the gamesmanship against rivals, the cut and thrust of debate, the cronyism of insider deals and camaraderie, and the applause of voters. He had entered politics to advance his business interests, but as politics became his first love Macdonald neglected his law firm and real estate investments, which turned sour. Meanwhile, he lived grandly despite soaring medical bills for Isabella, so his debts mounted. Only indulgent credit from a Kingston bank, where he served as a director, fended off bankruptcy. A contemporary marveled at how "a man of so much intellect and versatility" could become "such a child" about money matters.[72]

Macdonald's entry into politics had fortunate timing, for in 1844 the British Empire united the colonies of Canada West and Canada East into a union with equal representation for the two colonies. Imperial leaders imagined that balancing act as temporary, for they considered French Canadian culture inferior. The British architect of union, Lord Durham, referred to Francophone Canada East as "an old and stationary society in a new and progressive world" best led by Britons. In time, Durham assumed, French ways and words would fade away into British domination.[73]

Macdonald belonged to the Conservative Party, which entailed Anglophilia, reverence for law and order, and aversion to American influence. But Macdonald was a pragmatist open to new methods to facilitate economic development by using government funds to build canals, roads, and railroads. Seeking to reinvent and broaden his party as "Conservative-Liberal," Macdonald would have passed for a Whig in the United States.[74]

Rejecting the Francophobia of old-line Conservatives, Macdonald sought French Canadian partners for building a governing coalition. Treating them with respect, he rejected the folly of pressuring the Quebecois to abandon their language and culture—or of freezing them out of government patronage. "No man in his senses can suppose that this country can for a century to come be governed by a totally unfrenchified Gov[ernmen]t," Macdonald preached. Of the Quebecois, he advised, "Treat them as a nation and they will act as a free people usually do—generously. Call them a faction and they become factious." He worried as Anglophones became a majority in Canada, thereby rendering the French a defensive minority.[75]

Macdonald understood that only compromise could hold together a tenuous country divided by ethnicity, religion, language, and history. He had to navigate, he mused, through "the mingled interests and conflicting opinions of Catholic and Protestant, Upper and Lower Canadian, French and English, Scotch and Irish, constantly crossing and thwarting one another." The only solution was to rely on "the action of these very cross interests and these conflicting opinions" to prevent any group from dominating another. In 1854, Macdonald insisted that Canadians should "agree as much as possible" by "respecting each other's principles . . . even each other's prejudices" and thereby cultivate "a spirit of compromise and kindly feelings toward each other."[76]

Macdonald found a political partner in George-Etienne Cartier, who led the largest party, known as the *bleus*, in Canada East. The *bleus* competed for seats with the smaller, more liberal, and secular *rouge* party, which distrusted any partnership with Anglophones. A corporate lawyer and deft dealmaker, Cartier had much in common with Macdonald. Fluent in English, Cartier moved graciously and easily among Anglophone businessmen. He delighted in monarchy, British rule, and the pleasures of London. Saying that a French Canadian was an Englishman who spoke French, Cartier preferred the Canadian Union to the apparent alternative: annexation by the United States. Most Quebecois agreed with Cartier that a Canadian confederation would better protect French culture than absorption within the more domineering United

States. But Francophone support for the union hinged on preserving their equal power in Canada's parliament.[77]

Macdonald and Cartier confronted a rising opposition party, the Reformers led by George Brown, the editor of Canada's leading English-language newspaper, the Toronto *Globe*. Bright, charismatic, and resourceful, Brown was also tenacious, inflexible, and self-righteous. Tall (six feet, two inches), large, and strong, he dominated a room with his intense energy and flaming red hair. Brown irritated the usually unflappable Macdonald, who told his mother: "I am carrying on a war against that scoundrel George Brown and I will teach him a lesson." For eight years they crossed paths in parliament without speaking to one another.[78]

A liberal on many issues, including defending the rights of Black Canadians, Brown denounced the Catholic French as a supposed menace to the Protestant Anglophones of Canada. Catholicism, he thundered, "means tyranny, and has for its mission the subversion of the civil and religious liberty of the masses." In 1844, the 650,000 Quebecois of Canada East had outnumbered the 450,000 people of Canada West, but each region held forty-two seats in the Canadian parliament. During the late 1840s, however, immigration swelled the Anglophone population of Canada West, which by 1851 had 952,000 people compared to 890,000 in Canada East. Suddenly regional equality became, for Brown, "a base vassalage to French-Canadian Priestcraft." To increase the seats of Anglophone Protestants, Brown crusaded for "Representation by Population" (often shortened to "Rep by Pop"), which meant majority rule rather than provincial equality. Brown could not appreciate the existential threat that "Rep by Pop" posed to the Quebecois, who clung to equal provincial representation as essential to preserve their distinct culture.[79]

In 1857, Macdonald's coalition with Cartier won a general election, but the tenuous government confronted the contentious issue of selecting a permanent capital for the Canadian union. To mollify contending local interests, the capital had bounced between Toronto and Kingston in Canada West and Montreal and Quebec City in Canada East.[80]

Striving to take the divisive issue of the capital out of the Canadian parliament, Macdonald persuaded a majority to refer the question to Queen Victoria, who had never visited Canada. Canada's governor general helped Macdonald by privately advising the queen to choose a place equally disliked by all contenders: Ottawa, a crude, lumber-milling town of 300 sawmills and a couple of thousand shanties on the Canada West shore of the Ottawa River. The chief local entertainment consisted of drunken brawls between Irish and French-Canadian loggers. A journalist derided the new capital as "a sub-Arctic lumber village transformed by royal mandate into a political cockpit," and Brown's newspaper denounced Ottawa as best "abandoned to the moles and the bats." Macdonald's Quebecois allies in parliament were no happier, joining Brown's motion to reject Ottawa.[81]

In early 1858 Macdonald resigned, claiming that he protested an insult to the queen. For the first time in his life, Brown managed to form a governing coalition, but he did so on an unstable alliance with the Canadian *rouges* and his own anti-French Reformers. And, as usual, Macdonald had a trick up his sleeve to discredit Brown, whose government lasted only two days. Macdonald's friend, the royal governor general, refused Brown's request for a general election.[82]

Macdonald promptly formed a new government with Cartier as prime minister and Macdonald as attorney general for Canada West. Every member of the revived cabinet shifted portfolios—a gambit called the "double shuffle" by an outraged Brown. This trick enabled the new-old regime to avoid holding an election. A great admirer of his own ploys, Macdonald ridiculed Brown: "A prudent fish will play around with the bait some time before he takes it, but in this instance the fish scarcely waited till the bait was let down." By a narrow majority, the new government secured Ottawa as the new capital.[83]

As in the American Union, Canada's constitutional controversy pivoted on the power of a national majority over a minority region. In Canada, the unease derived not from rival systems of labor but instead from the cultural clash between Anglophone Protestants and Francophone Catholics. As Anglophone Canada West surged ahead in population, its leaders sought a political dominance that alarmed the Francophones of Canada East (Quebec).[84]

Francophone leaders pushed for "double majority" to pass any law in the Canadian parliament. This meant support of a majority of members in each half of Canada, a constitutional program resembling what John C. Calhoun pushed for on behalf of the American South. The Canadian problem was that parliamentary majorities were already unstable without having to seek them in both regions at once.[85]

Shepherd

Benito Juárez made an even better case for social mobility than Macdonald or Lincoln. Born in 1806 in a hut in the mountains of Oaxaca, Juárez grew up in a peasant family of Zapotec Indians. Malnourished as a child, Juárez grew to a height of just five feet. Orphaned at three years old, he served his harsh uncle as a shepherd. At age twelve, the boy walked to the city of Oaxaca to find work as a domestic servant and to attend school. Aided by a charitable patron impressed by his promise, Juárez learned Spanish and began to study for the priesthood. Bored by theology, he shifted to law, graduating in 1834.[86]

Prospering, Juárez won election to the city council and in 1843 married a white woman, Margarita Maza, from a prestigious family. "He is very homely, but very good," Maza explained. Four years later, Juárez became governor of Oaxaca, the first Native to govern a Mexican state. Rare in Mexico, such social ascent was impossible for an Indian in the race-obsessed United States.[87]

Firm, hard-working, dignified, courteous, sober, and honest, Juárez was soft-spoken and careful, watching and listening patiently while revealing little of himself. A friend recalled, "I never heard him depreciate anyone and, as for modesty, I have never known his equal." Fond of cigars, Juárez ate little and avoided alcohol. An American visitor, Agnes Joy Salm-Salm, recalled, "Juárez was a man a little under the middle size, with a very dark-complexioned Indian face, which was not disfigured, but . . . made more interesting, by a very large scar across it. He had very black piercing eyes and gave one the impression of being a man who reflects much and deliberates long and carefully before acting." Elite Mexicans attributed Juárez's serious manner to his Zapotec heritage, but he had to cultivate self-discipline because others watched him so closely, too ready to find flaws. Juárez could not afford the follies of men born into wealth and power.[88]

As governor, Juárez carefully accounted for every peso and dispensed with the pomp and parade that delighted other governors. Honest and devoted to his family, which grew to twelve children, he presented a sharp contrast to Mexico's serial dictator, the theatrical, selfish, and insincere Santa Anna. "I believe that the respectability of a ruler derives from the law and right conduct and not from costumes and martial accessories proper only for stage kings," Juárez explained. Personally devout, he attended religious services but refused to follow the political lead of Mexico's domineering bishops.[89]

Devoted to the rule of law as a means of improving society, Juárez wanted to help the poor majority by limiting the power of the church and by constructing new schools and better roads. He explained, "I am a son of the people and I will not forget it; on the contrary, I will stand up for their rights and take care that they learn, that they grow nobler and . . . create a future for themselves and abandon the path of disorder, vice, and misery." If Juárez had any vice, it was self-righteousness, but Mexico could do far worse for leaders—and had done so under Santa Anna.[90]

As a Liberal, Juárez challenged the dominant Conservative party. Defending Spanish traditions, Conservatives favored a centralized, hierarchical, and Catholic society that defended inequality of wealth as essential to social stability. A leading Conservative explained that Catholicism was "the only common tie that binds all Mexicans now that all others are broken, and the only one capable of maintaining the Spanish-American race and saving it from the great danger to which it is exposed"—meaning another invasion by the United States. Rejecting individualism and social mobility, Conservatives declared that "man had no rights, only the duty to serve God in the station in society in which the Almighty had placed him, by obeying his superiors, showing kindness to his inferiors, and believing and upholding the doctrines of the Catholic Church." Supported by landlords, generals, and bishops, Conservatives wanted to consolidate power in Mexico City, subordinating the nineteen states.[91]

Liberals favored decentralizing power in favor of the states and increasing the authority of legislators over the president. They also worked to weaken the Church, landlords, and army by promoting social mobility through individual competition for private property. Liberals expected market relations to reward merit and hard work, gradually softening Mexican inequality by uplifting the poor. Liberals meant to break up traditional solidarities, including Indian village communes, to force Natives to become modern on Liberal terms. One explained, "In order that the light of civilization can penetrate these [Native] towns, it is necessary to dissipate the clouds of their Indianism." The Liberal message appealed more to *mestizos* and the middle class in the towns than to the impoverished Indian majority in the countryside.[92]

With capitalism, individualism, and republicanism as their holy trinity, Liberals envied the political economy and civil society of the United States. Only by emulating American ways, Liberals believed, could Mexico sustain free government and develop a modern and vibrant economy. Their emphasis on civil liberties, economic development, and individual opportunity and responsibility made them philosophical fellow travelers with Lincoln. While Conservatives dreaded American investment as a Trojan horse, Liberals coveted that capital to kick-start Mexico's sluggish economy.[93]

Both Mexican parties struggled with the crisis wrought by the destructive American invasion of 1846–1848. Defeated and battered, Mexico suffered from a crushing foreign debt and raids by nomadic Comanches and Apaches crossing the new northern border to kill men and take women and children and horses, while leaving behind burned-out ranches and villages. Unable to afford sufficient garrisons to protect the long, mountainous, and arid frontier, the federal government had to rely on local power brokers—known as *caudillos*—to defend Mexico's northern states. But that devolution of authority deprived the nation of credibility and revenue.[94]

During the 1850s, Mexico's leaders faced crushing challenges far greater than those confronting Lincoln and Davis. While the United States seemed triumphant, Mexico faced an existential crisis posed by severe poverty, an immense national debt, internal divisions, and a powerful, covetous neighbor to the north. Many outsiders considered Mexico doomed to fail, but Juárez meant to save his country by perfecting liberalism there.[95]

Liberals

Lincoln, Macdonald, and Juárez shared a commitment to liberalism, the dominant and progressive ideology of the nineteenth century. Liberalism sought to perfect a new social order of equal individual rights. As free and competing individuals, rather than as members of local communities, people could demonstrate merit and fulfill potential by selling their labor or products on free markets. As equal citizens, they could share in the power of their republics. The nineteenth-century brand of liberalism promised to liberate people from the burden of the past that rewarded monarchs, aristocrats, and bishops.

By promising progress, liberalism battled the pessimism of traditional beliefs. Juárez denounced conservatives, who "do not have a profound belief in the principles of liberty and have no faith, therefore, in the progress of humanity, and do not strive to improve the condition of the people, removing the obstacles which prevent them from seeing their nakedness and misery." Juárez insisted that common people had "a natural instinct for liberty," so they would support "a decided partisan of liberal ideas . . . and that day will not be long in coming, given the irresistible impulse of the age."[96]

In nineteenth-century North America, liberalism had powerful enemies. In Mexico, class and race combined to empower a small white elite of generals, bishops, and landlords resistant to change. In Canada, liberalism faced distraction by the ethnocultural divide between Anglophone Protestants and Francophone Catholics. In the United States, the obsession with white supremacy clashed with the liberal promise of equal rights and opportunity for all. Americans relied on union to provide the internal peace and continental market essential for republican government and economic opportunity. But keeping that Union

depended on a constitutional pact with slavery: the country's great violation of liberal principles. As Democrats, Cazneau and Davis favored
liberal rights for all white men—but accepted or even celebrated the
power of that majority to keep Blacks enslaved and impoverished. At
mid-century, the Union relied on the illiberal bond of a racism shared by
North and South. While Democrats defended that cross-regional bond,
Lincoln and Swisshelm sought to perfect liberalism by weakening the
barriers of race. Could the Union survive that change?[97]

TWO ☙ FUGITIVES

All the powers of earth seem rapidly combining against [the
slave]. . . . One after another they have closed the heavy iron
doors upon him, and now they have him, as it were, bolted in
with a lock of a hundred keys, which can never be unlocked
without the concurrence of every key; the keys in the hands of a
hundred different men, and they scattered to a hundred different
and distant places; and they stand musing as to what invention,
in all the dominions of mind and matter, can be produced to
make the impossibility of his escape more complete than it is.

—ABRAHAM LINCOLN, 1857[1]

Tall, affable, charismatic, eloquent, and handsome, Franklin Pierce was the life of many parties, including the Democratic. More show than substance, Pierce read little and drank too much. Despising abolitionists as a menace to the Union, he purged them from the party in New Hampshire. Although a northern man, Pierce satisfied southern leaders as committed to defending slavery. "Pure, grand and good man, I never knew him to falter in the maintenance of sound principle," Jefferson Davis exulted. Pierce had served as an officer in the war against Mexico but reaped more mishaps than glory, so a wit mocked him as the "Hero of many a well fought bottle." In 1852, the Democrats nominated Pierce for the presidency on a platform that celebrated the Compromise of 1850, including the Fugitive Slave Law. The novelist Nathaniel Hawthorne wrote a campaign biography for Pierce, an old college friend. Hawthorne found it "a hard book to write" because the nominee had accomplished so little: "My heart absolutely sank at the dearth of available material."[2]

Yet Pierce trounced the Whig candidate, General Winfield Scott, by 254 to 42 in the Electoral College, carrying twenty-seven of the thirty-one states. Southern Whigs had deserted their party in disgust at Scott's pompous personality and ambivalence on slavery. He carried only two slave states, Kentucky and Tennessee. Whigs won no southern governorships and only fourteen of sixty-five congressional seats in the Deep South. "The Whig party is dead," declared congressman Alexander H. Stephens of Georgia. Even in the North, Scott inspired little enthusiasm. A Pennsylvania Whig lamented that rallying voters was "like pissing against the wind, when blowing sixty miles to the hour." An Ohioan noted, "General Apathy is the strongest candidate out here." In his inaugural address, Pierce vowed to silence all further "sectional or fanatical excitement" over slavery as a threat to "the durability of our institutions." But brave and resourceful fugitives would

PREVIOUS PAGE: *Anthony Burns (1829–1862), 1855, engraving by John Andrews.*

challenge Pierce's administration, intensifying agitation over slavery within the Union.[3]

Runaways

Although masters obsessed about the danger of a slave revolt, rebellions were few and local because anything larger seemed suicidal, for whites were better armed and organized for military conflict. Instead, slaves usually resisted through acts of deception by individuals or small groups. They slowed their work, pretended to misunderstand orders, faked sickness, broke tools, stole food, got drunk, burned down outbuildings, slipped poison into masters' food and drink, and ran away. To reach a northern state, fugitives had to overcome a gauntlet of slave patrols and bounty hunters with bloodhounds, but an informal network of sympathizers, later known as the "Underground Railroad," provided hiding places and sustenance. Most of the "conductors" were free Blacks assisted by white abolitionists, particularly Quakers.[4]

In 1849, Harriet Tubman escaped from slavery as a Maryland field hand, but she returned thirteen times to help another seventy people escape to freedom. Tubman reflected, "I grew up like a neglected weed—ignorant of liberty, having no experience of it; Now, I've been free, I know what a dreadful condition slavery is." Eloquent in prayer and prone to visions, Tubman seemed to communicate with the divine. Her success and deep faith led others to call her Moses, as her legend spread through the grapevine covertly nurtured by enslaved people. She had a large personality in a small body, just five feet tall. A friend recalled, "A more ordinary specimen of humanity could hardly be found among the most unfortunate-looking farm hands of the South. Yet in point of courage, shrewdness, and disinterested exertions to rescue her fellow-men, she was without equal."[5]

In the North, fugitives found limited freedom because of discrimination and segregation. Only the New England states allowed Blacks to vote. During the 1840s, northern states held nineteen referendums on enhancing the political rights of Blacks, but only two passed, and the rest lost by an average margin of five to one. Free Blacks became scapegoats villainized by Democratic politicians pandering to white prejudice. A sympathizer lamented attacks on "the unpopular and defenceless colored man. . . . We dislike them because we are unjust to them."[6]

Because the Federal Constitution required interstate cooperation in retrieving fugitive slaves, runaways had little security from bounty hunters in the North. In Pennsylvania, William Parker "found by bitter experience that to preserve my stolen liberty I must pay, unremittingly, an almost sleepless vigilance." Lewis Garrard Clarke did not feel safe until he reached British Canada, which did not extradite runaway slaves: "There was no 'free state' in America, all were *slave* states—bound to slavery, and the slave could have no asylum in any of them."[7]

During the 1840s, about a thousand runaways a year made it to the North (and often on to Canada). That seemed like a scant loss for a system that held three million people in bondage in 1850, but the fugitives had an impact far beyond their numbers. Masters insisted that any escape would become contagious, increasing into a massive wave, while provoking bloody revolts throughout the South. Runaways also published searing accounts of their sufferings, which contradicted proslavery propaganda about happy, lazy, and stupid slaves. A Virginia newspaper declared, "The continued existence of the United States as one nation depends upon the full and faithful execution of the Fugitive Slave Bill."[8]

Although southerners usually clamored for states' rights, the Fugitive Slave Law overrode northern state laws that protected the legal rights of accused runaways. The new law established federal commissioners to rule on cases where masters or their agents identified Blacks as runaways. The accused had no right to testify or to a jury trial. To bias rulings in favor of masters, the law awarded a commissioner $10 for everyone restored to slavery but only $5 when he ruled for freedom. In the 343 known cases, commissioners only freed 11. The law allowed no appeal of a commissioner's ruling.[9]

Federal officers and bounty hunters also could require citizens to assist in catching runaways—and to punish refusal with fines and six months in prison. Most Yankees did support the Fugitive Slave Law as a necessary evil to preserve the Union. Senator Daniel Webster of Massachusetts expected enforcement "if we would avoid rebellion, outbreaks, and civil war." President Millard Fillmore agreed that slavery was "guaranteed by the Constitution" and needed northern support to save the Union: "the last hope of free government in the world." Abraham Lincoln concluded that while he hated "to see the poor creatures hunted down, I bite my lip and keep quiet."[10]

Northern free Blacks denounced and resisted the Fugitive Slave Law. In Boston, six Black cooks refused to prepare a state dinner arranged by Webster; they would "see him in hell first." A New York convention of free Blacks

> Resolved: That the fugitive slave law is the law of tyrants.
> Resolved: That disobedience to tyrants is obedience to God.
> Resolved: That we will obey God.

Many free Blacks bought knives and revolvers to defend their homes. They also helped runaways flee across the border to British Canada. Frederick Douglass declared, "The only way to make the Fugitive Slave Law a dead letter is to make half-a-dozen more dead kidnappers."[11]

In September 1851, in Christiana, Pennsylvania, free Blacks did kill a Maryland slaveholder, who came with eight armed assistants to grab four runaways. Three leading rioters fled to Canada with help from Douglass along the way. "Civil War—The First Blow Struck," announced a Pennsylvania newspaper. President Fillmore sent federal troops to Christiana to arrest thirty Blacks and ten white supporters for treason. That inflated charge backfired, for a judge could see no evidence that the accused had waged war on the United States.[12]

Cabins

The pious daughter, sister, and wife of New England ministers, Harriet Beecher Stowe linked Christian faith to moral reform in society. In 1836, Harriet married Calvin Stowe, a Biblical scholar of slender means, so she began to write magazine articles to bring in money while aiding godly causes: temperance, Sunday schools, Bible distribution, and antislavery.[13]

For eighteen years, the Stowes lived in Cincinnati, Ohio, along the border with slavery, and Harriet watched in dismay as slave catchers returned to Kentucky with their human prey. Her housekeeper, Eliza Buck, a "very handsome mulatto girl" had escaped from slavery in Kentucky after repeated rapes by her master. Buck told Stowe of "poor slaves, who had been mangled and lacerated by the whip." Stowe linked their suffering to her own pain at losing an eighteen-month-old son, Charley, to cholera in 1849: "It was at *his* dying bed, and at *his* grave, that I learnt what a poor slave mother may feel when her child is torn away from her."[14]

In 1850 the Stowes moved to Maine, where Calvin became a professor at Bowdoin College. While attending church in February 1851, Harriet experienced a vision "blown into her mind as by the rushing of a mighty wind." In it, she saw a white man whipping a slave to death. The vision inspired her to write a novel, *Uncle Tom's Cabin, or Life among the Lowly*, which, Stowe recalled, "all came before me in visions, one after another, and I put them down in words." To help spark the reveries, she slept with an abolitionist compendium of fugitives' tales "under her pillow at night, till its facts crystallized into *Uncle Tom*."[15]

At a time when most Americans regarded abolitionists as dangerous fanatics, Stowe repackaged antislavery ideas in a vivid format that appealed to readers. Drawing on Christian scripture for prototypes, the novel featured Tom, a strong and humane slave with a Christ-like ability to suffer for the sins of others. Ultimately, he is whipped to death by a brutish master, Simon Legree. In the novel's other main plot, Eliza (modeled on Eliza Buck), her husband, and their daughter flee across an icy Ohio River to escape from slave hunters. The novel celebrated the heroism of the men and women, Black and white, who resisted brutish and drunken slave catchers, who bellow, "We have the law on our side, and the power." But for Stowe, the runaways had God on their side: the ultimate power.[16]

Published in 1852, *Uncle Tom's Cabin* sold 310,000 copies within a year (and three million eventually) to become the best-selling American novel. *Uncle Tom's Cabin* also became wildly popular in Britain and

Canada. By the end of 1852, two plays based on the novel and dozens of songs introduced Stowe's story to even more people.[17]

Uncle Tom's Cabin fulfilled Stowe's goal of promoting "a kindlier feeling toward the negro race" among northern readers. Congressman Joshua R. Giddings of Ohio insisted that Stowe "had done more for the cause of freedom . . . than any savant, statesman, or politician of our land."[18]

Stowe's novel both fascinated and angered southern readers, who bought thousands of copies to hurl down in disgust. The editor of the *Southern Literary Messenger* wanted a "review as hot as hellfire, blasting and searing the reputation of the vile wretch in petticoats who could write such a volume." A hostile reviewer accused Stowe of belonging "to the school of Women's Rights" that sought "political equality with men" while neglecting the duty "for which she was created—the high and holy office of maternity." Southern critics disparaged Stowe as "deficient in the delicacy and purity of a woman" because her novel discussed the sexual abuse of enslaved women. Defending gender and racial inequality as equally essential to social order, southern leaders felt outraged that a Yankee woman could challenge their way of life.[19]

Several southern states outlawed *Uncle Tom's Cabin*, alleging that it would instigate bloody slave revolts. A proslavery writer insisted that her "intense *love* of the *negro*" would provoke "the wholesale massacre" of white people and "envelop our dwellings in flames." One angry master mailed Stowe a severed ear apparently taken from a recaptured runaway.[20]

In Maryland, Samuel Green was a skilled blacksmith who had bought his freedom and that of his wife. But their master kept their children, and sold one far away to Missouri. Becoming a Methodist minister, Green covertly helped Harriet Tubman guide enslaved people to freedom in Canada. In 1857, Maryland magistrates arrested Green and searched his home, finding a copy of *Uncle Tom's Cabin*. Convicted of owning that dangerous book, he received ten years in prison. Maryland's governor refused to pardon Green: "I know Green. So far [as] his moral character goes, he is an honest man; but if I pardon him, I shall be called an abolitionist and mobbed."[21]

Within two years, proslavery writers produced fifteen novels to refute

Uncle Tom's Cabin. The authors depicted slave characters with happier lives than impoverished northern factory workers or Black fugitives freezing in Canada. These novels included *Uncle Robin in His Cabin in Virginia and Tom Without One in Boston.* A northern critic wondered why, given the "pictures of the intense happiness of the slaves," the southern novelists did "not make haste to sell their children to the slave traders." The contra-novels failed to match the sales or impact of *Uncle Tom's Cabin* for want of Stowe's ability to construct fast-paced plots with vivid characters.[22]

Wake-Up

Stowe's novel eroded northern support for enforcing the Fugitive Slave Law. A British visitor, Nassau W. Senior, noted that in 1850 and 1851 "the lower classes in New York and Boston enjoyed the excitement of a negro hunt as much as our rustics enjoy . . . a fox hunt." But that support had ebbed by 1854: "The sovereign people was converted; public sympathy turned in favour of the slaves. . . . As far as the Northern States are concerned, 'Uncle Tom' has repealed the Fugitive Slave Law."[23]

A growing number of Yankees felt subordinated by the Fugitive Slave Law. America's leading philosopher, Ralph Waldo Emerson, marveled that "this filthy enactment was made in the nineteenth century by people who could read and write. I will not obey it, by God." Senator William H. Seward of New York denounced the law as morally dead because an egalitarian God mandated "a higher law than the Constitution"—words that especially outraged southern leaders.[24]

In some cities, interracial mobs drove off slave catchers and liberated fugitives by breaking open jails or disrupting hearings. An antislavery man recalled rescuing Joshua Glover in 1854 from a jail in Milwaukee: "Twenty strong and resolute men seized a large timber some eight or ten inches square and twenty feet long and went for the jail door; bumb, bumb, bumb, and down came the jail door and out came Glover."[25]

Embarrassed when abolitionists rescued runaways in Boston, Daniel Webster denounced resistance to the Fugitive Slave Law as a traitorous madness that would destroy the Union. In April 1851, Webster sought

to make a point at the expense of Thomas Sims, a short, slight, young, and mixed-race fugitive from slavery in Georgia. In the bitter cold of February, Sims had survived a harrowing and hungry voyage for two weeks as a stowaway on a Boston-bound merchant ship. He landed safely, but his master sent an agent, assisted by two policemen, to arrest Sims. Hauled into a hearing, Sims burst out, "I will not go back to Slavery. Give me a knife, and when the Commissioner declares me a slave, I will stab myself in the heart, and die before his eyes!"[26]

Denied both freedom and a knife, Sims went away, escorted by hundreds of policemen through a howling crowd of Bostonians outraged at the betrayal of liberty in a city famous for launching the American Revolution. Back in Savannah, Sims suffered a public whipping staged by his master as a warning to others. President Fillmore wrote to thank Webster: "I congratulate you and the country upon a triumph of law in Boston."[27]

In March 1854, Anthony Burns escaped from Virginia, by stowing away in a Boston-bound ship. In May, slave catchers arrested Burns, and a federal commissioner ordered him restored to slavery. President Pierce sent hundreds of federal troops to help the Boston police escort Burns from prison through an angry crowd of 50,000 to the ship that took him back to Virginia. The effort cost the federal government $100,000—about a hundred times what Burns could sell for. Pierce meant to enforce the Fugitive Slave Law everywhere, even in antislavery Boston, but the spectacle alienated many watching moderates. The industrialist Amos A. Lawrence said that his family "went to bed one night old fashioned, conservative, Compromise Union Whigs," but after the Burns tragedy "waked up stark mad Abolitionists." Lawrence began to invest his fortune in the antislavery cause.[28]

Delany

After escaping from slavery in Maryland, Frederick Douglass settled in Rochester, New York, where he founded and edited a newspaper, the *North Star*, to promote abolition and women's rights. The paper had the motto "Right is of no Sex—Truth is of no Color—God is the Father of

Martin Robison Delany (1812–1885), 1865, lithograph by unknown.

us all, and we are all Brethren." After publishing a vivid memoir of his searing experiences as a slave, Douglass became a celebrated speaker, attracting rapt attention from large audiences.[29]

Douglass praised *Uncle Tom's Cabin* for rekindling "the slumbering embers of anti-slavery zeal into active flame," mobilizing thousands "who before cared nothing for the bleeding slave." Douglass concluded,

"The name of Harriet Beecher Stowe can never die while the love of freedom lives in the world."[30]

But another Black leader, Martin Delany, despised Stowe's novel as riddled with patronizing stereotypes of African Americans. Delany insisted that Stowe "*knows nothing about us* . . . neither does any other white person—and, consequently, can contrive no successful scheme for our elevation; it must be done for ourselves." Disgusted by the long-suffering Uncle Tom, Delany wanted to read of a bold Black protagonist who "buried the hoe deep in the master's skull." In a riposte to the pacifism of *Uncle Tom's Cabin*, Delany wrote and published his own novel, *Blake or the Huts of America*, which featured a defiant Black revolutionary leading slave revolts.[31]

Unlike Douglass, Martin Delany was born free—or as free as a Black person could be in the United States of 1812. Delany grew up in Charleston, Virginia (now West Virginia), the son of an enslaved field hand and a free Black seamstress. When Martin was ten, a white man tried to kidnap and sell him into slavery. Because Virginia criminalized teaching literacy to Blacks, magistrates threatened to arrest Pati for teaching her children to read, so she moved with her children to Pennsylvania.[32]

A brilliant student, Delany apprenticed as a doctor while editing a Black newspaper in Pittsburgh during the 1830s and early 1840s. A voracious reader of geography, history, politics, and medicine, Delany joined groups that helped runaways and pushed for civil rights in Pennsylvania. In 1843, Delany married Catherine Richards, and they had ten children named after Black heroes, including Toussaint L'Ouverture, the revolutionary leader of Haiti.[33]

In 1847, Douglass visited Pittsburgh and met Delany, who impressed him as a talented and "noble specimen of a man." Douglass recruited Delany to help edit his newspaper and to tour the Midwest, drumming up subscribers. In Ohio, Delany and a friend confronted a racist mob that howled, swore, and beat drums while vowing to tar and feather them before selling them into slavery. But Delany and friend barricaded their hotel's stairwell and displayed a hatchet and butcher knife to deter the attackers.[34]

In 1850 Delany left work with Douglass to become one of the first three Black students at Harvard Medical School. But their white peers complained "that we cannot consent to be identified as fellow students with blacks, whose company we would not keep in the streets, and whose Society as associates we would not tolerate in our houses." In early 1851, the dean of the medical school caved, compelling the Black students to leave Harvard. Moving to New York City, Delany became an inventor, but soon discovered that federal regulations barred Blacks from receiving patents because they were not considered American citizens.[35]

Infuriated by searing experiences, Delany rejected American society as incurably racist, blocking Blacks from developing their abilities and realizing their ambitions: "I am weary of our miserable condition, and heartily sick of whimpering, whining, and sniveling at the feet of white men." Irritated by subordination in white-led abolition societies, Delany warned Blacks: "Our elevation must be the result of *self-efforts*, and the work of our *own hands*." Challenging the pacifism of abolitionist societies, he endorsed armed revolts and migration to West Africa or Central America, where Blacks could govern themselves.[36]

Delany's Black nationalism clashed with the humanist universalism of his former mentor, Douglass, who claimed that Blacks could thrive in the United States once the nation renounced slavery and racism. With Black parents on both sides (unlike Douglass, whose father was his master), Delany dwelled on his racial purity as a source of superiority. That position offended Douglass, who rejected racial identities as obstacles to human equality: "I thank God for making me a man simply; but Delany always thanks him for making him a *black man*." Douglass added that Delany "has gone about the same length in favor of black, as the whites have in favor of the doctrine of white superiority." Douglass also charged that Delany's push for Black emigration would weaken the struggle for equality within the United States.[37]

Henson

To craft characters, Stowe drew on conversations with, and narratives by, fugitives from slavery. These included a memoir by Josiah Henson, published in 1849. Nine years later, Stowe praised Henson by writing a preface for his book's revised edition. That partial acknowledgment led Delany to claim that Henson was the primary source for the character of Uncle Tom. Although overstated, the connection seemed credible because Henson had shown a similar Christian endurance of suffering.[38]

Unlike Uncle Tom, Henson survived (if barely) life in slavery. Born in 1789 in Charles County, Maryland, Henson recalled his first memory as seeing his father with a bloodied back and an ear lopped off in punishment for opposing the master's rape of his wife. Young Henson passed through three owners and suffered a brutal beating by an overseer that crippled his right arm. Earning money as a preacher on Sundays, Henson offered to buy his freedom from his third master, Isaac Riley, for $450. Riley pocketed the money and then prepared to sell Henson into the even harsher slavery of a Louisiana cotton plantation. In 1830, Henson escaped with his wife and four children across Ohio to reach a safe haven in Canada West.[39]

In Canada, Henson worked hard, saving his small pay as a farm laborer, sharecropper, and minister to buy land. At a place they called "Dawn," Henson and his friends acquired 1,500 acres for a collective community of 500 people who sustained a trade school, farm, brickyard, gristmill, and sawmill. A century later, Henson's home in Dawn became a public museum called "Uncle Tom's Cabin Historic Site."[40]

By welcoming Black refugees, white Canadians claimed moral superiority over Americans, who boasted of freedom while keeping millions in slavery. In 1830, when some free Blacks from Ohio inquired about moving to Canada, the colonial governor replied, "Tell the Republicans on your side of the line that we do not know men by their color. If you come to us, you will be entitled to all the privileges of the rest of his Majesty's subjects." They could serve on juries, testify in court against whites, vote (provided they met the same property requirement as whites), and send their children to public schools. Canadian Blacks did not have to pay any special tax or post bond for good behavior—as so many American states required.[41]

American diplomats demanded that the British extradite runaway slaves as criminals who had stolen themselves from their owners. But colonial officials refused to extradite anyone for something that was not a crime in Canada. Even when a fugitive stole a horse to get away, Canadian courts and imperial officials declined to extradite, considering the animal essential to gaining freedom.[42]

In need of laborers, Canada West's landowners and entrepreneurs welcomed Blacks and offered good wages for clearing land and building roads. Land was abundant and cheap, enabling many newcomers to obtain small farms. Arriving poor, most refugees settled just within Canada near the border, usually along the Detroit River or lower Thames River in the towns of Amherstburg, Chatham, Colchester, Sandwich, and Windsor.[43]

Grateful for their haven, Black immigrants celebrated and defended British rule in Canada. After visiting Canada, the Black poet and activist Frances Harper wrote, "I have gazed for the first time upon a free land." Douglass insisted that in Canada a runaway could "nestle in the mane of the British lion, protected by the mighty paw from the talons and the beak of the American eagle." Black immigrants defended British rule to block their greatest fear: invasion and annexation by the United States. "The Natural hatred of the coloured people to the Americans would be a guarantee for their fidelity," a Canadian noted.[44]

Emigration to Canada surged after the Fugitive Slave Law of 1850 increased the peril to runaways within the United States. By 1860, about 40,000 former slaves lived in Canada West; two-thirds of them arrived during the 1850s. The governor general, Lord Elgin, worried that Canada was being "flooded with blackies who are rushing across the frontier to escape from the bloodhounds whom the Fugitive slave bill has let loose on their track."[45]

As Black numbers grew, white prejudice increased in Canada. Critics denigrated the fugitives as ignorant, drunken, lazy, and thieving—although, in fact, they committed fewer crimes than did poor white men. A hostile Canadian declared, "Let the slaves of the United States be free, but let it be in their own country. . . . In a word, let the people of the United States bear the burden of their own sins." Prejudice led local authorities to bar Black students from public schools, and most churches segregated Black worshippers in a back loft. Many hotels and steamboats refused to serve Blacks. The Conservative politician Edwin

Larwill pushed to limit Black immigration and civil rights in Canada— but Black voters helped to defeat him in two elections during the 1850s.[46]

Despite the regression in social conditions, Canada still offered greater freedom and opportunity for Blacks than did the United States. They could vote and openly organize to defend their rights. In 1853 John H. Hill wrote to a friend back home, "I want you to let the whole United States know [that] we are satisfied here because I have seen more Pleasure since I came here than I saw in the U.S. the 24 years that I served my master." Another fugitive concluded, "The mission of Great Britain is to extend freedom to all men; but that of the American Republic [is] to extend to only a part, while the rest is to be kept in the most degrading bondage."[47]

Dr. Alexander Milton Ross became a radical abolitionist after treating fugitives in Canada. Ross helped a young woman whose back was "still raw and seamed with deep gashes, where the lash of her cruel master's whip had ploughed up her flesh." He also found inspiration by reading *Uncle Tom's Cabin*: "To me, it was a command . . . that it was my duty to help the oppressed to freedom."[48]

Under the cover of birdwatching, Ross toured the South five times to lead at least thirty-one fugitives north to "Canada—the Land of Liberty for the slaves of the American Republic." Risking his life, Ross narrowly escaped from a lynch mob in Mississippi. Ralph Waldo Emerson praised Ross: "My brave Canadian knight is not only the deliverer of the slaves, but a lover of flowers, birds and old English poetry."[49]

Shadd

Many American Blacks worried that Canada might offer only a temporary haven before Americans annexed that land and imposed slavery there. In Delaware, Elizabeth Williamson feared for her relatives in Canada: "I am much afraid that Canada is not going to prove what it was cracked up to be. . . . American gold will buy it in time," and then it would "become the hunting ground for the American Bloodhound."[50]

Williamson wrote that letter to her niece, Mary Ann Shadd, who promoted Black emigration to Canada. Born free in 1823, Shadd belonged

to a mixed-race family who had fled from prejudice and segregation in
Delaware. During the 1830s, as Delaware's free Black numbers grew,
state legislators stripped them of civil rights, banned interracial marriage,
closed schools for Blacks, and fined any who came within half a mile
of a polling place on election day. The legislators explained, "We will
not permit them to associate with us. We will not tolerate any notion
of equality with them."[51]

Mary Ann's father, Abraham Shadd, was a shoemaker and antislavery
activist who moved his family in 1833 across the nearby state line to West
Chester, Pennsylvania, where Quakers ran a school for free Blacks. Hard
workers, the Shadds acquired a farm and sustained middle-class values
of self-improvement, moral discipline, and community engagement.[52]

Mary Ann Shadd taught at a school for Black children and emerged
as an eloquent public speaker for the antislavery cause. An admirer
described her as "a young (light colored) lady of fine diction, refined
address, and Christian deportment" with a formidable "energy of character." A friend recalled, "Miss Shadd's eyes are small and penetrating,
and fairly flash when she is speaking." Visiting New York City, Shadd
hailed a stagecoach, although the drivers refused to pick up Blacks. A
witness marveled that, although short and slender, Shadd displayed,
"such an air of impressive command . . . that the huge, coarse, ruffianly
driver" felt "suddenly seized with paralysis, reined up to the curb" and
took her on board.[53]

Impatient for progress, she regretted that many years of activist
speeches and conventions had accomplished so little: "We should do
more and talk less." Often African American men struggled to make
sense of a young woman who claimed a leadership role. They welcomed her talents but resented Shadd when she challenged them. Delany
deemed her "a very intelligent young lady and peculiarly eccentric."[54]

After the Fugitive Slave Law of 1850, Shadd despaired for Black prospects within the United States where runaways engaged in "a miserable
scampering from state to state, in a vain endeavor to gather the crumbs
of freedom that a pro-slavery [broom] may sweep away at any moment."
Terrified by the political power of the South, she predicted that very
soon "there will be no retreat from the clutches of the slave power."[55]

Shadd heeded the advice of another activist, James Theodore Holly, who urged Blacks to leave the United States and "swarm in a ceaseless tide to Canada West and hang like an ominous *black cloud* over this guilty nation." After visiting Toronto for an antislavery convention in September 1851, Shadd concluded that Canada West was "by far, the most desirable place of resort for colored people, to be found on the American continent." Settling in Windsor, she opened an interracial school. Her parents and siblings followed her to buy farms and set up a shoe-making shop.[56]

In 1852 Shadd published *A Plea for Emigration or Notes of Canada West,* which described most Canadians as open-minded: "There is more independent thought and free expression than among Americans." Attending Black rights conventions in the United States, she dazzled delegates with eloquent speeches pitching settlement in Canada. One delegate praised Shadd as "a superior woman; and it is useless to deny it . . . however much we may differ with her on the subject of emigration."[57]

At Windsor, she challenged the primary Black leader, Henry Bibb, a preacher who had escaped from slavery in Kentucky to found Canada's only Black newspaper, the *Voice of the Fugitive.* Bibb and Shadd clashed over how to respond to the increased racism in Canada during the 1850s. Bibb favored self-segregating into distinct communities, where Blacks could protect and help one another. Shadd, however, favored Douglass's strategy of demanding full integration as equals with whites. She disliked Bibb's segregated communities as bound to keep Blacks poor, dependent, and resentful. Shadd also denounced Bibb as a corrupt manipulator who skimmed donations from American philanthropists meant for fugitives. Counterattacking, his newspaper accused Shadd of lacking the decorum and deference of a proper lady, casting her as "the serpent that beguiled mother Eve, in the Garden of Eden." Bibb persuaded donors to withdraw funding for her school, obliging Shadd to close it in March 1853.[58]

To strike back, Shadd founded the *Provincial Freeman,* becoming the first African American woman to own and run a newspaper. By showcasing Black success stories in Canada, Shadd promoted emigration and refuted racists who insisted that freedom was wasted on African Americans. The *Provincial Freeman* also championed women's rights, reprinting essays by Harriet Beecher Stowe and Jane Grey Swisshelm. Shadd's newspaper denounced men who would "crush *a woman* whenever she attempts to do what has hitherto been assigned to men, even though God designed her to do it."[59]

After a fire consumed Bibb's printing office in October 1853 and he died in August 1854, Shadd turned her muckraking talents against the leaders of Dawn, including Josiah Henson. Shadd even challenged Frederick Douglass for opposing Black emigration to Canada.[60]

Shadd got along surprisingly well with Martin Delany, although she disliked his plan to resettle African Americans in a tropical country, where she warned that they would be "surrounded by big spiders, lizards, snakes, centipedes, . . . and all manner of creeping and biting things." In February 1856, Delany appeared to concede her point by moving to Canada, settling at Chatham. He wanted to spare his children from growing up in America: "They cannot be raised in this country without being stoop shouldered." A town of 4,000, a third of them Black, Chatham ranked second to Toronto as a center of Black culture and activism in Canada. In 1855, Shadd had moved the *Provincial Freeman* to Chatham, where her paper promoted Delany's medical practice, public lectures, and novel, *Blake or the Huts of America*. In turn, Delany praised her leadership and contributed essays to the *Provincial Freeman*.[61]

In September 1858, Delany and Shadd helped to rescue Sylvanus Demarest. About ten years old, Demarest was traveling with a white American who had kidnapped him. When their train stopped for water in Chatham, Shadd's brother Isaac led one hundred Blacks, armed with clubs, to storm the train and liberate Demarest. The railroad company prosecuted Isaac and six others for riot, but a Canadian court dropped the case against them.[62]

Mexico

Instead of looking to distant Canada for a haven, fugitives from Texas headed south and west across the Rio Grande to Mexico, which had outlawed slavery and granted citizenship to Blacks. In 1852 a San Antonio newspaper reported that a slave regarded Mexico as "his utopia for political rights and his Paradise for happiness." A fugitive, Felix Haywood, attested, "In Mexico you could be free. They didn't care what color you was, black, white, yellow, or blue." In 1854, the Yankee traveler, Frederick Law Olmsted, heard Texans complain that Mexicans actually believed "that good old joke of our fathers—the Declaration of Independence" with its notion of all men created equal.[63]

During the early 1850s, the journalist Jane Cazneau lived at Eagle Pass, on the Texas bank of the Rio Grande across from Piedras Negras. She marveled that Black fugitives in "Mexico have all the social rights and honors of the most esteemed citizens." This "equality of caste and color is a great allurement to the Africans on her border." She knew fugitives who had married "in the best families, and carry their honors with high dignity."[64]

The American government demanded that Mexico return the fugitives to American slavery—and threatened to retrieve them by force. At the port of Matamoros, the United States consul complained, "These people are, and always have been, deadly hostile to every American (unless he is a Negro or mulatto)." Rejecting the extradition of Black fugitives, the Mexican Senate asserted: "It would be most extraordinary that, in a treaty between two free republics, slavery should be encouraged by obliging ours to deliver up fugitive slaves to their merciless and barbarous masters of North America."[65]

Settled near the border, Black refugees could provide a highly motivated militia to repel raids by Comanche Indians and Texas Rangers. By defending the runaways, Mexicans defended their sovereignty. In 1852, in Guerrero, four town councilmen shot an American slaveholder trying to kidnap a Black man. Attentive to legal form, they dragged his corpse before a judge who certified that the man was, in fact, dead, "for not having responded when spoken to, and other cadaverous signs."[66]

Proximity to Mexico destabilized slavery in Texas. At El Paso, a master complained that his slaves worked slowly, but "I was afraid to chastise them, as we were right on the line where they could cross over into Mexico and be free." During the early 1850s, about 4,000 made it to Mexico, eluding bounty hunters. In 1855, a leading Texas Ranger, John Salmon Ford, complained "Something must be done for the pro-

tection of slavery property in this state. Negroes are running off daily."
If escapes drained Texas of slaves, Ford warned that the entire South
would suffer: "Let the frontier of slavery begin to recede and when or
where the wave of recession may be arrested, God only knows."[67]

In 1855, James Hughes Callahan led 111 Texas Rangers across the Rio
Grande to attack, loot, and burn the fugitive haven at Piedras Negras,
before Mexicans (including Blacks) drove the invaders back across the
border. A Mexican official reported, "Piedras Negras offers now a scene
of devastation. A multitude of innocent families are without shelter—
homeless and ruined." In Texas, the governor, public meetings, and
newspapers vindicated Callahan—as did the American ambassador to
Mexico. In 1857, the Texas Legislature honored Callahan by naming a
new county after him.[68]

Texans denounced Hispanics for fraternizing with Blacks and helping
some to escape. In 1854, Texans caught a Hispanic guiding a runaway to
the border, so they branded his forehead with a T for traitor and gave him
150 lashes. During the mid-1850s, armed vigilantes burned and lynched
to drive Hispanics out of at least four counties. In 1857, white teamsters
destroyed their competition by massacring seventy-five Hispanics.[69]

In south Texas, a rancher, Juan Nepomuceno Cortina, denounced
Americans as "flocks of vampires in the guise of men." Cortina rallied
fellow *Tejanos*, who had "been robbed of your property, incarcerated,
chased, murdered, and hunted like wild beasts, because your labor was
fruitful and because your industry excited the vile avarice which led
them." Ford considered Cortina intelligent, "fearless, self-possessed, and
cunning." Many Mexicans saw him as "destined to chastise the insolent
North Americans and restore Texas to the Mexican Union."[70]

In July 1859 in Brownsville, beside the Rio Grande, Cortina shot
and wounded a marshal who had pistol-whipped a Hispanic cowboy.
Declared an outlaw, Cortina lost his ranch. Seeking revenge, in September he rallied 500 armed supporters who seized Brownsville, where they
looted the stores and executed five Anglos accused of killing Hispanics.
In November, Cortina defeated a counterattack by Texas Rangers, but
they struck again in late December. Defeated, Cortina fled to Mexico,
eluding pursuit by federal troops led by Robert E. Lee. The Rangers

lynched his captured men and burned their homes. Still defiant, Cortina raided across the border to steal horses and cattle from ranches in south Texas. Ford conceded, "To the poor who heard him, Cortina was a sign of hope in a land where hope heretofore had no meaning."[71]

Frustration

Runaway slaves alarmed masters throughout the South. To protect their property, slaveholders demanded active support from the federal government and northerners. Virginia governor John Floyd declared, "The faithful execution of this law . . . is the only means now left by which the Union can be preserved with honor to ourselves and peace to the country."[72]

Northerners bristled at the southern demands for enforcement. The freedom of white men seemed compromised if compelled to help slave catchers. Lincoln complained that "the great body of the Northern people do crucify their feelings, in order to maintain their loyalty to the constitution and the Union." Several northern states passed "personal liberty laws" that gave accused fugitives the rights to testify in their own defense and to have jury trials. These laws also barred state officials from assisting slave catchers.[73]

Southerners felt especially outraged when northern Blacks used violence to help runaways. Henry Clay denounced obstruction from "African descendants; by people who possess no part, as I contend, in our political system." He wanted to know whether the "government of white men was to be yielded to a government by blacks."[74]

Abolitionist papers in the North exaggerated the number of runaways, and southern newspapers reprinted those reports to terrify their readers. Virginians, Kentuckians, and Missourians worried that slavery would erode in the Upper South as more enslaved people escaped. If the Upper South swung into the free state category, the Lower South would become more isolated within a hostile Union. Robert Barnwell Rhett of South Carolina warned that "the supporters of slavery [will] be forced further and further south until they make their last . . . stand on the shores of the Gulf" of Mexico.[75]

Southerners felt cheated of northern support for an institution deemed essential to their way of life. Without an effective Fugitive Slave Law, the Union became, a Virginian charged, an "instrument in the hands of one section for the oppression and injury of the other." An Alabama senator thundered that, if Yankees failed to return fugitives, "this government is and ought to be at [an] end."[76]

THREE ∞ DESTINIES

Let those who are sowing to the wind beware that they do not
reap to the whirlwind. —ELIHU B. WASHBURNE, 1854[1]

Federal census reports deepened southern alarm at losing power
to a growing northern majority. Seven-eighths of immigrants
settled in the northern states, and immigration surged during
the 1840s, when the North's population grew 20 percent faster than the
South's. Robert Barnwell Rhett of South Carolina mourned, "Every
census has added to the power of the non-slaveholding States and diminished that of the South. We are growing weaker, and they stronger by
the day." Already a minority in the House of Representatives, the South
lost parity in the Senate when the Compromise of 1850 added California as a free state. John C. Calhoun of South Carolina attributed "the
great and primary cause" of the "almost universal discontent" in the
South to the fact that "the equilibrium between the two sections, in

the Government as it stood when the constitution was ratified . . . has been destroyed."[2]

To regain power within the Union, southern leaders pushed to expand their society both westward, into federal territories, and southward, into Mexico, Central America, and Cuba. Senator John Slidell of Louisiana explained, "The South has desired the annexation of territory suitable to the growth of her domestic institutions in order to establish a balance of power within the Government that they might protect their interests and internal peace through its agency." Albert Gallatin Brown of Mississippi coveted Cuba and the "Mexican States; and I want them all for the same reason—for the planting and spreading of slavery."[3]

By seizing control of the Caribbean basin, southern expansionists dreamed of capturing the commerce of South America and building a railroad or canal across Central America to tap into the fabled trade of Asia. One southern journal proclaimed that the South "could control the productions of the tropics, and with them, the commerce of the world, and with that, the power of the world."[4]

Expansionists insisted that white Americans should dominate the colored people of subtropical lands by teaching them Protestant morality, modern commerce, and republicanism. Edmund Ruffin of Virginia claimed that an American "conquest of these mongrel and semi-barbarous communities" would be "a benefit to the conquered and to the world." Celebrating slavery as "a blessing alike to the master and the slave—a blessing to the non-slaveholder and the slaveholder," a Virginia politician hoped that "this mild, beneficent and patriarchal institution may cover the whole earth as the waters cover the great deep."[5]

While pushing American expansion southward, southern leaders opposed northern schemes to annex Canada, lest that further weaken the South in the Union. Congressman Lemuel D. Evans of Texas insisted that "emigration is repelled by the frozen snows of the wintry north, by

PREVIOUS PAGE: *(Left) William McKendree Gwin (1805–1885), c. 1860, photograph by Matthew Brady. (Right) David C. Broderick (1820–1859) c. 1859, photograph by unknown.*

its gloomy forests, the howling of its angry winds, and the thick-ribbed ice of its polar lakes," but people naturally felt drawn to "those sunny groves where the golden light lives forever on the grass, and the glory of fruit and flowers never fades." That southern stance irritated northern leaders. Senator John P. Hale of New Hampshire rejected manifest destiny because, he explained, it "always travelled South." Hale added, "If there is a geographical necessity for our expansion, let us go north. We have gone south long enough."[6]

Both antislavery and proslavery leaders felt threatened by the other—and feared subordination if they failed to contain their rivals. In 1854, the abolitionist Wendell Phillips warned, "The future seems to unfold a vast slave Empire united with Brazil & darkening the whole West." Free Soilers dreaded an alleged "Slave Power" plot against common men, while southerners complained of a supposed abolitionist conspiracy to destroy them by provoking slave escapes and revolts. Both sides clashed over expansion in the American West as well as around the Caribbean.[7]

Engine

Stephen A. Douglas hoped to ease sectional tensions by maximizing American expansion in every direction. A fellow politician described Douglas as "talented, ambitious, aspiring and reckless." Short and stout, he had the broad chest and big head of a much larger man. An irritated fellow senator complained that Douglas's legs were "too short, sir. That part of his body, sir, which men wish to kick, is too near the ground!" Admirers called him the "Little Giant," for his small size but large ego.[8]

Born in Vermont and obscurity in 1813, Douglas escaped apprenticeship as a cabinetmaker by heading west and studying law. After brief stops in upstate New York and northern Ohio, he settled in south-central Illinois, a frontier region where lawyers were few and lawsuits many.[9]

Running for office as a Democrat, Douglas impressed voters by his fiery charisma, gregarious bonhomie, and deep, melodious voice finely tuned to popularity. An admirer described the effervescent and energetic Douglas as a "perfect steam engine in breeches." Fueled by alcohol and chewing tobacco, Douglas won election to the state legislature in 1836, got appointed to the state supreme court in 1840, went to Congress in 1843, and became a U.S. senator in 1846.[10]

Douglas loudly championed "the rights of the people" against the "privileges of Property," primarily banks, but he made private exceptions for corporations that enriched him with stock and real estate. Douglas confessed that he "neither felt nor thought deeply on any question," which gave him a useful fluidity on political and moral questions. This man of the people lived grandly in a Washington, D.C., mansion, plying guests with pricey Havana cigars and rich Madeira wine.[11]

In 1847 Douglas married Martha Martin, a southern heiress, who brought him 150 slaves and a 2,500-acre plantation in Mississippi. For political reasons, he denied owning the plantation, but Douglas covertly managed the property and reaped its profits. He also pandered to voters by celebrating white supremacy in Illinois: "Our people are a white people; our State is a white State. We do not believe in the equality of the negro, socially or politically with the white man." Douglas defended slavery in the South because preserving "this political Union is worth more to humanity than the whole black race." The abolitionist Frederick Douglass complained, "No man of his time has done more to intensify hatred of the negro."[12]

Douglas promoted building a railroad from Chicago, where he owned prime real estate, across the continent to the Pacific. But no company could build a railroad across 2,000 miles of vast plains and high mountains without federal land grants and without settlers to buy those lands and provide crops for the trains to carry to market. To attract settlers, the federal government had to dispossess Indians and organize territories to provide law and local government. To satisfy settlers and get his railroad built, Douglas sought to organize two territories west of Missouri and Iowa: Kansas and Nebraska.[13]

Douglas claimed that his territorial and railroad plan would knit the country together, from ocean to ocean, with "continuous lines of settlement," bolstering the Union. Without a transcontinental railroad, Douglas warned, the United States would leave West Coast settlers isolated and alienated, ripe for secession to create their own country. In a contested and vulnerable Union, every schemer promised to produce the elusive unity needed to avert an impending collapse.[14]

But Douglas had a problem: southern congressmen would not cooperate because Kansas and Nebraska lay north of the Missouri Compromise Line of 1820, which barred slavery in northern territories. Southerners wanted no more territories to become free states that would compound the South's minority status in the Union. Missouri slaveholders also worried that free territories to the west would attract runaways from their plantations. A leading Missouri politician, Claiborne Jackson, concluded, "I say let the Indians have it forever. They are better neighbors than the abolitionists, *by a damn sight.*" But southern leaders might accept the new territories if Congress would abolish the Missouri Compromise line, for they hoped to rush in their own settlers to protect Missouri's western flank, and create more slave states.[15]

Adopting the slogan of "popular sovereignty," Douglas proposed an apparent compromise: he would repeal the Missouri Compromise line to allow settlers to decide whether to permit or outlaw slavery in each territory. This populist formula fit the Democratic faith in common voters and enabled Douglas to appeal for both northern and southern support for his Kansas-Nebraska territorial bill. A Pennsylvania senator agreed, "Who has a better right to settle this question than the hardy pioneer, who subdues the wilderness" and "substitutes the neigh of the horse and the bleating and lowing of the herds, for the howl of the wolf, [and] the scream of the panther?" Douglas insisted that "popular sovereignty" would at last drive agitation over slavery out of federal politics, restoring harmony to the country. In March 1854, the Senate passed the Kansas-Nebraska bill.[16]

Douglas relied on Alexander H. Stephens of Georgia to push the bill through the House of Representatives. Afflicted by colitis, a pinched nerve, chronic migraines, and rheumatoid arthritis, Stephens lived in pain, weighed less than 100 pounds, and looked pale as a cadaver. An observer mistook him for "a boyish invalid escaped from some hospital." Stephens described himself as "a malformed, ill-shaped, half-finished thing." Longing for "the highest places of distinction," he felt like "the most restless, miserable, ambitious soul that ever lived." Rejecting "sensuality and sexuality," Stephens never married. After a stint teaching school, he became a country lawyer, thriving through hard work and keen wit. Achieving the Georgia dream (for white men), Stephens bought a large plantation worked by dozens of enslaved people.[17]

During the 1840s, Stephens ran as a Whig to win a seat in Congress, where he befriended Lincoln, who shared his disgust at the Mexican War provoked by President Polk. Stephens then professed the old-school notions that slavery was a moral curse that the South had to endure rather than release millions of Blacks into freedom. Nor did he then favor expanding slavery elsewhere.[18]

But Stephens's views shifted after he nearly died on the piazza of an Atlanta hotel in September 1848. A leading Georgia Democrat, Judge Francis H. Cone, confronted Stephens, accusing him of treason to the South. In reply, Stephens struck Cone across the face with a cane. Pulling out a knife, Cone slashed the frail Stephens six times before bystanders separated them. The congressman barely survived and never regained full use of his right arm. Thereafter, he championed the expansion of slavery west and south.[19]

In 1850, Stephens left the Whigs in disgust when his northern colleagues, including Lincoln, worked to block southern expansion by reviving agitation for the Wilmot Proviso. In May 1854, Stephens helped pass the Kansas-Nebraska bill by a congressional vote of 113 to 100. "I feel as if the Mission of my life was performed," he exulted.[20]

Douglas, Stephens, and Pierce would reap the whirlwind for erasing the Missouri Compromise line. That erasure produced a political earthquake, rearranging the parties along sectional lines. Because northern Whigs had opposed the bill, their southern counterparts revolted and became Democrats, turning the Lower South into a one-party region. While Democrats dominated the South, they declined in the North, where most voters felt outraged by elimination of the Missouri Compromise line. One alienated northern Democrat called the Kansas-Nebraska Act a "firebrand that would set the whole Union on fire." An Albany, New York, newspaper mourned that the wall "to guard the domain of Liberty, is flung down . . . and Slavery crawls like a slimy reptile over the ruins to defile a second Eden." Protestors burned straw men labeled as Douglas, who wryly noted, "I could travel from Boston to Chicago by the light of my own effigy."[21]

In the fall of 1854, northern voters defeated most of the congressmen who had voted for the Kansas-Nebraska bill, costing the Democrats seventy-one of their ninety-three northern seats. In the next Congress, fifty-eight southern Democrats outnumbered their mere twenty-three northern colleagues. Dominant in all but two northern state legislatures in 1852, Democrats lost control of all but two in 1854. Exposed on the shrinking northern wing of that party, Douglas was pushed onto the defensive at home in Illinois and became dependent nationally on southerners, who expected him to serve as their errand boy.[22]

Dissident Democrats coalesced with Free Soilers and northern Whigs to form a new party, the Republicans. They claimed to defend free government against a southern "aristocracy" cast as "the most revolting and oppressive with which the earth was ever cursed, or man debased." Republicans blamed a "Slave Power conspiracy" for violating the Missouri Compromise, deemed a sacred covenant essential to "the Permanency of our Union." Vowing to reserve western lands for common white men, Republicans reasoned, "The effect of slave labor is always to cheapen, degrade, and exclude free labor."[23]

To fend off the Republican surge, northern Democrats doubled down on racism, playing up white supremacy in appeals to northern prejudices. Democrats accused "Black Republicans" of pushing for abolition to unleash "three to five millions of uncivilized, degraded, and savage men" to head north and steal jobs from white workers. Allegedly, Republicans would debase whites to equality with Blacks in political rights and social arrangements—including interracial marriage. Indiana Democrats organized a parade of young girls in spotless white dresses carrying banners labeled, "Fathers, save us from nigger husbands."[24]

Kansas

Antislavery and proslavery leaders competed to control Kansas, the new territory directly west of Missouri. Win in Kansas and the rest of the West would follow, both sides believed. Lose and face regional confinement. David R. Atchison of Missouri assured another southern senator: "We are playing for a mighty stake. The game must be played boldly. . . . If we win, we carry slavery to the Pacific Ocean. If we fail, we lose Missouri, Arkansas, Texas, and all the [western] territories." Congressman Preston Brooks of South Carolina agreed, "The fate of the South is to be decided with the Kansas issue." Accepting that challenge, Senator William H. Seward of New York declared, "God give the victory to the side which is stronger in numbers as it is in right." Rushing in the most settlers would win Kansas and so the West and so the Union.[25]

Initially, settlers went to Kansas enticed by fertile land offered by the federal government for just $1.25 per acre. But they faced the usual hardships of frontier life and a volatile climate. After praising Kansas as "the prettiest Co[untry] in the world," a settler lamented that it would "be warm enough to go naked in the bed, and the next hour it will be cold enough to freeze the tail off the dogs."[26]

Prior to 1856, most of the settlers came from the South, primarily nearby Missouri. Few owned slaves, but many hoped to become masters by prospering on new farms carved from the fertile prairie. To counter the southern settlers, antislavery activists organized and funded Yankee emigrants to Kansas.[27]

To preserve the southern advantage, Atchison rallied Missourians to rush into Kansas and unleash terror on the Yankee newcomers. One of his henchmen exhorted, "Mark every scoundrel among you that is the least tainted with free-soilism, or abolitionism, and exterminate him." Citing his previous experience driving Mormons out of Missouri, Atchison assured a fellow senator, "We are organizing. We will be compelled to shoot, burn & hang, but the thing will soon be over. We intend to 'Mormonize' the Abolitionists." He was right about the shooting, burning, and hanging, but the thing would not end soon in Kansas.[28]

In 1855, the proslavery men could have won a fair election for a territorial legislature, but they took no chances, bringing in hundreds of Missourians to scare away Free Soil voters and stuff boxes with illegal ballots. A proslavery society, the Blue Lodge, paid "a dollar a day & liquor" to recruit "Border Ruffians," described by a Free Soiler as "drunken, bellowing, blood-thirsty demons." Only a third of the 6,000 votes cast in the territorial election came from legitimate residents. The elected legislature consisted of thirty-six proslavery men and just three Free Soilers, who promptly resigned rather than dignify the charade.[29]

Convening their government at Lecompton, the victors legalized slavery and criminalized any criticism of it as subject to two years in prison at hard labor. Helping a slave to escape brought the death penalty. And no one could serve on a jury or vote in Kansas without swearing allegiance to the new territory's proslavery regime.[30]

When the federal territorial governor, Andrew Reeder, protested the electoral irregularities, a proslavery legislator knocked him from his chair and beat him up. Endorsing the proslavery regime in Kansas, Pierce sacked Reeder, who became a Republican. Pursued by Border Ruffians, Reeder fled eastward, crossing Missouri disguised as an Irish laborer. This became complicated when farmers tried to hire him to chop wood. But the disguised Reeder made it to Illinois and became a celebrity speaker on the Republican circuit through the Midwest.[31]

Despite the proslavery regime, Free Soil settlers kept arriving, and by early 1856 they had become the territory's majority. The New England Emigrant Society armed them with new rifles known as "Beecher's Bibles," after a leading abolitionist in New York, Reverend Henry Ward Beecher, brother of Harriet Beecher Stowe. Free Soilers organized militia units, framed their own free-state constitution, and elected a legislature and governor based in Topeka to challenge the proslavery regime at Lecompton. When President Pierce threatened to suppress the Topeka government with military force, Free Soilers vowed to defy "that ninney Frank Pierce."[32]

Some Free Soilers were abolitionists, but most just wanted to keep out all Blacks, free or enslaved. One Kansan explained that their "hatred to slavery was not as strong as their hatred to Negroes." The chief Free Soiler, James Lane, was a former Democratic politician from Indiana who organized a referendum that excluded free Blacks from Kansas by a vote of 1,287 to 453. Lane returned a runaway to his master, explaining "that we were not fighting to free black men but to free white men."[33]

The influx of armed Free Soilers outraged proslavery men as meant to cheat them out of Kansas. Atchison complained that Kansas hosted "an army of hired fanatics, recruited, transported, armed, and paid for the special and sole purpose of abolitionizing Kansas and Missouri." Border Ruffians harassed northern emigrants and seized arms shipments crossing Missouri bound for Kansas. Newcomers increasingly took the longer route via Iowa to avoid Missouri.[34]

In October 1855 a proslavery man murdered a Free Soil neighbor in a dispute over a land claim. In retaliation, Free Soilers burned the cabins of three proslavery men, including that of the murderer. The editor of a proslavery newspaper vowed to kill an abolitionist: "If I can't kill a man, I'll kill a woman, and if I can't kill a woman, I'll kill a child!"[35]

In late 1855, 1,500 Border Ruffians attacked Lawrence, the leading Free Soil town. After shooting a Free Soiler outside of town, the invaders backed off when they found the townspeople well armed behind new fortifications. In May 1856, Border Ruffians returned with five cannon to assault Lawrence. Outnumbered and outgunned, the Free Soil militia let the intruders sack the town, plundering shops and houses, demolishing two newspapers, and burning a hotel and the home of James Lane. A fiery and disheveled populist, Lane hid out, wearing a disguise of old clothes. That did not work, a friend recalled, because "the worse clothes [that] we put on [him], the more like Jim Lane he looked."[36]

The violence in Kansas spilled into Congress in May 1856, when Senator Charles Sumner of Massachusetts delivered a fiery speech entitled "The Crime Against Kansas." After denouncing the Border Ruffians as "the drunken spew and vomit of an uneasy civilization," Sumner insulted their congressional champions, including Andrew P. Butler of South Carolina. Listening in horror, Stephen A. Douglas muttered, "That damn fool will get himself killed by some other damn fool."[37]

Two days later, Butler's cousin, congressman Preston Brooks, stormed into the Senate with a gold-headed cane to beat the unarmed Sumner to a bloody pulp. Sumner survived, but barely, and could not return to work for more than two years. Brooks boasted,

> For about the first four or five licks he offered to make a fight, but I plied him so rapidly that he did not touch me. Towards the

last he bellowed like a calf. I wore my cane out completely save the head, which is gold. . . . It would not take much to have the throats of every Abolitionist cut.

Southerners celebrated Brooks for defending the honor of a relative and their region. They bought for him dozens of new canes to replace the one shattered over Sumner's head. One bore the inscription "Hit Him Again." Southerners justified repressing speech against slavery as essential to avoid a genocidal slave uprising. A Missourian asserted, "In a slaveholding community, the expression of such sentiments is . . . more criminal, more dangerous than kindling the torch of the incendiary [or] mixing the poison of the assassin."[38]

Northern whites felt outraged by the southern celebration of the bloody assaults on Sumner in Congress and on Free Soilers in Kansas. Most Yankees tolerated slavery in the South, but they refused to sacrifice their own free speech. Frederick Douglass concluded that free men "must either cut the throat of slavery or slavery would cut the throat of liberty."[39]

John Brown set out to cut the throats of proslavery men in Kansas. Born in Connecticut, Brown had tried almost everything to get ahead: working as a farmer, tanner, storekeeper, and banker. He embarked on twenty business ventures in six different states—and all failed. Something seemed fundamentally wrong with America, and Brown settled on slavery as the cause. In 1837, before his church, Brown publicly vowed, "Here, before God, in the presence of these witnesses, from this time, I consecrate my life to the destruction of slavery!" Brown impressed Frederick Douglass for acting "as though his own soul had been pierced with the iron of slavery."[40]

In 1855, Brown moved to Osawatomie in Kansas, "to help defeat SATAN and his legions." He survived the first winter on a diet of "bears with a very little milk." On the night of May 24–25, 1856, Brown and seven other armed men (four of them his sons) raided the proslavery hamlet at Pottawatomie Creek, taking five settlers from their beds to hack them to death with broadswords. Although none of the victims owned a slave, all had threatened Free Soilers. Brown declared, "I was doing God's service," reasoning that "Without the shedding of blood there is no remission of sin." He escaped pursuit, but proslavery men burned his home.[41]

As Brown intended, his massacre instigated a deadly civil war of ambushes and cabin looting and burning meant to drive out rivals. The partisans killed about thirty-eight men and destroyed property worth an estimated $2 million. The violence radicalized many of the Free Soilers, who began to assist Blacks escaping from slavery in Missouri. The latest territorial governor, Wilson Shannon, gave up trying to restore order: "Govern Kansas in 1855 and 1856? You might as well attempt to govern the devil in hell." His replacement, John W. Geary, was made of stronger stuff. A veteran of the war on Mexico and politics in San Francisco, Geary deployed federal troops to persuade both sides to stand down.[42]

Lecompton

Discarding Pierce as tainted by the congressional electoral defeats of 1854 in the North, the Democrats instead nominated James Buchanan as their presidential candidate. A sixty-five-year-old Pennsylvanian, Buchanan had long served in Congress and as a diplomat. Buchanan lacked charisma and intellectual curiosity, but he dressed elegantly, stood tall, and had a great stock of white hair. Many Americans thought he looked like a president, but not so former president Andrew Jackson, who derided the chatty Buchanan as "an inept busybody." Never marrying, Buchanan lived for thirteen years with William R. King of Alabama, a fellow bachelor, senator, and diplomat. Deeming the pair effeminate and intimate, Jackson called them "Miss Nancy" and "Aunt Fancy."[43]

Buchanan cultivated southern political friends and shared their insistence that emancipation would lead to a bloodbath: "Is there any man in this Union who could for a moment indulge the horrible idea of abolishing slavery by the massacre of the high-minded and chivalrous race of men in the South?" So, he insisted that northerners should shut up about slavery: "Touch the question of slavery and the Union is from that point dissolved."[44]

In 1856, Republicans ran the western explorer John C. Frémont for the presidency. In northern states they staged massive torchlight parades while chanting, "Free Soil, Free Speech, Free Men, Fremont!" That enthusiasm terrified southern leaders. Robert Toombs of Georgia declared, "The election of Frémont would be the end of the Union, and ought to be." Buchanan agreed that "Black Republicans" were to blame: "The Union is in danger, and the people everywhere begin to know it."[45]

Buchanan won the election by sweeping the South, save for Maryland, while taking five northern states: New Jersey, Pennsylvania, Indiana, Illinois, and California. Capturing 56 percent of the southern vote but only 41 percent in the North, Buchanan owed his victory to fears, especially in the Border States, of a civil war if Frémont won.[46]

As president, Buchanan favored the southern cause in Kansas, so he sacked Governor John W. Geary, whose even-handed efforts to keep peace had outraged the Border Ruffians. "I have learned more of the depravity of my fellow man than I ever before knew," Geary declared— and he had been in San Francisco at the riotous peak of the California gold rush. Denouncing the proslavery territorial legislators as "felons," Geary became a Republican, as had his predecessor Reeder. Kansas was making Republicans, one territorial governor after another. Next up was Robert Walker, a Mississippi planter and politician.[47]

In June 1857, the proslavery territorial legislators pushed forward with elections for a constitutional convention, which the Free Soil majority boycotted. In the June election, a mere 2,200 of 9,250 registered voters participated, selecting only proslavery delegates, who met at Lecompton in September. They wrote a constitution that guaranteed slavery in perpetuity, protected from any future legislative or constitutional change. Bypassing approval by a referendum, the delegates sent their constitution directly to Congress in application for statehood. Breaking with his southern friends, Walker denounced the Lecompton Constitution as "a vile fraud, a bare counterfeit."[48]

Southern leaders demanded that Buchanan accept the Lecompton Constitution and admit Kansas as a slave state. Southern governors and legislatures threatened to secede if Congress did not admit Kansas as a slave state. A Missouri politician warned, "If we cannot carry slavery into Kansas, it is quit[e] obvious that we cannot succeed anywhere else.

The result will be that no more slave states will be created. The majority of the North over the South will in a few years become overwhelming, in both houses of Congress." In February 1858, Buchanan endorsed the Lecompton Constitution and announced that Kansas was "at this moment as much a slave state as Georgia or South Carolina." Feeling betrayed, Walker resigned.[49]

The debacle embarrassed Stephen A. Douglas, who had championed popular sovereignty as the solution to the crisis over slavery in the Union. In 1858 Douglas also faced a tough reelection in Illinois, where fifty-five of fifty-six newspapers condemned the Lecompton Constitution. In a speech to the Senate, Douglas denounced admitting Kansas as a slave state as "trickery and juggle." Southern leaders howled with outrage, castigating Douglas as a backstabber "polluted with the leprosy of Abolitionism." Stephens complained: "Douglas was with us until the time of trial came, then he deceived and betrayed us."[50]

Despite Douglas's opposition, the Senate voted to admit Kansas as a slave state by 33 to 25, but Republicans and some northern Democrats defeated the bill, 120 to 112, in the House. A brawl broke out when a South Carolinian called a northern congressman a "Black Republican puppy." A New York newspaper reported, "There were some fifty middle-aged and elderly gentlemen pitching into each other like so many . . . savages." Stephens despaired, "The Union cannot and will not last long."[51]

The Buchanan administration belatedly submitted the Lecompton Constitution to a referendum in Kansas, where a fair election rejected it 11,300 to 1,788. The Free Soil majority had grown as northerners poured in while few southerners joined them, balking at taking slaves into an insecure territory. Free Soilers also captured the territorial legislature, which shifted the government from Lecompton to antislavery Lawrence. In 1859 a new constitutional convention abolished slavery and allowed free Blacks to settle in Kansas. A triumphant Free Soiler derided the declining proslavery men as "the Ruffians . . . who have not yet died of delirium tremens."[52]

Violence persisted along the border, but the tables had turned, with Kansas's Free Soil vigilantes, known as "Jayhawkers," taking the fight eastward into Missouri's western counties. In December 1858 John Brown and twenty men raided a farm in Missouri to kill a master, liberate eleven slaves, and lead them to freedom in Canada, a journey of 1,100 miles. In western Missouri, a militia commander reported, "A large strip of country within our state is almost entirely depopulated, our citizens driven from their homes and . . . threatened with death should they return." A civil war had begun in the borderland, and the South was losing—which seemed extra bitter after their hopes of 1854.[53]

With "popular sovereignty" Douglas had tried to push the slavery issue out of federal politics and thereby reunite and revitalize the Democratic Party for his own benefit. Instead, he deepened polarization along regional lines and diminished his party in the North, while southern leaders vilified him as treacherous. Nor did he even get his railroad built, as Congress was too bitterly divided to agree on a route. To revive his political fortunes, Douglas pandered to southerners who pushed for American expansion into Central America, Cuba, and Mexico. As expansion westward became more fraught, southerners increasingly favored rogue operations southward by armed volunteers known as "filibusters" (from a Spanish term for freebooters).[54]

Walker

Filibusters were bored and restless men, prone to drink, gamble, and brawl. Some were on the run from larceny, murder, or rape charges. Others had failed as attorneys, engineers, journalists, and doctors. Many were demobilized soldiers who could not readjust to civilian life. To restore their self-esteem, frustrated men sought to win battles, take booty, and seize *haciendas* from allegedly inferior peoples. A newspaper editor insisted that filibusters wanted "to wipe out the memory of a tainted life by a career of desperate and honorable adventure." Their adventures proved more desperate than honorable.[55]

Filibustering violated federal neutrality laws that barred attacks on peaceful countries. Presidents wanted American expansion to appear legal, consummated by diplomacy backed by the threat of federal military force—rather than driven by private adventurers. Federal leaders worried that filibusterers were reckless fools whose invasions outraged countries that might otherwise have been more receptive to American annexation. Filibustering also tainted the American reputation with European governments. In 1856, the British prime minister, Lord Palmerston, derided the United States as a "nation of Pirates . . . every day becoming a more formidable nuisance." To correct that impression, federal officials prosecuted filibusterers, but juries almost always acquitted them as manly adventurers spreading republicanism.[56]

Born in Tennessee, William Walker manifested the restless, shifting ambition of young men driven by a competitive society to seek elusive fame, influence, and money. Walker repeatedly failed but kept on striving, cycling through the three leading professions of white men: medicine, law, and journalism. In 1849, when his fiancée died of cholera, the broken-hearted Walker joined the California gold rush: that great outlet for ambitious and discontented men. Temperamental and contentious, Walker fought three duels, suffering severe wounds. He also spent time in jail for contempt of court.[57]

Failed as doctor, lawyer, and journalist, Walker became a filibusterer. Although slight (about 115 pounds), short (five feet, six inches), abundantly freckled, and draped in a preacher's frock coat, Walker commanded attention with bold words and reckless actions. He described his volunteers as "tired of the humdrum of common life, and ready for a career which might bring them the sweets of adventure or the rewards of fame." They resembled Walker: both victims and champions of a hypercommercial, competitive society.[58]

By seizing control of Central American countries, Walker vowed to introduce republican utopias for white men. But in practice he was a ruthless dictator who executed rivals and insubordinate followers and burned the towns and confiscated the property of people who defied him. An American diplomat noted that Walker treated other men as mere "pawns of the chessboard to be moved and sacrificed to advance the ambitious plans of [Walker]." A disillusioned follower derided Walker as a "freckled little Despot."[59]

In the fall of 1853, with just forty-five men, Walker invaded Baja California in Mexico. With some deft treachery, he seized the capital of La

Paz and proclaimed an independent republic with him as the president. Plundering the town, he alienated the inhabitants, so Walker crossed the Gulf of California to seize the state of Sonora, where the expedition collapsed from dissension, desertion, hunger, exposure, and Mexican resistance. Fleeing back to San Francisco to regroup, Walker faced trial for violating American neutrality laws, but no jury would convict him. A resident explained, "At that time in California it was as unpopular to be opposed to filibustering as it was to be opposed to African slavery, then our most cherished institution."[60]

In the spring of 1855, Walker resumed filibustering by targeting the troubled republic of Nicaragua, which offered tropical plantations and transit rights from the Caribbean Sea to the Pacific Ocean, a route that exploded in value as miners scrambled to reach gold-rich California. In 1851 the hard-driving capitalist Cornelius Vanderbilt of New York procured a monopoly for the key element of that transit corridor: steamboats across the country's large central lake.[61]

Vanderbilt's charter irritated the British, who sought to protect their investments in Central America from what they saw as American aggression. Lord Palmerston grumbled, "In dealing with vulgar-minded Bullies, and such unfortunately the people of the United States are, nothing is gained by submission to insult & wrong." Dependent on British loans, Nicaragua's government renounced their deal with Vanderbilt, so he solicited Walker's help in toppling that regime. With just fifty-seven men, Walker arrived in June 1855 to join Nicaraguan rebels.[62]

By October, the rebellion had won enough victories to compel the government to make a power-sharing agreement that gave Walker command of Nicaragua's army. A month later, he staged a coup, arresting and executing the president. Vanderbilt provided free passage for volunteers to join Walker in Nicaragua, raising his filibusterers to six hundred by the spring of 1856. Walker promised each 250 acres of land and $25 to $30 a month, four times what the U.S. Army paid enlisted men.[63]

Walker's success impressed Stephen A. Douglass, who speculated in Nicaraguan lands. In May 1856 the Pierce administration recognized Walker's government. The American queen bee of manifest destiny, Jane McManus Cazneau, moved to Nicaragua. In exchange for her formidable skills as a publicist, she and her husband procured silver mines and coffee plantations with Walker's help. American newspapers spread her praise of Walker as "the grey-eyed man of destiny."[64]

In September 1856, to attract more southern investors and volunteers, Walker legalized slavery and confiscated lands from Nicaraguans to endow American newcomers with plantations. The new emigrants included 160 Border Ruffians fresh from fighting in Kansas. Walker's measures alarmed Nicaraguans, who dreaded enslavement on the newcomers' plantations. Walker also made a powerful new enemy by double-crossing Vanderbilt, confiscating his ships to reward his rivals for the transit business through Nicaragua. Vanderbilt promptly cut off the flow of volunteers to Walker and subsidized military intervention by neighboring nations—Guatemala, Honduras, and San Salvador (now El Salvador)—whose leaders saw Walker's regime as a menace.[65]

In the spring of 1857, the forces funded by Vanderbilt closed in, inflicting heavy casualties on Walker's men, who were also depleted by a cholera epidemic. Desertion soared as Walker stinted on medical care and failed to pay his troops. One disgusted recruit declared that Walker paid "nothing a month, and six feet of earth." As his force collapsed, Walker fled to an American warship that sailed back to the United States.[66]

Defeated in Nicaragua, Walker returned to a hero's welcome in the American South, attracting throngs to hear him speak. In Georgia Walker asked if southerners would "permit yourselves to be hemmed in on the south, as you are already on the north and west." He promised to restore their power within the Union by reviving his conquest of Central America. A U.S. senator, Pierre Soulé of Louisiana, agreed that if "Nicaragua should become a part of this republic, the preponderance of the North is gone."[67]

But Walker bungled his cause, suffering a shipwreck in a foiled bid to return to Central America in January 1859. Trying again in the spring of 1860, Walker attracted only ninety-seven volunteers. Landing on the coast of Honduras, they suffered heavy losses in skirmishes with government troops. Walker fled to a British warship, but the Royal Naval captain turned him over to Honduran officials, who had him shot on

September 12. In death, Walker became a martyr of proslavery expansion, with Britons and Yankees cast as the villains.[68]

Cuba

Southerners especially coveted Cuba, a rich sugar-producing colony retained by the Spanish in defiance of the republican revolutions that had liberated the rest of Latin America early in the century. Many Americans invested in Cuba as planters or merchants, importing African slaves and exporting sugar and coffee. Cuba produced 60 percent of the sugar and 40 percent of the coffee imported into the United States.[69]

During the 1850s, southerners feared British pressure on Spain to abolish slavery in Cuba. They also dreaded that Cuban slaves might rebel to create another Black republic like nearby Haiti, which had become the great southern nightmare. Obsessing about a supposed British plot to "Africanize" Cuba, a southern leader claimed, "The question is, shall the African or the American Caucasian rule in that lovely island." Southerners extolled Cuba as a tropical paradise ideal for plantation slavery. An expansionist wanted to treat Cuba like a beautiful woman "breathing her spicy tropical breath, and pouting her rosy, sugared lips. . . . She is of age—take her, Uncle Sam."[70]

Some ambitious and well-educated young Cubans longed for independence as a republic to escape from Spain's heavy taxes, onerous regulations, and suppression of a free press. But they also worried that a revolution would weaken their control over the island's enslaved majority. These halfway revolutionaries sought American help to overthrow Spanish rule while averting efforts by slaves to seek freedom. But their American friends meant to exploit the Cuban republicans to annex the island as a slave state that would increase southern power within the United States.[71]

Cuba's leading revolutionary was Narciso López, who fled to the United States to escape arrest for plotting rebellion against Spain in 1848. Settling in New Orleans, López recruited hundreds of volunteers, a mix of Cuban exiles and American opportunists. He also benefited from support by the ubiquitous Jane Cazneau, who promoted American investment in Cuban filibustering. During the spring of 1850, López led 600 armed men in a steamship to land on the coast of Cuba, but they suffered heavy casualties and withdrew in disarray when the local people balked at joining them. Regrouping at New Orleans, López tried again in August 1851 with 400 men, but this invasion collapsed quickly and Spanish officials executed López and fifty other prisoners before cheering crowds in Havana.[72]

After López died, Governor John Quitman of Mississippi, took charge of efforts to invade and annex Cuba. Born a Yankee in New York in 1799, Quitman had taught school and studied law in Ohio, before ambition pulled him south to Mississippi in 1821. Three years later, Quitman married a southern heiress with a fortune in land and slaves that he expanded over the years. By 1850, Quitman owned at least 450 slaves on five plantations that totaled more than 7,000 acres. In a rare moment of reflection, he admitted, "I belong to the fortunate class of men. Whatever I undertake prospers and while some are laboring and toiling for reputation and fame without success, I obtain it without seeking or meriting it."[73]

Relishing his new life as a planter, Quitman derided Blacks as "a happy, careless, unreflecting, good-natured race" ruined by freedom but improved by slavery to "become the best and most contented of laborers." Impressed by his conversion, Mississippi's voters elected Quitman to the state legislature in 1827. After serving as a general in the American invasion of Mexico, he returned home to win election as governor of Mississippi in 1849. Capitalizing on outrage over the Wilmot Proviso and Compromise of 1850, Quitman warned that the South would be "hedged in by a wall of fire." But he overplayed his hand by prematurely pushing for secession from the Union. In 1851, public opinion in Mississippi turned against him, so Quitman quit his race for reelection.[74]

Quitman sought to rebuild his political fortunes by conquering Cuba. Tall, heavy, and muscular, with flowing curly hair, sweeping mustache, and fancy clothes, Quitman looked the part of an adventurer. In 1853, he agreed with prominent émigrés, known as the Cuban Junta, to lead their revolution in return for a bonus of $1 million if he succeeded. He cared little for Cubans, save for keeping most in slavery. Quitman saw

Cuba as the front line of a global struggle to preserve white supremacy through slavery: "Cuba is the battle ground. . . . The European policy is to establish near us negro or mongrel states. Such a result would be fatal to us. Our destiny is intertwined with that of Cuba. If slave institutions perish there, they will perish here."[75]

Alarmed by Quitman's preparations, the Spanish adopted radical countermeasures in Cuba. In 1853, a new captain general, Juan de la Pezuela, suppressed the slave trade and vowed to free slaves illegally imported. Pezuela legalized racial intermarriage (provided the husband was white); invited free Africans to immigrate; and armed a free Black militia to counter filibusterers and revolutionaries. Outraged by this "Africanization" of Cuba, southerners urged Quitman to strike fast, but he would not move until he had raised and trained 3,000 men for combat. He also wanted assurances of support from President Pierce.[76]

Pierce filled his cabinet with fellow expansionists, including Jefferson Davis, as secretary of war, and William Marcy, as secretary of state. Southern expansionists took over the key diplomatic posts: James Buchanan in London; Pierre Soulé in Madrid; and John Y. Mason in Paris. Pierce also consulted the great patroness of expansion, Jane Cazneau.[77]

In 1853 Marcy instructed Soulé to offer Spain $130 million for Cuba—more than six times what the United States had paid Mexico for 525,000 square miles of territory in 1848. But the Spanish clung to Cuba as a source of national pride and of revenue worth $10 million annually to the Crown. Soulé was also the wrong man for a sensitive diplomatic position. A verbose hothead, he had praised filibusters and denounced Spain in many speeches, vowing to speak "tremendous truths to the tyrants of the old continent." Within two months of arriving in Madrid, he shot the French ambassador in a duel and outraged the Spanish monarch by meeting with republicans plotting a coup.[78]

In October 1854, Buchanan, Mason, and Soulé convened in Ostend, Belgium, to coordinate a diplomatic campaign meant to pressure Spain to sell Cuba. Issuing an Ostend Manifesto, the American diplomats justified Cuban annexation as a security imperative. They vowed to protect "our internal peace and the existence of our cherished Union" by preventing "a second St. Domingo, with all its attendant horrors to the white race." Vowing to use force if Spain refused to sell, they concluded, "Cuba is as necessary to the North American republic as any of its present members."[79]

The Ostend Manifesto outraged Yankee and European leaders who expected more decorum from diplomats. American antislavery leaders linked the Ostend Manifesto to the Kansas-Nebraska Acts as the twin faces of militant expansion by the Slave Power. Marcy lamented, "The Nebraska question has sadly shattered our party in all the free states and deprived it of the strength which was needed, & could have been much more profitably used, for the acquisition of Cuba." He obliged Soulé to resign as scapegoat for the fiasco. Seeking to renew diplomacy with Spain, the Buchanan administration also moved to quash Cuban filibusters by prosecuting Quitman for violating the neutrality laws.[80]

Federal prosecution unraveled Quitman's filibustering force gathered at New Orleans. Investors stopped buying the bonds that he peddled to raise funds for Cuban revolution. As the money dried up, unpaid volunteers went home. Invading Cuba also seemed less urgent because Spain replaced Pezuela with a proslavery captain general. And the Cuban exiles withdrew their support because Quitman had subordinated their pursuit of independence to southern interests.[81]

In April 1855, Quitman resigned his command and returned to electoral politics. Quitman won a seat in Congress, but he died in July 1858 from "National Hotel Disease," an affliction that killed dozens of guests at that hotel in Washington, D.C. (They probably succumbed to a paratyphoid fever promoted by defective sewer pipes.) Meanwhile, Buchanan's bid for renewed negotiations to buy Cuba went nowhere.[82]

Santo Domingo

The Pierce and Buchanan administrations also coveted the Caribbean country of Santo Domingo (now the Dominican Republic), a former Spanish colony on the eastern two-thirds of the island of Hispaniola; Haiti held the rest. Most of Santo Domingo's 200,000 people lived in poverty as small farmers or worked on the estates of a richer and whiter elite. But the country had fertile land, promising mines, and good ports that attracted covetous Americans and Europeans. Above all, they lusted after Samana Bay, a deep harbor in a prime location for a naval base and coaling depot for steamships. Coveted by France, Spain, Britain, and America, Samana Bay remained Dominican only because the four powers so warily watched and checked one another.[83]

In 1853, the Pierce administration sent William Cazneau to Santo Domingo as a special agent to seek at least a commercial treaty and at best an annexation of the entire country. His wife, Jane, helped the cause by writing newspaper pieces praising Dominican potential if absorbed into the United States. William confronted "the jealousies of a suspicious people," who feared "that their domain will be seized, the native whites set aside, and the blacks enslaved if Americans gain a foothold."[84]

In 1854, Jefferson Davis sent a young U.S. Army engineer, George B. McClellan, to survey Samana Bay for a naval base. Angered by that survey, the French and British consuls warned Dominican leaders against selling any land to the Americans. In Washington, the British minister to the United States protested and cited the expansionist views of Jane Cazneau. Secretary of State Marcy lamely replied: "I assure you Mr. Crampton, I have had no dealings of any sort with that Lady." In fact, Marcy had sponsored her career since the early 1840s.[85]

William Cazneau had to settle for seeking a commercial treaty. But the Dominican Congress demanded that when visiting the United States, their people, including sailors, enjoy "the same rights and privileges which American Citizens would enjoy on their arrival here . . . without distinction of race or colour, throughout the States composing the Union." That demand would override the laws of southern states that jailed Black sailors while their ships were in port. Appalled by that demand, Cazneau sought to intimidate Dominicans by threatening an American naval attack. Marcy recalled Cazneau and the commercial treaty died.[86]

Slavery Road

Southerners resented that the Compromise of 1850 had hemmed them in to the west by making California a free state. But southern leaders sought, during the 1850s, to reverse that decision by converting California into a slave state while carving another one out of New Mexico. To enhance their western access, southern leaders wanted the federal government to build a railroad from Texas to the Pacific—and not to build one farther north to the benefit of their Yankee rivals, including Stephen A. Douglas. A southern route would enable planters to ship their cotton to the West Coast and across the Pacific to the fabled markets of Asia. Jefferson Davis also expected that such a railroad could flood California with southern settlers who could convert the state to slavery. A California supporter celebrated a southern transcontinental railroad as "emphatically the Southern, yea, what the abolitionists call the *great slavery road.*"[87]

As secretary of war, Davis authorized a survey of four routes across the continent, two northern and two southern. The survey crews submitted mixed reports, but Davis put his finger on the scale to declare that only the southernmost route, hugging the Mexican border, would do. That southern route, however, had a problem: it would dip across the Mexican border through the Mesilla Valley. In 1853, the Pierce administration sent James Gadsden of South Carolina to Mexico to demand a cession of the coveted valley. Gadsden warned Mexican leaders that they had to sell or "resort must be had to the sword, which will end in the absorption of the whole Republic." To avoid a fight, Mexico sold 46,000 square miles to the United States for $10 million in a deal called the Gadsden Purchase.[88]

With the potential railroad route secured, Davis next sought to solve the security problem posed by southwestern Native peoples, especially the Apache bands determined to preserve their homelands. Adapted to a harsh and arid environment of limited resources, Apaches raided their Hispanic neighbors and interloping Americans to take horses, cattle, sheep, and human captives. Their raids daunted travelers from making the crossing to California. Developed in the humid and forested east, the American army lacked the Apaches' ability to survive and fight in arid mountains. Cavalrymen struggled to keep their horses alive and working in an environment lacking fodder and water.[89]

To solve that security problem, Davis drew on the French success in using camels to transport men and supplies in the deserts of North Africa. In 1855, Congress authorized him to buy seventy-five camels. In the American Southwest, camels proved superior to horses and mules: able to travel more than 30 miles a day without water and with little fodder, while carrying heavier loads. But Americans never got over their distaste for camels as dirty, nasty, and ornery, so the army discarded them after Davis ceased to be secretary of war. A few feral camels survived in Arizona at least to 1901.[90]

Meanwhile, northern congressmen killed the southern railroad by blocking federal funding. To keep their dream alive, southern politicians diverted another federal initiative, for a subsidized mail road across the continent, starting in Missouri and ending in San Francisco. In 1857, the postmaster general, who came from Tennessee, directed that the route deviate by 600 miles from a direct shot across the continent, by dipping far to the south into Texas and across New Mexico to southern California before bending north again to reach San Francisco. He then awarded the lucrative mail contract to a firm favored by Democrats, the Butterfield Overland Stage Company, which built an infrastructure in the desert that might later be upgraded to accommodate a railroad: 200 fortified way stations with deep wells.[91]

Davis also sought to swing California into the proslavery camp by cultivating politicians with federal patronage. He found a promising ally in Dr. William M. Gwin. Born in Tennessee in 1805, Gwin had graduated from Transylvania University in Kentucky. Moving to Mississippi, he thrived as a doctor and became the federal marshal. Gwin speculated in land and acquired a large plantation worked by slaves.[92]

Entering politics, he lost his bid for Congress in 1844 and for the Senate in 1846, defeated both times by Davis. Frustrated in Mississippi, Gwin emigrated to California to "devote all my energies to obtaining and maintaining political power." A tall, robust man with a great shock of hair and a booming voice, Gwin exuded the brand of masculinity that played well in frontier politics. His timing was impeccable, for he helped lead the push for California statehood, winning in reward a seat in the U.S. Senate.[93]

In the Senate, he worked closely with Davis, his old rival become new friend, to promote American expansion southward into Cuba and Mexico—and to encourage California's conversion to a slave state. Retaining a large plantation in Mississippi, Gwin praised slavery as the "foundation of civilization." He championed the Fugitive Slave Act and Kansas-Nebraska bill. Granted a monopoly over federal patronage in California, Gwin built a network of ambitious men, almost all southern born, to dominate the state's primary party, the Democrats. They became known as the "Chivalry" because of their aristocratic southern style of life.[94]

The Chivalry dominated California politics during the 1850s. Thomas Butler King (from Georgia) boasted, "No antislavery man can be elected to any prominent office in the State or to Congress." Most voters supported the Chivalry as champions of white supremacy. Gwin declared, "Our people want none but the white race among us; we do not want Negroes or Chinese." California's laws barred Blacks and Chinese from voting, owning land, marrying whites, testifying in court, or attending public schools.[95]

Although the state's constitution forbade slavery, white Californians found plenty of loopholes to keep captive Indians as long-term indentured servants and Hispanic *mestizos* as peons trapped by debt. The Chivalry also indulged southern migrants who brought in enslaved Blacks. Laws against keeping slaves went unenforced, so masters advertised in newspapers to buy and sell them and to recover runaways. Enslaved Blacks remained few—perhaps 1,500 in 1855—but the Chivalry shaped a political and legal climate meant to increase that number.[96]

Slaveholders benefited from the California law that barred testimony by Blacks against whites—a ban that exposed African Americans to kidnappers. In 1858, Archy Lee went to court to claim his freedom, but the state supreme court ruled that his master could send him back to Mississippi for sale. California abolitionists appealed the case to a federal commissioner, who freed Lee. Angered by that ruling, a proslavery politician provoked a duel that killed the commissioner. Masters enjoyed greater legal protection in California than in any other ostensibly free state in the Union.[97]

In 1858–1859, about 500 free Blacks left for British Columbia, pushed by American prejudice and pulled by civil rights in a British colony. A Californian noted, "They are pleased with the idea of being allowed to vote, to testify in courts, & sit in juries." The migrants included Archy Lee.[98]

With Republicans weak in California, the primary challenge to the Chivalry came from Free Soil Democrats, a more plebeian lot known as "the Shovelry." Their Irish American leader, David C. Broderick, had been a New York City stonemason and saloon bouncer with a talent for brawling and a face scarred from a knife fight. Broderick appealed to fellow roughnecks who felt disdained by the Chivalry. Broderick opposed the state's fugitive slave law and discriminatory tax against Chinese immigrants.[99]

In 1859, Gwin and Broderick served as California's two federal senators. Dissatisfied with that power sharing, Gwin turned to his friend David S. Terry. An emigrant from Kentucky via Texas, Terry was a large, strong, and violent man. Serving as a judge on the state supreme court, he laid a pistol on his desk at the start of each session. To provoke a duel, Terry called Broderick a disciple of Frederick Douglass. Those were fighting words in racist California, so Broderick demanded a duel. As the challenged party, Terry got to choose the weapons. Playing a deadly trick meant to diminish Broderick's chances, Terry brought doctored pistols to the dueling ground south of San Francisco, where eighty spectators gathered. On September 13, 1859, Broderick's shot went off prematurely while Terry shot him in the chest. A California jury acquitted the judge of murder.[100]

With support from Gwin, southern California's leaders wanted to form their own state, provisionally called Colorado. Publicly they claimed to seek better representation and greater equity in taxation, but privately they assured Jefferson Davis that their new state would legalize slavery. In 1859, both houses of the state legislature approved, as did the voters in a referendum limited to southern California.[101]

But northern congressmen nixed the bid to divide California and add another state to the Union. This rejection alienated the Chivalry of California, who began to discuss breaking away to create their own nation along the Pacific coast. They would have that opportunity if

a Republican won the presidency in 1860—and that result provoked
southern secession.[102]

A parallel story played out in New Mexico, an arid land, where most
of the people were *Hispanos* living under a territorial government run
by southern Democrats. As in California, New Mexico's officials and
wealthiest *Hispanos* allied to maintain property rights, including the
ownership of captured Indians and indebted peons. Although New
Mexico only had a few dozen Black slaves, territorial leaders hoped to
attract masters bringing in many more to grow cotton beside the rivers
or to work the silver mines. In 1859 the territorial legislature adopted
a slave code written by territorial secretary Alexander Jackson (from
Mississippi), who boasted that he had "perfected the title of the South
to New Mexico."[103]

About 10,000 southern settlers concentrated in the southern reaches
of New Mexico, a region then known as Arizona (which was not then
defined as the western half of the territory), including the Mesilla Valley.
Most were Texans who came to ranch and develop the gold, silver, and
copper mines. By separating to form a distinct territory, they hoped to
revive the push for a southern railroad and obtain more federal troops
to dispossess and kill Apaches who got in the way.[104]

In April 1860, the Arizonans convened to draft a constitution and
select a provisional governor and territorial secretary, both from Texas.
Their proposed constitution included a slave code. The bid had strong
support in the Senate from Davis and Gwin, but northern politicians
killed it in the House of Representatives. That defeat frustrated and
alienated Arizonans, who would welcome an alternative to the Union
if offered by their southern friends.[105]

Serene Highness

Many southerners coveted northern Mexico: the states of Baja California, Chihuahua, Coahuila, Nuevo León, Sinaloa, Sonora, and Tamaulipas. One filibusterer claimed that the South could create twenty-five
slave states with fifty senators in Mexico, and thereby dominate the
Union to "prevent the further agitation of the slavery question." Expan-

sionists also wanted to seize the 125-mile-wide Isthmus of Tehuantepec in southern Mexico, where a railroad could facilitate transportation from the Gulf of Mexico to the Pacific Ocean.[106]

Filibusterers exploited the disordered politics of Mexico and the weakness of that government along its northern border. Blaming the victims for these miseries, American expansionists claimed that only their annexation could bring order to Mexico. Expansionists also argued that the United States had to act fast before the French or British seized the prize.[107]

Along the Rio Grande, filibusterers assisted the rogue "Republic of Sierra Madre" founded by a Mexican opportunist, José María Jesús Carvajal. Born in Texas when it was still a part of Mexico, Carvajal spent two years in the United States, working as a saddle maker in Kentucky before studying divinity in western Virginia. He became fluent in English and embraced Protestantism and slavery. Returning to Texas, Carvajal peddled bibles, surveyed land, and smuggled goods past Mexican border patrols. "His own countrymen call him a Norte Americano," a Texan noted.[108]

In 1851, at Tamaulipas, Carvajal launched a rebellion by posing as a liberator fighting against a military tyranny that unfairly exploited borderlands people. He recruited 300 Texans by promising pay and a free hand to seize fugitives from slavery within his breakaway republic. With their help, Carvajal attacked the key Mexican border town of Matamoros in October. By recruiting Texans, however, Carvajal alienated most Mexicans, who rallied to break his siege of Matamoros and disperse the insurgents. The leader of his Texan allies, John Salmon Ford, noted, "If there is one thing which will fill an average Mexican full to the brim of intense wrath it is the sight of an American." Carvajal fled back to Texas.[109]

Fed up with disorder, Mexico's Conservatives fell for the dangerous allure of their most charismatic and reckless leader, Antonio López de Santa Anna. After leading Mexican forces to many defeats during the American war, Santa Anna had been overthrown and exiled in late 1847. As an exile, he escaped the odium of the unpopular peace treaty extorted by the victorious Americans. A flamboyant opportunist, Santa

Anna insisted that Mexico needed a populist dictator to make the nation powerful and prosperous. In early 1853, a Conservative coup restored Santa Anna to power.[110]

Santa Anna's government dispensed with Congress, arrested and executed dissidents, and censored the press, closing over forty newspapers. The leading Conservative, Lucas Alamán, explained, "Santa Anna well-counseled—that will be the whole Constitution." Ruthlessly centralizing power in Mexico City, the regime eliminated state legislatures, appointed the governors, and monopolized taxation. Santa Anna jailed and later exiled the Liberal governor of Oaxaca, Benito Juárez, who relocated at New Orleans, where he supported his family by making cigarettes and cigars to sell in bars.[111]

For a while, Santa Anna became popular for executing bandits without civil trials, temporarily reducing crime. But soon people said that only Santa Anna was allowed to rob Mexicans. Fonder of sizzle than substance, Santa Anna spent lavishly on public ceremonies and parades, all closely regulated, including the length of mustaches permitted to civil servants. He increased taxes and borrowed money to enlist more soldiers dressed in flashy new uniforms. In a characteristic move, Santa Anna rewarded some teachers with shiny medals while he cut funding for their schools. Santa Anna erected many statues in his honor and had his picture displayed in every government building. A new national anthem sang his praises as he created two national holidays to celebrate "His most Serene Highness, Major-General, President of the Republic, National Hero, Knight Commander of the Great Cross . . . and Grand Master of the National and Distinguished Order of Guadalupe."[112]

Aware that his army was better for parades than fighting, Santa Anna dreaded another conflict with the United States, which the Pierce administration threatened in 1853 unless Mexico ceded the Mesilla Valley of southern Arizona. But Santa Anna also feared the political fallout of any new cession because he based his comeback on denouncing the Liberal politicians who had surrendered territory to the hated Americans.

To counter the northern threat, Mexican diplomats tried to draw

European monarchies into an alliance against the United States. The Mexican ambassador to France offered to exploit "the weak side of the United States—slavery." Aided by a French, Spanish, and British fleet, a Mexican army could land in the South to proclaim "the liberty of the Blacks," destroying plantation society. To entice European support, Santa Anna even offered to "resign his power into the hands of any foreign prince who would be supported on his throne against the rapacity of the United States." But European leaders considered Mexico too poor and weak to help them, and they worried that war with the United States would cost them their immense trade with the North Americans.[113]

Deprived of European help, Santa Anna had to cede the Gadsden Purchase to the United States. By selling more land to gringos, Santa Anna alienated his countrymen, for the cession exposed as hollow his bombastic claims to have made Mexico great again. Most of the American purchase money disappeared into his pockets and those of his cronies. His centralizing measures also threatened the *caudillos* who dominated many states and tenaciously clung to their private armies and control of local taxes.[114]

In March 1854, a revolution began at Ayutla in southern Mexico. A month later, Santa Anna attacked the rebel stronghold at Acapulco but suffered an embarrassing defeat. Enraged, the dictator burned villages and executed prisoners on his retreat to Mexico City. More people rallied to the rebels, including Juárez, who returned from exile. In August 1855 Santa Anna gave up and fled, while rioters sacked his property in the capital.[115]

Mexican disorder emboldened Henry Crabb, a boyhood friend of William Walker. In 1848 in Vicksburg, Mississippi, Crabb had killed a newspaper editor in a street brawl. Fleeing prosecution, he moved to California to become the Stockton city attorney and a proslavery state senator. In 1852 Crabb wrote the California law protecting slaveholders. Losing a bid for the U.S. Senate, Crabb became a filibusterer. In 1857, Crabb invaded Sonora with eighty-nine men to "erect another slave state." Crabb naively expected assistance from a *caudillo*, Ignacio Pesqueira. Distrusting the intruders, Pesqueira instead rallied resistance to them: "Long live Mexico! Death to the filibusters! . . . Let them die the death of wild beasts." Pesqueira crushed and captured the filibusters, executing all but one, a fourteen-year-old boy. The victors decapitated Crabb and pickled his head in vinegar for display.[116]

Knights

Born into a poor family in rural Virginia, George Bickley ran away from home at age twelve. During the following fifteen years, he wandered through four states while mastering phrenology: the pseudoscience of studying bumps in heads to assess character and predict futures. Moving to Cincinnati in 1851, Bickley forged medical credentials to become a professor at the Eclectic Medical Institute, which taught quack medicine to credulous students. Bickley married a wealthy widow, who provided his means to speculate in real estate and publish a newspaper. In 1857, however, his wife caught Bickley embezzling her funds, so she kicked him off the family farm and got a divorce. A publishing colleague described Bickley as "restless and scheming as he was shallow, very vain of his person, exceedingly fond of military display and constantly engaged either in devices to borrow money and crazy schemes of speculation."[117]

During the late 1850s, Bickley created a fantasy world for sale to others by founding a secret society with a very public profile: the Knights of the Golden Circle. This society promoted filibustering to acquire an arc of territories around the Caribbean, including Mexico. Calling that arc the Golden Circle, Bickley allured initiates with promises of wealth through American expansion. Declaring that "this is a selfish organization, which looks to the pecuniary interests of its friends," Bickley promised each initiate an officer's commission and 6,400 acres of Mexican land. But Bickley made out best of all by collecting initiation fees and monthly dues. Bickley urged every southern master to contribute a dollar per slave to promote "the Americanization and Southernization of the Republic of Mexico."[118]

Touring widely, Bickley gave proslavery speeches and organized chapters (known as "castles") throughout the South. Offering gaudy trappings of chivalry and plenty of military drill, the Knights appealed to southern men who indulged in violent fantasies couched as Christian duty. Bickley exhorted his followers, "Knights of the Golden Circle, let us be men—Christian and consistent men—energetic Anglo-Americans. Let us move boldly on in our labor of saving Mexico and of strengthening the South." Bickley promised to establish "a great Democratic monarchy—a Republican Empire, which shall vie in grandeur with the old Roman Empire." His recruits included a handsome young actor, John Wilkes Booth. Bickley's movement especially thrived in Texas, where he organized thirty-two castles scattered across twenty-seven counties.[119]

Bickley told supporters that the South had to seize Mexico before Yankees did so to hem in southern slavery: "No greater calamity could befall the South than the planting of free-soil colonies in Northern Mexico." Bickley meant to transform Mexico though ethnic cleansing:

> The Mexicans have just about finished the job of killing each other. . . . They are imploring the Americans to come in, finish the work, quietly bury them and take their country in payment for the job. Who will be the executioner—who will put this man out of his misery?

In 1859, an Arkansas reporter worried that Bickley was "a most dangerous man. . . . He is playing with the most dangerous passions of the southern people."[120]

Bickley could organize secret societies, shake down contributors, and disseminate proslavery and expansionist propaganda, but he could not actually lead men into combat. In March 1860 he invited his knights to assemble in south Texas for an invasion of Mexico. Two thousand arrived to find little of the provisions, arms, and ammunition that Bickley had promised. After stealing a few horses on the Mexican side of the Rio Grande, the knights dispersed homeward. Disgusted by the fiasco, they reduced Bickley to a figurehead role within the society that he had founded. Thereafter, the knights focused on promoting southern secession from the Union.[121]

Scorpion

To contain the South, some antislavery northerners wanted to preempt subtropical lands for free labor—just as they did with western territories. In 1858 Senator Seward warned southerners that the cause of free labor had "driven you back in California and Kansas; it will invade you soon in Delaware, Maryland, Virginia, Missouri, and Texas. It will meet you in Arizona, in Central America, and even in Cuba." By relocating American Blacks to free colonies, Republicans could reassure voters that former slaves would leave the United States, whitening the republic. By encircling the South with free territory, the promoters hoped to accelerate the collapse of slavery. They shared one conviction with proslavery men: that slavery had to expand to survive. The abolitionist James Redpath vowed to surround "the Southern States with a cordon of free labor within which, like a scorpion girded by fire, Slavery must inevitably die." He referred to trapped scorpions that sting themselves to death.[122]

But masters would fight for independence rather than sting their system to death. To justify secession, Robert Toombs of Georgia warned: "We are constrained by an inexorable necessity to accept expansion or extermination." But secession would lead to a civil war and that war might unravel slavery, as northern invaders recruited Black allies. Redpath understood that only war could kill American slavery: "Unless we strike a blow for the slaves—as Lafayette and his Frenchmen did" during the American Revolution, "or unless they strike a blow for themselves, as the negroes of Jamaica and Hayti, to their immortal honor, did—American slavery has a long and devastating future before it."[123]

FOUR ∽ THUNDER

The atmosphere of our Republic is getting foul and needs a
thunderstorm. A touch of war would do positive good.
—*MISSOURI REPUBLICAN*, JAN. 6, 1860[1]

M elchor Ocampo was a *mestizo* orphan adopted and raised by
a wealthy family in the central Mexican state of Michoacán.
Sent to Europe, Ocampo obtained an elite legal and scientific
education, which led him to analyze and denounce the hierarchies of
Mexican life. Blaming poverty and inequality on the wealth and power
of the Catholic Church, Ocampo wanted to abolish its legal privileges
(known as *fueros*) to allow freedom of conscience in a reformed society
where all religions were equal. Returning home, he became the Liberal governor of Michoacán, where his defense of individual freedom
horrified Conservatives as anarchic. They hated Ocampo as a traitor
to their class.[2]

After overthrowing Santa Anna, Ocampo and other radical Liberals

known as *Puros* sought to transform Mexico into a cohesive nation committed to legal equality, individual civil rights, social mobility, economic
development, and meritocratic government. That nation would enable
every individual to compete equally in the market for property and in
politics for influence. This new liberal order attacked the powerful men
and mediating institutions of the old regime: Church, army, and quasi-
feudal landlords. In contrast to the Catholic Church, which emphasized the original sin and fallen state of humanity, Liberals saw people
as improvable if empowered with equal rights and access to education.[3]

Liberalism appealed to Mexico's middle class in towns and cities,
especially to *mestizos*, who resented the traditional monopoly on wealth
and power exercised by a wealthy white elite. Liberalism advanced,
a supporter claimed, "the aspiration of all thinking men and of the
unfortunate classes that have the desire to better themselves." Liberalism had far less appeal to the Indian and rural majority, which distrusted individualism because it dissolved their corporate groups and
communal property.[4]

In 1856, the new Liberal government moved aggressively to write its
social vision into the law. In November, as minister of justice, Benito
Juárez drafted and secured passage of the *Ley Juárez*: a law reducing (but
not abolishing) the legal *fueros* of the Catholic Church and the army. The
minister of finance, Miguel Lerdo, wrote the *Ley Lerdo* to compel the
Church to sell its vast real estate holdings at discounted prices to tenants.
In Mexico City, the Church owned half the buildings. Nationwide, the
Church held about a fifth of the real estate.[5]

To consolidate and expand these reforms, the Liberals converted their
Congress into a constitutional convention. The delegates did take a
break to attend a theatrical performance of *La Cabana del Tío Tomas*
(*Uncle Tom's Cabin*). Led by Ocampo, *Puros* drafted a new constitution
that mandated freedom of conscience, speech, movement, and association. The constitution also prohibited any extradition of Black refugees

PREVIOUS PAGE: *(Left) John Brown (1800–1859), c. 1859, print by William Sartain.
(Right) Edmund Ruffin (1794–1865), c. 1859, photograph by unknown.*

from slavery in the United States. Seeking to expand the state and shrink the Church, Liberals terminated the *fueros* of the Catholic Church, including the right to conduct civil courts. To secularize education, the constitution promised government-funded schools for all Mexicans.[6]

The purest of the *Puros* worried that their constitution would not suffice to transform a country of extreme inequality where most people lived in poverty. Ponciano Arriaga worried, "Ideas are proclaimed and facts are forgotten. The Constitution should be the law of the *land*; but the condition of the *land* is not . . . considered. Are we to practice popular government and have a hungry, naked, and miserable people?" Arriaga sought radical land reform, taking property from wealthy landlords including the Church to bestow on the poorest peasants. But that went too far for most of his colleagues, many of them landlords or their lawyers. In February 1857, the convention proclaimed the new constitution and required all government officials to swear allegiance to their movement, known as *La Reforma*.[7]

The new constitution outraged Conservatives, especially Catholic bishops, who denounced *La Reforma* as "atheistic" and anarchic. A Conservative leader protested, "Placing sovereignty in the hands of the people means placing control in the hands of the ignorant." Instead, power "must rest in the hands of the just and learned." Denouncing Liberals as crypto-Protestants, Church leaders denied that Mexicans had a "freedom to err" by defying the Pope. Bishops excommunicated anyone who supported the new constitution. They even denied last rites and burial in consecrated ground to soldiers who remained loyal to the Liberal government. In the countryside, Conservatives launched the "War of the Reform" under the rallying cry of "religion and *fueros*."[8]

Implementing a radical constitution proved far more difficult than writing it. Lawyers and writers, the constitution's authors were intoxicated with words but unable to agree on deeds. Ocampo lamented, "We Liberals do not like leaders. . . . We always subordinate persons to ideas." Reacting against Santa Anna's dictatorship, the constitution empowered a unicameral Congress to control a weak president. *Puros* considered such a design more democratic, more responsive to the public will.[9]

President Ignacio Comonfort was a temporizer who sought an elusive

middle ground in Mexican politics. Noting his "absolute lack of character, [and] his great dearth of convictions," Ocampo declared, "I believe
that what is wanted is a hard hand. Time will tell who is right."But that
hard hand came from a general, Félix Zuloaga, who commanded the
garrison at Tacubaya, a suburb of the capital. In December 1857, Zuloaga
coerced Comonfort to renounce *La Reforma*.[10]

Feeling betrayed, Liberals denounced Comonfort. Dozens of Liberals resigned in Congress, and Liberal governors coordinated resistance to the coup. In January 1858, Zuloaga seized control of the capital
to sack Comonfort and make himself president. Benito Juárez fled to
Veracruz, where he declared himself the legitimate president, rallying
Liberal support.[11]

A brutal civil war erupted with the Liberals based at Veracruz, while
the Conservatives held Mexico City. Neither side had secure control
of the countryside, where a destructive banditry prevailed. In Mexico
City, the American ambassador, John Forsyth, lamented, "Evil & only
evil fills the land. . . . The prisons are filled with Liberals."[12]

Zuloaga did not last long, toppled in January 1859 in a coup by
another general, Miguel Miramón. Handsome, dashing, devout, and
ruthless, Miramón ordered captured Liberals executed as heretics and
traitors. His key subordinate, Leonardo Márquez, outdid his master. In
April 1859, Márquez crushed a liberal army at Tacubaya, taking hundreds
of prisoners. Thorough in his massacres, Márquez killed not only the
prisoners but the doctors and medical students who had treated wounded
Liberals rather than let them die. Márquez gloried in his new nickname,
"The Tiger of Tacubaya." Endorsing the massacre, Miramón hosted a
festive triumph for Márquez in Mexico City.[13]

The civil war radicalized Liberals, who destroyed church altars,
façades, and images of saints. To save Mexico, Liberals sought to separate church and state—and subordinate church to state while mandating
religious freedom for all. By setting up civil courts to handle births,
marriages, and deaths, Liberals challenged the Church's power over
key transitions in the lives of Mexicans. To shrink the public presence
of the Church in the streets, the government permitted only three religious festivals: Easter, Corpus Christi, and Christmas. By confiscating

Church properties, including monasteries and convents, Liberals hoped to break its political power—while raising funds for the government. By reselling church properties, the Liberals also hoped to redistribute land to ease inequality and spark economic growth.[14]

The American president, James Buchanan, worried that a European power would seize Mexican territory as collateral for unpaid debts. Both Americans and Europeans coveted the northern states of Mexico and the Tehuantepec transit corridor between the Gulf of Mexico and the Pacific. John Forsyth declared, "Mexican institutions are crumbling to pieces, and interposition to gather up the wreck, from some quarter, is as certain as it is indispensable. . . . Shall that interposition be American or European?" If France, Britain, or Spain intervened, Forsyth predicted that Mexico would become "the battleground for the maintenance of American supremacy in [North] America."[15]

In early 1859, Buchanan sent a special agent, William Churchwell, to Veracruz to assess conditions in Mexico. Churchwell sympathized with the Liberals as upholding "man's capability for self-government," while Conservatives sought "the restoration of monarchical rule or absolute despotism." Estimating that two-thirds of Mexicans favored the Liberals, he concluded that "the people of Mexico have exhibited a fidelity to the principle of constitutional Government scarcely to have been expected from their past history."[16]

Surprised to find "a full-blooded Indian" as the Liberal president, Churchwell underestimated Juárez as "a distrustful and timid politician . . . of a mild and benignant disposition; in his intercourse, modest like a child." The American assumed that real power lay with Melchor Ocampo, a more conventional leader: "Ocampo is a gentleman of great native intellect, and of considerable parts and learning, inflexible in his resolves, peremptory in his views, rather prompt in discourse and impatient of contradiction, but high-minded and, like his chief, incorruptible." In fact, the more dazzling Ocampo had learned to defer to Juárez as the steadiest of Liberals.[17]

Encouraged by Churchwell's reports, the Buchanan administration supported the Liberal government and sent a new ambassador, Robert McLane, to Veracruz. In December 1859, McLane and Ocampo concluded a treaty. In return for $4 million, the Liberal regime agreed to lease two tax-free transit corridors in perpetuity with permission for American troops to patrol: at Tehuantepec and across northern Mexico from the Rio Grande to the Pacific port of Mazatlán. Liberals hoped that these concessions would attract American investment to develop the railroads needed to exploit Mexico's resources. Conservatives, however, howled that Juárez had betrayed the nation by compromising the country's territory.[18]

Claiming an American protectorate over Mexico, Buchanan sought to tip the military scales of the civil war in favor of Juárez. The American president sent warships to seize vessels bearing munitions to supply the Conservative army besieging Veracruz. Deprived of ammunition, Miramón lifted his siege and withdrew back to the central highlands. That setback emboldened Zuloaga to try to reclaim the presidency, but Miramón imprisoned him, declaring, "I will show you how Presidents are made."[19]

In the American Senate, the McLane-Ocampo Treaty disappointed almost everyone. Designed, as one newspaper put it, to be "all things to all men so that it may catch some," that protean quality became a liability among senators consumed by mutual suspicion in 1860. Regarding Buchanan as corrupt, weak, and inept, few senators trusted anything he favored. Many senators balked at empowering a president to send troops into another country without a congressional declaration of war. Protectionists did not like the mutual lowering of tariffs. Many senators worried about entangling the United States in Mexico's apparently endless civil wars. Some southern senators disdained Mexicans as a mixed-race people unworthy of a treaty. Louis T. Wigfall of Texas "did not want Mexico or her mongrel population. Juárez and his Indian crew could not govern themselves, and if brought into contact with our people would contaminate them."[20]

Both southerners and Yankees worried that the treaty would weaken their home region by strengthening their rivals. A New Orleans newspaper noted, "The Republicans object" to adding Mexican land "because, they say, it will be slave territory, and the Southern democrats object to it because it will, they say, be free territory." A Georgia newspaper denounced the treaty for advancing the Yankee "object of hemming us in forever." In May 1860, the Senate killed the treaty by a vote of 27 to 18.[21]

Despite that diplomatic setback, Juárez's regime built a larger and better army. Defeating Conservative forces in the summer and fall of 1860, Liberals swept into Mexico City in January 1861. Miramón and other Conservative leaders fled to Cuba or Europe. United during the civil war, Liberals divided into factions once restored to national power. Ocampo lamented, "Unfortunately the Liberal Party is essentially anarchic, and will not cease to be so for many thousands of years" in contrast to the authoritarian Conservatives who "obey blindly and uniformly."[22]

Civilization

Prior to 1815, British officials had valued Indians as military allies needed to defend Canada against American invasion. Britons largely left Native cultures alone and treated chiefs with diplomatic respect, bestowing annual presents of goods and munitions. First Nations peoples regarded those presents from the Crown as their just deserts for guarding the colony against invaders and for sharing their land, fish, and game with colonists. Canada West (now Ontario) lacked the long, bloody history of settler wars that had generated so much fear and hatred of Natives in the United States. Canada also did not have the democracy for white men that, in the Union, favored wars to remove Indians. North of the border, the British Crown retained military power and gloried in a paternalism that provided more restraint in managing Natives.[23]

After 1815, however, imperial officials wanted to reduce spending on presents by discarding the Natives as allies. Those officials also meant to take Native land to accommodate an influx of immigrants seeking farms. In Canada West, colonial officials began to restrict First Nations people to enclaves known as "reserves" akin to American reservations. On those reserves, missionaries and officials could accelerate culture change by promoting Christianity and European ways, including private farms and domestic livestock. Natives resented the new policies designed to strip them of their language, traditions, and tribal identity and leadership.[24]

By 1850, the 15,000 First Nations people of Canada West were swamped by two million settlers. Claiming a monopoly on "civilization," Canadian leaders regarded Native cultures as inferior and doomed by nature and progress to collapse. John A. Macdonald declared, "All we can hope for is to wean them, by slow degrees, from their nomadic habits" and "absorb them or settle them on the land." Most Natives struggled with the total cultural change demanded of them. Macdonald rejected what Natives wanted: to remain distinct and sovereign nations, adapting at their own pace and in their own way to settler society.[25]

In 1857, as attorney general for Canada West, Macdonald drafted the key Canadian Indian policy for the century, the Gradual Civilization Act. It detailed a legal process for a Native to renounce tribal status by applying to a board of examiners, composed of white men. The applicant had to demonstrate education, freedom from debt, and good moral character. After a trial period of three years, he could receive private ownership of fifty acres, subtracted from his band's reserve. Then the former Native could become a full Canadian citizen with the same rights as a white man, including the vote.[26]

The Canadian Parliament passed Macdonald's bill with only a single dissenting vote. That dissenter wondered, "Why should this bill be pressed through without getting . . . the opinion of the Indians themselves or their chiefs?" Familiar with Natives, he added, "At their Council meetings, the Indian chiefs deliberated quite as sensibly as honorable members did in this house, and sometimes even more so." But the other members of parliament were paternalists who insisted that they knew what was best for Indians: to cease being Indians.[27]

First Nations chiefs denounced the new law as a threat to their cohesion, sovereignty, and culture. "There is nothing in it to be for their benefit, only to break them to pieces," a chief declared. First Nations also felt threatened in 1858, when the British Crown unilaterally dropped the traditional annual presents of trade goods. Two years later, the Crown transferred management of Native affairs entirely to the Canadian government, sacrificing imperial claims to protect their long-time allies. Referring to Queen Victoria, the chiefs declared, "They do not wish to be given over from . . . the Great Mother's care to the Provincial authorities."[28]

Gold

Far to the west, along the Pacific coast, the Hudson's Bay Company (HBC) ran a British colony based on Vancouver Island and the adjoining coast, then known as New Caledonia. A network of fur trading posts pivoting around Fort Victoria, in 1855 the colony had only 700 colonists, most of them company employees and dependents. Few Britons settled in a distant colony where they found, the governor confessed, "the absence of every thing like comfort." The newcomers lived beside many more Natives, subdivided into many nations, including the Nlaka'pamux.[29]

In 1856, the Nlaka'pamux discovered gold in the Thompson River. To protect their salmon-rich rivers and streams, they ordered American intruders to stay away. Found fishing for salmon, a barely literate miner reported, "The cheaf sed them fish was thar liven and we had no rite to take them and for us to pout them back. We dun so at once. . . . The brit American indins dident like the amaracans a toll."[30]

But nothing could stop the miner invasion that began in the spring of 1858. The great California gold rush had played out for common miners, leaving thousands underemployed and frustrated. Enticed by news from the north, a miner explained, "I have spent the best portion of my life in chasing after gold which has unfitted me for any other occupation, and to throw away the present chance appears to me like sacrificing all my past years of toil."[31]

In 1858, thirty thousand American miners poured into New Caledonia. Clad in red flannel shirts, blue jeans, heavy boots, and broad-brimmed hats, they brought metal pans and pickaxes for probing streams, sand bars, and hillsides for golden flakes and nuggets. Flimsy settlements of tents and wooden shanties popped up along the Thompson and Fraser Rivers. Gamblers, pimps, prostitutes, and storekeepers harvested gold from the miners. An English journalist described a new mining camp as "filthy and unsavoury—so exactly like its inhabitants." The newcomers polluted and dammed streams and rivers, ruining the salmon fishery essential to the Natives.[32]

The Hudson Bay Company struggled to cope with thousands of well-armed men. A Canadian reported, "Every man had his revolver & many a large knife also, hanging from a leather belt." Governor James Douglas worried that the newcomers would "establish an independent government, until by force or fraud, they became annexed to the United States."[33]

Born in Guyana (beside the Caribbean), Douglas was partially African in descent, and he had married a half-Cree woman: the sort of racial mixing that would have disqualified him from office in the United States. Douglas required miners to take out a license, limiting each claim to 144 square feet. For enforcement, he relied on a Royal Navy warship anchored at the mouth of the Fraser River.[34]

In 1858, to strengthen Douglas's hand, imperial authorities made him governor of a new crown colony—British Columbia—that included New Caledonia. Dispensing with any elected legislature, Douglas ruled by decree, declaring that "the best form of government . . . is that of a wise and good despotism." Polite but firm, Douglas impressed a colonist as "a glove of velvet on a hand of steel."[35]

During the summer of 1859, a pig broke into the potato patch of an American settler on San Juan Island, along the border. He shot the pig, which belonged to the HBC. When the company demanded compensation, the settler refused, and an American general sent troops to occupy the island under the command of Captain George Pickett, a fiery Virginian of later notoriety. British warships anchored off the island and landed a company of marines to hold one end. Both sides agreed to an armistice while diplomats sorted out ownership, which took a dozen years. During the interim, both garrisons drank and ate together to celebrate one another's national holidays. Only a single pig died in the brief "Pig War."[36]

Quirky and quaint, the Pig War attracts popular history writers, who neglect the bigger and grimmer Indian conflict provoked by invading miners within British Columbia. Confident in their superior numbers, the newcomers treated Indians as vermin, plundering, ousting, and killing them. At Okanogan Lake, miners found a Native village deserted. Breaking into caches of nuts and berries, the intruders gorged themselves and emptied the rest in the lake, a witness reported, "so that the Indians should not have them for provisions for winter." Then the armed miners waited in ambush for the Natives to return home. Seeing the ambush, the Indians fell on their knees to surrender, waving their arms to show that they were unarmed. The miners opened fire, and the lake ran red with blood from dozens of corpses. "It was a brutal affair," the witness reported, "but the perpetrators of the outrage thought they were heroes and were victors in some well-fought battle."[37]

Following American protocols, the miners held mass meetings to elect officers and organize companies before marching out of their camps, a trader noted, "in military formation, the stars and stripes at their head." Another witness reported, "The miners . . . went out to fight and kill all the Indians they could find, and found several camps of them, and just killed everything, men, women, and children." The victors burned villages and destroyed caches of food, while the starving survivors fled into the mountains, away from the rivers that had sustained them for centuries.[38]

Before the miner influx, Governor Douglas had treated Natives with diplomatic respect and had protected their villages from dispossession. In 1858, however, Douglas felt overwhelmed by the miner invasion, coming in numbers that he could not control. Confronting them risked an embarrassing defeat that would discredit his government. While Douglas stood down, the miners imposed their American solution on the Natives.[39]

Dred Scott

At the end of the eighteenth century, Roger B. Taney grew up in a rich family on a Maryland plantation worked by enslaved people. An idealistic young man, Taney freed the eight slaves that he inherited. Becoming a lawyer, he supported the American Colonization Society, which sought to purge the United States of Blacks, free as well as enslaved. As a young lawyer, Taney insisted that "the evil of slavery" was "a blot on

our national character, and every real lover of freedom confidently hopes
that it will be . . . wiped away." But Taney favored gradual, voluntary
emancipation by masters, so he opposed any government interference
with slavery.[40]

A lucid speaker with a sharp mind and polished manners, Taney
became Maryland's attorney general in 1827. A Democrat, he impressed
President Andrew Jackson, who tapped Taney to serve as his attorney
general and, later, as secretary of the treasury. In 1836, Jackson elevated
Taney to the Supreme Court as the chief justice, replacing the late John
Marshall. Where Marshall had been a staunch nationalist who expanded
federal authority, Taney championed states' rights.[41]

As he aged, Taney warmed to slavery and soured on Yankees, especially abolitionists, denouncing them as menacing fanatics. Regarding
the Federal Constitution as a limited compact between equal states to
protect all forms of property, including slaves, he dreaded the political
power of a northern majority. In 1855, Taney overruled his wife and
daughter who wanted to escape Maryland's summer heat and fevers by
vacationing in Newport, Rhode Island. Unwilling to concede any superiority to the North, Taney instead took the family to a resort in Virginia, where both wife and daughter died of yellow fever in September.
Taney channeled his grief into increased rage at critics of the South.[42]

The most important case in Taney's judicial career involved Dred and
Harriet Scott, an enslaved couple. During the 1830s, they belonged to an
army surgeon, John Emerson, who was posted to a fort in Minnesota,
then a free territory north of the Missouri Compromise line of 1820.
Emerson took them back to Missouri, where the Scotts sued for their
freedom, citing their sojourn in a free territory. After losing in the state
courts, the Scotts appealed to the U.S. Supreme Court.[43]

President Buchanan hoped for a Supreme Court decision that would
protect slavery in the federal territories and thereby discredit the antislavery Republicans. He privately assured one of the justices: "The great
object of my administration will be, if possible, to destroy the dangerous
slavery agitation, and thus to restore peace to our distracted country."
Without any sense of irony, Buchanan insisted that protecting slavery
would bolster the Union and thereby extend "civil and religious liberty

throughout the world." Taney also hoped to terminate "Northern insult and Northern aggression."[44]

In March 1857, by a seven-to-two vote, the Supreme Court ruled against Dred and Harriet Scott, forcing them to remain enslaved. Taney's decision argued that no federal court could hear the Scotts' appeal because no Black could ever be a citizen of the United States. The Chief Justice insisted that Blacks were an "inferior class of beings, who had been subjugated by the dominant race." According to Taney, even free Blacks "had no rights which the white man was bound to respect."[45]

Despite dismissing the case, Taney insisted on ruling against any federal restriction on slavery in the territories as an unconstitutional attack on private property rights. Determined also to strike down the popular sovereignty doctrine of Stephen A. Douglas, Taney claimed that no territorial legislature could restrict slavery. Two northern justices dissented, pointing out that Blacks in several northern states had long been citizens. They also vindicated federal restriction on slavery in territories, citing the Northwest Ordinance of 1787 and Missouri Compromise of 1820.[46]

Buchanan celebrated the Supreme Court decision and declared that every federal territory was open to slavery "by virtue of the Constitution." But the decision outraged most northerners. In New York, a Republican newspaper insisted that the ruling converted the Constitution into "a bulwark of inhumanity and oppression."[47]

In 1857, the United States, Canada, and Mexico adopted measures of citizenship that defined inclusion and exclusion. In the Dred Scott decision, the Taney Supreme Court limited civil and political rights to white men. In stark contrast, during the same year, the new Mexican constitution erased racial distinctions to render all citizens equal before the law. While Mexican Blacks welcomed that inclusion, Native peoples resented the erosion of their traditional rights as distinctive communities. So too did the Indigenous people of Canada who balked at becoming individual citizens under the Gradual Civilization Act of 1857. They clung to sovereignty as First Nations to preserve their distinctive identities and cultures. While American Blacks coveted inclusion in American society as equal, individual citizens, Native peoples wanted to be left alone in their own homelands.

During the late 1850s, the Buchanan administration denounced Mexican racial equality as a destabilizing threat to American slavery. The Mexican constitution of 1857 refused to return fugitives from the American South: "All slaves who tread the national soil recover their liberty by that very fact." The U.S. ambassador, John Forsyth, accused Mexicans of embracing "the mania of negrophilism" to betray "white blood . . . the master blood of the earth . . . which has conquered and civilized and Christianized the world." He threatened war if Mexico continued to "free our Slaves, as fast as they put foot on Mexican soil."[48]

Debates

In Illinois in 1858, Senator Douglas faced a tough reelection against the Republican candidate, Abraham Lincoln. Douglas worried, "I shall have my hands full. He is as honest as he is shrewd, and if I beat him my victory will be hardly won." Douglas considered Lincoln "the best stump-speaker, with his droll ways and dry jokes, in the West."[49]

Lincoln challenged Douglas to debates before hundreds and sometimes thousands of citizens, most of them common farmers. Dapper in an elegant suit, the short and stocky Douglas contrasted with the tall and rumpled Lincoln. Ignoring other issues, the candidates focused on the rights of Blacks and the future of slavery.[50]

Lincoln blamed the chaos in Kansas on Douglas's doctrine of popular sovereignty. Detecting a proslavery plot to dominate the country, Lincoln denounced the Dred Scott decision as a threat to freedom in every northern state: "I believe this government cannot endure, permanently half *slave* and half *free*. . . . It will become *all* one thing or *all* the other." He urged voters to favor Republicans, who "consider slavery a moral, social, and political wrong" over "the modern Democratic idea that slavery is as good as freedom, and ought to have room for expansion all over the continent."[51]

Counterattacking, Douglas relied on race baiting, denouncing Republicans as seeking social and political equality for Blacks. Lincoln, Douglas argued, "thinks that the Negro is his brother. I do not think the Negro is any kin of mine at all." Douglas insisted that the republic was "made by the white man, for the benefit of the white man, to be administered by white men." Casting whites and Blacks as competing in a zero-sum game, Douglas added, "I would not blot out the great inalienable rights of the white men for all the negroes that ever existed."[52]

Put on the defensive, Lincoln denied that he would allow Blacks to vote or marry whites. He just wanted them to enjoy the rewards of their own labor. By defending that right Lincoln protected laboring white men from an insidious southern plot to dominate them as well as Blacks. He rejected "all this quibbling" about racial inequality: "Let us discard all these things, and unite as one people throughout this land, until we shall once more stand up declaring that all men are created equal."[53]

Eager to run for president in two years, Douglas first needed to win reelection in Illinois, where most voters opposed the expansion of slavery, but he also had to avoid saying something that would offend southern Democrats. To exploit that vulnerability, Lincoln asked how Douglas could reconcile popular sovereignty with the Dred Scott decision that barred any territorial legislature from banning slavery. At their debate in Freeport, Douglas retorted that "slavery cannot exist a day or an hour anywhere, unless it is supported by local police regulations" to enable masters to recover runaways. This position became known as the "Freeport Doctrine."[54]

Douglas and Lincoln campaigned to influence elections for the state's legislature, which would select the U.S. senator. Republican legislative candidates won 125,430 votes to 121,609 for Democrats. But the latter had gerrymandered the districts to secure fifty-four seats to forty-six for the Republicans, assuring Douglas of reelection. National press coverage celebrated Lincoln's debate performance, and his edge in the popular vote impressed Republicans, for Illinois would be a key state in the next presidential election.[55]

The Freeport Doctrine infuriated southerners, who concluded that Douglas had tricked them with popular sovereignty and favored northern settlers in the federal territories. Accusing Douglas of enlisting "under the banner of that hideous fanaticism which threatens to crush the constitution and the South," Congressman Q. C. Lamar of Mississippi concluded, "Then perish the Democracy of the North! And, if need be, perish the Union!" Jefferson Davis derided Douglas as "our little grog drinking, electioneering Demagogue." Davis then rallied the southern majority in the senate's Democratic caucus to strip Douglas of his key chairmanship, of the Committee on Territories. To override popular sovereignty, Davis demanded a legal code to protect slavery in all the federal territories. Unacceptable to northern voters, such a code would, Douglas warned, destroy the northern wing of the Democrats, the only party that could hold the Union together.[56]

The rift between southern and northern Democrats threatened their prospects in the next presidential election. Douglas had wide and passionate support from northern Democrats, who saw him as the only candidate who could hold their region against the rising Republican tide. And northern Democrats resented southern domination of their party and the Union.[57]

Yancey

In 1808, the United States had banned the import slave trade from Africa. During the 1850s, however, some southerners pushed to lift that federal ban by arguing that slavery was a positive good for enslaved people as well as their masters. In Texas, a district judge told a grand jury, "I have no more doubt of the right of a civilized and Christian nation to capture the African wherever he may be found, and subject him to labor, enlightenment, and religion, than I have of one of our people to capture a wild horse on the prairies of the West and domesticate and reduce him to labor." A renewed slave trade would, another southerner added, offer "a sort of spite to the North and defiance of their opinion."[58]

An eloquent lawyer, planter, and editor, William Lowndes Yancey of Alabama led the push for reviving the import slave trade. At age thirty-four, Yancey had killed a white man for insulting him as a "damned liar." That man was his wife's uncle. After shooting the uncle, Yancey had clubbed him with the pistol and stabbed him for good measure. Convicted of manslaughter, Yancey served only three months in jail and paid a $1,000 fine. He remained defiant: "I have done my duty as a man, & he who grossly insulted me lies now, with the clod upon his bosom."[59]

Impressed by Yancey's deadly sense of honor, Alabama voters elected him to their state legislature in 1840. Four years later he joined Congress, but Yancey quickly soured on national politics. Returning home after two terms, Yancey barnstormed through the South to promote southern secession. A friend praised his speeches as "seasoned with the salt of argument, the vinegar of sarcasm, the pepper of wit, and the genuine champagne of eloquence." Those speeches became spicier as he dosed his neuralgia with alcohol and morphine.[60]

Deeming slavery just and foundational to southern society, Yancey demanded a reopening of the import slave trade. He asked, "If it is right to buy slaves in Virginia and carry them to New Orleans, why is it not right to buy them in Africa and carry them there?" He sought to "wipe out from our statute books the mark of Cain which has been placed upon our institutions."[61]

Reviving the overseas slave trade promised to halt the soaring price of slaves by increasing the supply for sale. Proponents worried that slavery would lose popular support if fewer white men could afford to buy Blacks. Supporters also hoped that thousands of new slaves would strengthen southern expansion: "With cheap negroes we could set the hostile legislation of Congress at defiance. The slave population . . . would overflow into the territories, and nothing could control its natural expansion."[62]

In the Senate, Jefferson Davis pushed to withdraw the federal ban and allow states to permit the slave trade. But the Senate balked, and no state government, not even in the Lower South, quite dared to risk international condemnation by reopening the import slave trade. And masters in the Upper South profited too much from the domestic slave trade to support reopening competition from Africa.[63]

But some southerners defied the federal ban with growing impunity. In 1858, Charles Augustus Lafayette Lamar of Savannah smuggled in 400 slaves from West Africa. A grand jury indicted Lamar, but a trial jury acquitted him. Mobs then harassed the grand jurors until they publicly renounced opposition to the slave trade as the "sickly sentiment of pretended philanthropy and diseased mental aberration of 'higher law' fanatics."[64]

Action

After five years of fighting slavery in Kansas, John Brown was fed up with the pacifism of most abolitionists: "Talk! Talk! Talk! That will never free the slaves. What is needed is action." Brown proposed to invade Virginia with an armed force to provoke a massive slave revolt. The rebels would then build a maroon society in the Appalachians as a bastion for wider attacks meant to destroy slavery and masters throughout the South. Most of Brown's financial backers balked at his scheme, citing "the manifest hopelessness of undertaking anything so vast with such slender means." But Brown counted on divine reinforcement: "If God be for us, who can be against us?"[65]

Brown did get support from Dr. Alexander Milton Ross, a Canadian abolitionist and ornithologist who had toured the South, where he helped at least thirty-one slaves escape to freedom. Ross found widespread networks of young men and preachers willing to assist escapes and keep his secrets. "On many occasions, I have placed my life in the hands of coloured men without the slightest hesitation or fear of betrayal," Ross recalled.[66]

Meeting Brown in Ohio in 1857, Ross admired his "intelligence, coolness, tenacity of purpose, and honesty. He appeared about five feet ten inches in height, slender, but wiry and tough." Ross concluded, "Never before or since have I met a greater or more remarkable man than Capt. John Brown," who was "a chosen instrument in the hands of God to let the oppressed go free."[67]

In 1858, Brown drafted a constitution for a new nation of racial equality meant to transform the United States. Refuting Taney's Dred Scott decision, Brown's constitution outlawed slavery and declared all people, of every race, equal citizens. In April 1858 Brown went to Canada to pitch his constitution and plan of attack to Black leaders. First and foremost was Harriet Tubman, the Underground Railroad conductor who had settled at St. Catherines to evade arrest under the Fugitive Slave Law. Calling her "the General," Brown praised Tubman as the toughest and bravest person that he had ever met. More impressed by

Brown than his plan, she agreed to raise funds for the cause but balked at joining the attack.[68]

After meeting with Tubman, Brown headed west to Chatham, a Canadian center for Black settlement and activism—and home to Martin Delany. As a rule, Delany disliked white abolitionists as paternalistic, but he admired Brown for treating Blacks as equals and fighting for them. In May 1858, Delany helped Brown convene thirty-four Black and twelve white abolitionists to hear and endorse his plans. Chaired by Delany, the convention chose Blacks to serve as president, vice-president, and cabinet officers of the provisional government. Brown became their military commander.[69]

Later in 1858, when Brown postponed his raid for another year, Delany lost interest and, instead, revived his dream of founding a Black nation far from the United States. In the summer and fall of 1859, Delany visited the Niger Valley of West Africa to locate his colony. When Delany returned to Canada to recruit emigrants, he found that Brown had followed his suggestion to seize the federal armory at Harpers Ferry. With guns from the armory, Brown meant to arm Black rebels whom he hoped to rouse from the countryside.[70]

Frederick Douglass rejected Brown's invitation to join the raid, deeming the target too dangerous. Douglass warned Brown that he would "never get out alive." Another former slave, Shields Green, also understood that the raid was suicidal but joined anyway: "I believe I'll go down wid de old man." Green deemed their sacrifice essential to provoking a final crisis over slavery in the United States.[71]

Brown led eighteen men into Harpers Ferry after dusk on October 16, 1859. At the arsenal they overwhelmed the lone guard, and then sent out scouts to look for slaves to join the revolt for freedom. Those scouts accidentally shot a free Black who was at the wrong place at the wrong time. Although no mass revolt erupted, some enslaved people set fire to barns and haystacks in support of Brown. "Night after night the heavens are illuminated by the lurid glare of burning property," the *Richmond Enquirer* reported.[72]

During the next day, hundreds of Virginia and Maryland militiamen converged on Harpers Ferry to besiege the firehouse of the arsenal, where Brown and his men holed up. A prolonged firefight killed two of Brown's sons. Another fatality was Dangerfield Newby, who had joined the revolt to help his enslaved wife and seven children escape from a nearby farm. After militiamen shot him down outside the firehouse, they mutilated his body and tossed it to pigs to eat. In Newby's pocket they found a letter from his wife, Harriet: "Oh dear Dangerfield, com[e] this fall without fail, monny or no Monny. I want to see you so much. That is the one bright hope I have before me."[73]

That morning Colonel Robert E. Lee was at home in Arlington, Virginia, supervising a wheat harvest by his slaves. Summoned to nearby Washington, D.C., Lee took charge of ninety Marines sent to Harpers Ferry. With a battering ram and bayonets, Lee's marines burst into the firehouse, killing more raiders and capturing five including Brown, who was badly wounded.[74]

Trials

Governor Henry A. Wise ordered Brown tried for treason against Virginia in Charles Town (now in West Virginia). Brown meant to turn defeat into victory by carrying a calm and dignified defiance to the grave. Brown assured his wife, "I can recover all the lost capital" by "hanging for a few moments by the neck, and I feel quite determined to make the utmost possible out of defeat." He added, "In my death I may do more than in my life." Brown told interrogators that he acted from "sympathy with the oppressed and the wronged that are as good as you and as precious in the sight of God." In response to those who called him mad, Brown declared, "I may be very insane. But if that be so, insanity is like a very pleasant dream to me."[75]

On November 2, when invited to make a final statement, Brown announced his own death sentence before a Virginia judge could do so: "I forfeit my life . . . and mingle my blood further with the blood of my children, and with the blood of the millions in this slave country whose rights are disregarded by wicked, cruel, and unjust enactments, I say, let it be done." On December 2, he went to the gallows, leaving a last note, "I, John Brown, am now quite *certain* that the crimes of this *guilty land will* never be purged *away* but with Blood." Lee commanded 264 federal troops and 1,000 state militia, who surrounded the gallows to prevent any last-minute rescue attempt. The witnesses included an actor named John Wilkes Booth, who said of Brown, "He was a brave old man" but a "traitor and terrorizer."[76]

Brown's grudging admirers included Governor Wise, who marveled, "He is a bundle of the best nerves I ever saw [although] cut and thrust and bleeding and in bonds. He is a man of clear head, of courage, fortitude, and simple ingenuousness. . . . He is a fanatic, vain, and garrulous, but firm, truthful, and intelligent." Wise praised Brown to warn southerners that abolitionists included resolute men who belied the stereotype of Yankees as cowards.[77]

Two weeks after Brown died, Virginians hanged four of his comrades, erecting separate gallows for the two whites and two Blacks. One of the Blacks, John Copeland, had written, "I am soon to stand and suffer death for doing what George Washington, the so-called father of this great but slave-cursed country, was made a hero for doing." White medical students took the Black bodies away for dissection at their school. A Yankee visitor marveled at Shields Green's "unclosed, wistful eyes staring wildly upward, as if seeking, in a better world, for some solution to the dark problems of horror and oppression so hard to be explained in this."[78]

One of the raiders, Osborne P. Anderson, escaped capture and returned home to Chatham, where Mary Ann Shadd helped compose and publish his story. Celebrating Brown as a martyr, African Americans held memorial services and draped their churches in black for mourning.[79]

Democrats blamed the raid on Republicans, particularly Seward for his "higher law" speech of 1850 and his 1858 insistence that the United States was on the brink of an "irrepressible conflict" over slavery. Stephen A. Douglas assured the Senate "that the Harpers Ferry crime was the natural, logical, inevitable result of the doctrines and teachings of the Republican Party," which he considered "an Abolition party under the name and disguise of a Republican party." Put on the defensive,

Republicans denounced Brown's raid as treasonous madness and reiterated their love of law and order and Union.[80]

A few Yankee freethinkers did defend and celebrate Brown's raid. The philosopher Henry David Thoreau declared, "John Brown's career for the last six weeks of his life was meteor-like, flashing through the darkness in which we live. I know of nothing so miraculous in our history." Thoreau's friend and mentor Ralph Waldo Emerson crafted an essay entitled "Courage" to praise Brown as a saint who would "make the gallows glorious like the cross."[81]

Ignoring the many northerners who disavowed Brown, southerners fixated on the few who praised him, concluding wrongly that most Yankees were foes. A Virginia legislator insisted that Brown's raid revealed to the "whole South as if by one vivid flash of light" the "true character of the danger before them" from a hostile North.[82]

Terror

Although sixty-five and in shaky health, Edmund Ruffin hastened to Charles Town to join the militia guarding Brown's execution. Ruffin hoped that abolitionists would try to rescue Brown: "If it is done, & defeated, everyone engaged will be put to death like wolves." Yet Ruffin felt moved by Brown's stoic dignity in the face of death. An extremist on the other side of slavery, Ruffin could see his reflection in Brown.[83]

Born in 1794, Ruffin came from a long line of Virginia tobacco planters. Ruffin pioneered and publicized the use of marl (deposits of ancient seashells) as a fertilizer to revitalize moribund fields. His method required intensive labor from many slaves. Setting aside youthful qualms about slavery, Ruffin launched a magazine that promoted slavery and agricultural improvement.[84]

Hypersensitive and needy for attention, Ruffin never felt satisfied that his work and views received enough praise. A friend and fellow agricultural reformer, James H. Hammond, declined to review a book by Ruffin lest it make him "mad as the devil if the whole article were not devoted to eulogizing him."[85]

In 1859 Ruffin obtained several of Brown's pikes as props to warn southerners of their peril. Ruffin took one to Washington, D.C., to impress southern congressmen and distributed others to southern governors for display in state capitols. Each bore Ruffin's label: "Sample of the favors designed for us by our Northern Brethren." Ruffin also wrote a novel, *Anticipations of the Future*, set in the mid-1860s, when a triumphant southern confederacy slaughtered Yankee invaders, an indulgent vision "amusing to my mind."[86]

Spooked by Brown's raid, southerners expected more abolitionist plots to provoke revolts, so they repressed internal dissent. An Atlanta newspaper declared, "We regard every man in our midst an enemy to the institutions of the South, who does not boldly declare that he believes African slavery to be a social, moral, and political blessing." Southern states or vigilantes banned Yankee newspapers, ousted teachers from the North, and drove out ministers who criticized slavery. A New York journalist thought that southerners were "going daft" and "no longer see anything as it is."[87]

Armed mobs searched for abolitionists, focusing on Yankee visitors and the occasional poor white deemed too friendly with enslaved people. A few suspects were lynched. In December 1859, the British consul at Charleston, Robert Bunch, reported:

> I do not exaggerate in designating the state of affairs in the Southern country as a reign of terror. Persons are torn away from their residences and pursuits; sometimes tarred and feathered, ridden upon rails, or cruelly whipped; letters are opened at the Post Offices; discussion upon slavery is entirely prohibited under penalty of expulsion, with or without violence, from the country. The Northern merchants and Travelers are leaving in great numbers.

Three weeks later, a British immigrant working as a stonecutter in Columbia, the state capital of South Carolina, spoke out against slavery. Seized by a mob, he suffered a brutal flogging followed by a coat of hot tar sprinkled with feathers, while the governor and legislators watched and applauded. Bunch could do nothing.[88]

Hinton Rowan Helper was the nightmare of southern planters: a common white who rejected slavery and publicized his views. Helper came from a farm family in a hilly county of North Carolina where plantations were few. After failing as a storekeeper and gold miner, he blamed Blacks and their masters for repressing social mobility by common whites. In 1857, in New York, he published *The Impending Crisis of the South*, which mustered census statistics to depict the southern economy as lagging far behind the North in everything except cotton cultivation.

Helper concluded that slavery distorted southern society, enriching and empowering an elite that exploited slaves and dominated common whites. Slavery, he reported, "makes us poor; poverty makes us ignorant; ignorance makes us wretched; wretchedness makes us wicked, and wickedness leads to the devil!" He insisted, "Nothing short of the complete abolition of slavery can save the South from falling into the vortex of utter ruin."[89]

A racist abolitionist, Helper summarized his creed as "Death to Slavery! Down with the Slaveholders! Away with the Negroes!" Seeking to whiten society, he favored deporting them after freeing them. Dreading bodily contact with Blacks as "a gross shame, a shocking indecency, and a glaring crime," Helper avoided hotels and restaurants that employed Blacks. He felt deeply disturbed by plantation masters who entrusted their children to Black wet nurses.[90]

Selling 150,000 copies by 1861, *The Impending Crisis* impressed Republicans, who produced a more concise version to distribute freely as a campaign document. Helper's case enabled them to claim that limiting slavery would help common whites in the South. That Republican embrace of Helper enraged southern leaders. A Virginia congressman accused Republicans of "stimulating my negroes at home to apply the torch to my dwelling and the knife to the throats of my wife and helpless children."[91]

Although Helper exaggerated the alienation of common whites, southern leaders wanted to take no chances. They denounced him as a race traitor who attacked a slave system essential to the security of all white people. Southern states banned and burned Helper's book. North Carolina mandated the death penalty for anyone importing the book more than once. Mobs beat or lynched those who praised Helper. In Buchanan, Texas, vigilantes burned alive a young peddler carrying copies of *The Impending Crisis*.[92]

Fire

In July 1860, in north Texas, suspicious fires destroyed the business districts of a dozen towns, including Dallas. Blaming slaves allegedly agitated by abolitionists, vigilantes rounded up hundreds of Blacks for brutal interrogation. A Texan reported, "In Dallis County they ar[e] Whipping about thirty Negros p[e]r Day. The Negros ar[e] Confessing all about the plot. They say that the Abolisionists have promised them there freedom if they would burne all the towns Down in the State." Allegedly, the plotters also poisoned wells with strychnine to eliminate white men and then force "their fair daughters into the embrace of buck Negroes for wives": the ultimate nightmare of southern white men.[93]

Dismissing the legal process as too slow and insufficiently deadly, Texans relied on vigilantes holding kangaroo courts enforced by lynch mobs. Community leaders—doctors, editors, lawyers, planters, and merchants—composed the vigilante committees. Mounted and armed men patrolled towns and counties at night to enforce a curfew on Blacks, whipping and sometimes lynching violators. Vigilantes tortured until they got confessions to confirm their suspicions: that a secret society of abolitionists known as "The Mystic Red" lay behind the plot. Most of the suspects were peddlers and preachers from the North.[94]

In Dallas County, many whites wanted to lynch every Black in the county: hundreds of people and, so, an expensive proposition that alarmed masters. In a compromise, the vigilante committee hanged three and whipped all the others. A witness said that hundreds "were rounded up like cattle" and "whipped without mercy." At least one died from the whipping. That did not satisfy hardliners, who burned two more Blacks to death.[95]

By the end of the summer, Texas vigilantes had killed at least fifty Blacks and twenty-five whites, including two men simply because they owned some rat poison. Two others died for receiving northern newspapers. A Texan attested, "The school boys have become so excited by the sport in hanging Abolitionists that the schools are completely deserted, they having formed companies, and will go 15 or 100 miles on horseback to participate." In the privacy of his diary, a minister lamented that as "savage deeds of blood and carnage" became routine "the most tender hearted naturally become relentless and cruel."[96]

In Fort Worth, a citizen's meeting focused suspicion on Anthony Bewley, a Methodist minister from Missouri who "had been seen perched on rail fences talking with negroes several times." Enticed by a thousand-dollar reward offered by the citizens, bounty hunters tracked Bewley down in Missouri and dragged him back to Fort Worth, where they hanged him on September 13. To the bitter end, Bewley proclaimed his innocence and denounced abolitionists. After a few weeks, the locals scraped the flesh from his bones so that they could display his skeleton on top of a store. Boys liked to go up on the roof to play "by bending the joints of the arms and legs" while mocking the fate of the "old abolitionist." There Bewley's sun-bleached bones remained until at least 1867.[97]

All the executed were innocent. The fires had erupted midday, when extreme August heat set off newly introduced phosphorus matches on store shelves. With daily temperatures often over 110 degrees, 1860 was the hottest and driest summer that anyone could remember. Some store clerks saw matches spontaneously ignite, but no one ever caught anyone setting a fire or poisoning a well. None of the executed had any ties to abolitionists. But the combination of heat, drought, and a pending presidential election ignited a mass panic. A Texan with the apt name of A. W. Sparks blamed "the conclusions of a mad people."[98]

Throughout the South, Democratic newspapers endorsed tales of poison and arson in Texas as a spreading menace, imperiling the lives of all white women and children. In October 1860, sixteen-year-old Sarah Lois Wadley of Vicksburg, Mississippi insisted,

> The Abolitionists have sowed the seeds of dissension and insurrection among us, those seeds are fast ripening and a bloody harvest seems impending; they have burnt our homesteads, killed our citizens, and incited our servants to poison us. . . . They shout

Freedom and Union, but they would take away our freedom and
give it to the negro.

This intense fear prepared most southern whites to accept secession as a
matter of life and death should a Republican become president.[99]

Fun

Southerners had long sought to silence discussion of slavery in Congress,
lest that talk reach enslaved people and inspire deadly revolts. Southern
members tried to intimidate Yankee critics by threatening to beat them
with canes or challenging them to duel. During the mid-1850s many
Republican congressmen responded in a more combative style. Defending their right to speak freely, these Republicans insulted slaveholders and
brawled with those who came at them. Fighting Republicans became
celebrities who attracted newspaper endorsements and adoring crowds.[100]

The fighting Republicans included John "Bowie Knife" Potter of
Wisconsin. Potter won his nickname by refusing to back down when
challenged to a duel by Roger Pryor, a Virginia Democrat. As the
challenged party, Potter got to choose the weapons, opting for bowie
knives. A Texan would have relished that duel, but Virginians valued their bodies and clothes too much, so Pryor backed down, rather
than employ such "vulgar" weapons. Now the Republicans could
crow that southerners were blustering frauds who dared not fight.
In 1860, the Republican national convention honored Potter with a
seven-foot-long "monster Bowie knife," inscribed "Will Always Meet
a Pryor Engagement."[101]

In 1860, armed confrontation became routine on the House and Senate floors. Senator James H. Hammond of South Carolina noted, "The
only persons who do not have a revolver and a knife are those who
have two revolvers." Hammond expected "a general fight in one or the
other House with great slaughter" because "no two nations on earth
are or ever were more distinctly separate and hostile than we are here."
Assuring Ruffin that a bloody end was near for the Union, Hammond
invited him to "come & see the fun."[102]

FIVE ❧ DISUNION

It seemed to me that the people were crazy, and we were
wild crazy. —H. W. BARCLAY, A GEORGIA SECESSIONIST, 1861[1]

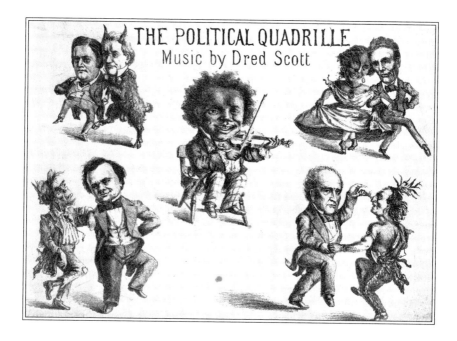

During the summer of 1860, the Prince of Wales, eighteen-year-old Albert Edward, the eldest son of Queen Victoria and Prince Albert and heir to the British throne, visited Canada. Prince Albert explained that his son went to serve "the Canadian wish to show the Americans how happy, free, and yet monarchical it is possible to be." Touring from Newfoundland to Canada West, the young prince attracted cheering throngs who celebrated belonging to the world's most powerful, prosperous, and stable empire. They cherished an imperial tie that kept at bay their numerous, powerful, and vulgar neighbors, the Americans. A Toronto newspaper claimed that without the protecting empire, Canada would "at once drop to the insignificance of Illinois or that dreary state, Vermont."[2]

To display their progress, Canadians dressed up towns with bunting, flags, banners, and triumphal arches made of wood but painted to look like stone. In Ottawa, the Prince supervised the ceremony to place a cornerstone for the new Canadian Parliament building. Displaying their Anglophilia, the architects adopted a neo-Gothic style in gray stone, thereby rejecting the neoclassical, white capitol buildings favored in the republican United States. By impressing imperial leaders, the Toronto *Globe* expected that Canada would be "looked upon as of greater importance, more interest will be taken in our welfare, more attention will be paid to our desires."[3]

But the royal visit encountered Canada's tensions between Catholics and Protestants. Banned in Britain for anti-Catholic rhetoric and violence, the Orange Order was legal and powerful in Canada West, where the Protestant majority resented Irish and French Catholics. Orangemen claimed that no men on earth loved the queen and empire more than they did.[4]

The Order controlled Toronto's city government, including the police. In 1855, an American circus visited Toronto and, after a performance, the clowns got drunk and visited a brothel claimed by Orangemen as their turf. A fight broke out, and the Americans won. Unwilling to accept defeat by a bunch of clowns, the Orangemen attacked the circus grounds, toppling tents, burning wagons, and pummeling performers. Their fellow Orangemen, the Toronto constables, looked on and claimed to know none of the rioters, who proved their prowess as the greatest clowns in Toronto.[5]

In September 1860, the prince's steamboat reached Kingston, where

OPPOSITE: *"The Political Quadrille, Music by Dred Scott," 1860, cartoon by unknown, mocking Breckinridge in the upper left paired with Buchanan as the devil; upper right shows Lincoln with a black woman; lower right presents John Bell with an Indian; lower left has Douglas with a ragged Irishman.*

two thousand Orangemen greeted him by bellowing anti-Catholic songs. Wearing orange ribbons, rosettes, and sashes, they erected two large arches decorated with symbols of their order. By claiming public space, Orangemen asserted their supremacy in Canada West. One exulted, "No other society or body of men could turn out in such strength, or with such an amount of flags, banners, regalia, and music as the Orangemen."[6]

But the prince had strict instructions from the imperial government to steer clear of the Order. His chaperone, the Duke of Newcastle, directed that the prince stay on board their ship. After two days of standoff, boat and prince steamed westward, leaving behind angry Orangemen singing destruction to Catholics. At the prince's next stop, the lake port of Belleville, hopes for a quieter welcome were dashed by two hundred persistent Orangemen arriving by train from Kingston to reenact their defiant welcome. Once again, the boat steamed away, to the dismay of local people who had prepared a lavish meal, decked houses with the Union Jack, and built ten arches "richly ornamented with garlands of flowers." Proceeding on to Cobourg, the prince could land, feast, and dance, because the local Orangemen agreed to appear as regular, peaceable subjects without regalia, flags, and provocative songs. A train loaded with pursuing Orangemen from Kingston broke down in a remote location that defied repair until the prince had left Cobourg. Accidents will happen when a railroad company and government agree to them.[7]

At Toronto, the Orangemen built a sixty-foot-tall arch at a key intersection, which the prince's party evaded upon entering the city. When the prince emerged from Sunday services, brawny Orangemen intercepted his carriage and tried to carry it and him under the arch, but the driver whipped the horses to gallop away. A day later, heading into the countryside by train, prince and duke thought they had left Orangemen behind—only to discover a bright orange arch newly erected over the rail line, which they could not avoid.[8]

In late September, the prince and entourage entered the United States at Detroit and spent the next month traveling through the Midwest and East. Making a grand impression, the prince drew immense crowds curious to see a real, "live Prince." Young women flocked to see, touch, and even pinch Edward, behavior that the Duke of Newcastle found "somewhat rough and vulgar." The worst experience came in Richmond, Virginia, where the locals felt irritated because the prince's visit led the city fathers to cancel an especially large, and much-anticipated, slave auction. They also felt offended when the prince declined an invitation to tour a plantation worked by slaves. The prince and duke did visit a statue of George Washington, but a white throng heckled, saying that Washington "socked it into you at the Revolution."[9]

Another irritation came in Albany, New York, at a dinner attended by Senator William H. Seward. Late in the evening and deep in his cups, Seward assured Newcastle that, for political advantage, he would insult and threaten the British with war. Newcastle bristled and replied "that if he carried it out and touched our honor, he would, some fine morning, find he had embroiled his country in a disastrous conflict." Seward miscalculated that baiting the British lion would distract Americans from their own internal strife.[10]

On October 22, prince and duke sailed away, headed home across the Atlantic. Their souvenirs included two gray squirrels and a mud turtle: gifts for the queen. Six weeks later, the British ambassador, Lord Lyons, wrote to the duke: "It is difficult to believe that I am in the same country which appeared so prosperous, so contented, and one may say, so calm when we travelled through it." Americans were, Lyons reported, "going ahead on the road to ruin with their characteristic speed and energy." The Union was unraveling because of the recent presidential election.[11]

Parties

Southern Democrats sought to sabotage Stephen A. Douglas's nomination for the presidency. In April 1860, the Democratic convention met in the worst place for Douglas: Charleston, South Carolina, the chief city of the state most hostile to Yankees. Addressing the convention, William L. Yancey demanded northern deference to southern interests: "Ours is the property invaded; ours are the institutions which are at stake; ours is the peace that is to be destroyed; ours is the honor at stake."[12]

When northern delegates rejected a territorial slave code, eight southern delegations bolted, depriving the convention of the two-thirds quorum needed to nominate a candidate. Northern delegates reconvened at Baltimore, where they chose Douglas. Most southern delegates met at Richmond, Virginia, to nominate John C. Breckinridge of Kentucky for president on a slave-code platform. By dividing, Democrats doomed their chances of winning the presidency. The British consul at Charleston, Robert Bunch, noted that, too late, southerners would "wake from their delusion to find the Democratic Party broken up and the whole power of the country thrown into the hands of the Republicans. When this shall happen, the days of slavery are numbered."[13]

In May, when the Republicans convened in Chicago, the leading candidate was Seward, an accomplished legislator and campaigner. Bright, talkative, outgoing, energetic, ambitious, and self-assured, Seward had a vibrant personality that dwarfed his small and slender frame—and compensated for his homely combination of big nose, bushy eyebrows, huge ears, reddish hair, and rumpled clothes. Bored by practicing law, Seward relished politics as "the important and engrossing business of the country." By the late 1850s, he had become the leading Republican in the U.S. Senate. But at the convention his wheeling and dealing political style troubled moralistic midwesterners, who also worried that his sometimes fiery antislavery speeches would alienate moderate voters.[14]

Seward's principal challenger was not much to look at. A British correspondent, William Howard Russell, described Abraham Lincoln as "a tall, lank, lean man, considerably over six feet in height, with stooping shoulders, long pendulous arms terminating in hands of extraordinary dimensions," and a head covered with a "thatch of wild republican hair" above "wide projecting ears." Yet Russell was "agreeably impressed with his shrewdness, humor, and natural sagacity." Packing the galleries, Lincoln's partisans bellowed their support. A deafened witness recalled, "Imagine all the hogs ever slaughtered in Cincinnati giving their death squeals together, [or] a score of big steam whistles going."[15]

Lincoln appealed to delegates for his humble origins; reputation for honesty and moderation; and folksy eloquence tinged with moral clarity. In a recent, celebrated speech, Lincoln had noted that southern leaders "want us to stop calling slavery wrong and join them, in acts as well as words, in calling slavery *right*" when their "thinking it right, and our thinking it wrong, is the precise fact upon which depends the whole controversy." He concluded, "Let us have faith that right makes might, and in that faith, let us, to the end, dare to do our duty as we understand it."[16]

To win, Republicans needed a virtual sweep of the free states, including five that had voted Democratic in 1856. Those swing states included Lincoln's home state, Illinois, and adjoining Indiana, where he had lived. Most of the delegates were pragmatists eager for victory. Abandoning Seward, the party nominated Lincoln. A southern Democrat, Louis T. Wigfall, of Texas dismissed Lincoln as "an ex-rail-splitter, an ex-grocery keeper, an ex-flatboat captain." Republicans relished that elitist contempt as proof that they promoted social mobility for common men.[17]

The Republican platform called for popular measures blocked by southern Democrats in Congress: a homestead act to provide free land for western settlers; federal support for a transcontinental railroad as well as river and harbor improvements; and a protective tariff for industry. The platform opposed the expansion of slavery and sought to end slavery in the District of Columbia, where the federal government held jurisdiction (unlike the states). But, to appeal to swing voters, Republicans promised to enforce the Fugitive Slave Law and leave slavery alone in the southern states.[18]

The Republicans left Chicago united, energized, and organized. Their boisterous, festive campaign featured brass bands and parades by hundreds, sometimes thousands, of men carrying torches and fence rails in honor of Lincoln. The marchers included quasi-military companies of uniformed young men known as "Wide-Awakes."[19]

Some old-school Whigs also ran a presidential candidate, John Bell of Tennessee. Carefully avoiding the divisive issue of slavery, Bell's platform offered pablum about loving the Federal Constitution and Union. Bell had little chance of winning, but he might take enough electoral votes to prevent any other candidate from securing a majority in the electoral college. Then the decision would be thrust into the House of Representatives, where the members were well armed with revolvers and bowie knives.[20]

The campaign divided Americans along regional lines, with Douglas pitted against Lincoln in the North while Bell competed with Breckinridge for the South. Northern Democrats sought to make the election pivot on race rather than slavery. One of their newspapers warned that Republicans would unleash millions of fugitive slaves to overwhelm northern whites, producing "African amalgamation with the fair daughters of the Anglo Saxon, Celtic, and Teutonic races." Although Lincoln carried New York State, a measure there to allow Blacks to vote lost badly, as even a third of Republicans voted no. Most northern voters were both racist and antislavery—and saw no contradiction there. They wanted to block the expansion of slavery without extending freedom and civil rights to Blacks.[21]

Election

The Union was in peril. On the eve of the election, a Mississippi newspaper declared, "The minds of the people are aroused to a pitch of excitement probably unparalleled in the history of our country." The election coincided with alarming rumors of an impending slave revolt, allegedly instigated by Republicans. Wigfall warned that the Republican Wide-Awakes were "over half million of men uniformed and drilled . . . to sweep the country in which I live with fire and sword." Jefferson Davis grimly declared that, if Lincoln won, "Mississippi's best and bravest should gather to the harvest-home of death."[22]

Southern threats of secession alarmed and energized Douglas, who claimed that he alone could save the Union. Although he was only forty-seven, his health was failing after years of heavy drinking, smoking, and eating. Traveling far and wide to speak long and hard, he became hoarser and sicker. In October, Douglas confided to a friend, "Mr. Lincoln is the next President. We must try to save the Union. I will go South." There Douglas declared that he would hang anyone who led a state into secession. Davis retorted that he would hang both Douglas and Lincoln if either invaded Mississippi to enforce the Union.[23]

On November 6, Lincoln learned that he had won. Walking home, he told his wife, "Mary, Mary, we are elected." Breckinridge secured eleven southern states but lost Missouri to Douglas, and Kentucky, Tennessee, and Virginia to Bell. That left all the free states (except half of New Jersey) for Lincoln. Winning almost no southern votes, he received 40 percent of the national popular vote, but got 54 percent in the North. Lincoln won big in the northeast but small in the midwestern and far western swing states, including by just 6,000 votes over his combined opponents in Illinois. But his states totaled 180 electoral votes, a clear majority. Lincoln would be the first president committed to containing and discrediting slavery.[24]

In Charleston, South Carolina, a great crowd celebrated the election results as justification for secession. White Carolinians erected a towering liberty pole to cheers and flew a dark banner inscribed "Here lies the Union, Born 4th July 1776, Died 7th Nov. 1860." Leaving Virginia, Edmund Ruffin rushed to Charleston to help celebrate secession as essential to "negro slavery, on which the social & political existence of the south rests." Hailed as a prophet by adoring crowds, Ruffin felt fulfilled at last: "The time since I have been here has been the happiest of my life."[25]

On December 20, 1860, a South Carolina convention voted unanimously for secession. A delegate explained, "Now a stand must be made for African slavery or it's forever lost." In January 1861, the other six states of the Lower South seceded: Mississippi, Florida, Alabama, Georgia, Louisiana, and Texas. To defend their new independence, those states stockpiled weapons and organized military units. Their governors seized federal forts, courts, post offices, customs houses, arsenals, and mints. A popular frenzy pushed the exhilarated secessionists. One reported, "People are wild. . . . You might as well attempt to control a tornado as to attempt to stop them."[26]

The lame-duck president Buchanan regarded secession as unconstitutional but insisted that he could do nothing to stop it. A New Yorker called Buchanan spineless: "Had this old mollusk become vertebrate, the theories of Darwin would have been confirmed." The corrupt secretary of war, John B. Floyd of Virginia, covertly shifted federal munitions and cannon southward, so that they could fall into Confederate hands.[27]

Southerners doubted that slavery could survive in a nation run by a party hostile to expanding human bondage. Mathew F. Maury of

Virginia warned, "The South is blocked to expansion and that itself is death." Wigfall bellowed that Republicans meant "to belt us round with free States, to starve us out or cause us . . . like poisoned rats, to die in our holes."[28]

Secessionists feared that Republicans would enable abolitionists to infiltrate the South and rally deadly slave revolts. In late 1860, a southern writer warned that "pillage, violence, murder, poison, and rape will fill the air with the demonic revelry of all the bad passions of an ignorant, semi-barbarous race urged to madness by the licentious teachings of our northern brethren." In Mississippi, vigilantes lynched a man wearing a red sash, the alleged mark of that supposed abolitionist club, Mystic Red. A mob beat a photographer for having a picture of Lincoln. Southerners lived in an echo chamber of alarms over impending race war.[29]

Disunionists also dreaded that Republicans could rupture the white solidarity needed to sustain slavery. They could do so by building a Republican party in the South, recruiting common whites with federal patronage: contracts and coveted jobs as customs collectors and postmasters. Then that party would permit the free circulation of abolitionist literature. William L. Yancey warned: "There will be free speech, as they call it, everywhere for the propagation of Abolition opinion. There will be a free press, as they call it, for the circulation of Abolition documents." He sought a southern nation composed of "a homogenous people, accustomed to slavery, holding it in reverence."[30]

Southern leaders asserted that only disunion could protect white supremacy. An Alabaman insisted that southern men would have to "submit to have our wives and daughters choose between death and gratifying the hellish lust of the negro!!" After centuries of sexually exploiting enslaved women, southern whites projected their behavior onto Blacks in the imagined future of southern nightmares.[31]

Wiggletail

Sam Houston was a tough and salty man of the frontier. In 1814, in combat against Creek Indians, Houston suffered three wounds that brought pain for the rest of his life. During the late 1820s he won election to

Congress and became governor of Tennessee. Suffering a breakdown after his marriage failed in 1829, Houston became an alcoholic drifter, moving west to Texas to live with Cherokees. In 1835 he sobered up just enough to command the Texan army that won independence from Mexico. As president of the new Lone Star Republic, Houston secured American annexation in 1845. A year later, the state legislature sent Houston to the U.S. Senate.[32]

Houston favored bondage as essential to economic development in Texas but considered slavery more secure within the Union rather than without. Relishing the bombastic, abusive politics of Texas, Houston mocked leading secessionists. John Marshall received the greatest insult in Texas: "a vegetarian; he won't eat meat; one drop of his blood would freeze a frog." Houston also warned voters to avoid listening to Louis T. Wigfall, dubbed "Wiggletail, . . . unless they were fond of lies."[33]

As the loudest secessionist in Texas, Wigfall sought to take down Houston as a traitor to the South. An eloquent and confrontational drunk, Wigfall dazzled a colleague with the "racy vehemence which poured from his limber lips." British correspondent William H. Russell marveled at Wigfall's feral face: "beetling, black eyebrows—a mouth coarse and grim, yet full of power, a square jaw—a thick, argumentative nose—a new growth of scrubby beard and moustache," and "eyes of wonderful depth and light, such as I never saw before but in the head of a wild beast."[34]

Born into a wealthy planter family in South Carolina in 1816, Wigfall bounced from one school to the next, excelling at drunken food fights rather than his studies. Clever enough to become a lawyer, Wigfall soon lost patience with his practice, turning to journalism and politics. After swapping insults with the elite Brooks family, Wigfall killed one in a brawl and fought two others in duels, suffering a bullet wound to his hip. But Wigfall's bullet also lamed Preston Brooks, who had to rely on canes, one of which he later smashed over Charles Sumner's skull.[35]

Wigfall fled from his creditors by moving to Texas, where he won election to the state legislature. In 1859, his fellow legislators elevated Wigfall to the United States Senate, where he insulted older colleagues and threw punches at younger ones. Opposing a Republican bill to provide free homesteads for settlers, Wigfall insisted that it was more important to provide "niggers for the niggerless" than "land for the landless."[36]

In early 1861 Houston was the governor of Texas. He warned Texans that Wigfall and other secessionists would swap the Union's prosperity and stability for "the anarchy and carnage of civil war." He added, "War is no plaything, and this war will be a bloody war. There will be thousands and thousands who march away from our homes never to come back." While he disliked Republicans, Houston wanted southerners to battle for states' rights within the Union.[37]

In January 1861 the state legislature overruled Houston, approving a special convention, which hastily met and voted 166 to 8 to hold a referendum for secession, deemed essential to preserve "the servitude of the African to the white race . . . in all future time." On February 23, Texans voted for secession by three to one, in part because armed men drove unionists away from the polls. At San Antonio's Alamo Plaza, a Unionist tried to address a crowd, but rowdies stormed the stage "six-shooters in hand, and with one wild yell . . . swept it clear." A witness added, "Then the shooting grew unpleasantly promiscuous." Triumphant secessionists burned the homes of several Unionists and one of their newspapers. As a frontier land crossed with a slave society, Texas was an especially violent place. A resident reflected that in Texas "a man is a little nearer death . . . than in any other country."[38]

On March 17, Texas's legislators sacked Houston as governor after he refused to swear allegiance to the new regime. Heading home, Houston stopped at the town of Brenham, where a crowd gathered and asked him to speak. When local secessionists vowed to stop him, an old friend sprang upon a table, drew out a revolver, and bellowed, "Now, fellow-citizens, give him your close attention; and you ruffians, keep quiet, or I will kill you." Houston warned the crowd, "The soil of our beloved South will drink deep the precious blood of our sons and brethren." But his speech changed few if any minds. In sorrow, Houston belatedly endorsed secession but privately still expected disaster: "Our people are going to war to perpetuate slavery," but "the first gun fired in the war will be the [death] knell of slavery."[39]

Despite the secession of Texas, Wigfall refused to leave the U.S. Senate, lingering through the winter and spring to gather military intelligence and buy weapons for the South. Wigfall assured Yankees that a civil war would end with him dictating their surrender at Faneuil Hall in Boston. Basking in the outrage of Unionists, Wigfall had never been happier. The wife of a South Carolina senator, Mary Chesnut, noted, "Wigfall chafes at the restraints of civil life. He likes to be where he can be as rude as he pleases."[40]

On a Texas plantation, an enslaved woman recalled her master as "the most hard hearted man I ever seen." But she praised his son, Walter Hyns, as "the best one of the family, and his father just hated him [be]cause he would take up for us niggers, so he made him go to war." On departing for the southern army, Walter defiantly told his parents that he would rather fight to free the slaves. His mother "told him [if] he thought so much of the niggers, he would be better off dead." Soon "he was killed, just blowed to pieces, they could not find enough to send him home." So Houston had warned.[41]

Confederacy

Southern Unionists tried to halt the popular momentum for secession by calling for a pause to hold an interstate convention to coordinate multiple states. They called this "cooperation"—which their foes called "submission." The cooperationists included Alexander H. Stephens of Georgia. A true conservative, Stephens dreaded secession as a revolutionary rupture that would spin out of control and into anarchy: "Instead of becoming gods, we shall become demons, and at no distant day commence cutting one another's throats."[42]

Stephens urged Georgians to wait to see what concessions Lincoln might make. Stephens wrote to the president-elect: "We both have an earnest desire to preserve and maintain the Union." In reply, Lincoln reassured his "once friend, and still, I hope, not an enemy" that he would never interfere with slavery in the states. But Lincoln clung to his core principle: "You think slavery is *right* and ought to be extended; while we think it is *wrong* and ought to be restricted. That I suppose is the rub." Yes, it was. When Georgia seceded on January 21, Stephens accepted disunion.[43]

In February, the seven seceding states sent delegates to Montgomery, Alabama, to form the Confederate States of America. Montgomery disappointed the British correspondent William H. Russell, who disliked the slave auctions and felt uneasy as the only white man in town without a loaded revolver. He concluded, "Their whole system rests on slavery, and as such they defend it." Russell found the delegates both impressive and alarming: "so earnest, so grave, so sober, and so vindictive."[44]

The delegates drafted and adopted a constitution that copied the U.S. Constitution with a few key changes to enhance state sovereignty, perpetuate slavery, and discourage partisan politics. The new constitution banned protective tariffs and federal funding for internal improvements. It also limited the president to a single term but stretched it to six years. The constitution upheld slavery as a fundamental property right. Slavery mattered more than states' rights in the Confederacy, for the new constitution barred any state from ever abolishing slavery—and no free state could join unless approved by two-thirds of both House and Senate.[45]

Confederates renounced the partisan techniques—conventions, parades, barbecues, treating, and stump speeches—that made nineteenth-century politics so festive and raucous, mobilizing large turnouts in hypercompetitive elections. By seceding, southerners could transcend the "universal liberty and equality, universal elections, absolute majorities, eternal demagogism and free competition [that] have leveled, degraded, demoralized, and debased Northern society."[46]

After an hour's discussion, the delegates chose Jefferson Davis as the Confederacy's president. Tall, dignified, and austere, with chiseled features and ramrod-straight posture, he looked the part of an idealized, masculine president. Russell described Davis as "a very calm, resolute man—slight, spare, a lean Cassius with extremely wrinkled, puckered skin on [a] thin, intellectual head, eye corner tic." With extensive political and military experience, including a stint as secretary of war, Davis seemed perfect to lead a new nation in the coming conflict.[47]

But Davis had many critics who found him arrogant, frosty, defensive, and impetuous. In stark contrast to Lincoln's humility, flexibility, and folksy humor, Davis was rigid, irritable, and quick-tempered. Holding grudges, he had to be right and rarely forgave contradiction. A former colleague in the U.S. Senate, Sam Houston, insisted "Jeff Davis is as ambitious as Lucifer and cold as a lizard."[48]

To reconcile reluctant secessionists, the delegates chose Stephens as vice-president. In March, at Savannah, he gave a celebrated speech declaring that the "cornerstone" of the Confederacy "rests upon the great truth that the negro is not equal to the white man; that slavery—subordination to the superior race—is his natural and normal condition." Stephens considered this a "great physical, philosophical, and moral truth."[49]

Southern leaders created the Confederacy with remarkable speed, taking just two weeks to craft a constitution, choose a president and vice-president, and organize a judiciary, treasury, postal service, and state department. They also began to raise troops. It took them much longer, five weeks, to settle on a new flag, considering more than 120 proposals. The most apt showed seven rattlesnakes tied by their tails, with a bale of cotton on one side and a jug of whisky on the other. But most members thought that design too frank. They settled on the "Stars and Bars," with two red stripes framing a white stripe, while the left corner had a field of blue with a circle of stars, one per state. Only later did the Confederacy supplement this with a battle flag, today called the Confederate flag.[50]

Confederates claimed to have restored the original, true republic allegedly created by the American Revolution. They took heart from citing that precedent of a victorious struggle against a powerful oppressor. Plastering George Washington's image on stamps and broadsides, Confederates damned Yankees as "Tories" and "Hessians." Confederates rewrote "The Star-Spangled Banner" as "The Stars and Bars," with a new chorus: "Oh! Say has the star-spangled banner become the flag of the Tory and vile Northern scum?"[51]

Crisis

During the winter of 1861, the Upper South states held back from secession. They had a smaller percentage of slaves (24 percent of their population compared to 47 percent in the Lower South) but suffered more escapes to the nearby North. So, their leaders clung to the protection (however limited) of the federal Fugitive Slave Law. But they also defended the right of any state to secede and threatened to join the Confederacy if the Union resorted to coercion.[52]

In 1861, North and South clashed over the meaning of the constitutional Union. James M. Mason of Virginia defined the United States as a mere "confederation of sovereign powers, not a consolidation of states into one people." Republicans countered that the Union was a majoritarian democracy superior to the states. Seward charged southerners with seeking "to convert the government from a national democracy, operating by a constitutional majority of voices, into a federal alliance, in which the minority shall have a veto against the majority." Both sides would fight to the death for their constitutional vision.[53]

Most Yankees feared that if some states left the Union, others would follow, until the country dissolved into several petty nations warring over a balance of power, until military dictators ruled them all. Indeed, some malcontents proposed breaking the Union into regional blocks, including one on the Pacific coast and another in the Midwest. An Illinois congressman protested: "Not only will states secede from the Union, but counties from states, and cities and towns from both" until "society and government will be ingulfed in one bottomless and boundless chaos of ruin."[54]

But what could be done to force the seceding states back? Coercion seemed implausible with a federal army of just 16,000 men scattered far and wide, mostly at small posts in the distant West. And attempted coercion would drive the wavering Upper South into disunion, weakening the federal government while strengthening the Confederacy.[55]

Senators from the Upper South hoped to entice Confederates back into the Union by offering concessions. Senator John J. Crittenden of Kentucky led a committee that proposed to amend the Federal Constitution to guarantee slavery in the states, the District of Columbia, federal properties in the South, and all territories south of a revived Missouri Compromise line. By stipulating that slavery could expand southward into any territory "hereafter acquired," Crittenden reassured southerners keen to seize lands around the Gulf of Mexico and Caribbean Sea. Crittenden's package also protected the interstate slave trade and compensated slaveholders who lost runaways to the North. Finally, Crittenden stipulated that his amendments were perpetual—unalterable by any future Congress.[56]

Seward supported Crittenden's amendments, but most Republicans balked at sacrificing their principles. Lincoln complained, "We have just carried an election on principles fairly stated to the people. Now we are told . . . the government will be broken up, unless we surrender to those we have beaten." He accepted the proposed federal guarantees for slavery in the South and District of Columbia—as well as strict enforcement of the Fugitive Slave Law. But Lincoln clung to the Republicans' core principle: that slavery could not expand into federal territories or new colonies. He dreaded that southern filibusters would seize Cuba and Central America "to put us again on the high-road to a slave empire." Rejecting the notion "that slavery has equal rights with liberty," Lincoln concluded, "If we surrender, it is the end of us."[57]

In January 1861 the senate narrowly rejected Crittenden's amendments. The whole exercise was pointless because Confederates declared that no concessions could draw them back into the Union. "We spit upon every plan of compromise," one insisted. Two South Carolinians told a Yankee, "We have a white man's government and will suffer death with all its horrors before we will exchange it for a negro government like yours."[58]

On March 4, in his inaugural address, Lincoln promised to enforce the Fugitive Slave Law and leave slavery alone in the South but to maintain federal authority there. To rebind the Union, he urged all Americans to heed "the mystic chords of memory" and "the better angels of our nature." Holding Lincoln's wind-blown hat during the ceremony, Stephen A. Douglas declared, "I am with him." But the Confederate Congress rejected Lincoln's appeal, authorizing an army of 100,000 men. There would be a war soon.[59]

Fort Sumter

To keep a potential rival close at hand, Lincoln offered his most coveted cabinet post, secretary of state, to Seward. The new secretary thought that he would dominate the administration on behalf of a country bumpkin in over his head as president. In love with his own talents and influence, Seward could not see their limits. William H. Russell described the secretary of state as "a subtle, quick man, rejoicing in power, given to perorate and to oracular utterances, fond of badinage [and] bursting with the importance of state mysteries, and with the dignity of directing the foreign policy of the greatest country—as all Americans think—in the world."

Once the fiery advocate of containing slavery, Seward now favored concessions to entice southerners back into the Union. This somersault appalled his antislavery wife, Frances, who opposed sacrificing "the liberty of nearly 4,000,000 human beings." Eager to score points and impress others, Seward boasted too much, cut corners, and gloried in small tricks. He lacked the moral depth that enabled Lincoln to understand rivals and share credit for success.[60]

On April 1, 1865, Seward proposed a plan to shock the country back together. He wanted to provoke a war with Spain and France for violating America's Monroe Doctrine by meddling in Latin America. Spain had begun to take over the Dominican Republic, and France was threatening to invade Mexico. Seward even proposed expanding the threats to Britain by renewing the border dispute over the San Juan Islands in the Pacific Northwest. Seward believed that war and expansion could best unite Americans, North and South.[61]

But Lincoln meant to govern as his own president, rather than serve as Seward's figurehead. In a polite but firm reply, Lincoln told Seward to focus on shrinking the domestic crisis rather than fabricating a bigger one overseas. Chastened, Seward submitted to the president's lead and soon became Lincoln's favorite advisor. In May 1861, Seward wrote to his wife in praise of Lincoln: "His Magnanimity is almost superhuman. . . . The President is the best of us, but he needs constant and assiduous cooperation."[62]

Lincoln hoped to avoid provoking a war but needed to sustain Fort Sumter, a rare base retained by the Union within the Confederacy. A granite fortress on a small island, Fort Sumter guarded the entrance to the harbor of Charleston—the most militant city in the new Confederacy. Lincoln decided to resupply but not reinforce the small garrison, hoping that the compromise would suffice for Confederates to hold fire.[63]

Confederates, however, regarded Fort Sumter as an unacceptable challenge to their independence. Confederate artillery opened fire just before dawn on April 12. Edmund Ruffin fired one of the first shots at the fort. Unable to match the destructive fire from Confederate batteries, the garrison (commanded by Robert Anderson) hunkered down for thirty-three hours. With the thunder of guns echoing in Charleston, Mary Chesnut scanned the faces of her slaves for their response to a war erupting over them. But, she noted, "They make no sign. Are they stolidly stupid or wiser than we are, silent and strong, biding their time?" Wiser, no doubt.[64]

In Fort Sumter the Union troops suddenly saw a beefy, hairy civilian in a frock coat, red silk sash, and top hat clambering through a casemate. He was the South's greatest glory-hound, Senator Wigfall. Without authorization from the Confederate commander, Wigfall had commandeered a small boat, a soldier, and three unlucky slaves to row him out to Sumter so that he could demand the fort's surrender. Anderson had little fight left, so he capitulated to Wigfall. Returning to Montgomery, the Confederate capital, Wigfall boasted that he had won the battle, while bitterly complaining that Anderson failed to praise him in a published report.[65]

Defining themselves as honorable and brave, southern leaders cast Yankees as cowardly money-grubbers who would never fight. Scoffing at southerners who feared a civil war, Senator James Chesnut of South Carolina boasted that he could drink all the little blood that would be shed. Robert B. Rhett went one better by offering to eat all the corpses slain in battle. One of those Yankees, William T. Sherman, lived in Louisiana as superintendent of a military academy. He warned secessionists, "This country will be drenched in blood." Sherman would help.[66]

The attack on Fort Sumter galvanized Yankee patriotism. The poet Walt Whitman recalled that the news "ran through the Land, as if by electric nerves." A Bostonian reported, "The whole population, men, women, and children, seem to be in the streets" waving Union flags. A

New Yorker exulted, "It seems as if we never were alive till now; never had a country till now." A day after Sumter surrendered, Lincoln called for 75,000 volunteers to suppress the southern rebellion. Four days later, he imposed a naval blockade along the southern coast and summoned federal troops from the West to head east for war. Military volunteers soon doubled what Lincoln had asked for.[67]

Upon learning of the attack, Douglas rushed to the White House to meet with Lincoln alone for two hours. Despite waning health, Douglas embarked on a grueling speaking tour to rally Democratic support for the Union. In Chicago, he told an immense crowd, "There can be no neutrals in this war, *only patriots—or traitors.*" A month later, cirrhosis of the liver killed the hard-drinking Douglas at the age of forty-eight. Lincoln ordered the White House draped in the black bunting of mourning. A leading Republican editor mourned, "The loss at this crisis must be regarded as a national tragedy."[68]

Upper South

In the Upper South, Lincoln's call for volunteers alienated most whites, for they refused to fight fellow southerners. Governor John Ellis of North Carolina assured Lincoln, "I can be no party to this wicked violation of the laws of the country, and to this war upon the liberties of a free people." Instead, Ellis waged war on the Union. Without waiting for his legislature to secede, he sent militia to seize three federal forts on the coast and an arsenal in Fayetteville. Tennessee's governor vowed that he would "not furnish a single man for the purpose of coercion, but fifty thousand if necessary for the defense of our rights and those of our Southern brothers."[69]

The fall of Fort Sumter stimulated Confederate nationalism in the Upper South. While bands played "Dixie," festive crowds lit fireworks, danced around bonfires, tore down the Stars and Stripes from public buildings, and raised Confederate flags. In North Carolina, William H. Russell saw "an excited mob" with "flushed faces, wild eyes, screaming mouths, hurrahing for 'Jeff Davis' and 'the Southern Confederacy.' . . . All was noise, dust, and patriotism."[70]

As the largest southern state in territory, wealth, and population, Virginia was pivotal. On April 17, three days after Sumter's surrender, Virginia's delegates voted to secede, submitting the decision to a referendum that, on May 23, approved disunion by 128,884 to 32,124 votes. A Richmond newspaper promised that secession would "emancipate" the state from northern "taxing and cheating and swindling the South" but conceded that the South faced a "civil war of gigantic proportions, infinite consequences and indefinite duration."[71]

That war had already begun in Virginia, as Governor Henry Wise sent armed volunteers to seize the naval dockyard at Gosport and the federal arsenal at Harper's Ferry. The victors hauled most of the arsenal's machinery back to Richmond to produce guns for the Confederacy. The navy yard provided invaluable cannon and the hull of the ship *Merrimack*, which the Confederates would remake into the celebrated ironclad warship, the C.S.S. *Virginia*.[72]

Virginia's Blacks rarely shared their true thoughts with masters, but Sam of Mecklenburg County was old and defiant. Apprised of Virginia's secession, Sam warned local whites that their slaves would "all be free pretty soon" because Lincoln would invade and "free everything as he goes." Those whites arrested, tried, and convicted him to serve at hard labor on the public works.[73]

Confederates felt thrilled to gain Virginia, which offered an industrial capacity that matched the original seven states of their new nation. Only Richmond's Tredegar Iron Works could produce the heavy cannon that the Confederates needed. As the premier state in the American Revolution and early republic, Virginia also endowed the Confederacy with prestige. Above all, Virginia's secession brought along the most talented and dignified officer in the United States Army, Robert E. Lee. In Texas, John Salmon Ford praised Lee: "He evinced an imperturbable self-possession, and a complete control of his passions. To approach him was to feel yourself in the presence of a man of superior intellect, possessing the . . . gift of controlling and leading men." Lee cherished the Union, but loyalty to Virginia trumped all, for he felt obliged to "go back in sorrow to my people & share [in] the misery of my native state."[74]

Lee's decision dismayed his patron, the Union army's commander,

Winfield Scott, a fellow Virginian who clung to the United States. Scott told Lee, "You have made the greatest mistake of your life, but I feared it would be so." Lee did worry that the conflict would be longer and harder than southerners recognized. He noted, "Above all, we shall have to fight the prejudices of the world, because of the existence of slavery in our country."[75]

Lee lost his family's cherished home in Arlington, close to Washington, D.C., for a Union general made the mansion his headquarters while troops dug trenches through the fields. A northern visitor found an elderly slave named Daniel weeding a bed of strawberries. Asked what he thought of the war, Daniel replied, "Well, massa, *it's all about things we've been so long a putting up with*."[76]

On May 6 Arkansas seceded, followed by North Carolina on May 20, and Tennessee on June 8, bringing the Confederate total to eleven states. Confederate leaders agreed to remove their capital from Montgomery, deep within the South, to Richmond, much closer to the front lines of a civil war with the Union. Much bigger than Montgomery, Richmond had 40,000 inhabitants, ranking second only to New Orleans among southern cities. The new capital also had booming factories, many railroad lines, and fashionable mansions, hotels, churches, and theaters.[77]

Causes

To win the war, Lincoln needed support from northern Democrats and border state folk, who would fight for the Union but not to free enslaved people. Although he despised slavery personally, Lincoln felt bound by political realities—as well as his reading of the Federal Constitution as protecting slavery within states. He told abolitionists: "My paramount objective in this struggle *is* to save the Union and is *not* either to save or to destroy slavery. If I could save the Union without freeing *any* slave, I would do it, and if I could save it by freeing *all* the slaves I would do it. . . . I have here stated my purpose according to my view of *official* duty; and I intend no modification of my oft-expressed *personal* wish that all men everywhere could be free."[78]

Lincoln saw the war as a test of free government for the entire world and the rest of history: "If we fail, it will . . . prove the incapability of the people to govern themselves." Committed to equal opportunity and social mobility, Lincoln insisted that only the United States sought "to elevate the condition of men—to lift artificial weights from their shoulders—to clear the paths of laudable pursuit for all—to afford all an unfettered start and a fair chance in the race of life."[79]

Lincoln's restraint angered abolitionists, who argued that the Union had to root out slavery to win the war. Blasting Lincoln's "inconsistent, vacillating, crooked and compromising advocacy of a good cause," Frederick Douglass said of slavery: "While the monster lives, he will hunger and thirst, breathe and expand. The true way is to put the knife into its quivering heart." The great conductor of the Underground Railroad, Harriet Tubman, likened slavery to a great snake that kept biting folk: "so he keep doing it, till you *kill him*. That's what master Lincoln ought to know."[80]

In 1861 Unionists fought to vindicate their republic by subduing the rebellion. A Union colonel accused southerners of seeking "the smoking ruins of the U.S. Government—that great gift of God to oppressed humanity." Unionists fought not just for themselves but for their posterity—and to set an example that could liberate the rest of the world. Defeat, however, would delight Europe's aristocrats and monarchs, who would control the world without a major republic to challenge them and inspire common people with hope. For Union soldiers, the stakes were global.[81]

In 1861 few Yankee soldiers meant to liberate Blacks as part of their fight for freedom. An Indiana sergeant, Samuel McIlvaine, defended "this Government which stands out to the rest of the world as the polestar, the beacon light of liberty & freedom to the human race." But when two runaways sought haven in his regiment's camp, they were grabbed by slave catchers "and taken back without molestation on our part." In 1861, a Massachusetts sergeant calculated that only one in a thousand Union soldiers was an abolitionist.[82]

Many immigrants rallied to the Union because they revered the United States as their haven and an inspirational example for reviving European struggles for republican liberation. An Irish-born recruit worried that if the Union failed, "the old cry will be sent forth from the aristocrats of Europe that such is the common end of all republics." Likening Confederates to aristocrats, a German immigrant turned Union soldier declared: "The freedom of the oppressed and the equality of human rights must first be fought for here!"[83]

Confederates insisted that they fought for Black slavery and white liberty as inseparable. Considering freedom as their due reward in a zero-sum, racial game, white southerners claimed that they faced enslavement if Blacks became free. Without Black slavery, southern men doubted that they could retain white supremacy and control over their own women. A Confederate recruit exclaimed, "Better, far better! [to] endure all the horrors of civil war than to see the dusky sons of Ham leading the fair daughters of the South to the altar."[84]

Confederates believed that slavery sustained their social order, including patriarchal families where men governed and protected dependent women and children. The defense of slavery, families, and homeland merged as Confederates braced for invasion. They insisted that northerners invaded to plunder, burn, rape, and kill, so that they could free enslaved people to join them in wreaking havoc. A Texas lieutenant agreed that he was "fighting against robbers and savages for the defense of my wife & family."[85]

North and South, men enlisted to show solidarity with friends and neighbors. Communities held recruitment rallies featuring bands, flags, crowds, rip-roaring speeches, and honored veterans of earlier wars. These civic revivals attracted young men who then felt social pressure to enlist. One recruit recalled, "It needed only the first man to step forward, put down his name, be patted on the back, placed upon the platform, and cheered to the echo as the hero of the hour, when a second, a third, a fourth would follow, and at last a perfect stampede set in to sign the enlistment roll, and a frenzy of enthusiasm would take possession of the meeting."[86]

Southern recruits dwelled on their masculine honor, for they dreaded shaming as cowards. A Virginian told his mother, "I intend to die *worthy of* the Mother that bore me and of the Father that taught me to be a *free man* & to have honor." A South Carolinian declared, "A man who will not offer up his life . . . does dishonor to his wife and children." Honor mattered so much to southerners because they denied that enslaved people had any. But a sense of duty to nation emerged as a secondary theme among Confederates just as appeals to honor appeared sprinkled in Yankee letters.[87]

Both sides regarded gender as a fundamental human division, dictating different roles for men and women in families and society. But the two regions varied in defining those differences. Northerners believed that men and women should operate in separate spheres of equal merit. In theory, northern men went out into society as breadwinners and citizens, while women sustained a clean and moral environment at home to sustain husbands and educate children. But some Yankee women did venture out to form and lead societies devoted to moral reforms and religious outreach. Most southerners believed in more traditional, patriarchal families, where men called the shots at home and beyond. They frowned on women taking any public role as a Yankee subversion of proper order. By practicing gender differently, each side saw the other as acting unnaturally.[88]

On both sides, women rallied men for war, celebrating recruits while damning shirkers. In Texas, Amelia Barr noted, "In a great many cases, it was the women of a family who compelled the men to enlist as soldiers." Few hesitated, for "what man could bear his family weeping over him, as if he was already dead in their love and respect?" Making flags for volunteer regiments, women presented them in public ceremonies that exhorted men to protect their women by defending that banner. A South Carolina recruit marveled, "It is astonishing what effect the waving of a woman's hand kerchief has upon a soldier. . . . I verily believe a woman with a hand kerchief could send one entire little army to perdition." And so they did.[89]

On the home front, women sewed uniforms, rolled bandages, made flags, assembled cartridges, and nursed the wounded. Newspapers, poems, and songs highlighted female contributions and sacrifices to assert the complete patriotism on their side. In the South, Kate Cumming declared, "A man did not deserve the name of man, if he did not fight for his country; nor a woman, the name of woman, if she did not do all in her power to aid the men."[90]

Coordinated by the male-led U.S. Sanitary Commission, northern women's associations helped sustain the well-being and morale of Union troops. About 20,000 Yankee women served as nurses, an occupation previously reserved for men. Participation in the war effort enabled many women to develop leadership abilities that made them more assertive thereafter in seeking political rights. By comparison, Confederate female associations remained smaller, localized, and poorly coordinated.[91]

Both Yankees and southerners insisted that they fought to defend true Christianity against dangerous heretics. But they defined Christianity differently. Favoring a patriarchal social order rooted in the Old Testament, Confederates felt disgusted by pious Yankees who sought to perfect society along Christian lines. "The Kingdom of Christ is not of this world," declared North Carolina Baptists. A Confederate claimed that he fought to "confound the whole set of Psalm singing 'brethren' and 'sistern' too. If it had not been for them . . . preaching abolitionism from every northern pulpit, I would never have been soldiering."[92]

Claiming favor from a just God, neither side could understand why the other fought. Confederates insisted that they just wanted to be left alone, so they cast Yankees as savage aggressors or the mercenary dupes of Republican demagogues. After one battle, a Confederate private came upon a mortally wounded prisoner, an immigrant, who explained, "I fight for the glorious Union and for the Flag which you have insult[ed]." The Confederate dismissed him as a "poor ignorant devil" and "a victim to the teachings of Lincoln & Seward."[93]

The Steedman family of South Carolina raged when their son and brother Charles, a naval officer, clung to the Union. His brother James rebuked Charles as "my Brother a Traitor to his Mother County . . . where lie the bones of his Father, Mother, & many dear relatives." Confederates often thought of allegiance in local and familial terms. In reply, Charles invoked a more abstract nationalism: "all that I know is my duty to flag & country under which I have served for the last 30 years." Many Unionists felt a bond with the nation and its symbols that transcended their family and local ties.[94]

James and John Welsh grew up as brothers in the Shenandoah Valley of Virginia, but James moved to Illinois, where he became a Republican and enlisted in a Union regiment in 1861. Back in Virginia, his brother John felt "pained to find . . . that I have a brother who would advocate sending men here to butcher his own friends and relations" on behalf of "black Republican rule." John accused James of betraying "home, mother, father, and brothers . . . all for the dear nigger." In reply, James denounced a brother who would "tear down the glorious Stars and Stripes, a flag that we have been taught from our cradle to look on with pride. . . . I would strike down my own brother if he dare to raise a hand to destroy that flag." Although James did not strike down his brother, John did die in combat in 1863.[95]

Union troops felt shocked by the rural poverty in southern hill country, where small farmers scratched out a living from a thin soil without the help of slaves. An Ohio officer regarded runaway slaves as "superior to the average of the uneducated white population," whom he deemed "unenterprising, lazy, narrow, listless and ignorant." Mixing pity with contempt, Yankee soldiers claimed a duty to liberate and uplift plain folk kept down by the slave-owning elite. A Maine soldier called the South "at least 100 years behind the north in improvements and all this difference is caused by slavery."[96]

Means

In 1861, neither side had a military sufficient to the massive challenge of either conquering or defending the vast Confederacy. Both nations relied on thousands of new volunteers, full of zeal but lacking training and discipline. They expected to win the war and return to civilian life as quickly as possible. States raised and organized the new regiments, each supposed to have about 1,000 men, but combat, disease, and desertion soon wore them down to much smaller numbers. Commanders clustered four or five regiments into a brigade led by a brigadier general. In the larger armies, two or three brigades formed a division, under a major general. In the largest forces, two or three divisions constituted a corps. About three-quarters of the recruits became infantrymen, supplemented by artillerymen who operated cannon and cavalrymen who rode about to scout for the enemy and harass enemy supply lines. The more industrialized North had the edge in artillery, while the Confederacy initially had far better cavalry.[97]

The North had a more industrialized economy and a larger population of free white men aged sixteen to forty-five: 2,500,000 compared to 900,000 for the Confederacy. The North had the luxury of enlisting only a third of its men—compared to three-quarters in the Confederacy, which left the southern home front starved for free labor. The North had twice as much railroad mileage, three times the bank capital, and ten times the manufacturing output of the South. The Union provided its troops with better weapons, lots of draft animals, sufficient clothing, and plenty to eat. Confederates had to rely on imported British weapons.[98]

To fund an expensive war, the United States had the immense advantage of an established treasury, a deep pool of American capitalists willing to loan money, and international credit. Lincoln's new secretary of the treasury, Salmon P. Chase, became a resourceful financier, pioneering the sale of government bonds to small-scale investors. A Philadelphia journalist praised every bond as "a bullet for a traitor's heart, and a nail for his coffin." Chase persuaded Congress to swell the money supply by issuing paper money, known as Greenbacks, in massive quantities, making them legal tender for all debts. Heavy new taxes, including the first American income tax, maintained their value.[99]

The South raised only 6 percent of its budget from taxes, compared to 21 percent for the North. To make up the gap, the Confederacy printed enormous quantities of paper money, which provoked an inflation that reached 9,000 percent, rendering the money worthless. As the southern economy eroded, Confederate troops suffered severely for want of enough clothing, food, and pay of any value. In June 1862, the French consul in Richmond, Alfred Paul, saw "an exhausted army, poorly fed, poorly clothed, burdened by want and disease, subjected to privations that exceed anything that human, physical, and moral strength can withstand." And yet Confederates fought on and won surprising victories.[100]

Paul predicted that the "horrific" civil war would expand to "proportions never before seen in history" and prove "long, fierce, and ruinous for the whole country." The North had superior resources, but they might not suffice for its more challenging war goal: to invade and conquer a vast Confederacy of 750,000 square miles, including a long spine of mountains, many broad rivers, and plenty of swamps. The South could win by holding on, repelling attacks long enough for northerners to grow weary of defeat and casualties—just as the American Revolutionaries had fended off the British. But staying on the defensive did not appeal to southerners certain that they could defeat twice their number of cowardly Yankees. Southerners clamored for offensives to drive invaders from their land and end the war fast. But these offensives would cost the Confederacy more men than it could replace.[101]

Canadian Union

In Canada, the 1861 census revealed that Anglophone Canada West had grown to a majority of 300,000 over Francophone Canada East. Because each province had an equal number of seats in parliament, a member of parliament from Canada West represented 20,000 constituents compared to 17,000 for an MP from Canada East. Led by George Brown, the Reform Party prevailed in Canada West by crusading for greater representation for their province. When rebuffed in parliament, Reformers threatened to rupture the Canadian Union. In a fiery speech of 1859 in parliament, Brown noted "the immense difficulties of governing two peoples, with two languages, two creeds, two systems of local institutions, under one general government." Weary of the "sectional and sectarian jealousy" (which he had done so much to promote), Brown thought it "better—a thousand times better [to] dissolve the connection."[102]

Fearing domination by the Anglophone Protestants of Canada West, Francophones rejected constitutional change as a threat to their language and Catholic faith. A newspaper editor explained: "We will consent to no compromise whatever on a principle so closely bound up with the existence of our nationality, of our religion, of all that remains of our heritage from our fathers." If denied equality in representation, they would dissolve the Canadian Union. Although he was an Anglophone from Canada West, John A. Macdonald sided with the Francophones as essential to his governing coalition. Angry Reformers cast him as a Judas who sold out his own province for selfish power.[103]

On April 17, a leading Reformer, William MacDougall, rose in the Canadian parliament to warn that Canadians of the "Anglo-Saxon Race" would "Look to Washington" for redress, which implied inviting American annexation. Macdonald pounced on these hasty words, making "No Looking to Washington" the slogan of his Conservative party in the next election. In July, voters rewarded Macdonald's Conservatives with a landslide victory in Canada West. MacDougall kept his seat, but the primary Reform leader, George Brown, suffered defeat in Toronto.[104]

Macdonald agreed with Lincoln that the American Civil War was a test of republicanism. But unlike the American president, the Canadian prime minister expected and hoped American republicanism would fail: "The fratricidal conflict now unhappily raging in the United States shows us the superiority of our institutions and of the principle on which we are based. Long may that principle—the Monarchial principle—prevail in this land."[105]

Indeed, American misfortune might become a Canadian windfall. Although Canadians disliked slavery, they feared American power even more. If the Union dissolved, the two (or more) new nations would be weaker, increasing the relative power of Canada in North America. In mid-1861, Macdonald dared to dream big: "that in consequence of the fratricidal war, Canada had every prospect of being the great nation of this continent." That seemed a tall order for a country of 3.1 million people, a tenth of American numbers. And Canadian leaders had to save their own faltering union.[106]

Canadians feared Seward's influence because he long had championed an American annexation of Canada. In early 1861, Canadian newspapers reprinted a column from the *New York Herald* declaring that the North, "being cut off from a Southern field of enterprise, must, by the law of their nature, expand northward and westward. Such is the decree of manifest destiny, and such the program of William H. Seward, Premier of the President elect." With the Republicans disavowing abolition, Canadians looked at the Union cause as an amoral drive for continental power. Most Canadian leaders hoped that the Confederacy would win and thereby divide the fearsome might of Americans.[107]

Agony

The American rupture affected all surrounding countries, including Santo Domingo (now the Dominican Republic), a former Spanish colony on the eastern two-thirds of the Caribbean island of Hispaniola. In 1859, the Buchanan administration had sent William Cazneau back to Santo Domingo as a special agent charged with reviving the American bid to buy Samana Bay, the great port on the northeast shore. Cazneau brought along his influential and talented wife, the journalist Jane Cazneau, who had coined the concept of an American "manifest destiny" to expand. The couple also served themselves by speculating in Dominican mines and plantations, which would soar in value after an American annexation. But their dreams crumbled as Dominican rulers rejected American overtures by instead inviting the Spanish to resume their colonial rule.[108]

During the early nineteenth century, Spain had lost almost all of her American colonies to republican revolutions. The Spanish retained only Cuba and Puerto Rico. During the 1850s, however, imperialists began to rebuild Spain's military might and colonial ambitions in hopes of joining Britain and France as a leading European power. By reclaiming Santo Domingo, the Spanish hoped to bolster the security of nearby Cuba against American aggression. Better still, they might use Santo Domingo as a base to rebuild their empire in Central and South America. Seward warned that Spain was "creeping out of her shell, and anxious to weave her web once more over her former possessions in America."[109]

In 1861, General Pedro Santana governed Santo Domingo on behalf of a light-skinned elite that dominated the poorer and darker peasants. Fearing invasion by Black-ruled Haiti to the west, the Dominican elite sought an external protector. Unable to sustain his bankrupt government, Santana favored submitting Santo Domingo to Spanish rule, provided he could remain as governor. In April 1861, 3,000 Spanish troops from Cuba occupied the capital of Santo Domingo and, a month later, the Spanish monarchy formally accepted Santana's gift.[110]

Preoccupied with civil war, neither the Union nor the Confederacy could interfere with Spain's intervention in the Caribbean. By doing little, Union leaders sought to keep Spain from recognizing or assisting the Confederacy, while southerners cultivated Spain as a potential ally that could provide munitions and, perhaps, deploy naval power to break the Union blockade. The Spanish ambassador to the United States, Gabriel García Tassara, welcomed disunion for sapping American power: "The Union is in agony, and our mission is not to delay its death for a moment."[111]

SIX ❧ MISERIES

Oh! What suffering, what misery, what untold agony this horrid
hell–begotten war has caused.

—JAMES HARRISON, CONFEDERATE SOLDIER, MAY 26, 1862[1]

In January 1861, the Mexican ambassador to the United States, Matías Romero, visited Springfield, Illinois, to meet president-elect Abraham Lincoln. Born in 1837 in Oaxaca, the home state of Benito Juárez, Romero became his protégé as a fellow Liberal. Entering the foreign service, he won appointment as Mexico's minister to the United States in 1860. Appalled by the proslavery Buchanan administration, Romero welcomed the Republicans as fellow Liberals committed to social mobility. He and Juárez also felt grateful for Lincoln's forceful opposition to the American war against Mexico during the 1840s.[2]

Meeting at Lincoln's home, Romero sought a new start for Mexico and the United States: "truly fraternal and not guided by the egotistic and antihumanitarian principles" of the Democratic administrations that had pillaged Mexico of "territory in order to extend slavery." Romero insisted that through trade and investment Americans could "obtain from Mexico all of the advantages" of annexation "without having to suffer any of the inconveniences."[3]

But Romero also had to explain away the financial woes and political turmoil of Mexico "which had already become proverbial here and were considered by many to be without remedy." The new American attorney general, Edward Bates, insisted that "the mongrel people of Mexico" were "wholly unfit to be our equals, friends and fellow citizens." If Mexico was a lost cause, Americans would further loot the country before Europeans could. So Romero pitched Juárez's Mexico as triumphant over a small minority of reactionaries, who had caused all the trouble but were now "unable to raise the standard of rebellion." Lincoln could not say the same for his country.[4]

Gracious and friendly, Lincoln impressed Romero as "a simple, honorable man," but too preoccupied with a rebellion in his own country to help Mexico. As the American civil war escalated, Romero often felt like the only sober man in a land of illusions. He marveled, "All federal cabinet members express very great and blind confidence in their army's

PREVIOUS PAGE: *"A Thrilling Scene in East Tennessee—Colonel Fry and the Union Men Swearing by the Flag,"* Harper's Weekly, *March 29, 1862.*

speedy reduction of the dissident states." As a Mexican, he knew much more about civil war than did any American.[5]

Combat

Dressed for parade rather than combat, in baggy red pants, feathered caps, and embroidered waistcoats, the new Union volunteers often resembled circus performers. The Confederates appeared almost as diverse but more gamy. In Virginia, a journalist marveled, "The volunteers were dressed in every imaginable style. . . . The only thing *uniform* about them was the *dirt*." By 1862, troops donned more standardized uniforms: dark blue for Yankees, and gray or brown for Confederates.[6]

At first, war seemed glorious to thousands of young men who had never known combat. A Mississippian enlisted "to fight the Yankees—all fun and frolic." Soldiers' heads swelled as they marched out of town while bands played patriotic tunes, women blew kisses, and cheering crowds waved flags. In June 1861, in Richmond, Mary Boykin Chesnut described the war as "all parade, fife, and fine feathers." A veteran Union officer, Ulysses S. Grant, reached a more sober conclusion, that "each side under-estimates the other and over-estimates itself."[7]

Proud of their freedom, volunteers balked at the hierarchy, regimentation, discipline, and punishments of military life. The adjustment proved especially hard and incomplete in the South, where white men thought that only slaves should take orders and abuse from superiors. Robert E. Lee lamented, "Our people are so little liable to control that it is difficult to get them to follow any course not in accordance with their inclination."[8]

Two-thirds of wartime deaths came from disease, which claimed 10 percent of Union recruits and 20 percent of Confederates. Soldiers ignored orders to keep clean camps, with latrines at a safe distance from their water supply. Lice, fleas, ticks, and rodents enlisted by the millions in both armies, conveying disease with their bites. Crowded together in filthy camps, soldiers suffered severely from dysentery and typhoid fever. "Our poor sick, I know, suffer much," but "they bring it on themselves by not doing what they are told. They are worse than children, for the latter can be forced," Lee complained.[9]

On long marches and in ramshackle camps, soldiers endured exposure to driving rain, severe heat, or bitter cold, which wore out their clothes and strength, increasing their vulnerability to pathogens. Soldiers subsisted on an unhealthy and often repulsive diet featuring rancid salt pork, seas of coffee, and a tough bread called "hardtack" that defied teeth but attracted worms. Nineteenth-century medical practice usually made matters worse, for ill-trained surgeons knew little about disease and usually could only issue opiates and amputate wounded limbs. A New Yorker concluded, "Our experience during the past year has dispelled all the novelty, mystery & glory of a soldier's life."[10]

Rapidly assembling massive armies, North and South made new officers of politicians, lawyers, doctors, merchants, and workshop or plantation managers. Many proved inept at training troops or leading them into the shock of combat. Over time, defeats weeded out incompetents, but not until many soldiers had lost lives and limbs.[11]

In 1861 and early 1862, when thrust into combat, cohesion eroded in a terrifying confusion of blood, sound, and fury, with men firing and moving almost randomly in a desperation to kill without getting killed. A New York soldier recalled, "Disintegration begins with the first shot, . . . months of drill apparently going for nothing in a few minutes." Most battles took place in an mix of forests, brush, and fields, where men became disoriented in the dense smoke and thunder of firearms and cannon. A Union general invited his family to imagine "the crash and thud of round shot through trees and buildings and into earth or through columns of human bodies" amidst "the uproar of thousands of voices," with "riderless horses rushing wildly about . . . and human frames thrown lifeless into the air" from explosions. After a day or two of this "man-slaughtering life," as one soldier called battle, even the supposed winners lacked the cohesion, will, and energy to pursue a retreating foe.[12]

Soldiers struggled to describe battles to civilians at home. After one bloody clash, an Alabaman noted, "When I go home it will take me months to describe what I saw on that terrible field." A Union general declared a battle was "too horrible to be real, and yet too real to forget." A Union surgeon reported, "My hands are constantly steaped in blood" from "arms shot off—legs shot off. Eyes shot out—brains shot out. Lungs shot through and, in a word, *everything* shot to pieces and totally maimed for all after life. The horror of this war can never be half told."[13]

As a South Carolina congressman, Lawrence Keitt had pushed for secession, naïvely believing that the war would be glorious and brief. Serving as a colonel, Keitt discovered the gory reality: "War in any aspect is cruel, but this war is robbed of chivalry, and is scarcely more than butchery. It is hate without manliness." A Confederate Don Quixote, Keitt sought to restore chivalry by charging on his gray horse directly at entrenched federal troops, who shot him dead. He was thirty-nine years old.[14]

Despite the horrors, men soldiered on into thunderous, smoky firestorms of shot. Often a mania gripped soldiers thrust into mass combat. A Wisconsin soldier recalled the anxious "eagerness to go forward, and a reckless disregard of life" by men "loading and firing with demoniacal fury and shouting and laughing hysterically." Addicted to the adrenaline rush of his new reality, Philip Kearny, a Union general, marveled, "I love war. It brings me indescribable pleasure, like that of having a woman." Was it worse to be Kearny's lover or soldier?[15]

Border States

To win the war, both sides needed to control four Border States, which sustained slavery counterbalanced by strong economic ties to the Union: Delaware, Maryland, Kentucky, and Missouri. Delaware readily stayed in the United States, but the other three waffled. Much was at stake, for Maryland, Kentucky, and Missouri could have increased the Confederacy's white manpower by 45 percent and its manufacturing capacity by 80 percent. And Yankees could not invade the Confederacy without getting through the Border States. Lincoln noted, "To lose Kentucky is nearly the same as to lose the whole game. Kentucky gone, we cannot hold Missouri, nor, as I think, Maryland. These all against us, and the job on our hands is too large for us." To woo their leaders, Lincoln promised to protect slavery within the states.[16]

In 1861, Maryland's governor was a tepid Unionist, and the state's legislators favored staying out of the war without leaving the Union just yet. Meanwhile, Confederate sympathizers kept busy sabotaging railway bridges and telegraph lines to cut off the national capital from the North. Rioters also attacked federal troops marching through Baltimore on April 19, slaying four of them. Returning fire, the troops killed twelve civilians. An angry city official told an officer that if his men fired again "there will be nothing left of you but your brass buttons to tell who you were." The boldest Maryland saboteur was Richard Thomas, a short, wealthy planter who cross-dressed as a pseudo-French woman called "Zarvona." Wearing her best petticoat and bustle, Zarvona seized a steamboat and took it away to Virginia. Unimpressed by the daring, a Union general considered Thomas "crack-brained."[17]

In May, Lincoln suspended the writ of *habeas corpus* in Maryland to enable federal army officers to arrest saboteurs. A War Department order explained, "In times of civil strife, errors, if any, should be on the side of the safety of the country." On May 25, federal troops arrested John Merryman, a wealthy slaveholder, for chopping down telegraph poles and burning bridges to keep federal troops out of Maryland.

His lawyers appealed to Chief Justice Taney, a fellow Marylander, who sympathized with the South. Defying Lincoln, Taney issued a writ of *habeas corpus*, requiring the local Union commander to bring Merryman into federal circuit court on May 27. The commander refused. A day later, Taney ruled that the Federal Constitution allowed only Congress, and not the president, to suspend the writ and thereby authorize soldiers to arrest civilians. Ready to paralyze the president's capacity to suppress dissidents, Taney favored "a peaceful separation" of the two regions as "far better than the union of all the present states under a military government, and a reign of terror preceded too by a civil war with all its horrors." Lincoln defied Taney's ruling, with support from the Republican majority in Congress.[18]

In September, federal troops arrested Baltimore's mayor and twenty-seven state legislators who supported secession. They stayed in jail through elections in November that replaced most with strong Unionists. The administration then released most of the jailed legislators, provided they took an oath of allegiance to the United States.[19]

To the west, Governor Claiborne Jackson rallied Missouri "to stand by her sister slave-holding States." Rejecting Lincoln's call for troops as "inhuman and diabolical," Jackson seized a federal arsenal at Liberty. He found support from the slaveholders clustered along the Missouri River, but the state's many small farmers elsewhere divided in their loyalties, while the German immigrants of St. Louis supported the Union. To spite the Germans, Jackson sent policemen to shut down their beer gardens. Jefferson Davis forwarded weapons to arm Jackson's militia for an attack on St. Louis.[20]

At St. Louis, a Union captain, Nathaniel Lyon, commanded 500 troops guarding a federal arsenal that housed 60,000 firearms and dozens of cannon coveted by Confederates. A Free Soiler from Connecticut, Lyon had a booming voice, intense blue eyes, and red beard, commanding attention despite his small stature. Brave, stubborn, resourceful, and profane, Lyon declared that rather than allow Jackson "to dictate to my government in any manner," he would see "every man, woman, and child in the State, dead and buried." Lyon recruited 4,000 volunteers from the city's immigrants.[21]

A master of improvisation, Lyon dressed as a genteel old lady with a shawl, veil, and wide sunbonnet to scout Jackson's militia encampment by riding through in a carriage. Returning to St. Louis, Lyon switched into his uniform and led his troops out to surround the militia camp, compelling surrender without firing a shot. But bullets flew in St. Louis that afternoon, when Confederate sympathizers rioted and Lyon's men shot back, killing twenty-eight. A boy recalled seeing a dead volunteer leaning against a wall: "My father said this was civil war." That night, rioters ruled the streets, burning African-American churches, wrecking a German newspaper office and beating, stoning, shooting, and lynching immigrants. In the morning, Lyon's men restored order, preserving St. Louis as a Union stronghold. Marching on Jefferson City, the state capital, Lyon drove out Jackson and his supporters in June. Fleeing to Arkansas, they set up a state government in exile.[22]

For his coup, Lyon won promotion to brigadier general. In August, he marched 6,000 men south to strike 10,000 Confederates camped at Wilson's Creek. Although outnumbered, Lyon reasoned that fortune favored the bold. "I will gladly give my life for a victory," he declared.

Instead, he gave it for a defeat, taking a bullet to the chest during a reckless charge. His discouraged men retreated, while the exhausted Confederates failed to pursue. The Union kept a shaky hold over most of Missouri.[23]

Kentucky was even more important than Missouri. Lincoln said that he hoped to have God on his side, but he must have Kentucky. Most Kentuckians sought to keep their state neutral, lest they divide and kill each other. Governor Beriah Magoffin tried to tip the scale by allowing Confederate officers to recruit Kentuckians, while he built up a force of state troops for a coup. Unionists countered by rallying their own armed men. Federal and Confederate armies camped just outside Kentucky, in southern Illinois and northern Tennessee, preparing to move in.[24]

The Confederates could not resist the temptation of seizing Columbus, a key position in western Kentucky on bluffs that commanded a rail line and the Mississippi River. By striking first, on September 4, 1861, the Confederates alienated most Kentuckians, including state legislators, who voted by three to one to embrace the Union. Federal troops moved in to occupy two-thirds of the state, including the capital. Magoffin fled into exile in the Confederacy, as did Senator Breckinridge, a presidential candidate of 1860. Kentuckians divided to fight on both sides: 40 percent with the Confederates versus 60 percent for the Union. As with Missouri, the Confederate government claimed Kentucky as a member state.[25]

The Union also prevailed in western Virginia: a poor and mountainous region of thirty-five counties with relatively few masters and slaves. The people traded more with nearby Ohio and Pennsylvania than with the rest of Virginia. For decades they had complained of underrepresentation in a state dominated by eastern slaveholders indifferent to western economic development. Clinging to the Union, western Virginians formed their own state government, which the Union recognized. It consisted of fifty counties and included Harpers Ferry, a strategic position beside the Potomac.[26]

The Lincoln administration needed western Virginia because it hosted a key east-west transportation link, the B&O Railroad, which connected the Midwest to Maryland and Washington, D.C. In June, Union troops from Ohio pushed in to seize the railway, driving back small Confederate forces. The region's most effective Union commander was William S. Rosecrans, but his superior, George B. McClellan, reaped the credit. Short but dapper, McClellan grew up in a wealthy family and received a prep school and Ivy League education. A star student in military engineering at West Point, McClellan had served ably in the war against Mexico before becoming a railroad executive to make more money. Upon taking command in western Virginia, McClellan flattered his men: "Soldiers! I have heard that there was danger here. I have come to place myself at your head and to share it with you. I fear now but one thing—that you will not find foemen worthy of your steel."[27]

To reclaim western Virginia, President Davis sent Robert E. Lee to rally Confederate troops, but he faced a logistical nightmare. Benefiting from transportation along the Ohio River and on the B&O Railroad, federal troops were well clothed, armed, and fed. Not so the Confederates sent to the far end of a long supply line over wretched roads, around mountains, and through winding valleys. Summer rains clogged those roads with mud, trapping supply wagons. Soggy Confederate troops became hungry, sick with measles, and demoralized. Lee grumbled that his undisciplined soldiers were "worse than children."[28]

After losing a few skirmishes, Lee returned to Richmond, where the newspapers turned against him as "Granny Lee" who had been "outwitted, outmaneuvered, and outgeneraled." Reaping the glory of victory, McClellan cultivated reporters who called him "the Young Napoleon." In 1861, it appeared that McClellan would become the war's greatest commander, eclipsing the overrated Lee. But looks proved deceiving.[29]

Parson

The Union faced its own logistical nightmare in attempting to reclaim mountainous east Tennessee. The region's only railroad ran from Virginia southwestward to Knoxville—good for sending in Confederate troops but useless for Union forces. As in western Virginia, most people in east Tennessee were small farmers who resented political domination by their state's planter elite. While the rest of Tennessee voted 86 percent for secession, only 31 percent did so in east Tennessee. East Tennesseans rallied around Andrew Johnson, the only U.S. senator from the South to cling to the Union. A former tailor, Johnson resented the "purse proud" planter as "not half as good as the man who earns his bread by the sweat of his brow."[30]

East Tennesseans also followed the lead of William G. Brownlow, an especially profane Methodist clergyman and newspaper publisher and editor. "Parson" Brownlow promised to "fight the Secession leaders till Hell freezes over and then fight them on the ice." Born poor into a life of farm labor, Brownlow had only a year's schooling, but he read everything he could borrow. A rival editor conceded that Brownlow "preached at every church and schoolhouse, made stump speeches at every crossroad, and knows every man, woman, and child, and their fathers and grandfathers before them, in East Tennessee."[31]

A fiery writer and speaker, Brownlow gloried in the nickname of "The Fighting Parson." He made many enemies: rival editors, Presbyterians, Baptists, Catholics, and Democrats. Brownlow boasted that "in point of severity, and wholesale abuse of individuals, our paper is without parallel in the history of the American Press." A staunch Whig, Brownlow called his Democratic rival, Andrew Johnson, a liar, coward, and the illegitimate son of a chicken thief. Brownlow's insulted foes tried, at various times, to lynch, shoot, cane, and club the parson, who courted combat despite his slight build and bookish appearance. Readers loved his performance, awarding the *Knoxville Whig* more subscribers than all other newspapers in the region combined.[32]

Like most people of east Tennessee, Brownlow despised Blacks as racial inferiors, and he hated abolitionists as menacing meddlers. In 1858, he had praised slavery as "a blessing to the civilized white race in general and a blessing to the negro slaves in particular." Outraged by *Uncle Tom's Cabin*, he blasted Harriet Beecher Stowe as "ugly as Original sin—an abomination in the eyes of civilized people: a tall, coarse, vulgar-looking woman—stoop-shouldered with a long yellow neck, and a long peaked nose—through which she speaks."[33]

But Brownlow opposed secession as a plot by elitist planters to exploit common white people: "Let Tennessee go into this *Empire of the Cot-*

ton States, and all poor men will at once become the *free negroes of the Empire*." When Tennessee did take the plunge, Brownlow kept the Stars and Stripes flying over his newspaper in a show of defiance. Emulating western Virginians, he organized a movement to separate east Tennessee into a new state that could remain in the Union.[34]

Eager to find and help southern Unionists, Lincoln exhorted his generals to make liberating east Tennessee a priority. In late 1861, however, the Union could spare only 4,000 men under General George H. Thomas, a Virginian who stayed loyal to the Union. Advancing to Mill Springs in southern Kentucky, Thomas routed a Confederate force in January 1862, but he could get no farther because winter weather blocked the roads through the twisting mountains.[35]

Thomas's halt came as bad news for east Tennessee partisans, who had torn down telegraph lines and burned nine railroad bridges to block Confederate resupply and reinforcement in the region. Declaring martial law and rushing in troops from Virginia, Confederates executed five bridge burners and left their bodies to dangle and rot beside the rebuilt bridges as a warning to others. Confederates jailed another thousand dissidents, and thousands more fled their homes to become refugees in Kentucky, where the men enlisted in Union regiments.[36]

Confederates arrested Brownlow and shut down his newspaper. Lacking evidence to convict him, they exiled him to the North in March 1862. There he greeted his old enemy Johnson as his new best friend, for they "rushed into each other's arms and wept like children." Touring the North, Brownlow addressed huge crowds, who paid well to hear him abuse Confederates and vow to hang their leaders with his own hands. For another $10,000, he published *Parson Brownlow's Book* to promote Unionism; it sold over 100,000 copies.[37]

Brownlow reinforced Republicans' wishful thinking that most southern whites would welcome Union armies as liberators who would rescue them from a despotic cabal of great slaveholders. Most Republicans ignored the abundant evidence that, outside of mountainous pockets like western Virginia and eastern Tennessee, almost all white southerners supported the Confederacy. By believing in a war of deliverance for common whites, most Unionists balked at crusading against slavery, lest that alienate potential southern supporters.[38]

Despite the Unionist edge in most of the border regions, they remained chaotic and bloody because Confederate guerrillas attacked Union outposts and supply lines and killed Unionist neighbors. Federal commanders countered by arming Unionists who treated Confederate civilians with equal brutality. Often the division emerged along older fault lines of neighborhood feuds that made the wartime violence brutally personal. A Confederate partisan said he committed a lynching "to see one union man shit his last dieing turd." A Missourian lamented, "Men seem to have lost their reason and gone mad." Night riders rousted civilians to shoot or hang men and older boys while the rest of their families watched and screamed. Then the raiders torched homes, barns, and sheds, consuming years of hard work to leave behind smoking ruins. A Missouri woman lamented, "Our farms are all burned up, fences gone, crops destroyed; no one escapes the ravages of one party or the other."[39]

The guerrilla warfare of the Border States spilled over into parts of the Midwest, as some Confederate partisans found haven among sympathizers in rural Illinois, Indiana, and Iowa. The partisans then helped their hosts and themselves by stealing from Unionist neighbors, leaving burned farms and lynched men in their wake. Union commanders had to divert troops from the front to suppress these bushwhackers.[40]

Young Napoleon

During the spring of 1861, the Union's elderly commanding general, Winfield Scott, proposed a methodical strategy that would slowly build up a trained army while the navy enforced a blockade on southern ports meant to suffocate the Confederate economy. Eventually, part of the army would advance down the Mississippi to reopen that trade corridor for the Midwest. Wits called his scheme the "Anaconda Plan," after a large snake that encircles and slowly crushes its prey.[41]

Scott's plan required a more patient people than the Americans.

Newspapers, citizens, and politicians (including Lincoln) clamored for a quick strike south from Washington, D.C., on Richmond, the new Confederate capital. Yankees wanted to believe that the Confederacy was an unpopular house of cards that would collapse if given a quick, hard push. Then all the Union troops could go home to celebrate.[42]

Unable to take the field, Scott relied on his subordinate, General Irvin McDowell, an able officer for a lesser assignment but unsuited to command a large army. On July 16, McDowell launched his move south with 30,000 men, targeting a Confederate army commanded by P. G. T. Beauregard at Manassas, a key railroad and turnpike junction in northern Virginia. Moving ponderously with excessive equipment, McDowell's troops lost any possibility of surprise, and Confederate reinforcements under Joseph E. Johnston arrived in time to raise the defenders' numbers to a parity with the invaders.[43]

Attacking on the morning of July 21, McDowell's troops gained ground until they ran into a fresh brigade commanded by Thomas J. Jackson, who earned the nickname "Stonewall" for holding firm under heavy fire on the battlefield's key hill. As the Union attack stalled, Beauregard counterattacked with troops screaming their piercing "rebel yell," which demoralized the northern troops. Exhausted by the heat of July and smoke of battle, the Yankees panicked and fled, throwing away guns and packs to make better speed. McDowell's army dissolved into a terrified, fleeing mob, but the Confederates were too disorganized and weary to pursue. Instead, they looted the dead and wounded Yankees. A Louisiana officer marveled at his men with "gold rings on their fingers, and their pockets filled with watches and money they had stolen." The victors included sixty-seven-year-old Edmund Ruffin, who helped operate a cannon and boasted of killing six Yankees.[44]

The costs of Manassas seemed shocking in July 1861: 400 Confederate and 625 Yankee dead. But these losses would soon seem quaintly low in a future of bigger, longer, and deadlier clashes. After the battle, a Georgian saw a comrade "weeping bitterly and wringing his hands over the stiff and blackened cor[p]se of his brother who fell on the other side." The witness concluded, "This civil war is a terrible thing." Another

Confederate was less troubled by Yankee corpses, sending a scalp to his aunt: "I could have sent a skull just dug up but it was too large."[45]

Confederates grew cocky, for Manassas seemed to confirm their superiority over the wretched Yankees. An Alabaman wrote a new song, entitled "Run Yank or Die," in which Union troops broke and fled whenever they heard the chorus "Hurrah for Slavery." The song became a hit in the Confederate army and on the home front. A Georgia congressman boasted that this one battle "has secured our independence." But Mary Chesnut aptly feared that the victory "lulls us into a fool's paradise of conceit."[46]

Manassas ignited bitter feuds between Beauregard, Johnston, and Davis as each claimed credit for the victory and blamed the other two men for hindering a triumphant advance to seize Washington, D.C. Davis rebuked Beauregard for trying "to exalt yourself at my expense." Mary Chesnut concluded that Johnston's "hatred of Jeff Davis amounts to a religion." Beauregard and Johnston became the favorites of Confederate congressmen who despised Davis.[47]

The stunning Union defeat undercut American credibility abroad. The editor of the London *Times* scoffed at the United States as "a so-called Power that can scarcely defend its capital against its fellow-citizens." Irritated by Yankees, a Canadian woman exulted when Manassas "caused all Canadians to scorn and laugh at them." Canada's governing Conservatives staged a champagne party to celebrate the Union defeat. For once in his life, the premier, John A. Macdonald, avoided a party, deeming this one in bad taste.[48]

On the Union side, initial panic quickly passed, replaced by greater determination to fight a longer war against formidable foes. A day after the defeat, Lincoln sought to enlist another 500,000 men for three-year terms. Lincoln replaced McDowell with McClellan, the hero of West Virginia, who came to Washington to rebuild the Army of the Potomac. Only thirty-four, he had become the second-ranking general in the Union.[49]

Masterful at training and supplying soldiers, McClellan was a fussy perfectionist who resisted and resented political pressure to lead them into combat. A lifetime of achievement had robbed McClellan of humility. Handsome and attentive to his troops, McClellan gloried in their cheers as he rode by. "You have no idea how they brighten up now when I go among them. . . . I believe they love me," he told his wife. McClellan insisted that only he could save the Union but only if the president, Congress, and General Scott got out of his way. He fancied that with a few victories, "I could become Dictator or anything else that might please me." Pushing Scott into retirement in November, McClellan became general-in-chief. "I can do it all," McClellan assured Lincoln.[50]

McClellan meant to focus the war narrowly on reasserting federal authority with few casualties and little destruction to property. He opposed emancipation as a threat to restoring the old Union: "I will not fight for the abolitionists." Although he disliked slavery in principle, McClellan disdained Blacks: "I confess to a prejudice in favor of my own race, & can't learn to like the odor of either Billy goats or niggers." Vowing "with an iron hand [to] crush any attempt at insurrection" by enslaved people, McClellan ordered his troops forcibly to return fugitives to their masters. He kicked out of his camp a popular musical group, the Hutchinson Family Singers, for performing abolitionist songs. Confident in the racism of most soldiers, McClellan insisted that the army would dissolve rather than fight for emancipation. Initially, he deemed Lincoln "really sound on the nigger question."[51]

Wedded to limited war, McClellan would only advance in overwhelming force meant to overawe the enemy without the dangerous uncertainties of massive battles. His life of repeated success had bred a phobia of risk, lest a single defeat sour his aura of always winning. McClellan talked big of inevitable triumph, but acted small, repeatedly insisting that Confederates outnumbered him. In August 1861 he had twice as many troops as the Confederates in northern Virginia, but McClellan claimed that they had "from 3 to 4 times my force." So he demanded more time and ever more reinforcements from the government.[52]

By November, Republican congressmen were losing confidence in McClellan, who seemed more show than substance. "'Young Napoleon' is going down as fast as he went up," one wrote. Another congressman added, "Action, action is what we want and must have," to sustain morale on the home front. The British correspondent William H. Russell concluded, "I like the man, but I do not think he is equal to his occasion or his place."⁵³

Inexperienced with criticism, McClellan raged in private against Republicans, including Lincoln, who had patiently supported his general. McClellan assured his wife, "I am becoming daily more disgusted with this imbecile administration. . . . The pres[i]d[en]t is nothing more than a well-meaning baboon." In November, Lincoln and Seward visited McClellan's home to discuss strategy, but the general refused to see them, instead retiring to bed. The president serenely said, "I will hold McClellan's horse if he will only bring us success." McClellan, however, kept preparing excuses for failure: "If it is so, the fault will not be mine."⁵⁴

In December, Republicans in Congress set up a special Joint Committee on the Conduct of the War. Holding hearings to interrogate executive officials and military officers, the committee humiliated those deemed too weak in prosecuting the war. After a botched attack on a Confederate outpost at Ball's Bluff beside the Potomac, the committee scapegoated General Charles P. Stone, a Democrat and disciple of McClellan. Accused of treason, Stone spent six months in prison without trial.⁵⁵

The chair of the committee, Benjamin F. Wade of Ohio, privately accused Lincoln of "murdering your country by inches" with a "blundering, cowardly, and inefficient" prosecution of the war. Seeking better relations, Lincoln invited Wade and his wife to a dinner and ball at the White House. Wade replied, "Are the President and Mrs. Lincoln aware that there is a civil war? If they are not, Mr. and Mrs. Wade are, and for that reason decline to participate in feasting and dancing."⁵⁶

Lincoln needed respites of festivity, for he felt intensely anxious over the faltering Union offensives, the heavy casualties of mass war, and bitter political divisions in the North. Every week he received anonymous letters threatening his assassination in vivid detail. One angry critic wrote, "Do you ever realize that the desolation, sorrow, [and] grief that pervades the country is owing to you?" Lincoln also worried about his volatile wife, Mary Todd Lincoln, whose extravagant tastes exceeded his income, so she drew recklessly on government funds. Both Lincolns nearly suffered breakdowns in February 1862, when typhoid fever killed their cherished son, Willie, aged eleven. Profoundly depressed, Lincoln neglected to eat and could not sleep, haunting the telegraph room of the War Department through the night in desperate hope of better news from his generals. When he did sleep, nightmares of funerals, sometimes his own, tormented Lincoln. A friend worried that Lincoln was wasting away into a living corpse with "a sunken, deathly look about the large, cavernous eyes."[57]

Blockade

The Union did adopt a key part of Scott's Anaconda Plan: to cripple the southern economy by blockading its ports. An effective blockade could prevent the export of cotton and the Confederate import of munitions from Britain. But a blockading fleet had to contend with 3,500 miles of coastline, 10 major ports, and another 180 smaller ones. In April 1861, the United States had only forty-three warships, most of them then in distant oceans. But the new secretary of the navy, Gideon Welles, proved a master administrator who leased scores of merchant ships, armed them with a few cannon, and sent them south. By the end of 1861, Welles had 260 warships on duty, with another 100 under construction. The small, new Confederate navy could not compete, allowing Union warships free movement along the coast.[58]

Samuel F. Du Pont commanded the South Atlantic Blockading Squadron, which watched ports from Florida to Virginia. Born and raised in wealth in Delaware, he had been a conservative Democrat who defended American slavery as a paternalistic system that benefited enslaved Africans. But during the 1850s, shore visits to the Deep South opened his eyes: "The degradation, overwork, and ill treatment of the slaves in the cotton states is greater than I deemed possible, while the capacity of the Negro for improvement is higher than I believed." As a wartime admiral, he helped enslaved people to escape.[59]

In May 1862, Robert Smalls was enslaved, twenty-three years old, married with three children, and an expert pilot employed on the *Planter,* a steamer that transported Confederate troops and supplies from Charleston to forts at the mouth of the harbor. Before dawn on May 13, the *Planter* sat at a city wharf loaded with cannon for shipment to Fort Sumter. While the white officers slept, Smalls slipped onto the unguarded ship with his family and eleven other enslaved people. They steamed out of the harbor, raised a white flag, and raced to the blockading squadron to turn over ship and cargo to the Union. The federal government rewarded Smalls and his companions with prize money and took the *Planter* into the U.S. Navy to help enforce the blockade. Becoming a pilot for the squadron, Smalls impressed Du Pont: "His information is thorough and complete as to the whole defenses of Charleston."[60]

To tighten the blockade, Du Pont seized southern ports to serve as Union bases for resupply and repair. Union forces also sought to capture cotton for shipment to Europe to reduce the pressure from French and British diplomats to lift the blockade. The Union already controlled the mouth of Chesapeake Bay thanks to Fort Monroe at Hampton Roads, Virginia. In the largest operation (held in November 1861), seventeen warships and nearly 13,000 men seized Port Royal, South Carolina, liberating 10,000 enslaved people in the vicinity. By April 1862, these amphibious operations reduced the Confederacy to possession of just two major ports on the Atlantic coast: Charleston, South Carolina, and Wilmington, North Carolina.[61]

To evade Union warships, Confederates (and British collaborators) developed smaller, sleeker, faster vessels with shallower drafts and gray paint for lower visibility. Favoring moonless, foggy, or stormy nights, these "blockade runners" darted in and out of southern harbors bound to and from the British-held islands of Bermuda and the Bahamas or Spanish Havana. There they could obtain coal for fuel and exchange cotton for European manufactures. With cotton soaring in price on European markets (owing to the reduced supply arriving there), blockade runners and their crews made great profits. During the war, five out of six blockade runners got through, but the shift to smaller vessels dramatically reduced cargo capacity. The volume of goods reaching the South fell to a third of prewar levels. The high cost of imported goods contributed to the spiraling inflation that sapped the southern economy.[62]

Seeking a new weapon to break the blockade, Confederates converted the captured hulk of a Union warship into an ironclad gunboat, the CSS *Virginia,* then a novelty in American waters. Covered with iron plates four inches thick, the ironclad could repel the cannon shot that wrecked wooden warships. The Confederates mounted ten cannon on the vessel, four on each broadside and one each at bow and aft. An iron ram at the waterline on the bow provided another means to take out wooden hulls. Two old steam engines propelled the ironclad. On March 8, 1862, CSS *Virginia* ventured out of Norfolk harbor to attack five Union warships blockading that port, blowing up one, sinking another, and driving a third onto the shore. The battle killed 361 Union sailors but only two on the *Virginia* thanks to the superior protection of her iron shell. Calling it a day, the Confederate crew returned to port, planning to finish off the Yankee squadron in the morning.[63]

The next day, CSS *Virginia* steamed out to find that the Union had countered with its own ironclad, USS *Monitor,* just arrived from New York City. Escaping from slavery in Norfolk, a woman had brought word to Welles of the Confederate ironclad project. Her information hastened construction on the *Monitor* as a counter. An innovative design, the *Monitor* presented a limited target above water in the form of a single revolving gun turret with eight inches of armor and two rifled cannon. Although lacking the bulk and firepower of *Virginia,* the smaller *Monitor* was more maneuverable, thanks to a shallower draft and stronger engine. For two hours, the ironclads exchanged fire, with neither able to penetrate the other's shell. Losing power from its balky engines, *Virginia* returned to port and stayed there until May 1862, when Union troops captured Norfolk. Retreating Confederates blew up their prize warship to keep it from falling into Yankee hands.[64]

The Confederates built twenty-one more ironclads on the *Virginia* model, and the Union countered with fifty-eight, primarily of the *Monitor* sort, although some had two, and even three, gun turrets. As Union armies seized ports and advanced along rivers, Confederates destroyed most of their ironclads, which had failed to break the blockade.[65]

Seeking another wonder weapon, Confederates also experimented with submarines, primarily CSS *Hunley,* built at Charleston. For power, the crew of seven men turned a crank connected to the propeller. A torpedo on a wooden spar projecting from the bow was the sole weapon. In February 1864 the *Hunley* attacked and sank the USS *Housatonic*, in the first kill by a submarine in history. But the explosion also crippled the *Hunley*, which collapsed, killing the crew, and that loss terminated the Confederate submarine program.[66]

The Confederates had more luck with commerce raiders built for them by British shipyards, whose owners evaded neutrality laws by pretending that the buyers were Italians. Powered by both sails and steam engines, the raiders were sleek and fast. Over the heated protests of U.S. diplomats, the British allowed eight new ships to sail away without weaponry in early 1862. Heading to remote islands, they received guns and Confederate names, including CSS *Alabama*, CSS *Florida*, and CSS *Shenandoah*. The raiders sailed the oceans to seize 261 Union merchant ships, burning most and ransoming others. These losses drove up insurance costs to prohibitive levels, shrinking the American merchant marine to a third of its prewar size.[67]

To hunt for the elusive raiders, the Union navy diverted seventy-seven warships from blockade duty. For over two years, the hunters had no luck, reaping abuse from Yankee newspapers. "What vexes me," Admiral Du Pont complained, "is that so few people know or understand what a needle in a haystack business it is to chase a single ship on the wide ocean." At last, in June 1864, a Union warship tracked the CSS *Alabama* to the French port of Cherbourg. The flamboyant Confederate captain, Raphael Semmes, could not resist the challenge to fight a single ship combat, but he lost and *Alabama* sank.[68]

Trent

To break the Union blockade, Confederates needed European allies with powerful fleets: Britain, France, and Spain. The South did find sympathizers among European aristocrats, who despised American republicanism as an anarchic threat to their power and world order. The British prime minister, Lord Palmerston, derided American politicians as "men who have no sense of Honor and who are swayed by the passions of irresponsible masses." Privately, he relished disintegration of "the *Dis-*united States."[69]

In 1848, Europe's rulers had got a scare from a spate of republican revolutions. Although suppressed, the revolutions lingered in the troubled minds of monarchs and aristocrats, who blamed the American example. So they welcomed a civil war that would divide and weaken the United States while discrediting republics as too volatile to endure. Sir John Ramsden assured Parliament, "We are now witnessing the bursting of the great republican bubble which had so often been held up to us as a model on which to recast our own English Constitution." A French cabinet minister assured an American, "Your Republic is dead, and it is probably the last the world will see."[70]

Kings and aristocrats disdained Yankee politicians as vulgar upstarts. Mocking Lincoln as an ape, the French empress, Eugénie, urged scientists to call off "searching Africa for the missing link when a specimen was brought from the American backwoods." Confederate diplomats pandered to European aristocrats by embracing elitism and deriding northern democracy as mob rule. The Belgian king, Leopold, celebrated "the monarchical-aristocratic principle in the Southern states."[71]

The Union had potential admirers among middle-class Europeans. In France, a liberal politician declared, "The future of republicanism in Europe depended upon the success of republicanism in America." But European liberals wanted the United States to abolish slavery, so they felt disappointed in 1861, when Union leaders balked. A British abolitionist complained, "Neither Lincoln nor Seward has yet spoken an antislavery syllable since they took office." It became easy for Europeans to dismiss the American conflict as all about economic self-interest and regional power. Offering a general's commission to the great Italian revolutionary Giuseppe Garibaldi, a Union diplomat insisted "that the fall of the American Union . . . would be a disastrous blow to the cause of Human Freedom equally here, in Europe, and throughout the world." Although intrigued by that pitch, Garibaldi declined so long as the Union failed to fight for emancipation.[72]

In May 1861, Britain formally recognized the Confederates as "belligerents" rather than rebels. Under international law, belligerents could contract loans and buy arms in neutral countries, such as Britain and France. That status took the Confederacy a key step closer to full diplomatic recognition as a sovereign nation. American leaders also seethed when the British foreign minister, Lord Russell, met with Confederate envoys in London. Seward blustered, "We will wrap the whole world in flames! No power is so remote that she will not feel the fire of our battle and be burned by our conflagration." Considering republics volatile and reckless, the British ambassador, Lord Lyons, complained, "It is the business of Seward to feed the mob with sacrifices every day, and we happen to be the most grateful food he can offer." In August 1861, a Canadian visiting the United States marveled at Yankee belligerence: "What a strange race of madmen—only fit for a lunatic asylum—our old, calm, calculating, and sagacious friends in the North . . . have become!"[73]

Southern diplomats exploited the tensions fomented by an Anglophobic northern press and Seward's fiery rhetoric. To appease Europeans, Confederate diplomats were supposed to downplay slavery and instead cast the South as a plucky underdog fighting for free trade and national self-determination. That pose seemed more plausible given the Republican vow to protect slavery within the states. Confederate diplomats assured British leaders that Lincoln "proposes no freedom to the slave but announces subjection of his owner to the will of the Union, in other words, to the will of the North." Confederates benefited from European disgust at the Republicans' protectionist trade policies that jacked up tariffs on imports.[74]

The Union blockade also troubled Europeans by reducing the flow of cotton to their factories and of their manufactures to the Confederacy. Britain and France derived at least three-quarters of their cotton from the South, and cotton textiles served as their leading industrial sector, employing directly or indirectly at least four million people in Britain and nearly one million in France. Over half of British exports by value consisted of cotton textiles. A London newspaper warned that if Britain lost her cotton supply "a thousand of our merchant ships would rot idly in dock, two thousand mills must stop their busy looms; two thousand thousand mouths would starve for lack of food."[75]

Confederates believed that the French and British economies so depended on cotton that their leaders would intervene to break the Union blockade of southern ports. The South's leading magazine, De Bow's *Commercial Register*, preached: "To the slave-holding states [cotton] is the great source of their power and their wealth, and the main security for their peculiar institution. Let us teach our children to hold the cotton plant in one hand and a sword in the other, ever ready to defend it as a source of commercial power abroad and, through that, of independence at home." Never one to understate, Louis T. Wigfall declared that southern cotton so ruled the transatlantic economy that even Queen Victoria must "bend the knee in fealty and acknowledge allegiance to that monarch."[76]

In mid-1861, to pressure Europeans, southerners imposed an embargo on cotton exports until the French and British recognized their independence. During 1861, however, that embargo had little impact on European textile manufacturers, who had exploited the bumper crop and low prices of 1860 to import more than usual, building up reserves. Those reserves gave them time to seek other sources of supply from Algeria, Egypt, and especially India. European leaders also resented the effort to coerce them with an embargo. The lead Confederate diplomat in Britain, William L. Yancey, sadly reported that "important as cotton is, it is not King in Europe."[77]

An eloquent hothead, Yancey made a poor diplomat, particularly in Britain, where the people opposed the African slave trade that he had championed. Contrary to his instructions, Yancey praised slavery to British leaders as essential to civilization and global commerce. Irritated by Yancey's blustering, Lord Russell retorted that the "stain of slavery" made the Confederate cause "loathsome to the civilized world." Yancey blamed Harriet Beecher Stowe: "The anti-Slavery sentiment is universal. *Uncle Tom's Cabin* has been read and believed." Fed up with diplomacy, Yancey asked for, and got, permission to resign and return home, where he warned Confederates, "We cannot look for any sympathy or help from abroad."[78]

In the fall, President Davis sent two new ambassadors to Europe: James M. Mason of Virginia for Britain and John Slidell of Louisiana for France. In October, they slipped through the blockade to Cuba, where they boarded a British mail packet, the *Trent*, for passage to Britain. Acting on his own, without orders from Washington, Captain Charles Wilkes of USS *San Jacinto* intercepted the *Trent* after it steamed out of Havana in November. A boarding party arrested and removed Mason and Slidell, whom Wilkes carried away to a military prison in Boston. The captures thrilled Lincoln and the northern press and public as a rare Union victory in 1861. As the author of the Fugitive Slave Law, Mason seemed a great catch for antislavery men, and Slidell came a close second for pushing filibustering in the tropics. Congress honored Wilkes with a gold medal.[79]

But the British press, public, and leaders denounced the violation of their sovereign flag by Wilkes. "The people are frantic with rage," a British friend informed Seward. In December, Lord Lyons delivered an ultimatum from his government: the United States must apologize and release Mason and Slidell or face war. With "Mr. Seward at the helm of the United States, and the mob and the Press manning the vessel," the Duke of Newcastle expected war. Anticipating an American invasion of British North America, Britain sent more warships and 11,000 troops across the Atlantic to reinforce Canada, where the people displayed a great burst of British patriotism.[80]

Beleaguered by one war, the Union could not afford a second with the world's premier naval power—and with the French probably joining the fight as British allies. To everyone's surprise, Seward became the voice of reason in the cabinet, pushing the president to give way. Taking that advice in late December, Lincoln ordered Mason and Slidell released and sent off to London. Blaming Wilkes as a rogue operator, Seward provided political cover by insisting that the British were embracing the long-held American position on neutral rights. A relieved British soldier in Montreal remarked, "We had good times; we had no care; we had our beer." The British rulers agreed to forget about an American apology.[81]

Expecting future trouble from the Americans, British leaders wanted Canadians to pay more for their own defense by training and funding 100,000 militiamen to guard the long border with the United States. Despite their British patriotism, most Canadians balked at the high cost of defending themselves against the mighty Americans. Britons should protect them, Canadians reasoned, because the imperial tie alone made them a target for invasion when Anglo-American relations soured. It did not sit well with British leaders when the mayor of Montreal praised Canada as "the land of freedom, the land free from taxes, protected at the expense of the Mother Country." Already suffering from a budget deficit, many Canadians doubted that they could afford to build up a force sufficient to repel an American army. Better, they thought, to avoid offending the Yankees by keeping a low profile. "Canada's best defence was no defence," declared a politician.[82]

As the Canadian premier, John A. Macdonald felt obliged to seek at least a modest increase in defense funding. In the spring of 1862, he proposed a bill to train 30,000 men for a month each year at a cost of $1.1 million—a tenth of Canada's annual revenue. The plan also provided for conscription, an unpopular prospect particularly in Quebec, where French Canadians opposed serving under British officers. In May 1862, this Militia Bill failed after Macdonald did little to promote it, evading most of the debate. The British governor general reported that Macdonald's absence was "nominally by illness, but really, as everyone knows, by drunkenness." Expecting his bill to lose, Macdonald preferred to indulge in one of his epic benders. Blamed for the unpopular budget deficit, Macdonald's government was already teetering, so he exploited the militia bill defeat to resign—exiting as a martyr of British patriotism. The Militia Bill defeat irritated British leaders as proof of Canadian irresponsibility. Why, they wondered, should British taxpayers and soldiers defend Canada?[83]

Debts

The Lincoln administration cultivated good relations with Mexico's Liberal government led by Benito Juárez. Lincoln helped by appointing an able ambassador: Thomas Corwin, a tall, robust, and gregarious former congressman from Ohio. His antislavery convictions and opposition to the American invasion of Mexico impressed Juárez and his ambassador to the U.S., Matías Romero. Corwin reported that Liberals "entertain[ed] a sad and profound conviction that our failure will be the doom of free government everywhere on earth." Juarez approved Corwin's request to allow California volunteers to cross Mexican territory to reach Arizona.[84]

By contrast, Jefferson Davis chose an offensive ambassador: John T. Pickett, a veteran filibusterer who had invaded Cuba and Nicaragua. Unable to mask his aggression, Pickett contradicted the official Confederate party line of renouncing expansion. Regarding Mexico as "our natural inheritance," Pickett derided the "gross ignorance and superstition of the people (if Mexico may be said to have a people)." Angered by Mexico's transit for Union troops, Pickett told Juárez to expect "30,000 Confederate diplomats" coming across the Rio Grande. In Mexico City, Pickett often got drunk and insulted Mexicans, observing that once captured by Confederates, Mexicans would "for the first time in their lives" be "usefully employed" by "hoeing corn and picking cotton" on southern plantations. Juárez's agents intercepted and decoded Pickett's intemperate dispatches, sharing copies with Corwin. Then Mexican authorities arrested and expelled Pickett for punching and kicking a Yankee visiting Mexico City—and for warning a Union diplomat to stay "out of the reach of the toe of my boots."[85]

The Confederacy did better in northern Mexico thanks to a more tactful agent, Juan A. Quintero, who dealt with a more receptive regime, that of the *caudillo* Santiago Vidaurri. A Cuban who had lived in Mexico, Quintero understood Hispanics far better than did Pickett. Educated at Harvard, Quintero had practiced law and edited Spanish-language newspapers in New York City and San Antonio. In June 1861 he visited Vidaurri, who governed the states of Nuevo León and Coahuila as a fiefdom, displaying only nominal allegiance to Juárez. As "Lord of the North," Vidaurri arbitrarily merged his two states, built up a private army, and appropriated customs duties collected at the border with Texas. Handsome and charismatic, he was popular for running an efficient government that boosted economic growth.[86]

In 1862 Vidaurri grabbed another state, Tamaulipas, which included the city of Matamoros, the primary port for exporting cotton procured from Texas. In exchange, Confederates obtained European munitions imported through Matamoros. Visited by sixty to eighty ships a day, that port boomed as it enabled Confederates to work around the Union blockade. In a year, the city's population more than doubled, reaching 50,000 as ramshackle tenements, gambling houses, brothels, and saloons multiplied. The cross-border trade generated robust customs revenues—about $175,000 a month—for Vidaurri's regime. He also skimmed profits from his large stake in the borderland's leading import-export firm run by his son-in-law.[87]

Vidaurri felt drawn to the Confederate assertion of states' rights, so he proposed to join the Confederacy. The Davis government, however, balked for fear of undercutting its European diplomacy, which had renounced expansion southward. So Quintero settled for brokering a commercial treaty with Vidaurri.[88]

Some Unionists fled from Texas to seek haven at Matamoros, where they were led by Edmund J. Davis and William W. Montgomery. In March 1863, however, Confederate troops swept into Matamoros, grabbing Davis and Montgomery. A delighted Quintero reported that the captives would "not commit treason again in this world. They are permanently located in the soil of the Country" after lynching at Brownsville. While Confederates did kill Montgomery, they spared Davis because his daughter had married a Confederate official, and she vouched for him.[89]

An accomplished thief, Vidaurri could not resist the temptation posed by $16 million in Confederate bullion shipped to Matamoros for forwarding to Texas to pay troops. In November 1863 Vidaurri grabbed the money, ostensibly to pay Confederate debts owed to his import firm. Calling Vidaurri's bluff, the Confederate commander in Texas, General Kirby Smith, suspended cross-border trade. In return for 2,000 bales of cotton delivered, Vidaurri released the money and once again became the great borderland friend of the Confederacy.[90]

In addition to Vidaurri's wayward regime, the Juárez government suffered from Conservative guerrillas in the mountainous countryside. In May 1861, they swept into Michoacán to seize Melchor Ocampo at his *hacienda*. The Conservative commander, Leonardo Márquez, had Ocampo shot. Juárez sent troops to find and punish Márquez, but they blundered into an ambush that routed them and killed their general.[91]

The Juárez government also faced a financial and diplomatic crisis over Mexico's immense national debt. Before losing power to Juárez, the Conservative regime of Miguel Miramón had borrowed 7.5 million pesos from a Swiss banker based in Paris, Jean-Baptiste Jecker. Desperate for funds to pay his army, Miramón accepted outrageous terms that set the principal owed by Mexico at 15 million pesos. In part, Miramón made that deal because of Jecker's ties to the Duc de Morny, the half-brother of the French emperor, Napoleon III. After the Liberals returned to power, Napoleon's government demanded payment of the 15 million pesos in full and with interest.[92]

Mexican Conservatives sought to entice France to intervene in Mexico by promising to replace their republic with a monarchy headed by a European prince. That scheme intrigued the French ambassador to Mexico, the Duc de Saligny, an elitist addicted to alcohol and egotism. As a protégé of the Duc de Morny, Saligny enjoyed a clout with Napoleon far beyond his limited talents. In Europe, the prime mover was a wealthy Mexican expatriate, José María Gutiérrez Estrada, a staunch Conservative and devout Catholic. Estrada insisted that only monarchical displays of power could impress common Mexicans to support traditional institutions and inequalities. He worked closely with the French empress, Eugénie de Montijo, an ultraconservative Catholic who despised republicans, Mexican as well as American. The empress assured her husband, "Sooner or later, war will have to be declared on the Americans."[93]

Napoleon III aspired to rebuild the imperial power of his megalomaniacal uncle, Napoleon I. Like him, the new Napoleon regarded military power wrapped in theatricality as the essence of glory—and considered glory essential to dazzle and rule the French. Only victories abroad could sustain an imperial regime that relied on periodic popular plebiscites for validation. Convinced that his monarchy had stabilized France, Napoleon sought to do the same for Mexico. Because his British allies would not accept direct French rule over Mexico, Napoleon endorsed Estrada's scheme of recruiting a Catholic prince from another country. For that role, Napoleon began to cultivate the Archduke Maximilian, the younger brother of the Austrian emperor, Franz Josef.[94]

By making Mexico a French protectorate, Napoleon III hoped to contain the United States and restore "to the Latin race its power and prestige," rescuing Hispanics from Protestant and republican heresies. "Never will any achievement have grander results, for the task is to rescue a continent from anarchy and misery," supplanting "dangerous Utopias and bloody confusion" with "the standard of monarchy."[95]

Overly imaginative, Napoleon confused wishes with reality—and lacked the self-discipline to work through inevitable difficulties. His flamboyant schemes both bemused and alarmed the conventional rulers of Europe. Austria's ambassador to France regarded Napoleon's Mexican intervention as "one of those fancies which the happy optimism of the Emperor thinks up, one does not know how." Britain's prime minister, Lord Palmerston, distrusted Napoleon as "the crafty spider," whose imperial "mind seems as full of schemes as a warren is full of rabbits." Often Napoleon made plans without informing his own foreign ministry, which took a more sober view of international relations. His exasperated foreign minister declared, "The Emperor has immense desires and limited abilities. He wants to do extraordinary things but is only capable of extravagances." Most extravagant of all was Napoleon's grand design to rework the Americas by taking over Mexico.[96]

As an excuse to intervene, Napoleon exploited Mexico's national debt, which Europeans calculated at about $80 million—far more than the impoverished, war-torn country could pay. In July 1861 the Juárez government suspended debt payments for at least two years. Begging for patience from its creditors, the government needed the hiatus to restore order and bolster its revenue. But the European powers refused to wait. In October, the leaders of Britain, France, and Spain agreed to send warships and troops to seize Veracruz so that they could divert Mexico's customs revenue into their own treasuries.[97]

To avert that invasion, the American ambassador, Thomas Corwin, proposed that the United States assume responsibility for paying the annual interest on the Mexican debt to the Europeans for five years. With eleven million American dollars, Corwin hoped to buy time for Juárez to restore Mexico's finances (and so repay the United States). As collateral, however, he demanded that Mexico stake its northern provinces so long coveted by Americans: Baja California, Chihuahua, Sinaloa, and Sonora.

If Mexico failed to pay, the American benefactor would turn crocodile to swallow the northern provinces and so keep them out of Confederate and European hands. Despite that risk, Romero saw the American deal as the lesser of two evils: "We find ourselves [facing] the hard alternatives of sacrificing our territory and our nationality at the hands of [the United States] or our liberty and our independence before the despotic thrones of Europe. The second danger is immediate and more imminent."[98]

Trusting neither Juárez nor Americans, the Europeans rejected Corwin's proposal. Seeking the payment of principal, not just interest, they coveted the same Mexican lands that the Americans wanted as their security. And the American Senate rejected Corwin's proposed loan from an unwillingness to confront the European powers during their own civil war. Senator Charles Sumner told Romero, "We have too many foreign complications to look for new ones." Romero warned his government to "expect nothing from this country in our hour of trial."[99]

Cinco de Mayo

In December 1861 a Spanish fleet of twenty-six warships landed 6,000 troops to occupy Veracruz. The disgraced Confederate ambassador, John T. Pickett, hastened from Mexico City to Veracruz to welcome the Spanish and help them humble Mexico. Because the Spanish sustained slavery in Cuba and Puerto Rico, Pickett declared, "The Spaniards are now become our natural allies and jointly with them we may own the Gulf of Mexico and effect a partition of this magnificent country."[100]

In January 1862, 800 British and 2,600 French troops joined the Spanish in occupying Veracruz, but the allies soon divided over their goals. The Spanish and British balked at the excessive French demands for Mexican payments on the notorious Jecker loan—as well as the French push to overthrow Juárez. In February 1862 the Spanish and British made a deal with the Juárez government to ensure Mexico's payments to them. Then they withdrew their troops and warships from Veracruz.[101]

Unwilling to make a similar deal, Napoleon sent another 4,500 French troops to Veracruz and ordered an advance inland to seize Mexico City. The French general, Comte de Lorencez, assured Napoleon, "I am already master of Mexico" because "we are so superior to the Mexicans in race, in organization, in discipline, in morality, and in elevation of feeling." Per usual with invaders, they posed as liberators bringing law, order, and justice to Mexico. A disgusted Liberal retorted, "Even if we have revolutions, if our roads are unsafe, if we are uncivilized barbarians, we say, leave us alone!"[102]

With 6,000 French troops, Lorencez besieged the key city of Puebla, about midway on the road to Mexico City. The Liberal general, Ignacio Zaragoza, had 5,000 men to defend strong fortifications, but the French ambassador to Mexico, Marquis de Saligny, assured Lorencez that the inhabitants were Conservatives who would overwhelm the garrison and open the city gates: "The barricades will fall as if by magic. You will make your entrance under a rain of flowers, to the confusion of Zaragoza and his gang." On May 5, 1862, the French attacked Puebla but suffered a bloody defeat subsequently celebrated in Mexico as Cinco de Mayo.[103]

The French fell back to Orizaba, near Veracruz, to regroup. Lorencez blamed Saligny for misleading him about the ease of capturing Puebla: "He has no other aptitude than the deplorable talent for writing lies." But Saligny was Napoleon's favorite, so the emperor rebuked and sacked Lorencez, replacing him with Louis Forey.

Embarrassed by losing to Mexicans, Napoleon rushed reinforcements across the Atlantic, raising the French expeditionary force to 30,000 men. French honor and glory demanded victory. Napoleon advised Forey to proceed with "boldness and caution," which seemed idiotic if not uttered by an emperor. A French critic rued Napoleon's "senseless enterprises, these theatrical visions . . . these ambushes on the independence of peoples."[104]

Napoleon could pursue his Mexican fantasy because a civil war divided Americans, blocking both the Union and the Confederacy from interfering. Seeking a French alliance, Confederates renounced their own long-standing ambitions to expand into Mexico and the Caribbean. Instead, they pandered to Napoleon by endorsing his Mexican intervention. Slidell told Napoleon that Lincoln was "the ally and protector of your enemy Juárez," so the Confederacy would "make [a] common cause with you against the common enemy." Southerners reasoned that, in the short term, self-containment was better than losing their war for independence.[105]

A Confederate alliance tempted Napoleon, who relished dividing the United States into two hostile nations, both too weak to expand into Latin America. Then the Confederacy could serve as "an intermediate balancing power between the Federals and the Hispanic-Americans." But Napoleon's foreign ministers doubted that Confederates could be trusted to stay within their boundaries, so they delayed recognizing the Confederacy. The American ambassador in Paris, William Dayton, asked the French foreign minister to clarify Napoleon's policy. "He has none; he awaits events," the minister replied. Dayton told Seward: "Truthfulness is not, as you know, an element in French diplomacy or manners." To be fair, truthfulness also lagged in Seward's priorities.[106]

While Seward and Lincoln restated American opposition to a monarchy in Mexico, they tacitly agreed not to interfere with Napoleon's intervention. Seward explained, "This is not the most suitable time we could choose for offering idle menaces to the Emperor of France. . . . Why should we gasconade about Mexico when we are in a struggle for our own life?" In return, Americans expected Napoleon to stay out of their civil war—an understanding that the emperor accepted. Consequently, the Mexican Liberals felt abandoned by the Yankees. A Mexican leader noted, "We should not fool ourselves; we are alone, completely alone."[107]

SEVEN ◌ REVOLUTIONS

If it is true that the continued existence of slavery requires the destruction of the Union, it is time to ask if the existence of the Union does not require the destruction of slavery.

—GOVERNOR CHARLES ROBINSON OF KANSAS[1]

Up to now we have witnessed only the first act of the Civil War—the constitutional waging of war. The second act, the revolutionary waging of war, is at hand.

—KARL MARX, AUGUST 1862[2]

I n early 1862, Republican leaders pressured Mexico to cede land for the United States to resettle American Blacks. Anticipating the fall elections, Republicans sought to reassure northern voters that their states would not fill up with Black refugees from the South. Instead, Republicans would promise to offload those refugees to a subtropical colony. In February, the postmaster general, Montgomery Blair, met with the Mexican minister Matías Romero to seek the cession of Cozumel Island and adjoining Yucatán. Blair reasoned, "These regions are destined to be populated by Negroes. We need to rid ourselves of them." The Union's ambassador, Thomas Corwin, also urged Mexico to "give us an asylum . . . for the colonization of such people of color as we may wish, from any cause whatever, to get rid of."[3]

Republicans sought to take advantage of Mexico's official position of racial equality. Noting that Mexicans "believe all human beings are endowed with the same rights without distinctions about their place of birth or the color which nature painted their faces with," Blair conceded that Americans did not. Corwin agreed that Mexico had "the only people of the white race known to us" willing to "treat the black man and woman on a footing of perfect equality." Accepting the moral weakness of their own citizens, Republicans sought to exploit Mexican principles to pry open land for colonization.[4]

The Republicans' pressure put Romero and Juárez in a bind, for their Liberal government coveted good relations with the United States but could afford no more land cessions to Yankees. Assuring Blair that "the people of Mexico were firmly decided against alienating another inch of national territory," Romero urged Americans to renounce their old "policy of constant aggressions against our territory . . . absolutely and permanently." Black immigrants were welcome in Mexico as citizens but not as colonial pawns of the United States.[5]

Colonization remained a dangerous folly, for the United States lacked the means to relocate four million enslaved people. The fantasy served a political purpose: to enable whites to oppose slavery while claiming that they could deport all Blacks. In August 1862, Lincoln invited five Black preachers to meet him at the White House, something no other president had done. But once they had assembled, Lincoln assured them that racial difference was too great to permit coexistence with whites:

PREVIOUS PAGE: *"Stampede among the Negroes in Virginia—Their Arrival at Fortress Monroe,"* Frank Leslie's Illustrated Newspaper, *June 8, 1861.*

"Your race are suffering in my judgment, the greatest wrong inflicted on any people," but they could never achieve "equality with the white race" in the United States. He even blamed Blacks for the Civil War: "But for your race among us there could not be war." Lincoln concluded, "It is better for us both, therefore, to be separated." So, he sought their help in colonization "for the good of mankind." To reject this, he charged, would be "extremely selfish." Lincoln rushed his words into newspapers, for he meant to reach white voters rather than Blacks with his pitch for colonization.[6]

Most Blacks wanted freedom and equality as fellow Americans in a multiracial democracy. A. P. Smith wrote to the president, "Pray tell us, is our right to a home in this country less than your own, Mr. Lincoln? . . . Are you an American? So are we. Are you a patriot? So are we." Confident that Blacks and whites could coexist, Frederick Douglass denounced Lincoln's "pride of race and blood, his contempt for Negroes, and his canting hypocrisy." Douglass dreaded any discussion of mass Black emigration as tending "to awaken and keep alive and confirm the popular prejudices of the whites against us."[7]

Contrabands

To maintain support for the Union cause from Democrats and the Border States, Lincoln had balked at moving against slavery. Enforcing the Fugitive Slave Law, the federal government returned more runaways to their masters in 1861 than the proslavery Buchanan administration had done in four years. Even federal troops served as slave catchers.[8]

Invasion, however, disrupted the southern system of policing that kept Blacks enslaved. Once war began, every federal fort or army camp in the South became an alternative sovereignty that enticed enslaved people to try their luck as runaways. When enslaved people did push into federal lines, their initiative put moral pressure on Union commanders. They included General Benjamin F. Butler at Fort Monroe, near the mouth of Chesapeake Bay. In May 1861, Butler commanded just sixty-three acres surrounded by hostile Confederates. Their commander, Col. Charles K. Mallory, employed enslaved people for the dirty work of digging trenches and building fortifications. That labor policy reassured white recruits averse to menial labor. "Our negroes will do the shoveling while our brave cavaliers will do the fighting," a Richmond newspaper boasted. These Confederates saw no irony in the regimental flag that flew over their laboring slaves: "Give me Liberty, or give me Death."[9]

Perhaps the flag inspired three slaves to steal a boat and row to the federal fort on the night of May 23. Frank Baker, Shepard Mallory, and James Townshend took a brave and desperate gamble, for the Federals might send them back to their angry master. Claiming the three men as his property, Colonel Mallory demanded that Butler return them per the Fugitive Slave Law. Butler said the law obliged the return of runaways to U.S. citizens, so he would do so if Mallory took an oath of allegiance to the Union. Of course, that sly proposal outraged the Virginia colonel as an insult.[10]

A veteran lawyer and race-baiting Democratic politician from Massachusetts, Butler was an unlikely emancipator. At the Democratic national convention in 1860, Butler had supported Jefferson Davis for the presidency. In the fall election, Butler voted for John Breckinridge, the champion of slavery. But Butler despised secession, so he rallied to the Union war effort and landed a general's command as Lincoln sought to sustain a bipartisan war.[11]

Ever shrewd, Butler declared the three runaways "contraband of war," liable to seizure by the federal government because employed by Confederates to support their rebellion. The northern press enjoyed Butler's contraband ploy as a neat lawyer's trick played at Confederate expense. Even conservatives could abide a ruling that kept Blacks as property—but transferred them into federal hands, potentially for future sale to pay for the war. An abolitionist marveled, "The venerable gentleman, who wears gold spectacles and reads a conservative daily, prefers confiscation to emancipation. He is reluctant to have slaves declared freemen but has no objection to their being declared contrabands." Most northern whites could support emancipation if presented as punishing rebels rather than as uplifting Blacks. Without publicly endorsing the "contraband policy," the president tacitly approved Butler's ploy in late May. Thereafter, whites referred to Black fugitives as "contrabands."[12]

Word of the new federal policy spread rapidly, leading a visitor to Fort Monroe to marvel at "the mysterious spiritual telegraph which runs through the slave population." Enslaved people overheard indiscreet masters rage against federal efforts to take their property. Mary Chesnut noted that whites "talk before them as if they were chairs and tables."[13]

By the end of July, over 850 runaways had reached Fort Monroe, which they called "the freedom fort." Fed, clothed, and paid, the men helped build defenses while the women mended and washed clothes. A correspondent reported that they "labored steadily through the long, hot day; a quiet, respectable, industrious" people. But he also noted that Blacks kept their thoughts private, having "a weird, solemn aspect . . . as if they, the victims, had become the judges in this awful contest." Insightful about Confederate dispositions and the local landscape, fugitives helped the Union as scouts and spies—but not yet as soldiers.[14]

Harry Jarvis escaped to the freedom fort by crossing thirty-five miles of Chesapeake Bay alone in a canoe. Jarvis boldly went up to General Butler to enlist as a soldier—but that was a political bridge too far in 1861. Jarvis recalled that the general "said it warn't a black man's war. I tol' him it would be a black man's war 'fore dey got fru." He was far more prescient than the general. Two years later, the army enlisted Jarvis, and he would lose a leg in combat.[15]

During the summer of 1861, the Union allowed every military commander leeway to decide what to do with runaways. General McClellan arrested runaways in western Virginia, while the federal commandant at Fort Pickens in Florida announced that he would never return "a poor wretch to slavery." A naval officer added, "If negroes are to be used in this contest, . . . they should be used to preserve the Government not to destroy it."[16]

Fugitives' scars and stories gradually educated northern troops, who previously had known enslaved Blacks only through the distorting prism of minstrel shows or political screeds. Blacks appeared in a new light as people with families torn apart by sales and brutalized by violence. "There is a universal desire of the slaves to be free," a soldier noted. Appalled by a master who sold his own mixed-race child, an Iowa sol-

dier promised, "By G[o]d I'll *fight* till hell *freezes* over and then I'll cut
the ice and fight on."[17]

Confiscation

Called into a special session starting on July 4, Congress debated what
to do about escaped slaves. Many Democrats insisted that the military
had no constitutional power to interfere with southern slavery. They
also feared that such interference would harden southern resistance to
reunion. Republicans countered that slavery caused secession and war,
so only by shattering that system could they restore a Union that could
endure. In August 1861 the Republican majority passed a confiscation
act authorizing federal troops to seize any property, including slaves,
employed by rebels to assist military operations. In further instructions
to generals, the War Department specified that all slaves coming to
federal lines became free. Although Lincoln signed off on both the law
and instructions, he doubted their constitutionality in private: "I do
not see how any of us now can deny and contradict all we have always
said, [that] the Congress has no constitutional power over slavery in
the states."[18]

The emancipation of fugitives only applied to the rebel states, for
the Union continued to protect slavery in the Border States. John C.
Frémont challenged that restraint. A national hero for his western explo-
rations during the 1840s, Frémont was a loose cannon and self-promoter
who benefited from a brilliant, charming, and well-connected wife,
Jessie Anne Benton Frémont, daughter of a leading U.S. senator from
Missouri. She was the brains and the will in their partnership. A leading feminist, Lydia Maria Child declared, "What a shame that women
can't vote. We'd carry our Jessie into the White House on our shoulders." Instead, Jessie tried to carry John there, helping him to win the
Republican nomination in 1856. Although defeated, Frémont remained
an influential politician, so Lincoln gave him command in Missouri.
An inept general, Frémont failed to organize an offensive or curtail
corruption by military contractors. Instead, in August 1861, he issued

a proclamation that declared martial law and emancipated all slaves of disloyal masters within Missouri.[19]

Border State Unionists howled that Frémont undercut their cause by alienating all slaveholders. In September 1861 Robert Anderson, the former Fort Sumter commander, warned Lincoln that unless the proclamation was "immediately disavowed and annulled, Kentucky will be lost to the Union." The president canceled Frémont's order, which outraged Radical Republicans, including the fiery editor Jane Grey Swisshelm, who accused Lincoln of "imbecility or treachery" for inflicting "the most terrible calamity that has ever befallen our nation."[20]

Insisting on civil government's control over generals, Lincoln replaced Frémont in November, and the new commander rounded up those he had freed for return to their masters. Confronted by Jessie Frémont at the White House, Lincoln declared, "It was a war for a great national idea, the Union, and . . . General Frémont should not have dragged the Negro into it." Of course, keeping Blacks out of political sight in this war required a great sleight of hand—which the president felt obliged to play in 1861.[21]

Save for the special case of fugitives who belonged to rebels and fled to federal forces in wartime, Lincoln believed that the Federal Constitution left emancipation within the states to their own governments. All he could do was to incentivize those states to emancipate. In the fall of 1861, Lincoln lobbied Border State leaders to accept federal compensation for a very gradual process, lasting until 1893, with masters receiving about $400 per slave. In 1861 this plan was radical, for no previous president had pushed for emancipation within states.[22]

In March 1862 Lincoln sought congressional funding for his gradual emancipation program. A Democratic congressman from Illinois protested against tapping taxpayers to buy slaves and "turning them loose in their midst." Although the Republican majority passed the program, no Border State would take the bait, not even Delaware, which had only 587 masters and 1,800 enslaved people. Kentucky's legislature voted to disenfranchise any resident who "may advocate the doctrine of the abolition or emancipation of slavery."[23]

Republicans did claim the constitutional power to abolish slavery in the District of Columbia, a federal territory which had 3,185 enslaved people. Republican congressmen insisted on immediate emancipation, but did offer $300 per slave in compensation to masters: well below the market price. Congress also allocated $100,000 to subsidize colonization by Black volunteers from the district. In April 1862 Republicans passed and enacted their law over the opposition of all Border State and almost all Democratic congressmen.[24]

The District's former slaves celebrated obtaining "that dearest of all earthly treasures—Freedom." Nothing came of the colonization option, as only one Black agreed to leave. The local colonization society noted that freed Blacks instead expected "changes which will make their condition here as good as that of white men." Jane Grey Swisshelm reported that that the capital's freed Blacks were hard-working and orderly: "The colored folks of this District are quietly solving the great problem of the age and putting to shame all the much ado about finding a place to which they can be sent. . . . The despised colored man will tax the ingenuity of his maligners to find apologies for their hatred and persecution."[25]

As masters feared, and abolitionists hoped, freedom in the District invited escapes from adjoining Maryland and Virginia. Soldiers blocked attempts by masters to retrieve their former slaves by invoking the Fugitive Slave Act. Although that law persisted on the books until 1864, it became moribund almost everywhere by late 1862.[26]

On July 12, 1862, at the White House, Lincoln met with twenty-nine Border State congressmen. Citing the swelling tide of escapes, Lincoln warned them that "the institution in your states will be extinguished by mere friction and abrasion—by the mere incidents of the war." The president again advocated compensation and gradual emancipation, but twenty-one of the twenty-nine congressmen adamantly opposed any "radical change of our social system." Denouncing the plan as an unconstitutional interference with states' rights, they lectured the president: "Confine yourself to your constitutional authority; confine your subordinates within the same limits; conduct this war solely for the purpose of restoring the constitution to its legitimate authority." Exasperated by Border State resistance, Lincoln privately shifted toward the alternative pushed by Radical Republicans: to use his war powers as president to emancipate all slaves in rebel areas immediately. Lincoln explained, "I conceive that I may in an emergency do things on military grounds which cannot be done constitutionally by Congress." But Lincoln needed military victories to pitch emancipation as a winning program.[27]

Rivers

At the start of the war, Confederates praised Albert Sidney Johnston as their finest general, hailed by a Texan as "a Military Messiah." Jefferson Davis called Johnston "the greatest soldier, the ablest man, civil or military, Confederate or Federal." Yes, Davis thought Johnston a better commander than Robert E. Lee. Born in Kentucky and educated at West Point, Johnston had befriended Davis, then a fellow cadet. During the Mexican War, Johnston performed well and won promotion to command federal forces in California after that conflict. Tall, handsome, muscular, and charismatic, Johnston looked the part of an inspirational general. In 1861, Davis gave him command of Confederate forces in Tennessee. Davis's devotion proved a mixed blessing, for he thought Johnston able to defend a larger region with fewer troops than those concentrated in Virginia to defend Richmond.[28]

Johnston faced a tougher challenge than any commander in Virginia, where the rivers ran west to east, providing barriers to a northern invader. In Tennessee, the major rivers flowed south to north, inviting a northern foe to penetrate deep into the Confederacy, disrupting a key region for growing grain, raising horses, and producing copper, lead, iron, and gunpowder. And a political imperative drove Union leaders to prioritize seizing the Mississippi Valley to reopen the Midwest's commercial access to the Gulf of Mexico. General William T. Sherman described the Mississippi as "the great artery of America, and whatever power holds it, holds the continent." With it, the Union could divide the Confederacy. Without it, the Midwest might seek a separate peace with the South. At St. Louis, the Union assembled transports and gunboats to command the rivers and haul thousands of troops and their supplies.[29]

To block the Union armada, Johnston built three forts in western Kentucky and northwestern Tennessee. The strongest held the town of Columbus beside the Mississippi. Fort Henry defended the Tennessee River, and Fort Donelson controlled the Cumberland River. Behind thick earthworks, batteries of heavy cannon were supposed to shatter Union ships that tried to pass, but the forts were badly designed and poorly built. By pinning most of his troops down in frontline forts, Johnston sacrificed a strategic reserve within Tennessee to deploy in a more mobile manner. His priority would benefit an aggressive Union commander who could concentrate his force to target one fort after another. Once Union gunboats and troops punched through the forts, they could race upstream deep into Tennessee.[30]

Ulysses S. Grant seemed no match for the renowned Confederate commander. Born into a family of modest means on an Ohio farm in 1822, Grant graduated from West Point with a mediocre record. "A more unpromising boy never entered the Military Academy," recalled his fellow cadet William T. Sherman. Grant seemed more dutiful and persistent than brilliant. As a lieutenant, he performed well during the war against Mexico despite his political opposition to that conflict as unjust. After the war, Grant went to St. Louis to marry Julia Dent, the daughter of a wealthy, slaveholding Democrat. Grant's best man at the wedding was James Longstreet, a West Point classmate and a future Confederate general.[31]

Posted at small and isolated western posts far from his beloved wife, Grant became bored and depressed. Escaping into heavy drinking, he neglected his duties. In 1854, he resigned under pressure from a harsh superior officer. Although Grant sobered up, he did little better in civilian life, reaping debts instead of profits as a farmer in Missouri and a tanner in Illinois. But Grant developed a patient persistence and empathy for others who struggled in life. Disgusted by the slavery he saw in Missouri, Grant became a Republican in 1860.[32]

When the Civil War broke out, and the federal army needed thousands of new officers, Grant got a new start as a colonel in command of a volunteer regiment. In August 1861 he won a quick promotion to brigadier general thanks to patronage by a Republican senator and

Grant's skill at training raw recruits. Eager to vindicate himself, Grant had little to lose, and much to gain, by pushing his troops into decisive combat. Although a poor student of conventional tactics and strategy at West Point, Grant mastered the improvisational style of a new war with large forces of volunteers. He explained, "The art of war is simple enough. Find out where your enemy is. Get at him as soon as you can. Strike him as hard as you can, and keep moving on." Grant showed confidence in his soldiers, so they trusted him. He made a stark contrast to the golden boys of command—George B. McClellan and Albert Sidney Johnston—who worried too much about losing battles to win them.[33]

In February 1862, Grant's 18,000 men bypassed the strong Confederate post at Columbus on the Mississippi to target, instead, the weaker Fort Henry beside the Tennessee River. The garrison fled, exposing Fort Donelson on the nearby Cumberland River to Grant's next strike. Although bigger, stronger, and better garrisoned, Fort Donelson was commanded by John B. Floyd, a corrupt politician turned inept general. Because he had betrayed the Union as Buchanan's secretary of war, Floyd dreaded capture, so he fled, forsaking his men. A more professional officer, Simon Bolivar Buckner, stayed to surrender on Grant's unconditional terms, which delighted the northern public, so eager for a resolute war hero. Some people even thought that Grant's initials, U. S., stood for Unconditional Surrender. When a newspaper reported Grant's fondness for cigars, grateful citizens sent him eleven thousand. Lincoln promoted Grant to major general.[34]

In addition to capturing 14,000 Confederates, Grant's victories bore rich strategic fruit. Columbus became redundant and vulnerable, so the garrison retreated southward, sacrificing the northern gateway to the Mississippi Valley. By capturing the Confederate forts, Grant opened the Cumberland and Tennessee Rivers for Union gunboats to steam deep into Tennessee and even northern Alabama. "The rebels all have a terror of the gunboats," exulted a Union officer.[35]

Lacking troops to replace those lost at Henry and Donelson, Johnston could not defend Nashville, the Tennessee state capital. The city's masters also hampered defense by refusing to lend their slaves to build earthworks, and common white men balked at that job. On February 23, Johnston abandoned Nashville, withdrawing to northern Mississippi. Dismayed by defeats and retreats, the Confederate press and congressmen blamed Johnston. But Davis stood by his man: "If Sidney Johnston is not a general, we had better give up the war, for we have no general."[36]

Lincoln set up a Unionist government for Tennessee to serve as a showplace for redeeming the South rapidly by converting repentant rebels into loyal citizens. By succeeding in Tennessee, Unionists hoped to encourage other Confederate states to submit and rejoin the Union. Parson Brownlow helped by visiting Union prison camps to persuade captured Tennesseans to swear renewed allegiance to the Union. The president appointed Andrew Johnson as the military governor of Tennessee. Zealous and dictatorial, Johnson shut down pro-Confederate newspapers, jailed prominent men who refused to swear allegiance to the Union, and imposed punitive taxes on them. Johnson asserted, "We have all come to the conclusion here that treason must be made odious and traitors punished and impoverished."[37]

To the west, in Missouri, Samuel R. Curtis replaced Frémont in command of Union troops. A West Point graduate and former Iowa congressman, Curtis was dull but competent: a stark contrast to his flamboyant Confederate opponent, Earl Van Dorn, praised by a subordinate as "a dashing soldier, and a very handsome man, and his manners were graceful and fascinating." Intoxicated by his own charm, Van Dorn boasted, "Soldiers, behold your leader! He comes to show you the way to glory and immortal renown." But Van Dorn was better at seducing other men's wives than in managing troops. Davis's brother complained that "when Van Dorn was made a General it spoiled a good Captain."[38]

Both armies had about 11,000 men in early March, when they clashed at Pea Ridge in southwest Missouri. Curtis's artillery blunted the Confederate charge, and then a Union counterattack spooked Van Dorn, who withdrew, to the disgust of his men. Abandoning Missouri to the Union, Van Dorn headed eastward across the Mississippi to join Johnston's army. The following May, an enraged doctor stormed into Van Dorn's headquarters to shoot the general dead for seducing his wife. Sympathizing with the killer, local magistrates did not prosecute the murder.[39]

Shiloh

General Grant became careless as he moved up the Tennessee River to threaten Johnston's base at Corinth. Reaching Pittsburgh Landing, near a church called Shiloh, Grant neglected to fortify his encampment, for he considered Johnston's troops too few and too demoralized to attack. In fact, Johnston had rallied his men and brought in reinforcements from Missouri and New Orleans. With 42,000 men, Johnston surprised Grant's 43,000 at dawn on April 6. The Yankees fell back toward the river, but the Confederate attack lost momentum when a bullet severed an artery in Johnston's leg, and he bled to death. Pierre G. T. Beauregard took command and called off further attacks at nightfall. Success had disordered his army as hungry and ragged troops broke ranks to plunder the captured Yankee camp.[40]

That night, Grant refused to retreat, counting instead on 20,000 reinforcements who arrived under the command of Don Carlos Buell. On the morning of April 7, the Union army counterattacked, surprising and driving back the Confederates, who lost all the ground gained the day before. In mid-afternoon, Beauregard pulled his battered men back to Corinth. The Union lost about 13,000 men and the Confederates 10,000 in the bloodiest battle of the war to date. Indeed, more men fell during the two days of Shiloh than in combat in all American conflicts before the Civil War. After seeing "piles of dead soldiers' mangled bodies," many "without heads and legs," Sherman concluded, "The scenes on this field would have cured anybody of war." But neither Sherman nor Grant took that cure, for both had a bloody resolve to see the war through to a Union victory.[41]

The northern press focused on the casualties and the initial disarray of Grant's army on April 6. When a Republican leader pressed Lincoln to fire Grant, the president replied, "I can't spare this man; he fights." For Lincoln, Grant was the anti-McClellan. But Grant answered to Henry Halleck, who commanded Union forces west of the Appalachians. A gifted administrator with an abrasive style, Halleck felt jealous of Grant's victories and critical of the army's performance at Shiloh. Taking direct command over Grant's army, Halleck subordinated his best general.[42]

Grant seethed as Halleck took his sweet time assembling 100,000 soldiers before inching forward toward the Confederate base at Corinth. Entrenching his camp every night to avoid another surprise attack, Halleck took a month to advance twenty-two miles. On the night of May 29–30, the Confederates evacuated Corinth, leaving Halleck with "a dirty, filthy town" but without any prisoners; a half-victory when the Union needed more. Halleck lacked Grant's killer instinct to trap and destroy Confederate armies.[43]

Contrary to his critics, Grant had won a great strategic victory by repulsing Johnston's high-stakes attack at Shiloh. To concentrate a large force for battle at Shiloh, Johnston had weakened Confederate garrisons on the Mississippi. These included Island No. 10, which protected the northern approach to the city of Memphis. On April 7, John Pope led 12,000 Union troops, supported by ironclads, to cut off the island, compelling the surrender of 7,000 Confederates and fifty-two heavy guns. The victorious Union force headed downstream to destroy a Confederate flotilla and seize Memphis, which became the key Union base on the Mississippi River.[44]

Johnston also had withdrawn most of the Confederate troops from New Orleans, leaving that city vulnerable to an amphibious Union assault from the Gulf of Mexico. Home to 170,000 people, New Orleans was the greatest southern city and the key port for the Mississippi watershed. To keep Union warships from ascending the river to attack New Orleans, the Confederates relied on two forts seventy-five miles below the city. But the Union deployed a powerful flotilla commanded by a talented admiral, David G. Farragut, a Tennessean who stayed loyal. Farragut was supported by 15,000 soldiers commanded by Benjamin Butler, the former commander at Fort Monroe. On April 23, after pounding the forts with mortar fire, Farragut's ships bypassed them to steam upstream. Appearing beside the wharves of the city on April 25, he dictated a surrender. A witness recalled, "The crowds on the levee howled and screamed with rage."[45]

Butler commanded the Union occupation of New Orleans. He described the inhabitants as "all hostile, bitter, defiant, explosive . . . a spark only needed for destruction." So, he took a hard line at the first signs of trouble. In late April, when a leading citizen tore down a Union flag on top of the city's mint building, Butler had him tried for treason and executed.[46]

Butler especially worried about the city's elite white women: "bejewelled, becrinolined and laced creatures calling themselves ladies," who insulted, spat upon, and emptied chamber pots on Yankee troops. He considered the women two-faced for indulging in street politics while expecting feminine immunity from punishment. In May, Butler issued his notorious "women's order," warning them to leave Union troops alone or risk treatment as common prostitutes. The order worked: white women restrained their contempt for the city's occupiers so troops did not arrest any elite women as prostitutes. But Butler's order outraged Confederates, who denounced him as a "beast." President Davis ordered Butler's execution as a war criminal if captured.[47]

During the first half of 1862, the Union won impressive victories in the Mississippi watershed: Forts Henry and Donelson, Pea Ridge, Shiloh, Island No. 10, and New Orleans. They secured most of Tennessee, including the key cities of Memphis and Nashville, as well as the core of Louisiana around New Orleans. In Richmond, Mary Chesnut lamented, "Battle after battle, disaster after disaster. . . . New Orleans gone—and with it the Confederacy. Are we not cut in two?" She worried about worse to come because McClellan's massive Army of the Potomac was, at last, on the move against Richmond. After so many disasters in the west, losing the Confederate capital would shatter the southern cause by demoralizing soldiers and civilians while losing half the new nation's industrial capacity.[48]

Peninsula

In March 1862 McClellan embarked 100,000 soldiers on boats to descend Chesapeake Bay to the peninsula between the James and York Rivers for a strike upstream at Richmond. His strategy avoided the overland challenge of crossing multiple rivers, where Confederate defenders could inflict long delays and heavy casualties. But the scheme risked exposing the national capital to a Confederate overland thrust while McClellan's men sat in their boats. Lincoln and Secretary of War Edwin M. Stanton compelled McClellan to leave 50,000 men behind to defend Washington. Of course, McClellan cited that force reduction as his excuse for likely defeat by supposedly superior Confederate numbers.[49]

In late March, McClellan's 100,000 men landed on the Peninsula to confront just 13,000 Confederates entrenched at Yorktown. But their commander, John Magruder, was a showman who shifted troops and cannon to create an illusion of a larger force—so McClellan settled down to a slow siege instead of pushing through to Richmond. Magruder's superior, General Joseph Johnston, marveled, "No one but McClellan could have hesitated to attack."[50]

When Magruder did retreat on May 5, McClellan followed gingerly, taking three weeks to advance eighty miles. At last, in late May, McClellan's army came within six miles of Richmond. The French ambassador to the United States, Henri Mercier, reported, "I think we have finally come to the decisive moment of the crisis. Before long the Federals will be in Richmond, there is no longer the shadow of a doubt."[51]

But Mercier did not reckon with McClellan's fears. Although Johnston had only 60,000 men, McClellan insisted that he faced 200,000 rebels and needed massive reinforcements. When the president demanded an attack, McClellan raged that no one understood his true plight with "the rebels on one side, & the abolitionists & other scoundrels on the other." If Lincoln wanted a breakthrough, "he had better come & do it himself."[52]

Exploiting McClellan's latest delay, Johnston struck first on May 31, hitting part of the Union force at Seven Pines. The Union troops held firm, displaying the fruits of McClellan's training and organization. But he was no battlefield commander, lacking Grant's ability quickly to exploit an advantage. Despite mauling the Confederates, McClellan pulled back a few miles.[53]

At Seven Pines, Johnston had suffered a severe wound, so President Davis turned command over to Robert E. Lee. This shift delighted

Davis, who despised Johnston as insolent and secretive. McClellan also thought Lee more to his own taste as an adversary. Conceited because of small victories over Lee in West Virginia in 1861, McClellan misjudged his opponent as "timid & irresolute in action." He would soon discover otherwise.[54]

Lee reorganized the Confederate defenders to ensure better food, tents, and medical care. But he also pushed those men harder to upgrade the city's defensive earthworks—work that southerners resented as the duty of slaves. "Our people are opposed to work. Our troops, officers, Community, & press, all ridicule & resist it," Lee lamented. He sent guards into the "brothels, gambling saloons & drinking houses of Richmond" to round up "thousands of skulkers," returning them to the ranks.[55]

To the west, in Virginia's Shenandoah Valley, the Confederacy got a boost from a brilliant campaign waged by Thomas "Stonewall" Jackson during May and early June. Quiet and eccentric, he struck many as a religious fanatic: "Old Tom Fool," some called him. But Jackson knew what McClellan never learned: that an army can work wonders if led decisively. Jackson described his strategy as "always mystify, mislead, and surprise the enemy." Through rapid marches and sudden attacks, Jackson's men repeatedly shocked and routed larger Union forces. Jackson's fast-moving men became known as "foot cavalry," getting their food by plundering the forsaken camps of defeated foes. As his victories accumulated, Jackson developed an aura, which inspired his men with confidence while spooking their foes. Jackson's Valley campaign tied down 60,000 Union troops, depriving McClellan of reinforcements.[56]

Exploiting McClellan's passivity, Lee launched a daring cavalry raid, led by the dashing J. E. B. Stuart, attired in gray uniform, red cape, yellow sash, and felt hat with an ostrich-feather plume. In mid-June, Stuart's 1,200 troopers rode around McClellan's inert army, taking prisoners, disrupting supply lines, and discerning weak points before returning to Richmond. Armed with Stuart's insights, Lee brought Jackson's troops by railroad from the Shenandoah Valley for a counteroffensive. While pinning down the main Union army of 75,000 men posted south of the Chickahominy River with just 27,000 Confederates, Lee sent

Jackson with 60,000 rebels to strike at the weaker Union position, 30,000 men posted north of that river.[57]

Despite Lee's deft plan, the June 26 attack at Mechanicsville went badly, costing the Confederates 1,500 dead to just 360 for the Federals. Jackson proved oddly disengaged, delaying his advance with fatal consequences for the other Confederate division sent to hit the entrenched Union troops. Having sustained a manic energy for six weeks of marching and fighting in the Valley, Jackson and his men were worn out and needed a break that Lee did not afford them.[58]

But McClellan was the beaten man, calling off his offensive to begin a slow, painful retreat to his supply base at Harrison's Landing on the James River. For the next six days, Lee hounded the larger, lumbering Union army. These attacks cost more Confederate than Union lives, but McClellan kept falling back while sending hysterical telegraphs to the secretary of war. On June 28, McClellan wrote, "I have lost this battle because my force was too small . . . If I save this army now, I tell you plainly that I owe no thanks to you or to any other persons in Washington. You have done your best to sacrifice this army." A disgusted subordinate blasted McClellan's retreat as "prompted by cowardice or treason."[59]

While McClellan shrank, Lee swelled. Ordinarily a soft-spoken, courteous Virginia gentleman, he became puffed with an angry resolve. Snapping at subordinates, Lee demanded a faster pace meant not just to defeat McClellan but to destroy his army. Lee's aggression wore down his own men, fighting day after day in summer's heat. But once McClellan's army reached Harrison's Landing in early July, Lee called off further attacks.[60]

The Seven Days' Battles embroiled soldiers in the horrors of modern warfare by thousands armed with rifled muskets and heavy artillery. The two armies lost 36,000 men, more than the war had cost in all battles during the first six months of 1862. Sent out on burial duty after a battle, a Confederate found "corpses swollen to twice their original size, some of them actually burst asunder with the pressure of foul gases. . . . The odors were nauseating and so deadly that, in a short time, we all sickened and were lying with our mouths close to the ground, most of us vomiting profusely." At a field hospital of surgeons cutting off limbs and casting them in heaps, a Union soldier saw "the Hogs belonging to the Farm eating arms and other portions of the body." Jackson took a morbid delight in this: "I knew a hog was not particular about what it ate, but I gave them credit for having better taste than to eat a Yankee."[61]

In Staunton, Virginia, Joseph Waddell overheard a neighbor, "a poor woman," receive the news that a cannonball had killed her husband during the Seven Days: "Her wailings were heard at our house for an hour or two." Lee had saved Richmond but at a human cost that the Confederacy could not sustain in the long run. The issue remained whether Union morale could persist long enough to defeat the Confederacy.[62]

Lessons

By saving Richmond, Lee became the greatest Confederate hero, far more than any other general, President Davis, or the Confederate Congress. Fortunately for the Confederacy, Lee took George Washington, rather than Napoleon, as his model in political life, deferring to, rather than toppling, civil authority. Back in the capital with a respite from battle, he reverted to stoical restraint in public. Mary Chesnut wished that she could know him better: "He looks so cold and quiet and grand." In peaceful interludes, his one apparent passion was, Lee explained, "fried chicken. Not one fried chicken or two—but unlimited fried chicken."[63]

Things were less festive at Harrison's Landing, where McClellan sulked with his army rendered useless in a cul-de-sac. Giddy with expectations of capturing Richmond, the northern public felt crushed with disappointment by his retreat. Republican congressmen demanded that Lincoln replace McClellan with a more aggressive commander, which meant a Republican. But Lincoln visited the army in mid-July to find that the troops still adored McClellan, believing that he had extricated them from a trap. Bristling at calls for a harder war to liberate more enslaved people, McClellan lectured the president "Military power should not be allowed to interfere with the relations of servitude. . . . A declaration of radical views, especially upon slavery, will rapidly disintegrate our present armies."[64]

Had McClellan swept into Richmond to rout the Confederate government, he might have ended the war in 1862 as the Union's great savior. Such a victory would have restored the Union without ending slavery. Instead, McClellan's failed campaign prolonged the conflict and discredited his limited-war strategy. Most Yankees sought a harder war meant to punish the Confederates for their stubborn resistance.[65]

Many Union officers began to push for emancipation as the means to victory: by undermining the southern economy while transferring Black labor to strengthen the federal cause. General Grant sought African Americans' help "as teamsters, hospital attendants, company cooks and so forth, thus saving soldiers to carry the musket. I don't know what is to become of these poor people in the end, but it weakens the enemy to take them from them." Southern Blacks provided Union commanders with their best intelligence of Confederate positions and resources. In northern Alabama, General Ormsby Mitchel relied on them for early warning of Confederate guerrilla attacks: "Without their help, it would be impossible for me to hold my position."[66]

After McClellan's failure on the Peninsula, Republicans in Congress adopted harder war measures. In July 1862 Congress authorized a draft to expand the army—and invited the president to accept "persons of African descent," at least as laborers but potentially as soldiers: a horrifying prospect to most Democrats. Congress also passed a much tougher confiscation act authorizing troops to seize more property from rebels, including enslaved people who "shall be deemed captives of war and shall be forever free." Federal troops interpreted the measure as free license for them to plunder Confederate homes and stores.[67]

While McClellan retained command of the Army of the Potomac, Lincoln transferred many of his troops to a newer army based in northern Virginia with a more aggressive commander, John Pope, the victor at Island No. 10 on the Mississippi. Arriving in northern Virginia, Pope assured his new troops: "I have come to you from the West, where we have always seen the backs of our enemies." Posing as the anti-McClellan, Pope resolved to wage a hard war on civilian property as well as Confederate troops: "War means desolation and death, and it is neither humanity nor wisdom to carry it out upon any other theory. The more bitter it is made for the delinquents, the sooner it will end." Pope directed his men to "subsist upon the country": a euphemism for looting.[68]

Most Union troops welcomed Pope's invitation to wage a harder war against southern civilians, who increasingly seemed irredeemable. The profane insults of southern women especially shocked federal soldiers. A New York private reported, "They give a fellow invitations to kiss them in localities that I never thought of applying that token of affection." Another soldier concluded that southern women were "little more to be respected than she wolves or rattlesnakes." Confederate guerrillas enraged Union troops by killing teamsters, couriers, and sentinels, so those troops sought revenge by looting and burning the farms of civilians within their grasp. A Pennsylvania soldier noted, "Our boys have born[e] with this damning mode of warfare and suffered their comrades picked off until forbearance has ceased to be a virtue. . . . No more prisoners is the watch word."[69]

Union soldiers especially enjoyed plundering the Virginia farm of the arch-secessionist Edmund Ruffin. Taking or ruining his provisions, books, furniture, and tools, they vandalized Ruffin's home with graffiti: "You did fire the first gun on Sumter, you traitor son of a bitch," and "You old cuss, it is a pity you go unhanged." A Confederate insisted that "a party of malicious monkeys let loose in the house" could not match Yankees in vandalizing Virginia homes. They even defaced churches with slogans that included, "Death to all traitors, thus saith the Lord."[70]

Pope's troops undermined slavery in northern Virginia, as slave patrols collapsed, many masters fled, and enslaved people bolted to federal camps. A Virginian protested, "We could do nothing but look on and see our property skedaddle," some in stolen carriages. "Men went to bed rich and got up poor." Ruffin felt stunned that his slaves ran away, "for nowhere were they better cared for, or better managed & treated, according to their condition of slavery." He did not understand that they wanted no further management by him.[71]

Confederates longed to crush and kill Pope. With McClellan's troops sidelined while withdrawing in boats back to Washington, Lee led 55,000 men against Pope's 60,000 camped near Manassas in northern Virginia. Lee sent Jackson around behind Pope's army to threaten his supply line. The Union general fell back to seek the elusive Jackson— rather than strike forward against Lee and Richmond. Jackson wheeled around to block Pope, while Lee pushed up from behind to hit the disorganized Union army, inflicting a savage defeat in the Second Battle of Manassas on August 30. Pope's shattered army fled to seek haven within the fortifications of Washington, leaving behind 16,000 dead and most of his wounded: more than a quarter of his army. "Their dead were strewn over a space 5 miles long and three wide, piled up in many places— sometimes in long lines," a Confederate noted. To show contempt, the victors refused to bury the Union dead.[72]

Antietam

Despising Pope as a rival, McClellan had undermined him by withholding reinforcements, contributing to the debacle at Manassas. Writing to his wife, McClellan reasoned that if "Pope is beaten, they may want me to save Washington again. Nothing but their fears will induce them to give me any command of importance."[73]

Lincoln called McClellan's conduct "unpardonable," but did pardon him. Sending Pope away to fight Indians in the West, Lincoln merged the two Union armies in northern Virginia into the single Army of the Potomac under McClellan's command. With the Union soldiers demoralized by defeat, Lincoln concluded, "We must use what tools we have. There is no man in the Army who can lick these troops of ours into shape half as well as he." When McClellan reappeared before the army with renewed authority, an officer reported, "Men threw their caps high into the air, and danced and frolicked like school-boys."[74]

In July, Lincoln privately had concluded "that it was a military necessity absolutely essential for the salvation of the Union, that we must free the slaves or be ourselves subdued." On July 22, Lincoln convened his cabinet to propose an emancipation proclamation that would declare free all enslaved people then under rebel control. As an emergency act under his executive war powers, the proclamation would require no congressional legislation. The cabinet approved, but Seward advised keeping it secret "until you can give it to the country supported by military success," lest Americans and Europeans see the measure as pure desperation. Lincoln agreed, so Pope's defeat kept the proclamation in Lincoln's desk. Thereafter, the proclamation depended on success by the undependable McClellan.[75]

Short on supplies, Lee's army could not linger in northern Virginia, which Union troops had picked clean of crops, provisions, and farm animals. Although victorious, most of the Confederates were shoeless, ragged, hungry, and dirty—for want of soap. A sympathetic woman described

> the gaunt starvation that looked from their cavernous eyes. All day they crowded to the doors of our houses, with always the same drawling complaint: "I've been a-marchin' and a-fightin' for six weeks stiddy and I ain't had n-a-r-thin' to eat 'cept green apples an' green cawn, an' I wish you'd please to gimme a bite to eat."

In September Lee marched north to extract provisions from farmers in Maryland and Pennsylvania. His troops longed to invade the North to make Yankees suffer a measure of what they had done to Virginia.[76]

Domestic politics also drove Lee's offensive into Union territory. He and Davis hoped to satisfy a southern press and public that clamored for an offensive meant to win the war fast. Lee and Davis also calculated that victories in Maryland and Pennsylvania would discredit the Republicans and sway northern voters in the approaching November election. If Democrats could sweep Republicans out of state governments and Congress, the Union war effort would falter.[77]

Lee expected to rally enough civilian support to wrench Maryland out of the Union and into the Confederacy. By isolating Washington, D.C., such a transfer would impress British and French diplomats with Confederate might, persuading them to intervene and dictate a peace settlement. French and British leaders wanted to propose an armistice that would lift the Union blockade, followed by binding mediation

to define peace terms. Because such a settlement could only end with
southern independence, Confederates welcomed mediation, while
Union leaders rejected it as a hostile act. With Lee marching north, the
British prime minister, Lord Palmerston, expected another Confederate victory that would put Union leaders in "a more reasonable state of
mind" regarding mediation.[78]

But Lee's late-summer offensive did not go as expected. He found
scant civilian support when his army entered western Maryland, a land
of small farms and many Unionists. Instead of gaining recruits, Lee lost
thousands of stragglers. After eating green corn and apples, many were
too sick with dysentery to keep up on the hard march. A Yankee civilian
followed the track of Lee's army "by the thickly strewn belt of green
corn husks and cobs, and . . . a ribbon of dysenteric stools just behind."[79]

Everything seemed set up for McClellan to win big, for he faced a
Confederate army weakened by hunger, sickness, and straggling—with
a tenuous supply line and men deflated by a lack of civilian support in
Maryland. McClellan also had 80,000 men versus just 50,000 for Lee—
although the Union commander claimed that he faced 120,000. Then
McClellan got a godsend, as his scouts found a copy of Lee's marching
orders inadvertently dropped by a staff officer. The orders revealed that
Lee had divided his force, sending Jackson westward to attack Harper's
Ferry. But McClellan advanced in his usual methodical, plodding manner, more afraid to lose than determined to win. That delay allowed
Jackson time to capture Harpers Ferry, taking immense stores of valuable
munitions plus 11,000 prisoners, the largest haul taken by Confederates
during the war. Jackson then hastened his men back in time to rejoin
Lee's army in Maryland.[80]

At last, on September 17, at Antietam, McClellan launched poorly
coordinated attacks, allowing Lee to shift reserves to receive each blow on
different parts of his line. A Union soldier marveled, "We have a desperate foe to contend with who comes at us in tatters and rags [but] fight[s]
like Devils from Hell." Unwilling to risk his own reserves, McClellan
held back, costing the Union a chance to break through. As night fell,
both commanders called off their attacks to reassess and reorganize armies
that jointly had suffered about 6,000 dead and 17,000 wounded, evenly

split between the two sides. It was the bloodiest single day of the war to date. One Confederate general, John Bell Hood, told Lee, "I have no division. They are lying on the field where you sent them, sir." While McClellan asked too little of his army, Lee risked too much.[81]

On September 18, Lee refused to retreat, but McClellan declined to attack, satisfied that he had "fought the battle splendidly & that it was a masterpiece" that had "defeated Lee so utterly and saved the North so completely." Possessed of a rich fantasy life, McClellan did not want to lose his masterpiece by fighting the next day. A relieved Confederate officer marveled that McClellan lacked "the commonest kind of every day common sense" for failing to renew his attack on a battered army "backed against a river, with no bridge & only one ford." That night, Lee's army escaped across the Potomac to Virginia. A Union soldier complained that McClellan's failure to pursue "prolongs this horrid war." Both commanders had botched the campaign: Lee by advancing into Maryland and seeking battle from a weak position; McClellan by failing to make Lee pay for his mistakes.[82]

European diplomats interpreted Antietam as a strategic victory for the Union, which at least and at last had blunted Lee's run of victories. Inclining to caution, French and British leaders thought it best to hold off trying to impose mediation. Those leaders still doubted that the Union could conquer the South, but who knew, given the many twists and turns of an uncertain and chaotic war? The French ambassador, Henri Mercier, warned his superiors that the conflict often seemed "about to reach its climax, only then to rush off in one direction or another." Better, he thought, to wait and see the results of the approaching November election in the United States.[83]

Proclamation

Antietam was the biggest victory McClellan could deliver—so Lincoln had to make the most of it. On September 22, Lincoln convened his cabinet to announce the Preliminary Emancipation Proclamation that they tentatively had approved in July—pending a victory, which Antietam barely provided. Effective January 1, 1863, the proclamation

exempted the Border States. It also did not apply to Tennessee and
Louisiana, where federal troops had reclaimed the state capitals and
sought slaveholder support. Still the proclamation was a radical turn,
seeking immediate emancipation without compensation to Confederate masters. By freeing many slaves, Lincoln would revolutionize the
war. "The South," he declared, "is to be destroyed and replaced by new
propositions and ideas."[84]

Initially, the proclamation did not impress British leaders, who saw it
as desperate and hypocritical. A London newspaper mocked, "The principle is not that a human being cannot justly own another, but that he
cannot own him unless he is loyal to the United States." The British tide
began to turn in December, when Union sympathizers organized huge
rallies and mass petitions in an unexpected quarter: the working-class
neighborhoods so affected by the blockade of southern cotton. Workers
rallied to defend the Union as a republic that offered dignity to common
men—and a model for reforming their own hierarchical society. They
also saw the Emancipation Proclamation as an essential step toward a
complete abolition of American slavery. Pressured by public opinion,
British leaders abandoned proposing mediation, compelling their ally,
the French emperor Napoleon III, to back away as well.[85]

Angry Confederates interpreted the Emancipation Proclamation as
meant to provoke slave revolts: the long-standing southern nightmare,
always imagined as a massacre of white women and children. If that
imagined revolt did not eliminate whites, they would slaughter Blacks
in revenge. Jefferson Davis denounced the proclamation as "a measure
by which several millions of human beings of an inferior race, peaceful
and contented laborers in their sphere, are doomed to extermination,
while at the same time they are encouraged to a general assassination of
their masters." After learning of the proclamation, an Arkansas soldier
awoke from a nightmare: "I had to eat by the side of a negro." Worse
still, the Black "had a plate to eat on and I had none." Playing a zero-
sum racial game, Confederates fought on in grim determination to
maintain white supremacy.[86]

Most northern Democrats blasted presidential emancipation as an
unconstitutional grab for executive power that would alienate the Border

States and deepen the Confederate resolve to fight. Kentucky's governor warned that the proclamation would "fire the whole South into one burning mass of inexhaustible hate." Democrats insisted that emancipation sacrificed the "old Union," by which they meant a loose confederation, substituting the more centralized nation favored by Republicans. McClellan assured fellow Democrats that Lincoln had turned "our free institutions into a despotism." And Democrats claimed that emancipation alienated Union soldiers: "A large majority can see no reason why they should be shot for the benefit of niggers and Abolitionists."[87]

In the November election, Democrats expected to win big by hammering away at Lincoln's encroachments on civil liberty; the mounting casualties of an apparently endless war; and emancipation cast as betraying white supremacy. They warned northern voters of a coming invasion by freed Blacks to take their jobs, homes, and daughters. Democrats did capture key governorships in New York and New Jersey, and legislative majorities in Illinois and Indiana, plus they added thirty-four seats in Congress. But Democrats had expected even bigger gains. In the nineteen states within the Union, Republicans still controlled seventeen governorships and sixteen state legislatures. They also retained a majority of twenty-five seats in the House and even added five seats to their edge in the Senate. Having weathered the electoral storm, Republicans could forge ahead with a harder war against the South.[88]

Once the election was over, Lincoln moved quickly, on November 7, to sack McClellan from command of the Army of the Potomac. Already soured by the general's conduct at Antietam, the president became fed up when McClellan dithered instead of taking the war to the enemy—as a Lee or Grant would do. Lincoln insisted that McClellan and his followers "have no idea that the war is to be carried on and put through by hard, tough fighting that will hurt somebody, and no headway is going to be made while the delusion lasts." The president wanted a military team fully committed to a hard war that included emancipation.[89]

To command the Army of the Potomac, Lincoln replaced McClellan with Ambrose E. Burnside, who had done well with smaller commands but had botched his troops' attack in the recent battle at Antietam. Advancing south to the Rappahannock River at Fredericksburg with

120,000 men, Burnside found Lee's 75,000 Confederates holding the high ground behind the town. Angered by snipers sheltered within Fredericksburg, Burnside had eighty-seven cannon bombard the town with 100 shells per minute on December 11. "I was reminded of a Sunday school picture I had once seen of the burning of Sodom," a soldier marveled. Most of the inhabitants fled into the countryside with what little they could carry. Union troops occupied and looted the ruins. One exulted that "secession families have been made to feel the awful horrors of a war brought on by their treason." Watching from the nearby heights, a Confederate officer seethed: "I hate them worse than ever. . . . It seems to me that I don't do anything from morning to night but hate them worse and worse."[90]

On December 13 Burnside ordered frontal assaults uphill against Confederates sheltered by a stone wall on the heights west of town. Thousands of Yankees paid with lives and limbs for their commander's folly. Thrust into the deadly fire of "a complete slaughter pen" (as one Confederate said), the Union troops suffered 13,000 casualties to just 5,000 for the Confederates. Afterward, witnesses could walk across the battlefield from Union corpse to corpse without touching the ground. Many were "mashed into one complete jelly." The victors looted and stripped the dead of money, watches, and clothing. A Confederate said the denuded dead "looked like hogs that had been cleaned."[91]

The costly defeat demoralized Union troops and deflated civilian support for the war. A soldier wrote, "I am sick and tired of disaster and the fools that bring disaster upon us." Another Union soldier reported that many of his peers were so depressed that only "the thought of their families keeps them from suicide." Lincoln also felt disheartened, "We are now on the brink of destruction. . . . If there is a worse place than Hell, I am in it." Any military hope lay to the west, but even there the Union cause had faltered.[92]

Guerrillas

In the Mississippi Valley, Union forces lost the momentum gained in the winter and spring of 1862. Their next prime target was Vicksburg,

Mississippi, a fortified town on bluffs that towered 200 feet above a sharp bend in the river. In June 1862, Farragut brought his fleet upstream from New Orleans to bombard Vicksburg, but his guns struggled to hit the Confederates' batteries on top of the bluff. Then typhoid, dysentery, and malaria incapacitated most of the Union sailors and soldiers, so Farragut steamed back to Louisiana in frustration.[93]

Farragut had expected support from Henry Halleck's army based at Corinth in northern Mississippi. But Halleck stayed put, immobilized by the Confederate threat to his overland supply routes from the North. As Union forces penetrated deeper into the South, they relied more on railroads to bring reinforcements and supplies. Long rail lines invited disruption by guerrillas, especially fast-moving cavalry who swept in behind the Union army to tear up track, burn bridges, ambush trains, topple telegraph poles, and shoot sentries. Often it took Union forces weeks to repair a rail line, halting their army during the wait. General Sherman complained, "Railroads are the weakest things in war" when "running through a country where every house is a nest of secret, bitter enemies."[94]

In early 1862, the Union seemed to have conquered 50,000 square miles in eastern Tennessee and northern Mississippi and Alabama, but northern troops could not patrol and control all of that terrain. Large garrisons secured Nashville, Memphis, and Corinth, but in the broad hinterland hostile civilians helped guerrillas attack Union outposts and supply trains. A Union general lamented, "Scarcely a day passes without some attack upon our bridge guards, our trains, or telegraph wires." Sherman noted, "Our armies pass across & through the land," but "the war closes in behind and leaves the same enmity behind."[95]

Many southerners preferred to serve as guerrillas rather than in the regular Confederate army. Although usually unpaid (save by plunder) and obliged to subsist and arm themselves, guerrillas relished freedom from drill, discipline, and superiors. An Arkansan explained, "I wanted to get out where I could have it more lively; where I could fight if I wanted to, or run if I so desired. I wanted to be my own general." Disdaining so-called civilized warfare, guerrillas cultivated an aura of savagery meant to terrify their foes. A Virginia guerrilla vowed "to hunt Yankees as I would wild beasts" and expected his men to "live & fight like Indians."[96]

For the Confederacy, guerrillas were a mixed blessing. They disrupted Union supply lines but resisted control and coordination by Confederate commanders. Many guerrillas were draft dodgers or deserters, denying regular Confederate armies of desperately needed reinforcements. Preferring to fight on their own terms closer to home, some insisted that they had "enlisted for the defense of their homes & for no other purpose." Here Confederate appeals to enlist for defense of hearth and home came back to bite the new nation's leaders. With the Confederacy unable to keep invaders out, much of the southern countryside became a war zone, drawing homeward the most discontented troops. As guerrillas, they could claim to defend their homes and stay true to the Confederate cause. But their indiscriminate violence often alienated civilians.[97]

Guerrillas infuriated Union troops, who never knew when snipers or raiders would strike, killing and maiming with sudden fury. Seeking a respite between grim battles, troops resented their relentless unease when occupying hostile communities. Even battle seemed better than the random violence inflicted by "bushwhackers." Regulars derided guerrillas as treacherous cowards who hit, ran, and hid—often posing as Unionists. Or they tricked Yankees by wearing captured blue uniforms before spinning to attack. Many guerrillas mutilated their victims, leaving decapitated heads and disemboweled bodies beside the road to terrify others—to the special fury of Unionists and Union troops.[98]

After losing a few comrades to guerrilla butchery, federal troops longed for revenge. Often they gave prisoners an apparent chance to run and then shot them down for attempting to escape. Northern troops also vented their fury on southern civilians suspected of aiding and abetting guerrillas. A Union colonel explained, "Every time the telegraph wire was cut, we would burn a house; every time a train was fired upon, we should hang a man." Guerrilla conflicts always frustrate occupying armies into inflicting collective punishment on civilians, who are easier to catch than the elusive culprits.[99]

A former champion of restraint, Sherman became hardened by guerrilla attacks. In July 1862 he began collectively punishing communities that apparently aided the irregulars. In October, he said of southern civilians: "They cannot be made to love us, but they can be made to fear us, and dread the passage of our troops through their country." He burned towns and hamlets suspected of harboring snipers who fired on trains and riverboats. In January 1863 Sherman reported, "Our armies are devastating the land. . . . Farms disappear, houses are burned and plundered, and every living animal killed and eaten."[100]

But there were limits. Both Union and Confederate generals distinguished between their organized, rule-bound regular regiments, on the one hand, and the chaotic, brutal irregulars, on the other. Seeking higher moral ground in a propaganda competition, the generals on each side boasted of their good conduct, while highlighting every violation by their foes. Regular troops did execute suspected guerrillas—and looted and torched the houses of their civilian supporters. But conventional commanders and troops avoided the massacre of civilians and captured regulars. For all their differences, Yankees and Confederates treated one another as fellow whites speaking the same language and sharing many customs. So they spared white civilians from the slaughter inflicted on Indians and Mexicans by Americans—or on captured Blacks by Confederates. At its core, in the movement of vast armies, generals conducted a civil war that fell far short of total—but the brutal margins of irregular war kept growing as the conflict dragged on.[101]

Buell

During the summer of 1862, Halleck sent troops eastward to take Chattanooga, a railway juncture and the gateway to eastern Tennessee, a Unionist stronghold under a harsh Confederate occupation. But Halleck entrusted that campaign to Don Carlos Buell, a ditherer in the mold of his friend McClellan. It took Buell three weeks to move his army ninety miles, irritating Lincoln, who complained of an "apparent want of energy and activity." Just 2,500 Confederate cavalry rode rings around Buell's hapless 40,000, destroying his railroad supply lines. The alternative was to cut loose from the supply line by having troops forage hard on the civilian population for supplies—a hard-war technique ruled out by the conservative Buell.[102]

In central Tennessee, Buell confronted a Confederate army commanded by Braxton Bragg. A stickler for discipline, from soldiers as well as slaves, Bragg had a dim view of human nature and democracy. To explain Confederate defeats, he insisted, "Universal suffrage, furloughs & whiskey have ruined us." He made examples by shooting a few soldiers for deserting or looting. Dyspeptic and abrasive, Bragg bickered with his subordinate generals, who came to despise him. It did not help that Bragg often lost confidence during battles. But he had a close and protective friend in Jefferson Davis.[103]

Rather than wait for Buell at Chattanooga, Bragg hard-marched his 48,000 men in two columns northward to invade Kentucky—living off the land as Buell refused to do. Bragg believed that Kentuckians felt oppressed by Yankees and would rally to his army. Alarmed by the Confederate offensive, Halleck told Buell that the threat of the guillotine had motivated French generals to move faster during their revolution, so perhaps the Union should follow suit. That grim humor seemed to work, for Buell led 60,000 men northward, pursuing Bragg into Kentucky. On October 8, Buell's army caught up with Bragg at Perryville, where the two forces pummeled one another in a disordered battle without any decisive advantage. The Confederates suffered 3,400 casualties, but the Union lost 4,200. Discouraged because so few Kentuckians rallied to help him, Bragg retreated to Tennessee, while his subordinates denounced him as a bungler. When Buell failed to pursue the retreating Confederates, Lincoln replaced him with William S. Rosecrans.[104]

Further west, Grant tried to revive Union fortunes by attacking Vicksburg, 250 miles southwest of his base at Corinth in northern Mississippi. But on December 20, Confederate cavalry swooped in behind Grant's army, destroying his key supply depot at Holly Springs. In disgust, Grant returned to Corinth. His key subordinate, Sherman, forged ahead down the Mississippi River thanks to the more secure support provided by ironclad gunboats. At Chickasaw Bluffs, three miles north of Vicksburg, 16,000 Confederates entrenched on high ground to block Sherman's advance. Attacking with 32,000 men on December

29, Sherman suffered a humiliating defeat, with 1,800 Union casualties to fewer than 187 for the Confederates. He too had to withdraw northward for the winter. With even the best northern generals—Grant and Sherman—stymied, the Union cause was faltering in the West as in the East in late 1862.[105]

The year's last hope for a Union victory lay with Rosecrans's army in middle Tennessee. In late December, Rosecrans advanced southward to attack Bragg at Stones River. Camping near each other, the two armies held an impromptu battle of the bands with the federals playing "Yankee Doodle" to try to drown out the Confederates' "Dixie." Wearied of this, one band switched to the sentimental "Home, Sweet Home," which the other side picked up as thousands of Yankees and Confederates sang along across their lines. The next day they resumed killing one another. The episode highlighted the sentimental culture shared by both sides—and the competing nationalisms dividing them.[106]

On December 31, the Confederates struck first and hardest at the Union left flank, "like a whirl-a-gust of woodpeckers in a hail storm," said Sam Watkins, a southern soldier. Rosecrans rallied his men, despite wearing a splatter of blood and brains from an aide decapitated beside him by a cannonball. As Union resistance stiffened, Bragg's attacks faltered. Neither side renewed combat on January 1, but Bragg made one last, desperate bid a day later. In a badly devised assault, he sent John Breckinridge's division charging into intense artillery fire that cost 1,500 Confederate lives in an hour. The survivors broke and fled. Disengaging the rest of his army, Bragg pulled back twenty-five miles to the south. Rosecrans did not pursue. The battle cost both sides dearly: 31 percent of the Union force and 33 percent of the Confederates.[107]

Although the barest of Union victories, Stones River relieved Republicans, desperate for any good news after Burnside's demoralizing debacle at Fredericksburg three weeks earlier. Lincoln wired Rosecrans, "God bless you, and all with you. I can never forget, whilst I remember anything. . . . You gave us a hard earned victory which, had there been a defeat instead, the nation could hardly have lived over." Every major battle contributed to the ebb and flow of national morale that ultimately would determine whether one side or the other could hang on long enough to win.[108]

Emancipation

On January 1, 1863, Lincoln finalized and implemented his Emancipation Proclamation. "I never, in my life, felt more certain that I was doing right than I do in signing this paper," Lincoln told Seward. The final version still exempted Tennessee, Louisiana, parts of eastern Virginia, and all the Border States: collectively home to a million slaves (a quarter of the American total). But the final proclamation authorized the enlistment of Black Americans for military service and vindicated runaways who used violence in self-defense.[109]

Formerly skeptical with cause, African Americans now praised Lincoln as a liberator, singing a new verse to an old hymn:

Go down, Abraham, away down in Dixie's land,
Tell Jeff Davis to let my people go.

At a refugee camp on the Sea Islands of South Carolina, a Union colonel and abolitionist, Thomas Wentworth Higginson, watched a ceremonial reading of the Emancipation Proclamation to former slaves dressed in their Sunday best. Claiming the United States as, at last, their own, they began singing the anthem "My Country, 'Tis of Thee." Higginson recalled, "I never saw anything so electric; it made all other words cheap; it seemed the choked voice of a race at last unloosed."[110]

The Emancipation Proclamation committed Union troops to liberating Blacks as northern armies penetrated deeper into the Confederacy. Frederick Douglass exulted, "Every general and every soldier that now goes in good faith to Old Virginia goes there for the very purpose that sent honest John Brown to Harper's Ferry." Word of the proclamation spread like wildfire among enslaved people deep within the South. When masters talked about politics and war, enslaved people overheard. In South Carolina, a Black refugee explained, "We's can't read, but we'se can listen." At Fort Monroe in Virginia, 3,000 refugees

had arrived during the eighteen months before January 1863, but 10,000
did so in the first three months of 1863. In Richmond, two of Jefferson
Davis's slaves fled to the Yankees, and a third tried to burn down the
Confederate White House.[111]

Only a prolonged southern rebellion could have ended slavery in a
Union previously committed to preserving that system in the states. The
frictions of war enabled thousands of enslaved people to seek freedom
through escape to Union lines. Then fierce Confederate resistance pro-
tracted the war and angered Unionists, who sought revenge by liberating
more slaves to ruin the southern economy and armies. Salmon P. Chase
noted, "If the slaveholders had stayed in the Union, they might have
kept the life in their institution for many years to come," but "they had
madly placed [slavery] in the very path of destruction." In Tennessee,
a Unionist slaveholder lashed out at secessionists: "I warned you years
ago that when you began this rebellion you would destroy slavery. You
rebels . . . are the very ones who have struck a death blow to the heart
of slavery."[112]

In March 1863, Halleck assured Grant that the war had
been transformed:

> There is now no possible hope of a reconciliation with the rebels.
> The union party in the South is virtually destroyed. There can be
> no peace but that which is enforced by the sword. We must con-
> quer the rebels or be conquered by them. The north must either
> destroy the slave oligarchy or become slaves themselves.

Yankee prospects gained strength from thousands of Black recruits,
fighting for their freedom and for the Union—while Confederates
steadily lost the enslaved labor that sustained their cause. The revolutionary stage of this civil war had begun.[113]

EIGHT ଓ WEST

You build big houses, big ships, big towns. . . . Then, after
you have got them all, you die and leave them behind. Now
we call that slavery. You are slaves from the time you begin
to talk until you die; but we are free as air . . . Our wants are
few and easily supplied. The river, the wood, and plain yield
all that we require, and we will not be slaves. Nor will we
send our children to your schools, where they learn only to
become like yourselves.

—CADETE, AN APACHE CHIEF,
ADDRESSING AN AMERICAN CAPTAIN, 1865[1]

The journalist Jane Grey Swisshelm crusaded for equal rights for
Blacks, but she disdained Native peoples as "lazy, impudent beggars" and thieves. Devoted to the Republican gospel of social
mobility through free labor, Swisshelm saw both slaveholders and Indians as parasites, exploiting the labor of others.[2]

Swisshelm's hatred for Indians deepened in 1862, when Dakotas (also called the Sioux) attacked and killed hundreds of settlers, some within a dozen miles of her home at St. Cloud in Minnesota. She became unhinged by exaggerated reports that warriors had raped white women and butchered their children. Concluding that "a Sioux has just as much right to life as a hyena," Swisshelm wanted to exterminate "these red-jawed tigers whose fangs are dripping with the blood of the inno-cents. . . . If they have any souls, the Lord can have mercy on them if he pleases! But that is His business. Ours is to kill the lazy vermin and make sure of killing them." Touring the east in late 1862, Swisshelm gave public lectures promoting genocide against Indians: "Our people will hunt them, shoot them, set traps for them, put out poisoned bait for them—kill by every means we would use to exterminate panthers." These deadly words carried extra punch because delivered by a slight and short matron in a genteel dress.[3]

Claiming to be civilized, Americans cast Indians as their opposites, as savages. In 1863, a federal official defined Native peoples as "ignorant, deluded, superstitious, and wicked creatures, degraded and brutal in all their habits and instincts." By casting Natives as treacherous brutes, Americans justified attacking them as proper revenge. In March 1863, at the White House, Lincoln told visiting chiefs: "Although we are now engaged in a great war between one another, we are not, as a race, so much disposed to fight and kill one another as our red brethren." That claim seemed odd given that Americans were slaughtering one another in a massive civil war far deadlier than any Indian conflict.[4]

The Civil War spread throughout the West in an imperial form. Republicans drew the West more fully within the Union's economic and political orbit by dispossessing Indians and fending off Confederates asserting their own claims. Unionists also sought to contain a challenge by Mormons who had settled in the Great Basin, where they offered an alternative society that included polygamous marriage. Ulysses S. Grant

saw the West as entangled with the civil war in Mexico as well as the one
tearing apart the United States. So he sought to send troops "for duty
in the Territories of Utah & New Mexico & Arizona for the purpose
of squelching out Polygamy, quieting hostile Indians, and watching the
French in Mexico."[5]

Prize

Nineteenth-century Americans saw their national future unfolding west
of the Mississippi River as settlers created new farms, mines, ranches,
and towns. Recognizing the high stakes involved, northern and southern
leaders clashed over what form of society—slave or free labor—should
prevail in the West and thereby claim the American future. Because
frontier settlement could tilt the Union's balance of power, the West
was the contested prize that sparked the Civil War.[6]

Save for the humid Pacific coast north of San Francisco, the West was
an arid land intersected by long chains of towering mountains and a few
rivers and streams. At two million square miles, the West comprised
most of the nation's territory, but it was lightly developed and weakly
controlled by the United States in 1860. The region both allured and
alarmed as a wilder landscape of canyons, deserts, salt lakes, vast plains,
and the nation's highest peaks. Americans saw opportunity and challenge in a strange land of bison herds, grizzly bears, and defiant Indians.
Danger and distance made the West a special land of imagined freedom
beyond the social constraints of eastern crowds. "Eastward I go only
by force; but westward I go free," declared Henry David Thoreau. But
how could Americans be free and still make a living in such a daunting
land? They coveted individual freedom but were bound together by
market transactions—and most settlers wanted enough government to
protect their private property.[7]

The vast scale and demanding landscape complicated American efforts
to control the West. In 1861, no railroad line extended beyond western
Missouri, compelling travelers and teamsters to rely on horses, oxen, and
wagons to cross the continent. With American settlement concentrated
on the distant Pacific coast, nearly 3,000 miles west of Washington, D.C.,

most mail and goods arrived by a long ocean route via Panama. In Kansas, Iowa, and Minnesota, farmers lived close enough to rivers and railroads to get their crops to market, but farther west they had to depend on the limited consumption provided by nearby miners and soldiers. Those miners boosted western development by finding gold and silver, which could bear the cost of long-distance transportation to eastern cities.[8]

In 1861, only 700,000 American citizens, about 2 percent of the nation's total, lived west of Kansas. Most of them (433,000) dwelled in distant California and Oregon, where Americans found tons of gold. The vast, intervening interior of Great Plains, Rocky Mountains, Great Basin, and Southwest remained largely unsettled by Americans save for four pockets: Mormons near the Great Salt Lake; old Hispanic communities along the Rio Grande in New Mexico; and newer mining camps in Arizona and Colorado.[9]

But Americans meant to exploit and dominate the region, so the federal government sprinkled the West with sixty forts garrisoned by about 10,000 troops in 1861. By then, Congress had subdivided the region into three states—Kansas, California, and Oregon—and seven territories: Colorado, Dakota, Nebraska, Nevada, New Mexico, Utah, and Washington. An eighth territory—Indian Territory (now Oklahoma)—received displaced Natives from the East. They preferred to govern themselves, and Americans would not share federal power with them.[10]

In the West's interior, about 300,000 Native peoples retained an independence that alarmed Americans. In a vicious cycle, miners and ranchers surged into a region to harvest and deplete the natural resources that Indians needed to subsist. Without compensating Natives, newcomers took timber, pastured livestock, killed game animals, and transformed their habitat into ranches, mines, and farms. Reduced to starvation, Natives stole horses and cattle from the intruders. Outraged by those losses, settlers attacked Indians, who retaliated in kind.[11]

Settlers promoted genocide. A Colorado major declared, "I think and earnestly believe the Indians to be an obstacle to civilization, and [they] should be exterminated." To enjoy their vision of western freedom, Americans killed Indians. In Washington Territory, settlers declared, "God never intended the survival of the Indian race. The Indian is in the way; and the sooner he is put out of his misery and out of the way, the better." During the 1850s, Californians slaughtered Native men and enslaved women and children, reducing that state's Indian numbers from 150,000 in 1850 to just 30,000 in 1860.[12]

As an alternative to genocide, federal officials proposed confining Indians on reservations, while taking their best lands for settlers to develop as private property. An entrepreneur preached, "It is certainly for the interest of all citizens to have these lands settled by enterprising white settlers rather than have them remain in the hands of the indolent, improvident Red Man." Federal officials sought to save Indian lives by killing their cultures, transforming Natives into American citizens through education and hard labor. An official said of the Indian: "His whole nature must be changed. He must have a white man's ambition" by becoming "more mercenary and ambitious to obtain riches." Once remade into competitive, acquisitive individuals, "tribal relations would be broken down," as Natives lost their traditions, languages, and identities.[13]

Federal policy demanded that Natives become American-style farmers on lands that Americans rejected as too poor. Taking most of the best land, settlers left the dregs for reservations, where corrupt officials embezzled funds and supplies promised to Natives. Resisting confinement on bleak reservations, Natives defended their homelands and rejected the American way of life as soiled by greed, deceit, and arrogance.[14]

In 1861, many Native peoples saw an opportunity to fight back as federal garrisons withdrew eastward to fight the Confederate rebellion. Natives raided stagecoaches, mining camps, and ranches in hopes of driving away the intruders. These attacks alarmed Union men, for those lines of communication and transit seemed critical to national unity in a troubled time. By keeping the lines open, Union leaders could tap western resources to help contain and defeat the Confederacy.[15]

Despite the pressing need for manpower to fight in the East, the Union committed 20,000 volunteers to control and conquer western Indians. That surge of volunteers doubled the 10,000 regulars posted in the West before the war. Often recruited from mining camps, the volunteers doubled as prospectors, employed by commanders to seek gold and silver in streambeds and hillsides. Their officers calculated that a gold and silver strike would attract thousands of new settlers, hastening local development and confining Indians.[16]

Pacific Republic

During the Civil War, the Union worked to confine the South with a naval blockade to the east, but Confederates meant to break out westward from Texas across the Southwest to the Pacific. Convinced that slavery had to expand to survive, southern leaders seceded from the Union once persuaded that Yankees meant to claim the West entirely for themselves. But southerners imagined a grand future for slavery if they could claim the Southwest and southern California. "We are now the nucleus of a growing power which, if we are true to ourselves, our destiny, and high mission, will become the controlling power on this continent," Alexander H. Stephens declared at the dawn of the Confederacy.[17]

California offered gold, sending to the east about $3 million every month, which kept the federal government afloat as it built a massive military. Grant noted, "I do not know what we would do in this great national emergency were it not for the gold sent from California." Desperate for funds, Confederates longed to snatch that golden goose away from the Union. California allured national imaginations, promising to empower either Union or Confederacy with boundless future possibilities—while confining the other to a geopolitical claustrophobia.[18]

In California, Confederate leaders counted on support from the state's proslavery Democrats called "the Chivalry" and led by William M. Gwin, a transplanted Mississippi slaveholder turned U.S. senator. Dominant in California during the 1850s, Gwin's Democrats were losing ground to the Republicans at the start of the new decade. In an upset, Lincoln carried California in 1860 with just 32 percent of the votes because three other candidates split the rest. In early 1861, Free Soil

Democrats (called "the Shovelry") and Republicans united to form a majority in the state legislature.[19]

The Chivalry recoiled as Lincoln replaced California's postmasters, mint workers, customs collectors, and federal marshals with Republicans. In 1861, California's proslavery Democrats sought to secede to form an independent "Pacific Republic" with boundaries extending eastward to the Rocky Mountains. In speeches and newspaper essays, they dwelled on the vast natural resources and economic potential of the West Coast as best developed by an independent republic that could expand across the Pacific and into Latin America. A visitor noted that the Chivalry sought "to fascinate the restless, fortune-hunting people of California with prospects of conquests in Mexico and Oceanica." Favoring neutrality in the Civil War to the east, the Chivalry warned that staying in the Union would saddle Californians with heavy taxes and battlefield corpses. One state senator declared, "I will die before I will contribute a dime to prosecute a wicked, unholy, unjust, black-hearted abolition war upon my southern brethren."[20]

Republicans denounced the Pacific Republic scheme as too risky and expensive. The West might be rich in resources, but it remained too thinly populated to fund its own national government. Better to stay in the Union, which heavily subsidized the West through military, transportation, and postal expenditures. Then news of Fort Sumter swung popular emotions decisively against the Confederates as aggressors, leading to mass rallies and fiery speeches in support of the Union. In late April, the legislatures of California, Oregon, and Washington endorsed the Union cause, as did most of the region's newspapers. Daunted by that popular surge, the leaders of the Chivalry dropped their Pacific Republic scheme while waiting for Confederate victories to discredit the North.[21]

In April 1861 a few pro-South hotheads sought to jump-start California secession by organizing a military coup to seize San Francisco, the chief port for exporting California's gold. The leader, Asbury Harpending, had run away, at age fifteen, from his old Kentucky home to join William Walker's filibuster in Nicaragua. Moving to California, Harpending got rich from gold mining. In 1860, he boasted, "I wasn't quite 20, couldn't vote, couldn't make a contract, yet, I had over a quarter of a million in hard cash." Young, rich, and stupid made for a dangerous combination. In 1861, Harpending meant to rally California's abundance of "reckless human material"—frustrated miners, runaway debtors, and demobilized soldiers—"all eager to engage in any under- taking that promised adventure and profit."[22]

Able to raise only 100 men, Harpending turned to the Texan in command of federal troops in California in early 1861: Albert Sidney Johnston. But Johnston refused to cooperate, seeing a military coup as disreputable. Instead, he resigned from the U.S. Army so he could head east to fight and die for the Confederacy with honor on a battlefield. In late April, General Edwin V. Sumner, took command in California, and he aggressively deployed federal troops to intimidate the plotters.[23]

Unrepentant, Harpending headed east to pitch a piracy scheme to the Davis administration, which commissioned him as a captain in the navy—although Harpending had no naval experience, and the Confed- eracy had no ship for him. In late 1862 he slipped back to San Francisco to buy a schooner and recruit twenty desperadoes armed with rifles, revolvers, and cutlasses. They planned to attack Union ships leaving San Francisco laden with California's gold. But Harpending and his men boasted of their plans at taverns. Alerted to the plot, the government arrested and jailed Harpending and his gang. After a year behind bars, he won release by swearing allegiance to the Union.[24]

In September 1861 California voters had elected a Republican, the railroad tycoon Leland Stanford, as governor, and his party controlled the state legislature. The state government rallied to the Union by raising ten regiments of volunteers employed to suppress Indians and Confederate sympathizers in California. That political turn spooked the leaders of the Chivalry—William Gwin, David Terry, and Joseph Lancaster Brent—who fled from California to join the Confederacy. In November 1861, federal officials intercepted and arrested Gwin on suspicion of spying for the South. Lacking sufficient evidence to con- vict, the Union released Gwin, who returned to his plantation in Mis- sissippi. Southern sympathizers persisted in southern California, where they openly flew the Confederate flag. Some became bandits preying on stagecoaches until captured or shot by Unionists.[25]

New Mexico

Foiled within California, the Confederates turned to a Texan invasion of New Mexico that could, then, push westward to the Pacific. A Confederate officer noted, "The objective, aim, and design of the campaign was the conquest of California." In late 1861, the federal commander in California reported that southern sympathizers were "congregating in some force in the southern counties, in the hope of receiving support from Texas." In revolutions and border lands, men dreamed of leveraging small forces into grand schemes of empire.[26]

But the Confederate invaders struggled to overcome New Mexico's arid environment of spiky mountains and broad deserts around thin agricultural stretches beside a few rivers. A soldier lamented that New Mexico "was very poor, very broke, and some parts desolate of water, grass, timber, and everything else save rattlesnakes and prairie dogs." Invaders could not find much food for themselves or fodder for their horses. For lack of any railroad, the Confederates had to haul their provisions and ammunition around on creaky wagons and balky packhorses.[27]

The invaders could not count on much help from the New Mexicans. Most were Spanish-speaking *Hispanos* clustered along the Rio Grande, from El Paso on the south to Taos at the foot of the Rocky Mountains to the north. A few of the richer ranchers and merchants supported slavery and felt drawn to the Confederacy, but the common *Hispanos* just never much liked Texans.[28]

Confederates did find support in the territory's southern quarter, around Mesilla, Tubac, and Tucson, where many southerners had settled in mining boom towns. Claiming the best sources of water and timber, the intruders pushed aside the native Apaches, who fought back. To suppress them, miners welcomed Confederate help. They also felt frustrated by Republican congressmen who had defeated the miners' bid for their own territorial government, called "Arizona," to consist of the southern half of the future states of New Mexico and Arizona (below the thirty-fourth parallel).[29]

In early 1861, Texans sent Philemon T. Herbert into southern New Mexico to rally miners for the Confederacy. Born in Alabama, Herbert had practiced law in Texas before migrating to California during the gold rush. As a member of the Chivalry, he won election to Congress in 1854. Two years later, Herbert became enraged at a hotel in Washington when the head waiter, an Irish immigrant, refused him breakfast after the posted time. So, Herbert shot the waiter dead. Yankees denounced Herbert as a ruffian, while southern newspapers said that the Irishman got what he deserved. Prosecuted for manslaughter, Herbert won acquittal but left Congress for Texas, where he felt more at home. In March 1861, Herbert convened the leading Arizonans to secede from New Mexico and the Union.[30]

To support the new territory, Texas sent 300 mounted men led by Col. John Baylor, a legislator, rancher, rustler, and journalist. Baylor had founded and edited a newspaper, aptly named *The Whiteman*, to urge genocide for Indians. Practicing what he preached, Baylor led armed vigilantes to massacre peaceful Indians living on reservations in 1858 and 1859. In July 1861 Baylor's men advanced up the Rio Grande from El Paso, defeating federal troops, who burned their fort and fled northward. Suffering from dehydration and heat prostration in the desert, the soldiers surrendered to the pursuing Confederates. To celebrate, Baylor appointed himself governor of Arizona. Although the Mesilla newspaper was pro-Confederate, the editor criticized Baylor. Confronting the editor in the street, Baylor knocked the man down and shot him dead. A jury of his troops acquitted their commander.[31]

President Davis sent a more veteran officer, Henry H. Sibley, to take command in New Mexico. From Louisiana, Sibley had graduated from West Point and fought in the American war against Mexico. After that war, Sibley served in New Mexico, developing a local expertise that intrigued Davis. Resigning from the federal army in April 1861, Sibley headed to Texas, yelling at his former men: "Boys, if you only knew it, I am the worst enemy you have." In October, he returned to New Mexico with 2,700 Confederate soldiers.[32]

Confederates sought to help *Hispano* ranchers and Anglo miners in their conflicts with Apaches, who waged war as raiders, taking livestock and captives. Subdivided in many small bands, they dwelled in brush and grass huts, called *wickiups*, in small villages deep within the canyons between mountains clad in piñon and mesquite trees. Highly mobile, Apaches were adept at guerrilla warfare in a demanding environment.[33]

Seeking to exterminate Apaches, Baylor instructed a subordinate to entice them in for a peace parlay "and when you get them together kill all the grown Indians and take the children prisoners and sell them to defray the expense of killing the Indians. . . . Allow no Indian to escape." Baylor provoked an international incident by charging across the Mexican border in pursuit of Apaches. Unable to find any, he seized and lynched three peaceable laborers of Indian descent who worked at a Mexican mine. Two of them were women. This atrocity was too much for Davis, who sacked Baylor as military officer and territorial governor. Returning to Texas, Baylor won election to the Confederate Congress.[34]

The Confederates in Arizona were too few to defeat Apaches, who ambushed and destroyed small patrols. A Texan recalled one attack: "We was going along, free and easy. Then, without no warning at all, the Indians come hellity-larrup, just swarming outen the rocks. There was a whole cloud of them." During that summer, Confederates suffered heavier casualties to Apaches than to federal troops.[35]

In New Mexico, Union forces were commanded by Col. Edward R. S. Canby, a forty-four-year-old Kentuckian who remained loyal to the Union. Energetic and resourceful, Canby supplemented his small regular force with four regiments of New Mexico volunteers raised by Christopher "Kit" Carson, a fellow Kentuckian who had become a renowned trapper, hunter, rancher, and scout. Although illiterate, Carson spoke English, Spanish, and several Native languages. He also had a quiet resolve and intelligence that impressed others, save for one of his Indian wives, who cast him out.[36]

In February 1862, Sibley defeated Canby's federal force at Valverde beside the Rio Grande, but the Confederates suffered heavy casualties and failed to dislodge the Union garrisons at Fort Craig and Fort Union. Bypassing them, Sibley headed north to occupy Albuquerque and Santa Fe, where his supply line from Texas became dangerously long and vulnerable. To strike back, Canby counted on Union volunteers coming south from Colorado. They had an especially powerful second-in-command, Major John Chivington, a bellowing, burly, Methodist minister who preached while armed with pistols to deal with hecklers.[37]

In March 1862, at Glorieta Pass north of Santa Fe, Chivington outflanked the Confederates to surprise and burn their supply train of eighty wagons. The loss of horses, mules, wagons, and provisions compelled Sibley to withdraw his discouraged men southward on a long retreat to Texas. Drinking heavily, Sibley neglected his troops, who suffered severely from heat, hunger, thirst, and Apache ambushes. About 500 Texans died on the hard journey homeward, and they littered their trail with broken weapons, shattered wagons, and dead horses. Taking out their frustrations on *Hispanos* who refused to supply them, Confederates burned a village and killed twenty civilians. Sibley reported that his men had developed an "irreconcilable detestation of the country and the people." They also detested Sibley.[38]

The New Mexico campaign had involved small armies, but the stakes were large. The Confederates had dreamed so big, and so far beyond their means, that the crash proved depleting and discrediting to potential supporters in the West. The Union would retain the great resources of California, including gold reserves essential to its monetary system. For the time being, the Union had contained the Confederacy to the west. But to retain western support, federal leaders would have to succeed where Confederates had failed: by suppressing Indian resistance.[39]

Jayhawkers

In addition to their foray into the Southwest, Confederates sought to break out of containment by pushing west from Arkansas into Indian Territory (now Oklahoma). The governor of Arkansas noted, "Negro slavery exists in the Indian Territory, and is profitable and desirable there, affording a practical issue of the right of expansion, for which the war began."

From Indian Territory, Confederates might strike northward to reclaim Kansas for the South. During the late 1850s, conflict had created a bloody borderland along the margins of eastern Kansas and western Missouri. Rival antislavery and proslavery partisans had plundered, dispossessed, and expelled hundreds of families, generating intense hatreds on both sides.[40]

The withdrawal of southern senators from Congress enabled the Republican majority to admit Kansas as a free state in January 1861. The new governor of Kansas, Charles Robinson, meant to escalate the border war: "Missouri must be taught a lesson & I should be glad of an opportunity to give it." But many Missourians sought to teach the same bloody lesson to Kansans. A Union general reported, "It is the old border hatred intensified by the rebellion and by the murders, robberies, and arson" of "irregular warfare."[41]

Kansas's new U.S. senators included the populist firebrand Jim Lane. A charming and enterprising rogue, Lane cultivated Lincoln, calling on the president almost daily to offer advice and seek favors. In other Union states, governors organized volunteers and commissioned their officers, but Senator Lane did so for Kansas. Lane's political rival, Governor Robinson, protested that Lincoln had empowered "an insane fanatic to run riot, independent of all authority." The president replied that Lane "knocks at my door every morning. You know he is a very persistent fellow and hard to put off. I don't see you very often and [I] have to pay attention to him."[42]

Glorying in the nicknames "Grim Chieftain" and "Bloody Jim," Lane rallied irregular volunteers, known as jayhawkers, to seek revenge and loot in western Missouri. During the summer of 1861, they stole

"A Rebel Guerilla Raid in a Western Town," wood engraving by Thomas Nast, Harper's Weekly, *Sept. 27, 1862.*

livestock, plundered and burned farms and stores, liberated slaves, and executed foes. A supporter exulted in "that joyous time of springtide when, with flags and banners flapping, the jayhawkers . . . swooped across the state line to crush the rebellion for God and the Union and in the process pluck old Missouri clean for God and themselves."[43]

Indiscriminate in theft and brutality, the jayhawkers alienated many civilians in Missouri, which disgusted regular Union officers. One denounced the jayhawkers as "a mere ragged, half-armed, diseased, and mutinous rabble" whose camps were "little better than pig-pens." In January 1862, General Henry Halleck blamed their atrocities for turning "against us many thousands who were formerly Union men." But Lane's brutality in Missouri enhanced his popularity in Kansas, where he raised many men for the Union.[44]

In 1862, Lane recruited hundreds of Blacks—quite contrary to the then official federal policy banning their service. He even commissioned some as officers. "This war is for slavery," Lane reasoned, so the Union ought to "make [war] the mighty engine for slavery's destruction." Plus,

he needed every man he could get, and former slaves were highly motivated fighters. Lane declared, "I would like to see every traitor . . . die
by the hand of his own slave."[45]

Lane expressed a racist brand of antislavery that thrived among midwestern Republicans. While eager to smite the Confederacy with Black
troops, he did not want them as neighbors or fellow citizens. Lane
initially recruited Blacks as "squires" to support his white "knights"
in a "glorious Crusade of freedom." Every knight was "entitled to his
squire to prepare his food, black his boots, load his gun, and take off his
drudgery." Lane wanted to conquer Texas to provide a postwar haven
where Black squires and their families could settle, far from the white
knights of Kansas.[46]

To counter Lane's jayhawkers, pro-Confederate Missourians fought
back as guerrillas, who also blurred the line between war and crime.
They included William Quantrill, a slight young man who looked like
the Yankee schoolteacher that he had been in Ohio. Moving to Kansas
in 1857, Quantrill initially sided with the Free Soilers, but they turned
on him after discovering his sideline as a burglar. In 1860, Quantrill
defected to Missouri, where he made money by tracking runaway slaves
for bounties.[47]

Charismatic, and a deft rider and crack shot, Quantrill attracted followers, growing his command from fifteen men in 1861 to four hundred in August 1863. Quantrill's chief lieutenant, William Anderson,
became known as "Bloody Bill" because he butchered captured Yankees
to decorate his bridle and saddle with their scalps. Another disciple was
Sarah "Kate" King, who rode and fought with the gang as Quantrill's
common-law wife. She was thirteen when their relationship began in
1861. Quantrill assured his men and women plenty of loot and free rein
to kill captured Yankees.[48]

In 1863, Quantrill's greatest raid hit Lawrence, Kansas. Hated as a
base for abolitionists, including Jim Lane, and a haven for escaped slaves,
Lawrence also enticed raiders as a prospering commercial town rich in
potential loot. "We can get more revenge and more money there than
anywhere else in the state," Quantrill said. The raiders felt enraged by
the recent collapse of a brick jail in Kansas City holding many women

arrested for aiding their relatives in Quantrill's gang. Five women died, including a sister of "Bloody Bill" Anderson. On August 21, Quantrill's four hundred raiders surprised, looted, and burned Lawrence, killing at least 180 people, most of them men and boys rounded up and executed. The raiders threw some victims into burning buildings to die. One was a Black baby. "We are fiends from hell!" they screamed. Lane escaped death by fleeing from bed in his nightshirt. After the raiders retreated to Missouri, a Kansan reported, "Commotion, confusion, terror, and vengeance all blended into one indescribable feeling."[49]

Embarrassed by Quantrill's raid, Union general Thomas Ewing, Jr., issued an order on August 25, evicting 20,000 inhabitants from four Missouri counties within fifteen days. Union troops shot a few who resisted removal, and jayhawkers poured in to plunder and burn thousands of empty homes, leaving only charred chimneys.[50]

But the mass dislocation failed to daunt Quantrill, who ambushed and massacred ninety Union troops at Baxter Springs in southeastern Kansas in October. The slaughter troubled a Confederate general, who wrote, "We cannot, as a Christian people, sanction a savage, inhuman warfare, in which men are shot down like dogs after throwing down their arms and holding up their hands supplicating for mercy." Taking refuge in north Texas, the raiders kept busy robbing southerners, lynching one who resisted. Missouri's Confederate governor in exile, Thomas Reynolds, denounced them: "These bands are *utterly* useless as military organizations. They war not on the enemy, but on our own people."[51]

Although too brutal for Reynolds, Quantrill was too soft for "Bloody Bill" Anderson, who broke away with most of the gang, including the brothers Frank and Jesse James. In September 1864, Anderson's men stopped and robbed a train in Centralia, Missouri, butchering and scalping two dozen unarmed Union soldiers heading home on furlough. The raiders put some corpses across the tracks to run over them with the locomotive. Union cavalry pursued Anderson's fleeing men but fell into an ambush. All 116 cavalrymen died, most after trying to surrender. Frank James vindicated the massacre: "What is war for if it isn't to kill people for a principle?" A month after the butchery at Centralia, Union soldiers shot Anderson dead in a skirmish. Quantrill survived until the spring of 1865 when, on a raid into Kentucky, he suffered a paralyzing shot in the back. In June, Quantrill died after a month of searing pain—although not as great as that of the baby that his men had cast into a fire.[52]

Indian Territory

The border violence spread into Indian Territory, where most of the Natives had been relocated by force from the southern states during the 1830s. Known as the "five civilized nations," the Cherokees, Chickasaws, Choctaws, Creeks, and Seminoles had adopted many ways from their white neighbors: Christianity, literacy, national governments, private property in land, and agriculture with livestock and, in some cases, enslaved people. A social fault line cast the poorer Natives, generally "fullbloods" in ancestry and traditional in customs, against more prosperous "mixed-bloods" with larger farms raising cotton with slave labor. A Confederate captain considered the mixed-blood leaders "nearly as white as I am; they are educated gentlemen and are [as] polite as any of our own race." He thought that they "would certainly stand the test of civilization" better than most people in Arkansas.[53]

At the start of the Civil War, most Indian Territory chiefs wanted to be left alone. But neither belligerent could afford to bypass their strategic location. If the five nations supported the Union, they could harry Confederates in Missouri and Arkansas. But if enlisted for the Confederacy, the Indians could assail Kansas to their north, thereby lifting the jayhawker pressure on Missouri. Because Americans dreaded Natives as (supposedly) ruthless, scalping savages, they posed a psychological threat disproportionate to their numbers. A Confederate insisted, "One regiment of Cherokees or Choctaws, well mounted, would inspire more wholesome terror . . . than a vast army of Americans from the States."[54]

In January 1861 Governor Henry Rector of Arkansas invited the chiefs to join "the common brotherhood of the slaveholding states." More ominously, a southern general warned Natives that the Confederacy would "never consent to see their country *settled or governed by abolitionists.*" In May, the Confederate government sent Albert Pike, an Arkansas lawyer, poet, planter, and politician, to Indian Territory as a special commissioner. Bright and adaptable, Pike had cultivated ties with Native peoples, learning their languages and customs, developing friendships and influence.[55]

Giving priority to war to the east, the Lincoln administration withdrew federal garrisons from Indian Territory in May 1861. Southerners happily filled the vacuum, sending troops to occupy the evacuated forts. Annexing Indian Territory to the Confederacy, southern leaders provided each Native nation a nonvoting seat in Congress, which was more political access than the Union ever had offered. Pike also proposed treaties that pledged mutual defense, payment for Native soldiers, and assumption of the annuities owed to them by the federal government. These promises seemed credible because Pike generously doled out $100,000 in presents to Native chiefs. Residing closer to Texas and Arkansas, the Choctaws and Chickasaws felt especially exposed to southern attack, so they quickly joined the Confederates. Located a bit farther north, the Cherokees, Creeks, and Seminoles divided into pro-Union and pro-Confederate factions.[56]

With 21,000 people, the Cherokees were the most numerous and powerful of the five nations and, therefore, pivotal to controlling Indian Territory. Their primary chief, John Ross, favored neutrality: "We do not wish . . . our homes to be rendered desolate and miserable by the horrors of civil war." But his chief rival, Stand Watie, rallied many Cherokees for the Confederacy. In August 1861, after the Confederate victory at Wilson's Creek in nearby Missouri, Ross reluctantly joined the southern cause. Raising two Cherokee regiments, Watie rose in rank to brigadier general: the only Native so honored by either side. Although dark in complexion, Watie impressed a Confederate general as having "more brains than nine tenths of the white race" as well as "energy and fixedness of purpose—unquestioned patriotism and courage." But Ross's wife Mary hated Watie and secession, so she fled after tearing down a newly raised Confederate flag at the Cherokee council house.[57]

Creeks, Seminoles, Choctaws, and Chickasaws also raised cavalry regiments for the Confederacy. Sent to support them, a Texan reported,

"A ring was filled with painted Indians, all marching in a side-like manner, stepping high and fast, while they chanted a strange song. Some
of the Texans got the spirit and joined their Indian allies, dancing and
whooping under the dark skies of the Indian Territory." In late 1861 the
allies attacked pro-Union Natives, primarily Creeks, scattering them and
destroying their farms. The survivors fled north to Kansas, where the
10,000 sick, ragged, and hungry refugees strained resources and patience.
Kansans wanted to subtract Indians, not add them to the state. In early
1862 Lincoln agreed to organize a counterattack to reclaim Indian Territory, so that the refugees could go home. Impressed by that gathering
offensive, Ross and his supporters defected from the Confederacy to
join the Union. Taking revenge, Watie burned Ross's mansion and the
Cherokee capitol in Tahlequah.[58]

In June 1863 the Union counteroffensive began as General James Blunt
led Union troops and Indian allies south from Kansas into Indian Territory.
In mid-July, at Honey Springs, Blunt's better-armed Union force routed
pro-Confederate Natives and burned their farms. The losers fled southward into Texas. But the federal hold on Indian Territory remained shaky
thanks to raids by Watie on Union supporters and Yankee supply wagons
and steamboats. By late 1864, Indian Territory had become a wasteland as
Native peoples suffered from a civil war imposed by outsiders.[59]

Deseret

The Union faced another western challenge in Utah Territory, where
Mormon settlers had fled from the Midwest to create their own independent domain called Deseret. During the 1850s, the Mormons (who
called themselves "Saints") reluctantly accepted federal jurisdiction with
outsiders (whom Mormons called "gentiles") as the territorial governor
and judges. But the Saints usually ignored the official government, preferring rule instead by their church led by a formidable president and
prophet, Brigham Young. The Saints sought statehood, but Congress
distrusted them and disliked their practice of polygamy in marriage.[60]

When the Civil War erupted, Saints denounced both sides as oppressors who richly deserved mutual destruction. The Mormon newspaper gave little coverage to the Civil War save as evidence for the bloody madness of Americans. Because Mormons had endured persecution in Illinois, Young blasted such "cursed scoundrels as Abe Lincoln and his minions who have sought our destruction from the beginning." Young opposed the Emancipation Proclamation and insisted that abolitionists "would let the negroes loose to massacre every white person." Like Canadians, Deseret's people welcomed southern secession because it weakened the United States, which they saw as a more powerful menace.[61]

In 1861 Young adopted neutrality for Deseret, announcing that Saints would neither pay federal taxes nor contribute soldiers to fight for the Union: "They are fighting in the East; let them fight and be d[amne]d! They cannot get any assistance from Utah!" Just ninety-five Mormons served as federal volunteers and only for ninety days within Deseret during 1862. Deseret's autonomy surged in July 1861, when federal troops pulled out, marching east to war.[62]

In early December, Lincoln's appointee as territorial governor, John W. Dawson, arrived in Utah and promptly vetoed a new bid by the legislature for statehood. The veto doomed Dawson's governorship. After just twenty-four days in office, Dawson fled in fear for his life after he allegedly propositioned a Mormon widow, who chased him away with a shovel. Seven pursuing vigilantes caught the runaway governor and beat him nearly to death.[63]

Exploiting the governor's absence, Mormon legislators framed a state constitution in January 1862. Although congress rejected that bid for statehood, Young persisted in acting as governor and convened a legislature in April. When a new federal governor arrived in the summer of 1862, Young told him "that a Government administered by one man . . . appointed by God, would be far better than a Government of the United States." When the territorial governor refused to leave, Young denounced him as "a nigger worshiper," a "black-hearted abolitionist," and a sack of "cow shit." During the 1860s, Deseret and Utah were distinct governments: the first effective and the second nominal.[64]

In June 1862 Congress moved toward confrontation by passing the Morrill Act (after Vermont senator Justin Morrill), which banned polygamy in federal territories and barred churches there from owning real estate worth more than $50,000. In July Lincoln signed the bill into law, but the territorial officials could not enforce it in Utah. Preoccupied with fighting the Confederacy, Lincoln could accept Mormon autonomy in Utah for the time being. Invoking a folksy story about plowing around a log too big, heavy, and wet to move, he assured a delegation from Deseret: "That's what I intend to do with the Mormons. You go back and tell Brigham Young that, if he will let me alone, I will let him alone."[65]

But Lincoln's War Department did not leave the Mormons alone. Suspecting them of aiding and abetting Indian attacks on Americans traveling through Utah to the West Coast, Union generals ordered Col. Patrick Edward Connor to occupy that territory with 850 California volunteers. An Irish-born immigrant to the United States, Connor had served in the war against Mexico with courage and zeal. After the war, Connor settled in California, where he thrived as a surveyor and rancher. A staunch Unionist in 1861, Connor recruited and commanded a volunteer regiment. Marching into Utah in August 1862, he declared, "Traitors shall not utter treasonable sentiments in this district with impunity but must . . . receive the punishment they so richly merit." The regiment's chaplain added that "those who resist their march because of polygamy, are as real traitors as those who resist because of slavery."[66]

To intimidate Mormons, Connor built a fort on a hill just three miles outside Salt Lake City. This proximity infuriated Young, who denounced the California volunteers as profane heathens. The Deseret militia mounted fifteen cannon to defend Salt Lake City and fortified Young's house to deter any federal attempt to arrest him. In response, Connor denounced Mormons as "a community of traitors, murderers, fanatics, and whores." Despite the fury of their words, the two men avoided each other and armed conflict. Nearby Indians were not so fortunate.[67]

Connor's volunteers patrolled the overland trail to the north, where starving Shoshones raided emigrants and stagecoach stations for livestock, killing people who resisted. Seeking massive retributive violence, Connor rejected overtures from Shoshones seeking a negotiated settlement. Instead, in January 1863 he attacked a large encampment at Bear River about 140 miles north of Salt Lake City. Hunkered down in the deep snow and bitter cold, the Shoshones repulsed the initial attack but ran low on ammunition. Overwhelming the Shoshones, the volunteers killed men, women, and children: about 250 in total. Connor's men suffered twenty-two dead. By burning the camp, including the winter food supply, the victors sentenced the scattered survivors to exposure and starvation. The Union rewarded Connor with promotion to general.[68]

The new general employed his soldiers as prospectors to seek veins of silver and gold. Connor hoped to initiate a mineral rush that would swamp the Mormon population in Utah with a new majority of gentiles. Connor invested $80,000 in a mining company and launched a newspaper, the *Union Vedette*, to attack Mormonism and urge Americans to flock in to get rich in Utah. "Silver in the Mountains—Silver in the Streets—Silver Everywhere," the paper exaggerated.[69]

Connor's mining initiative horrified the Mormons, who dreaded an influx by thousands of greedy outsiders, who might corrupt the weakest among the Saints. Young preached, "It behooves us, brethren and sisters to live near to God . . . rather than to become insane after gold." To discourage intruders and backsliders, Young, his bishops, and their newspaper tried to discredit reports of gold and silver discoveries as "humbugging" nonsense. But some Mormon bishops preempted promising mining sites by staking their own claims. Gentile prospectors did find silver, but the ore proved unmarketable (in the short term) for want of smelters or railroad transportation. Because no rush of gentile numbers ensued, Mormons remained about 90 percent of Utah's population.[70]

The failure of Connor's mines reduced tensions between volunteers and Saints. Best of all, from a Mormon perspective, the Union promoted Connor to major general and sent him away to the Great Plains to fight

Indians. In 1865 Young toned down his own fiery rhetoric as events failed to fulfill his prophecy of a doomed Union. Young collaborated with a new territorial governor who proved more conciliatory than his predecessors. Having outlasted Connor's provocations, Young retained control over Deseret.[71]

Canyons

While fending off Confederate forays into the West and accepting Mormon neutrality, the Union escalated warfare against Indians in the Southwest. In New Mexico in June 1862, as the Confederate invasion receded, Union forces received a boost from 2,350 volunteers arriving from California under the command of General James Carleton, a lean and mean disciplinarian. Taking command of New Mexico in September, Carleton organized a mining company that employed troops as prospectors and guards. "If I can develop the mineral wealth in this country," he declared, "I shall have fulfilled my mission." But his men disliked their new assignment and pined for the milder climate of California. One junior officer said that it was so hot in southern Arizona (often over 110 degrees) that when a soldier died and went to hell, he found it too cold and asked for extra blankets.[72]

Carleton's intrusive miners antagonized Apaches and Navajos, who increased their raiding. After rousting them from their high-country homelands, Carleton planned to consolidate them at one reservation, Bosque Redondo, in the desert to the east. Carleton described Bosque Redondo as a "reformatory" where "the old Indians would die off, and the younger ones would take their place." Carleton regarded Natives as wild game: "An Indian is a more watchful and a more wary animal than a deer. He must be hunted with skill." Unless they submitted to reservation life, he expected to render Indians extinct like "the races of mammoths and mastodons, and the great sloths."[73]

In January 1863, federal troops captured the Apache chief Mangas Coloradas. One night in prison, he awoke to searing pain in his feet because troops had heated bayonets in a fire to torment him. When he howled with anger, they shot him dead, alleging that he was trying to escape. Severing the chief's head, the fort's surgeon plunged it into boiling water to strip off the flesh. He sold the skull to the Smithsonian Institution, where the chief's defiance persisted, for his brain capacity measured larger than that of almost all whites—refuting the prevailing pseudoscience that claimed Natives had smaller brains.[74]

Later in 1863 Carleton shifted his focus to the 12,000 Navajos inhabiting canyons in northwestern New Mexico. Although related to Apaches, Navajos had adopted a more settled mode of life, building substantial homes called hogans, cultivating gardens, tending orchards, and keeping flocks of sheep. But they also raided Hispanic ranches to take captives (usually women and children) and livestock. *Hispanos* returned the favor, sustaining a persistent interplay of raid and counterraid. Carleton also wanted to remove Navajos to secure a road from his mining company to the new mines.[75]

Carleton sent "Kit" Carson and his New Mexico volunteers into the Navajo canyons to destroy hogans, crops, flocks, and orchards. By January 1864 Carson had reduced the survivors to starvation. During the winter, 8,000 Navajos surrendered, accepting forced relocation to Bosque Redondo, 300 miles to the east.[76]

Confined to that bleak reservation in a desert, Navajos pined for their beloved mountains and mesas. For want of trees, wood was scarce for fuel, fences, and homes. The inmates had to work long, hard days digging irrigation ditches while suffering from searing heat and epidemics of measles, dysentery, and smallpox. Their crops often failed from alternating bouts of cutworms, frost, heat, and hail. Disarmed and confined, the Navajos were vulnerable to slave-raiding by Comanches, their Native enemies who remained free on the plains to the east.[77]

Adamant and uncompromising, Carleton ran New Mexico as a military fiefdom, with Bosque Redondo as his showplace: home to "the happiest people I have ever seen." In fact, his reservation cost taxpayers more than a million dollars a year, and at least 10 percent of the inmates died annually. Carleton vowed, "The Navajos should never leave the Bosque, and never shall if I can prevent it." But by 1867, Carleton had alienated almost everyone in New Mexico, so the federal government reassigned him and, a year later, permitted Navajos to relocate to a reservation in their homeland.[78]

Little Crow

In Minnesota, the home of Jane Grey Swisshelm, most of the Natives were Dakotas, known to Americans as the "Sioux." During the 1850s, as thousands of settlers poured into Minnesota, the primary Dakota Chief, Little Crow, considered resistance futile: "The white men are like the locusts when they fly so thick that the whole sky is a snowstorm. . . . Kill one—two—ten, and ten times ten will come to kill you." By 1860, Minnesota's 172,000 whites were twenty-five times the 6,500 Dakotas.[79]

The newcomers cleared the forest, plowed the soil, and hunted game animals, depleting resources that Dakotas had relied on. With his people impoverished, Little Crow agreed to exchange land for annuity payments from the federal government. In 1851 and 1858, treaties reduced the Dakotas to a long, narrow reservation, 10 miles by 150 miles, along the Minnesota River. Pouring into the ceded lands, settlers treated their Indian neighbors with contempt, calling them beggars and thieves. Making the best of the bad situation, Little Crow adopted many American ways: cutting his long hair; adopting settler's clothes; moving into a frame house; and farming with domesticated livestock.[80]

For their massive cessions, Dakotas received just thirty cents per acre, less than a tenth of the land's market value. The federal government promised to pay them 6 percent interest annually in a mix of cash, provisions, and goods, primarily cloth and clothing. But poverty obliged many Dakotas to seek food on credit from local traders, who then collected most of the annual payment.[81]

Federal officials were supposed to ensure fair play, but they shared in the corruption, allowing their trader friends to supply reservations with rotten food while charging the government premium prices. In Minnesota the biggest operators were two traders, politicians, and friends: Henry Hastings Sibley (no relation to the Confederate general) and Alexander Ramsey. Despite belonging to rival political parties, they collaborated to cheat the Dakotas. A critic insisted, "The cohesive power of public plunder cements rogues together stronger than any party." Ramsey became the governor, while Sibley commanded the state militia. In early 1862 a federal inspector reported that Dakotas had been "robbed & defrauded of the little miserable pittance granted them by Congress." But Minnesota's congressmen blackballed the inspector and got him reassigned.[82]

In 1862 federal officials delayed delivering the annuities due in June. That delay reduced many Dakotas to starvation, but the leading trader at the reservation, Andrew Myrick, refused to advance any more food: "If they are hungry let them eat grass or their own dung." Sarah Wakefield, the wife of the reservation's doctor, marveled, "Suppose the same number of whites were living in the sight of food, purchased with their own money, and their children dying of starvation, how long, think ye, would they remain quiet?" The starving Dakotas noted the withdrawal of most federal troops to fight Confederates to the east. A chief recalled, "It began to be whispered about that now would be a good time to go to war with the whites and get back the lands."[83]

On the morning of August 17, 1862, four young Dakotas killed five settlers. The killings put their chiefs on the spot. Would they support the young men or surrender them for trial and execution? Fed up with their miseries, most of the chiefs demanded that Little Crow lead them to war. To preserve his authority, he reluctantly agreed but predicted that they would all "die like the rabbits when the hungry wolves hunt them."[84]

On August 18, armed Dakotas ravaged the reservation agency and nearby settlements, killing, plundering, and burning. One of their first victims was Myrick, whom they shot and then stuffed grass into his dead mouth. Other dead traders had their mouths filled with cash, as Dakotas said "to them, you have stole our money, now take all you will." By the end of the week, Dakotas had killed 400 settlers, most of them women and children. In a panic, thousands abandoned their farms, fleeing eastward, depopulating a zone 50 miles wide by nearly 200 long.[85]

Governor Ramsey entrusted the counterattack to his friend Sibley. Having provoked the war by profiteering at Dakotas' expense, the two men set out to crush them. With 1,500 volunteers, Sibley ascended the

Minnesota River, attacking and routing the fleeing Dakotas at Wood Lake in September. Dispirited by defeat, about 2,000 Dakota surrendered in October, while the rest fled westward to the Great Plains or northward across the border to the British colony of Assiniboia (Red River).[86]

Dakotas released their prisoners, including a woman denounced by Sibley as a race traitor. He alleged that she "had become so infatuated with the redskin who had taken her for a wife, that although her white husband was still living . . . she declared that were it not for her children, she would not leave her dusky paramour," and, if he "should be hung, she will shoot those of us who have been instrumental in bringing him to the scaffold and then go back to the Indians. A pretty specimen of a white woman she is, truly!"[87]

Sibley distorted the story of Sarah F. Wakefield. Born and raised in Rhode Island, she had married a doctor posted at the reservation in 1861. A year later, she was thirty-two and the mother of two, a boy and a girl. Unhappy in her marriage, she felt sensitive to the sorrows of others, including Dakotas, treating them with a generosity unusual among her neighbors: "Not a day passed but some of the Indians were at my house, and I had always pitied them and given them food." Wakefield hired some women to sew and do housework "and began to love and respect them as well as if they were whites."[88]

Her reputation for generosity saved Wakefield's life on August 18, when Dakotas attacked the agency. A warrior named Chaska spared her from death by claiming Sarah as his captive and new wife. Going along with the ruse, she slept in Chaska's lodge—but did not become his lover. Committed to assimilation, Chaska had gone to school, adopted American dress, and farmed like a settler. Sarah later recalled, "If it had not been for Chaska, my bones would now be bleaching on that prairie."[89]

In September, at his own peril, Chaska brought Wakefield to Sibley's military camp, where she vouched for his protection and kindness. She recalled: "I was a vast deal more comfortable with the Indians in every respect, than I was during my stay in that soldiers' camp, and was treated more respectfully by those savages, than I was by those in that camp." Contrary to their promises, the troops arrested Chaska and charged him with murder. Wakefield confronted an officer, "Captain Grant, if you hang that man, I will shoot you." Her attempts to vindicate Chaska fed camp gossip that he was her lover. Dismissing Wakefield's testimony on his behalf, a military commission sentenced Chaska to hang.[90]

Although the Indians had surrendered under a flag of truce, Sibley treated them as criminals rather than prisoners of war. His military tribunal convicted 303 Natives of murder or rape and sentenced them all to die—although most had done no more than fight in battles. Sibley promised enough executions "to satisfy the longings of the most bloodthirsty" Minnesotans and to provide "a great example which would strike terror into all Indians."[91]

But President Lincoln worried that executing hundreds of Indians would cause an international scandal as Europeans charged Americans with vindictive cruelty. He also learned that corrupt officials and traders had provoked the Dakota uprising. Reviewing the military tribunal's records, the president and his legal staff saw a travesty of justice, so he approved only thirty-eight executions, sparing 265 men, one of them Chaska. But the spared remained in a prison camp, where sixty-seven died of hunger and disease by April 1864: more than expired on the gallows.[92]

Outraged by Lincoln's relative clemency, Minnesotans threatened to massacre every Indian captive: man, woman, and child. A U.S. senator warned Lincoln: "Either the Indians must [all] be punished according to law, or they will be murdered without law." A member of Lincoln's cabinet regarded Minnesota's vengeful congressmen as "but slightly removed from the barbarians they would execute." When Governor Ramsey protested that presidential clemency angered voters, Lincoln replied that he would not "hang men for votes."[93]

Hanged at Mankato on the day after Christmas, the thirty-eight Dakotas constituted the largest mass execution conducted by the United States. Although Lincoln had spared Chaska, his captors confused him with another Dakota of the same name, who was meant to die. Chaska was one of three executed for mistaken identity.[94]

Death brought them no peace, for a day later grave robbers exhumed and butchered the thirty-eight corpses for trophies. A celebrated doctor, William W. Mayo, took some for medical research, leaving the rest for common robbers. Later Mayo's Indian skeletons became the property of the internationally celebrated clinic in St. Paul named for him. The grave robber who scalped Chaska turned his hair into a watch chain worn for twenty-five years—until 1887, when the robber donated it to the Minnesota Historical Society for display to memorialize "that great hanging event."[95]

Shocked by Chaska's death, Sarah Wakefield felt that her attempts to defend him "just cursed me and killed the man." Visions of Chaska's mother tormented Wakefield's nights: "I can see her sorrowful face in my dreams as I saw her last sitting on the bank of the Yellow Medicine River all alone; such a moan as escaped from her was heart rending . . . for she blamed me, as I do myself, for not letting him go with Little Crow." Wakefield wrote an anguished letter to President Lincoln: "I am abased already by the world as I am a Friend of the Indians." Her husband rebuked Sarah for submitting to life among the Indians rather than killing herself. "He says I have brought my trouble upon myself and now I must bear it."[96]

To mollify most Minnesotans, who wanted more vengeance, Lincoln revoked the annuities owed to Dakotas and confiscated the rest of their homeland. The survivors had to move westward to a new reservation on the bleak plains of the Dakota Territory. The uprooted included those who had kept the peace and helped to release the white captives, including Sarah Wakefield. Although the Winnebago people had not attacked anyone, the United States also evicted them simply because Minnesotans distrusted all Indians and coveted their fertile lands. Lincoln might not hang hundreds of Indians for votes, but he would dispossess thousands of them so that Minnesota would remain a Republican state.[97]

Lincoln appointed a new secretary of interior from Minnesota, and he rewarded his friends with contracts to supply the 8,000 Dakotas forced to move westward. To maximize their profits, the contractors tormented the dispossessed with rotten food, wretched shelter, and scant clothing. In prison camps or on the forced march, hundreds died of exposure, disease, and malnutrition. Dumped on an arid reservation, the refugees struggled to raise crops and suffered attacks from local Indians who resented competition for bison from the newcomers. American military guards also treated the refugees with brutality, shooting seven of them rather than sorting out which one had stolen a single horse. Disgusted by the abuse of Natives who had surrendered, their missionary wrote, "If I were an Ind[ian], I would never lay-down the war-club while I lived. They are right, to be savages is the only hope of the Indian."[98]

Little Crow and another 500 Dakotas escaped across the border into the British colony of Assiniboia along the Red River of the North. Fearing the refugees, many of the colony's settlers wanted to cooperate with American troops sent to the border in pursuit. Some settlers lured two chiefs, Shakopee and Medicine Bottle, into a house and plied them with free liquor spiked with laudanum and chloroform. Then the hosts tied the victims to a toboggan and dragged them over the border to the federal commander, who had them hanged. In despair, Little Crow returned to Minnesota. Starving, he stopped at a farm to pick raspberries on July 3, 1863, when the farmer shot and killed Little Crow. His scalp and skull went on display at the Minnesota State Historical Society until returned to his family for burial in 1971.[99]

Sand Creek

In September 1862, Lincoln had sent General John Pope to take command in Minnesota and the northern Great Plains. Disgraced by defeat at Manassas and irritated by reassignment, Pope longed to redeem his reputation by crushing Indians in the West. He vowed "utterly to exterminate the Sioux. . . . They are to be treated as maniacs or wild beasts." With the Dakotas already defeated by Sibley, Pope sought another enemy, so he targeted a related people, Lakotas, who lived to the west on the Great Plains. As a pretext, he insisted that they had welcomed Dakota refugees and attacked Americans traveling westward to new gold mines in Idaho. Gifted at hysteria, Pope assured his superiors: "It is not only the Sioux with whom we have to deal. All the Indians—Sioux, Chippewas, and Winnebagoes, are on the verge of outbreak along the whole frontier."[100]

During the spring of 1863, in an excessive and expensive display of force, Pope led 4,200 troops westward onto the Great Plains, to the delight of Minnesotans who wanted to eliminate all Indians within striking distance. A Lakota chief, Sitting Bull, then thirty-three, confronted Pope's scouts: "The Indians here have no fight with the whites. Why is it the whites come to fight the Indians?" Pope's indiscriminate attacks spread war throughout the Great Plains as alarmed Natives took revenge on travelers and settlers.[101]

Pope and other Union commanders practiced total war on the Great Plains, seeking to destroy entire Native communities and the environment that sustained them. In the fall of 1864, Union troops in Nebraska set fire to the central Plains by having horses drag burning bales of hay across the grass. A captain reported, "The fire rolled on and on, leaving in its train only blackness and desolation. All night the sky was lighted up. The fire swept the country clean." Spreading across thousands of square miles, the massive blaze drove away the bison that sustained Natives and torched the grasses needed by their horses. The flames also consumed Native encampments along with the dried meat stored to sustain Indians through the winter. A Union colonel boasted, "Universal consternation has spread among the Indians, to whom this mode of warfare is apparently new. . . . They begin to dread the white man's power." That was the point.[102]

Pope's war drew in the Cheyenne who lived in eastern Colorado. In 1858, thousands of miners and ranchers had pressed into Colorado after the discovery of gold at Pike's Peak. The newcomers depleted the streamside timber and vast herds of bison to the dismay of Native peoples, who suffered from hunger. Dreading the superior numbers and weapons of the intruders, the elderly chief Black Kettle agreed to sacrifice lands by signing the Fort Wise Treaty of 1861. That treaty obliged Native peoples to stay south of the Arkansas River, away from the main transportation corridor for Americans bound to and from the mining district. But most other Cheyenne chiefs and their Arapaho allies refused to sign the treaty and continued to attack settlers.[103]

Native resistance infuriated the territorial governor, John Evans, who sought to accelerate Colorado's development and thereby enrich his speculations in lands and railroads. To fight Indians, the governor relied on Col. John Chivington, a former Methodist preacher and the hero of Union victory at Glorieta Pass in New Mexico in 1862. By crushing Indians, Evans hoped to accelerate Colorado statehood, allowing him to become a senator and Chivington to win a seat in Congress. But a subordinate officer distrusted the glory-seeking and Indian-hating Chivington as "a crazy preacher who thinks he is Napoleon Bonaparte."[104]

Chivington's volunteers looked for Indians to attack on the Great Plains. The easiest to find belonged to Black Kettle's band, for they expected no trouble. At a recent meeting with the chiefs, Evans and Chivington had assured Black Kettle that his people would be safe if they camped at Sand Creek. Privately, however, Evans asked, "What shall I do with the Third Colorado Regiment if I make peace? They have been raised to kill Indians, and they must kill Indians."[105]

At dawn on November 29, 1864, Chivington ordered his 700 men to attack Black Kettle's camp and to take no prisoners. Black Kettle displayed an American flag to try to stop the attack—but in vain. He survived, but the attackers slaughtered about 150 Natives, most of them women and children. Returning to Denver as conquering heroes, the volunteers displayed scalps to thunderous applause in a theater. "Colorado soldiers have again covered themselves with glory," a local newspaper boasted.[106]

But Indian attacks surged thereafter, as Cheyennes, Lakotas, and Arapahos sought revenge. A Native survivor from Sand Creek helped destroy settlements along the Platte River: "At night the whole valley was lighted up with the flames of burning ranches and stage stations." Blaming the surge on Chivington's treachery, U.S. senators investigated Sand Creek. Their findings led the president to sack Evans as governor and order Chivington court martialed, but he dodged that trial by resigning his commission. Eastern leaders wanted to conquer the West—but without the spectacular atrocities that called so much attention to Sand Creek.[107]

Empire

The Union won a double victory in the West, keeping the Confederacy confined while dispossessing, relocating, and restricting many

Native peoples. The Superintendent of Indian Affairs in Utah meant to teach Indians "that the Americans are the master of this country." A federal commissioner noted that "the freedom of territorial and industrial expansion, which is bringing imperial greatness to the nation, to the Indian brings wretchedness, destitution, [and] beggary." Spreading through the West, federal volunteers explored thousands of square miles, identifying mines and promising routes while building forts. By demystifying the vast land, American troops weakened Native resistance. As prospectors found new veins of gold, silver, and copper, eastern men surged westward, hoping to get rich. For protection, they demanded that Union troops rout and confine Indian peoples.[108]

During the Civil War, Republicans accelerated American settlement and exploitation of the West. In 1862, Lincoln urged Congress to adopt "extraordinary measures" to develop the West's "immense mineral resources . . . as rapidly as possible." A market society of competitive Americans would supplant the Indians. The survivors would be confined on reservations, where schools and workshops could compel them to forsake their independence and culture. In California, a great orator of nationalism, Thomas Starr King, insisted, "There is something both natural and heaven-sent about the integrity of the Union . . . and that integrity includes filling up the continent" with settlements.[109]

In October 1861, the Union completed a telegraph line across the continent to California, drawing the nation closer through instantaneous communication. Lincoln celebrated completion as "auspicious of the Stability & Union of the Republic." Republicans also hastened the organization of western polities linked to the Union. In 1861 Congress organized the Dakota, Colorado, and Nevada territories, followed by Arizona and Idaho in 1863, and Montana in 1864. In that last year, Congress also promoted Nevada to statehood. With slavery banned in western territories and states, the North gained even greater dominance in the Union.[110]

During the Civil War, Republicans could pass bills that southern Democrats had blocked during the 1850s. In 1862 Congress approved a Homestead Act, Land-Grant College Act, and Pacific Railroad Act. All three measures used western lands as capital to promote social engineering along Republican lines. In effect, Indians paid in land to improve the lot of citizens, who got free farms, higher education, and better transportation.[111]

In the past, the United States had sold frontier land to settlers and land speculators. For the first time, the Homestead Act of 1862 promised free land to settlers. Every citizen could apply for 160 acres—deemed sufficient for a small farm—and receive title after occupying and working the premises for five years. The congressional sponsor, Galusha Grow of Pennsylvania, championed the "grand army of the sons of toil, whose lives from the cradle to the grave are at constant warfare with the elements, with the unrelenting obstacles of nature and the merciless barbarities of savage life." But Congress put settlers in harm's way, for most homestead land lay west of the 100th meridian of longitude, which ran through the Great Plains and marked a rough boundary between sufficient rainfall to the east for farming and too little to the west. And Indians defended their homelands by attacking settlers.[112]

Authored by Justin Morrill of Vermont, the Land-Grant Act stimulated state public universities by offering the first federal subsidies: 30,000 acres of western land for each senator and representative in a state's delegation. By selling that land (taken from Indians), a state could endow new universities that taught agricultural science. By enhancing farm productivity, scientific methods would raise the rural standard of living. To advance that goal, Congress also created the Department of Agriculture.[113]

In the Pacific Railway Act, Congress subsidized wealthy capitalists to build a transcontinental railroad meant to link the Pacific coast to the Midwest, thereby accelerating settlement of the vast zone in between. Capitalists balked at relying on their own money to build a railroad across harsh terrain that was so thinly settled. For hundreds of miles and many years much of the Great Plains, Rocky Mountains, and Great Basin would provide too few passengers and too little produce to generate profits for the railroads. So, the federal government had to kick-start the enterprise by offering millions of acres of western land that the railroad companies could sell or use as collateral for loans. A company received a corridor 400 feet wide as the right-of-way—the

prime zone for building railway stations and other commercial enterprises. The railroads also got 6,400 acres of public land for every mile of
construction, plus a loan of $16,000 per mile, rising to $48,000 a mile in
the mountains. Lavish gifts of corporate railroad stock helped persuade
key congressmen to be generous with public land and money. In 1863,
the Central Pacific Railroad company began construction at Sacramento
in California, while the Union Pacific Railroad Company commenced
laying tracks westward from Omaha in Nebraska. Ultimately, the Central Pacific laid enough track to get federal land equal to the area of
Maryland while the Union Pacific reaped acreage equivalent to New
Jersey and New Hampshire combined.[114]

The Civil War erupted over the western expansion of slavery, and the
conflict enabled the Union to triumph by reshaping that vast region as
the ultimate prize. By accelerating and shaping western development,
the Union imposed its liberal vision for the American future, one where
market competition, free labor, and republican elections determined
winners and losers. The federal government would dispossess Indians
and confine them until they became detribalized as individual citizens.

But the Republican vision produced contradictions. Although initiated to enhance social mobility for common men, the Republican
program in the West actually compounded the advantages of wealthy
corporations. They had the greatest power in the market and superior
influence with federal officials. During the Civil War, the Republican
Party became more devoted to growing the economy by favoring big
business with public resources.[115]

NINE ⟨ INVASIONS

Of all the whole creation in the east and west,
the glorious Yankee nation is the greatest and the best.
Come along! Come along! Don't be alarmed,
Uncle Sam is rich enough to give you all a farm.

—HARRIET TUBMAN, SINGING TO ESCAPED SLAVES, 1863[1]

In 1863, invading armies pushed deep into North America in two civil wars, one American, the other Mexican. The Confederate general, Robert E. Lee, pressed northward into Pennsylvania, threatening to envelop Washington, D.C. Along the Atlantic Coast, Union forces assaulted the southern port of Charleston, South Carolina. To the west, the Union general Ulysses S. Grant renewed his attack on

Vicksburg, the great Confederate bastion beside the Mississippi River. Another Union army targeted the key railroad junction at Chattanooga in southeastern Tennessee. Farther south, a reinforced French army, commanded by Louis Elie Frederic Forey, threatened the Mexican city of Puebla on the road to Mexico City. The five offensives—one Confederate, one French, and three Union—sought to sway momentum in wars mired in bloody stalemates.

Waged in civil wars, the invasions had the highest political stakes. Forey sought to topple the Liberal republic led by Juárez, substituting a monarchy run by Conservatives. By defeating the Union army on northern territory, Lee meant to discredit the Lincoln administration and sway northern elections in favor of Democrats who might make peace on Confederate terms. Grant wanted to bolster the Republicans, particularly in the Midwest, by completing the Union's control of the Mississippi Valley, the key corridor for trade within the continent. Conquering Chattanooga would enable Yankees to liberate eastern Tennessee, a haven for Unionism. By taking Charleston, the cradle of southern defiance and independence, Union forces could thrill Yankees and demoralize Confederates. American Republicans and Mexican Liberals saw all these campaigns as intertwined and laden with global stakes: to vindicate republicanism and equal rights against an unholy alliance of slave-lords, aristocrats, and monarchists. The fate of republican government hung in the balance as the armies lurched forward.

Regency

In North America, the French made the first big move of the 1863 campaign. A year before, they had suffered a humiliating defeat at Puebla, but the French emperor Napoleon III doubled down by sending 25,000 reinforcements and two accomplished generals to renew the offensive.

PREVIOUS PAGE: *"Raid of Second South Carolina Volunteers among the Rice Plantations of the Combahee, from a Sketch by Surgeon Robinson," wood engraving,* Harper's Weekly, *July 4, 1863.*

Forey commanded with assistance from François Achille Bazaine. After seizing Puebla, Napoleon expected his army to crush Juárez's republican army and take Mexico City.[2]

The emperor fantasized that most Mexicans would welcome French troops as liberators restoring order to an anarchic country. Early and often, Napoleon assured diplomats that he would let Mexicans choose their own government. Privately, he instructed General Forey, "You must be master in Mexico without appearing to be." A captain noted the farce: that Mexico was "completely free to choose provided it decrees a monarchy" dominated by the French. Despite promising a government of national unity, the invaders relied on Mexican reactionaries, including the generals Juan Nepomuceno Almonte and Leonardo Márquez, who had fearsome reputations for atrocities. They were the favorites of the French political advisor to the expedition, the Marquis de Saligny.[3]

In March 1863, Forey's 26,000 men marched westward into the central highlands to renew the French assault on Puebla. At a fearsome cost in casualties, they captured the perimeter forts and broke into the city, where it took eight days to advance seven blocks in hand-to-hand combat. A French officer marveled at a defense "perfectly organized and conducted" by "the Mexicans who in there are not the Mexicans we know." But the defenders ran low on food and ammunition. Their commander, Jesús González Ortega, tried but failed to break out, so he surrendered his 12,500 men on May 17. Almonte and Márquez wanted to execute all the captured officers, but Forey insisted on treating them well in honor of their able defense of Puebla. Many escaped, including Ortega and his most able lieutenant, Porfirio Díaz.[4]

The defeat at Puebla left Juárez with only 6,000 soldiers to defend Mexico City against the advancing French force of 25,000. On May 31 the Mexican Congress adjourned after granting emergency powers to Juárez to rule as a dictator. In early June, Juárez shifted north by 200 miles to a provisional capital at San Luis Potosí. Starting on June 7, French and Conservative troops marched into Mexico City to cheers from the wealthy few but sullen silence of the common many.[5]

Almonte and Saligny organized a government that imposed Conservative policies, including fines and jail time for people who did not attend Catholic mass on Sundays or who failed to kneel during religious processions through the streets. The new regime replaced the Liberal Congress with an "Assembly of Notables": 231 in number, almost all Conservatives. A triumvirate shared executive power: Almonte; another general, José Mariano Salas; and Archbishop Pelagio Antonio de Labastida. Almonte deferred to Labastida, while Salas was a doddering nonentity dismissed by a French captain, Pierre Henri Loizillon, as "a mummy unearthed for the occasion." Despising the leading Conservatives as "thieves, immoral and incompetent," Loizillon blamed Saligny: "a rascal but a very fine and accomplished one, who only toys with General Forey."[6]

To validate the new regime, Napoleon wanted a national plebiscite in Mexico. But Saligny, Forey, and the Conservatives insisted that such a plebiscite was impossible in a vast country with bad roads and illiterate voters, and when the new regime controlled only the narrow corridor from Veracruz to Mexico City. Forey derided most Mexicans as "totally ignorant, like wild beasts living almost like savages." So he accepted as sufficient a vote by the Assembly of Notables on July 11 to invite the Austrian archduke Maximilian to rule Mexico as an emperor. A former British ambassador scoffed that most of the Notables represented "places inhabited by two Indians and a monkey." According to Captain Loizillon, Conservative troops celebrated the new monarchy by firing "a hundred rounds of cannon in the square, amid the complete indifference of the population." The Notables declared themselves a "Regency," to govern until their new emperor arrived from Europe. They sent a delegation across the Atlantic to deliver their invitation to Maximilian.[7]

Disliking the Regency as too openly reactionary, Napoleon blamed Saligny and Forey. The emperor recalled both men, replacing them with Bazaine. A stocky and clever general fluent in Spanish, Bazaine had counterguerrilla experience fighting in Algeria. Brave in combat, he was more popular with the troops than Forey. Deft at military politics, Bazaine took credit for successes while shunting blame onto Forey for any failure. Another officer described Bazaine as "what he has been all his life, ambiguous and sly." Napoleon instructed his new commander to

CLOCKWISE FROM TOP LEFT:
Abraham Lincoln (1809–1865).
Jefferson Davis (1808–1889).
Benito Juárez (1806–1872).
John A. Macdonald (1815–1891).

CLOCKWISE FROM TOP LEFT:
Mary Ann Shadd Cary (1823–1893).
Jane Grey Cannon Swisshelm (1815–1884).
Harriet Tubman (1822–1913).
Harriet Beecher Stowe (1811–1896).

CLOCKWISE FROM TOP LEFT:
Stephen A. Douglas (1813–1861).
Alexander H. Stephens (1812–1883).
John A. Quitman (1798–1858).
William Walker (1824–1860).

CLOCKWISE FROM TOP LEFT:
Roger B. Taney (1777–1864).
William H. Seward (1801–1872).
Louis T. Wigfall (1816–1874).
Samuel Houston (1793–1863).

CLOCKWISE FROM TOP LEFT:
Robert E. Lee (1807–1870).
Parson William G. Brownlow (1805–1877).
Frederick Douglass (1818–1895).
George B. McClellan (1826–1885).

CLOCKWISE FROM TOP LEFT:
Albert Sidney Johnson (1803–1862).
Ulysses S. Grant (1822–1885).
Thomas "Stonewall" Jackson (1824–1863).
William Tecumseh Sherman (1820–1891).

CLOCKWISE FROM TOP LEFT:
James Longstreet (1821–1904).
Henry Hopkins Sibley, CSA (1816–1886).
William Quantrill (1837–1865).
James Henry Lane (1814–1866).

CLOCKWISE FROM TOP LEFT:
John Ross (1790–1866).
Stand Watie (1806–1871).
Patrick Edward Connor (1820–1891).
Brigham Young (1801–1877).

CLOCKWISE FROM TOP LEFT:
Little Crow (1810–1863).
Gen. Henry Hastings Sibley, USA (1811–1891).
Red Cloud (1822–1909).
James H. Carleton (1814–1873).

CLOCKWISE FROM TOP LEFT:
Matías Romero (1837–1898).
Thomas Corwin (1794–1865).
Leonardo Márquez (1820–1913).
Miguel Miramón (1831–1867).

CLOCKWISE FROM TOP LEFT:
Napoleon III (1808–1873).
François Achille Bazaine (1811–1888).
Empress Carlota of Mexico (1840–1927).
Emperor Maximilian of Mexico (1832–1867).

CLOCKWISE FROM TOP LEFT:
Joshua L. Chamberlain (1828–1914).
Clement Vallandigham (1820–1871).
Joseph E. Johnston (1807–1891).
Braxton Bragg (1817–1876).

CLOCKWISE FROM TOP LEFT:
Jubal A. Early (1816–1894).
Philip H. Sheridan (1831–1888).
Sterling Price (1809–1867).
John Bell Hood (1831–1879).

CLOCKWISE FROM TOP LEFT:
Patrick Cleburne (1828–1864).
George H. Thomas (1816–1870).
Lew Wallace (1827–1905).
Francis Preston Blair, Sr. (1791–1876).

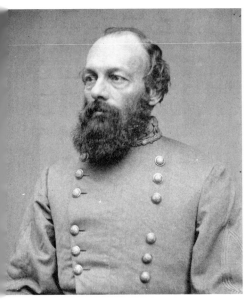

CLOCKWISE FROM TOP LEFT:
E. Kirby Smith (1824–1893).
Matthew F. Maury (1806–1873).
Felix Constantin Alexander Johann Nepomuk Salm-Salm (1828–1870).
Agnes Elizabeth Winona Leclerq Joy Salm-Salm (1844–1912).

CLOCKWISE FROM TOP LEFT:
Santiago Vidaurri (1809–1867).
Porfirio Díaz (1830–1915).
George Brown (1818–1880).
Thomas D'Arcy McGee (1825–1868).

impose moderation: "Do not become reactionary; do not retract the sale of clerical property; finally try to keep peace in the country while using mostly Mexican troops to do it." But Forey stayed until early October—and Saligny lingered until Christmas—to Bazaine's irritation.[8]

Dominated by Labastida, the Regency defied Bazaine's advice to reconcile with moderate Liberals. The archbishop demanded the return of every atom of Church property taken and sold by the Juárez government. Then the cleric wanted the government to prosecute, imprison, and fine many of the purchasers. Labastida also expected French troops to enforce public submission to Catholic processions and ceremonies—and to bar Protestant services in Mexico. When Bazaine balked, Labastida insisted that Pope Pius IX—and not Napoleon—was the ultimate ruler of Mexico. Although Catholic, French officers preferred the more tolerant tone of their government at home, so they regarded the Mexican archbishop as a bigoted bully restoring a backward society. A French general derided Labastida as "youthful, fat, with a blooming pink face trimmed by a triple chin . . . the type of the papistical churchman, unctuous, saccharine, and false."[9]

Throwing off the mask of restraint, Bazaine marched 200 French troops into a Regency meeting in October to demand submission. Almonte and Salas agreed, but Labastida refused, so Bazaine sacked him from the triumvirate. Lashing back, the archbishop denied sacraments to French soldiers and Mexican officials who supported them. Labastida also organized mass street protests and circulated leaflets calling for a revolt against the French as "enemies of religion and order." By threatening to blow open the cathedral with cannon, the French garrison compelled Labastida to stand down. A French general described the archbishop as "a little dense and very dangerous."[10]

To resolve the political tension in Mexico City, Bazaine and Napoleon wanted to hasten Archduke Maximilian's arrival to rule Mexico as emperor. But Maximilian balked, seeking reassurance that the French had subdued resistance and that most Mexicans favored his monarchy. For credibility in Europe, Napoleon also coveted the appearance of popularity in Mexico, which the partisan Assembly of Notables failed to provide. Maximilian's wariness and Napoleon's chagrin compelled

Bazaine to take an offensive meant to conquer more territory so the French could stage a more plausible referendum of Mexican opinion. In Mexico and the United States, battles and elections kept looping together in the intense politics of civil wars.[11]

Mexican politics got even messier in February 1864, when Santa Anna suddenly returned from exile to Veracruz. Loudly professing devotion to Maximilian, the old dictator angled to become his prime minister by rallying public support. But Almonte did not relish submitting to his old boss, so he proclaimed, "Santa Anna does not come back today to govern, nor to do as he damn well pleases, he comes back to obey." When Santa Anna kept on politicking, Bazaine sent him packing back into exile in March.[12]

Dreams

Martin Delany and Mary Ann Shadd Cary had settled in Chatham, the largest Canadian community for Black refugees from American slavery. Delany practiced medicine while Shadd edited a newspaper and ran a private school. Delany meant to have only a brief stay while he launched his colony for African Americans in West Africa. But Shadd Cary believed in Canada as the best place for Blacks to fulfill their potential by integrating with the white majority.[13]

Shadd Cary's confidence in Canada weakened at the start of the 1860s as white racial prejudice increased, eroding the official laws mandating equality. Blacks faced greater segregation in public accommodations and schools. Shadd lamented that Canadian whites "will not permit a colored child to enter a school where white children are taught." She also felt unmoored after the death of her husband, Thomas Cary, in November 1860.[14]

In January 1863, Lincoln's Emancipation Proclamation galvanized Delany and Shadd Cary with a new hope that the United States could become a true homeland for African Americans. Rather than lurk on the northern sidelines in Canada, they returned to America to help rally Black men for military service in a special new corps, the "United States Colored Troops." Mocking Chief Justice Taney's rhetoric, Canada's Black Methodist ministers exhorted young men "to put down the ungodly man-stealers, who, in this war, have no rights which coloured men are bound to respect." About 2,500 Black Canadians crossed the border to enlist in the Union army or navy.[15]

Delany became a star recruiter initially in New England, later expanding his operation into the Midwest. He impressed a witness as having "a commanding voice and a confident air. His laugh was full of jollity." Eager for Black recruits to help fill quotas needed to avert a draft of white men, northern states offered generous bounties: $250 to $300. After meeting Delany, President Lincoln sent a note to Secretary of War Edwin Stanton: "Do not fail to have an interview with this most extraordinary and intelligent black man." Stanton commissioned Delany as a major: the highest rank of any Black in the army.[16]

Delany persuaded Shadd Cary to become his assistant recruiter. He admired her energy, eloquence, and integrity—all valuable for a role that demanded speeches, visits to homes, and handling federal money. From riding the abolitionist lecture circuit, she had developed widespread contacts to introduce her to Black communities and shelter her from racist mobs.[17]

Another Canadian refugee, Harriet Tubman left her home in St. Catherines, traveling south to the Union-occupied Sea Islands of South Carolina in 1862. While assisting at a hospital and refugee camp for fugitives, Tubman served as a spy, slipping behind Confederate lines to gather information. She also recruited and led a company of Black rangers to scout and raid the hinterland. Tubman worked with Colonel James Montgomery, a devout abolitionist who had fought beside John Brown against slaveholders in Kansas and Missouri. Sharing her zeal for a hard war against slavery, Montgomery declared that "Southerners must be made to feel that this was a real war, and that they were to be swept away by the hand of God." Another Union officer declared that Montgomery believed in "praying, shooting, hanging and burning [as] the true means to put down the Rebellion."[18]

In June 1863, Tubman planned and helped lead a raid by her rangers and Montgomery's troops along the Combahee River in South Carolina. Destroying bridges and warehouses and burning fifty plantations, the raiders also freed 750 enslaved people. She recalled, "We laughed, an[d] laughed" as hundreds defied overseers to flee to the Union gunboats while carrying away children, pigs, and chickens. After the raid, a newspaper correspondent praised the "speech from the black woman who led the raid, and under whose inspiration it was originated and conducted. For sound sense and real native eloquence, her address would do honor to any man, and it created a great sensation."[19]

In early 1863, Martin Delany's oldest son, Toussaint L'Ouverture Delany, left Canada for New England to enlist in the 54th Massachusetts, one of the first Black regiments and a key test of the concept. The regiment drew recruits from throughout the North and Canada. They included two sons of Frederick Douglass from Rochester, New York. Lewis Douglass assured his fiancée, "I am striking a blow for the welfare of the most abused and despised race on earth." Completing their training in May, the men paraded through cheering crowds in Boston before embarking on a steamer taking them south to attack Charleston, South Carolina. The writer Henry Wadsworth Longfellow marveled, "Saw the first regiment of blacks march through Beacon Street, an imposing sight, with something wild and strange about it, like a dream. At last, the North consents to let the Negro fight for freedom."[20]

Black troops sought to vindicate their race by serving with ability and courage. A Louisiana recruit vowed to "fight as long as I can, if only my boy may stand in the street equal to a white boy." By demonstrating their manhood, Blacks pressured their states and nation to treat them as equal citizens. "I felt like a man with a uniform on and a gun in my hand," a Black recruit declared. In early 1863 most of the recruits were free Blacks from northern states that denied them the right to vote or send their children to public schools. In effect, they fought a double war: for equality in the North as well as to smash slavery in the South. As Union forces pressed deep into the Confederacy, more slaves escaped and enlisted in the Black regiments. One of the new recruits, Sergeant Prince Rivers, reasoned, "This is our time. If our fathers had had such a chance as this, we should not have been slaves now."[21]

Initially, Democrats derided the Black troops as too cowardly and stupid to fight, alleging that serving beside them disgraced white troops.

Democrats denounced recruiting Blacks as meant to promote "the fanatical idea of negro equality." Opponents claimed that emancipation hardened Confederate resistance, ruining prospects of negotiating peaceful reconciliation—a fantasy still cherished among Democrats. Kentucky's governor insisted that Black soldiers would "fire the whole South into one burning mass of inexhaustible hate."[22]

White men in the Union army divided over emancipation and Black troops. A Wisconsin officer warned Lincoln that most soldiers "hate the Negro more than they love the Union." Some did desert in disgust, but others accepted that they needed Black reinforcements to win the war. An Illinois soldier said that his comrades "like the Negro no better now than we did then, but we hate his master worse. . . . I am henceforth an *Abolitionist* and I intend to practice what I preach."[23]

Many Union commanders assigned Black troops to menial tasks behind the front lines to free up more white troops for combat. Deeming a Black "not the equal of the white man," General Sherman employed Blacks "as pioneers, teamsters, cooks, and servants" or, at most, a "local garrison." Although considered demeaning, these support roles became more important as the Union pushed their supply lines deeper into the South.[24]

Union bureaucrats and congressmen added insult to injury by deeming Blacks second-class soldiers qualified only for the lower pay of laborers. Promised equal pay at enlistment, Black troops discovered in July 1863 that the government would only allow them $7 per month, regardless of rank. By contrast, a white private got $13 a month, rising to $21 for a sergeant. Demanding equality, many Black troops refused to accept their pay for eighteen months, fighting for a principle despite the hardship imposed on their families. One recruit wrote to the president, "Now your Excellency, we have done a Soldier's duty. Why can't we have a Soldier's pay?" At last, in June 1864, Congress authorized equal pay for most Black troops.[25]

Black soldiers also resented that so few could become officers. Whites claimed that Blacks lacked command ability and that White officers would not associate with them. So white men led the Black regiments. Colonel Thomas W. Higginson noted the folly: "There were more than a hundred men in the ranks who had voluntarily met more dangers in their escape from slavery than any of my young captains had incurred in their lives." Confessing to a change of heart, Colonel Robert Gould Shaw felt "perfectly astonished at the general intelligence these darkeys display."[26]

Rope

Convinced that southern fighting men were invincible, many Confederates sought a scapegoat for defeats, often blaming Jefferson Davis. With the Confederacy shorthanded and attacked from multiple directions, every congressman and governor demanded local reinforcements—and faulted the president for failing to deliver them. Congressman Lawrence Keitt complained, "To see a great cause lost, and a great people butchered by gross and criminal incapacity strikes like a dagger to the heart." Calling Davis a coward and imbecile, Keitt urged him "to get a rope and hang himself." Davis's political foes in congress also included the formidable Senator Louis T. Wigfall of Texas. Another critic, General Joseph E. Johnston, recuperated from his wounds at Wigfall's house in Richmond. Their collaboration deepened the president's fury toward both men as treacherous. A Davis supporter, Mary Chesnut, sighed, "Wigfall, . . . from whom we hoped so much, has only been destructive."[27]

Thin-skinned, Davis treated critics as perverse fools. He lacked Lincoln's capacity to work with rivals in a common cause and endure their criticism. Tenacious and self-righteous, the Confederate president had to win every argument. In a rare moment of self-criticism, Davis sighed, "I wish I could learn just to let people alone who snap at me." But the president usually got his way, for his opponents were divided on principle, with some defending the old states' rights but others, including Wigfall, favoring a nationalization of power but longing for a different president. The divided opponents proved more annoying than effective at challenging Davis's administration.[28]

Hard-pressed by superior Union forces in early 1862, Davis felt compelled to coerce more resources out of the people. With the support of most in congress, he remade the Confederacy into a more consolidated nation than southerners had bargained on at the start of the war. The government raised taxes; took over railroads and the munitions industry; and impressed produce and livestock from farms for the troops. In return, farmers received nominal payment at less than market value in paper money of declining value. To discourage desertion, the government required passes for people to travel across state lines. Confederate senators protested that they could not go home "without obtaining a pass like a negro." An official confessed, "The iron is gone deep into the heart of society."[29]

In February 1862, the Confederate Congress authorized Davis to suspend the writ of habeas corpus and impose martial law in any city or district facing imminent attack. Two days later, Davis put Richmond under martial law. The Confederate commander there banned the sale of liquor, confiscated privately owned firearms, and initiated a passport system to control people moving in and out of the city. He rounded up dissidents, including the pastor of Richmond's Universalist Church. The sudden restriction on civil rights seemed especially jarring because Confederate leaders had denounced Lincoln as a tyrant who imposed arbitrary arrests and military law.[30]

On April 16, 1862, the Confederate Congress enacted the first national conscription law in American history. Centralizing control over recruitment (formally a state prerogative), the law arbitrarily extended the enlistments of volunteers already in the army, obliging them to serve for another two years. The Conscription Act also imposed a draft on all able-bodied white men between the ages of eighteen and thirty-five, compelling them to serve for three years. The new law exempted Confederate and state officials, including local militia officers, teachers, newspaper editors, and laborers in munition workshops. Men could buy their way out by hiring a substitute, but that cost soared to $6,000 in Confederate money ($300 in gold) by late 1863. Priced out of hiring a substitute, many plain folk called the conflict a rich man's war but a poor man's fight.[31]

Plain folk also bristled at planters who evaded Confederate efforts to requisition slaves to build fortifications and haul goods. Most masters resented and resisted any interference with their human property. They also rightly worried that their slaves more readily escaped to the Yankees if moved and gathered near the front lines to assist Confederate troops. A Georgia congressman asked: "Have you ever noticed the strange conduct of our people during this war? They give up their sons, husbands, brothers & friends . . . to the army, but let one of their negroes be taken, and what a howl you will hear." A Confederate official lamented, "The sacrosanctity of slave property in this war has operated most injuriously to the Confederacy."[32]

Confederate soldiers believed that they fought to protect hearth and home from larcenous and emancipating Yankees. But what were they to do when their government inflicted hardships on their families? Having promised protection, the government seemed to have defaulted, becoming a predator on the autonomy and property of common white men. Feeling betrayed, some evaded the draft or deserted to flee homeward. A Virginia soldier declared, "I love my country but I love my family better."[33]

Draft dodging and desertion thrived in hilly and mountainous counties inhabited by plain folk with doubts about the Confederacy. In these refuges, deserters and draft dodgers formed outlaw bands that ventured out to rob plantations and towns. In September 1863 a Confederate official warned that "the condition of things in the mountain districts of North Carolina, South Carolina, Georgia, and Alabama menaces the existence of the Confederacy as fatally as either of the armies of the United States." Governors and generals had to divert troops from the front to deal with armed dissidents at home.[34]

Just as women had mobilized their men for war, so wives and mothers could summon them to desert. In April 1863, a North Carolina wife explained, "we wiimen will write our husbands to come . . . home and help us [if] we can't stand it." Another woman declared, "What do I care for patriotism? My husband is my country. What is country to me, if he be killed?" In central Mississippi, a Confederate judge deemed local women "rotten hearted . . . far worse than the men" and "responsible" for the surge in desertions by common soldiers.[35]

Those deserters brought down the wrath of authorities whose violence ruined many families. By enforcing the draft and retrieving deserters with military force, Confederate officials escalated the pressure on wavering civilians, treating any reluctance as criminal. Probing the countryside, cavalry ventured deep into the hills and mountains, scouring for deserters and draft dodgers. When unable to find men hiding in the woods, the enforcers targeted their families, plundering, burning, torturing, and raping. In North Carolina, a woman reported that home guards took children to "Hange them until they turn Black in the face trying to make them tell whear there fathers is."[36]

In Jones County, Mississippi, Newton Knight led a formidable gang of southern deserters. A common farmer who owned no slaves, Knight had opposed secession, but he volunteered for the Confederate army in 1861, when so many young men proved their manhood by enlisting. Two years later, Knight deserted in outrage over the impact of conscription and impressment on his kinfolk. He declared, "If they had a right to conscript me when I didn't want to fight the Union, I had a right to quit when I got ready." Hiding out with help from his common-law wife, a former slave named Rachel, Knight boasted of having seceded from the Confederacy to form the "Free State of Jones."[37]

In 1863, Knight's merry men robbed, abused, and killed tax collectors and conscription officers. In at least fourteen skirmishes, they battled Confederate troops sent to arrest and execute them. "We stayed out in the woods minding our own business, until the Confederate Army began sending raiders after us with bloodhounds. . . . Then we saw we had to fight," Knight explained. Local women provided food, nursing, and an early warning system, blowing horns to warn of approaching Confederates. Some women, including Rachel Knight, took up arms to join the fight or poisoned the bloodhounds used to track deserters.[38]

The pressures of war corroded the southern economy, producing shortages and soaring inflation, hitting the plain folk especially hard. By early 1863 a Confederate dollar had only a seventh of its 1861 value. As the Union blockade tightened, consumer goods vanished from store shelves. And military demands sucked up surplus labor and food and commandeered railroads, undermining the interstate flow of commerce.

Meanwhile, rampaging armies ravaged thousands of farms and depleted their livestock and produce. Class tensions increased as common people complained that the rich were getting richer at their expense—and that government officials did too little to help.[39]

In the cities, food became scarce and expensive, leading to bread riots by poor people, often the wives and mothers of soldiers. In Richmond, in April 1863, a thousand people marched on the governor's mansion to demand bread. "This is little enough for the government to give us after it has taken all our men [for the army]," one woman explained. When the governor refused to help, they smashed open and looted bakeries, shops, and warehouses. "Our children are starving while the rich roll in wealth," the rioters shouted. President Davis joined the governor and mayor to rally militia against the rioters. Officials gave the mob five minutes to go home before the troops opened fire. After four tense minutes, the rioters dispersed. To discourage another riot, Richmond's city fathers began to provide food relief for the poor.[40]

Some southern leaders opposed Davis's centralizing measures as corrosive to the rights of states and individuals. The malcontents included Vice-President Alexander H. Stephens, who resented that Davis froze him out of important meetings and decisions. Denouncing the draft, impressment, and suspension of habeas corpus, Stephens declared, "Far better that our country should be overrun by the enemy, our cities sacked and burned, and our land laid desolate, than that the people should thus suffer the citadel of their liberties to be entered and taken by professed friends." Stephens spent most of his term sulking at home in Georgia.[41]

Georgia's governor, Joseph Brown, accused Davis of acting like a Republican to consolidate federal power. Brown denounced the draft as a "dangerous usurpation by Congress of the reserved rights of the States" and "at war with all the principles for which Georgia entered into revolution." To shelter many Georgians from the draft, Brown appointed hundreds of new officers in the state militia. Davis replied that he had the constitutional power to adopt any measure for defense "when our very existence is threatened by armies vastly superior in numbers."[42]

Resolve

Despite their many complaints, most southerners supported Davis and the Confederacy because submitting to the Union seemed far worse. "The Yankees must be whipped, if it takes every dollar & every man in the Confederate States to do it," declared a Mississippian. An Alabama soldier reasoned that "we are ruined if we do not put forth all our energies, & drive back the invaders of our slavery South." Most Confederates believed that a Yankee victory would bring humiliation, ruin, and Black equality, which they cast as "Slavery for the White Man!"[43]

Through defeats and hardships, southerners proved remarkably resilient. In diaries, letters, and newspapers, they praised one another for sacrificing and enduring for their cause. Sarah Morgan of Louisiana declared, "I have lost my home and all its dear contents for Southern Rights, have stood on the destroyed hearth stone and looked at the ruin of all I loved without a murmur, almost glad of the sacrifice, if it would contribute its might towards the salvation of the Confederacy." Another southern woman wrote of Yankees, "A sea rolls between them and us—a sea of blood. Smoking houses, outraged women, murdered fathers, brothers, and husbands, forbid such a union. . . . How we hate them with the whole strength and depth of our souls!"[44]

Some Union soldiers recognized that the harder war hardened their enemies. A northern officer reflected, "Were low, ignorant ruffians to visit my home while I was away fighting, burn my house, lay waste [to] my property, insult mother and sisters, beggar the little children I might love, taunt the gray hairs I might respect, leave starvation in the place of plenty, I should feel singularly strengthened in my early delusion." An Illinois soldier wrote to his wife, "Our army is doing some very disrespectful and disgraceful things. A perfect reign of terror, starvation, and hatred we leave behind us as we go."[45]

For Davis, hating the Union's hard war was personal as well as political. In June 1862, Yankees raided the Davis Bend plantations of Hurricane and Brierfield, the homes of the brothers Joseph and Jefferson Davis. Raiders and liberated slaves vented their rage at the absent Confederate president by stealing or smashing dishes, mirrors, books, furniture, and windows. After slashing to shreds a portrait of Davis, they burned Hurricane and left Brierfield a hollow wreck. Disgusted by "the appalling atrocities," Davis denounced Yankees for waging "a campaign of indiscriminate robbery and murder."[46]

By focusing on Yankee depredations, southerners obscured similar abuses by their own troops, who became unruly when denied the provisions and clothing promised by recruiters. In July 1862, in Virginia, a Confederate general lamented, "Our own army is as destructive as the enemy's, & nearly one half the State is a desert." Another general complained, "We have no discipline in our army, it is but little better than an armed mob. . . . Where our army marches & camps, desolation follows."[47]

Gettysburg

In early 1863, Lincoln sacked the bungling commander of the Army of the Potomac, Ambrose Burnside, replacing him with Joseph Hooker, who had an aggressive combat reputation. But Hooker was also a hedonist and egotist, who kept a headquarters that a critic called "a combination barroom and brothel." Indeed, "hookers" became a synonym for prostitutes who followed the army. The general also had undermined Burnside, faulted Lincoln, and speculated that Hooker might save the Union by becoming a dictator. Hearing the rumors, Lincoln admonished Hooker: "Only those generals who gain successes can set up [as] dictators. What I now ask of you is military success, and I will risk the dictatorship."[48]

At first, Hooker did well, restoring morale by improving food, sanitation, and hospitals while reorganizing the cavalry. In the spring, he invaded northern Virginia, declaring, "May God have mercy on General Lee, for I will have none." With 120,000 men opposed by just 60,000 Confederates, Hooker insisted that Lee's army faced "certain destruction." But Hooker's bluster hid a fatal flaw: a nervous insecurity in a crisis.[49]

Despite his smaller numbers, Lee seized the initiative by attacking

Hooker's advance in a dense forest near Chancellorsville on May 1. Spooked by the attack, Hooker pulled his troops back to a defensive position but left his right flank exposed. Detecting that flaw, Lee sent Stonewall Jackson to strike the vulnerable position, exploiting the cover provided by the forest. "O! tomorrow, Death will hold high carnival," a Confederate officer wrote to his wife. Attacking late on May 2, Jackson's men surprised and routed the Yankees, but, in pursuit, Jackson took three bullets in his arms, all fired by his own men mistaking him for a Union officer in the dark. Pneumonia set in to kill Jackson, costing Lee his best general. On May 3, Hooker failed to counterattack, instead pulling back, to the disgust of his generals. The Union force suffered 17,000 casualties to 13,500 for the Confederates. Many wounded men died in flames when the forest caught fire.[50]

Routed yet again by Lee with a smaller army, Union troops and civilians became restive. Horace Greeley's newspaper expressed horror that 120,000 "magnificent soldiers" had been "cut to pieces by . . . 60,000 half-starved ragamuffins." Lincoln lamented, "My God! My God! What will the country say?" It would say that an incompetent ran the Army of the Potomac. In late June, the president sacked Hooker in favor of George Meade. A grumpy man, Meade lacked charisma and imagination, but he was more of a fighter than the poseur Hooker.[51]

With Union forces pressing forward in Mississippi and Tennessee, Davis favored shifting some Virginia troops westward. But Lee rejected that plan in favor of his own: to invade the North to get into Pennsylvania. Such an invasion could, Lee claimed, best relieve the Union pressure on Vicksburg and Chattanooga. By defeating Yankees on their own turf, Lee could discredit the Lincoln administration and bolster the Democrats in elections: "If [we are] successful this year, next fall there will be a great change in public opinion at the North. The republicans will be destroyed." Lee's offensive thrilled southerners who believed that he could never lose, no matter the odds.[52]

Sweeping northwestward around the slow Army of the Potomac, Lee's men reached southern Pennsylvania, where they stripped the farms and stores of alcohol, provisions, and livestock. When a farm woman protested, General James Longstreet retorted, "Yes, madam, it's very sad—very sad; and this sort of thing has been going on in Virginia more than two years—very sad."[53]

Lee's troops seized hundreds of Blacks to send them south for sale into slavery. A Pennsylvanian, Rachel Cormany, noted that rebel cavalrymen were "hunting up the contrabands & driving them off by droves. . . . They were driven by just like we would drive cattle." In Chambersburg, a Confederate officer proclaimed "that they would burn down every house which harbored a fugitive slave, and did not deliver him up within twenty minutes." To escape capture, thousands of Blacks fled. One explained that he feared "de Rebels kotchin' us an[d] takin[g] our chill[dr]en fum us and sellin[g th]em . . . an[d] we wud nevah see dem ag[a]in."[54]

Lee's troops converged on the town of Gettysburg July 1. Pushing Union cavalry back, Confederates seized and looted the town. Withdrawing to high ground south of Gettysburg, the Union force rallied and received reinforcements overnight. Meade consolidated a strong position on a two-mile arc from Cemetery Hill on the northeast, along Cemetery Ridge, to Little Round Top at the southwestern end. Sizing up that strong position, Longstreet favored moving around the Yankees, but Lee meant to smash them headlong to win a decisive victory. Given the Union army's superior numbers (88,000 to Lee's 70,000), he took an immense risk.[55]

On July 2, Lee's attacks hammered the two flanks of the Union arc, but the Yankees held firm. At the critical position on the south end, a Maine regiment commanded by Joshua L. Chamberlain weathered assaults on Little Round Top. Despite the day's setbacks, Lee had the blood lust, convinced that he had softened up the Yankees for a devastating punch at the center of their line on Cemetery Ridge on July 3. "I could see the desperate and hopeless nature of the charge and the hopeless slaughter it would cause," Longstreet recalled.[56]

Longstreet concentrated 150 cannon to bombard the Union center for two hours. A Connecticut soldier marveled, "All at once it seemed as though all the artillery in the universe had opened fire and was belching forth its missiles of death and destruction." But most of the shot flew high over the heads of Yankees sheltered behind stone walls and breastworks. Finally, at mid-afternoon, Longstreet sent forward 12,000 men, led by George Pickett. A mile wide, Pickett's charge had to cover over 700 yards of open fields to reach the strongly posted Union troops. Searing fire devastated the attackers, killing and wounding nearly half of them before the charge collapsed. The three days of combat cost the Confederates 28,000 casualties to 23,000 for Meade's army.[57]

Late on July 4, Lee's weary and battered army began to retreat southward for Virginia. A Georgia soldier reported, "I have been cold, hot, wet, dry, ragged, dirty, hungry & thirsty, marched through clouds of dust, waded mud knee deep & suffered from fatigue & loss of sleep." Used to winning against superior numbers, the Confederates felt shaken by defeat. One soldier mourned, "the Armey is Broken harted," for "it Don't look like that we will Ever whip the Yankees [because] they have got too many men for us."[58]

Disgusted by press criticism, Lee offered to resign: "I cannot even accomplish what I myself desire, how can I fulfill the expectations of others?" Of course, Davis refused the offer, for the Confederacy needed Lee more than ever. A female diarist exulted, "Gen. Lee has *not* resigned and as long as so good and great a man has charge of our army in Virginia, we will not despair." Lee had eclipsed Davis and every other general as the unifying leader of an embattled nation.[59]

Lee's army escaped back to Virginia because Meade was so slow and hesitant in his pursuit, squandering a chance to hammer a battered foe. Detecting "a dreadful reminiscence of McClellan," Lincoln seethed, "We had them within our grasp. We had only to stretch forth our hands and they were ours." Meade spent the rest of the summer and fall marching about in northern Virginia, failing to jostle Lee's army into a major battle. Lincoln concluded that he needed a new commander drawn from the West, where Union forces won more decisive victories.[60]

Vicksburg

Henry Halleck directed Grant to renew his offensive against Vicksburg because "the opening of the Mississippi River will be to us of more advantage than the capture of forty Richmonds. . . . The eyes and hopes of the whole country are now directed to your army."[61]

But Vicksburg bristled with cannon within fortifications set on high bluffs above the river, and the town was buffered by dense swamps and clouds of mosquitoes. In February and March, Grant's troops and runaway slaves dug canals through the mud to enable riverboats to bypass Vicksburg's heavy guns. Two months of backbreaking work proved futile, souring morale, particularly as the swampy work exposed the men to venomous water snakes and epidemics of malaria, measles, pneumonia, and dysentery.[62]

The stalemate in the mud renewed rumors that Grant was too drunk to lead his men. Brushing aside critics, Lincoln insisted that he needed Grant's fighting persistence. Indeed, the president joked that he wanted other generals to drink the same brand of whiskey. But, just to be sure, he sent a special agent, Charles A. Dana, to investigate. Impressed by Grant, Dana declared him "the most honest man I ever knew, with a temper that nothing could disturb. . . . not an original or brilliant man, but sincere, thoughtful, deep and gifted with courage."[63]

By comparison, John C. Pemberton was a poor choice to command at Vicksburg. A Pennsylvanian who married a Virginian, Pemberton chose the Confederacy over the Union in 1861. Because two of Pemberton's brothers fought for the Union, many southerners distrusted his allegiance and disliked his cranky manners. But Jefferson Davis called Pemberton "one of the best Generals in our service"—although he had never led an army in combat. Tenacious in his loyalties and hatreds, Davis resented criticism of Pemberton as treacherous to him.[64]

The Confederate forces suffered from poor coordination. To appease critics in Congress, Davis reluctantly sent his own enemy, Joseph E. Johnston, to assume overall command west of the Appalachians as far as the Mississippi River: a daunting territory of 180,000 square miles. Lacking his own army, Johnston was supposed to supervise Pemberton's and Braxton Bragg's forces despite the three hundred miles between them. Worse still, Johnston had no authority over the Confederate troops west of the Mississippi although their cooperation was essential to defending

Vicksburg. Seething as Davis ignored his recommendations, Johnston did little as Grant seized the initiative.[65]

Grant's chief subordinate, William T. Sherman, advised pulling back to Memphis to regroup, but Grant better understood the political context: "The country is already disheartened over the lack of success on the part of our armies," so his troops had "to move forward to a decisive victory or our cause was lost." On the night of April 16, Grant ran his gunboats down the Mississippi past the guns of Vicksburg, suffering only light casualties. Then Grant could cross the river thirty miles south of the city to get his troops onto dry land.[66]

Rather than march north to attack Vicksburg directly, Grant swung his army of 29,000 eastward to block Johnston from coming to Pemberton's rescue. Breaking from his supply line along the Mississippi, Grant had his men live off the land by plundering farms and plantations. His troops brushed aside small Confederate forces to hit Jackson, the state capital, where Grant dispersed 6,000 defenders and destroyed much of the city. Then in mid-May, Grant turned westward to pin Pemberton in his entrenchments at Vicksburg. In seventeen days, Grant had marched 180 miles and fought five battles, inflicting 7,200 casualties while suffering 4,300.[67]

Johnston urged Pemberton to evacuate Vicksburg and unite their forces for a more mobile attack on Grant. Recognizing the Confederacy's shortage of troops, Johnston reasoned that saving an army trumped preserving control of any place. But Pemberton clung to Davis's orders to hold Vicksburg at all costs. A woman in that town pitied the defenders, "Wan, hollow-eyed, ragged, foot-sore, bloody, the men limped along . . . humanity in the last throes of endurance."[68]

Reinforced to a strength of 75,000 men, Grant besieged Vicksburg, enclosed by twelve miles of Union trenches and bombarded by 220 heavy guns. As the town burned, starving defenders and civilians dug caves for shelter and ate dogs, cats, and rats for food. While pinning Pemberton in, Grant posted Sherman's men to the east to fend off any renewed attack by Johnston. But the Confederate commander stayed put, assuring his superiors "I consider saving Vicksburg hopeless."[69]

After a siege of forty-seven days, Pemberton surrendered his 30,000 starving men on July 4. Watching Grant's troops march into the town, a woman marveled: "What a contrast [between these] stalwart, well-fed men, so splendidly set-up and accoutered" and "the worn men in gray, who were being blindly dashed against this embodiment of modern power." The coincidence of victories at Gettysburg and Vicksburg on July 4 thrilled Unionists.[70]

Five days later, the Confederate commander at Port Hudson, the last southern bastion on the Mississippi, surrendered his 7,000 men. At last, the valley was in Union hands, isolating Texas and Arkansas from the rest of the Confederacy. Lincoln declared, "Grant is my man, and I am his [for] the rest of the war." Meanwhile, Johnston and Davis blamed one another for the debacle at Vicksburg: "the darkest hour of our political existence," as Davis put it. Suspending that general, Davis left the overmatched Bragg to cope with the Union advance on Chattanooga.[71]

Respect

In addition to Vicksburg and Gettysburg, July 1863 featured a third critical battle, this time deep within the Union: in New York City, where rioters confronted policemen and troops enforcing a draft. Because the rioters chanted support for the Confederacy, a prominent New Yorker concluded, "Jefferson Davis rules New York today." The fissures of civil war ran through both regions rather than neatly dividing them into North and South.[72]

As the war dragged on into a third year, white volunteers lagged, obliging the U.S. Congress to impose a draft, but a conscript could buy his way out by paying $300 or hiring a substitute. Of 207,000 men drafted, 87,000 paid the fee and another 74,000 hired substitutes, leaving only 46,000 conscripts who entered the army. The system did prod more men to volunteer and thereby avoid the stigma of being a conscript.[73]

The draft law seemed unfair to poorer men, who could not afford to pay the fee or hire a substitute. Alienation became violent in New York City, where thousands of Irish immigrants lived in filthy slums and worked for low wages, often in competition with Black laborers.

The immigrants became Democrats who resented the city's leading businessmen, most of them Protestant Republicans. Many Irish immigrants concluded that Republicans drafted them as cannon fodder to benefit Blacks.[74]

On July 12, 1863, eight days after the Union victories at Gettysburg and Vicksburg, hundreds of rioters attacked and destroyed the draft offices in New York City. For the next four days, armed mobs terrorized the city, attacking Republican newspapers, homes of abolitionists, and Black neighborhoods. Rioters tortured and lynched Blacks or cast them in the river to drown. Pushing aside outnumbered policemen, the insurgents looted stores and burned Protestant churches, police stations, the homes of Blacks, and an orphanage for their children.[75]

The War Department rushed thousands of Union troops from Gettysburg to New York to suppress the riots. On July 15 and 16 soldiers killed enough rioters to disperse the rest. With 20,000 troops patrolling the streets, the draft resumed on August 19. But the Democratic city council appropriated funds to pay commutation for all the conscripts.[76]

The Black victims in New York City included a seven-year-old boy stoned and clubbed to death. He was the nephew of a sergeant in the 54th Massachusetts regiment, Robert J. Simmons. Another soldier in that regiment, James Gooding, learned that the mob had burned his home. Unlike the rioters, Simmons and Gooding fought for the Union, presenting a contrast that impressed Republicans.[77]

Two days after the New York City rioting ended, the 54th regiment went into battle near Charleston, South Carolina. Both opponents and supporters saw the attack as a key test of Black troops. The skeptics included their own commander, General Truman Seymour, who sent the 54th to assault Fort Wagner, a formidable thicket of earthworks and palmetto logs bristling with fourteen cannon and held by 1,700 men. Seymour told another general, "Well, I guess we will . . . put those d[amne]d niggers from Massachusetts in the advance; we may as well get rid of them one time as another."[78]

At night on July 18, the Black troops charged into deadly fire, reaching the top of the parapet. "Not a man flinched, though it was a trying time. A shell would explode and clear a space of twenty feet, [but] our men would close up again," recalled Sergeant Lewis Douglass. The regiment's commanding colonel, Robert Gould Shaw, fell dead, shot through the chest. Confederate reinforcements poured into the fort to drive back the attackers. A mile away, Harriet Tubman watched and heard the cannon fire, which resembled lightning and thunder, "and then we heard the rain falling, and that was the drops of blood falling; and when we came to get in the crops, it was the dead that we reaped." She helped nurse the wounded survivors. The 54th lost 42 percent of its men as casualties, including Douglass, wounded in the hip by a bullet.[79]

News of Fort Wagner came shortly after a battle at Milliken's Bend, beside the Mississippi River, where Black troops drove off an attack by a much larger force of Texans. A Union captain declared, "I never more wish to hear the expression, 'The niggers won't fight.'. . . They fought and died defending the cause that we revere." A Wisconsin officer marveled, "I never believed in niggers before, but by Jasus, they are hell for fighting." After Fort Wagner and Milliken's Bend, most of the northern press, Republican politicians, and Union generals accepted Black troops as invaluable for winning the war. "The truth is they have fought their way into the respect of all the army," a Union officer concluded.[80]

Despite stereotyping Blacks as happy-go-lucky cowards, southerners dreaded facing them in combat. After Milliken's Bend, a southern matron protested, "It is terrible to think of such a battle as this, white men and freemen fighting with their slaves, and to be killed by such a hand, the very soul revolts from it." A Union officer reported that captured Confederates "told me that they would rather fight two Regiments of White Soldiers than one of Niggers. Rebel Citizens fear them more than they would fear Indians."[81]

Confederates hated Black troops for defying their assigned place as docile slaves. Indeed, southerners saw U.S. Colored Troops as their greatest nightmare: Blacks armed and organized for a bloody slave revolt to kill white people. After one battle, a North Carolinian reported that captured Blacks were "either bayoneted or burnt. The men were perfectly exasperated at the idea of negroes opposed to them & rushed at them like so many devils." Southerners also slaughtered captured Union officers who led Black regiments. After one battle with Black troops, a

Texas officer reported, "We took no prisoners, except the white officers, fourteen in number; these were lined up and shot after the negroes were finished."[82]

In April 1864, General Nathan Bedford Forrest and 1,500 Confederates attacked Fort Pillow, beside the Mississippi River in Tennessee. Half of the 600 defenders were Blacks. A former slave trader, Forrest meant to "demonstrate to the Northern people that negro soldiers cannot cope with Southerners." Overwhelming the fort, the Confederates massacred two-thirds of the Black defenders, most while trying to surrender. A Confederate sergeant recalled, "Their fort turned out to be a great slaughter pen. . . . Human blood stood about in pools, and brains could have been gathered up in any quantity." The victors cast forty wounded Blacks into a trench and buried them alive.[83]

Confederates did take some Black prisoners, usually consigning them to slavery. The captors refused to exchange Blacks to recover their own men. Southerners would "die in the last ditch," a Confederate official asserted, before "giving up the right to send slaves back to slavery as property recaptured." Under pressure from Black leaders to retaliate, the Union suspended prisoner exchanges in mid-1863. Over the next eighteen months, on both sides, thousands of prisoners accumulated in wretched prisons meant to accommodate hundreds.[84]

Union prisoners suffered the most, as Confederate logistics withered under the pressure of war. Unable to feed and clothe its own troops adequately, the Confederacy struggled to cope with thousands of imprisoned federals. The grimmest conditions prevailed at Andersonville in Georgia, a stockaded camp of twenty-six acres holding over 33,000 men by August 1864. Suffering from starvation, exposure, filth, and disease, a third of the Andersonville prisoners died compared to about 12 percent of the southerners confined by the Union during the last three years of the war.[85]

Home Front

By the end of the war, 178,000 Blacks had reinforced the Union army, while another 18,000 bolstered the navy. Primarily former slaves, they enabled the United States to achieve the two-to-one edge in soldiers needed to overwhelm the Confederacy. Grant declared that Black recruits comprised "the heaviest blow yet given to the Confederacy. By arming the negro, we have added a powerful ally. . . . and taking them from the enemy weakens them in the same proportion [that] they strengthen us."[86]

As federal troops pressed deeper into the South, they attracted thousands of runaways, who assisted as spies, guides, nurses, laundresses, teamsters, laborers, and soldiers. A Confederate colonel warned, "They know every road and swamp and creek and plantation in the country and are the worst of spies." General Kirby Smith lamented, "The policy of our enemy in arming and organizing negro regiments, is being pushed to formidable proportions. . . . Our plantations are made his recruiting stations." Smith concluded, "Every sound male black left for the enemy becomes a soldier whom we have afterwards to fight."[87]

The advance of Union troops undermined slavery. In Chattanooga, a Confederate noted that the spirits of Black people "rise and fall with the ebb and flow of this tide of blue devils." When "the whites are depressed and go about the streets like mourners," the Blacks became as "glad as larks." Masters felt shocked by the escapes, claiming betrayal by people who had been well treated. "I have seen the favourite and most petted negroes [be] the first to leave in every instance," Honoria Cannon declared, adding that "learning to do our own work would be hard." During the war, 500,000 slaves escaped, about one-seventh of the enslaved people in the South.[88]

Southern leaders diverted soldiers from the front lines to patrol country roads and intercept runaway slaves. With the war becoming more desperate, patrols executed captured fugitives and displayed their heads on posts beside the roads as a warning to others. "It is *we* or *they* [who] must suffer," explained a white woman in Georgia. The terror helped Confederates to keep most enslaved people working on farms and plantations.[89]

With so many white men away in Confederate service, the burden of watching and punishing enslaved people often fell on women. One wife lamented, "My Slaves will not work without some man to make them." A North Carolina soldier replied: "my advice to you about that, when they begin their Slack jaw, take something & Shoot Branes & leave them for the dogs to eat." Savvier planters had to compromise by stopping whippings in favor of more positive incentives, including a share of the crop as labor compensation.[90]

When masters fled from advancing Union troops, enslaved people took over farms and plantations as their own. A Natchez planter complained, "They are practically free—going, coming, and working when they please." He added, "The most of them think . . . that the plantation and every thing on it belongs to them." Confederates raided those plantations to abduct and kill Blacks. "The ferocity of these guerrilla massacres has rivaled everything in savage warfare short of cannibalism," a Union official declared.[91]

Former slaves wanted to come and go as they wished; to live without fear of the whip or sale; to learn to read and write; and to worship when and how they chose. "I wuz glad ter git free," Charles Barbour recalled, "cause I knows den dat I won't wake up some mornin' ter fin'd dat my mammy or some ob de rest of my family am done sold." Long deprived of learning, adults and children flocked to new schools sponsored by northern abolitionists. A chaplain noted that for Black troops, their "cartridge box and spelling book [were] attached to the same belt."[92]

Freed people expected to own and run small farms carved out of the plantations of their former masters. Blacks saw this as overdue compensation for their labor and essential to sustain true freedom. A freedman declared, "Gib us our own land and we take care of ourselves; but widout land, de ole massas can hire us or starve us, as dey please." Freed people insisted that a new middle class of Black farmers could sustain a true republic in the South by fending off resurgent power by an oligarchy of wealthy planters. A Union officer, James A. Garfield of Ohio, agreed, "If we want a lasting peace, if we want to put down this rebellion so that it shall stay forever put down . . . we must take away the platform on which slavery stands—the great landed estates of the armed rebels of the South."[93]

At Davis Bend, enslaved people liberated the Hurricane and Brierfield plantations of Jefferson Davis and his brother Joseph. Young Black men enlisted in the Union navy or army while their kin cut firewood to fuel steam engines and raised cattle to feed sailors and soldiers. In return, the freed people received pay and guns for self-defense. In September 1863, they fought off Confederate raiders, who hanged a retarded boy to express their frustration. By 1864, Davis Bend attracted 3,000 Black refugees from the hinterland. As tenant farmers, they thrived, raising good crops and improving their properties. In 1865, an army officer reported, "The Freedmen have built houses, and expended money on the land, with the expectation that the Government would sustain their claim to it in preference to that of the rebel owners."[94]

In January 1865, General Sherman turned over to freedmen the coastal islands of Florida, Georgia, and South Carolina, where they set up 20,000 small farms and organized schools and their own militia. Sherman considered the arrangement temporary, for he could not, and did not, issue them legal title to the land, leaving that question to the government. But his own views remained stingy: "The negro on his becoming free, has no right to the property of his former owner."[95]

Davis Bend and the Sea Islands were exceptions to the rule, for federal officials preferred to lease confiscated lands to capitalists who could revive the plantations to produce the cotton coveted by northern manufacturers and French and British importers. Those capitalists included Edward S. Philbrick, who complained that former slaves refused to work for low wages. One of them explained, "We wants land—dis bery land dat is rich wid de sweat ob we face and de blood ob we back." Philbrick felt frustrated, declaring that "no people on the face of the earth of their rank in civilization" were "so independent as they are." But a sympathetic general insisted that the speculators "cared nothing how much flesh they worked off of the negro provided it was converted into good cotton"—and then into money.[96]

In occupied districts, the Union government hoped to wean southern planters from supporting the Confederacy by confirming their lands in exchange for oaths of allegiance. Federal officials exulted when some Louisiana planters declared, "We are ready to give up the name of 'slavery,' we care nothing about the name. But we must have certain control over these men." These planters obliged Blacks to enter annual contracts to work at subsistence wages – thereby replacing slavery with a sort of serfdom. In Louisiana, General Nathaniel Banks ordered former slaves to provide "continuous and faithful service" with "respectful deportment, correct discipline, and perfect subordination." Republicans like Banks devoutly believed in contracts as training for economic responsibility.[97]

Immigrants

The Union also derived military strength from immigrants, for most arrived poor, needed work, and felt enticed by uniforms and pay. Because only 6 percent of prewar immigrants lived in the South, the Union had an immense advantage in recruiting them. By the end of the war, immigrants or their sons made up a third of the Union army and navy, with the largest numbers coming from Germany (243,000) and Ireland (234,000).[98]

Union leaders worried as the flow of immigration dried up at the start of the war. During the mid-1850s about 500,000 Europeans arrived annually, but that number fell below 92,000 in 1861 owing to alarm about the upheaval in North America. Secretary of State Seward assured Union diplomats: "This civil war must be a trial between the two parties to exhaust each other. The immigration of a large mass from Europe would of itself decide it." In August 1862 he sought to boost immigration by publicizing America's high wages and the free farms offered by the Homestead Act. Immigration rose in 1863 to more than 176,000, with further increases in 1864 and 1865. Thousands of the men enlisted in Union forces, each receiving at least a $500 bounty: more than a laborer could make in two years.[99]

Seeking European help in suppressing the foreign recruiting, southern diplomats insisted that Union agents enticed and deceived immigrants before compelling them to enlist. But French and British leaders declined to interfere. So, Confederates turned to Pope Pius IX, who despised American republicanism as too liberal and secular. Defending an ancient faith as eternal truth, he refused to "reconcile himself to progress, liberalism, and modern civilization." Mourning the deaths of so many Catholics in the Union forces, Pius IX urged American bishops to oppose the war. In Ireland, Confederate agents circulated a papal letter that denounced Union recruiting of Catholic immigrants. Those agents also publicized atrocities allegedly committed by Protestant Union troops against Catholics in Louisiana, including exposing a priest to "Alligators and Snakes!"[100]

Chattanooga

After the fall of Vicksburg, the next Union target was Chattanooga, the key railroad junction in southeastern Tennessee. The War Department assigned that advance to the Army of the Cumberland commanded by William S. Rosecrans. A methodical commander (and devout Catholic), Rosecrans spent the first half of 1863 training, supplying, and organizing his army while Lincoln and Secretary of War Stanton seethed at the delay. Once he did move, in late June, Rosecrans waged an efficient and clever campaign that advanced without a major battle. Through a ballet of shifting columns, he repeatedly feinted at Bragg's entrenched army, only to shift around to a flank to threaten the Confederate supply line. Unnerved by Rosecrans's movements, Bragg fell all the way back to Chattanooga, muttering "This is a great disaster." Losing only 570 Union casualties in eleven days, Rosecrans advanced eighty miles to threaten Chattanooga. Abandoning that city on September 8, Bragg withdrew into the hills of northern Georgia. His retreat enabled another Union army to seize Knoxville, liberating Unionist east Tennessee from a harsh Confederate occupation. Parson William G. Brownlow returned home to Knoxville to revive his anti-Confederate newspaper.[101]

Bragg and his subordinate generals despised one another. Although indecisive in real combat, Bragg was resolute in internal feuds. His grumpy manner and strict discipline also soured morale among his enlisted men. One recalled that Bragg "wanted always to display his tyranny and to intimidate his privates as much as possible." To rally Bragg's discouraged army, Davis urged Robert E. Lee to go west to assume command. Lee declined but did send James Longstreet with 12,000 men to reinforce Bragg. Traveling over the rickety Confederate railroad system, Longstreet's men began reaching northern Georgia on September 18, nine days after they started.[102]

Reinforced, Bragg turned about to attack Rosecrans's advance at Chickamauga Creek on September 19. In a rarity for this war, a Confederate army of 68,000 outnumbered the 58,000 Union troops. During the first day, the Union army held on in heavy fighting, but on the next day a renewed Confederate assault broke through a gap in the Yankee line. Misreading the disposition of his troops, Rosecrans had made a fatal mistake, ordering a division to abandon the very place where the Confederates then struck. Panicked by the rupture, Rosecrans and a third of his army broke and fled eight miles back to Chattanooga. The second-ranking Union general, George Thomas, rallied the rest of the troops to hold firm, blunting Longstreet's repeated assaults. That night, Thomas joined the retreat to Chattanooga. Shaken by heavy losses (18,000 for the Confederates to 16,000 for the Union), Bragg was slow to pursue, dismaying his many critics, who now included Longstreet.[103]

Rosecrans entrenched his battered troops at Chattanooga beside the Cumberland River, conceding the high ground to the west and south—Lookout Mountain and Missionary Ridge—which the Confederates occupied and fortified. Calling Rosecrans "confused and stunned like a duck hit on the head," Lincoln sent Grant to assume command and reinforced him with Joseph Hooker and 13,000 men drawn from the Army of the Potomac. Dismissing Rosecrans, Grant retained Thomas to command the Army of the Cumberland. Then Grant opened a new supply route to bring in provisions for the hungry federal troops. "We began to see things move. We felt that everything came from a plan," a Union officer noted.[104]

While Grant seized the initiative, Bragg and his officers bickered. Informed by her husband on Bragg's staff, Mary Chesnut reported that Bragg had "a winning way of earning everybody's detestation. Heavens how they hate him." Paralyzed by distrust, the army stayed inert in the hills overlooking fortified Chattanooga. Longstreet assured the secretary of war that "nothing but the hand of God can save us or help us as long as we have our present commander." To cope with the crisis, Jefferson Davis visited the army in early October, but he foolishly stuck with his friend Bragg. To reduce conflict, Davis sent Longstreet off with 15,000 men to attack Knoxville, thereby depriving Bragg of a quarter of his force just as Grant prepared to strike.[105]

While Bragg's army shrank to 36,000 men, Grant's swelled to 80,000 as Sherman arrived with 20,000 more troops. Lacking confidence in the soldiers defeated at Chickamauga, Grant assigned Thomas's army to feint an attack at the Confederate center, on Missionary Ridge, while Hooker and Sherman assaulted the two flanks. On November 24 Hooker's troops drove the Confederates from Lookout Mountain, but Sherman's men suffered a bloody repulse inflicted by Bragg's best subordinate general, Patrick Cleburne, on November 25. To help Sherman, Grant ordered Thomas to increase the sound and fury of his feint. Doing much more, Thomas's 18,000 men erupted in a spontaneous and apparently suicidal assault on their entrenched foes. To everyone's surprise, the attackers swept up the hill and over the top, routing the stunned Confederates, in what a witness called "one of the greatest miracles in military history."[106]

Losing 6,000 men as prisoners, the defeated Confederates fled twenty-five miles southward into Georgia. A southern soldier recalled, "I felt sorry for General Bragg. The army was routed, and Bragg looked so scared," while his fleeing troops heckled him as a coward and bully. Shaken by the debacle, Bragg confessed, "The whole responsibility and disgrace rest on my humble head." But then he resumed blaming his subordinates as drunks and incompetents. Davis had no choice but to replace Bragg with Joseph E. Johnston.[107]

The Confederate hope provided by Chickamauga dissolved at Chattanooga, compounding southern dismay and Union delight. Grant's reputation soared even higher, and Lincoln summoned him east to take command of the fight against Lee. Meanwhile, on November 29, Longstreet suffered a bloody defeat at Knoxville. After a hard winter in the mountains, he retreated eastward to rejoin Lee's army in the spring of 1864.[108]

Copperheads

Hindsight casts Gettysburg, Vicksburg, and Chattanooga as decisive turning points that doomed the Confederacy. Although shaken by those defeats, Confederates expected the South to rise again. A year before, southerners remembered, they had suffered defeats in winter and spring only to rally dramatically that summer and fall under Lee's leadership. Convinced that they had a greater resolve than their foes, Confederates expected to win the war by inflicting heavy casualties and growing expense on the Yankees. If they could hold on for another year, Confederates expected northern voters to cast out the Republicans in favor of Democrats. In this political war, victory depended on elections as well as battles.[109]

In August 1863, Lincoln rebuked Democrats for opposing Black emancipation and recruitment: "You say you will not fight to free negroes. Some of them seem willing to fight for you." The president concluded that after the war, Black veterans would recall how "they have helped mankind on to this great consummation, while, I fear, there will be some white men, unable to forget that, with malignant heart, and deceitful speech, they have strove to hinder it." The president especially referred to the provocative Clement Vallandigham of Ohio.[110]

Proud of his southern descent, Vallandigham was an eloquent populist who represented a congressional district dominated by "Butternuts," the name for southern migrants who disliked slavery but hated Blacks. Sharing their prejudices, Vallandigham damned Republicans for allegedly conspiring to bring "stinking niggers" north to take away the jobs and daughters of common white men, multiplying "black babies" through the land.[111]

Breaking with Stephen A. Douglas and other War Democrats, Vallandigham led Peace Democrats, who opposed restoring the Union by force. Against all evidence, he insisted that the South could be lured back by concessions that guaranteed slavery forever. In 1861 Vallandigham proposed to rearrange the country into four regions—Pacific, Northeast, Midwest, and South—each with a veto over congressional laws and the choice of president: a formula for political paralysis.[112]

Hammering Republicans for trampling on civil liberties, Vallandigham accused Lincoln of creating a "vast centralized military despotism" to erase the rights of states and citizens. Vallandigham asserted that Republicans waged a bloody, expensive, inept, and apparently endless war for a fanatical goal: to free Blacks rather than simply restore the old Union. Charging Republicans with "the enslavement of the white race by debt and taxes and arbitrary power," he wanted an armistice followed by a peaceful reunion with slavery preserved. Vallandigham ignored Confederates' insistence that they would never reunite with Yankees on any terms.[113]

Republicans demonized all Peace Democrats as "Copperheads," deadly, insidious, secretive, and treasonous snakes within the North. Although sincerely alarmed, Republicans exaggerated the number of Democrats who joined secret, violent societies within the Union. Wrapping themselves in the Union cause, Republicans urged Democrats to suspend partisan competition during the war. The governing party published a pamphlet with the revealing title *No Party Now, but All for Country*. Republican officers encouraged their troops to attack Democratic newspapers and their editors. A Union soldier said of Copperheads: "Morally they are so low that their highest ambition is to get drunk on bad whiskey."[114]

Vallandigham got a boost from an overreaction by the Union commander in Ohio, Ambrose Burnside, who blamed a spike in army desertion on the congressman's fiery antiwar speeches. On May 5, in the middle of the night, 150 Union troops broke down Vallandigham's door with axes and hauled him away. Denied a civil trial, Vallandigham faced a military tribunal that convicted and imprisoned him for treason. Glorying in the role of political martyr, Vallandigham insisted that he suffered from a Republican military dictatorship. Many War Democrats agreed, which alarmed Lincoln, who commuted Vallandigham's sentence to banishment. Turned over to the Confederates, Vallandigham advised them to "hold out this year," to enable Peace Democrats to win political control in the North.[115]

In June, Vallandigham slipped out of the Confederacy on a blockade-runner bound to Canada. Settling in Windsor, across the river from

Detroit, he conducted a campaign in exile to become governor of Ohio. Highlighting racial fear, his proxies in Ohio exhorted, "Let every vote count in favor of the white man, and against the Abolition hordes, who would place negro children in your schools, negro jurors in your jury boxes, and negro votes in your ballot boxes!" Ohio Democrats staged a parade featuring sixty white girls wearing white dresses and red sashes beneath a banner: "Give Us White Husbands or None at All."[116]

To oppose Vallandigham, Republicans supported a War Democrat, John Brough. To help the cause, Lincoln publicly justified exiling Vallandigham: "Must I shoot a simple-minded soldier boy who deserts, while I must not touch a hair of a wiley agitator who induces him to desert?" Union victories at Vicksburg and Gettysburg undermined claims by Peace Democrats that the war was lost. The old-time racism also receded among swing voters after the horrors of the New York riot and the courage of U.S. Colored Troops. In the November 1863 election, Brough won by over 100,000 votes (61 percent of the overall vote). Union candidates also won impressive victories in the gubernatorial races in Kentucky and Pennsylvania, defeating Peace Democrats. Republicans captured two-thirds of the seats in the New York legislature. The fall elections demonstrated that most northerners remained committed to fighting the war—and now accepted emancipation as essential to victory.[117]

While the November elections bolstered Lincoln, Jefferson Davis felt weakened by Confederate voters. Many southerners were dismayed by defeats, the draft, impressment of food and animals, the government's virtual bankruptcy, and hyperinflation. They clung to a war for independence but doubted that Davis was the right man to lead them. The lead critic, Joseph E. Brown, won reelection in Georgia by a landslide. Davis did retain majority support in both houses of the Confederate Congress, but his majority slipped as opponents increased their seats to 41 (from 26) of the 106 seats in the lower house and to 12 of the 26 senators. Davis's edge in Congress depended on unelected congressmen from areas occupied by Union troops: Kentucky, Missouri, Tennessee, Arkansas, and parts of Louisiana and Virginia. Desperate to reconquer their states, those congressmen favored Davis's centralizing measures.[118]

Address

After the fall elections, Lincoln delivered a speech at Gettysburg to help dedicate a new cemetery for the Union dead. In Biblical cadences, the president described a crusade to perfect a nation dedicated to freedom and equality. Drawing on the philosophical imperatives of the Declaration of Independence, Lincoln rooted the Union struggle in the country's revolutionary origins:

> Four score and seven years ago our fathers brought forth on this continent, A new nation, conceived in Liberty, and dedicated to the proposition That all men are created equal. Now we are engaged in a great civil war, testing whether that nation, or any nation so conceived and so dedicated, can long endure.

After honoring the sacrifice by the dead, Lincoln imagined a victorious future:

> That we here highly resolve that these dead shall not have died in vain—That this nation, under God, shall have a new birth of freedom—and that government of the people, by the people, for the people, shall not perish from the earth.

Without explicitly mentioning slavery, the president linked emancipation ("a new birth of freedom") to saving the Union and republican government. In just 272 words uttered within three minutes, Lincoln depicted a moral crusade that could permit no negotiated sacrifice of freedom to buy a tenuous restoration of the old Union of semi-sovereign states.[119]

Lincoln expressed American exceptionalism, but the theme of embattled free government with global stakes also applied to Mexico. While Confederates mourned their defeats at Gettysburg, Vicksburg, and Chattanooga, they took heart from French victories in Mexico. Because Confederate resistance shielded French troops from Yankee interference, southerners expected Napoleon to join their fight against the Union. In 1863 the two civil wars became more intertwined.[120]

TEN ❧ ELECTIONS

> Abe Lincoln, beast as he is, should be elected.
> —JOHN A. MACDONALD, 1864[1]

> There is one thing which is beyond the reach of perversity, and
> that is the tremendous verdict of history. History will judge us.
> —BENITO JUÁREZ TO MAXIMILIAN, 1864[2]

North America had four pivotal elections in 1864. In Mexico, the French invaders held plebiscites meant to persuade Europeans that most Mexicans welcomed rule by an imported monarch. In Canada, an election seemed inevitable because the weak and unstable governing coalition risked losing a parliamentary vote of no confidence. But few wanted that election given the growing tensions between Francophone and Anglophone Canada—and a dread that the American civil war would spill across the border. In 1864, the Confederacy had no national election, but North Carolina's gubernatorial contest was a key test of resolve in the South. The Union would host the most important election as the Lincoln administration defended a war fought to end slavery as well as to reunite the country. If Peace Democrats prevailed, the war effort would collapse, culminating in southern independence and the perpetuation of slavery.

After suffering major military defeats in 1863, the South's hopes lay in swaying the Union's elections in the fall of 1864. By inflicting heavy battlefield losses on the Yankees, Confederates could promote war-weariness in the North. Confederates cherished every report of northern discontent over emancipation, conscription, taxes, and limits on free speech. Southern newspapers reprinted antiwar speeches by Democrats as allegedly true measures of northern sentiment. A Georgia senator, Benjamin H. Hill, declared, "The Presidential election in the United States in 1864 . . . must determine the issue of peace or war, and with it the destiny of both countries."[3]

While counting on northern war-weariness, Confederates had their own discontents as supplies became scarce, inflation soared, slaves escaped, refugees proliferated, and casualties mounted. Struggling to cope, civilians felt numb. In Texas, in April 1864, a woman noted, "People do not mourn their dead as they used to. Everyone seems to live only in the present—just from day to day—otherwise I fancy many would go crazy." In June, she added, "We cannot bear to think of the past and so dread the future."[4]

North Carolina's gubernatorial election tested the extent of Confederate discontent. Slow to embrace secession, North Carolinians had been quick to criticize the Davis administration for bungling the war and demanding too much of them. Impressment, taxation, conscription, and casualties bore especially hard on the small farmers of North Carolina. They supported southern independence and slavery but wanted a more competent and less coercive Confederate government. Although overtly a Davis critic, Governor Zebulon Vance conducted a shrewd balancing act. While demanding concessions for North Carolina from

PREVIOUS PAGE: *"Sherman's March to the Sea," 1868, engraving by Alexander Hay Ritchie after F. O. C. Darley.*

Davis, Vance championed the war effort, pursued deserters ruthlessly, and marginalized louder critics of the war. He claimed that defeatists "would leave their children a heritage of shame, to feed upon the bitter husks of subjugation."[5]

The owner and editor of the state's most influential newspaper, William W. Holden took a stronger position against the war. The bloody defeats at Gettysburg and Vicksburg persuaded Holden that no more North Carolinians should die for a lost cause. He appealed to common farmers who resented the wealth, power, and draft-exemption of leading planters. During the summer of 1863, Holden rallied over a hundred local meetings in thirty counties to demand peace. Holden sought to bypass both the Union and Confederate governments by holding a state convention to reconcile with northern states willing to adopt the same strategy. He claimed that his plan would boost the electoral chances of Peace Democrats in the North, thereby ending the war with southern independence intact. But Holden would accept reunion if that alone could restore peace—and if slavery survived. Vance disavowed Holden as a traitor who undercut the southern war effort and might provoke civil war within the Confederacy. In September 1863, Confederate troops vandalized Holden's newspaper office. Striking back, Holden challenged Vance in the gubernatorial race of 1864.[6]

Insisting that reunion would doom slavery and impose Black equality, Vance charged that Holden's peace plan would compel North Carolinians to join Lincoln's "negro troops in exterminating the white men, women, and children of the South." Energetic and clever, the burly Vance was a far better campaigner than Holden. Winning three-quarters of the vote, Vance affirmed that the Confederacy would hang tough, even in North Carolina, putting the burden on Union voters to follow suit.[7]

Plebiscite

Young, ambitious, and idealistic, the Archduke Maximilian had served in northern Italy as a viceroy for his older brother, the Austrian emperor Franz Josef. When radical unrest broke out in Lombardy, Franz Josef blamed his brother as too liberal and indulgent. The Austrian emperor shifted Maximilian into a more ceremonial role as an admiral. Blocked from top power in Austria, Maximilian longed to find his own empire to rule. Tall and handsome, with blue eyes, golden hair, and immense charm, he could perform an imperial role with panache. His greatest asset was his beautiful, imperious, and brilliant wife Carlota, the daughter of Europe's savviest monarch, Leopold of Belgium. Upon meeting Carlota, an American marveled at "her dazzling teeth and eloquent dimples, the light of genius beamed from her expressive eyes, and her whole face seemed luminous with intelligence." She had a stronger will and brighter mind than Maximilian, who dithered and waffled in a crisis.[8]

Ruling Mexico appealed to Maximilian's sense of tradition, for his Habsburg family had reigned over the Spanish Empire, including Latin America, during the sixteenth and seventeenth centuries. But Maximilian also fancied himself a modern, liberal monarch whose good deeds earned love from his people. As a benevolent autocrat, Maximilian meant to bring unity and prosperity to all Mexicans. So the archduke coveted proof that he was Mexico's choice rather than a French puppet or Conservative dupe. "A sham vote would produce nothing but a phantom monarchy," he declared.[9]

Waiting for a proper plebiscite in Mexico, Maximilian spent late 1863 and early 1864 dickering with Franz Josef, Napoleon, and British leaders to seek diplomatic, military, and financial assistance for his new empire in Mexico. Maximilian hoped that broad European support would persuade the Union to accept his regime. He also worried about relying solely on the fickle and manipulative French ruler. But the British balked at entanglement in Mexico, leaving Maximilian to depend on the undependable Napoleon for troops and money.[10]

In return for keeping at least 28,000 French troops in Mexico through 1865, Napoleon dictated extortionate financial terms. Mexico would have to pay 270 million francs for the intervention so far; another 25 million in damages owed to French civilians resident in Mexico; and the controversial Jecker debt set at 75 million francs. After the summer of 1864, Mexico would pay another 1,000 francs annually per French soldier in Mexico. Such a burden would crush that country, dooming Maximilian's regime, but he naïvely agreed. A diplomat for Juárez sneered that the deal confirmed that Maximilian "is what we call a cabbage head."[11]

To hold a Mexican plebiscite sufficient to impress Maximilian, the French commander, François Achille Bazaine, needed to control more of the country. In October 1863, the French-Conservative regime held only the central corridor from Veracruz, on the Gulf Coast, through Puebla to Mexico City. Three times the size of France, Mexico defied central rule because a mountainous terrain alternated with torrid lowlands (in the south) and high deserts (to the north). Lacking railroads, people relied on mules and horses to pull wagons along wretched roads that became mud pits in winter and dustbowls in summer. A diverse and mostly poor people clung to a localism that distrusted any regime based in Mexico City—especially one dominated by foreigners. Mexico's terrain favored guerrillas who relied on peasant support for provisions and on looting their foes for money and arms.[12]

The French organized *contra-guerrillas*, who committed atrocities meant to intimidate Mexicans. The *contra-guerrillas* executed their prisoners and seized village leaders as hostages for shooting if their neighbors did not deliver supplies. A *contra* noted, "Anyone suspected of having had relations with the enemy was put to death by us; the guerrillas did the same thing on their side, so that the poor devils who lived there had only one prospect in life: the noose."[13]

The ruthless Colonel Charles Du Pin commanded the *contra-guerrillas*. Adopting flamboyant Mexican garb, Du Pin resembled a murderous Santa Claus, with a long, white beard; wide, embroidered sombrero; red and black coat festooned with medals; white pants; yellow riding boots; and sword and pistols. A mix of Mexicans, French, and Americans, his *contra-guerrillas* received higher pay and lower discipline. They revered Du Pin as a fellow rogue who encouraged their brutality. He declared, "Every Mexican is a guerrilla, or has been one, or will be one. By shooting those in our custody, there is no risk of making a mistake."[14]

In early 1864, while Du Pin terrorized the countryside along the coast, Bazaine pushed northward to seize the major cities of populous north-central Mexico: Queretaro, Guanajuato, Guadalajara, and San Luis Potosí. With smaller forces of ill-trained and poorly armed men, the Liberal generals withdrew from the main roads into the hills, waiting for chances to pounce on French outposts, patrols, and supply wagons. In the exception that proved the rule, a Liberal army led by José López Uraga attacked an *Imperialista* (Conservative) army led by Leonardo Márquez but suffered a rout in mid-December at Morelia. Several Liberal generals died in combat, including the former president, Ignacio Comonfort. Others, including Uraga, lost faith and defected to join the *Imperialistas*.[15]

Routed from San Luis Potosí, Juárez fled northward onto treacherous turf: the domain of the *caudillo* Santiago Vidaurri, who ruled the northeastern states of Coahuila, Nuevo León, and Tamaulipas. Vidaurri profited from the expanding cotton trade with Confederates across the nearby border in Texas. Wagons carried cotton to the Mexican port of Matamoros, which became a booming and teeming "city of strange denizens" (as one Texan said) paying exorbitant rents for shacks to do business worth millions of dollars. After losing Veracruz and Mexico City to the French, Juárez needed to tap the robust revenue of the cross-border trade.[16]

Clinging to his autonomy, Vidaurri paid only lip service to the Liberal government, resisting Juárez's effort to claim Monterrey as his new capital. In August 1864, with *Imperialista* help, Vidaurri defeated Juárez, who fled northward across a desert to find a haven in the distant state of Chihuahua. Accompanied by a few true believers, the refugee president relied on his dignity and stoic sense of duty to keep alive the Liberal cause. The U.S. consul in Chihuahua reported, "The situation is very bad and would bring despair upon any mind less faithful and hopeful than President Juárez." With his regular army scattered, the republican cause depended primarily on guerrillas in the countryside.[17]

By securing the cities in central and eastern Mexico, Bazaine could arrange a sort of plebiscite, but it took the form of French troops collecting signatures to petitions inviting Maximilian to become Mexico's emperor. This method excluded the illiterate majority, primarily Indians. Claiming to have secured the consent from all "the reasonable people of Mexico," Bazaine rationalized, "the Indian masses have never been sincerely consulted by any party, and the pretext is simple, they are regarded as creatures without reason." To include them, "one would have to change the whole social organization of the country." A French general claimed that most Mexicans "would have acclaimed the devil or the Grand Turk, if we had presented their candidature at the end of our swords and bayonets."[18]

Conservatives claimed to have secured for Maximilian an implausible 6.5 million votes in a nation of 8 million. They did so by counting all the people of a state as committed by petitions subscribed by a few local notables in towns with French garrisons. The farce did not impress Charles Wyke, a former British ambassador to Mexico: "The poor archduke will now be told that the majority of the population has declared in his favor, and thus be induced to go out to a country where his presence will only have the effect of prolonging a civil war with all its attendant horrors."[19]

Empire

In the spring of 1864, Maximilian and Carlota prepared to sail for Mexico over the protests of her grandmother, the former French queen Marie Amelie. When they ignored her warnings to stay in Europe, she burst into tears and shrieked, "They will be murdered." In late May, as their ship entered Veracruz harbor, a retiring French general sailed out, headed for home. He thought: "Poor Maximilian! . . . What are you going to do in that atrocious country" where a divided people "have been tearing one another apart for more than forty years?"[20]

The imperial couple aspired to play contradictory roles. On the one hand, they became fluent in Spanish and posed as Mexican patriots embracing and defending the nation's independence and interests. Carlota assured the French empress: "We dress *a la Mexicaine*. I wear a sombrero when riding. We eat *a la Mexicaine*, we have a carriage with many mules and bells, we are always wrapped in *sarapes*. . . . In everything external and childish we conform to Mexican customs and amaze the Mexicans themselves."

On the other hand, the imperial couple sought to impose a regal style modeled on European protocols. On the voyage across the Atlantic, Maximilian wrote a 600-page compendium to define proper costumes, manners, and ceremonies for servants and courtiers. He mandated a palace guard of men at least six feet, six inches tall, all wearing silver braid and silver helmets topped with an imperial eagle. At great expense, Maximilian rebuilt a summer palace on the heights of Chapultepec, which offered stunning views of Mexico City, lakes, and two volcanoes. Believing in the triumph of style over substance, Carlota declared, "It is not reform that changes men, it is the way it is done."[21]

The couple spent lavishly on palaces, court, and travels despite a staggering national deficit. The regime's annual expenses of 48 million pesos nearly tripled the 17 million in revenues. Liberal governments had practiced far greater economy on annual budgets of 15 million pesos. Before the invasion, Juárez had received a salary of $30,000 (converted into American dollars of that time), with another $41,000 for expenses, while Maximilian and Carlota spent $1,900,000 in one year to display and consume the glories of monarchy. Liberal presidents made do with two carriages, while Maximilian acquired thirty-three. In 1865, Maximilian served 700 bottles of wine per month. The imperial parties were glorious—while they lasted.[22]

At first, the royal act worked because it was novel and entertaining. Carlota and Maximilian hosted balls, receptions, parades, operas, and plays, attracting curious throngs intrigued by the razzle-dazzle of royalty. By sparing no expense, emperor and empress meant to please and be pleased. Initially, many in the capital city's elite thought that an imperial style could bring a new start to Mexico, rescuing the nation from conflict and poverty. One Mexican recalled his first sight of Maximilian, "His long, golden beard, parted in the center, gave him such an aspect of majesty that it was impossible to see him without immediately being attracted and fascinated." Maximilian projected sunny optimism: "The present is gloomy, but the future will be splendid." But sometimes the sound of gunfire spoiled the festive mood as guerrillas raided a nearby suburb.[23]

Close observers recognized that Maximilian lacked substance behind his glitter and optimism. Noting that the emperor spoke "with much cleverness and great fluency but. . . . little to the purpose," a British diplomat concluded. "All his arguments were based either on his hopes or on his good intentions." A French journalist reported, "Promises multiplied without being kept and project followed project without a chance of realization."[24]

Although Maximilian respected and loved Carlota, it was the love of a brother, for they rarely slept together. For nocturnal company, he preferred a shifting cast of young ladies of the court. Maximilian said that Carlota never came into his private quarters "unless I send for her. She knows my weak point and adapts herself to it, and harmony has never been disturbed."[25]

Dedicated to *noblesse oblige*, Maximilian sought to help Mexico's Native peoples, so long exploited by landlords and previous regimes: "The more I study Mexico, the more I am convinced that the regeneration of the country must be based on the Indians, who make up the vast majority of the population." He meant to "lift up this fascinating and easily governable race" by providing public education and liberating them from debt peonage. Natives preferred Maximilian's program over the Liberal drive to dissolve traditional communities and force them to compete as individuals in a market society. Maximilian also celebrated Mexico's indigenous history by collecting, preserving, and displaying Aztec antiquities. In his travels around Mexico, the emperor attracted adoring throngs of Indian peoples. Carlota, however, thought that her husband went too far when he took a seventeen-year-old Native girl as his favorite mistress.[26]

Maximilian hoped to rise above party, uniting Liberals with Conservatives to end the civil war. While the Liberal *Puros* held back, he had some success recruiting moderates. To attract them, the emperor appointed a moderate, José Fernando Ramírez, as his foreign minister and, in July 1864, freed all political prisoners. Maximilian also sidelined two especially brutal Conservative commanders, Leonardo Márquez and Miguel Miramón, sending them away to Europe as diplomats.[27]

Bazaine's victories and Maximilian's concessions persuaded many moderate Liberals to forsake Juárez as a lost cause. They also felt enticed by Maximilian's vision of a technocratic government freed, at last, from violent partisanship. Perhaps a stable monarchy could kick-start economic development, spearheaded by railroad construction. Moderates liked that the emperor spent lavishly on streetlights, parks, monuments, and tree-lined boulevards to make over Mexico City in the Parisian style that asserted modernity. They also warmed to his efforts to rationalize and centralize the bureaucracy, where functionaries had to show up for work, follow rules, and obey superiors. But the reforms proved fleeting and rarely stretched beyond the capital.[28]

Above all, the emperor conciliated moderates by upholding the Liberals' confiscation of church lands. Given that thousands of people had procured ecclesiastical properties, taking them back would have disrupted the economy and produced massive resistance. Instead, Maximilian sought to make the Catholic Church a branch of the government. Priests and bishops would receive salaries, but would have to cede their other revenues to the empire. As servants of the government, the church would lose autonomy and power.[29]

Conservatives, especially bishops, despised Maximilian's outreach to moderates. Denouncing the emperor's religious policies as "Juarism without Juárez," bishops championed Catholic supremacy as essential to restoring order in an anarchic society. In December 1864, a papal emissary (known as a "nuncio"), Monsignor Pietro Francesco Meglia, arrived to demand that Maximilian nullify Juárez's Reform Laws and restore ecclesiastical properties and power. "As a perfect, independent, and sovereign society" ruled only by the Pope, the church would monopolize education and suppress other religious groups. Disgusted, Carlota wanted "to throw the papal nuncio out of the window" and described her meeting with him as hell, "for hell is no more nor less than a blind alley with no way out." Maximilian concluded that Catholic bishops "have honey in their mouth and ice in their hearts." In late December and early January, the emperor issued decrees mandating religious freedom and reaffirming the former confiscation of church property.[30]

Thereafter, a cold war persisted between the imperial regime and

Catholic leaders who had summoned that government into being. In scandalous leaflets, bishops derided the emperor as a philanderer whose syphilis prevented Carlota from bearing children, rendering her a bitter harridan. The imperial couple believed that a conniving Mexican clergy kept the masses in ignorance, the better to dominate them. A French official worried, "The clerical party is furious. On whom is the Emperor now going to lean?"[31]

In his greatest delusion, Maximilian thought that he could convert Juárez. The emperor invited the president to give up the fight and return to Mexico City to serve as prime minister in a government of national reconciliation. Astonished by the proposal, Juárez politely but firmly refused to sacrifice his principles. Despite defeats and retreats, Juárez remained defiant: "Above all is the independence and dignity of our country" which would never accept Maximilian's interference "in our affairs with his bayonets."[32]

Neutrality

Preoccupied with fighting its own rebellion, the Union could not block the advent of Maximilian's empire in Mexico. Biding his time, Lincoln bit his tongue: "My policy is, attend to only one trouble at a time. If we get well out of our present difficulties and restore the Union, I propose to notify Louis Napoleon that it is about time to take his army out of Mexico. When that army is gone, the Mexican people will take care of Maximilian." The chair of the Senate's foreign affairs committee, Charles Sumner, agreed: "Let the Rebellion be overcome, and this whole continent will fall naturally, peacefully, and tranquilly under the irresistible influence of American institutions." Seward assured the French that Americans would "practice in regard to Mexico . . . the non-intervention which they require all foreign powers to observe in regard to the United States."[33]

To preserve the Union's neutrality in Mexico, Napoleon and Maximilian rejected Confederate bids for an alliance. Reneging on promises to southern diplomats, Napoleon's government seized warships purchased by the Confederacy. Previously Maximilian had spoken of his empire and the Confederacy as a common cause, but in early 1864 he refused to meet with southern emissaries—from a naïve hope that the Union would recognize his regime. Seward toyed with that hope to string France and imperial Mexico along, keeping both sidelined in the American Civil War.[34]

Juárez's minister to Washington, Matías Romero, resented the Union's neutrality as a threat to his country, which desperately needed arms and reinforcements. To pressure the Lincoln administration, Romero worked to sway public opinion in favor of the *Juaristas* as engaged in a kindred struggle for republican independence. He planted favorable stories in newspapers and cultivated leading businessmen, congressmen, and journalists with lavish receptions and dinners. But he had to struggle against American prejudices that most Mexicans were too violent, poor, indolent, ignorant, racially mixed, and Catholic for a proper republic. An American consul at Matamoros considered them "no more capable of self-government than the animals."[35]

By procuring American arms to smuggle across the border into northern Mexico, Romero played cat and mouse with French consuls out to detect and intercept covert shipments of munitions that violated American neutrality laws. In San Francisco in 1864, a French consul concluded, "In this country everything has its price," so he could only stop arms shipments "by means of 'gratifications' at the right moment to certain officials, and especially the chief of police," who wanted more than "pretty words." Mexicans had no monopoly on corruption—contrary to American stereotypes.[36]

Blaming Seward for the neutrality policy, Romero cultivated Congress's Radical Republicans, who also disliked the secretary of state as a temporizer with too much influence over Lincoln. They shared the *Juarista* insistence that the Mexican and American civil wars were linked in a global struggle between republican liberalism and reactionary monarchy. A leading radical, Thaddeus Stevens, warned that if the Confederacy and Maximilian won, "The Old World would shape our institutions, regulate our commerce, and . . . finally dictate the rulers who should sit upon our thrones." Stevens concluded, "The approaching fate of Mexico should be our warning."[37]

In early 1864, the Radical chair of the House Committee on Foreign Affairs, Henry Winter Davis of Maryland, introduced a resolution denouncing "any monarchical Government erected on the ruins of any republican Government in [North and South] America under the auspices of any European Power." Romero assured congressmen that the resolution would rally Mexicans behind Juárez and Frenchmen against Napoleon. Passed unanimously by the House on April 4, 1864, the resolution embarrassed Seward, who resented congressional interference with his diplomacy.[38]

Coalition

The Canadian union also seemed imperiled as politicians struggled to form a government sufficiently broad and confident to address the tensions between Francophone (and Catholic) Canada East and Anglophone (and Protestant) Canada West. In early 1864, John Sandfield Macdonald led an administration formed of fellow mediocrities drawn by patronage away from the three main parties: the Conservative-Liberals of John A. Macdonald, the Reformers of George Brown, and the French-Canadian *bleus* of George-Etienne Cartier. The unstable government seemed doomed to collapse, leading to a general election, which John A. Macdonald predicted would be a "war to the knife."[39]

In the spring, when the John Sandfield Macdonald government did dissolve, Brown emerged in the surprising role of a peacemaker. He had long pushed for a more representative Parliament that would empower the larger population of Canada West to dominate the Canadian Union at the expense of Francophones. Frustrated in that ambition, Brown tried a new tack in 1864. He proposed dissolving Canada's union in favor of a looser confederation, in which each half would enjoy greater autonomy for conducting domestic policy, including control over education and family law. The unitary parliament would persist to preserve free trade, good relations, and mutual security between the two Canadas. Brown's new plan appealed to Cartier of the *bleus*, who wanted to spare Canada East from meddling by Brown and his Protestant ilk of Canada West.[40]

John A. Macdonald preferred a stronger and more centralized Canadian union on the British model, but he could live with a federation if it expanded by taking in the Maritime provinces to the east and the Pacific colonies of Vancouver and British Columbia to the far west. Macdonald thought that a bigger confederation would improve the security of every province against the threat of an American invasion. He warned, "We were liable, in case England and the United States were pleased to differ, to be cut off, one by one."[41]

British leaders favored such a transcontinental confederation so that they could reduce their troops posted in Canada. Those leaders wanted to prepare for a potential war in Europe provoked by the rising power of Prussia or persistent tensions with Russia. Britain's rulers also disliked the costs and difficulties of defending distant Canada when Canadians spent so little for their own protection. A British leader, William Gladstone, declared, "Canada is England's weakness, till the last British soldier is brought away & Canada left on her own."[42]

Brown agreed to work for a transcontinental federation, but he doubted that the fractious leaders of diverse colonies could pull that off. In case of failure, he demanded, and Macdonald accepted, the fallback goal of federating just Canada East and West. On June 21, Brown, Cartier, and Macdonald announced their grand coalition committed to transforming Canada's constitution. By combining, the three leaders sought, Brown explained, "the power of settling the sectional troubles of Canada forever." The coalition enabled the three governing parties to postpone a general election that none wanted. Brown exulted at the "unanimity of sentiment" as "without example in this wooded country."[43]

The new political partners wanted to crash a party planned by Maritime provincial leaders, who would gather in Charlottetown, on Prince Edward Island, in September. The Maritimers meant to discuss forming their own regional union. Fortunately for the Canadians, many Maritimers might prefer a larger country over a smaller union dominated by Nova Scotia, whose capital was Halifax. A New Brunswick politician noted that Maritimers "hate each other, and they all unite in hating Halifax."[44]

On August 29, seven Canadian leaders, including Brown, Cartier, Macdonald, and Thomas D'Arcy McGee, boarded a steamer at Quebec bound down the St. Lawrence and into the Gulf to reach Charlottetown on September 1. Macdonald assured his peers, "Everything, gentlemen, is to be gained by union, and everything to be lost by disunion. . . . If we allow so favourable an opportunity to pass, it may never come again." Fueled by plenty of festivity at the meeting, the Maritimers agreed to join a Canadian confederation.[45]

To hash out the details, the leaders reconvened at Quebec City in October. In just two weeks, Canadians and Maritimers defined a new constitution meant to unite them (although the Prince Edward Islanders dropped out). The new Canadian parliament would have two houses, with an elected lower house representing population, thereby increasing the clout of Canada West. Appointed by the Crown, the upper house would offer equality to all three charter regions, Canada East, Canada West, and the Maritimes. Macdonald crafted most of the constitution by day, while he drank and cavorted at night. Delegates found a drunken Macdonald "in his night shirt with a railway rug thrown over him, practicing Hamlet before a looking-glass."[46]

In early 1865, the Canadian parliament debated the plan drafted at Quebec. Most of the opposition came from French Canadian *rouges*, who charged that an enlarged confederation would threaten their culture. One declared, "The [Canadian] union having failed to produce assimilation, they have turned to a more powerful, more terrible instrument: federation." To weaken opposition, Macdonald demanded a vote on confederation as a package—precluding debates on, and amendments to, particular clauses.[47]

Macdonald also persuaded a majority that they need not submit confederation to any popular referendum. Brown shared that aversion to "the risk of allowing political partisanship to dash the fruit from our hands." By avoiding a referendum, McGee claimed that Canadians would "resist the spread of this universal democracy doctrine" generated by Americans. As in forming the parliamentary coalition in June 1864, the scheme advanced by avoiding an election. On March 11, 1865, the Canadian parliament approved confederation by 99 to 33. But there were still miles to go, for many Maritimers had developed cold feet—and the deal needed final approval by the British Parliament. Plus no

one had consulted the colonists on the Pacific coast to draw them into
the confederation.[48]

Crater

Lincoln knew that his reelection hinged on the fortunes of Union
armies, especially that commanded by Ulysses S. Grant. To maximize
the impact of superior Union manpower, weapons, and supplies, Grant
sought to coordinate simultaneous invasions across the entire Confederacy. Universal pressure would prevent Confederates from exploiting
their interior lines to shift forces to different fronts as they had done in
1863 to win at Chickamauga. In Virginia in 1864, Grant accompanied
and supervised General George G. Meade's Army of the Potomac to
attack Lee's army defending Richmond. In the other main offensive,
Sherman was to strike south from Chattanooga to take Atlanta, a strategic railroad hub and industrial center. By devastating the southern heartland and crippling railways, Sherman would weaken logistical support
for Lee's army. Other Union forces targeted the Shenandoah Valley of
Virginia and Mobile Bay, Alabama, while Grant counted on Benjamin
Butler to drive up the James River to threaten Richmond.[49]

Taking charge of the Army of the Potomac, Grant found many officers spooked by their many defeats by Lee's army. "Oh, I am heartily
tired of hearing about what Lee is going to do," Grant vented. "Some of
you always seem to think he is suddenly going to turn a double somersault and land in our rear and on both flanks at the same time. Go back
to your command and try to think what we are going to do ourselves,
instead of what Lee is going to do." Eastern officers thought that Grant
had never fought a general as formidable as Lee.[50]

In early May in northern Virginia, Grant's 120,000 men crossed the
Rapidan River to attack Lee's 64,000. But the terrain, known as "the
Wilderness," favored defenders as the attackers became confused in the
din and smoke of battle in dense woods. Blazing shells set trees on fire,
burning wounded men to death. Although he had lost 17,500 casualties
to Lee's 11,000, Grant refused to retreat, surprising his own troops. A
friend to Grant before the war, General James Longstreet warned his

fellow Confederates, "That man will fight us every day and every hour till the end of the war."[51]

Pushing his army farther south and east, Grant tried to get between Lee's army and Richmond, as that would force a battle on Union terms. To disrupt Lee's railroad supply line, Grant sent 10,000 cavalrymen commanded by Philip H. Sheridan, an able and feisty general. Then thirty-three years old, Sheridan was not much to look at. Just five feet, five inches tall, Sheridan struck Lincoln as a "chunky little chap, with a long body, short legs, not enough neck to hang him, and such long arms that, if his ankles itch, he can scratch them without stooping." Plus, his head seemed too big and bumpy, but Sheridan had piercing eyes and a forceful charisma that galvanized troops. A subordinate likened Sheridan's leadership to "an electric shock . . . whose personal appearance in the field was an immediate and positive stimulus to battle." Armed with new rapid-fire carbines, Sheridan's troops defeated the outnumbered Confederate cavalry at Yellow Tavern on May 11, felling their dashing commander, Jeb Stuart.[52]

But Lee intercepted Grant's advance at Spotsylvania Courthouse, where the Confederates fought from behind earth-and-log barricades. By the start of 1864, both armies had learned to erect hasty but effective trenches and barriers that made attacks almost suicidal. On May 10, a Union attack breached the Confederate line at an exposed salient, but Lee's men rallied, sealing off the gap. On May 12, an even larger Union thrust again seemed to break through in vicious hand-to-hand combat, but a Confederate counterattack drove back the Yankees. After the battle, a witness found "horses and men chopped into hash by the bullets" and appearing "like piles of jelly."[53]

Northerners mourned the soaring human costs: 36,000 Union casualties in a single week of massive battles. Still Grant pressed on, vowing "to fight it out on this line if it takes all summer." He waged a war of grinding attrition, for the North could generate more reinforcements than the South. But the almost continuous fighting and marching wore on Grant's troops. "Many a man has gone crazy since this campaign began from the terrible pressure on mind & body," lamented Captain Oliver Wendell Holmes, Jr.[54]

In late May, Grant again pushed his army farther south and east, in a bid to outflank Lee. But the Confederates moved faster, for they had a shorter route. At Cold Harbor, Lee blocked Grant's advance by erecting a thicket of trenches and barricades. Underestimating those defenses, Grant ordered a frontal assault that slaughtered his men on June 3. "It was not war, it was murder," a Confederate general stated. In less than an hour, Grant lost 7,000 men to just 1,500 for the sheltered rebels. Too late, Grant saw and mourned his mistake. General Meade wrote to his wife, "I think Grant has had his eyes opened, and is willing to admit now that Virginia and Lee's army is not Tennessee and Bragg's army."[55]

Still Grant kept pushing, this time bypassing Richmond and crossing the James River to strike at Petersburg, a critical rail hub twenty-three miles south of the Confederate capital. At last, Grant confused Lee, enabling 15,000 Union troops to reach Petersburg on June 15, when only 2,000 Confederates defended the city. But the Union soldiers balked because, after Cold Harbor, they felt "a great horror and dread of attacking earthworks again," an officer explained. The opportunity passed, enabling Lee to arrive with his army to reinforce Petersburg. Grant settled in for a siege, while Lee hunkered down within his trenches, unable to move without sacrificing Richmond to the enemy. "Where are we to get sufficient troops to oppose Grant? . . . His talent & strategy consists in accumulating overwhelming numbers," Lee wrote.[56]

The human cost threatened to turn time against the Union. In seven weeks of intense combat, Grant had suffered 65,000 casualties, about half of his original army, so that he had to rely on many new recruits for his Petersburg siege. In those seven weeks, the Army of the Potomac lost as many men as it had in the preceding year of the war. A Union general, Gouverneur K. Warren, mourned, "For thirty days it has been one funeral procession past me, and it has been too much." It also had become too much for the northern public. A general on sick leave found "great discouragement over the North, great reluctance to recruiting, strong disposition for peace." By denouncing Grant as a "butcher," Democrats scored points with war-weary voters.[57]

To break the stalemate, Grant sought to blow a hole through the

Confederate line. Coal miners from a Pennsylvania regiment dug a 500-foot tunnel under the Confederate trenches and packed the end with four tons of gunpowder. On July 30, the blast blew a crater 170 feet long, 80 feet wide, and 30 feet deep, destroying a South Carolina regiment and artillery battery. Union infantry charged into the opening, but Grant entrusted that assault to General Ambrose Burnside, who had botched most of his previous assignments in the war; the crater was no exception. Rather than shift around the hole, Union troops plunged into the crater, where they were sitting ducks for the Confederate counterattack.[58]

With a special zeal, Confederates slaughtered the Black troops that they found in the crater. An Alabama general boasted that his men "literally mowed down the enemy, piling up Yankees and Negroes on each other." Another Confederate described the victory as "the jubilee of fiends in human shape and without souls." By the end of the day, the Union had suffered 3,800 casualties, twice those of the enemy. "It was the saddest affair I have witnessed in the war," Grant lamented. More lives and time had been lost, blighting Lincoln's chances for reelection.[59]

Grant counted on another Union army, led by General David Hunter, to devastate the Shenandoah Valley, a prime source of produce and livestock for Lee's army. In June, Hunter's 18,000 men took over the valley, looting and burning farms, towns, and railroads while liberating hundreds of slaves. A Union soldier declared himself as "happy as a big sunflower." To reclaim the valley, Lee sent 14,000 men under Jubal Early, a fiery, disheveled, and hard-drinking general eager to kill Yankees. Low on ammunition and courage, Hunter fled westward through the mountains into West Virginia.[60]

By abandoning the valley, Hunter violated Grant's orders to keep constant pressure on the Confederates. Indeed, the runaway general opened an invasion route for Early to advance northeastward down the valley into Maryland. Crossing the Potomac River on July 6, Early's army threatened Washington, provoking panic there. With just 14,000 men, Early had turned the tables on the Yankees. Instead of taking Richmond, they might lose their own capital, which lacked enough defenders

because Grant had withdrawn almost all the garrison for his siege at
Petersburg. Scrambling to meet the threat, Grant sent soldiers rushing
back to Washington just in time to dissuade Early from attacking.[61]

Withdrawing on July 12, Early took revenge on Maryland and Pennsylvania towns for the destruction wrought by Union forces in Virginia. He sent two cavalry brigades commanded by John McCausland
into Pennsylvania to demand $500,000 from Chambersburg. When the
inhabitants refused to pay, Early's men burned 278 homes and another
271 barns and stables. The people heard "the screams and sounds of
agony of burning animals, hogs, and cows and horses."[62]

In an election that swung on the fortunes of war, Early boosted
the Democrats, who blamed the Lincoln administration for provoking
Confederates with brutality and for incompetence in defending Pennsylvania. Gideon Welles, the secretary of the navy, concluded, "The
waste of war is terrible, the waste from imbecility and mismanagement
is more terrible. . . . It is impossible for the country to bear up under
these monstrous errors and wrongs." In July, Lincoln's call to conscript
another 500,000 men compounded his unpopularity in a weary nation.
Dubbing conscription the "Lottery of Death," a Democratic newspaper
editor declared, "Lincoln is deader than dead" in his electoral prospects.
On August 23, Lincoln sent a memorandum to prepare his cabinet for
his almost certain defeat in the approaching election.[63]

Atlanta

During the spring and summer of 1864, Sherman also struggled in
his offensive against Atlanta, for he faced a wary and wily adversary,
Joseph E. Johnston. With only 65,000 men to oppose Sherman's 98,000
men, Johnston avoided risky attacks, instead entrenching at key passes
and fords to block the Union advance. Feinting at Johnston's strong
positions, Sherman sent his favorite subordinate, James B. McPherson,
with 25,000 men to outflank the Confederates and threaten their supply
line. Johnston would then fall back to find another place to fortify in
Sherman's path.[64]

On June 27, Sherman lost patience with the war of maneuver, order-

ing a direct assault at Kennesaw Mountain, Johnston's latest stronghold. But that ill-conceived attack lost 3,000 men (to 600 Confederate
casualties) and failed to budge Johnston's line in searing summer heat
and humidity. After the battle, a Confederate recalled, "I never saw so
many broken down and exhausted men in my life." He was "wet with
blood and sweat . . . and many of our men were vomiting with excessive
fatigue, over exhaustion, and sunstroke, our tongues were parched and
cracked for water, and our faces blackened with powder and smoke."
Reverting to a flank movement on July 2, Sherman sent McPherson's
army southwestward, compelling Johnston to fall back to the Chattahoochee River near Atlanta.[65]

Maneuvers took time, which Johnston thought favored the Confederacy, running out the clock for the fall election in the North. But as
Johnston gave ground, Yankee troops swarmed over Georgian farms
to loot and burn. A Yankee general said his men left north Georgia "as
though all the locusts of Egypt had been upon it." The invasion also
disrupted slavery, as enslaved people ran away to help their liberators. To
halt that destruction and disruption, Jefferson Davis wanted Johnston to
attack Sherman and drive back his army. Davis relied on an informant
among Johnston's subordinates: General John Bell Hood, a Texan whose
reckless courage had crippled his left arm at Gettysburg and cost him a
right leg at Chickamauga. His attacks also got a lot of his men killed,
but Davis thought that Hood was just the sort of aggressor needed to
crush the Yankees.[66]

Fearing that Johnston would abandon Atlanta without a fight, Davis
sacked him on July 17 and appointed Hood to that command. Davis
ignored Lee's warning that Hood was too reckless and pigheaded to lead
an army: "All lion, none of the fox." Sherman welcomed the change
in command as a godsend, while many Confederate congressmen felt
outraged at the displacement of their favorite, Johnston. The change
rattled Confederate soldiers, who cherished Johnston for improving
their food, clothing, and morale—while avoiding the heavy casualties
of rash attacks.[67]

During eight days in late July, Hood launched three attacks, all fail-
ures that cost 15,000 Confederate casualties compared to 6,000 for the

Union. With dwindling manpower, the Confederacy could not afford to squander so many lives. Hood's soldiers did kill Sherman's favorite subordinate, McPherson, shot down when he mistakenly rode into Confederate lines on July 22.[68]

After driving Hood back into Atlanta, Sherman slowly extended his forces to cut off railroads that supplied the city, but his progress seemed far too slow for impatient Yankees. With Grant stymied at Petersburg and Jubal Early threatening the national capital, northern morale reached a low ebb in August. Desertion and draft-dodging soared, depleting the Union force needed to win the war. Civilians balked at their higher taxes and wanted their boys to come home. A leading Republican operative, Thurlow Weed, concluded that Lincoln's reelection was "an impossibility. . . . The people are wild for peace."[69]

Parties

Democrats expected to win the fall election, but the party was divided between War Democrats, who supported fighting for reunion, and Peace Democrats opposed to any further loss of life. Casting Lincoln as a bloodthirsty tyrant and "widow maker," some Peace Democrats longed, as one put it, "that some bold hand will pierce his heart with a dagger point for the public good." The two Democratic factions united in denouncing emancipation as an obstacle to either winning the war or making peace.[70]

In August, the Democrats held their national convention in Chicago. To split their differences, they adopted a peace platform primarily written by Clement Vallandigham, but they nominated a War Democrat, General George B. McClellan, for the presidency. The platform denounced the war as a bloody failure and indulged in the fantasy that Democrats could reunite the nation with an armistice followed by peace negotiations conducted by a convention of delegates from the states.[71]

McClellan opposed the platform's proposed armistice with the Confederates lest that lead to southern independence. McClellan also refused to label the war a failure: "I could not look in the face[s] of my gallant comrades of the army and navy, who have survived so many bloody battles, and tell them that their labor and the sacrifice of our slain and wounded brethren had been in vain." Regarding Blacks as inferior, McClellan did favor abandoning emancipation: "The Union is the one condition of peace. We ask no more."[72]

Republicans had their own divisions, for radicals disliked Lincoln, considering him too weak in running the war and too soft toward the South in his plan for reconstruction. In December 1863 Lincoln had proposed to hasten southern reincorporation within the Union. Once 10 percent of the white voters took an oath of allegiance to the Union and accepted emancipation, a state could apply for readmission. Those who took the oath received a full pardon including a restoration of property taken from them—save for slaves and any lands already sold. Lincoln's plan denied pardons only to the top leaders of the Confederacy. As a further enticement to white southerners, Lincoln's plan promised that restored states could regulate the "laboring, landless, and homeless class" of Blacks. A leading radical, Wendell Phillips, charged that Lincoln's policy "makes the freedom of the negro a sham and perpetuates slavery under a softer name." In July 1864 Lincoln further angered radicals by vetoing Congress's stricter "Wade-Davis plan," which would have delayed a southern state's readmission until half of its white men had sworn allegiance to the Union.[73]

In early 1864, the hyperambitious secretary of the treasury, Salmon P. Chase, sought radical support to bid for the presidency. But Chase's egotism rankled many of his fellow radicals. Benjamin Wade concluded, "Chase is a good man, but his theology is unsound. He thinks there is a fourth person in the Trinity." Lacking support even in his home state of Ohio, Chase withdrew his candidacy. As a reward, in the fall Lincoln nominated Chase to replace Taney, who had recently died, as Chief Justice of the Supreme Court. A Republican celebrated that "old Roger B. Taney has earned the gratitude of his country by dying at last. Better late than never."[74]

With Chase sidelined, some radicals turned to a disgruntled Union general, John C. Frémont, as their presidential candidate. But even Frémont recognized that he was no more than a spoiler who might siphon off enough Republican votes to ensure victory for McClellan.

On September 22, Frémont withdrew in favor of Lincoln, but the president had to mollify the radicals by sacking the conservative Postmaster General Montgomery Blair. A Lincoln supporter sighed that the party had to appease "the impracticables . . . the better-than-thou declaimers, the long-haired men and the short-haired women."[75]

To attract War Democrats, Lincoln's Republicans rebranded their party as the "National Union Party." To give that reinvention credibility, the president discarded his loyal vice-president, Hannibal Hamlin, in favor of a War Democrat, Andrew Johnson of Tennessee. But the party's platform was staunchly Republican, demanding an unconditional surrender by the Confederates and a constitutional amendment to abolish slavery. Emancipation and Union, one and inseparable, was the campaign credo of Lincoln's reinvented party. Republicans cast all Democrats as defeatists, at best, and traitorous "Copperheads" at worst. The *New York Times* warned voters that the Democrats would "entail upon our children a dissevered Union and ceaseless strife."[76]

Confederates hoped to disrupt the northern election by sending money and agents to rally true Copperheads for an armed uprising in the Midwest. In Canada the agents recruited Confederate prisoners-of-war who had escaped from federal camps. The agents brought sixty of these veterans in civilian attire to Chicago in August, during the Democratic convention. They expected thousands of Copperheads to help them break open a nearby prisoner-of-war camp at Camp Douglas and then seize arms from a federal arsenal to spread the revolt. But Union officials had anticipated trouble, so they sent troops to watch the city, camp, and arsenal. The frustrated agents canceled the operation.[77]

Copperheads instead made trouble in rural areas of the Midwest. Some attacked local Republicans, burning barns, homes, and mills to drive them out. In July, a traveler found in southern Illinois "among neighbors . . . a feeling of enmity, hatred & general conduct bordering almost upon insanity." In Iowa, a Republican woman worried, "We have not only an open foe to contend with, but a secret foe at home in our very midst, rebel sympathizers, peace men, traitors, copperheads . . . are daily plotting treason, to overthrow the government. O how sad it is to think of it." Republican troops returned the abuse by roughing up Copperheads and smashing their printing presses. Midwesterners felt on the edge of their own civil war during the summer and fall of 1864.[78]

Democrats hoped to win the election by dwelling on the war's casualties and frustrations—as well as the burdens of taxes, conscription, and restraints on civil liberties. Democrats also alleged that Republicans sought to dissolve racial difference through marital "miscegenation" to produce "the blending of the white and the black." A Democratic newspaper warned that in Washington, "Filthy black niggers, greasy, sweaty, and disgusting, [were] now jostling white people and even ladies everywhere, even at the President's levees."[79]

Lincoln retorted that he fought for the Union, "But no human power can subdue this rebellion without using the Emancipation lever as I have done." The Union needed thousands of Black soldiers and sailors to defeat the rebellion. Disgusted by Democratic proposals to abandon emancipation, Lincoln asked of Black troops: "Why should they give their lives for us, with full notice of our purpose to betray them?" But the president expected to lose, remarking in August, "I am going to be beaten, and unless some great change takes place *badly beaten*."[80]

Victories

Great changes did favor the Republicans in late summer, just in time to save Lincoln's bid for reelection. On August 5, Admiral David Farragut led his Union fleet of four ironclads and fourteen wooden warships into Mobile Bay, pushing through heavy fire from two powerful forts and past many mines, three gunboats, and a Confederate ironclad. Badly battered by Union fire and ramming, the Confederate gunboats and ironclad capitulated. Federal troops landed to isolate and bombard the forts, which the Confederates surrendered on August 18 and 23. The Union victory shut down Mobile as a port for blockade runners.[81]

In late August, Sherman renewed cutting the roads and railroads that sustained the Confederate defenders of Atlanta. On September 1, Hood evacuated the city after destroying the factories, railyard, and massive stocks of munitions that the Confederacy so desperately needed. News of the victory ignited wild celebrations in the North. Confederates felt depressed both by the loss of Atlanta and by Yankee exultation. In Georgia, a newspaper lamented, "The fickle and besotted multitude but recently clamoring for peace, now elated by a single success after a multitude of defeats, is shouting with mad enthusiasm for the subjugation of the South." In Richmond, Mary Chesnut wrote in her diary, "We are going to be wiped off the earth."[82]

Confederates got more grim news from the Shenandoah Valley, where Grant sent the able and aggressive Philip Sheridan to command 43,000 men, including 8,000 cavalrymen. On September 19, Sheridan's troops overwhelmed Jubal Early's 15,000 men at Winchester. Early fell back twenty miles to a strong defensive position on Fisher's Hill, but Sheridan attacked and won again on September 22.[83]

Fleeing fifty more miles southward, Early exposed the valley's farms to destruction by advancing Yankee troops following Grant's orders to turn the Valley into "a barren waste." Sheridan later explained, "The people must be left [with] nothing but their eyes to weep with over the war." In two weeks, his troops destroyed seventy-one flour mills, thirteen other mills and manufactories, 947 miles of railroad, and 2,000 barns containing 20,000 tons of hay. They also killed 3,000 sheep and 4,000 cattle, dead animals that attracted great flocks of buzzards. "We could always tell when the Yankees were coming by the birds rising high up and sailing around," a Confederate recalled. A soldier from Vermont claimed that the devastation was "teaching the people to have some respect for Yankee power." But a Confederate blamed the "smoky trail of desolation" on "the government of Satan and Lincoln." Confederates executed Union foragers when caught, and the Yankees did the same to guerrillas.[84]

In mid-October, Sheridan left his army to visit the capital for a strategy conference with the secretary of war. Exploiting his absence, Early hurried north to hit the Union force encamped at Cedar Creek. Surprised at dawn on October 19, the Yankees panicked and fled. Prematurely gloating, Early relaxed his guard, calling off pursuit to indulge his men in looting the Union camp and dead. But that afternoon Sheridan

returned to rally his men in a dramatic ride to the front line. His counterattack dissolved Early's army into a "routed, disorganized rabble" of
fleeing men, terminating Early's ability to resist Sheridan in the valley.[85]

Far to the west, Sterling Price led 12,000 Confederate cavalry northward from Arkansas to invade Missouri, in hopes of recovering the
state and affecting the Union's national election. On September 27,
Price attacked Pilot Knob, a strongly fortified supply base seventy-five
miles south of St. Louis. After suffering heavy losses, Price gave up
his advance on St. Louis, instead swinging westward along the Missouri River to destroy railroads, bridges, and small Union outposts.
Price assembled a train of 500 wagons laden with loot, stretching for
eight miles and slowing his progress. Drinking heavily, he lost control
over his men, who looted far and wide and renamed their commander
"Goddamn Price."[86]

In October, as Union reinforcements poured into the state, Price
faced entrapment by converging forces in western Missouri. Fleeing
southward, Price suffered heavy losses in two defeats. Deaths, captures,
and desertion reduced his force to just 3,500 men (of an original 12,000)
by November 7, when the survivors escaped beyond the Arkansas River.
A Confederate officer derided the bombastic Price for having "the roar
of a lion but the spring of a guinea pig." His failed raid had influenced
the election—but in Lincoln's favor.[87]

The ultimate Union victory came at the polls in November, when
news of military victories boosted the National Union Party. Lincoln
won 55 percent of the popular vote and carried the electoral college by a
landslide of 212 to 21. He captured every state save Kentucky, Delaware,
and New Jersey, and only those three states elected Democratic governors and state legislatures. Gaining thirty-seven congressional seats,
Republicans would dominate both the House (149 to 42) and Senate (42
to 10). By voting 78 percent for Lincoln, Union soldiers helped turn his
victory into a rout. The percentage ran high because many Democrats
in the ranks declined to vote in disgust at the Vallandigham platform.
Regarding a military victory as within reach, most soldiers preferred to
fight on rather than risk an armistice that would let the Confederacy and

slavery survive. Addressing a crowd outside the White House, Lincoln celebrated "that a people's government can sustain a national election in the midst of a great civil war. Until now it has not been known to the world that this was a possibility."[88]

Republicans in Congress celebrated by pushing a Thirteenth Amendment to the Federal Constitution, banning slavery throughout the country, including the Border States exempted from the Emancipation Proclamation. Unless it was written into the constitution, Lincoln feared that his emancipation policy might not survive a court challenge or the twists of politics after the war ended. Most Democratic congressmen still opposed such an amendment as violating states' rights and white supremacy, while precluding southern reunion. But eleven Democrats broke ranks to vote aye. One of them, James S. Rollins, explained, "We can never have an entire peace in this country as long as the institution of slavery remains." Lincoln helped swing votes with generous helpings of patronage positions. Rollins got to appoint a federal judge back home in Missouri.[89]

On January 31, 1865, the amendment passed the House by 119 to 65, just two votes above the two-thirds threshold. The floor and gallery erupted in joy. Charles Douglass (son of Frederick) reported, "Such rejoicing I never before witnessed, cannons firing, people hugging and shaking hands, white people I mean, flags flying all over the city." But ratification still required approval by three-quarters of the states (27 of 36).[90]

Vulnerable Point

Born in Ireland, Patrick Cleburne prospered in Arkansas as a druggist and land speculator before becoming one of the Confederacy's best generals. In January 1864, as Cleburne brooded over mounting defeats, he pitched a radical proposal to his fellow generals of the Army of Tennessee. He argued for enlisting Blacks to counteract the thousands aiding Union forces. Noting their ability "to face and fight bravely against their former masters," Cleburne warned that slavery was "our most vulnerable point, a continued embarrassment," and "a source of

great strength to the enemy." He favored emancipation, for only freedom could motivate Blacks to fight for the South: "The negro has been
dreaming of freedom. It has become the paradise of his hopes." Cleburne
contradicted the Confederate insistence that slaves accepted and thrived
in their assigned lot.[91]

After Cleburne finished speaking, the other generals erupted,
denouncing his proposal as treasonous and "revolting to Southern sentiment, Southern pride, and Southern honor." That army's commanding general, Joseph E. Johnston, suppressed word of the proposal, lest
it undermine morale in the ranks. President Davis directed Cleburne
to keep quiet, for the Confederacy needed to appear united for slavery.
Despite his superior abilities, Cleburne was passed over for promotion
repeatedly after his scandalous proposal.[92]

In November 1864 Davis belatedly endorsed part of Cleburne's plan
as the only way to save the Confederacy's shrinking forces under intense
Union pressure. He urged Congress to buy 40,000 male slaves to employ
as military laborers—and perhaps serve as a reserve force in an emergency. "We are reduced to choosing whether the negroes shall fight for
us or against us," Davis sighed. He even proposed freeing those who
served well—but not the many more slaves who remained on farms and
plantations. Davis meant to emancipate only the bare minimum needed
to win a war still meant to preserve slavery.[93]

Davis's proposal ignited an angry debate in the Confederate Congress,
newspapers, state legislatures, and public meetings. Most southern leaders rejected his plan for violating the prime purpose of the Confederacy.
Henry Chambers of Mississippi declared, "The negro race was ordained
to slavery by the Almighty. Emancipation would be the destruction of
our social and political system." Howell Cobb of Georgia insisted, "If
slaves will make good soldiers our whole theory of slavery is wrong."[94]

Confederate troops threatened to desert if compelled to serve beside
Blacks. A North Carolina soldier declared, "I did not volunteer my
services to fight for a free negroes' country but to fight for a free white
man's country and I do not think I love my country well enough to
fight with black soldiers." In Virginia, a private denounced the proposal as demoralizing: "I think we have disgraced ourselves; . . . the

idea of having negroes fighting to enslave their offspring is mor[e] than redicalous."[95]

Even in early 1865, with their country on the ropes, most Confederates preferred to fight shorthanded rather than admit that slavery was wrong. Emancipating any Blacks as a reward for military service would concede that the abolitionists were right: enslaved people would fight to be free. Proslavery men alleged that Blacks could never become good soldiers, yet also insisted that arming them would lead to the massive, bloody slave revolt of whites' nightmares. Created to avert such an imagined revolt in 1861, southern independence seemed pointless without slavery.[96]

Although stymied in Congress, Davis played the emancipation card in diplomacy. In early 1865, Davis sent Duncan F. Kenner, a Louisiana sugar planter, to Europe on a special mission. Kenner could promise gradual emancipation in return for British and French recognition of southern independence. But that promise was hollow, for the Confederate constitution entrusted slavery to the states, and they were unlikely ever to emancipate. Smelling the desperation, French and British leaders rejected the Kenner proposal as far too little, far too late for the failing Confederacy.[97]

Back in Virginia, Lee tried to revive Davis's stalled plan by writing to the Confederate Congress. Going beyond the president, Lee recommended gradually emancipating all southern slaves. Despite Lee's prestige, the Congress stalled for another month. At last, in mid-March 1865, it narrowly (by three votes in the House and one in the Senate) approved a tepid version of Davis's proposal. The president could ask owners and states for permission to enlist their slaves as soldiers—and none of them could be freed without the consent of their masters. A supporter likened the measure to throwing some cargo overboard to save a ship: "If we triumph in the end, the institution will be preserved."[98]

Because few masters would cooperate, only about sixty Blacks began to drill as Confederate soldiers in Richmond and Petersburg. At night they were confined at a military prison. By day they were mocked and abused in the streets by whites. None of the Black recruits saw combat, and they were vastly outnumbered by the thousands who aided the Union.[99]

Howl

Sherman had captured Atlanta, but Hood's cavalry disrupted Sherman's railroad supply line back to Chattanooga. Weary of chasing the elusive cavalry, Sherman proposed to abandon Atlanta and forsake his supply line by marching southeastward across Georgia to the port of Savannah. He explained that by "smashing things to the sea . . . instead of being on the defensive, I would be on the offensive." His troops could feed themselves and devastate farms, plantations, and towns while discrediting the Confederacy as incapable of defending its people. "I can make the march and make Georgia howl," Sherman announced.[100]

Hood howled in an angry letter, blasting Sherman for exceeding "in studied and inglorious cruelty, all acts of war ever before . . . in the dark history of war." In a blistering reply also meant for public consumption, Sherman rebuked Hood for invoking God:

> You who in the midst of peace and prosperity have plunged the nation into dark and cruel war. . . . If we must be enemies let us be men, and fight it out, as we proposed to do, and not deal with such hypocritical appeals to God and humanity. God will judge us in due time.

Sherman meant to punish Confederates for disrupting the Union essential to keeping peace among Americans. "We are not only fighting hostile armies, but a hostile people, and must make old and young, rich and poor, feel the hard hand of war" and "make them so sick of war that generations would pass away before they would again appeal to it."[101]

Rather than oppose Sherman's advance, Hood turned his army northward, heading into Tennessee to attack the weaker Union force there. With the two armies marching in opposite directions, Sherman's 62,000 men faced only token resistance from Joseph Wheeler's 3,500 cavalry supplemented by some erratic Georgia militiamen. Advancing about a dozen miles per day, the Yankees could fan out in four columns to cover a front from 40 to 60 miles wide during a march of 285 miles from Atlanta to Savannah. A soldier boasted that they "destroyed all we could not eat, stole their niggers, burned their cotton & gins, spilled their sorghum, burned & twisted their R[ail] Roads and raised Hell generally." But they spared most homes and massacred no people, so Sherman's March fell well short of the total wars of our own grim time. Launched in mid-November, the march culminated a month later, when Sherman's troops drove Confederates out of Savannah and obtained supplies from the Union fleet.[102]

While marching to the sea, Sherman entrusted the defense of Tennessee to General George Thomas, a thorough and methodical commander underestimated by Grant and Sherman as too slow, better at defending a position than at leading an offensive. Thomas had 60,000 men to counter Hood's 38,000, but the Union troops were scattered among many garrisons stretching from Memphis to Knoxville. Most of Thomas's troops were men that Sherman did not want, including Black troops. A former slaveholder from Virginia, Thomas also doubted that he could rely on Blacks in combat. With Hood heading for Nashville, Thomas had to consolidate and prepare an army.[103]

Hood needed to move fast to hit Nashville before Thomas could assemble his scattered forces. But Hood took his time to gather supplies and repair railroads, while his barefoot infantry moved slowly through rains and cold mud. In late November, Hood hoped to slip behind Thomas's advance force, commanded by John M. Schofield, to cut it off from Nashville. When Schofield escaped Hood's first trap, he blamed his troops, alleging that Joseph Johnston's caution had made them soft.[104]

Seeking to toughen his men, Hood ordered one of his suicidal assaults, this time upon Schofield's fortified position at Franklin, thirty miles south of Nashville. Ignoring protests from his subordinate generals, Hood sent 38,000 Confederates headlong across two miles of open fields into the withering fire of Schofield's 28,000 men, well supported by cannon. Schofield lost about 2,300 men, but Confederates took 7,000 casualties, including six dead generals. A southern soldier, Samuel Watkins, reported, "It was a grand holocaust of death. . . . The dead were piled one on the other all over the ground. I never was so horrified and appalled in my life." Watkins counted forty-nine bullet holes in one general: Patrick Cleburne, who had pushed for Black emancipation. Already plenty tough, Hood's men learned a different lesson at Franklin: that their inept commander cared little for their lives.[105]

A day later, Schofield's troops slipped away to reinforce Thomas at Nashville. Hood followed to encamp south of the strongly entrenched Yankees within the city. Not even Hood dared to attack, for he had too few men, all of them badly spooked by the bloodbath at Franklin. So he waited for two long weeks for Thomas to attack him. Irritated by Thomas's delay, Secretary of War Edwin Stanton complained, "[This] looks like the McClellan and Rosecrans strategy of do nothing and let the rebels raid the country." Grant prepared to head west to replace Thomas. Neither Grant nor Stanton understood that Thomas needed time to prepare an attack meant to overwhelm, rather than just dislodge, the enemy.[106]

At dawn on December 15, Thomas unleashed his attack, pinning down Hood's right wing with one division, while multiple divisions hammered the left. Outnumbered two to one by 50,000 Yankees, Hood fell back to form a new line between two hills. "I have never seen an army so confused and demoralized," Watkins recalled. After a night's rest, Thomas renewed his attack on December 16, when Hood's position collapsed as his men panicked. Over 4,000 surrendered, while many of the rest threw away their weapons and packs to run faster.[107]

The Black troops suffered heavy casualties in courageous assaults on Hood's army. Impressed, Thomas abandoned his former prejudices, assuring his staff: "Gentlemen, the question is settled; negroes will fight." Some Confederate prisoners protested to Thomas about having Black guards, claiming to prefer death. Thomas replied, "Well, you may say your prayers, and get ready to die." The prisoners reconsidered their position.[108]

The dissolution of Hood's ragged, hungry army continued during the long, hard retreat through cold, pouring rain. Watkins pitied Hood, a "feeble and decrepit" man "pulling his hair with his one hand . . . and crying like his heart would break." Watkins concluded, "The once proud army of Tennessee had degenerated to a mob." Hood had begun with 38,000 men, but had only 14,000 on December 28, when the survivors crossed the swollen Tennessee River to find safety in northern Alabama. Half of the troops no longer had weapons, and none had enough to eat or wear. Their wagons and artillery were long gone. Hood resigned his command on January 13, 1865.[109]

The crushing defeat at Nashville demoralized southerners. In January, the Confederacy's chief logistical officer, Josiah Gorgas, mourned, "No money in the Treasury—no food to feed Gen. Lee's army—no troops to oppose Gen. Sherman. . . . Wife and I sit talking of going to Mexico to live out there the remnant of our days." Mary Chesnut concluded, "The deep waters are closing over us."[110]

Terror

Hard-pressed by superior Union forces—and frustrated by a lack of European help—Confederate leaders became desperate. In 1864 they sought to leverage their limited manpower through sabotage and terrorism meant to demoralize northern civilians. They also hoped to thrill southerners who demanded retaliation for Union ravages on Confederate farms and towns. The Davis government sent agents to Canada to prepare operations meant to sow "anarchy and civil strife" within the Union. Early in the war, Davis had avoided provocative actions from Canada lest that irritate British leaders. By 1864, however, Confederates despaired of British help, unless they could provoke a border war between the United States and Canada by implicating Canadians in cross-border sabotage missions. "A [Yankee] war with England would be our peace," noted a Confederate official.[111]

In September 1864, John Yates Beall, a former Confederate soldier, led twenty men from the Canadian shore to seize a ferryboat on Lake Erie. From that platform, they meant to surprise, board, and commandeer an American armed vessel, the USS *Michigan*. Then the raiders would head to Johnson Island, a Union prisoner-of-war camp off the Ohio shore, to liberate thousands of Confederates. But when Canadian officials alerted American naval officers, Beall aborted the mission, scuttling the steamer while his men scattered. Trying again, he crossed the border to try to derail a train bearing captive Confederates bound to a prison. But Union agents arrested Beall in December and, two months later, a military tribunal convicted him of sabotage and treason—and a hangman ended the agent's life.[112]

Other Confederate agents sought to burn down New York City on November 25, 1864. They hoped to kill thousands by planting bottles of incendiary material in nineteen hotels, two theaters, and P. T. Barnum's museum. They targeted places crowded with civilians, rather than the city's military shipbuilding yards and arms factories. The six arsonists botched the job, for their fires damaged some rooms without consuming buildings. The agents escaped by train to Toronto, leaving behind a mass panic in New York City. By imperiling thousands, the arson plot enraged New Yorkers—most of them Democrats—against the Confederacy and Canada.[113]

The raid with the biggest impact came in October 1864, when another Canadian-based agent, Bennett Young, led twenty armed Confederates across the border into Vermont. They surprised and robbed the three banks of St. Albans, extracting $200,000. One raider declared, "We represent the Confederate States of America, and we come here to retaliate for acts committed against our people by General Sherman." Riding out of town on stolen horses, they shot and killed one civilian and wounded another. The dead man was a Copperhead in the wrong place at the wrong time. The raiders also tried but failed to burn the commercial district before fleeing back to Canada. Young hoped to provoke an American invasion of Canada, bringing on a border war that would divert Union troops from attacking the South.[114]

Declining to take that bait, Seward and Lincoln settled instead for pressing Canadians to arrest and extradite the raiders to the United States for trial as criminals. Canadian authorities did jail Young and thirteen of his men, but in early December, a magistrate, Charles J. Coursol, freed them on a technicality. That liberation outraged the Yankee press and politicians, who demanded the invasion and conquest of Canada "as a St. Bernard would throttle a poodle pup."[115]

Coursol's ruling angered Canada's leading politician, John A. Macdonald, who feared an American invasion. Embarking on damage control, Macdonald suspended Coursol and ordered the suspects pursued and rearrested, securing Young and four others. Macdonald also created a border police to keep an eye on troublemakers. The Canadian parliament granted $50,000 to compensate the St. Alban's banks and, in February 1865, toughened its neutrality law to authorize the arrest, fining, and expulsion of any alien plotting to attack the United States. The law froze further Confederate activity in Canada. In response, Lincoln and Seward lifted newly imposed restrictions on cross-border travel. Union leaders did not want a Canadian crisis to distract them from finishing off the Confederacy.[116]

The Lincoln administration could not stop Congress from rescinding the Reciprocity Treaty of 1854 made with British North America. Negotiated by a Democratic administration committed to free trade, that treaty had liberated most cross-border trade from customs duties. The treaty produced a boom in trade between Canada and the United States to the benefit of both. But reciprocity did not sit well with most Republicans, who favored protectionism and thought that termination would pressure Canadians to accept American annexation. Congress killed the treaty in early 1865.[117]

In response, Canadian leaders sought to build a bigger confederation less reliant on trade with the United States—and better prepared to resist American invasion. A cynic in parliament, Christopher Dunkin, scoffed that not even the biggest Canadian confederation could defeat the powerful Americans: "The best thing Canada can do is to keep quiet and give no cause for war," laying out the true Canadian foreign policy to the present day.[118]

Stakes

The year of elections confirmed the high stakes of the civil wars ravaging North America. By building a confederation, Canadian leaders sought to keep the whole bloody mess south of their border with the United States. Farther south, the French imposed a foreign monarch on

Mexico. In that foreign interference, Unionists saw their future if they failed to destroy the Confederacy.

Yankees fought for Union not as an abstraction but from dread of the alternative. Only that Union, they believed, spared them from repeated wars between rival countries spawned from the wrecked and subdivided nation. Inevitably, Unionists predicted, repeated civil wars would invite foreign interventions and culminate in military despotisms to the ruin of republican self-government. General Sherman explained to John Bell Hood: "You cannot have peace and division of our country. If the United States submits to a division. . . . it will not stop but will go on until we reap the fate of Mexico, which is eternal war." Agreeing with Sherman, northern voters reelected Lincoln to finish the job of rebuilding the Union by crushing the Confederacy.[119]

ELEVEN ⚔ BORDERS

It is hard to tell who is who, and what is what, on that
border. The state of affairs is about as mixed as the river is
indefinite as a boundary line.
—PHILIP H. SHERIDAN (ON THE RIO GRANDE)[1]

If I owned hell and Texas, I would rent out Texas and live
in hell. —PHILIP H. SHERIDAN[2]

In January 1865, General Grant had his hands full besieging Lee's army at Petersburg. Yet he took the time to write a secret letter to the Union commander in California, Irvin McDowell, about alarming news from Mexico. A Confederate agent, Dr. William Gwin, sought to colonize Sonora, a mineral-rich state along the American border. Grant warned, "The Dr. is a rebel of the most virulent order," who would "entice into Sonora the dissatisfied spirits of California" to "organize them and invade the State." By rallying in Mexico, Confederates might prolong the war and perhaps still win it. Haunted by that prospect, Grant wrote to McDowell, "without having discussed this question with anyone," not even the president, "to put you on your guard against what I believe may prove a great danger." If Gwin's Confederates did attack California, McDowell was to invade Sonora and assist the republican regime of Benito Juárez against the *Imperialistas*.[3]

During the 1850s, Gwin had been California's most powerful politician, leading pro-southern Democrats known as the Chivalry. In 1861, he had pushed for California to secede as part of a new Pacific-coast republic. Foiled, he fled to Mississippi, but Grant's troops burned his plantation there in 1863. Slipping out of the Confederacy on a blockade runner, Gwin reached Paris, where he pitched French officials on a colonizing scheme to attract 15,000 armed miners to Sonora by recruiting Confederate sympathizers from California and Arizona. Gwin assured the French that Sonora had more gold and silver than California—which had been the richest mineral strike in history. By taking a hefty cut from the bullion, the French could collect on the immense debt allegedly owed to them by Mexico. In return, Gwin sought a large land grant and the governorship of Sonora.[4]

Gwin impressed the emperor's conniving half-brother, the Duc de Morny, who invested in the Sonora scheme and secured Napoleon's support. Confiding in that support, Gwin sailed for Mexico, arriving in June 1864. Another expatriate described him as a "tall, broad, squarely built man, with rough features—which seemed hewn out of a blow with an ax—ruddy skin, and a wealth of white hair brushed back from his brow." But Gwin was gambling on two unstable and intertwined empires, French and Mexican.[5]

In no mere coincidence, Grant wrote to McDowell on January 8—the same day that Francis P. Blair, Sr., departed from Grant's headquarters at City Point with a flag of truce to cross Confederate lines for secret negotiations with an old friend, Jefferson Davis. A conservative Repub-

OPPOSITE: *"Mexican Firing Squad for the Emperor Maximilian," 1867, photograph by unknown.*

lican, Blair persuaded Lincoln to let him seek peace by offering Davis a bold alternative: to dissolve the Confederacy and merge southern and northern forces to invade Mexico and crush the French and *Imperialistas*. Under this plan, Davis would resign as Confederate president to command 20,000 troops for the Mexican expedition with Robert E. Lee and William T. Sherman as his chief subordinates. While declining the proposal, Davis gave Blair a letter for Lincoln with an offer to negotiate further.[6]

Blair's proposal resembled Seward's effort in 1861 to avert civil war by uniting North and South for a foreign invasion. But reconciliation was even harder in 1865, after four years of bloodshed had generated intense hatreds. Plus the Union was abolishing slavery. By aborting the North's bid to conquer the Confederacy, Blair's peace would leave open the process of reconstructing the South. Such an inconclusive ending appalled most Republicans, including Grant, who distrusted Blair.[7]

Grant's friend Lew Wallace shared that distrust. During the war of the late 1840s, Wallace had served in Mexico, becoming fond of the country and fluent in Spanish. "You know Mexico is Lew's *darling*," his wife sighed. After that war, Wallace had become a politician in Indiana and a general in the Union army. Writing to Grant in early 1865, Wallace proposed a secret mission to the Union post of Brazos de Santiago, at the mouth of the Rio Grande. Wallace would contact the Confederate commander at nearby Brownsville to persuade him to defect with his troops to help Juárez: "I'll wager you a month's pay that I win, and that Blair & Co. lose." Wallace and Grant were playing a high-stakes game to head off Blair's rival bid to end the Civil War. A week later Grant sent Wallace to the Rio Grande but admonished him to keep the mission secret from secretary of state Seward.[8]

Seward favored strict neutrality in the Mexican conflict. In July 1864, Grant had told Seward, "I feel the reestablishment of republican government in Mexico would really be a part of our present struggle." Seward replied, "Yes, we want to get Napoleon out of Mexico, but we don't want any war over it; we have certainly had enough of war." Fearing that Grant would produce "irritation and annoyance" with French forces along the Rio Grande, Seward sought through diplomacy to find a face-saving way for the French to withdraw.[9]

Wallace ventured to a region called "Kirby-Smithdom," in honor of the Confederate commander of Texas and western Louisiana. Kirby Smith acted as de facto president of his vast (about 600,000 square miles) but thinly populated realm that was isolated by Union control of the Mississippi Valley. In 1864, Smith's troops had repelled a Union invasion, but his district suffered from shortages of supplies and pay—and from a surplus of generals who feuded with one another.[10]

The Davis government used Kirby-Smithdom as a dumping ground for disgraced commanders, including John B. Magruder, a bon vivant who had disgusted Lee as unreliable. In Texas, Smith discovered that Magruder would obey no "order unless it chimed in with his own plans and fancies." Living large despite hard times, Magruder irritated his hungry troops.[11]

In March 1865 Wallace reached the Union outpost at the mouth of the Rio Grande to woo the Confederate commanders at Brownsville: Colonel John S. Ford and General James Slaughter. Wallace pressed them to surrender and join him in invading Mexico to oust the French. Unwilling "to see his state invaded & Ruined, and the war decline into guerilla murders," Slaughter agreed, but his immediate superior, General John Walker, accused Ford and Slaughter of flirting with "the blackest treason to the Confederacy."[12]

By turning down Wallace, Walker bought time for Kirby Smith to seek a deal with Maximilian and Napoleon. In the press, Smith floated trial balloons promoting the annexation of Texas and Louisiana by the French or Mexican empires. In January 1865, he sent a French general in Confederate service, Camille de Polignac, on a secret mission to Paris. A friend of the Duc de Morny, Polignac enjoyed access to the highest levels of Napoleon's government. To evade the Union blockade, Polignac traveled via Mexico, Cuba, and Spain, so he did not reach Paris until late March. By then Morny was dead and Napoleon was unimpressed by Kirby Smith's military prospects.[13]

Meanwhile back in Richmond and Washington, Blair's initiative prompted Davis and Lincoln to consider negotiations to end the war.

Both presidents wanted to appease public discontent with mounting casualties, but neither could budge on the central points of the conflict: slavery and sovereignty. Writing to Lincoln, Davis sought "to secure peace to the two Countries." Lincoln replied that he hoped to restore "peace to the people of our one common country" and to end slavery. Despite the chasm between their positions, they agreed to hold more talks—if only to probe one another for signs of weakness.[14]

On February 3, aboard a Union ship moored at Hampton Roads, three Confederate representatives, including Vice-President Alexander H. Stephens, met with Lincoln, Seward, and Grant. During four hours of discussion, the two sides made no progress. Lincoln pressed for emancipation and Confederate surrender, while Stephens pushed for Blair's joint war in Mexico as a team-building exercise so that "the passions on both sides might cool." Brushing away Blair's plan as a nonstarter, Lincoln offered but one concession: to pay millions in compensation to masters if the Confederacy surrendered by April 1. But the Confederates could accept no deal that dissolved slavery and their independence.[15]

By confirming Lincoln's firm position, the discussions discredited southern critics of the war, who had broached the fantasy of making a quick peace that preserved Confederate independence. As Davis had hoped, the southern press demanded a redoubled commitment to fight. In a fiery speech of defiance, Davis predicted victory within a year, which astonished Stephens as "the emanation of a demented brain." Meanwhile, Lincoln's cabinet rejected his proposal to compensate Confederate masters for emancipated slaves.[16]

The End

Grant's massive army of 120,000 men was slowly suffocating Lee's 60,000 at Petersburg and Richmond by cutting supply lines from farther south. That constriction got a boost in mid-January 1865, when another Union force under Admiral David Porter and General Alfred Terry bombarded and stormed Fort Fisher, a powerful coastal base that guarded the approach to Wilmington, North Carolina. That victory closed the last major port enabling blockade runners to send supplies to Lee's army.[17]

The Yankee invasion of North Carolina increased desertion by Confederates desperate to go home to protect their families—and get something to eat. North Carolina's Governor Zebulon Vance lamented "the general despondency and gloom which prevails among us." In a single month, Lee's army lost 8 percent of its men. Deserters responded to urgent appeals from wives and mothers. A military doctor noted "that the women were the cause of nearly all the desertions." In a Richmond street, Mary Chesnut saw troops taking away a recaptured deserter while his wife yelled after him: "You desert agin, quick as you kin—come back to your wife and children. Desert, Jake! Desert agin, Jake!"[18]

In February, Sherman's troops marched northeast from Savannah into South Carolina to destroy everything of military value in their path. As in Georgia, Sherman meant to deplete southern provisions and demoralize civilians by demonstrating the inability of the Confederacy to defend them. Longing to punish that state for starting the whole bloody war, Sherman vowed to "smash South Carolina all to pieces."[19]

Building long bridges across broad swamps and rivers swollen by winter rains, Sherman's 60,000 men pushed deep into South Carolina, brushing aside weak resistance by 20,000 Confederates. Making a feint toward Charleston, Sherman instead turned inland to seize Columbia, the state capital, on February 17. By the next day, half of the city had burned down, with Yankees and Confederates blaming one another.[20]

Sherman's advance cut the Confederate supply line to Charleston, obliging its defenders to withdraw on February 18. They left behind a city battered by artillery bombardment by Union coastal forces. A visitor found a "city of ruins, of desolation, of vacant houses, of widowed women, of rotting wharves, of deserted warehouses," but also of Blacks jubilant at liberation by U.S. Colored Troops, who led the way into the city. They included Major Martin Delany, who recruited hundreds of Black Carolinians eager to join the Union army.[21]

In mid-March Sherman advanced into North Carolina, where he confronted a familiar adversary, Joseph E. Johnston, who had only

21,000 poorly supplied men to resist Sherman's 60,000. As blunt and pessimistic as ever, Johnston assured Lee: "Sherman's course cannot be hindered by the small force I have. I can do no more than annoy him."[22]

While Sherman ravaged the Carolina hinterland that supplied Lee's troops, Grant extended his massive army westward to snap off the rail lines that sustained Petersburg's defenders. On April 1, at a crossroads called Five Forks, Philip H. Sheridan's men captured the last railroad by overwhelming Confederates led by the luckless George Pickett. Half of the defenders surrendered while the rest fled, casting their weapons aside in a panic. On April 2, Grant ordered his forces to attack all along Lee's line of entrenchments.[23]

As Confederate defenses crumbled, Lee pulled his army out of Petersburg, heading westward. He informed President Davis, then attending church, that Richmond was doomed. Davis and his officials scrambled for wagons and trains to haul away records and gold. To deprive Yankees of spoils, retreating Confederates burned factories, flour mills, tobacco warehouses, and military supplies, but the flames spread to torch many homes and stores. As the last Confederate troops departed, mobs ruled the streets, breaking open shops in a "demonical struggle for the countless barrels of hams, bacon, whisky, flour, sugar, [and] coffee."[24]

Early on April 4, Union troops marched into Richmond to restore order and put out the flames, while freed people cheered liberation. A Black chaplain addressed the "vast multitude" to proclaim "for the first time in that city freedom to all mankind." While singing, "Slavery chain done broke at last," Blacks smashed open the slave traders' pens, and the liberated inmates "came out shouting and praising God" and Lincoln. Apprised of the victory, Lincoln exulted, "Thank God I have lived to see this. It seems to me that I have been dreaming a horrid dream for four years, and now the nightmare is gone." On April 5, he visited Richmond, to the delight of joyous Blacks.[25]

With 50,000 men, Lee retreated westward, heading for Danville to seek provisions and trains to take them south into North Carolina to join Johnston's army for a combined assault on Sherman. Stinted on rations for months, the malnourished men struggled to keep up on their march through rain and mud. And they were hounded by pursuing Union cavalry led by the aggressive Sheridan.[26]

Winning the race to Danville, Sheridan's troops compelled Lee's army to slog on farther westward toward Lynchburg, another railroad junction and base for supplies. On April 6 Sheridan attacked the Confederates at Sailor's Creek, inflicting 1,700 casualties and taking 6,000 prisoners, among them eight generals. Many more Confederates deserted, heading home or surrendering to Yankees, who could feed them. With victory within grasp, a Union officer mourned his side's losses: "So near the end and yet men must die."[27]

On April 8 Sheridan's cavalrymen pulled ahead and swung around to block Lee's retreat at Appomattox Courthouse, a rural village. Soon Union infantry arrived to bolster the cavalry. Outnumbered five to one, Lee surrendered on April 9. He rejected the alternative of dispersing to sustain a guerrilla war, because that would provoke savage retribution against civilians by Union forces. Sharing that dread of partisan conflict, Grant offered generous terms meant to persuade Confederates to accept that their war was over. Rather than heading to prison camps, they would have paroles to go home and could take horses and mules with them for their farms.[28]

Lee's surrender doomed the Confederacy. For three years, his brilliance had sustained southern morale through many defeats elsewhere in the war. "Our only hope is in Lee the Invincible," a Texan woman declared in 1863. On April 6, 1865, Henry A. Wise assured Lee that "there has been no country, general, for a year or more. You are the country to these men. They have fought for you." But the corollary was that his surrender led most Confederates to despair. In Georgia, Eliza Andrews mourned: "Everybody feels ready to give up hope. 'It is useless to struggle longer,' seems to be the common cry, and the poor wounded men go hobbling about the streets with despair on their faces."[29]

On the evening of April 9, news of Lee's surrender reached Washington, D.C., igniting a rapturous celebration in the streets, as throngs rang bells, fired guns, waved flags, and sang patriotic songs while hugging and kissing one another. The eruption expressed the enormous relief felt after four years of suffering and disappointment. A crowd gathered outside the White House, where Lincoln gave a brief speech and had a band play his favorite tune, "Dixie," which he claimed that Grant had captured along with Lee. Two days later, the president gave a longer speech that endorsed civil rights for freed Blacks. The speech disgusted a stage actor and Confederate agent named John Wilkes Booth: "That means nigger citizenship. Now, by God, I'll put him through. That is the last speech he will ever make."[30]

On April 14, Lincoln and his wife Mary went to the theater to see a comedy. At mid-performance, Booth slipped into the back of the presidential box, pressed his pistol to Lincoln's head, and pulled the trigger. While the president blacked out, Booth jumped onto the stage to yell his last theatrical line to the shocked audience—"Sic semper tyrannis"—this is the fate of tyrants. The leap broke his leg, but Booth hobbled off-stage and mounted a waiting horse for his escape. Never regaining consciousness, Lincoln died nine hours later. A grieving cabinet member, Gideon Welles, noted the crowd around the house: "The colored people . . . were painfully affected."[31]

On that night of April 14, one of Booth's co-conspirators broke into Seward's home and stabbed him repeatedly with a knife. Although scarred and hospitalized, Seward lived. Worried attendants tried to keep word of Lincoln's death from Seward, lest he plunge into deadly despair. One morning, Seward looked out the window to see a flag at half-mast. "The President is dead," he muttered. Attendants denied it, but Seward noted that Lincoln had never visited—and would have if alive. Then Seward broke down sobbing. Begun in rivalry, their partnership had become a deep friendship before ending in tragedy.[32]

In death, Lincoln became a martyr for the Union and emancipation. For so long, critics had mocked his appearance, posture, and folksy humor; or they had cast him as a bloodthirsty tyrant. Belatedly but powerfully, northerners recognized his dignity, endurance, and wisdom. Noting that he had visited Richmond on Palm Sunday and died on Good Friday, many Americans saw Lincoln as the savior of the nation. Grant declared that Lincoln was "incontestably the greatest man I have ever known." In Mexico, Benito Juárez mourned: "I have felt this disaster profoundly, for Lincoln, who was working with such constancy for the full freedom of his fellow men, merited a better fate than the [bullet] of a cowardly assassin."[33]

Grieving millions turned out for Lincoln's long, rolling funeral, which began at the national capital and then traversed 1,700 miles in a railcar with stops at more than 100 towns and cities, concluding in Springfield, Illinois, for his burial. There was plenty of grief far away from the railroad. In Mississippi, an army officer reported that the former slaves of Jefferson Davis mourned Lincoln's death: "All the colored people, men, women, and children, have crape, black string or mourning of some kind."[34]

For years, Frederick Douglass had clashed with Lincoln in frustration over his temporizing about slavery. But Douglass came to admire the president's moral growth during the terrible war. Called on to address the people of Rochester, white and Black, Douglass felt a new bond with all of them as fellow Americans: "We shared in common a terrible calamity, and this touch of nature made us more than countrymen, it made us Kin." Never could Douglass have experienced this before the Civil War.[35]

That bond of racial unity did not prevail throughout a land still troubled by prejudice. In the fall, Harriet Tubman boarded a train in Philadelphia bound to New York, but the conductor ordered her to leave a coach that he reserved for whites. "We don't carry niggers," he bellowed. When she refused to move, other passengers helped the conductor wrench her from her seat. Casting her into a second-class car, they broke Tubman's arm.[36]

Too little had changed for Tubman—but too much for Edmund Ruffin, Virginia's arch-secessionist. Despairing over Lee's surrender, Ruffin hoped that Napoleon's France and Maximilian's Mexico would send troops to save the Confederacy. Ruffin insisted that southerners "would rather, by ten thousand times, be the subjects of the Emperor of France, than of Abraham Lincoln."

When that desperate hope faded, Ruffin retreated to his room, where he prepared a suicide note of over seven thousand words: "I here declare my unmitigated hatred to Yankee rule—to all political, social & business connection with Yankees—& to the Yankee race." He hoped that the rebellion would revive if his family published his words. But Ruffin concluded that note more aptly than he knew with "The End." Putting the muzzle of a gun in his mouth, Ruffin pressed the trigger with a forked stick, ending his life on June 17, 1865. Hearing the shot and finding the body, a son told his children, "The Yankees have killed your Grandfather."[37]

Grand Review

In mid-April, Jefferson Davis spouted defiance as he fled southward from Virginia to North Carolina, seeking out Joseph Johnston's army. Promoting guerrilla warfare to the death, Davis declared, "Nothing is now needed to render our triumph certain but the exhibition of our own unquenchable resolve," for the enemy would fail at the "impossible task of making slaves of a people resolved to be free." A Confederate soldier muttered, "Poor President, he is unwilling to see what all around him see."[38]

The president should have seen the rampant evidence of chaos and despair. Deserters were looting government warehouses, and outlaw bands were robbing farms. Often foraging armies had burned up the fences and consumed all the livestock on those farms. The roads were littered with dead horses, smashed wagons, and discarded weapons. Friends warned Davis, "I fear the spirit of the people is broken," and "We are falling to pieces."[39]

After learning of Lee's surrender, Johnston wanted no part of Davis's perpetual war. The general assured the fugitive president: "It would be the greatest of human crimes for us to attempt to continue the war" because partisan warfare would "complete the devastation of our country and ruin of its people." The news from Appomattox had demoralized Johnston's troops, who deserted in droves and ransacked warehouses. "It was nothing more than a howling mob," a witness noted. Johnston lamented that his army was "melting away like snow before the sun."[40]

But Johnston drew Sherman into negotiations that violated Union orders for generals to avoid political questions. Sherman worried that, without a prompt and formal surrender, Johnston's men would scatter into the hills to prolong the war "in its last and worst shape, that of assassins and guerrillas." Aspiring to "produce Peace from the Potomac to the Rio Grande," Sherman sought a political settlement that would apply to all remaining Confederate forces, including those in distant Alabama and Texas. On April 18, Sherman agreed to compromise Union plans for reconstruction by recognizing Confederate state governments, extending amnesty to all Confederates, and restoring properties confiscated from them. Rather than surrender their weapons, the soldiers could turn them over to arsenals controlled by those state governments. The deal's silence about emancipation implied that those governments would decide the matter. The terms were so indulgent that even Davis was prepared to accept them.[41]

But Sherman's deal required approval by the new American president, Andrew Johnson, and his cabinet. They were shocked by its political terms. Secretary of War Edwin Stanton raged that Sherman had "relieved rebels from the pressure of our victories and left them in [a] condition to renew their efforts to overthrow the United States government." Sharing that dismay, Grant traveled to North Carolina to supervise Sherman in negotiating Johnston's surrender along the Appomattox lines. Davis ordered Johnston to resume fighting. Instead, on April 26 at Greensboro, he surrendered on Grant's terms "to avoid the crime of waging hopeless war." Johnston's remaining 12,000 men could go home on parole after receiving Union rations. Davis denounced Johnston's surrender as but the latest of many treacherous acts. On May 4, the Confederate forces in Alabama surrendered by accepting paroles and rations. Organized resistance persisted only to the west, in Texas.[42]

Fleeing southward through the Carolinas into Georgia, Davis sought to reach Texas, to revive the Confederate military cause there. But on May 10 in southwest Georgia, Union troops captured Davis, who had donned his wife's shawl, enabling the northern press to mock his masculinity by claiming that he wore drag as a disguise. His captors hustled Davis off to a military prison to await trial as a traitor.[43]

On May 23 and 24, 1865, Union forces celebrated victory by marching down Pennsylvania Avenue in Washington, D.C., in a parade known as the Grand Review. A hundred thousand spectators attended, including the president, his cabinet, and generals Grant and Sherman. But there was a glaring absence from the reviewing podium: General Philip H. Sheridan, who had done so much to win the war. Never short on ego, Sheridan had longed to lead his parading troops through the cheering throngs. But on May 17 he had received secret and imperative orders from Grant to head west with 50,000 men to subdue the last Confederate army in Texas.[44]

Meeting privately with Sheridan, Grant had explained that Kirby Smith's domain might host a Confederate revival because nearby *Imperialista* Mexico could provide military support. Grant worried, "I see nothing before us but a long, expensive and bloody war" as "tens of thousands of disciplined soldiers, embittered against their Government" joined the *Imperialistas.* Sheridan recalled that Grant "looked upon the invasion of Mexico by Maximilian as part of the rebellion itself . . . and that our success in putting down secession would never be complete till the French and Austrian invaders were compelled to quit the territory of our sister republic." Exploiting Seward's incapacitation by an assassin, Grant and Sheridan could make trouble for Maximilian.[45]

Sheridan's mission emerged from secret meetings between Grant and Juárez's ambassador, Matías Romero. During the late 1840s, as a junior officer serving in the war against Mexico, Grant had developed an empathy for the Mexican people. Regretting his role in that unjust war, Grant longed for the chance to do right by republican Mexico in 1865. Romero said of Grant that, "although he is tired of war, his major desire is to fight in Mexico against the French, that the Monroe Doctrine has to be defended at any price." Romero trusted Grant as a rare American who meant to help Mexico: "Grant could not do more if he were a Mexican." They decided that he could best help by staying in Washington to influence Johnson, while sending Sheridan to crush Kirby Smith's army and then "fight in Mexico to expel the French." The next day, Grant wrote his orders to Sheridan.[46]

Fragments

In Texas, Kirby Smith's army collapsed before Sheridan arrived as word of Appomattox triggered mass desertions by men who had lost hope.

At Galveston a defiant private told his local commander: "We are ready
to admit that times will Be hard if we are subjugated. But it wont Bee
any harder on me than it will on my wife and children with [me] kild
and the country intir[e]ly Burnt out and devastated." A federal general
marveled, "The thing is going to pieces so fast that one cannot count
the fragments." Deserting soldiers looted government warehouses and
stables. At Austin, Amelia Barr reported, "Confederate soldiers, without
officers or order, are coming in every hour, and there is nothing but
plunder and sack going on—and the citizens are as bad as the soldiers."
Barr mourned, "The dream is over. No Southern independence now."[47]

But Blacks hoped to fulfill their dream of freedom. Barr added, "Had
to iron; the negro won't work. . . . Both men and women have deserted
their homes, and are hanging about the streets, watching the white men
plundering, but too much afraid of the white man to take a hand in the
work." A week later, she added, "My negro servant comes home to eat,
then she runs into the city again. I have all her work to do, but she is
waiting for her *freedom*. I cannot blame her." Two days later, Barr asked
her servant, "Will you hire yourself to me, Harriet? I will give you six
dollars a month." Harriet replied, "Six dollars [is] too little. . . . I [be]
long to myself now. I want eight dollars now. When a nigger [becomes]
free, they worth more." Barr agreed but three days later noted, "Harriet
had gone forever."[48]

Embarrassed by his army's collapse, Smith hid for thirty-six hours "to
escape the mob of disorderly soldiers thronging the roads." On May 30
he announced, "Soldiers! I am left a Commander without an army—a
General without troops. You have made your choice. It was unwise &
unpatriotic, but it is final. I pray you may not live to regret it." On June
2, Smith boarded a federal steamer at Galveston to capitulate, but he
then fled to Mexico, claiming that he could bring along 19,000 defiant
Confederates. Rejecting "vassalage to the Federal government," they
"would rally around any flag that promises to lead them into battle
against their former foe."[49]

Many Confederates vowed that they would go to Mexico rather than
submit to the hated Yankees and their Black allies. John R. Baylor, of
Arizona infamy, rejected living with "thousands of idle, thieving &

impudent niggers among us with a standing army over us to protect their pets." In the spring, Union policy toward the defeated seemed so uncertain that some Confederate generals and officials fled to avoid anticipated imprisonment. A young woman in Georgia reported, "The men are all talking about going to Mexico and Brazil. If all emigrate who say they are going, we shall have a nation made up of women, negroes, and Yankees."[50]

But only about 2,000 Confederates did go to Mexico during the spring and summer of 1865. Despite their bluster, most soldiers went home to wives and children to rescue neglected farms. By limiting arrests and calling off trials of Confederates, the Union reduced the number who felt pressured to leave for Mexico. Many veterans were too poor to bear the expense of a long, hard, and dangerous journey across Texas and into Mexico. In Texas, Smith reported, travelers confronted "bands of robbers and plundering deserters with which the roads were infested." Guerrillas added to the dangers once a traveler crossed into Mexico. In September in Nuevo León, they killed Confederate general Mosby M. Parsons, three of his staff officers, and a former congressman.[51]

Before the war, Joseph Shelby had prospered in Missouri as a rope manufacturer and plantation owner. During the 1850s, he fought as a proslavery Border Ruffian in Kansas, participating in the first sack of Lawrence. During the Civil War, Shelby's aggression and intelligence made him the best cavalry commander in the west. Refusing to surrender in June 1865, he led three hundred men of his Iron Brigade across Texas bound for Mexico. Having committed many atrocities in Missouri, Shelby's men could not return in safety to a state dominated by vengeful Unionists. Instead, they took munitions from the arsenals in Texas, crossed the Rio Grande, and fought their way through Liberal guerrillas to reach the French garrison at Monterrey in northern Mexico.[52]

To bypass the overland dangers, many Confederate refugees went by sea via Cuba to reach the Mexican port of Veracruz. They included the fiery, profane, and verbose Jubal Early, who vowed "to get out from [under] the rule of the infernal Yankees," adding that he "could scalp a

Yankee woman and child without winking my eyes." Reaching Mexico City in the fall, he offered to help Maximilian attack the Union. When the emperor refused, Early complained, "I went to Mexico hoping there might be a war with the U.S., but I found the Empire an infernal humbug and no chance in that quarter." Early was reduced to waging a war of words against Sheridan in the English-language *Mexican Times.*[53]

Maximilian welcomed the refugees as colonists who could help develop Mexico—but he wanted them to keep a low profile, lest they provoke an invasion by the United States. Seeking to cultivate goodwill with the United States, the emperor compelled the refugees to renounce attacks north of the border. Barring them from serving in their own cohesive units, Maximilian sought to disperse them within *Imperialista* regiments. The emperor also worried that Confederates would turn filibusterers if allowed to settle and concentrate in Mexico's northern states. So he settled them in central Mexico.[54]

Few women and too many governors and generals went to Mexico. They included the inept Sterling Price and his fiercest critic, former Missouri governor Thomas C. Reynolds. Mexico also attracted the Chivalry leader (and deadly duelist), David S. Terry, who had become a Confederate officer. General John McCausland went to Mexico to avoid prosecution or murder for burning Chambersburg, Pennsylvania, in 1864. Dismayed by falling from grace, the bigwigs were a bitter and squabbling lot who blamed one another for defeat. Smith described his peers as "Confederate censorians, fault finding & dissatisfied."[55]

Once a distant vision to romanticize, the Mexican Empire came into sharper and grimmer focus for the immigrants. Exotic customs, Catholic ceremonies, and subtropical rains and fevers stressed their morale as did bad roads and many bandits. Clinging to English words and one another, the newcomers were disgruntled expatriates. They did not like the locals, who returned the disfavor. A Yankee in Mexico City mocked southern expats, who "fought over their battles, fought each other . . . shirked the payment of debts, insulted strangers, insulted citizens, bullied and boasted," earning a reputation for "whisky, braggadocio, rudeness, dishonesty, and indolence."[56]

Fearful Crisis

In early May 1865, William Gwin reached Mexico City to find that the Confederate collapse had shocked and imperiled Maximilian's regime:

> We arrived here at a fearful crisis in the affairs of this continent. Everything is shaken here, as elsewhere, by the surrender of Lee, and the death of Lincoln. . . . This country is paralyzed by the news. The Liberals are rejoicing at the prospect of the speedy appearance of the Yankees to exterminate the empire and restore them to power.

Only the American Civil War had permitted Napoleon and Maximilian to pursue their Mexican empire. The southern implosion stripped away the Confederate buffer that had kept the powerful Union away from Mexico. The French minister to Mexico considered Maximilian's regime doomed "all at once by the taking of Richmond, the surrender of Lee, and the reconstruction of the Great American Union."[57]

Gwin considered returning to the United States to submit to the victors, but his son worried that "all traitors should be hung, and as we are all traitors, there's nothing left for us but hanging." In June 1865, *Juaristas* intercepted letters from Gwin boasting of his plan to colonize Sonora with Confederate refugees. Obtaining the incriminating letters, Matías Romero shared copies with the American government, which filed a protest with France. The publicity embarrassed French leaders, who had come to suspect Gwin of conning them with exaggerated tales of Sonora's mineral wealth. In a cruel trick, Napoleon gave Gwin, then visiting Paris, a sealed letter for Maximilian, ostensibly in support of the Sonora plan. When Maximilian opened the letter, he read Napoleon's advice to discard Gwin as a liability.[58]

Maximilian already had soured on Gwin as a filibusterer out to exploit Sonora for himself. Mexicans recalled that his political protégé, Henry Crabb, had died attempting to seize Sonora in 1857. When someone praised Gwin as a pioneer, Maximilian retorted, "Yes, a pioneer for the South." On June 28, 1865, Maximilian's official newspaper, *El Diario*, disavowed the Sonoran scheme. Feeling betrayed, Gwin assured his wife: "Fear of the United States seems to be the prevailing sentiment all over the world. We cannot escape that power; its long arm reaches every country. Then why not submit at once?" Gwin rode north into Texas and on to New Orleans, where he was arrested and held in a military prison for eight months, while Congress investigated his efforts to draw Confederates into Mexico.[59]

With the American Civil War over, Juárez hoped that the Yankees would confront France and openly assist the republican cause in Mexico. Juárez instructed Romero to seek American help "as a friend and not a master" by offering "soldiers or money, without exacting humiliating conditions or the sacrifice of a single inch of our territory." Bypassing Seward, Romero met privately with President Johnson at the White House to argue that *Juaristas* "defend the interests of the masses against the privileged classes" by "fighting in defense . . . of the republican form of government and liberal institutions."[60]

Maury

Born into a prestigious family in Virginia, Matthew F. Maury became a naval officer and an international celebrity as a pioneering navigator, astronomer, and oceanographer. During the late 1850s, Maury corresponded with Maximilian over shared interests in navigation. In 1858, the archduke arranged for Maury to receive an Austrian gold medal for scientific achievement. In 1861, Maury joined the Confederacy, helping the war effort by developing torpedoes and procuring warships in Britain. Linking the Confederacy and the Mexican Empire, Maury offered his services to Maximilian in 1863: "I can be more useful to the common cause under your banner than I am permitted to be under my own." Overestimating Maximilian's finances, Maury urged him to buy ironclad warships from a British shipyard for a Mexican navy meant to master the Pacific and conquer California. Mexico tended to inspire exotic fantasies among credulous Americans.[61]

When the Confederacy collapsed, Maury left Britain for Mexico, where he was welcomed by Maximilian and appointed imperial astronomer for an observatory not yet built. To help the common cause, Maury proposed a program to recruit Confederate refugees: "The wreck of the Southern Confederacy is rich in the materials of Empire" that could "surround the throne with the elements of an elegant aristocracy." Long dubious of democracy as vulgar and divisive, Maury embraced monarchy as noble and unifying. He dreamed of transforming Mexico into the nexus of global trade, linking Europe and Asian trade—and thereby eclipsing the United States.[62]

In September 1865, Maximilian appointed Maury commissioner for immigration—assisted by the flamboyant John Magruder, who ran a land office charged with making surveys and locating colonists on farms. Maximilian promised to subsidize immigrants, allow them to import property without paying duties, and exempt them from other taxes for a year. Poor men would receive free grants of 160 to 320 acres each, while the prosperous could purchase land for a dollar per acre.[63]

Hoping to attract 200,000 immigrants to build a "New Virginia," Maury appointed recruiters in seven southern states and California. He also published and circulated a promotional pamphlet depicting Mexico as a tropical paradise where a little labor would produce riches and leisure. Maury's enthusiasm did not impress his Virginia relatives, who declined to join him in Mexico. A son-in-law refused to circulate the pamphlet because "everyone would think Maury insane" by reading it. A Dutch friend agreed, assuring Maury, "I never met a man of such high intellect who was so much led astray by his own imagination as you are."[64]

Maury claimed that slaves directed by masters offered the best labor system to realize Mexico's agricultural potential. To evade that country's laws against slavery, Maury proposed, and Maximilian accepted, a system of supposed "apprentices" who could not be sold but had to serve their master for at least five years. Maximilian insisted that masters would "care for them in a patriarchal and paternal manner during their apprenticeship" and keep them from "idleness and vice."[65]

The apprentice system failed. Few masters could persuade or coerce freed Blacks to go to Mexico. "They are all turned loose and are as wild as zebras," lamented Maury's nephew in Virginia. Those who did join their masters soon escaped, exploiting the wartime chaos and antislavery ethos of Mexico. A former Confederate general complained, "All our Negroes decided to leave us upon our arrival here. . . . Negroes are worse than worthless in this country." One refugee marveled at seeing a former Louisiana judge doing his own work: "He blacks his own shoes and feeds and curries his own horse."[66]

Maury located the chief Confederate colonies in a valley near the road between Veracruz and Mexico City. To honor the empress, the colonists named their leading town "Carlota." Its prime location and fertile soil attracted Sterling Price, Joseph Shelby, and former governors of Louisiana and Texas. But the town was not much to look at, according to a surveyor: "The low walls, the iron grates of the windows, and the dull, rusty red of the tile-covered roofs make it look like an immense collection of private jails."[67]

Southern immigration fell far short of Maury's fantasy of attracting 200,000. At best, he brought in another 3,000, on top of the 2,000 who had come on their own earlier in 1865. Many of the refugees quickly soured on a country that refuted Maury's glowing descriptions. It did not help that Maximilian could not afford his expensive promises of subsidies. And Maury was an inept administrator, running what one subordinate called "Maury's absurd colonization bureau." Many newcomers could not get land grants for lack of surveys and proper records. News of the chaos reached the South, daunting further immigration. Southern newspapers and magazines urged people to stay home to help the region recover from the war. When Maury invited Robert E. Lee to Mexico, forsaking the South, the general replied: "I prefer to struggle for its restoration and share its fate rather than give up all as lost." Maury complained that Virginians had become "humble pie-eaters."[68]

Although Maury was failing, Sheridan refused to believe it. Writing inflammatory reports to his superiors, the general exaggerated Maury's success as a menace to the United States. Sherman agreed, vowing to "break up [Maury's] nest of Confederates which was agitating the public mind in the South and preventing the people there from quietly submitting to subjugation." Sheridan deployed troops at New Orleans and along the Rio Grande to obstruct and even arrest emigrants. Ginned up by Sheridan's and Sherman's alarm, Congress investigated Maury for reviving slavery in Mexico. That unwanted attention gave Maximilian second thoughts about promoting a Confederate influx that he could no longer afford.[69]

Wolves

In June 1865 Sheridan reached Texas to find the chaos and looting that followed the dissolution of Kirby Smith's army. Sheridan denounced the Confederate surrender in Texas as "a swindle on the part of Kirby Smith & Co, as all the Texas troops had been disbanded. . . . Everything on wheels, artillery, horses, mules, etc., have been run over into Mexico." Sheridan assured Grant, "We never can have a fully restored Union, and give a total and final blow to all malcontents, until the French leave Mexico." Like Grant, Sheridan regarded the American and Mexican civil wars as linked parts of "the old contest between Absolute-ism and Liberalism."[70]

Along the lower Rio Grande, Sheridan waged psychological warfare against *Imperialistas* on the other bank. Marching troops along the river and assembling boats, he made a show of imminent invasion with an overwhelming force. Sheridan boasted, "Affairs on the Rio Grande are getting beautifully mixed up." He dispatched an emissary to Juárez, "taking care not to do this in the dark," so that word spread "like wild-fire." Sheridan's scouts probed deep into northern Mexico to prepare for invasion by seeking sources of food and fodder; locating French garrisons; and contacting Liberal guerrillas. But his lead scout died in a firefight with "a party of ex-Confederates and renegade Mexican rancheros." To rattle the *Imperialistas*, Sheridan sent belligerent notes to General Tomás Mejía, demanding the return of all Confederate munitions taken to Matamoros. If refused, Sheridan could assert an "ample excuse for crossing the boundary." Sheridan later claimed that he would have toppled Maximilian by late 1865 "had not our government weakened. . . . A golden opportunity was lost."[71]

The opportunity dwindled once Seward recovered from his wounds and returned to the State Department. In mid-June, he demanded a cabinet meeting to discuss what Grant, Romero, and Sheridan were up to. At that meeting, Grant argued for invading Mexico with American troops to round up Confederate refugees and drive out the French. According to Romero, Seward responded by "ably refuting Grant's ideas and making his own policy prevail," warning that an American invasion "would wound French pride and produce a war with France." Diplomacy, Seward insisted, could persuade Napoleon to withdraw his troops. Averse to more war, the cabinet preferred Seward's caution. Secretary of the Navy Gideon Welles concluded that Seward "acts from intelligence, Grant from impulse."[72]

A deft political infighter, Seward charmed Johnson, who entrusted foreign affairs entirely to the secretary of state, restricting Grant to his military command. In late July, Seward exploited his clout to forbid Romero's private visits with Johnson. On Seward's advice, the president also enforced the neutrality laws that banned the export of arms to belligerents. In July, at Johnson's request, the secretary of war ordered Sheridan to stand down and remain neutral along the Rio Grande. Privately, Grant blasted Seward as "a powerful practical ally of Louis Napoleon, but I am strongly in hope that his aid will do the Empire no good." Juárez insisted that he expected little "from the powerful, because they respect each other, [and] because they fear each other. . . . Wolves do not bite each other, they respect each other."[73]

While blocking Grant in cabinet meetings, Seward shrewdly exploited the general's threat to pressure the French. Toughening his diplomatic language with a touch of menace, Seward urged Napoleon to withdraw before Union generals and American public opinion demanded war.[74]

Passing time favored Seward's policy of military restraint. In May, at the peak of Union power and alarm over fleeing Confederates, Romero had urged the United States to invade Mexico quickly "before mustering out its army," which was massive and well supplied. But he underestimated the American politics that demanded a rapid demobilization. Composed of volunteers raised to fight the Confederacy, the big army could not endure for long in peacetime. Neither Congress nor the president meant to disappoint so many voters who wanted to go home. By December, 900,000 troops had mustered out, leaving just 125,000 to serve, stretched thin to fight Indians in the West and protect Blacks in the South. The military means for intervening in Mexico had vanished—to Seward's relief.[75]

Denied the regular army to invade Mexico, Romero and Grant shifted to raising 10,000 volunteers from demobilized federal troops. Seeking an inspirational and able general to attract and organize recruits, Grant chose General John Schofield (who had bloodied Hood's Confederate army at Franklin, Tennessee, in November 1864). Meeting with Romero and Grant, Schofield welcomed the challenge and a $100,000 bonus to serve as a Mexican major general. The secretary of war helped the cause by giving Schofield a year's leave of absence from the U.S. Army. Romero was ecstatic, assuring Juárez, "We will soon have realized all our desires and expectations for victory."[76]

In August, however, Seward invited Schofield to join him on a family vacation at the New Jersey shore. Plying the general with charm, wine, and flattery, Seward persuaded Schofield to accept an alternative mission. Instead of fighting in dusty Mexico, he could sip champagne in gay Paris as Seward's special emissary sent to tell Napoleon that "he must get out of Mexico." Once Schofield accepted that diplomatic mission, Seward delayed his departure until November. Reaching Paris in December 1865 and lingering until May 1866, Schofield never got a private meeting with Napoleon because Seward's ambassador, John Bigelow, never set one up. Delighting in the sights and pleasures of Paris, Schofield did not mind. Seward boasted that he had "squelch[ed] the wild scheme" of Grant.[77]

With Schofield diverted, Romero and Grant turned to Lew Wallace to recruit and command American volunteers raised for their covert war in Mexico. Ever enthusiastic, Wallace expected to raise at least 10,000 veterans "as soon as they are somewhat wearied of the monotony of home." Wallace felt that way, which exasperated his long-suffering wife Susan: "Mexico is uppermost in Lew's mind at present—when he dies, Mexico will be found written on his heart." She wanted him to stay home rather than risk death in a Mexican civil war: "Surely we have made graves enough there without marching an army against Maximilian." In addition to his romance with Mexico, Wallace pursued the golden dreams of easy wealth ignited by Mexico in the fancies of gringo adventurers.[78]

Wallace assembled fellow dreamers as recruiting officers. They included some former Confederates, among them Virginia's guerrilla chieftain John S. Mosby and John S. Ford, the Texan who had conspired with Wallace at Brownsville. But the recruiters could raise only a few hundred men, and upon reaching the Rio Grande most of them balked at the hardships of Mexico. Sheridan reported that Americans "could not subsist on tortillas and frijoles as the Mexican soldier does." Better then, Sheridan concluded, to arm Mexicans to win their civil war.[79]

Ignoring American neutrality laws, Grant and Romero covertly procured American weaponry for Juárez's men. With the end of the Civil War, American arms manufacturers were keen for foreign business to reduce their robust inventories of top-of-the-line weapons refined in the recent bloodbath. Sheridan stockpiled munitions along the Rio Grande and then tipped off nearby *Juaristas* to cross the river at night to retrieve their windfall. The weapons included 30,000 modern rifles drawn from the federal arsenal at Baton Rouge. By mid-1866, *Juaristas* had obtained a parity in firepower with their foes.[80]

In July 1865, Sheridan instructed his commander at Brownsville on the Rio Grande to "annoy the French authorities as much as you can through others without provoking actual hostilities or without making it too apparent." In January 1866, a company of Wallace's volunteers and 100 Black U.S. troops surprised, captured, and looted the *Imperialista* garrison at Bagdad, a suburb of Matamoros. A day later a French warship bombarded the Americans, who returned fire, leaving two dead on each side. Alarmed by the Bagdad clashes, General Bazaine pulled French troops southward, away from the border. He left behind an *Imperialista* garrison commanded by Mejía. Outgunned and outnumbered, Mejía abandoned Matamoras, which the *Juaristas* reclaimed in June 1866.[81]

Black Decree

In 1865 the Mexican civil war was a shifting contest of long-distance probes and counters across an arid and mountainous land that stretched thin the 47,000 French soldiers. A French general lamented, "The distances which the troops are made to cover are simply insane. My division has traveled 19,000 miles in seventeen months." A soldier complained, "We are running like crazy people after an enemy that cannot be caught." The French could capture large towns, an officer noted, but guerrillas held the countryside:

> No one sees any escape from our situation. We cannot find any pretext to leave; we have not advanced a step. The Mexican armies . . . use a very good system, always keeping clear of us and never engaging [in] battle; they retreat as we advance, and *when* we withdraw, since we are not numerous enough to occupy every position, they return quietly and settle down again in the places they occupied. The territory is so vast that they can go on playing that little game as long as they like.

Scattered in scores of dusty towns, French troops felt bored with their lot and enraged by persistent and elusive foes. Seeking revenge, soldiers burned villages and massacred civilians. The most brutal officer remained Charles Du Pin of the *contra-guerrillas*. At Tampico, an American saw Du Pin's men decapitate prisoners to play football with their heads.[82]

In September 1865, Bazaine sent French troops northward into Chihuahua to drive Juárez from his refuge at that state's capital. Juárez fled across 230 miles of high desert to El Paso del Norte, beside the Rio Grande. Despite Juárez's desperate position, another Liberal, General Jesús González Ortega, coveted it. The president's four-year term of office would expire at the end of November 1865. Under the constitution of 1857, in the absence of an election the chief justice would succeed to the presidency—and Ortega had become chief justice. This claim put Juárez in a tough spot, as he had been the stickler for legal forms. But he also believed that he alone could save the republic—and Mexico's congress had made him president for the duration of the civil war. Most Liberals supported Juárez, so Ortega left for the United States, where he charged the Mexican president with becoming a dictator.[83]

Lew Wallace made the long, arduous ride through mountains from Monterrey to seek Juárez. He found the classic juxtaposition of *Juarista* resistance: ragged troops serving a surprisingly confident and dignified president. Wallace assured his wife: "My opinion of the president grows better every day. Without doubt he is a true patriot and a great man; and as to his cabinet, it is composed of abler men than ours."[84]

Although Bazaine had not finished the job of pushing Juárez out of Mexico, the French general pretended that his victory was complete. In October 1865 he persuaded Maximilian to issue his infamous "Black Decree," which announced that, because Juárez had been crushed and evicted, any lingering armed resistance was mere banditry subject to death within twenty-four hours of capture. Bazaine ordered his men to take no prisoners: "This is a war to the death, a war without quarter between barbarism and civilization." The decree changed little in practice except to put Maximilian's name to the standard practice of *Imperialistas* and French contras. Why, then, issue the special decree? Bazaine wanted to stop Maximilian from pardoning any prisoners.[85]

Maximilian and Carlota needed an heir to their throne. Despite eight years of marriage, they lacked children, so the imperial couple adopted a grandchild of Agustín de Iturbide, the original Mexican emperor of the early 1820s. Such a link asserted a Mexican pedigree for the imported monarchs. To procure the two-year-old boy named Agustín, Maximilian promised his parents 150,000 pesos annually—money the indebted country could ill afford. In return, the family accepted exile in Europe, so that they could not interfere with the boy's education. His mother, Alice Green Iturbide, was an American who had married a son of the late emperor. In September 1865, she signed over her son, but regretted her decision nine days later and sought to reclaim him. Maximilian sent a carriage with troops ostensibly to bring Alice Iturbide to the palace. Instead, they took her away to Veracruz and forced her onto a ship bound for France.[86]

Refusing to accept defeat, Alice returned to the United States, where she shared her story with the press, which happily villainized the Mexican monarch. "Maximilian Charged with Kidnapping an American Child," ran a headline in the *New York Times*. Congress condemned Maximilian, and the American ambassador in Paris protested to the French government. Although Napoleon declined to interfere, he was none too happy with the embarrassing fiasco.[87]

Maximilian's regime was dying for lack of money, for he could collect little in taxes from a poor country ravaged by war, and Napoleon was busy milking Mexico to enrich French bankers and other creditors. The French emperor expected payment in full of Mexico's massive prewar debt, including the notoriously inflated Jecker loan made to the illicit Conservative regime in 1859. Then Napoleon exceeded even that scam by persuading the cash-strapped Maximilian to sell new bonds on the French market, adding another 534 million francs to Mexico's national debt. But his regime received only 6 percent of the funds because the bonds sold at a 63 percent discount and Napoleon claimed almost all the proceeds to pay for his military expenditures. Still, Napoleon demanded more collateral, including half of the customs revenue from Veracruz and control of the silver mines in Sonora.[88]

General Bazaine disdained Maximilian as irresponsible and unreliable. But so was Bazaine, who was supposed to train a Mexican army, but he refused to arm the recruits lest they desert with their weapons to join Juárez. In early 1865, when French treasury officials forced Maximilian to slash his budget, the emperor discharged most of his Mexican troops. Many became guerrillas fighting for loot and nominally for Juárez. The demobilization kept Maximilian dependent on the French troops that Napoleon wanted to bring home. Of such contradictions are empires made and unmade.[89]

Maximilian's regime was a gilded but flimsy façade. Both weak and stubborn, Maximilian struggled to make up his mind and then took bad advice. The French ambassador reported that the inconsistent emperor "reasoned well and acted entirely to the contrary." His paternalism waffled between indulgence and authoritarianism. "The more I study the Mexican people," Maximilian wrote, "the more I am led to the conclusion that we have got to try to make them happy without their help, and perhaps against their will." In mid-1865, Maximilian fired his cabinet as "incapable and lazy men, who . . . don't really know why they exist." But the emperor neglected his own duties to travel the countryside, collecting birds, butterflies, flowers, and antiquities while basking in the forced cheers of his people. William Gwin complained that, with "the emperor wandering through the country stuffing birds, public business is at a standstill." Gwin derided Maximilian as "of all men living, probably the least qualified to govern Mexico." A French journalist concluded, "Mexico is on a volcano; the Emperor and Empire used up; the insurrection triumphant."[90]

Madness

Fleeing debts and seeking glory, a young Prussian prince, Felix zu Salm-Salm, emigrated to fight for the Union, taking command of a volunteer regiment from New York in 1861. When the volunteer regiments demobilized in mid-1865, Salm-Salm declined to stay in the regular army at a reduced rank, feeling "horrified at the idea of living a dreary life in some little garrison beyond the pale of civilization." His wife thought that Salm-Salm "had the pugnacious instincts of a fighting cock." Seeking action, he hastened south to Mexico to offer his services to Maximilian, "for whose person and civilizing task I had always felt great sympathy." Salm-Salm would find more chaos than civilizing in Mexico.[91]

Salm-Salm's chief asset was his beautiful, forceful, and clever wife, Agnes Le Clercq Joy, renowned for her conversational and riding skills. Boldly moving among men as their equal, Agnes generated romantic and contradictory stories. She either came from Quebec or northern Vermont and her birth was in 1840, 1844, or 1845. Perhaps she was French Canadian and maybe an Indian. Because she rode so well, surely she had performed in a circus—or had been an actress on the New York stage. Rather than correct the stories, Agnes wrapped herself in a mystery that drew more attention. Adept at self-promotion, she invented a close friendship with Lincoln and boasted of commanding a Union company in combat. Neither was true. She charmed generals and politicians to get promotions for her prince, whom she married in 1862. She exploited her new cachet as a princess among Americans, who only despised aristocrats in principle.[92]

Prince Salm-Salm was a rare Union officer to support Maximilian's empire rather than Juárez's republic. During the 1850s, the prince had met the future emperor and, like so many others, mistook his charm for competence. As in the Union's war, the princess went along, arming herself with a revolver. An admirer praised "Princess Salm-Salm, in her gray-and-silver uniform sitting her horse like a female centaur." Little did the couple realize that they had defeated one lost cause in America only to join another in Mexico.[93]

In 1865, General Bazaine and other French officials wrote sobering reports about Maximilian's chaotic administration, while the press and legislature in Paris attacked the French occupation of Mexico as an expensive quagmire of folly. Fearing a war with the powerful Americans, Napoleon wanted to bring his 47,000 troops back home to cope with the rising threat within Europe from Prussia.[94]

On January 22, 1866, Napoleon addressed the French legislature to announce mission accomplished in Mexico. Having stabilized Maximilian's government, the troops could come home with honor in three stages: October 1866, March 1867, and October 1867 (later Napoleon amended that to one big withdrawal in March 1867). The visiting American general John Schofield marveled at the emperor's "audacity in the creation of convenient facts" to extricate himself from the Mexican "farce."[95]

Napoleon's announcement undercut Maximilian and Carlota. The French ambassador to Mexico, Alphonse Dano, described their position as "sad and painful beyond anything they expected. They are desperate and frightened." Urging Napoleon to reconsider, Maximilian warned, "If the guerrilleros return, everyone who has declared for the empire will be hanged or shot without mercy." Getting nowhere, Maximilian blamed Bazaine. In turn, that general insisted that Maximilian told "more lies than the biggest Mexican liar," while Carlota was "proud, disagreeable, vain, and believes herself a superior statesman." In fact, she was superior to Bazaine and Maximilian.[96]

Anticipating the disaster to come, Napoleon sought to save some face by persuading Maximilian to abdicate. If he returned with the French troops, Europeans could not blame Napoleon for abandoning Maximilian. Tempted by abdication, he began to pack, filling crates with his collection of 600 specimens of tropical beetles, butterflies, and plants. But his cabinet ministers insisted that Maximilian stay put, fearing a more rapid collapse and their own executions if he left. They were bolstered by their chief generals, Leonardo Márquez and Miguel Miramón, just returned from diplomatic posts. Ultimately, Maximilian heeded Carlota, who rejected abdication as cowardly, humiliating, and "only admissible in old men and idiots." She warned, "There is just one step from pathetic to ridiculous." But that step had already been made.[97]

In January 1866, Carlota became depressed by news of the death of her beloved father, the Belgian king Leopold I. The blow was political as well as emotional, for Leopold had provided troops, money, and diplomatic support—which her brother as royal heir revoked. Alarmed by Carlota's depression, the Mexican court doctor slipped morphine into her tea. Discovering that trick, Carlota dismissed him and became obsessed with a dread of poison.[98]

In August 1866, Carlota went to Paris on a desperate mission to lobby Napoleon to cancel the withdrawal: "He has a generous heart and he will listen to me." In fact, the French emperor was polite, charming, and noncommittal. Frustrated and furious, Carlota deemed Napoleon "the devil in person," and she denounced the French court, "It is all slime from beginning to end. Here every word is a lie."[99]

Humiliated by failure, Carlota snapped, becoming paranoid and delusional. Visiting the Pope in September, she sought refuge at the Vatican from French agents allegedly out to poison her food. The Pope lamented, "Nothing is spared me in this life—now a woman has to go mad in the Vatican." Obliged to stay in a hotel, Carlota would only eat chickens brought to her room alive for killing and cooking by her maidservant. Thinking that she could eat only food untouched by others, she scalded her hand reaching into a boiling pot. On October 1, Carlota wrote her last letter to Maximilian, "Dearly beloved treasure, I bid you farewell. God is calling me to Him."[100]

Rather than return to Mexico, Carlota went into seclusion at an Austrian palace near Trieste, where she was tended by servants and doctors. Obsessed with her failure to bear children, Carlota insisted that she was "nine months pregnant by the redemption of the devil, nine months by the Church, and now I am pregnant by the army." A doctor concluded, "The Empress had fallen victim to Mexico."[101]

Crushed by Carlota's breakdown, Maximilian felt alone and unmoored as his regime tottered. Reliant on her resolve and insights in a crisis, he suffered from her absence. Without Carlota, Maximilian saw no point in keeping Agustín Iturbide as their adopted son, so the emperor sent the boy back to his long-suffering mother, Alice.[102]

Queretaro

Abandoning outposts, Bazaine consolidated his troops in fewer and larger garrisons in central Mexico. Seizing the forsaken towns, *Juaristas* took revenge on Mexican collaborators and French civilians. A French captain despaired, "It is a complete fiasco, and very sad because of all the personal misfortunes. French and Mexicans alike curse the French intervention. Everything that is happening is so appalling that I cannot believe we left Mexico in such a shameful way." Mexican *Imperialistas* were supposed to fill the gap, but most were too poorly trained and motivated to resist the *Juarista* surge.[103]

As guerrillas took over more of the countryside, the Confederate colonies suffered increased robberies, kidnapping for ransom, and rustling of livestock. Despairing of their prospects, many colonists bolted for Cuba, Brazil, Canada, Britain, or even Japan. But most expatriates went home to the American South to take an oath of allegiance and seek a federal pardon. They included Kirby Smith, who got a pardon with help from his West Point classmate, General Grant.[104]

Even Matthew Maury departed, forsaking Mexico's failing immigration office in February 1866. That spring, Maximilian closed the office to save money. When an audit revealed missing funds, the *Mexican Times* blasted Maury's management as "conducted in utter defiance of common sense and with not much regard for truth or honesty." Abandoned by Maury, colonists cursed him for enticing them into anarchy.[105]

In June 1866 a thousand guerrillas seized the Confederate town of Carlota, looting, burning, and killing. Most of the colonists returned home, where a South Carolina newspaper noted, "The sight of these broken, hungry, desolate people as they straggled back into a hundred communities across the South became the best argument against emigration."[106]

Once the French troops completed their withdrawal, Bazaine expected Maximilian's regime to collapse within a few "days and hours." Anticipating a *Juarista* massacre of Conservatives and French expatriates, Bazaine wrote to President Andrew Johnson, urging him to send American troops to occupy and pacify Mexico: "The moral influence of the United States has destroyed the Empire, and thus the obligation rests upon the United States to keep Mexico from anarchy and protect the thousands of foreigners residing there."[107]

Seward shared Bazaine's alarm but opposed sending American troops to Mexico. Instead, the secretary of state sent General Sherman on a diplomatic mission to meet with Maximilian and hasten his abdication. Sherman was also supposed to consult with Juárez to secure his protection for American and European expats during the transfer of power. But the blunt and fiery Sherman was no diplomat. Reaching Veracruz in November 1866 on an American steamship, the cranky general was miffed when Maximilian rejected abdication. And Sherman deemed Juárez too far away in Chihuahua: "I have not the remotest idea of riding on mule back a thousand miles in Mexico to find the chief magistrate." In a huff, Sherman ordered his crew to take him and their ship back to New Orleans after less than a week at Veracruz harbor. The secretary of the navy derided the mission as "a miserable, bungling piece of business."[108]

In fact, Juárez was moving southward, following his victorious armies. During the spring and summer of 1866, the Liberals liberated the periphery of the country, including the southern states of Chiapas, Guerrero, and Tabasco, as well as the northern states of Baja California, Chihuahua, and Sonora. By recovering the seaports of Guayamas,

Mazatlán, Matamoros, and Tampico, Liberals gained prime sources of customs revenue subtracted from the empire.[109]

In the fall, *Juarista* troops pressed into central Mexico, retaking Guanajuato, San Luis Potosí, and Zacatecas. Commanded by Mariano Escobedo, a Liberal army routed withdrawing *Imperialistas* at San Jacinto, killing or capturing three-quarters of them. *Imperialista* control shrank to the narrow corridor from Mexico City via Puebla to Veracruz with one major outpost at Queretaro, 100 miles northwest of the capital.[110]

In February 1867, French troops abandoned Mexico City, marching eastward to Veracruz, where warships and transports would take them home. On March 16, the last French soldiers boarded their ships. Rejecting Bazaine's renewed pleas to abdicate and join the evacuation, Maximilian doubled down on his pose as a Mexican patriot relieved to get rid of foreign troops. He declared, "At last, we are free!" but Maximilian was whistling past his own graveyard.[111]

Prince and Princess Salm-Salm stuck with Maximilian. As romantics, they expected that their loyalty and courage could turn the tide against overwhelming odds. Little did they realize that their emperor was a fool leading a suicide mission. While the princess stayed in the capital, the prince joined the staff of General Santiago Vidaurri, the *caudillo* who had fled from his northern states.[112]

Maximilian went to Queretaro, a city defended by 9,000 *Imperialistas* led by generals Márquez, Miramón, Mejía, and Vidaurri. But Queretaro was a deadly cul-de-sac in a valley exposed to artillery fire from 35,000 Liberals in the surrounding hills. Too late, Maximilian realized that "the Republican forces, which have been so unjustly characterized as disorganized, demoralized and motivated only by the desire to pillage, prove by their acts that they are a unified army."[113]

Desperate for reinforcements, Maximilian sent Márquez and Vidaurri back to Mexico City to organize a relief expedition for Queretaro. Instead, they betrayed the emperor by grabbing power in the capital. Rather than march north to relieve Queretaro, Márquez and Vidaurri headed east to attack the Liberal army of Porfirio Díaz besieging Puebla. But Díaz captured that city, routed Márquez's army, and drove the survivors back to Mexico City.[114]

Trapped at Queretaro, defenders suffered from artillery fire that wrecked buildings and killed dozens. As morale declined, hungry *Imperialistas* deserted, reducing the garrison to 5,000 men. When Miramón gave a meat pie to Maximilian's starving staff, who called it delicious, the general revealed that he had plenty of cats to make more.[115]

Maximilian placed his trust in Colonel Miguel López by giving him command of the imperial bodyguard—and the emperor became godfather to the colonel's child. On the night of May 14–15, however, López accepted 7,000 golden pesos from Escobedo to let *Juarista* troops into the city to surround Maximilian's headquarters and compel the surprised defenders to surrender. Escobedo confined Maximilian, Salm-Salm, Miramón, and Mejía to prison cells in a former convent. Contrary to Bazaine's fears and *Imperialista* propaganda, the disciplined victors committed no massacre and little looting. But they did want revenge on the leaders of their enemies.[116]

Hastening to Queretaro, Princess Salm-Salm tried to help her prince and emperor escape by offering bribes of $100,000 each to the two colonels in command of the prison guards. Lacking cash, she could offer only promissory notes for future payment, which did not impress the colonels, who tipped off Escobedo. He ousted her from the city.[117]

In mid-June, a court martial tried and convicted Maximilian, Miramón, and Mejía for treason against the Republic of Mexico. The court sentenced them to die. Defense lawyers, diplomats, and Princess Salm-Salm lobbied Juárez to pardon Maximilian. But Juárez refused, citing the letter of the law and the fury of his troops and generals who demanded revenge for their many comrades executed under the emperor's notorious Black Decree. And if Maximilian survived, he might remain a rallying point for *Imperialistas* waging civil war. By executing him, Juárez reasoned, he could more easily spare the lives of the emperor's misguided followers: "The tomb of Maximilian and the others will be the redemption of the rest of the misled."[118]

By defying foreign pressure to pardon, Juárez asserted Mexico's sovereign dignity. He told a sobbing Princess Salm-Salm, "If all the kings and queens of Europe were in your place, I could not spare that life. It is not I who take it, it is the people and the law; and if I should not do its will, the people would take it and mine also." A firing squad executed Maximilian, Miramón, and Mejía on June 19.[119]

The executions helped to end resistance in Mexico City, which surrendered on June 20 after seven weeks of bombardment by Díaz's army. Márquez went into hiding after looting the treasury of a million dollars. Initially, he hid in an empty mill, then a newly dug grave, before escaping in disguise to Veracruz and on to Havana, where he lived in exile. Despite having committed more atrocities than any other general, Márquez evaded Liberal justice at the end. Vidaurri was not so lucky. Captured in hiding, he suffered a severe beating, was taken to a dump at the edge of the city, forced to kneel in horse dung, and shot in the back while a band played a mocking song, "The March of the Crabs." On July 15, Juárez entered the capital in triumph.[120]

During the fall of 1869 the former American secretary of state, William H. Seward, visited Mexico for three months. Both hosts and guest flattered one another with pretty lies. Seward claimed credit for the Liberal triumph, and his gracious hosts—Juárez and Romero—agreed, feting him as their greatest friend. Seward declared that during the Mexican civil war "the United States became for the first time, in sincerity and earnestness, the friend and ally of every other Republican state in America and all the Republican states became, from that hour, the friends and allies of the United States." Despite later American military interventions and Latin American resentments, the United States had shown greater solidarity with Mexico than ever before—and had belatedly contributed to Juárez's victory with diplomatic support and covert arms shipments. The French ambassador to the United States, Jules Berthemy, agreed: "What happened in Mexico is first of all a defiance of Monarchical Europe from Republican America."[121]

Juárez

Civil wars had devastated all of Mexico—in contrast to the United States, where the South bore the brunt of destruction while the North prospered. Mexico's conflict featured more executions and massacres, claiming thousands of civilian lives. That civil war left more enduring havoc as many demobilized soldiers and guerrillas could find scant work in a depressed economy. Rampant banditry discouraged foreign investment in Mexico.[122]

Unlike the United States, Mexico had suffered the violent dislocation of its legitimate government, kept on the run for four years. While the Union had retained credit internationally, the Juárez government had to renounce the inflated national debt incurred by the illegitimate regimes of Miramón and Maximilian. Also alienated by Maximilian's execution, Europeans treated Mexico as a pariah nation, unfit for the foreign investment so desperately needed for recovery and development. Desperate for capital, Mexico depended on American investors, who demanded and secured ownership of key assets: mines, oil fields, and railroad routes.[123]

Liberals favored a market economy of equal opportunity that would reward merit, uplifting poor strivers while eroding concentrations of inherited wealth and power. But to win his civil war, Juárez had relied on regional *caudillos* and some wealthy *hacendados* (landlords), who expected to keep the peasants poor and docile. Unable to reform the countryside (where most Mexicans lived), Liberals concentrated on changing towns and cities, where a middle class supported a market society. By investing in secular schools and a federal bureaucracy, Liberals enhanced social mobility. Linking free minds to free markets, a Liberal official insisted, "The diffusion of knowledge, like the circulation of money, frees many minds of the proletariat; and instruction bears fruit in free minds as does capital in free hands." Liberals were thoroughly bourgeois reformers.[124]

Rather than provide free farms to poor peasants, the revenue-starved Juárez regime sold properties confiscated from *Imperialistas* to Liberal *hacendados*. And the regime dared not enforce the laws against the debt peonage that provided cheap labor for *haciendas*. Instead, the government privatized and sold the lands of Native communities, obliging thousands more to become wage laborers. The land policies provoked several regional rebellions by peasants, but Juárez deployed troops to suppress them on behalf of their landlords.[125]

Years on the run had made Juárez suspicious of others and convinced that he alone could lead Mexico. Necessary for wartime survival, those qualities became liabilities when he needed to collaborate with other ambitious men in a restored republic. For his cabinet, Juárez favored older men who had clung to him through thick and thin, but that cronyism frustrated younger politicians.[126]

The harsh experiences of war had led Juárez away from the core Liberal commitments to strong states, limited federal government, and a weak president. "It is not possible to govern in these conditions, no one obeys, no one can be obliged to obey," Juárez complained. In August 1867, he ran for the presidency, abandoning an earlier pledge not to seek reelection. He also asked voters to approve sweeping constitutional changes to strengthen the presidency at the expense of congress and the states.[127]

Critics howled that Juárez took illicit means to alter a constitution that they had defended so devoutly through two civil wars. Although Juárez won reelection with 72 percent of the ballots, voters rejected his constitutional changes.[128]

Juárez's tenacious hold on power alienated his most able, ambitious, and impatient general, Porfirio Díaz, who wanted to be president. The Princess Salm-Salm remembered him as "a man of medium height, with a rather handsome face, and brilliant, dark, and very intelligent eyes." Charismatic and courageous, Díaz had fought in thirty-seven battles, suffered many wounds, and twice dodged execution as a prisoner. In November 1867, Díaz's brother Félix won the governorship of Oaxaca over a candidate favored by Juárez.[129]

In 1871, Porfirio Díaz ran for president against Juárez, as did Sebastián Lerdo, who felt it was his turn to lead. Díaz and Lerdo split 53 percent of the electoral vote, enabling Juárez to claim victory with 47 percent. In November, the Díaz brothers rebelled, denouncing Juárez's "indefinite, imposed, and outrageous re-election" as a betrayal of republicanism. But congress and the federal army sided with Juárez, routing the rebels in January 1872. The victors captured and executed Félix Díaz. Ever a survivor, Porfirio Díaz escaped in disguise to Veracruz, where he caught a ship to exile in New York City.[130]

The Díaz revolt took a toll on Juárez, then sixty-five years old. In

July 1872 he died after his third heart attack of the year. By resolve and
endurance, Juárez led the triumph of a liberal republic over a conservative monarchy imposed by foreigners. Although he failed to break the
regional power of *caudillos* or reduce inequality, Juárez did promote a
stronger sense of national identity, a market economy, and a secular government freed from domination by the Catholic Church. Aside from his
electoral irregularities, he sustained the rule of law, freedom of the press,
public education, and religious pluralism—establishing new norms for
civic culture in Mexico. Juárez had overcome longer odds and greater
dangers than even Lincoln during the great North American struggles
of the mid-nineteenth century.[131]

Fates

After leading French troops in Mexico, General Bazaine returned to
France, where he suffered a crushing defeat and surrendered his army
to Prussian invaders in October 1870. Disgusted by that defeat, the
French overthrew Napoleon III, replacing his empire with a republic.
That new republic court-martialed Bazaine and exiled him to a small
island in the Mediterranean. In 1874, he escaped in a sailboat chartered
by his Mexican wife, who took him away to Spain, where he spent the
rest of his life in genteel poverty.[132]

The victorious Prussian army included Prince Felix zu Salm-Salm,
who had returned home after serving Maximilian in Mexico. Bitter at
the French for abandoning the Mexican emperor, Salm-Salm delighted
in helping to defeat Bazaine. But the prince died in combat and left massive debts to his American-born widow, Princess Agnes zu Salm-Salm.
In despair, she sought to become a nun, but the Pope quite rightly ruled
that she lacked "a vocation for a nunnery." She did have a vocation for
melodrama, obtaining a surprise inheritance from an American relative
and admirer. The bequest enabled her to buy a modest home on the
Rhine, where she died in December 1912.[133]

Of the major figures in the Mexican struggle, the longest survivor
was the most surprising: the empress Carlota, who had gone mad in
1866. In July 1867 the king of Belgium brought his sister home to live

for nearly sixty years in royal castles. In happier moments she played
the piano, read, sewed, took walks, rowed on a lake, and conversed
with her rag doll, thinking it was Maximilian. She experienced World
War I, a conflict provoked by the blundering diplomacy of the elderly
Franz Joseph, Maximilian's brother and emperor of Austria and Hun-
gary. Carlota watched as German planes dropped bombs on a nearby
village. "It will be a final catastrophe, sir," she announced. In January
1927, Carlota died of pneumonia at the age of eighty-six. "It is all for
naught. We shall not succeed," were her last words.[134]

TWELVE ⅏ RECONSTRUCTIONS

> Our population is destined to roll its restless waves to the icy
> barriers of the north . . . The monarchs of Europe are to have no
> rest while they have a colony remaining on this continent.
> —WILLIAM H. SEWARD (AMERICAN)[1]

> We must qualify ourselves to fulfill the spirit of tolerance and
> forbearance. It is our only means to make a great nation of a
> small people. —THOMAS D'ARCY MCGEE (CANADIAN)[2]

As with Mexico's *Imperialistas*, the Union's military triumph alarmed Canadian leaders in the spring of 1865. On April 11, John A. Macdonald warned, "The surrender of Lee & the Close of the War bring matters to a crisis between England & Canada" because "the United States, flushed with success with their armies full of fight" might invade Canada to spite the British. Union newspapers and congressmen accused the British of coddling Confederates and allowing them to exploit Canada as a base for exporting terrorism. Yankee leaders blustered that taking Canada would compensate the Union for its grievances against Britain.[3]

During the fall of 1865, Canadian fear of an invasion receded as the United States demobilized its volunteer regiments and became preoccupied with reconstructing the South. But then Canadians worried about the thousands of demobilized troops who were Irish immigrants. Having fled from British misrule in Ireland, they might strike back by invading Canada. Irish radicals, known as Fenians, hoped that such an invasion would provoke war between Britain and the United States, improving the prospects for revolution in Ireland. Fenians sang,

Many battles have been won
Along with the boys in blue
And we'll go and capture Canada,
for we've nothing else to do.

Union commanders reported that Fenians were mustering and drilling along the border, but Grant told his subordinates to stand down unless an actual invasion began. Federal leaders wanted to avoid alienating Irish Americans, a major voting bloc in American politics.[4]

Although nearly a third of Canadians were of Irish descent, most were too busy with farms and jobs to promote revolution. The most radical preferred to make trouble in Ireland rather than invite it into Canada. Irish Catholics would brawl with Orangemen in the streets of Toronto, but immigrants wanted no part of helping Americans conquer Canada. In general, they rather liked Canada as a land of opportunity and freedom compared to Ireland. The Catholic Church denounced Fenian agitators as reckless and immoral—as did Canada's leading Irish politician, Thomas D'Arcy McGee. A radical agitator when young in

PREVIOUS PAGE: *"Battle of Ridgeway, June 2, 1866," 1869, by unknown.*

Ireland, McGee had emigrated to the United States, where he soured on republicanism as corrupt, demagogic, and tainted by slavery. Moving to Canada in 1857, McGee embraced the British empire and became a politician with a quick wit, rich singing voice, and a capacity for alcohol that impressed even John A. Macdonald.[5]

Lacking support in Canada, Fenian invaders would have to win on their own. To attract followers willing to fight or contribute money, leaders had to talk big: of growing thousands of supporters and immense stockpiles of weapons, of subverted Irish troops willing to betray British garrisons, and of thousands of Irish Canadians longing for liberation. Fenian leaders hoped to strike on St. Patrick's Day, March 17, 1866, but they struggled to organize and arm enough men along the border. In April, about 500 armed Fenians did assemble in Eastport, Maine, to attack the nearby island of Campobello, New Brunswick. Tipped off by informers, the British sent warships while New Brunswick mustered militiamen to block the raid. After burning a Canadian customs office on a smaller island, the Fenians dispersed homeward.[6]

The Fenian debacle at Eastport encouraged Canadian authorities to let down their guard, assuming that the worst had passed. But on June 1, about 800 armed Fenians rushed across the Niagara River to land near Fort Erie. Advancing into the interior, they defeated hastily assembled and ill-trained militia at the village of Ridgeway and won another firefight near Fort Erie. Fenian leaders had expected that news of a victory or two in Canada would enthuse thousands of Irish Americans to join the invasion. Hearing crickets instead, the Fenians withdrew back to the American side of the border on June 3. No British garrisons had mutinied, few Canadians showed support, and most Irish Americans stayed home.[7]

Making few arrests and no convictions, American authorities instead offered Fenians free railroad passes to return to their homes. A belated presidential proclamation denounced cross-border attacks, but that did nothing for Canada's dead militiamen. Outraged at the weak American response, George Brown accused Americans of wearing "the mask of sympathy for Irish wrongs" to provoke Canada's annexation "by means of border troubles." Most Canadians sought a stronger and larger confederation to protect them against threats from the United States. Fenians did more to build Canada than to liberate Ireland.[8]

In March 1865 the Canadian parliament had approved a confederation, but the Maritimers also had to approve. Although few in number—250,000 in New Brunswick, and 350,000 in Nova Scotia— Maritimers occupied the crucial eastern approaches to Canada. Reliant on oceanic commerce and fisheries, the Maritimers dealt more with Britain across the Atlantic than overland with Canada. Independent from one another, the small Maritime colonies feared being swallowed up in a larger country dominated by Canadian strangers. Many Maritime politicians preferred to remain big fish in their small ponds. Why then gamble on what one Nova Scotian called "this crazy Confederacy with a mongrel crew, half-English, half French"? But British leaders meant to reduce their defense commitments and costs by pushing the Maritimers to join Canada.[9]

In 1865 many Maritimers distrusted confederation as a conniving scheme hatched from the "oily brains of Canadian politicians." In early March, voters in New Brunswick cast out the pro-confederation provincial government led by Leonard Tilley. Nova Scotians also appeared poised to reject confederation under the leadership of Joseph Howe, who preferred "the rule of John Bull to that of Jack Frost," for he disdained Canada as a land of "wilderness and ice." Spooked by Howe's popularity and New Brunswick's election, Nova Scotia's premier, Charles Tupper, backed away from confederation as "impractical."[10]

John A. Macdonald, George Brown, and Alexander T. Galt led a Canadian delegation to London to lobby imperial leaders to pressure the balky Maritimers. Delighted by the warm welcome from Britain's rulers, including Queen Victoria, Galt exulted: "We were treated as if we were ambassadors and not as *mere Colonists*." Galt reported attending "games of all kinds, menageries of savage animals, and shows of Irishmen disguised as savage Indians."[11]

As the Canadians had hoped, British leaders took their side, informing the Crown's lieutenant governors in New Brunswick and Nova Scotia "to turn the screw as hard as will be useful, but not harder" to persuade Maritimers to get on board. The British insisted that funding for the intercolonial railroad coveted by Maritimers would depend on confederation. Noting their "great jealousy of Canada," the colonial secretary, Edward Cardwell, advised: "While Imperial influence may be pressed, Canadian predominance must be *sup*-pressed."[12]

Crown influence helped to swing New Brunswick, as did secret Canadian money sent by Macdonald to support pro-confederation candidates for the provincial legislature. New Brunswick voters also reacted against the April 1866 raid by Fenians along their border—which made the case that the province would benefit from defense by a larger confederation. In June 1866, pro-confederation candidates won thirty-three of the colony's forty-one legislative seats. With New Brunswick back on board, Charles Tupper persuaded Nova Scotia's legislature to authorize negotiations for that province to join the confederation. But he needed to complete a final deal with the other provinces and British Parliament before May 1867, when Nova Scotia would hold a new legislative election. Considering Nova Scotian voters a fickle lot, Tupper urged Macdonald to hasten a Canadian delegation back to London to close the deal there.[13]

Then Macdonald became the problem, for his alcoholism had worsened, often preventing him from attending in parliament. Part of the problem was Macdonald's effort to outdrink his boon companion, Thomas D'Arcy McGee. When colleagues denounced their public drinking as disgraceful, Macdonald allegedly took his friend aside: "Look here McGee, this Cabinet can't afford two drunkards, and I'm not quitting." But neither would McGee.[14]

Macdonald also had a shrewd, political reason for delaying his visit to London. He meant to shrink the period for negotiations to reduce the risk that critics at home would learn about last-minute tweaks in the constitution, lest they make trouble by reopening the entire question. In October, Macdonald explained: "No echo of it must reverberate through the British provinces until it becomes law. . . . The Act once passed and beyond remedy, the people will soon be reconciled to it." At last, in late November, Macdonald led a Canadian delegation back to London, where they joined Tupper, Tilley, and other Maritime leaders. Meeting in a London hotel, the Canadians accepted the chief demand of the Maritimers: to pay for a railroad connection and to start work within six months.[15]

The delegates also had to choose a name for their new country. Macdonald favored the "Kingdom of Canada," with a royal prince to serve as governor general—as that title would elevate Canada to a parity with Ireland in the imperial constellation. At the last minute, the delegates instead adopted the "Dominion of Canada." The change reflected a concern that "kingdom" would anger Americans, who opposed monarchy in the Americas.[16]

Macdonald led the discussions with his usual savvy charm, attentive to the complex interests of four differing provinces. A French-Canadian delegate, Hector Langevin, marveled, "Macdonald is a sharp fox. He is a very well-informed man, ingratiating, clever, and very popular. He is *the man* of the conference." A British official admired Macdonald's ability to manage jealous politicians of rival provinces, all acting "as eager dogs watch a rat-hole; a snap on one side might have provoked a snap on the other; and put an end to all the concord."[17]

But Macdonald drank too much and sometimes could not attend sessions. One night he nodded off without tending to his candle, which ignited a newspaper and then bed and clothing. Macdonald suffered severe burns to hair, head, and hands before he sobered up enough to put out the blaze. But for a thick flannel night shirt, he noted, "I would have burned to death."[18]

Macdonald decided that he needed a nocturnal keeper. On February 16, 1867, he married Susan Agnes Bernard, the thirty-year-old sister of his secretary. She was bright, well-read, strong-willed, and fluent in French and English. They had been acquainted for nine years, but their intense courtship began right after the nearly fatal fire. They had profound differences, for she was pious, temperate, and moralistic. But she shared his love of politics and became as fiercely protective as he would let her be. She made Macdonald promise to drink less—he could not and would not promise abstinence. His reduced drinking proved entirely relative and slight, which caused friction. A colleague reported, "John A. was carried out of the lunch room, hopelessly drunk. What a prospect Mrs. John A. has before her."[19]

In late December, the delegates reached agreement and Parliament then finalized the British North America Act in March 1867. Unlike American constitutions, which dwelled on individual rights to liberty, the Canadian version included the British colonial formula that mandated "Peace, Order, and good Government." Still tethered to Great Britain, which would manage foreign policy, the Dominion was half colony and half nation, but wholly committed to avoiding becoming American. Britain's colonial secretary defined "Canada as a quasi-independent country, primarily responsible . . . for its own defence, though assured of the powerful support of England when doing its duty to itself & to her." Proud of the British Empire, Canadians cherished parliamentary government as superior to American democracy, which they saw as demagogic and unstable.[20]

On July 1, 1867, the new Canadian government formally commenced with a festive celebration at Ottawa around the newly completed Parliament Buildings. Through her governor general, Queen Victoria knighted Sir John A. Macdonald and named him the first prime minister of Canada. The Dominion was pulled together by a few politicians not previously known as visionaries—above all by Macdonald, who cajoled, pressured, and wooed others to gamble on a bigger Canada.[21]

There was trouble in Nova Scotia, where confederation's critics had prevailed in the spring election, capturing eighteen of the province's nineteen seats in the Dominion's parliament. But Macdonald placated Nova Scotians by reducing tariffs on their imports, assuming the province's debt of nearly $2 million, and awarding an annual subsidy of $85,000. Disgusted by some Nova Scotian hotheads promoting American annexation, Howe preferred to accept Macdonald's deal. In the 1868 Nova Scotian election, Howe's moderates prevailed, and he joined the cabinet in Ottawa.[22]

While adding Howe, Macdonald lost Thomas D'Arcy McGee, targeted by Fenians for death as a traitor to Ireland. In early 1868, McGee had ominous nightmares: "If ever I were murdered, it would be by some wretch who would shoot me from behind." On April 6, 1868, after an evening session of parliament, McGee shared drinks and cigars with Macdonald at a bar before each headed home. At 2:00 a.m. McGee reached his lodging and, as he opened the door, was shot in the back of the head. He was forty-three years old. Learning of the murder, Macdonald hurried to the scene and helped carry McGee's corpse from the street to a sofa in the boarding house.

The police arrested Patrick James Whelan, a twenty-eight-year-old tailor and Fenian. A search revealed the murderous revolver in his pocket. Convicted in September, Whelan died on the gallows in February 1869 still professing innocence and defiance. After the bloody American Civil War, McGee had warned Canadians: "The days of the colonial comedy of Government were over and gone" because "politics had become stern and almost tragic for the New World."[23]

Sandwich

Because the Dominion was new and tenuous, Canadians worried that Americans would continue to seek their annexation. In April 1867, Macdonald complained, "A brilliant future would certainly await us were it not for those wretched Yankees who hunger & thirst" for Canada. To hold their own in North America, Canadians needed to expand westward by adding the Pacific colony of British Columbia—and the vast intervening land of prairie, plains, and mountains known as Assiniboia or Red River. Macdonald explained, "If Canada is to remain a Country separate from the United States, it is of great importance that they should not get behind us by right or force and intercept the route to the Pacific."[24]

But Canadian expansion westward might provoke conflict with Americans who coveted the same territory. Rather than seeing Canada as a kindred free government, Americans perceived a watered-down British monarchy that threatened republicanism. A bellicose American senator, Zachariah Chandler of Michigan, declared that a transcontinental Canada would become "a standing menace . . . that we ought not to tolerate and will not tolerate." He added, "This North American continent belongs to us and ours it must be." No one thought that Canadians could put up much of a fight against the United States. With just four million people, Canada had a tenth of the American population—and most Canadians lived within a hundred miles of the American border, beside, the London *Times* declared, "the most powerful and aggressive state in the New World."[25]

After the Civil War, Seward pushed for northern expansion, beginning with Alaska. On March 30, 1867, he concluded a treaty with Russia for the United States to buy Alaska for $7.2 million. The Russian empire needed money and did not value Alaska, where few Russians and more Natives lived. The seal and sea otter trade had collapsed from overhunting, making the colony a financial liability. With American mariners nosing around Alaska's harbors, Russians feared a settler takeover like those that had annexed Texas, California, and Oregon. By selling instead, Russians preserved good relations with the United States. At odds with most of the European powers, the Russians needed diplomatic friends.[26]

In April the Senate quickly approved the deal. Americans did not expect much from Alaska's vast, frosty interior of forests, mountains, and tundra, dismissed by a leading Republican as a "desolate, dreary, starved region" where "otters and seals and so forth are yearly persecuted toward extermination." But Americans did covet Alaska's ports to serve as fishing and whaling bases and to facilitate trans-Pacific commerce. In October, Russia formally transferred Alaska to the United States.[27]

Americans celebrated the acquisition as a squeeze play on Canada, now bracketed by Alaska to the northwest and Washington Territory to the south. Seward declared that "Nature designs that this whole continent. . . . shall be, sooner or later, within the magic circle of the American Union." As a start, he assured senators that Alaska would "help the United States to acquire British Columbia." In May 1867, British Columbia's leading newspaper warned that American Alaska "places the whole of Her Majesty's possessions on the Pacific in the position of a piece of meat between two slices of bread, where they may be devoured in a single bite."[28]

British Columbia was a mountainous, heavily forested colony with only about 10,000 colonists, most of them American miners who arrived during the gold rush of the late 1850s. By 1867, the gold was played out, leaving depression behind. The governor described his capital as a "melancholy picture of disappointed hopes" manifest in boarded-up shops and hotels. To shed the colony's massive public debt, most of the colonists favored American annexation. British Columbians traded down the Pacific Coast with the United States rather than overland with distant Canada on the far side of the daunting Rocky Mountains and Great Plains. By joining the United States, British Columbians could gain full access to the California market for their lumber, fish, and furs.[29]

In 1867, Seward wanted Great Britain to deliver British Columbia as compensation for Americans' "*Alabama* claims." These claims derived from the losses suffered during the war by merchant shipping from British-built Confederate commerce raiders, including CSS *Alabama*. Senator Charles Sumner wanted even more: all of Canada as compensation for the American war debt of $2 billion incurred after the raiders went to sea.[30]

Invested in the Dominion, British leaders instead pushed the British Columbians to join Canada. In 1870, a delegation from that colony traveled to Ottawa to negotiate a deal, but to get there they had to go south to California to take the Americans' new transcontinental railroad. The delegates reasonably concluded that they could not join the Dominion without a Canadian railroad connection across the continent. Canada's leaders promised to build one within ten years, although no one had surveyed a route through the toughest mountains on the continent. Buying agreement, Canada's leaders also consented to pay British Columbia's public debt plus generous subsidies every year. Displaced colonial officials got Canadian pensions, and the province received disproportionate representation for its then small population. On July 20, 1871, British Columbia joined the Dominion.[31]

For an overland rail route to British Columbia, Canadians needed the vast hinterland west of Lake Superior. But in 1870 the region belonged to Native peoples and their Metis relatives, with a small sprinkling of colonists concentrated around Winnipeg along the Red River. A Crown charter had awarded that territory, known as Assiniboia, to a London-based fur-trading enterprise: the Hudson's Bay Company. That arrangement satisfied the Natives and Metis, who relied on fur trading. But the colony's 1,600 white settlers were Anglophones who favored joining either Canada or the United States. They wanted to accelerate economic development by dispossessing Natives and Metis, whom they saw as ignorant, indolent, and superstitious barbarians.[32]

Initially, Americans had an advantage because Minnesota's merchants had drawn Assiniboia into their economic orbit. Taking produce to Minneapolis was far easier than getting to Canada across hundreds of miles of granite barrens sprinkled by scrubby trees. In 1868 Macdonald noted that the inhabitants had "become so Americanized in interest and feeling" that Canada had to act fast. To head off an American land grab, Canadians made a deal with the Hudson's Bay Company in March 1869. Canadians bought the core of the region for £300,000 and agreed to share the revenue from selling land to settlers. The HBC kept its northern territories, which still had some value for the fur trade. In June 1869 Canada established a territorial government for the acquired land.[33]

But Canadian leaders had failed to consult the Metis, who distrusted a Canadian takeover as a threat to their rights. To block a hasty annexation, they relied on a talented young man, Louis Riel, the son of a French-Canadian mother and Metis father. A devout Catholic, Riel graduated from a Jesuit college in Montreal and then practiced law. In 1868 he returned home to Red River to organize and lead a provisional government. At Winnipeg, an American described Riel as "ambitious, quick of perception, though not profound, of indomitable energy [and] daring, [but] excessively suspicious of others."[34]

Disdaining subordination in a territory, the Metis wanted immediate and full provincial status as "Manitoba," with special protection for their land rights and culture as Francophone Catholics. In December 1869 Riel's partisans seized control of Fort Garry, which dominated nearby Winnipeg. They also blocked the entry of Canada's territorial governor, William McDougall, a poor choice given to little thought and hasty bombast. Thereafter, wits dubbed him "William the Conquered." Riel explained that the Metis resented being "treated as if they were more insignificant than they really were."[35]

In February 1870, Anglophone settlers tried to kill Riel and grab Fort Garry. Defeating them, Riel's government tried and convicted one, Thomas Scott, for treason. Shot by a firing squad in March, Scott became a martyr to the settlers and their champions, the Protestant expansionists of Ontario (the former Canada West). One of them said of the dimwitted Scott: "His mental gifts may have been few—yet he died for us."[36]

Macdonald worried that Riel was a pawn for Minnesota's annexationists. Although ungrounded, that fear seemed credible because the American consul at Winnipeg, Oscar Malmros, bought the region's lone newspaper, the *Nor'Wester*, which then published his manifesto, "Annexation Our Manifest Destiny." Winnipeg's leading hotel took down the Union Jack, replaced by the Stars and Stripes. Alarmed, Macdonald ordered 1,200 troops to head west to Manitoba, where they found no armed resistance.[37]

Offering a carrot as well as a stick, the Canadian parliament passed the Manitoba Act in May 1870. As Riel had demanded, Canada established a provincial (rather than a territorial) government for Manitoba—and protected the French language and Catholic faith. Canada also reserved 1.4 million acres for the Metis and provided the province with a generous annual subsidy until the population reached 400,000. Canadians promised amnesty to Riel's supporters—save for a few (including Riel) accused of killing Scott. To escape prosecution, Riel fled into exile. Through back channels, Macdonald used secret-service funds to pay Riel to stay in the United States for a few years.[38]

Canada had secured Manitoba but at a high cost to relations between Quebec and Ontario. Quebec's leaders denounced the military expedition as an Anglo-Protestant land and power grab at the expense of Francophones. If denied a share of the West, the Quebecois feared containment and stagnation—as had American southerners during the 1850s. In response, Ontario's expansionists accused Quebec's leaders of plotting to seize the region through Catholic priests who allegedly manipulated the credulous Metis. An Ontarioan declared, "Manitoba has been . . . the battle-ground for our British and French elements with their respective religions, as Kansas was the battle-ground for Free Labour and Slavery. Ontario has played a part . . . analogous to New England, Quebec to that of the southern States."[39]

To compete with the United States, Canadians wanted to build a stronger nation with a larger population. They sought to attract European immigrants to settle the vast western lands of Manitoba and British Columbia. That Canadian geopolitical ambition threatened First Nations with dispossession.

By terminating aboriginal cultures and governments, Dominion leaders meant to absorb Natives as individuals into Canadian society. An official declared, "I want to get rid of the Indian problem. . . . Our objective is to continue until there is not a single Indian in Canada that has not been absorbed into the body politic." Claiming benevolence, Canadians insisted that they were lifting primitive peoples into civilization. But most Natives wanted to be left alone. In British Columbia, some Natives told intruding lumbermen: "We do not want the white man. He steals what we have. We wish to live as we are."[40]

Volcanoes

Americans were too busy reconstructing the South to interfere with Canadian confederation. Devastated by war, the South faced a long, hard recovery. The conflict had killed or wounded an eighth of southern white men of military age. Rampaging Union forces had destroyed a third of the South's livestock, at least half of the prewar capital, and two-thirds of the railroads. Liberated slaves accounted for $4 billion in property lost. Plus, millions of dollars in Confederate bonds and currency became worthless, wiping out the savings of thousands. Returning home, veterans found gutted homes, burned barns, toppled fences, and few livestock. A Confederate lamented, "Now the present is dreary and comfortless, we can but mourn our dear lost cause, and sicken at the remembrance of the sea of blood shed in vain." In Louisiana, Braxton Bragg told a friend, "We sowed & we have reaped. We enjoyed four years of license and are now paying for it."[41]

During the spring and summer of 1865, outlaws preyed on farms and travelers. A Georgia woman lamented, "We have no currency, no law, save the primitive code that might makes right." In hilly and mountainous counties, Unionists had scores to settle with Confederate persecutors. In August, a Knoxville woman reported "more shooting in town today between Rebs and Union men." A month later, she lamented "We certainly live in horrible times. Scarcely a day passes [when] someone is not killed."[42]

Shock and despair gripped Confederates compelled to accept defeat. Obliged to do her own work, a South Carolinian concluded that white women had fallen from "being queens in social life" to "mere domestic drudges." Another South Carolina woman thought that "all of us are Volcanoes with a crust outside & the only way of judging the secret fires consuming others is to look within ourselves." Perhaps they would erupt with deadly consequences.[43]

As an antidote to despair, former Confederates could hate. A southern innkeeper raged after Yankees killed his sons, torched his house, and freed his slaves: "I git up at half past four in the morning, and sit up til twelve at night, to hate 'em." A woman added, "Oh how I hate the Yankees! I could trample on their dead bodies and spit on them." That rage did not bode well for reconciliation—particularly when Yankee troops occupied the South to help freed Blacks. White southerners especially despised the public presence of Black troops. A Georgian declared, "When I see a black guard goin' around the streets with a gun on his shoulder, . . . I hate the whole Yanky nation." A South Carolina Unionist warned that his Confederate neighbors "have learned nothing and forgotten nothing."[44]

Liberated Blacks felt both ecstatic and uneasy about what freedom would bring. Testing their new liberty, thousands took to the roads, seeking some new place, far from harsh memories of old farms and plantations. In Virginia, a former slave recalled, "Just think of whole droves of people, that had always been kept so close, and hardly ever left the plantation before, turned loose, all at once, with nothing in the world, but what they had on their backs, . . . walking along the road with nowhere to go." A Florida planter noted, "The negroes don't seem to feel free unless they leave their old homes, just to make sure they can go when and where they choose." Many looked for family members sold away by masters. Others gravitated to southern towns, seeking safety in numbers. Between 1865 and 1870, the urban Black population in the South doubled.[45]

In the countryside, Blacks wanted better treatment. Women withdrew from field work to tend homes and sent their children to school. Freed men and women aspired to own at least forty acres to support their families and claim the dignity of independent citizens. In 1865 a former slave told a traveler, "What's de use of being free if you don't own land enough to be buried in?"[46]

Freed people claimed land as their right. Alabama Blacks said of southern whites, "The property which they hold was nearly all earned by the sweat of *our* brows." In Virginia, Bayley Wyatt agreed, "Our wives, our children, our husbands, has been sold over and over again to purchase the lands we now locates upon; for that reason we have a divine right to the land." Wyatt added that enslaved labor had built more than southern plantations: "Didn't dem large cities in the North grow up on de cotton and de sugars and de rice dat we made? . . . I say dey has grown rich, and my people is poor."[47]

An ambitious former slave, Henry Adams, struggled to get ahead in the South of 1865. Working hard as a freedman, Adams invested his savings to buy a wagon and team to haul produce in Louisiana. But rural whites could not stand the sight of a prospering Black man. In December, vigilantes waylaid and robbed Adams of all he had. Moving on, Adams passed by a Black corpse hanging from an oak tree; then the ashes of a wagon "belonging to a colored man. . . . with all his things: even his mules were burned." Next, Adams found "the head of a colored man lying on the side of the road." Persistent, Adams purchased a horse, only to fall into another ambush, this time by five former Confederates, who demanded, to whom did he belong? Adams replied that he did "belong to God but not to any man." Infuriated by that reply as insolence, the white men retorted that no Blacks could travel through their parish without acknowledging a master. Spurring his horse, Adams narrowly escaped through a hail of bullets. Black freedom remained embattled in a violent land.[48]

Black Codes

Victorious in war, the Union risked defeat in reconstructing the South. Federal troops faced a daunting task: to occupy about 800 counties spread across 750,000 square miles. A tough assignment at full strength in the spring of 1865, the job became even harder as the Union army demobilized in the summer and fall. In June 1865, 202,000 federal troops occupied the South; that number fell to 18,000 by October 1866. Concentrated in the larger towns and along key railroads and rivers, federal troops were stretched thin in the rural South.[49]

In Congress, Radical Republicans distrusted former Confederates, who seemed unrepentant and defiant. Restoring them to the Union would bolster Democrats in American politics. By driving Republicans from federal power, the Democrats could unravel the wartime consolidation of a stronger Union. Indeed, southern states stood to gain political power from abolition of the constitution's three-fifths clause, which would add twenty-eight congressional seats and electoral college votes.[50]

Rather than reward recent Confederates with readmission, Radicals wanted to punish them as traitors and transform southern society. A Republican general and politician, Carl Schurz, insisted, "the whole organism of southern society . . . must be reconstructed, or rather constructed anew, so as to bring it into harmony with the rest of American society," premised on free labor and social mobility. Radicals claimed revolutionary power because, they insisted, southern secession had been "state suicide," reducing those states to federal territories until reconstructed. Exploiting the war as a constitutional rupture, Thaddeus Stevens wanted to cleanse "all our institutions . . . from every vestige of human oppression, of inequality of rights, of the recognized degradation of the poor, and the superior caste of the rich."

By awarding the vote to Blacks, Radicals hoped to keep former Confederates out of state power. By confiscating land from wealthy Confederates, Radicals could endow freed Blacks with farms, thereby rebuilding southern society. By promoting greater equality between classes and races, Radicals would keep a slave-owning oligarchy from reemerging to menace the Union again. When Democrats demanded the Union "as it was" and the Constitution "as it is," a Radical retorted, "I want the Union as it wasn't and the Constitution as it isn't."[51]

Initially, President Johnson favored a hard line against Confederate leaders. Touchy about his humble origins and poor education, Johnson resented the many slights that he had received before the war from wealthy planters. During the war, his fiery speeches denounced the leading Confederates as traitors who deserved death. As president, he pushed for the rapid trial, conviction, and execution of four people accused of plotting Lincoln's assassination. They did not include John Wilkes Booth, who had died resisting arrest by Union troops in Virginia. The executed four did include a woman who ran the boardinghouse where Booth had lodged. Johnson also kept Jefferson Davis in a military prison without trial for two years as the administration dithered about what to do with him.[52]

In late May, Johnson abruptly shifted toward a policy of reconciliation. With Congress out of session for eight months, Johnson issued two proclamations on May 29. The first restored civil rights to former Confederates who swore allegiance to the United States—but withheld those rights from the wealthiest planters and leading politicians and generals of the rebellion. Those excluded men could apply directly to the president for his pardon. To the surprise of all, Johnson proved a soft touch, flattered when prominent men solicited his good will. Soon hundreds of southerners flocked to the White House, and Johnson pardoned 13,500 of the 15,000 who applied. Johnson counted upon the southern elite to help deliver their states for his bid for reelection in 1868.[53]

In his second proclamation, Johnson revealed that he remained a Democrat committed to states' rights and a weak federal government rather than the consolidated nation favored by Republicans. Uneasy with military occupation, he made it easy for southern states to draft new constitutions and rejoin the Union. Although Johnson had freed his five slaves during the Civil War, he insisted that Blacks possessed less "capacity for government than any other race of people." Convinced that Black voting would ignite a genocidal race war, Johnson asserted, "White men alone must manage the South."

When Frederick Douglass led a Black delegation to the White House to protest, Johnson urged them to emigrate. After the meeting, Johnson angrily told his secretary, "I know that d[amne]d Douglass; he's just

like any nigger, & he would sooner cut a white man's throat than not."
Stubborn and self-righteous, Johnson clung to his prejudices, and he
lacked Lincoln's humor, tact, and ability to compromise.[54]

To supervise reconstruction in each state, Johnson appointed governors who were southern Unionists with conservative views on restricting Blacks and protecting private property. The president also barred
Blacks from voting for the delegates to conventions charged with writing
new state constitutions. Johnson did expect the delegates to revoke ordi-
nances of secession, renounce Confederate public debts, and ratify the
Thirteenth Amendment abolishing slavery—but he did nothing when
some conventions balked. No new state constitution allowed Blacks
equal civil rights, much less the vote. A Mississippi delegate reasoned,
"Tis nature's law that the superior race must rule, and rule they will."[55]

Blacks denounced the empowerment of recent Confederates at the
expense of African Americans who had fought for the Union. In North
Carolina, Blacks declared, "It seems to us that men who are willing
on the field of danger to carry the muskets of the republic, in the days
of peace ought to be permitted to carry its ballots." Martin Delany
reminded Johnson that Black troops had "saved the nation from destruction." Douglass added, "Slavery is not abolished until the black man
has the ballot."[56]

Southern leaders, however, felt relieved and thrilled by the president's indulgence. A South Carolina politician recalled that Johnson
"held up before us the hope of a 'white man's government,' and . . . it
was natural that we should yield to our old prejudices." In the elections of 1865, former Confederates became governors, state legislators,
congressmen, and senators. In Georgia, a Unionist muttered, "Our
people are yet crazy."[57]

Southerners insisted that any "elevation of the blacks will be the
degradation of the whites." Enraged by Blacks moving around, southern whites meant to pin them down on plantations. Living in a ruined
country, whites insisted that their own economic recovery demanded
cheap and tractable Black labor. A Mississippi newspaper preached,
"The true station of the negro is that of a servant. The wants and state
of our country demand that he should remain a servant." Planters

believed that Blacks would accept their lowly lot if denied hope of owning a farm.[58]

The southern state governments adopted "Black Codes" that subordinated freed people by requiring them to stay put and work on annual contracts for low wages regulated by white officials. A Black person who roamed instead of working faced arrest as a vagrant, followed by whipping and sale to serve as an unpaid apprentice for up to ten years. A Kentucky newspaper sought to teach the former slave "that he is *free*, but free only to labor." A northern visitor noted that a master may have "lost his individual right of property in the former slaves," but southern laws maintained that "the blacks at large belong to the whites at large."[59]

White vigilantes disarmed, whipped, lynched, and shot Blacks who resisted the restored order. Georgia's Blacks had to submit to labor contracts by Christmas, or militiamen threatened to "make the woods stink with their carcasses." Grand juries indicted over 500 Texans for murdering Blacks in 1865 and 1866, but the courts convicted not a single suspect. "Murder is considered one of their inalienable states' rights," noted a Yankee visitor. Southern states denied Blacks the right to testify, exposing them to abuse and theft by whites. Southern courts convicted thousands of Blacks for petty crimes and then leased the convicts to work on chain gangs for businesses, particularly to build railroads.[60]

During the war, some Union generals had enabled Blacks to claim small farms carved out of plantations. In March 1865, Congress created a Freedmen's Bureau to help Blacks recover from slavery by providing free schools and protecting free labor. The Bureau began to divvy up confiscated lands into farms of forty acres for distribution among freed people. In August, however, Johnson ordered the Bureau to stop redistributing land. Instead, the president returned confiscated properties to former Confederates, including the Davis Bend plantations of Jefferson and Joseph E. Davis.[61]

In early 1865 most Yankees cared little about voting rights for southern Blacks. Indeed, only five northern states then allowed Blacks to vote. In 1865, state referendums defeated attempts to allow Black men to vote in Connecticut, Minnesota, and Wisconsin. Johnson delighted in tweaking northern politicians who pushed for Black voting in the South: "You complain of the disfranchisement of the negroes in the Southern States, while you would not give them the right of suffrage in Ohio today." Of course, the president did not want Blacks to vote anywhere, giving him a sort of immoral consistency.[62]

By late 1865, however, Republicans worried that former rebels were stealing the Union victory by reclaiming power and restoring quasi-slavery in the South. Had thousands of northern men given their lives to permit former Confederates to make a mockery of that sacrifice? Denouncing the Black Codes, a Chicago newspaper thundered that Yankees would convert a southern state "into a frog pond before they will allow such laws to disgrace one foot of soil in which the bones of our soldiers sleep and over which the flag of freedom flies." The showdown with the president came in December 1865, when Congress reconvened and refused to seat southern congressmen elected under Johnson's lenient reconstruction policy.[63]

Blunderland

In early 1866 congressional hearings documented the widespread torture and murder of Blacks by white vigilantes in the South. In February, to protect Blacks, Congress strengthened and renewed the Freedmen's Bureau, but Johnson vetoed the bill as allegedly unfair to southern whites. In Ohio, a Democratic newspaper exulted, "Great Victory for the White Man. Rejoice, White Man, Rejoice! The Hour of Your Deliverance has Come."[64]

A month later, Congress passed a civil rights bill that declared American-born Blacks to be free citizens with the same legal rights as whites. Overriding the traditional power of states to regulate rights, the bill created a national citizenship meant, a sponsor said, to "protect our citizens, from the highest to the lowest, from the whitest to the blackest, in the enjoyment of the great fundamental rights which belong to all men." Those rights included making contracts, owning property, testifying in court—but not voting, which was then considered a political rather than a civil right.[65]

On March 27, Johnson vetoed the civil rights bill, alleging that it discriminated against white men and violated states' rights. But Congress overrode this veto, enacting the Civil Rights Law on April 9. Emboldened by that success, Congress renewed the Freedmen's Bureau, again overriding a presidential veto.[66]

Concerned that the Supreme Court might invalidate the Civil Rights Law, Republicans in Congress passed a Fourteenth Amendment in June 1866. By creating a national birthright citizenship, the amendment required states to respect civil rights for all people born in the United States. The amendment also nudged southern states to enfranchise Blacks by threatening to reduce congressional representation (and electoral college votes) for states that restricted the vote. Congress required ratification of the Fourteenth Amendment by any state seeking readmission to the Union. Per the Constitution, the president could not veto an amendment, but Johnson did urge southern states to reject it.[67]

In the spring and summer of 1866, southern riots exposed the failure of Johnson's reconstruction policy. In early May, in Memphis, whites rioted for three days, looting and burning African-American homes, schools, and churches. The rioters raped at least five women and killed forty-six people, many of them Union veterans. An investigator reported, "Defenseless old men and women were butchered in the streets and their own houses. Dwellings were burned by the dozen, and in one instance a young woman dying was thrown into the flames of a burning house and consumed."[68]

In July, in New Orleans, former Confederates, including policemen, attacked a Unionist convention. In what General Sheridan called "an absolute massacre," the rioters killed thirty-four Blacks and three white Radicals, including a former state treasurer, Anthony P. Dostie, who was stabbed and shot multiple times, then trampled. Exulting in his death, a New Orleans newspaper advised boiling his body to make soap for distribution in "bars to Yankee 'school marms.' Delicious will be the kisses by those angular females from ebony cheeks, late lathered with sweet scented Dostie."[69]

Outraged by the riots, Republicans denounced the president as an alcoholic Copperhead who betrayed the Union's victorious soldiers. In

Tennessee, his former collaborator, Parson William Brownlow, dismissed Johnson as "the dead dog of the White House."

Fighting back, the president went on a speaking tour around the country, hoping to swing the fall congressional elections in favor of his fellow Democrats. When his speeches attracted hecklers, Johnson lost his cool, unleashing angry diatribes. The president likened himself to Jesus, longed to hang Thaddeus Stevens, and blamed southern bloodshed on Radicals. Johnson's outbursts fed rumors that he was a drunkard too undignified for the presidency. "Andy's Adventures in Blunderland," wrote one observer. A friend worried: "He was regularly mad . . . & couldn't talk like a reasonable being." Grant denounced Johnson's conduct as "a National Disgrace." In the fall election, Republicans won every governorship and increased their majority in Congress. Fear of former Confederates had trumped prejudice against Blacks with northern voters.[70]

Despite the electoral debacle, Johnson refused to compromise with Congress. Returning to session in December, Congress enabled Blacks to vote in the District of Columbia, a federal enclave, where states' rights did not apply. In January 1868 the president vetoed the bill, siding with the district's white voters, who had rejected Black suffrage by 7,400 to 36 in a referendum. Johnson insisted, "The will of the people must be obeyed." He did not consider the will of Black people. Congress again overrode his veto, for they meant the District to serve as a model for a reconstructed South.[71]

Disgusted by Johnson's stubborn and confrontational conduct, moderate Republicans joined the Radicals to mandate a reconstruction program controlled by Congress. They readmitted Tennessee, the lone southern state to ratify the Fourteenth Amendment. In March 1867 Congress subordinated the other ten southern state governments within five military districts commanded by Union generals with occupying troops. The generals would supervise elections for conventions to write new state constitutions that ratified the Fourteenth Amendment and empowered Black men as voters. Johnson vetoed the law, but Congress again overrode him.[72]

Congress also limited Johnson's power to interfere with its new program of reconstruction. Passed over his veto, a Tenure of Office Act barred the president from dismissing any major federal official, including members of his cabinet, without the senate's approval. Congress especially sought to protect Secretary of War Edwin Stanton and the generals commanding southern districts.[73]

During the summer, while Congress was on vacation, Johnson struck back. Despite the Tenure of Office Act, he sacked Stanton, ostensibly suspending rather than replacing him as a legalistic pretext. Grant reluctantly accepted an interim appointment as secretary of war, pending the return of Congress. The president also replaced four district commanders, including Philip H. Sheridan.[74]

In January 1868, when Congress returned to session, the Senate reinstated Stanton as secretary of war. Carefully considering his own political future, Grant sided with the Republicans by resigning as the interim secretary, which infuriated Johnson. Each called the other a liar. Encouraged by Radicals, Stanton reclaimed and barricaded his office, posting armed guards around the building. In February, the House impeached the president by a party-line vote of 126 to 47.[75]

Per the Constitution, the Senate would try the impeached president, with a two-thirds majority required for conviction and removal. Begun on March 30, the trial lasted nearly two months and induced a new moderation by Johnson, reining in his venomous bombast. In April he nominated a new secretary of war, John Schofield, a general acceptable to most Republicans. Johnson even accepted radical state constitutions for Arkansas and South Carolina that allowed Black men to vote.[76]

In May, Johnson's show of moderation swayed just enough Republican senators to forestall conviction in his Senate trial. All twelve Democrats would vote for acquittal, but the other forty-two senators were Republicans, more than enough for the thirty-six needed to convict. But seven moderates broke with their party brethren. With just six months left before the next presidential election, the straying seven preferred to leave Johnson's fate to the voters.[77]

Johnson's political survival thrilled southern Democrats but terrified their Republican rivals, who faced a surge in violence. "I see little hope for the Republic," muttered Thaddeus Stevens. Johnson could claim victory: he had bought time for defiant conservatives to preserve the South as a "white man's country."[78]

Farces

After his narrow escape, Johnson reverted to pugnacious defiance, again casting himself as the Federal Constitution's defender against Republican defilers. Although the president had approved the new Arkansas and South Carolina constitutions in early May, he vetoed their readmission to the Union on June 20. Five days later, he rejected six other states that adhered to Congress's required process. Johnson insisted, "The subjugation of the States to negro domination would be worse than the military despotism under which they are now suffering." Congress overrode all the vetoes.[79]

With these vetoes, Johnson appealed to southern Democrats on the eve of that party's nominating convention. But most northern Democrats still would not forgive him for helping Lincoln win reelection in 1864. To Johnson's dismay, the delegates nominated Horatio Seymour, a former governor of New York who had been a wartime Peace Democrat. His running mate, Francis Blair, Jr., had the usual reactionary obsession with interracial sex. Blair vowed to save the South from the power of "a semi-barbarous race of blacks" eager to "subject the white women to their unbridled lust." Republicans mocked that "Seymour was opposed to the late war, and Blair was in favor of the next one."[80]

In May, Republicans nominated Grant, a war hero who seemed to rise above partisanship. A leading Republican praised Grant for having a "genius for silence." By keeping quiet about political issues, Grant cultivated popularity as all things to all voters. His campaign slogan declared, "Let us have peace." That appealed to Americans eager to avoid another civil war and weary of partisan bickering. In the campaign, Republicans dwelled on Grant's military victories and the threat of a renewed southern rebellion.[81]

Many southern Blacks acquired guns and organized self-defense companies, but racist whites interpreted those measures as preparations to attack them. A French journalist in America, Georges Clemenceau, marveled that, in southern news stories, "There is always a band of heavily armed negroes attacking a handful of harmless whites. Then when it comes to counting the dead," all were Black.[82]

A secret society, the Ku Klux Klan, rallied angry white men, most of them former Confederate soldiers. They were led by a "Grand Wizard," the former slave trader and general Nathan Bedford Forrest, whose troops had massacred Black and white Unionists at Fort Pillow in 1864. Well-armed, and concealed by white robes and garish masks, Klansmen whipped and often killed Blacks and white Republicans. In one Louisiana parish, Klansmen staged a "Negro hunt" that slaughtered at least 162. A congressional investigation later concluded that 1,081 Blacks died violently in Louisiana during the election of 1868. Klansmen also burned Republican newspapers and Black schools and churches. Only a single Black dared to vote Republican in one parish; he was killed later that night. Spread thin, federal troops could not control the vast countryside beyond the major towns.[83]

Despising Grant, Johnson campaigned for Seymour. By ignoring pleas for military aid from Unionist governors confronting Klan terror, Johnson helped swing Louisiana and Georgia for the Democrats. Thanks to courageous Black voters, however, Republicans carried six of the other eight reconstructed states. In the end, Grant won the popular vote with 53 percent and got 214 of the 294 electoral votes.[84]

Republicans sought to consolidate their southern gains by adopting a Fifteenth Amendment to provide a constitutional guarantee for African-American voting. "It must be done. It is the only measure that will really abolish slavery," declared a Nevada senator. By federalizing the protection of voting rights, the amendment overrode the power of states to define their electorate. An Indiana senator insisted, "I assert that we are one people and not thirty-seven different peoples."[85]

But Republicans could not pass their amendment without limiting it to satisfy senators who feared that a broad definition of citizenship would include women or Chinese immigrants. Rather than guaranteeing the right of all adults (or all men) to vote, the amendment simply barred states from disenfranchising on the basis of race or previous servitude. In February 1869, Congress passed that amendment over the usual protests of Democrats that Black voting would lead to mixed-race children.[86]

To reach approval by three-quarters of the states, the Fifteenth Amendment depended on the reconstructed southern states, where Congress required ratification for readmission. On March 30, 1870, the secretary of state certified the Fifteenth Amendment as the law of the land. Blacks gathered to celebrate "the final seal of God in the condemnation of American slavery."[87]

In the South many Blacks became county and state officials, both elected and appointed. The new Black politicians included Mary Anne Shadd Cary's younger brother Isaac Shadd, who moved to Mississippi, settling at Davis Bend, where Jefferson Davis had owned a plantation. Winning a seat in the state house of representatives, Shadd became the speaker, 1874–1875. The South's newly integrated state governments funded public schools and adopted fairer laws regulating labor relations. But whites still dominated southern businesses and land ownership, and most of them despised paying taxes to fund schools and aid Blacks. So Democrats sought to topple the Reconstruction governments by redoubled efforts to terrorize Black voters (and their white Republican allies).[88]

During the mid-1870s, this southern violence (and a Democratic surge in the 1874 mid-term election) put northern Republicans on the spot. They recognized that most northern voters found reconstruction tiresome. Becoming more conservative, many Republicans accepted criticism of reconstructed regimes as expensive, corrupt, and demagogic. At the same time, they decided that white southerners had done enough to regain power by accepting emancipation and the perpetual Union. A Republican politician recalled, "It was all over—the war, reconstruction, the consideration of the old questions. . . . The nation had done its part; it had freed the slaves, given them the ballot, opened the courts to them, and put them in the way of self-protection and self-assertion." Nothing more could or would be done: no free land and no more troops to protect them. Blacks would have to make do as oppressed minorities in southern states.[89]

Defeated in the war and again in Mexico, Jubal Early meant to win the peace in the South. Returning from exile in 1869, Early settled in Lynchburg, Virginia, where he practiced a little law and much myth making. In many speeches, books, and essays, Early devoted the last twenty-five years of his life to developing the Lost Cause ideology, which denied that defeat was a moral judgment against the Confederacy. Cast as a noble defense of constitutional rights (with little to do with slavery), the Lost Cause had nearly triumphed thanks to the courage of southern men and noble leadership by Robert E. Lee. Only a massive Yankee superiority in numbers of men, dollars, and weapons had enabled Grant to overwhelm Lee's army.[90]

For most southern whites, Early framed the historical memory of the Civil War. Early's success infuriated a wartime foe, General George H. Thomas, a Virginian who remained loyal to the Union. After the war, Thomas had his hands full supervising Reconstruction in Tennessee, and he blamed the Lost Cause mythology for empowering vigilantes who terrorized Republicans, especially Blacks. He denounced Early's version of the Civil War "as a species of political cant, whereby the crime of treason might be covered with a counterfeit varnish of patriotism."[91]

The decay of reconstruction forced Martin Delany to make difficult choices. During the war, Delany recruited Blacks for the Union army and became an officer. After the war, as a Freedmen's Bureau agent based at Hilton Head, South Carolina, he insisted that Blacks would never have won freedom "had we not armed ourselves and fought for our independence." Indeed, he favored a further armed struggle to seize land. "We have now two hundred thousand of our men well drilled in arms and used to warfare, and I tell you it is with you and them that slavery shall not come back again."[92]

By 1870, however, Delany shifted toward favoring Black accommodation to annual labor contracts and white leadership in South Carolina. Assuring Blacks that property would rule South Carolina as it did everywhere, he dreamed of "a union of the whites and blacks" to develop "the wealth of the South." Leaving the Freedmen's Bureau in

1869, Delany settled in Charleston, where he developed a real estate business and sought acceptance by the state's leading Democrats. He adopted their criticism of poor Blacks as ignorant pawns of corrupt Republican demagogues.[93]

In 1876, Delany campaigned for the Democratic candidate, Wade Hampton III, a wealthy planter and former Confederate general. Fooled by Hampton's lip service to racial harmony, Delany overlooked violence by white Democrats against Black Republicans. Heckled by Black women calling him a race traitor, Delany retorted that "it was the duty of those who had education to teach them that their best interests were identical with the white natives of the State." By stuffing ballot boxes and intimidating Black voters, Democrats elected Hampton in what they boasted was "one of the grandest farces ever seen." Hampton rewarded Delany with a minor judicial post, but the state legislature fired him and all other Black officials in 1879.[94]

If he could not lead Blacks in South Carolina, Delany meant to lead them into exile in West Africa. He founded the "Liberian Exodus Joint-Stock Steamship Company," but that expensive scheme took only 200 passengers across the Atlantic before collapsing into bankruptcy. Giving up, Delany moved to Wilberforce, Ohio, where he died in January 1885 at the age of seventy-two.[95]

In Jones County, Mississippi, the collapse of Reconstruction came as a shock to Newton Knight, a white man, and his wife Rachel, a former slave. In 1865, the northern triumph had seemed to vindicate Knight and his fellow deserters for resisting the Confederacy. During the 1870s, however, Democrats regained state power by playing the race card to discredit whites who, like Knight, defended Black rights. In 1882 Democrats elected as governor Robert Lowry, who had pursued and executed members of Knight's company during the war. Newton and Rachel helped build a local school, but the teacher dismissed their children because of their color. That night Newton burned down the school that he had built. When he died in February 1922, at the age of ninety-two, the local newspaper declared that Knight had "ruined his life and future by marrying a negro woman."[96]

Storms

When the Civil War began, the great promoters of American expansion, Jane and William Cazneau, lived in Santo Domingo (now the Dominican Republic), the eastern two-thirds of the island of Hispaniola, with Haiti to the west. Although poor, Santo Domingo was a beautiful land of lush valleys between green mountains. The country also lay beside busy sea lanes from Latin America through the Caribbean to the Atlantic and on to Europe or the United States. Purchasing plantations and mines, the couple hoped to attract settlers by promoting American annexation of Santo Domingo. In 1861, however, Spain reclaimed the country as its colony, with support from Dominican leaders who sought a European protector against Haiti.[97]

Accusing the Cazneaus of helping rebels against Spanish rule, the colonial regime burned their home and confiscated their businesses, while the couple fled to Jamaica. Losing the war in the countryside, Spanish control shrank to the capital and its suburbs by late 1864. After the Union victory in April 1865, Seward demanded a Spanish evacuation, which promptly followed in July. A Dominican general took power as president, and the Cazneaus returned to reclaim their properties and rebuild their fortunes.[98]

Quick to exploit any opportunity, the Cazneaus got a lucky break in January 1866, when Seward toured the Caribbean to investigate potential coaling stations for steam-powered warships. In Santo Domingo, the Cazneaus made themselves his chief hosts and interpreters, urging Seward to annex at least the harbor at Samana Bay and perhaps the entire country. But the administration was distracted by impeachment and the next presidential election, so nothing came of annexation until Grant supplanted Johnson in March 1869.[99]

Seward left office before he could be pushed, but Grant also wanted to annex Santo Domingo. Rather than keep Santo Domingo as a dependent colony, Grant proposed welcoming it into the Union as a state. In late 1869, the Dominican president and Congress accepted annexation in return for payment of their national debt plus bonuses to them of $1.5 million.[100]

But most American senators balked at adding a tropical state with a Black majority. Opponents also showed that William Cazneau had bribed leading Dominicans and secured sweetheart land deals to a full tenth of the country. To rescue the cause of annexation, a supportive senator displayed a large block of salt derived from Santo Domingo. Many of his colleagues came by his desk to lick it. Despite the tasty salt, the Senate rejected annexation in June 1870.[101]

In January 1871, Grant tried to revive annexation by sending three white commissioners to investigate, with Frederick Douglass in a subordinate role as secretary. It was a halfway invitation into the Republican elite for Douglass. Impressed by the natural beauty and economic potential of the island, the commissioners returned home in March to submit a favorable report.

The prospect of a new state with Black residents in the majority especially appealed to Douglass as a way to strengthen political support for equality within the Union. There was all too much evidence that America remained racially unequal. Grant hosted the returning commissioners for dinner at the White House, but he did not invite Douglass to attend.[102]

By promoting annexation, Douglass clashed with the powerful Senator Charles Sumner of Massachusetts. In part, the prickly Sumner opposed annexation to spite Grant, who had refused to defer to the senator's longer experience with foreign affairs. Secretary of State Hamilton Fish thought Sumner "a monomaniac upon all matters relating to his own importance." But Sumner also claimed to act on principle: to protect Haiti and Santo Domingo as independent republics. To support that principle, however, Sumner resorted to racist clichés that the tropics best suited Blacks, while Whites belonged in the temperate zone. Out to win, Sumner cultivated support from conservative senators with more overtly racist views, and they helped defeat annexation again in April 1871. Douglass mourned, "Santo Domingo is opposed mainly, if not wholly, because her people are not white. If they were of the pure Caucasian race all parties would jump at the acquisition." The Civil War might have killed slavery, but racial prejudice persisted and intensified during the late nineteenth century.[103]

Abandoning Santo Domingo in 1872, William and Jane Cazneau returned to their plantation in Jamaica, where he died in January 1876. Falling sick, Jane Cazneau recovered with help from a Black nurse. Setting aside her old racial prejudices, Cazneau resolved to promote Black education in the West Indies. To raise funds, she visited New York City, where Cazneau attended services conducted by Reverend Henry Ward Beecher, a prominent abolitionist and brother of Harriet Beecher Stowe. Impressed by the sermon, Cazneau told him, "Fifteen years ago, . . . I would have deemed it doing service to God to put a bullet through your head." A Democrat during the 1850s, she had considered an abolitionist "a fearful agitator—an enemy of the Nation."

In December 1878 Cazneau boarded a ship bound for Santo Domingo. Like so many vessels hastily built during the Civil War, the *Emil B. Souder* had weak timbers and shoddy nails. On December 10 the ship broke up and sank in a storm. Only two crewmen survived, by clinging to wreckage until rescued. They last saw Cazneau holding to the rigging of a sinking ship in a howling wind and driving rain. She was seventy-one and blind.[104]

Shining

For most Yankees, freeing slaves had not been the prime goal of the civil war and reconstruction. Instead, northerners fought to restore the Union. In 1862, they belatedly adopted Black liberation once it seemed essential to defeat the Confederate rebellion. After winning the war, Unionists feared losing the peace if former Confederates returned to power in southern states. So, for a decade Congress promoted Black civil and political rights as essential to fend off a Confederate revival in the South. By the mid-1870s, however, most Yankees lost patience with Reconstruction. Retreating to a restored Union as the sole goal, Republicans joined Democrats in enabling southern states to restore white supremacy. In 1880 Douglass mourned, "There was more care for the sublime superstructure of the republic than for the solid foundation upon which it could alone be upheld."[105]

But that sublime superstructure did matter. By 1865 most Republicans regarded the original Federal Constitution as tainted by excessive states' rights and immoral protections for slavery. Exploiting their majority in Congress, Republicans grafted three radical new amendments—the Thirteenth, Fourteenth, and Fifteenth—onto the Constitution. Collectively, they reworked the original constitution to empower the nation to protect equal civil rights for all citizens. During the 1870s, however, Republicans backed away from the radical implications of their reworking of the Constitution.[106]

Liberal dreams of equality did survive the long period of retreat— and sometimes they emerged among surprising people. A slaveholder in Missouri and Border Ruffian in Kansas, Joseph Shelby became a Confederate general who fled to Maximilian's Mexico to avoid surrendering to Yankees. But in 1867 Shelby returned from Mexico a changed man, disgusted by his former delusions. Settling in Kansas City, he became a Republican and a federal marshal who appointed a Black deputy over the protests of local whites. Regretting his violent past in bleeding Kansas, Shelby confessed,

> I am now ashamed of myself. I had no business there. . . . The policy that sent us there was damnable, and the trouble we started on the border bore fruit for ten years. I ought to have been shot there. . . . Those were days when slavery was in the balance, and the violence engendered made men irresponsible.

Deciding that his old foe, the abolitionist John Brown, had been, in fact, the greatest man of his generation, Shelby wanted a statue erected in his honor.[107]

In 1859 Governor Henry A. Wise of Virginia had hastened John Brown's trial and execution. After the Civil War, however, one of Brown's daughters came south to set up a school for Blacks, including Wise's ex-slaves. He welcomed her. When a white neighbor protested, Wise asserted, "John Brown was a great man, sir. John Brown was a great man." Wise had forsaken slavery: "God knew that we could be torn away from our black idol of slavery only by fire and blood and the drawn sword of the destroying angel of war." That angel had destroyed much, including Mexican monarchy and American slavery, but what would rise on the ruins?[108]

During the late 1870s, Frederick Douglass remained a Republican despite the party's retreat from enforcing Reconstruction in the South. Republicans rewarded him with patronage in the District of Columbia as U.S. marshal and recorder of deeds, and he became America's first Black ambassador, serving in Haiti from 1889 to 1891. Upon returning to the United States, Douglass reclaimed his voice as an activist to denounce southern lynching of African Americans. "Rebel rule is nearly complete in many states," Douglass mourned.[109]

The older generation of activists was fading. During the Civil War, Jane Grey Swisshelm sold her newspaper in St. Cloud, Minnesota, and moved to Washington, D.C., to help the Union cause. Working as a clerk in a federal office for pay, she devoted spare hours to nursing wounded soldiers and helping Black orphans. A military boomtown, Washington was crowded, noisy, and filthy, depressing Swisshelm as "plentifully besprinkled with dead horses, dead dogs, cats, rats, rubbish and refuse." She thought it "a matter of national pride that the President is to have more mud, and blacker mud, and filthier mud in front of his door than any other man can afford." But she also found moral growth among men and women striving to help Black refugees and wounded soldiers: "Our Government and people were very imperfect but had developed a sublime patriotism—made an almost miraculous growth in good."[110]

But she saw a grave threat in Andrew Johnson's presidency. In December 1865 Swisshelm launched another newspaper, *The Reconstructionist*, which promoted the Radical cause and attacked Johnson for betraying the Union victory. Two months later, she lost her day job as a government clerk, which she saw as retribution by Johnson. Worse came in March 1866, when an arsonist set her press ablaze. She put out the fire to save her newspaper, but, for the first time in her life, Swisshelm backed down from a fight, shutting down *The Reconstructionist*. Retiring as an editor and publisher, she left the capital to live in rural Pennsylvania. Soon Swisshelm wearied of her rustic neighbors and moved to Pittsburgh, where she died of an ulcer in July 1884 at the age of sixty-eight. A journalist reflected, "In her time she was a tiger."[111]

Mary Ann Shadd Cary remained a tiger for civil rights. After the war, she left her Canadian home to settle in Washington, D.C., where many African-American leaders congregated. Offering more jobs and better political rights than most of the country, Washington attracted 40,000 Black newcomers during the 1860s. Shadd Cary called the capital "the Mecca of the colored pilgrim." Becoming a school principal, she supervised twenty-five teachers and two hundred students during the early 1870s. Shadd Cary also gave public lectures, sang temperance songs, and attended meetings of labor, gender, and racial reformers.[112]

Setting aside old debates over Canadian emigration, Shadd Cary and Frederick Douglass collaborated during the 1870s. His newspaper in the capital, *New National Era*, published her essays while she toured the country to raise funds for that press. On the eve of one trip, Douglass sent her a note: "Go to the South, my friend, go with words of cheer—go with words of wisdom to our newly emancipated people and help them in their travels through the wilderness."[113]

To enhance her public voice, Shadd Cary attended the law school of Howard University, recently established in the city to provide higher education for African Americans. She was the first Black woman to enter an American law school, and the only one in her Howard class of forty-six. For want of money and time (as she continued to work as a school principal), she did not receive her degree until 1883. Despite her degree, Shadd Cary could find few clients willing to employ a Black woman.[114]

Shadd Cary had to navigate the fractures of race, class, and gender that divided American reformers after the Civil War. White feminists felt dismayed that Republicans declined to extend civil and political rights to their gender in the Fourteenth and Fifteenth Amendments. In response, some feminists alienated their Black sisters by arguing that educated white women deserved to vote more than did poor Black men. Shadd Cary kept trying to bridge the growing gap. In 1871 she was one of sixty-three women who called the bluff of voting officials in the District of Columbia by marching to city hall to demand registration. The officials refused. In 1880 she was one of just two Blacks attending a suffrage convention of 2,000 women in Washington.[115]

In 1878 Congress terminated electoral government in the District of Columbia, substituting rule by three appointed commissioners. District whites preferred to disenfranchise all voters (including themselves) rather than permit Black political participation. During the 1880s, the commissioners repealed local civil rights laws, segregated public facilities, and empowered the police to abuse Blacks. The great possibilities of 1865 had withered for African Americans in the capital.[116]

In 1893, at the age of seventy, Mary Ann Shadd Cary died of stomach cancer. She owned no real estate and had only $150 in personal property, primarily her law books. The historian and civil rights activist W. E. B. Du Bois paid tribute to Shadd Cary: "Well-educated, vivacious, with determination shining from her sharp eyes . . . she became teacher, editor, and lecturer," pushing "through crowd and turmoil to conventions and meetings." She had kept the faith through the hardest of times.[117]

EPILOGUE ∞ SLEEPING GIANTS

A government that has for nearly a century enslaved one race
(African), that proscribes another (Chinese), proposes to
exterminate another (Indians), and persistently refuses to
recognize the rights of one-half of its citizens (women), cannot
justly be called perfect. —CORA TAPPAN, 1869[1]

On May 10, 1869, railroad executives celebrated completing the
American transcontinental route at Promontory Summit in
Utah. They had the Civil War and Reconstruction on their
minds as they drove a final, golden stake inscribed: "May God continue
the unity of our Country as this Railroad unites the two great oceans of
the world." Those corporate barons considered their railroad an essential

bond of Union in the region that could best fulfill national ideals: the West. But the completion ceremony also demonstrated racial limits to western dreams by excluding the thousands of Chinese laborers who had helped build the railroad.[2]

After the Civil War, Union officials felt empowered to apply their liberal philosophy throughout the land. They envisioned a nation composed of individuals all free to buy and sell labor as well as free to vote. By subduing southern rebels, Republicans believed that they had smashed the greatest threat to the land of free men: southern slavery. The great reward of victory lay in control over the West, where hard-working strivers could exploit mineral, timber, and agricultural riches. Americans thought of the West as a wilderness where they shaped their future by creating private property and new towns. In fact, the region already had diverse peoples, Natives and newcomers from Latin America, Asia, and the eastern United States. The West was a multiracial borderland.[3]

Native nations still held and defended much of the western interior. In 1866–1867 the great flashpoint was a set of new forts along the Bozeman Trail through the Lakota country to the goldfields of Montana. The intrusion lacked the legal cover of any treaty, and the soldiers and teamsters took a toll on the bison herds that sustained Native communities. Led by a war chief called Red Cloud, Lakotas harried soldiers venturing out to hunt, harvest timber, or tend cattle. In December 1866 warriors ambushed and killed Captain William J. Fetterman and eighty soldiers. In 1868, the United States admitted a rare defeat, abandoning the Bozeman Trail and burning the forts.[4]

But Americans expanded a more important transit corridor: across the Great Plains along the Platte River. This east–west corridor offered the prime overland route across the continent and included the transcontinental railroad. But that intrusion ran through prime bison hunting territory—to the dismay of Native peoples. To push them into reservations, Union leaders relied on their most flamboyant hero from the

OPPOSITE: *"The First Vote," 1867, cartoon by Thomas Nast based on an A. R. Waud drawing,* Harper's Weekly, *Nov. 16, 1867.*

Civil War, George Armstrong Custer. Brave, reckless, and egotistical, Custer longed to win more fame by crushing Indians. In November 1868, Custer drove his men hard through a blizzard in search of a Cheyenne encampment, finding one along the Washita River far south of the corridor and in a zone reserved for Natives seeking to avoid war. At dawn on November 27, 1868, Custer's regiment charged, surprising and butchering the Natives, including Black Kettle, a chief who had survived a similar massacre four years earlier at Sand Creek.[5]

Despite the Republican vision of free society, westerners continued to capture and sell Indian women and children. Especially in New Mexico and Arizona, land barons retained cheap labor through debt peonage, with many of the laborers descended from enslaved Indians. Enslavers insisted that they alone had worked hard to make property, casting slaves and peons as racial inferiors undeserving of freedom.[6]

In 1865 Secretary of the Interior James Harlan ordered western officials to suppress Indian slavery for such "unrequited labor should not be tolerated in a country professing to be free." In 1867 Congress passed an Anti-Peonage Act with fines of up to $5,000 and prison terms of up to five years. But enforcement relied on lawsuits in New Mexico courts, where many jurors held peons and defended the system as paternalistic. Thanks to unenforced laws, thousands persisted in debt peonage until the twentieth century.[7]

Between 1840 and 1880, nearly 300,000 Chinese people moved to the western United States. Employers, especially railroad companies, cherished cheap and diligent workers, but white laborers hated the competition. Calling the Chinese "coolies," critics cast them as alien and docile automatons who undercut wages and work standards for Americans. Denied citizenship, the Chinese received no protection from the Fourteenth and Fifteenth Amendments. During the 1870s, Chinese immigrants suffered from violent pogroms meant to drive them out of western communities. In 1882, the federal government barred further immigration from China.[8]

As in the South, federal authority in the West ran thin beyond the major towns and occasional forts. Locally powerful people were well armed and ready to use violence to preserve unequal, coercive relationships justified in racial terms. Although a powerful player in the West, the federal government was most successful when meeting, rather than challenging, settler demands. Those settlers were voters, and the Chinese, Indians, and most Hispanics were not. So federal officials defaulted on their liberal vision. In 1869 a reformer named Cora Tappan noted, "A government that has for nearly a century enslaved one race (African), that proscribes another (Chinese), proposes to exterminate another (Indians), and persistently refuses to recognize the rights of one-half of its citizens (women), cannot justly be called perfect."[9]

Treaty

Certain of their own superior government, Americans liked to believe that Canadians inevitably would come to their senses and join the Union. So why fight a war for annexation now? Instead, annexationists counted on economic pressure to bring Canadians around. In 1865, the United States terminated the reciprocity treaty of 1854, which had promoted free trade and allowed Americans to fish in Canadian waters. Americans then assured Canadians that only annexation could restore their full access to the American market. Seeking their own leverage, Canadians barred all foreign vessels from fishing near its shores. They believed that Americans valued fishery access enough to cave on trade reciprocity.[10]

In early 1871 Macdonald joined a British delegation sent to Washington, D.C., to negotiate with five Americans, led by Grant's secretary of state, the aptly named Hamilton Fish. The leaders of both nations hoped to reduce tensions generated by the Civil War. Alarmed by the rising power of Germany in Europe, British leaders wanted to bring their troops home from Canada. To do so, they needed a secure peace with the Americans. A British leader lamented, "It is the unfriendly state of our relations with America that . . . paralyses our action in Europe."[11]

Eager for a deal with the Americans, Britain's rulers expected Macdonald to cooperate. London directed its other commissioners to "speak strongly to Sir John Macdonald . . . that with all due regard for the interests of Canada, we cannot allow our friendly relations with foreign countries to be affected by unreasonable opposition from the Dominion." Duty bound to participate in the conference, Macdonald expected nothing but political trouble at home: "My share in the Kudos will be but small, and if anything goes wrong, I will be made the scapegoat."[12]

The British commissioners accepted American access to the fisheries without restoring reciprocity for Canada. Britons also agreed to the American refusal to compensate Canadians for damages inflicted by Fenian invaders. A British leader told Canadians to become more resigned to the bad manners of Americans: "When you have to deal with a powerful and most unreasonable nation . . . the first requisite is to keep one's temper."[13]

In return for those Canadian concessions, the Americans gave what the British most wanted: international arbitration of the *Alabama* claims and of the contested boundary through the San Juan Islands in the Pacific Northwest (which had occasioned the Pig War of 1859). In 1872, the *Alabama* claims mediators required the British to pay $15.5 million, all in money and none in Canadian land. In a separate 1872 arbitration, the German emperor awarded the San Juan islands to the United States. In a third mediation, however, Canadians won $5.5 million from the Americans in compensation for access to the fisheries: a sum considered excessive by the U.S. Congress.[14]

Concluded in May 1871, the Treaty of Washington certified American dominance in North America as the price of Canadian survival. When Macdonald signed the treaty, he grumbled, "Well, here go the fisheries." But the treaty did secure a continental boundary between the United States and Canada along the 49th parallel, preserving British Columbia and Manitoba for the Dominion. In November 1871, the British withdrew almost all of their troops from Canada.[15]

By guaranteeing £2.5 million for the transcontinental railroad, British leaders helped persuade Canadians to ratify the treaty in May 1872. In August the federal election pivoted on that treaty, which Liberals continued to attack. But voters awarded 126 seats in parliament to Macdonald's Conservatives compared to 77 for opponents. Formerly disappointed in the treaty, Macdonald could now announce that his tombstone would honor him for making that deal.[16]

North America

During the late 1860s and early 1870s, Canada, Mexico, and the United States had transformations that strengthened their federal governments. Defeating a foreign monarchy, Mexican Liberals restored a republic with enhanced nationalism. Canadians constructed a transcontinental Dominion that drew both Atlantic and Pacific provinces into a new confederation, with Ontario and Quebec at the core. Triumphant in a civil war, the United States became, at last, a nation ruled by a majority—rather than a loose confederation of quasi-autonomous states. According to Thaddeus Stevens, Radical Republicans made a "revolution to correct the palpable incongruities and despotic provisions of the Constitution," and thereby sought to transform "this nation into a perfect Republic." A strengthened, consolidated nation could reconstruct the South and more fully exploit the vast American West, often by subsidizing big business. All three North American reconstructions fed on a liberal dream of unifying nations composed of equal individuals—reducing the clout of intermediary groups and states.[17]

All three national transformations nearly failed. The Union war effort had often faltered and might have collapsed but for Lincoln's reelection after key military victories in the fall of 1864. The Mexican republic was nearly dead until revived by the Union triumph over the Confederacy—which led Napoleon to withdraw French troops. And Canadian confederacy was a Humpty Dumpty that kept falling—but had to be put back together again because the Union triumph made it impossible for small and separate British colonies to survive in North America. Each of the three national consolidations fed on the other two, which shaped what leaders in each saw as feasible and essential.[18]

The three consolidations occurred within a continental asymmetry of power. Victory in the Civil War saved the republican Union and enhanced its imperial power. The United States emerged from the war with a stronger federal government and greater military potential. Intimidated by that enhanced power, Russians sold Alaska, the Spanish bolted from Santo Domingo, and the French withdrew from Mexico. After 1867, the United States no longer faced any European challenge in North America. Canadians and Mexicans had to defer to the United States, which eclipsed them in population, economic wealth, and military strength. Canadians built a confederation designed to enable them to persist in a continent dominated by Americans and virtually abandoned by the British. Just as carefully, Mexicans appeased Americans by welcoming investors who increasingly owned and controlled Mexico's resources. To keep some sovereignty, Canadians and Mexicans had to avoid antagonizing their powerful neighbor. With concessions they soothed Americans into accepting a continental order that they could sway without governing directly.[19]

Ending American slavery, ousting a European monarchy, and building a transcontinental Canada were great achievements unmatched by any other twenty-year period in the nineteenth century. But those transformations still fell short of the utopian promises of that century's form of liberalism. They all confronted limits set by powerful interests that sustained local inequalities primarily defined by race. Mexico remained wracked by peasant rebellions and regional *caudillos* who resisted national consolidation. Francophone Canadians clung to their distinctive identity and provincial autonomy, remaining suspicious of the Dominion as a vehicle for Anglophone domination. Resistance to national might was most violent within the United States, especially in the South. Despite enhanced federal power, American leaders ultimately failed to transform southern society and politics. Restoring the Union ultimately came by excluding southern Blacks from the liberal dream of equal opportunity.[20]

But revolutions plant possibilities that can later revive. During the 1870s, Senator Charles Sumner predicted that the constitutional amendments of Reconstruction would become "sleeping giants" to "create a more just social order." During the first half of the twentieth century about three million Blacks fled repression and bleak conditions in the South to resettle as industrial workers in northern cities. Thanks to the Fifteenth Amendment, which applied to the North as well as the South (and was taken more seriously in the northern states), the migrants could vote, developing an influence with federal leaders. During the mid-twentieth century, northern Black pressure prodded the federal government to uphold civil rights in the South.[21]

ACKNOWLEDGMENTS

I dedicate this book to Gary Gallagher and Joan Waugh, who have set such high standards for friendship and scholarship—and to our mutual friends Roy Ritchie and Louise Nocas, who have been such generous friends and inspirational examples. I also honor the memory of my late friend Roland Grillon, who died as I was completing the book. A Parisian with epic stories to tell, Roland sustained a bond formed on a tropical island, where we created a tennis court on cracked concrete, rigged up a derelict fishing net, and scavenged waterlogged balls from a cove. My sister Carole is guilty of many loving acts, including introducing me to Roland. Another of those acts was bringing her husband, Marty Goldberg, into my life, for every Red Sox fan should find a Yankee fan to love.

The book manuscript benefited from close and helpful readings by Liz Varon, Ari Kelman, and Andres Resendez—and especially from Gary. Those who know Gary will not be surprised that he upheld precision in the English language and gave no ground on his view of the West and Confederate internal conflict as equally marginal to the Civil War. So, he bears no responsibility for any of my errors on those scores (or any other). But he is fully responsible for teaching me many lessons on the pool table.

I was introduced to Civil War history at Colby College by my mentor, Harold B. "Hal" Raymond. Without his guidance and encouragement, I never could have become a historian. I am also grateful to his successor, Elizabeth D. Leonard, who has remarkable energy and conviction. Hal and Elizabeth have jointly vindicated Colby's most controversial graduate, Benjamin F. Butler.

I learned much about the Civil War from Bill Blair, who generously included me in his insightful tours of Antietam, Gettysburg, and Harpers Ferry. I remain in awe of his thick notebooks filled with information for each site. And few experiences are more enjoyable and rewarding than talking history with Bill Blair and Ari Kelman at the Lincoln Diner in Gettysburg.

I also thank Caroline Janney for her exceptional leadership of the University of Virginia's John L. Nau III Center, dedicated to the history of the Civil War era. The Nau center sustains a vibrant community of scholars, and I am grateful to all of them for sharing their research and insights. Reading and talking with Ed Ayers has been a recurrent and essential part of my continuing education in all things Southern.

Pablo Ortiz persists as an exceptional spiritual guide. Chris Reynolds and Alessa John have been the best of friends—despite Chris's violent devotion to senior discounts at restaurants. And Emily Albu remains the kindest and most generous of human beings. For unmatched expertise on pirates, I am grateful to the legendary Kevin R. Convey.

Andrew Wylie and his assistants provided exemplary literary representation. Throughout the writing and production of this book, I benefited from the wisdom and support of a consummate editor, Steve Forman of W. W. Norton. His lone flaw is an enduring devotion to baseball's Evil Empire.

Finally, I thank the many historians who have produced so much superb scholarship on the United States, Canada, Mexico, and Native nations during the nineteenth century. Reading their work has widened my horizons.

NOTES

EPIGRAPH

1. Barr, *All the Days of My Life*, 95.

INTRODUCTION: UNSETTLED

1. Henry Clay quoted in Hendrickson, *Union, Nation, or Empire*, 200.
2. Lang, "Limits of American Exceptionalism," 183–204.
3. Gallagher, *Union War*, 1–2; Henry Clay quoted in Harrold, *Border War*, 11; Hendrickson, "Escaping Insecurity," 216–42; Hendrickson, "First Union," 40–42; James Shields quoted in Hendrickson, *Union, Nation, or Empire*, 209 ("Sir").
4. Freeman, *Field of Blood*, 10–11; Daniel Webster quoted in Hendrickson, *Union, Nation or Empire*, vi; McCurdy, "Prelude to Civil War," 5–6, John Quincy Adams quoted on 5.
5. Hendrickson, *Union, Nation, or Empire*, 132–39; Hietala, *Manifest Design*, 10–11, 25; Benjamin Milam quoted in Schwartz, *Across the Rio to Freedom*, 9.
6. Hendrickson, "First Union," 40–42; Henry Clay quoted in Hendrickson, *Union, Nation, or Empire*, 200; St. John, "Unpredictable America of William Gwin," 57, 61.
7. Hendrickson, *Union, Nation, or Empire*, 203–204; Levine, *Half Slave and Half Free*, 59–60; McPherson, *Battle Cry of Freedom*, 9.
8. Levine, *Half Slave and Half Free*, 52–54; McPherson, *Battle Cry of Freedom*, 25–26, 33–34.
9. Howe, *What Hath God Wrought*, 536–37; Larson, *Market Revolution in America*, 89–90, 101–2.
10. C. Clark, *Social Change in America*, 167–68, 180; Larson, *Market Revolution in America*, 75–76; Levine, *Half Slave and Half Free*, 69–70.
11. Foreman, *World on Fire*, 27–30, Alexis de Tocqueville quoted on 28 and Sydney Smith quoted on 28; Haynes, *Unfinished Revolution*, 24–25, 36–37, 40–50.
12. Karp, *Vast Southern Empire*, 8, 12, 15–21, 41–42, *Richmond Enquirer* quoted on 20 ("the center"), Francis Pickens quoted on 105 ("Our systems"); Schoen, *Fragile Fabric*, 160–61.
13. Fehrenbacher and McAfee, *Slaveholding Republic*, 156–68; Karp, *Vast Southern Empire*, 4–7, 25–26, 90.
14. Careless, *Union of the Canadas*, 128–31; Wilton, *Popular Politics*, 233–34; Wise and Brown, *Canada Views the United States*, 49–73, Fredericton *Headquarters*, quoted on 71.
15. Careless, *Union of the Canadas*, 3–19; Wilton, *Popular Politics*, 194–95, 218.
16. Careless, *Union of the Canadas*, 20–32.
17. Gwyn, *Man Who Made Us*, 14–16; Morton, *Critical Years*, 4–6.
18. Morton, *Critical Years*, 1–7.
19. Bourne, *Britain and the Balance of Power*, 171–83, Earl Grey quoted on 171; Lord Palmerston quoted on 182–83; Careless, *Union of the Canadas*, 58–70, 115–26.
20. Stuart, *United States Expansionism*, 127–37.

21. Clary, *Eagles and Empire*, 128–38; DeLay, *War of a Thousand Deserts*, 282–88; Fowler, *Santa Anna*, 283–84; Guardino, *Dead March*, 6–17, 170.

22. Lynch, *Spanish American Revolutions*, 295–302, Manuel Abad y Queipo quoted on 298; Russell, *History of Mexico*, 113.

23. Fowler, *Santa Anna*, 284; Guardino, *Dead March*, 6–10, 67–69, 89–90, 169–74; A. Greenberg, *Manifest Manhood*, 25–26, Jane Grey Swisshelm quoted on 25.

24. Feldberg, *Turbulent Era*, 55–61; Freeman, *Field of Blood*, 10–16; Hahn, *Nation Without Borders*, 61–64; Ignatiev, *How the Irish Became White*, 160–61.

25. Baker, *Affairs of Party*, 22–24, 51–52; Levine, *Half Slave and Half Free*, 134–35.

26. Downs, *Second American Revolution*, 11–12.

27. Kersh, *Dreams of a More Perfect Union*, 109; Levine, *Half Slave and Half Free*, 81–85.

28. Feldberg, *Turbulent Era*, 11–14, 35–36; Ignatiev, *How the Irish Became White*, 148–49; Levine, *Half Slave and Half Free*, 66–67, 85–86.

29. Baker, *Affairs of Party*, 19–20, 130–31, 143–48; Feldberg, *Turbulent Era*, 76–80; Watson, *Liberty and Power*, 33–35, 50–51, 185–86, 194–95.

30. Feldberg, *Turbulent Era*, 41–42; Ignatiev, *How the Irish Became White*, 75–81, 124–30.

31. Holt, *Franklin Pierce*, 87–88; Levine, *Half Slave and Half Free*, 200–6; Potter and Fehrenbacher, *Impending Crisis*, 248–59.

32. Levine, *Half Slave and Half Free*, 60–61, Frederick Douglass quoted on 61.

33. Foner, *Fiery Trial*, 20–21; Stauffer, *Black Hearts of Men*, 1–2; Varon, *Disunion*, 95–97.

34. Kolchin, *American Slavery*, 194–96; Virginia planter quoted in Levine, *Half Slave and Half Free*, 25; D. G. White, *Ar'n't I a Woman*, 57–58.

35. Campbell, *Empire for Slavery*, 218–20; Jefferson Davis quoted in Freehling, *Road to Disunion*, vol. 1:82; Oakes, *Ruling Race*, 109–10, 132–33; Schoen, *Fragile Fabric*, 187.

36. James Henry Hammond quoted in Egerton, *Year of Meteors*, 37; Foner, *Fiery Trial*, 16–17; Horton and Horton, *Slavery*, 71–72; Schoen, *Fragile Fabric*, 3–4, 167–68.

37. Beckert, *Empire of Cotton*, 104–105, 119–21, 205–206; Schermerhorn, *Business of Slavery*, 7–8; Schoen, *Fragile Fabric*, 1–2.

38. Beckert, *Empire of Cotton*, 107–108, 158; Deyle, *Carry Me Back*, 16–21, 34–38; Horton and Horton, *Slavery*, 78–79, 83–84; W. Johnson, *Soul by Soul*, 5–8, 19–20.

39. Beckert, *Empire of Cotton*, 110–11, 115–16; W. Johnson, *Soul by Soul*, 191–93; Joseph Acklen quoted in Levine, *Half Slave and Half Free*, 34.

40. Faust, *James Henry Hammond*, 103; Frederick Douglass quoted in Levine, *Half Slave and Half Free*, 29; Oakes, *Ruling Race*, 110–11.

41. Karp, *Vast Southern Empire*, 2–4, 57–58, 70–71, 81, William Lowndes Yancey quoted on 101 ("immense superiority"); Alabama agricultural society quoted in Levine, *Half Slave and Half Free*, 18 ("Our condition"); Schoen, *Fragile Fabric*, 169–70.

42. Beckert and Rockman, eds., *Slavery's Capitalism*, 181–82, 223–24, Charles Sumner quoted on 181 ("unhallowed"); Karp, *Vast Southern Empire*, 100–101; James Hammond quoted in McPherson, *Battle Cry of Freedom*, 100.

43. Mexican Liberal constitutional delegate quoted in Roeder, *Juárez*, vol. 1:133.

ONE: LIVES

1. Benito Juárez quoted in Roeder, *Juárez*, vol. 2:617.

2. Cott, *Bonds of Womanhood*, 63–100; Ryan, *Womanhood in America*, 113–18.

3. Levine, *Half Slave and Half Free*, 71–76.

4. Hudson, *Mistress*, 7–15.

5. Hudson, *Mistress*, 11–16, Jane McManus quoted on 15–16.

6. Hudson, *Mistress*, 15–19, 21–23, 29–40, Aaron Burr quoted on 18–19; May, "Lobbyists for Commercial Empire," 387.

7. Hudson, *Mistress*, 45–46, 50–53, William Marcy quoted on 75.

8. Hudson, *Mistress*, 41–43, 45–46, 50, 53–60; May, "Lobbyists for Commercial Empire," 388–90.

9. "Annexation," *Democratic Review*, vol. 17 (July 1845): 5; Hietala, *Manifest Design*, 8–9; Howe, *What Hath God Wrought*, 705–6; Hudson, *Mistress*, 45–46, 60–62. Hudson makes the case for McManus as the author of "Annexation."

10. Guardino, *Dead March*, 326–27; Hudson, *Mistress*, 71–75, 79–84, 90–93, Jane McManus quoted on 75 ("I would not see"), and 84 ("There is danger").

11. Hudson, *Mistress*, 95–96, 112–14, 137; May, "Lobbyists for Commercial Empire," 390–91.

12. [Cazneau], *Eagle Pass*, 17–20, 23–24, 42, 134–35, quotes on 20 ("for what it is," "abstract question"), 23 ("leave emancipation"), 23–24 ("highly absurd"), and 134–35 ("stupid," and "even in"); Cazneau quoted in Downs, *Second American Revolution*, 71 ("Who can").

13. [Cazneau], *Eagle Pass*, 50, 179–83, 186–88, quotes on 97 ("leave room"), 179 ("Wherever"), 183 ("leave the matchless").

14. Hoffert, *Jane Grey Swisshelm*, 1–3, 15–25; Larsen, *Crusader and Feminist*, 1–2.

15. Hoffert, *Jane Grey Swisshelm*, 1–3, 33–51, 68–73, Swisshelm quoted on 33 ("mockery"); Larsen, *Crusader and Feminist*, 2–8, Swisshelm quoted on 8 ("drunken").

16. Hoffert, *Jane Grey Swisshelm*, 2–4, 133–40, Mrs. P. Lorton quoted on 133; Larsen, *Crusader and Feminist*, 3–4.

17. Hoffert, *Jane Grey Swisshelm*, 26–27, 46–49, 79–93, Swisshelm quoted on 109 ("wipe off"), and 130 ("woman's right"); Larsen, *Crusader and Feminist*, 4.

18. Hoffert, *Jane Grey Swisshelm*, 1–3, 29–32, 136–37, Swisshelm quoted on 29 ("immediate"), *Pittsburgh Post* quoted on 61 ("one of"), George D. Prentiss quoted on 107 ("a man") and Swisshelm quoted on 107 ("Perhaps"); Larsen, *Crusader and Feminist*, 5–7, acquaintance quoted on 31 ("slight figure").

19. Hoffert, *Jane Grey Swisshelm*, 4, 53–59, 113–16, 139–40; Larsen, *Crusader and Feminist*, 1, 9–14, *St. Cloud Visiter* quoted on 10 and 13.

20. Hoffert, *Jane Grey Swisshelm*, 116–21, James Shepley quoted on 116; Larsen, *Crusader and Feminist*, 14–21.

21. Hoffert, *Jane Grey Swisshelm*, 188–89, Swisshelm quoted on 188.

22. *Chicago Tribune* quoted in Hoffert, *Jane Grey Swisshelm*, 103; Larsen, *Crusader and Feminist*, 30–31.

23. Donald, *Lincoln*, 19, 76, Lincoln quoted on 19 ("undistinguished" and "short and simple'); Foner, *Fiery Trial*, 114–16; Lincoln quoted in McPherson, *Battle Cry of Freedom*, 28 ("not ashamed").

24. Carwardine, *Lincoln*, 7–8, 14–15, 20, 26; Foner, *Fiery Trial*, 34–35; Lincoln quoted in McPherson, *Battle Cry of Freedom*, 28.

25. Donald, *Lincoln*, 21–24; Foner, *Fiery Trial*, 3–5, 37; Goodwin, *Team of Rivals*, 46–47; Richardson, *To Make Men Free*, 3–4.

26. Foner, *Fiery Trial*, 7–8; Richardson, *To Make Men Free*, 4–5; Woods, *Arguing Until Doomsday*, 36–39.

27. Carwardine, *Lincoln*, 4–7; Donald, *Lincoln*, 29–33; Goodwin, *Team of Rivals*, 48–49, 51–53, Lincoln quoted on 48; Richardson, *To Make Men Free*, 5.

28. Carwardine, *Lincoln*, 5–6; Donald, *Lincoln*, 29–33, Lincoln's neighbors quoted on 33; Foner, *Fiery Trial*, 14, 36–38.

29. Donald, *Lincoln*, 25–40; Goodwin, *Team of Rivals*, 47–49, Lincoln quoted on 47 ("All that"), Redmond Grigsby quoted on 49 ("sat down"), and John W. Lamar quoted on 49 ("he was"), Lincoln quoted on 56 ("It isn't"), Joshua Speed quoted on 57 ("never saw").

30. Carwardine, *Lincoln*, 4–9, 14; Donald, *Lincoln*, 25–43, James Quay Howard quoted on 43; Foner, *Fiery Trial*, 40–41.

31. Carwardine, *Lincoln*, 4–7, 9–10, 13–16, William Herndon quoted on 4; Donald, *Lincoln,* 44–67; Goodwin, *Team of Rivals*, 54–57.

32. Carwardine, *Lincoln*, 19; Donald, *Lincoln*, 84–93, William Herndon quoted on 84; Foner, *Fiery Trial*, 12–13.

33. Carwardine, *Lincoln*, 10–12, 22–23, Lincoln quoted on 23 ("foul"); Donald, *Lincoln*, 113–15, 119–32, Lincoln quoted on 124 ("the blood"), Democrats quoted on 125.

34. Carwardine, *Lincoln*, 20–21, 24–25; Delbanco, *War Before the War*, 229–32; Foner, *Fiery Trial*, 5–8, 15–19, 24–28, 31, 48–50, Lincoln quoted on 19.

35. Carwardine, *Lincoln*, 21–22; Foner, *Fiery Trial*, 10–12, Lincoln quoted on 11-12.

36. Donald, *Lincoln*, 133–33, Lincoln quoted on 134 ("I hold"); Foner, *Fiery Trial*, 17–19, 21–24, 27–32, 42–43; Alexander H. Stephens quoted in Guelzo, *Fateful Lightning*, 9; Lincoln quoted in Guelzo, *Lincoln and Douglas*, 33–34 ("No man" and "our duty").

37. Donald, *Lincoln*, 134–35, Lincoln quoted on 134 ("natural death"); Foner, *Fiery Trial*, 34–35; Lincoln quoted in McPherson, *Battle Cry of Freedom*, 28 ("free labor system").

38. McCurry, *Masters of Small Worlds*, 34–36, 43–48, 53–59, 71–72; Oakes, *Ruling Race*, 123–24, John Mills quoted on 123 ("A man's merit"); Oakes, *Slavery and Freedom*, 83–84, 94–95, J. D. B. DeBow quoted on 95 ("The non-slaveholder").

39. Delbanco, *War Before the War*, 240–41, James Hammond quoted on 240; Abel P. Upshur quoted in Lepore, *These Truths*, 236 ("However poor"); McCurry, *Masters of Small Worlds*, 241–49; Oakes, *Ruling Race*, 40–41, 132–33, 138–47, Richmond Enquirer quoted on 141; Schoen, *Fragile Fabric*, 5–6, 147–48.

40. Hermann, *Pursuit of a Dream*, 6–7; Kolchin, *American Slavery*, 174–80; Levine, *Half Slave and Half Free*, 40–44; McCurry, *Masters of Small Worlds*, 27–30, 42–43, 72–74; Oakes, *Ruling Race*, 38–40, 58–59, 65–67, 83–86; Schoen, *Fragile Fabric*, 155–57.

41. Stephen Duncan quoted in Baptist, *Half Has Never Been Told*, 208 ("We will"); J. Rothman, *Flush Times*, 2–11, Joseph H. Ingraham quoted on 5 ("one vast") and 10 ("to sell"); Woods, *Arguing Until Doomsday*, 15–20.

42. Cooper, *Jefferson Davis*, 14–21, 23–27; Woods, *Arguing Until Doomsday*, 20–21, 24.

43. Cooper, *Jefferson Davis*, 28–38; Hermann, *Joseph E. Davis*, 41; Woods, *Arguing Until Doomsday*, 24–25.

44. Cooper, *Jefferson Davis*, 38–40; Woods, *Arguing Until Doomsday*, 25–27, Davis quoted on 27.

45. Cooper, *Jefferson Davis*, 41–72; Hermann, *Joseph E. Davis*, 70–71.

46. Cooper, *Jefferson Davis*, 72–80, 226–31; Hermann, *Joseph E. Davis*, 70–71; Hermann, *Pursuit of a Dream*, 6–7; Woods, *Arguing Until Doomsday*, 28–29.

47. Cooper, *Jefferson Davis*, 173–74, Jefferson Davis quoted on 174 ("happy"); Davis quoted in Hermann, *Pursuit of a Dream*, 32 ("for the benefit") and in Woods, *Arguing Until Doomsday*, 100 ("entered").

48. Cooper, *Jefferson Davis*, 173–74, 229–39; Freehling, *Road to Disunion*, vol. 1:498–99; Hermann, *Pursuit of a Dream*, 10–14, 28–32.

49. Cooper, *Jefferson Davis*, 90–97; Hermann, *Joseph E. Davis*, 71–72; Woods, *Arguing Until Doomsday*, 66, 68.

50. Cooper, *Jefferson Davis*, 84–88, 98–109, Davis quoted on 103 ("We of the South") and 107 ("May our Union"); Woods, *Arguing Until Doomsday*, 64–70, European quoted on 101.

51. Cooper, *Jefferson Davis*, 115–26, 130–61, John A. Quitman quoted on 145; Woods, *Arguing Until Doomsday*, 78–80.

52. Earle, *Jacksonian Antislavery*, 129–31, 135–39, David Wilmot quoted on 138 ("white man's"); Hietala, *Manifest Design*, 122–25, Wilmot quoted on 125 ("sympathy" and "fair country"); Wilentz, *Rise of American Democracy*, 596–97, Free Soiler quoted on 627.

53. Cooper, *Jefferson Davis*, 169–72, 190–91, Davis quoted on 190 ("an institution"); Davis quoted in Freehling, *Road to Disunion*, vol. 1:499 ("that the South").

54. Cooper, *Jefferson Davis*, 169–72, 181–82, Davis quoted on 170 ("consent"), and 172 ("lust of power" and "staining"); Varon, *Disunion*, 192–93.

55. Foner, *Fiery Trial*, 51–52; A. Greenberg, *Wicked War*, 196; Hietala, *Manifest Design*, 126–27, 133, 220, 231–32, 250–54; Richards, *Slave Power*, 153–54, 159–60.

56. Foner, *Fiery Trial*, 54–55; Holt, *Rise and Fall of the American Whig Party*, 461–62, 474–76; Varon, *Disunion*, 207–8.

57. Hendrickson, *Union, Nation, or Empire*, 195; Holt, *Rise and Fall of the American Whig Party*, 463–65; Schoen, *Fragile Fabric*, 197–200; Varon, *Disunion*, 209–11.

58. Delbanco, *War Before the War*, 259–60; Holt, *Rise and Fall of the American Whig Party*, 517–52; Varon, *Disunion*, 227–28; Woods, *Arguing Until Doomsday*, 100–101.

59. Delbanco, *War Before the War*, 260–61, John C. Calhoun quoted on 261; Holt, *Rise and Fall of the American Whig Party*, 459–60, 476–84; Horton and Horton, *Slavery*, 146–47; Sinha, *Slave's Cause*, 490–91; Varon, *Disunion*, 207, 225–26.

60. Gwyn, *Man Who Made Us*, 1–14; Martin, *John A. Macdonald*, 17–19; Phenix, *Private Demons*, 4–10.

61. Creighton, *John A. Macdonald*, vol. 1:2–3, 8–10, 24; Gwyn, *Man Who Made Us*, 19–28, T. R. Preston quoted on 24; Lower, "Character of Kingston," 17–35; Martin, *John A. Macdonald*, 21–22; Phenix, *Private Demons*, 10–12.

62. Gwyn, *Man Who Made Us*, 28–33, 57, 204–5; Martin, *John A. Macdonald*, 17–18, 22–23; Phenix, *Private Demons*, 12–14, 22–23.

63. Gwyn, *Man Who Made Us*, 34–46, John Langton quoted 45; Martin, *John A. Macdonald*, 24–25; Phenix, *Private Demons*, 24–29.

64. Gwyn, *Man Who Made Us*, 36–44; Lower, "Character of Kingston," 32–33; Martin, *John A. Macdonald*, 19–20, 29.

65. J. K. Johnson, "John A. Macdonald," 141–47; Martin, *John A. Macdonald*, 26–27, 31–32, 34–36; Phenix, *Private Demons*, 29–30, 39–42, 46–47, Macdonald quoted on 29.

66. John A. Macdonald quoted in Ducharme, "Macdonald and the Concept of Liberty," 162; Martin, *John A. Macdonald*, 39–40, 55–56.

67. Gwyn, *Man Who Made Us*, 210–11, Sir John Willison quoted on 211; Martin, *John A. Macdonald*, 23, 27–28.

68. Gwyn, *Man Who Made Us*, 104–12, 122, Macdonald quoted on 112 ("long game," "If I don't"), and 198 ("When fortune"); Macdonald quoted in Martin, *John A. Macdonald*, 9–10 ("Only"); Moore, *1867*, 206–7 ("cabinet").

69. Gwyn, *Man Who Made Us*, 166–67; Moore, *1867*, 199–201, Robert Dickey quoted on 200 ("whenever"), Macdonald quoted on 200 ("Anyone") and 207 ("highly"); Dr. John Workman quoted in Phenix, *Private Demons*, 4 ("Macdonald indeed").

70. Gwyn, *Man Who Made Us*, 164–65, Richard Cartwright quoted on 165 ("Ah, John"); Martin, *John A. Macdonald*, 28–29, James Porter quoted on 28 ("There wasn't").

71. Gwyn, *Man Who Made Us*, 74–86, 118–19, 183–86; Martin, *John A. Macdonald*, 45–46, 50–55, 62, 67, 69, 76; Phenix, *Private Demons*, 65–66, 68–79, 84–88, 90–94, 98–104, 130–31, Maria McPherson quoted on 94.

72. Martin, *John A. Macdonald*, 55–56, 60, contemporary quoted on 76.

73. Curthoys, "Dog That Didn't Bark," 34–35, Lord Durham quoted on 35.

74. Ducharme, "Macdonald and the Concept of Liberty," 141–47; Gwyn, *Man Who Made Us*, 61–73, 120–27; J. K. Johnson, "John A. Macdonald," 151–55; Martin, *John A. Macdonald*, 30, 41–44, 49–50; Phenix, *Private Demons*, 63–68.

75. Gwyn, *Man Who Made Us*, 127–33, Macdonald quoted on 128; Phenix, *Private Demons*, 110–11.

76. Macdonald quoted in Gwyn, *Man Who Made Us*, 212–13 ("mingled interests" and "the action"); Macdonald quoted in Martin, *John A. Macdonald*, 33–34 ("agree," "respecting," and "spirit of compromise").

77. Moore, *1867*, 136–46.

78. Careless, *Brown of the Globe*, vol. 1:248–50; Gwyn, *Man Who Made Us*, 137–39, Macdonald quoted on 137; A. Levine, *Toronto*, 74–75 ; Martin, *John A. Macdonald*, 49–50, 56–57, 62–63.

79. Careless, *Brown of the Globe*, vol. 1:250–52; Gwyn, *Man Who Made Us*, 93, 139–44, George Brown quoted on 143 ("base vassalage"); Brown quoted in A. Levine, *Toronto*, 75 ("means tyranny"); Martin, *John A. Macdonald*, 36–37, 57–58.

80. Careless, *Brown of the Globe*, vol. 1:223.

81. Careless, *Brown of the Globe*, vol. 1:239, 263–64; Gwyn, *Man Who Made Us*, 174–75, 401–2, Goldwin Smith quoted on 421; Martin, *John A. Macdonald*, 63–65, 69–70, Toronto *Globe* quoted on 70; Morton, *Critical Years*, 12–16.

82. Careless, *Brown of the Globe*, vol. 1:264–77; Martin, *John A. Macdonald*, 70–73; Messamore, "Macdonald and the Governors General," 254–57.

83. Careless, *Brown of the Globe*, vol. 1:277–80; Gwyn, *Man Who Made Us*, 175–77, Macdonald quoted on 177; Moore, *1867*, 20–23.

84. Careless, *Brown of the Globe*, vol. 1:219–20, 224.

85. Careless, *Brown of the Globe*, vol. 1:256–57, 293–95.

86. Krauze, *Mexico*, 160–63; McAllen, *Maximilian and Carlota*, 41–42; Roeder, *Juárez*, vol. 1: 5–13, 44–47; Wasserman, *Everyday Life and Politics*, 94–95.

87. Ridley, *Maximilian and Juárez*, 25; Roeder, *Juárez*, vol. 1: 66–67, Margarita Maza quoted on 67; Wasserman, *Everyday Life and Politics*, 95.

88. Krauze, *Mexico*, 163–66; Roeder, *Juárez*, vol. 1:169–70, Guillermo Prieto quoted on 169 ("I never heard"); Salm-Salm, *Ten Years of My Life*, 188 ("Juárez was").

89. Roeder, *Juárez*, vol. 1: 142–43, Juárez quoted on 143.

90. Krauze, *Mexico*, 166–67, Benito Juárez quoted on 167 ("I am a son"); Olliff, *Reforma Mexico*, 19; Ridley, *Maximilian and Juárez*, 32–33.

91. DeLay, *War of a Thousand Deserts*, 23–25; Guardino, *Dead March*, 13–14; Ridley, *Maximilian and Juárez*, 8–11, 20, Conservatives quoted on 10–11 ("man had no"); Lucas Alaman quoted in Roeder, *Juárez*, vol. 1:102 ("only common tie").

92. Russell, *History of Mexico*, 145–46; Vanderwood, *Disorder and Progress*, 36–37, Liberal legislator quoted on 36.

93. Olliff, *Reforma Mexico*, 3–12; Vanderwood, *Disorder and Progress*, 35–36.

94. Delay, *War of a Thousand Deserts*, 317–40; Reséndez, *Other Slavery*, 219–30; St. John, *Line in the Sand*, 31–32.

95. Olliff, *Reforma Mexico*, 3–4; Pani, "Juárez vs. Maximiliano," 169.

96. Benito Juárez quoted in Roeder, *Juárez*, vol. 2:546.

97. R. White, *Republic for Which it Stands*, 57–59.

TWO: FUGITIVES

1. Abraham Lincoln quoted in Delbanco, *War Before the War*, 335.

2. Cooper, *Jefferson Davis*, 242–48, Davis quoted on 248; Freeman, *Field of Blood*, 177–82, Nathaniel Hawthorne quoted on 182; Holt, *Franklin Pierce*, 5–11, 17–18, 22–24, 28–30, a Whig wit quoted on 45.

3. Holt, *Franklin Pierce*, 44–46, 52–53, Pennsylvania Whig quoted on 45 ("like pissing"), Ohioan quoted on 45 ("General Apathy"), Pierce quoted on 53 ("sectional"); McPherson, *Battle Cry of Freedom*, 117–18, Alexander H. Stephens quoted on 118 ("Whig party"); Woods, *Arguing Until Doomsday*, 116–18.

4. Camp, *Closer to Freedom*, 2–4; Franklin and Schweninger, *Runaway Slaves*, 2–6, 11–15; Hahn, *Nation Under Our Feet*, 42–60; Horton and Horton, *Slavery*, 119–21, 132–34, 137–38; Sinha, *Slaves' Cause*, 382–93, 438–39.

5. Dunbar, *She Came to Slay*, 24–60; Horton, *Harriet Tubman*, 5–28; Oertel, *Harriet Tubman*, 14–49; Quarles, "Harriet Tubman's Unlikely Leadership," 43–49, Tubman quoted on 43 ("I grew up"), William Still quoted on 49 ("more ordinary").

6. Baker, *Affairs of Party*, 243–44; J. Jones, *Dreadful Deceit*, 100–101, 140–41, James Freeman Clarke quoted on 141 ("the unpopular"); Ryan, *Women in Public*, 22–27; Watson, *Liberty and Power*, 50–53.

7. Hahn, *Political Worlds of Slavery and Freedom*, 1–3, Lewis Garrard Clarke quoted on 2, William Parker quoted on 36; Horton and Horton, *Slavery*, 79–80, 89–90; Sinha, *Slave's Cause*, 422–23.

8. Camp, *Closer to Freedom*, 101–102; Fehrenbacher and McAfee, *Slaveholding Republic*, 231–33, *Southern Literary Messenger* quoted on 233 ("continued existence"); Foner, *Gateway to Freedom*, 6–27; Varon, *Disunion*, 95–97, 99–100.

9. Delbanco, *War Before the War*, 42, 227–28; Foner, *Gateway to Freedom*, 25–26; Horton and Horton, *Slavery*, 148–49.

10. Delbanco, *War Before the War*, 227–28, 252–55, Daniel Webster quoted on 264; Millard Fillmore quoted in Fehrenbacher and McAfee, *Slaveholding Republic*, 233; Lincoln quoted in Foner, *Gateway to Freedom*, 26.

11. Delbanco, *War Before the War*, 263–70, Black cooks quoted on 264; Huebner, *Liberty & Union*, 70–72, New York State Convention of Colored People quoted on 71–72; K. Jackson, *Force and Freedom*, 7–8, 39–43; Wilentz, *Rise of American Democracy*, 645–50, Frederick Douglass quoted on 650.

12. Delbanco, *War Before the War*, 286–92; Harrold, *Border War*, 153–55; H. Jackson, *American Radicals*, 182–88; K. Jackson, *Force and Freedom*, 43–47; Wilentz, *Rise of American Democracy*, 645–50, Pennsylvania newspaper quoted on 647.

13. Reynolds, *Mightier than the Sword*, 1–21.

14. Reynolds, *Mightier than the Sword*, 14–18, 28–29, 38–39, 59, 97–98, Harriet Beecher Stowe quoted on 59 ("very handsome"), and 88 ("It was at"), Eliza Buck quoted on 98 ("poor slaves").

15. Reynolds, *Mightier than the Sword*, 33–35, Charles Beecher quoted on 33 ("blown") and Harriet Beecher Stowe quoted on 33–34 ("It all came") and 93 ("under her pillow").

16. Reynolds, *Mightier than the Sword*, 35–47, 67, 98–100, 112–14, 118–24, *Uncle Tom's Cabin* quoted on 123; Varon, *Disunion*, 243–44.

17. Foreman, *World on Fire*, 26–27; Reynolds, *Mightier than the Sword*, 45, 126–28, 136–37, 145; Winks, *Blacks in Canada*, 184–86.

18. Blight, *Frederick Douglass*, 218–19, 226–27; Reynolds, *Mightier than the Sword*, 90–93, 116, 129–31, Harriet Beecher Stowe quoted on 130; Varon, *Disunion*, 244–45, Joshua R. Giddings quoted on 245.

19. Glymph, *Out of the House of Bondage*, 53; McPherson, *Battle Cry of Freedom*, 89–91, unnamed editor quoted on 90 ("review"); Reynolds, *Mightier than the Sword*, 44–45, 114, *Southern Literary Messenger* quoted on 44 ("the school"), *New Orleans Daily Picayune* quoted on 44 ("deficient"); Varon, *Disunion*, 136–37, 254–55.

20. Delbanco, *War Before the War*, 305; Reynolds, *Mightier than the Sword*, 150–52, Henry Field James quoted on 151–51.

21. Reynolds, *Mightier than the Sword*, 150–51; Thomas H. Hicks quoted in *The Liberator*, Aug. 15, 1862 ("I know Green").

22. McPherson, *Battle Cry of Freedom*, 89–91, book title quoted on 90; Reynolds, *Mightier than the Sword*, 152–58; Varon, *Disunion*, 136–37, 245–48, *New York Independent* quoted on 247 ("pictures" and "not make haste").

23. Nassau W. Senior quoted in Reynolds, *Mightier than the Sword*, 147.

24. Harrold, *Border War*, 146–47, Jane Grey Swisshelm quoted on 147; H. Jackson, *American Radicals*, 171, 184–8; McDaniel, *Problem of Democracy*, 196–97; Ralph Waldo Emerson quoted in Levy, "Sims' Case," 60; Varon, *Disunion*, 217–221, William H. Seward quoted on 220–21.

25. Delbanco, *War Before the War*, 288–89, 317–18, C. C. Olin quoted on 318 ("Twenty strong"); Harrold, *Border War*, 53–54, 155–56.

26. Delbanco, *War Before the War*, 273–81, 284–85; H. Jackson, *American Radicals*, 183; Levy, "Sims Case," 42–68, Thomas Sims quoted on 68.

27. Delbanco, *War Before the War*, 281–82, Millard Fillmore quoted on 282; H. Jackson, *American Radicals*, 183–84, 194; Levy, "Sims' Case," 68–69.

28. Delbanco, *War Before the War*, 308–14, Amos A. Lawrence quoted on 310; Link, *Roots of Secession*, 109–10; Varon, *Disunion*, 240–41.

29. Blight, *Frederick Douglass*, 87–173, 188–95, 291–92; Ottilie Assing quoted on 291–92; Horton and Horton, *Slavery*, 145–46; Lepore, *These Truths*, 248–50, *North Star* quoted on 250; Sinha, *Slave's Cause*, 425–28.

30. Blight, *Frederick Douglass*, 247–48; Levine, *Martin Delany*, 72–80, Douglass quoted on 89 ("The name"); Douglass quoted in Reynolds, *Mightier than the Sword*, 129–30 ("the slumbering embers" and "who before").

31. Levine, *Martin Delany*, 72–90, Delany quoted on 78 ("*knows nothing*") and 80 ("buried the hoe").

32. H. Jackson, *American Radicals*, 165–66; Painter, "Martin R. Delany," 150–51; Sterling, *Making of an Afro-American*, 6–23.

33. H. Jackson, *American Radicals*, 166–67; Painter, "Martin R. Delany," 151–52; Sterling, *Making of an Afro-American*, 24–28, 33–62, 76–92.

34. Blight, *Frederick Douglass*, 186, 191–92, Douglass quoted on 186; Painter, "Martin R. Delany," 152–53; Sterling, *Making of an Afro-American*, 92–121.

35. Dorsey, *Reforming Men & Women*, 160–61; Levine, *Martin Delany*, 61–62; Sterling, *Making of an Afro-American*, 122–39, Harvard students quoted on 130.

36. K. Jackson, *Force and Freedom*, 47; Levine, *Martin Delany*, 2–7, 55–56, Delany quoted on 70 ("I am weary"), 78 ("Our elevation"); Painter, "Martin R. Delany," 153–56; Reynolds, *John Brown*, 255–56, Delany quoted on 256 ("Our elevation").

37. Blight, *Frederick Douglass*, 238–39; Levine, *Martin Delany*, 6–12, Douglass quoted on 6.

38. Delbanco, *War Before the War*, 306–7; Reynolds, *Mightier than the Sword*, 87–90, 103–5; Winks, *Blacks in Canada*, 187–89, 193–94.

39. Reynolds, *Mightier than the Sword*, 105–6, 114; Winks, *Blacks in Canada*, 181–82.

40. Silverman, *Unwelcome Guests*, 54–57; Winks, *Blacks in Canada*, 180–84.

41. L. Campbell, "Northern Borderlands," 200–2, 220; Silverman *Unwelcome Guests*, 21–28, Sir John Colborne quoted on 27; Winks, *Blacks in Canada*, 149–56, 251–52, 262.

42. Silverman, *Unwelcome Guests*, 36–43; Winks, *Blacks in Canada*, 168–75.

43. A. Levine, *Toronto*, 79–82; Rhodes, *Mary Ann Shadd Cary*, 29–30; Silverman, *Unwelcome Guests*, 23–24; Winks, *Blacks in Canada*, 142–45, 245.

44. H. Jackson, *American Radicals*, 179–81, Frances Harper quoted on 180 and Frederick Douglass quoted on 181; Silverman, *Unwelcome Guests*, 35–36; Winks, *Blacks in Canada*, 149–50, Canadian quoted on 151.

45. Lord Elgin quoted in A. Levine, *Toronto*, 83; Rhodes, *Mary Ann Shadd Cary*, 27–31; Silverman, *Unwelcome Guests*, 61–62, 151; Winks, *Blacks in Canada*, 162–63, 240.

46. L. Campbell, "Northern Borderlands," 197–98, 204–8, 215–16; Silverman, *Unwelcome Guests*, 33–35, 62–73, Walter McCrae quoted on 65–66; Winks, *Blacks in Canada*, 142–49, 248–51.

47. Anonymous quoted in Downs, *Second American Revolution*, 75 ("The mission"); A. Levine, *Toronto*, 82–83; Radforth, *Royal Spectacle*, 73–74; Silverman, *Unwelcome Guests*, 160–61; John H. Hill quoted in Winks, *Blacks in Canada*, 246–47 ("I want").

48. Reynolds, *John Brown*, 257; Ross, *Recollections and Experiences*, 1–3, quotations from 2 ("marks"), 2–3 ("To me"), and 17 ("still raw").

49. Reynolds, *John Brown*, 257–58, Emerson quoted on 257; Ross, *Recollections and Experiences*, 3–18, 34–39, quotation from 3 ("Canada"); Winks, *Blacks in Canada*, 260.

50. Elizabeth Williamson quoted in Sterling, *We are Your Sisters*, 231–32; Winks, *Blacks in Canada*, 162–63, 238.

51. Rhodes, *Mary Ann Shadd Cary*, 4–10, Delaware legislature quoted on 10.

52. Rhodes, *Mary Ann Shadd Cary*, 13–19.

53. Rhodes, *Mary Ann Shadd Cary*, 19–23, 26–27, William J. Watkins quoted on 27 ("such an air"), Alexander McArthur quoted on 38 ("a young"), William

J. Watkins quoted on 110 ("Miss Shadd's"); Silverman, "Mary Ann Shadd," 87–88.

54. Rhodes, *Mary Ann Shadd Cary*, 22–23, Shadd quoted on 21, Martin Delany quoted on 23.

55. Rhodes, *Mary Ann Shadd Cary*, 52; quotes from Shadd, *Plea for Emigration*, 44.

56. Rhodes, *Mary Ann Shadd Cary*, 32–46, Shadd quoted on 34, James T. Holly quoted on 53; Shadd, *Plea for Emigration*, 17–20; Silverman, "Mary Ann Shadd," 89–90; Sterling, *We are Your Sisters*, 170–71.

57. Rhodes, *Mary Ann Shadd Cary*, 35–46, 66, William J. Watkins quoted on 109; Shadd, *Plea for Emigration*, 5–11, 14–17, 26–28, 34–36, quote from 34; Silverman, "Mary Ann Shadd," 91–92; Sterling, *We are Your Sisters*, 168.

58. Rhodes, *Mary Ann Shadd Cary*, 34–35, 41–43, 49–587, 66–69; Shadd, *Plea for Emigration*, 31–33; Silverman, *Unwelcome Guests*, 58–60, 110–12; Winks, *Blacks in Canada*, 206–7, 218–19.

59. Rhodes, *Mary Ann Shadd Cary*, 62–63, 70–76, 91–94, 108–9, 118–19, *Provincial Freeman* quoted on 103; Silverman, "Mary Ann Shadd," 92–93; Sterling, *We are Your Sisters*, 168–69.

60. Rhodes, *Mary Ann Shadd Cary*, 81–85, 90–94, 125; Silverman, "Mary Ann Shadd," 93–94; Silverman, *Unwelcome Guests*, 115–16.

61. Levine, *Martin Delany*, 180–81; Painter, "Martin R. Delany," 157; Rhodes, *Mary Ann Shadd Cary*, 86–89, 101–2, 112–20, Shadd quoted on 87; Sterling, *Making of an Afro-American*, 159–60, Delany quoted on 160.

62. Leonard, *Honorable Elijah Leonard*, 47–48; Rhodes, *Mary Ann Shadd Cary*, 132–33.

63. Baumgartner, *South to Freedom*, 120–21, 173; Campbell, *Empire for Slavery*, 62–63, *San Antonio Ledger* quoted on 180; Felix Haywood quoted in Marten, *Texas Divided*, 30; Schwartz, *Across the Rio to Freedom*, 23–28, Frederick Law Olmsted quoted on 28.

64. All quotations from [Cazneau], *Eagle Pass*, 138–40; Schwartz, *Across the Rio to Freedom*, 42–43.

65. Baumgartner, *South to Freedom*, 165–67, 179–81; Nichols, "Line of Liberty," 417–18; Schwartz, *Across the Rio to Freedom*, 11–18, 24–25, 31–32, 50–51, Mexican Senate quoted on 14, R. Fitzpatrick quoted on 54.

66. Baumgartner, *South to Freedom*, 167–68, 173–79, 219–20, Jesus Flores quoted on 179 ("for want"); Nichols, "Line of Liberty," 414, 417–19; Schwartz, *Across the Rio to Freedom*, 18–23; Tyler, "Fugitive Slaves," 2–4, 9–10.

67. Campbell, *Empire for Slavery*, 63–64, N. B. Hawkins quoted on 180; Ford, *Rip Ford's Texas*, 214; May, *Southern Dream*, 136–37, John S. Ford quoted on 137.

68. Nichols, "Line of Liberty," 427–31; Schwartz, *Across the Rio to Freedom*, 32–36; Shearer, "Callahan Expedition," 438–51, Emilio Langberg quoted on 442; Tyler, "Fugitive Slaves in Mexico," 5–10.

69. Kelley, "Mexico in His Head," 718; Manuel Robles Pezuela to Lewis Cass, Oct. 14, 1857, in Manning, ed., *Diplomatic Correspondence of the United States*, vol. 9:944–45; Nichols, "Line of Liberty," 424–26.

70. G. C. Anderson, *Conquest of Texas*, 322–24; Ford, *Rip Ford's Texas*, 261–62 ("fearless"), 276 ("destined"); Marten, *Texas Divided*, 30–31; Montejano, *Anglos and Mexicans*, 32–33, Juan Nepomuceno Cortina quoted on 32.

71. Carrigan and Webb, *Forgotten Dead*, 108–13, John S. Ford quoted on 111; Ford, *Rip Ford's Texas*, 264–309; Haley, *Sam Houston*, 365–66.

72. Harrold, *Border War*, 138–46, John Floyd quoted on 144; Varon, *Disunion*, 226–29, 235–37; Woods, *Arguing Until Doomsday*, 8–9.

73. Delbanco, *War Before the War*, 295, 314–15, Lincoln quoted on 295; Foner, *Gateway to Freedom*, 216–17, 220–21.

74. Delbanco, *War Before the War*, 234–35, Henry Clay quoted on 272 ("African"); Clay quoted in Levy, "Sims' Case," 41 ("government").

75. Deyle, *Carry Me Back*, 86; Harrold, *Border War*, 4–6, 12, 194–95, Robert Barnwell Rhett quoted on 195; Link, *Roots of Secession*, 99–100.

76. Fehrenbacher and McAfee, *Slaveholding Republic*, 246–51, Jeremiah Clemens quoted on 246 ("this government"); Levy, "Sims' Case," 42; Harrold, *Border War*, 148–49, 154; Link, *Roots of Secession*, 100–108, Richard A. Carter quoted on 113 ("instrument").

THREE: DESTINIES

1. Elihu B. Washburne quoted in Varon, *Disunion*, 255.

2. John Forsyth quoted in Bonner, *Mastering America*, 186 ("If we allow"); Delbanco, *War Before the War*, 244–46; Hendrickson, *Union, Nation, or Empire*, 202–204, Robert Barnwell Rhett and John C. Calhoun quoted on 202; Varon, *Disunion*, 257.

3. Downs, *Second American Revolution*, 55–57, 69; Johnson, *River of Dark Dreams*, 14–16; John Slidell quoted in P. J. Kelly, "Cat's Paw," 59 ("The South"); May, *Southern Dream*, 8–11, 37–38, Albert Gallatin Brown quoted on 9 ("and I want"), *Texas Republican* quoted on 11 ("restore").

4. Brettle, *Colossal Ambitions*, 28–30; Guterl, *American Mediterranean*, 5–7; Majewski and Wahlstrom, "Geography as Power," 346–47; *Southern Standard* quoted in McPherson, *Battle Cry of Freedom*, 106.

5. John B. Baldwin quoted in Ayers, *In the Presence of Mine Enemies*, 125; Karp, *Vast Southern Empire*, 2–4, 57–58, 70–71, 81; Edmund Ruffin quoted in Stampp, *America in 1857*, 189.

6. May, *Southern Dream*, 12–13, Lemuel D. Evans quoted on 13, and John P. Hale quoted on 174 ("always traveled"); Hale quoted in Downs, *Second American Revolution*, 88 ("If there is").

7. Downs, *Second American Revolution*, 56–59, Wendell Phillips quoted on 56; Karp, *Vast Southern Empire*, 4–7, 48–49, 88–89; Schoen, "Calculating the Price," 194–200.

8. Guelzo, *Lincoln and Douglas*, 3–9, Thomas Hart Benton quoted on 7 ("too short"); Woods, *Arguing Until Doomsday*, 29–32, politician quoted on 30 ("talented").

9. Egerton, *Year of Meteors*, 18–19.

10. Doyle, *Social Order*, 170–71; Guelzo, *Lincoln and Douglas*, 3–9, admirer quoted on 9; Woods, *Arguing Until Doomsday*, 35, 40–41, 57–59.

11. Guelzo, *Lincoln and Douglas*, 6–9, Stephen A. Douglas quoted on 6 ("rights" and "privileges"), and 7 ("neither felt"); Woods, *Arguing Until Doomsday*, 41, 54–55.

12. Egerton, *Year of Meteors*, 7, Frederick Douglass quoted on 7; Stephen A. Douglas quoted in Guelzo, *Lincoln and Douglas*, 11–12 ("Our people"); May, *Slavery, Race, and Conquest*, 22, 53–54, Douglas quoted on 22 ("this political Union").

13. Etcheson, *Bleeding Kansas*, 9–10; Holt, *Franklin Pierce*, 72–73; Morrison, *Slavery and the American West*, 142–43; Woods, *Arguing Until Doomsday*, 60–63, 81–84, 128–30.

14. Stephen A. Douglas quoted in Woods, *Arguing Until Doomsday*, 131.

15. Ashworth, *Slavery*, vol. 2:55–61; Etcheson, *Bleeding Kansas*, 11–12, 16, Claiborne Jackson quoted on 11; Harrold, *Border War*, 162–63; Morrison, *Slavery and the American West*, 145–46; Woods, *Arguing Until Doomsday*, 131–35.

16. Etcheson, *Bleeding Kansas*, 12–19; Morrison, *Slavery and the American West*, 143–47, Richard Brodhead quoted on 144; Potter and Fehrenbacher, *Impending Crisis*, 157–75; Varon, *Disunion*, 252–53; Woods, *Arguing Until Doomsday*, 90–94, 98–103.

17. Schott, *Alexander H. Stephens*, 9–30, Joseph LeConte quoted on 20 ("boyish"), Stephens quoted on 20 ("malformed"), 25 ("the highest" and "most restless), and 26 ("sensuality").

18. Freehling, *Road to Disunion*, vol. 1:442; Schott, *Alexander H. Stephens*, 31–82.

19. Schott, *Alexander H. Stephens*, 91–93.

20. Holt, *Franklin Pierce*, 81–82; Schott, *Alexander H. Stephens*, 163–73, Stephens quoted on 173; Woods, *Arguing Until Doomsday*, 129–30, 135–36.

21. Etcheson, *Bleeding Kansas*, 22–24, Stephen A. Douglas quoted on 23; Freeman, *Field of Blood*, 182–83, Benjamin Brown French quoted on 183; Morrison, *Slavery and the American West*, 154–55, *Albany Evening Journal* quoted on 154.

22. Holt, *Franklin Pierce*, 82–83; Varon, *Disunion*, 251–52.

23. McPherson, *Battle Cry of Freedom*, 126–27, Michigan Republicans quoted on 126; Morrison, *Slavery and the American West*, 149–51, *Illinois State Journal* quoted on 150; Varon, *Disunion*, 255–57, "Appeal of the Independent Democrats" quoted on 253 ("Slave Power" and "Permanency").

24. McPherson, *Battle Cry of Freedom*, 143–44, 159–60, Ohio Democrats quoted on 143, Indiana Democrats' banner quoted on 159; Foner, *Fiery Trial*, 117–18.

25. Etcheson, *Bleeding Kansas*, 26–27, 46–47; McPherson, *Battle Cry of Freedom*, 145–49, David Atchison quoted on 145, and Preston Brooks quoted on 149; William H. Seward quoted in Potter and Fehrenbacher, *Impending Crisis*, 199.

26. Etcheson, *Bleeding Kansas*, 28–29, George Spivey quoted on 40–41; Reynolds, *John Brown*, 143–44.

27. Ashworth, *Slavery*, vol. 2:63–64; Etcheson, *Bleeding Kansas*, 28–42; Potter and Fehrenbacher, *Impending Crisis*, 202–4.

28. McPherson, *Battle Cry of Freedom*, 145–47, David Atchison quoted on 145–46; Woods, *Arguing Until Doomsday*, 140–41.

29. Earle, "Beecher's Bibles and Broadswords," 50–51; Etcheson, *Bleeding Kansas*, 31–33, 47–48, 53–62, Blue Lodges quoted on 32; Harrold, *Border War*, 164–65; Thomas H. Webb quoted in Reynolds, *John Brown*, 141.

30. Earle, "Beecher's Bibles and Broadswords," 55; Etcheson, *Bleeding Kansas*, 63–65; Holt, *Franklin Pierce*, 91; Reynolds, *John Brown*, 141–42.

31. Etcheson, *Bleeding Kansas*, 66–68, 105–6.

32. Earle, "Beecher's Bibles and Broadswords," 51–54; Etcheson, *Bleeding Kansas*, 91–93, H. Miles Moore quoted on 93; Harrold, *Border War*, 166–67.

33. Etcheson, *Bleeding Kansas*, 36–39, 65–66, 69–78, *Herald of Freedom* quoted on 71; James Lane quoted on 120; Reynolds, *John Brown*, 142–43.

34. Ashworth, *Slavery*, vol. 2: 70–74; Etcheson, *Bleeding Kansas*, 91–93, 118–19, David Atchison quoted on 47; Harrold, *Border War*, 166–70.

35. Earle, "Beecher's Bibles and Broadswords," 58–59; Reynolds, *John Brown*, 145–47, Robert S. Kelley quoted on 198.

36. Etcheson, *Bleeding Kansas*, 79–105, Albert D. Richardson quoted on 120; Harrold, *Border War*, 167–69; Varon, *Disunion*, 266–67.

37. Freeman, *Field of Blood*, 217–19, Stephen A. Douglas quoted on 219; Varon, *Disunion*, 268–69, Charles Sumner quoted on 269; Walther, *Fire-Eaters*, 173–74.

38. Etcheson, *Bleeding Kansas*, 1–4, Benjamin Stringfellow quoted on 34; Freeman, *Field of Blood*, 219–26; Reynolds, *John Brown*, 161–62, Preston Brooks quoted on 161; Varon, *Disunion*, 270–71, cane inscription quoted on 270.

39. Morrison, *Slavery and the American West*, 157–59; Reynolds, *John Brown*, 161–62; Frederick Douglass quoted in Stauffer, *Black Hearts of Men*, 21.

40. Blight, *Frederick Douglass*, 280–85, 288–89, Douglass quoted on 281; Reynolds, *John Brown*, 168–69, Brown quoted on 65 ("Here, before God").

41. Blight, *Frederick Douglass*, 293–95, John Brown quoted on 293 ("to help defeat" and "Without shedding"); Etcheson, *Bleeding Kansas*, 107–12, Oliver Brown quoted on 107 ("bears"), J. Brown quoted on 111 ("I was doing"); Reynolds, *John Brown*, 133–37, 154–67, 171–74; Varon, *Disunion*, 267–68.

42. Earle, "Beecher's Bibles and Broadswords," 60–62; Etcheson, *Bleeding Kansas*, 120–26, 131–35, Wilson Shannon quoted on 131; Harrold, *Border War*, 171–72.

43. Baker, *James Buchanan*, 25–26, Andrew Jackson quoted on 25 ("Miss Nancy") and 31 ("inept").

44. Baker, *James Buchanan*, 30–33, Buchanan quoted on 30 ("Is there") and 33 ("Touch"); Morrison, *Slavery and the American West*, 177–81.

45. Baker, *James Buchanan*, 71–72, Buchanan quoted on 71; Foner, *Fiery Trial*, 80–82; McPherson, *Battle Cry of Freedom*, 155–61, Republicans quoted on 161; Potter and Fehrenbacher, *Impending Crisis*, 262–63, Robert Toombs quoted on 262.

46. Foner, *Free Soil*, 197–203; Morrison, *Slavery and the American West*, 185–86; Potter and Fehrenbacher, *Impending Crisis*, 260–65; Varon, *Disunion*, 286–87.

47. Etcheson, *Bleeding Kansas*, 136–43, John W. Geary quoted on 143 ("I have learned"); McPherson, *Battle Cry of Freedom*, 161–63, Geary quoted on 163 ("felons").

48. Etcheson, *Bleeding Kansas*, 143–45, 151–53; McPherson, *Battle Cry of Freedom*, 163–65, Robert J. Walker quoted on 165 ("vile fraud"); Morrison, *Slavery and the American West*, 196–97; Varon, *Disunion*, 305–6.

49. Etcheson, *Bleeding Kansas*, 147–49, 158–60, 171–72, William B. Napton quoted on 148; Harrold, *Border War*, 172–73; McPherson, *Battle Cry of Freedom*, 164–66, James Buchanan quoted on 167.

50. Egerton, *Year of Meteors*, 41–43, *Charleston Herald* quoted on 43; McPherson, *Battle Cry of Freedom*, 166–68, Alexander H. Stephens quoted on 167; Morrison, *Slavery and the American West*, 197–98, Stephen A. Douglas quoted on 198.

51. Etcheson, *Bleeding Kansas*, 153–58, 168–74, 179–82; McPherson, *Battle Cry of Freedom*, 168–69, Lawrence Keitt quoted on 168 ("Black Republican"), *New York Weekly Tribune* quoted on 168, Alexander H. Stephens quoted on 168.

52. Ashworth, *Slavery*, vol. 2:75–76; Etcheson, *Bleeding Kansas*, 153–64, 183–84, 190–218, Thomas Ewing, Jr., quoted on 164.

53. Burke, "Scattered People," 74–75, Gustavus Parsons quoted on 74; Etcheson, *Bleeding Kansas*, 190–218; Harrold, *Border War*, 172–73.

54. Downs, *Second American Revolution*, 85–87; Etcheson, *Bleeding Kansas*, 184–85; May, *Slavery, Race, and Conquest*, 88–89, 134–36, 148–49.

55. May, *Manifest Destiny's Underworld*, 3–4, 82–83, 91–97, 197–98; *United States Democratic Review* quoted in Stampp, *America in 1857*, 191.

56. Bourne, *Britain and the Balance of Power*, 182–202, Lord Palmerston quoted on 195; W. Johnson, *River of Dark Dreams*, 322–23, 385–90; May, *Manifest Destiny's Underworld*, 161–67, 231–33, 240–41; May, *Southern Dream*, 27–28, 113–26.

57. Hahn, *Nation Without Borders*, 165; W. Johnson, *River of Dark Dreams*, 381–82; May, *Southern Dream*, 78–79.

58. Freehling, *Road to Disunion*, vol. 2:161–62; May, *Manifest Destiny's Underworld*, 40–41, 79–80; May, *Southern Dream*, 79–80, 90–93, William Walker quoted on 91.

59. W. Johnson, *River of Dark Dreams*, 366–67; May, *Southern Dream*, 80–83, John Wheeler quoted on 82 ("pawns") and Louis Schlessinger quoted on 83 ("freckled").

60. May, *Manifest Destiny's Underworld*, 40–42; Matthews, *Golden State in the Civil War*, 29–30, Horace Bell quoted on 30; May, *Southern Dream*, 83–85.

61. W. Johnson, *River of Dark Dreams*, 367–68; May, *Southern Dreams*, 85–90.

62. Bourne, *Britain and the Balance of Power*, 170–72, Lord Palmerston quoted on 182; W. Johnson, *River of Dark Dreams*, 368; May, *Manifest Destiny's Underworld*, 238.

63. Hahn, *Nation Without Borders*, 165–66; W. Johnson, *River of Dark Dreams*, 368–69; May, *Southern Dream*, 90–99.

64. Hudson, *Mistress of Manifest Destiny*, 159–60, Jane Cazneau quoted on 160; May, *Slavery, Race, and Conquest*, 118–29; May, *Southern Dream*, 96–103.

65. Etcheson, *Bleeding Kansas*, 137–38; Hahn, *Nation Without Borders*, 166–67; W. Johnson, *River of Dark Dreams*, 369–71, 390–91; May, *Manifest Destiny's Underworld*, 240–41, 263–65.

66. May, *Slavery, Race, and Conquest*, 133–34; May, *Manifest Destiny's Underworld*, 196–97, 200–205, Joseph Hall quoted on 202; Stampp, *America in 1857*, 190–91.

67. Freehling, *Road to Disunion*, vol. 2:161–62, William Walker quoted on 161; May, *Manifest Destiny's Underworld*, 264–67, Pierre Soulé quoted on 264; May, *Slavery, Race, and Conquest*, 130–31, 136–37; May, *Southern Dream*, 111–16.

68. May, *Southern Dream*, 131–32; McPherson, *Battle Cry of Freedom*, 115.

69. Chambers, *No God but Gain*, 18–20, 24–25, 83–84, 92–96, 121–22; Downs, *Second American Revolution*, 59–61; Karp, *Vast Southern Empire*, 60–61.

70. Chambers, *No God but Gain*, 105–6, 109–11, 121–23, 166–68; John Quitman quoted in Freehling, *Road to Disunion*, vol. 2:165; W. Johnson, *River of Dark Dreams*, 319–21; May, *Southern Dream*, 6–7, 32–33, Louisville *Daily Courier* quoted on 7.

71. Downs, *Second American Revolution*, 59–66; Hudson, *Mistress of Manifest Destiny*, 96–98; May, *Manifest Destiny's Underworld*, 86–87; May, *Southern Dream*, 25–26.

72. Downs, *Second American Revolution*, 66–67, 71–72; Guterl, *American Mediterranean*, 17–18; Hudson, *Mistress of Manifest Destiny*, 95–96, 104, 135–36; Johnson, *River of Dark Dreams*, 304–6, 324–26, 339–51; May, *Southern Dream*, 27–29.

73. Freehling, *Road to Disunion*, vol. 2:162–63; May, *Southern Dream*, 46–47; Walther, *Fire-Eaters*, 83–85, John Quitman quoted on 92.

74. Cooper, *Jefferson Davis*, 134–38, 145–46, 210–23; Freehling, *Road to Disunion*, vol. 1:525–27, John Quitman quoted on 525 ("hedged"); Walther, *Fire-Eaters*, 85–86, 94–98, Quitman quoted on 85 ("a happy" and "become").

75. Downs, *Second American Revolution*, 75–76, John Quitman quoted on 76 ("Cuba is"); Guterl, *American Mediterranean*, 24–25; Walther, *Fire-Eaters*, 102–8.

76. Downs, *Second American Revolution*, 74–75; Johnson, *River of Dark Dreams*, 361–62, *DeBow's Review* quoted on 362; May, *Manifest Destiny's Underworld*, 254–57.

77. Downs, *Second American Revolution*, 72–74; Hahn, *Nation Without Borders*, 161–62; May, *Southern Dream*, 40–41.

78. Cortada, *Spain and the American Civil War*, 11–13; Hietala, *Manifest Design*, 211–12, 247–48; Holt, *Franklin Pierce*, 59–63; Potter and Fehrenbacher, *Impending Crisis*, 180–85, Pierre Soulé quoted on 184.

79. Bourne, *Britain and the Balance of Power*, 184–86; Hendrickson, *Union, Nation, or Empire*, 198–99; May, *Southern Dream*, 68–70; Potter and Fehrenbacher, *Impending Crisis*, 189–91, Ostend Manifesto quoted on 190.

80. William Marcy quoted in Hendrickson, *Union, Nation, or Empire*, 198; May, *Southern Dream*, 59–62, 69–71; Potter and Fehrenbacher, *Impending Crisis*, 191–92.

81. Downs, *Second American Revolution*, 76–79; W. Johnson, *River of Dark Dreams*, 363–65; May, *Manifest Destiny's Underworld*, 34–35, 259; May, *Southern Dream*, 63–71.

82. Freehling, *Road to Disunion*, vol. 2:166–67; May, *Slavery, Race, and Conquest*, 165–69; May, *Southern Dream*, 72–75, 163–89; Stampp, *America in 1857*, 60.

83. Cortada, *Spain and the American Civil War*, 30–31; Hudson, *Mistress of Manifest Destiny*, 150–53; Tansill, *United States and Santo Domingo*, 125–36, 172–75.

84. Cortada, *Spain and the American Civil War*, 31; Hudson, *Mistress of Manifest Destiny*, 150–53; Tansill, *United States and Santo Domingo*, 175–76, 185–88, William Cazneau quoted on 185 and 188.

85. Rafuse, *McClellan's War*, 61; Tansill, *United States and Santo Domingo*, 188–93, William Marcy quoted on 193.

86. Tansill, *United States and Santo Domingo*, 195–204, Dominican Congress quoted on 197–98.

87. Waite, *West of Slavery*, 1–11, 28–32, 41–44, 139, Thomas Jefferson Green quoted on 41; Woods, *Arguing Until Doomsday*, 120.

88. Berbusse, "Two Kentuckians Evaluate the Mexican Scene," 502–3, James Gadsden quoted on 503; Fowler, *Santa Anna*, 305–8; Potter and Fehrenbacher, *Impending Crisis*, 153–54, 178, 182–83; Waite, *West of Slavery*, 50–54.

89. Nelson, *The Three-Cornered War*, 16–18; Utley, *Indian Frontier*, 55–58.

90. Cooper, *Jefferson Davis*, 277; Waite, *West of Slavery*, 73–78; Woods, *Arguing Until Doomsday*, 122–25.

91. Waite, *West of Slavery*, 62, 64, 78–85.

92. W. H. Ellison, ed., "Memoirs of Hon. William M. Gwin," 1–6; St. John, "Unpredictable America of William Gwin," 57.

93. W. H. Ellison, "Memoirs of Hon. William M. Gwin," 14–15, 24; St. John, "Unpredictable America of William Gwin," 57, 60; Gwin quoted in Stanley, "Senator William Gwin," 243.

94. Keehn, *Knights of the Golden Circle*, 129–30; Matthews, *Golden State in the Civil War*, 34–35, 205–6; Richards, *California Gold Rush*, 37–41; Stanley, "Senator William Gwin," 245–48, Gwin quoted on 245 ("foundation").

95. Coleman, "African American Women," 103–5; Reséndez, *Other Slavery*, 246–65; Gwin quoted in Stanley, "Senator William Gwin," 247; Waite, *West of Slavery*, 93–95, 107–8, 111–12, Thomas Butler King quoted on 111.

96. De Graaf and Taylor, "Introduction," 8–9, Robert Givens quoted on 9; McCurdy, "Prelude to Civil War," 8–9; Waite, *West of Slavery*, 98–105.

97. Matthews, *Golden State in the Civil War*, 68–73, 203–5; L. Thomas, *Between Two Empires*, 173–74; Waite, *West of Slavery*, 99–100; Winks, *Blacks in Canada*, 272–73.

98. Matthews, *Golden State in the Civil War*, 205–6; Waite, *West of Slavery*, 118–21, Californian quoted on 118; Winks, *Blacks in Canada*, 273–77.

99. Matthews, *Golden State in the Civil War*, 34–35, Californians quoted on 65; Quinn, *The Rivals*, 40–47, 99–103; Waite, *West of Slavery*, 108–17.

100. Matthews, *Golden State in the Civil War*, 28–29, 36, 38–40; McCurdy, "Prelude to Civil War," 8, 24; Quinn, *The Rivals*, 256–76; Richards, *California Gold Rush*, 5–7, 219–21; Smith, *Freedom's Frontier*, 77–79; Waite, *West of Slavery*, 119–21.

101. Matthews, *Golden State in the Civil War*, 39, 216–18; Waite, *West of Slavery*, 102-3, 106, 110, 155–58.

102. Richards, *California Gold Rush*, 215–16, 225; Waite, *West of Slavery*, 158–60.

103. Reséndez, *Other Slavery*, 2, 6, 245–46; Waite, *West of Slavery*, 123–25, 134–42, 144–46, Alexander Jackson quoted on 125.

104. Waite, *West of Slavery*, 150–53.

105. Waite, *West of Slavery*, 154–55.

106. Keehn, *Knights of the Golden Circle*, 54–55; May, *Southern Dream*, 136–46, 150, George Bickley quoted on 150; Olliff, *Reforma Mexico*, 26–27.

107. May, *Southern Dream*, 136–46.

108. Ford, *Rip Ford's Texas*, 195–96; May, *Manifest Destiny's Underworld*, 36–38; May, *Southern Dream*, 147–48; Olliff, *Reforma Mexico*, 57–60; Shearer, "Carvajal Disturbances," 201–4, Stephen F. Austin quoted on 202 ("His own countrymen").

109. Ford, *Rip Ford's Texas*, 196–205, quote on 204; Schwartz, *Across the Rio to Freedom*, 33–34; Shearer, "Carvajal Disturbances," 205–20, 230n93.

110. DeLay, *War of a Thousand Deserts*, 71–72; Fowler, *Santa Anna*, 279–85, 291–92; Krauze, *Mexico*, 133–35; Russell, *History of Mexico*, 146–47.

111. Bazant, "From Independence to the Liberal Republic," 25–28; Fowler, *Santa Anna*, 292–98, 310; Olliff, *Reforma Mexico*, 35–36; Roeder, *Juárez*, vol. 1:101–5, 108–11; Sinkin, *Mexican Reform*, 28–29, 32–33, Lucas Alamán quoted on 29.

112. Fowler, *Santa Anna*, 298–304; Krauze, *Mexico*, 149–50, for Santa Anna's title, see 149; Roeder, *Juárez*, vol. 1:113–14.

113. Baumgartner, *South to Freedom*, 190–93, Mexican minister to France quoted on 190; Fowler, *Santa Anna*, 304–5, Santa Anna quoted on 305; James Gadsden to William L. Marcy, Sept. 2, 1854, in Manning, ed., *Diplomatic Correspondence*, vol. 9:728–30.

114. Sinkin, *Mexican Reform*, 33–34, 51–52.

115. Bazant, "From Independence to the Liberal Republic," 30–32; Fowler, *Santa Anna*, 297, 308–16; McAllen, *Maximilian and Carlota*, 42–43; Olliff, *Reforma Mexico*, 10–11, 31–32; Ridley, *Maximilian and Juárez*, 26–27; Roeder, *Juárez*, vol. 1:114–17.

116. Masich, *Civil War in the Southwest Borderlands*, 32–33; May, *Manifest Destiny's Underworld*, 43, 88, 90, 191, 262, William Allen Wallace quoted on 262 ("erect"); St. John, *Line in the Sand*, 42–50, Ignacio Pesqueria quoted on 48–49.

117. Keehn, *Knights of the Golden Circle*, 8–10, anonymous colleague quoted on 10; May, *Manifest Destiny's Underworld*, 45, 261–62.

118. Keehn, *Knights of the Golden Circle*, 9–11, 23–26, 37, George Bickley quoted on 23 ("This is selfish") and 73 ("Americanization"); May, *Manifest Destiny's Underworld*, 261–62.

119. Buenger, *Secession and the Union in Texas*, 155–56; Frazier, *Blood & Treasure*, 13–14; Keehn, *Knights of the Golden Circle*, 28–29, George Bickley quoted on 28 ("great Democratic monarchy"); May, *Southern Dream*, 149–50, Bickley quoted on 150 ("Knights").

120. Keehn, *Knights of the Golden Circle*, 1–3, 18–27, 39, George Bickley quoted on 19 ("The Mexicans"), and 72 ("No greater calamity"), and *Arkansas True Democrat* quoted on 24; May, *Southern Dream*, 151–54.

121. Keehn, *Knights of the Golden Circle*, 41–53; May, *Southern Dream*, 151–54; Potter and Fehrenbacher, *Impending Crisis*, 466–67.

122. Cornell, "Citizens of Nowhere," 358–60; Downs, *Second American Revolution*, 57–58, William H. Seward quoted on 57; May, *Slavery, Race, and Conquest*, 102–3, 181–86; Oakes, *Scorpion's Sting*, 25–27, James Redpath quoted on 26.

123. James Redpath quoted in Hunt, *Haiti's Influence*, 149; Oakes, *Scorpion's Sting*, 27–28; Robert Toombs quoted in Waite, *West of Slavery*, 183.

FOUR: THUNDER

1. *Missouri Republican* quoted in Ponce, "'As Dead as Julius Caesar,'" 364.

2. Bazant, "From Independence to the Liberal Republic," 32–33; Ridley, *Maximilian and Juárez*, 23–25; Roeder, *Juárez*, vol. 1:105–8; Sinkin, *Mexican Reform*, 47–48.

3. Fowler, *Independent Mexico*, 230–34; Sinkin, *Mexican Reform*, 7–8, 11, 18–20, 115–17.

4. Sinkin, *Mexican Reform*, 18–20, 54, 78–79, Francisco Zarco quoted on 78 ("the aspiration").

5. Knapp, *Life of Sebastián Lerdo de Tejada*, 34–38; Krauze, *Mexico*, 158–59; Ridley, *Maximilian and Juárez*, 27–28; Roeder, *Juárez*, vol. 1:119, 121, 123–24; Scholes, *Mexican Politics*, 1–8, 15–18; Sinkin, *Mexican Reform*, 98–99, 117–18, 122–25.

6. Bazant, "From Independence to the Liberal Republic," 34–36; Olliff, *Reforma Mexico*, 61–62; Pani, "Juárez vs. Maximiliano," 169–70; Roeder, *Juárez*, vol. 1:126, 129–35; Sinkin, *Mexican Reform*, 55–59, 62–63, 67–68, 128–30, 133–34.

7. Roeder, *Juárez*, vol. 1:127–29, Ponciano Arriaga quoted on 127–28; Sinkin, *Mexican Reform*, 72–73, 134–35.

8. Catholic bishops quoted in Pani, "Juárez vs. Maximiliano," 170–71; Roeder, *Juárez*, vol. 1:121–22, 138–39, 144–45, 151; Scholes, *Mexican Politics*, 17–22, J. J. Pesado quoted on 19 ("Placing" and "must rest").

9. Roeder, *Juárez*, vol. 1:140–62, Melchor Ocampo quoted on 141.

10. Fowler, *Independent Mexico*, 235–37; John Forsyth to Lewis Cass, Dec. 17, 1857, in Manning, ed., *Diplomatic Correspondence*, vol. 9:962–63; Roeder, *Juárez*, vol. 1:117–19, 145–56, Melchor Ocampo quoted on 118 ("I believe") and 141 ("absolute lack"); Wasserman, *Everyday Life and Politics*, 105–6.

11. Fowler, *Independent Mexico*, 237–38; Roeder, *Juárez*, vol. 1:l48, 153, 155–57.

12. Fowler, *Independent Mexico*, 238–39; John Forsyth to Lewis Cass, Aug. 1 and 31, 1858, in Manning, ed., *Diplomatic Correspondence*, vol. 9:1016–18, 1091–20, quotation on 1016–17.

13. Robert McLane to Lewis Cass, Apr. 21, 1859, and Melchor Ocampo to McLane, Apr. 22, 1859, in Manning, ed., *Diplomatic Correspondence*, vol. 9:1058–62 and 1063–64; Ridley, *Maximilian and Juárez*, 29–36.

14. Roeder, *Juárez*, vol. 1:161–62, 173, 183–86, 205; Scholes, *Mexican Politics*, 43–55; Sinkin, *Mexican Reform*, 100–1, 135–45.

15. John Forsyth to Lewis Cass, Nov. 18, 1857, and Nov. 25, 1857, in Manning, ed., *Diplomatic Correspondence*, vol. 9:946 and 959–60 ("Mexican institutions"); Roeder, *Juárez*, vol. 1:179–192, Forsyth quoted on 191 ("battleground").

16. Berbusse, "Two Kentuckians Evaluate Mexico," 510–11; William Churchwell to Lewis Cass, Feb. 8, 1859, in Manning, ed., *Diplomatic Correspondence*, vol. 9:1024–25.

17. William Churchwell to James Buchanan, Feb. 22, 1859, in Manning, ed., *Diplomatic Correspondence*, vol. 9:1033–34; Roeder, *Juárez*, vol. 1:192–94.

18. Robert McLane to Lewis Cass, Apr. 7 and 21, 1859, in Manning, ed., *Diplomatic Correspondence*, vol. 9:1037–43, and 1050–56; Olliff, *Reforma Mexico*, 19–21; Ponce, "'As Dead as Julius Caesar,'" 345–47; Roeder, *Juárez*, vol. 1:175–76, 212–18; Scholes, *Mexican Politics*, 29–37.

19. Roeder, *Juárez*, vol. 1:220–24, Miguel Miramón quoted on 223; Scholes, *Mexican Politics*, 37–42.

20. Ponce, "'As Dead as Julius Caesar,'" 347–75, Louis Wigfall quoted on 355, *New York Herald* quoted on 375; Roeder, *Juárez*, vol. 1:225–27.

21. May, *Southern Dream*, 160–62, *Macon Daily Telegraph* quoted on 162; Ponce, "'As Dead as Julius Caesar,'" 342, 357–76, *New Orleans Daily Picayune* quoted on 376.

22. Pani, "Juárez vs. Maximiliano," 171–72; Ridley, *Maximilian and Juárez*, 42, 58–61, Melchor Ocampo quoted on 59; Roeder, *Juárez*, vol. 1:263–65.

23. Schmalz, *Ojibwa of Southern Ontario*, 120–25, 143–46; Surtees, *Canadian Indian Policy*, 33–34.

24. Dickason, *Canada's First Nations*, 200–4; Schmalz, *Ojibwa of Southern Ontario*, 148–49, 167–75.

25. Gwyn, *Man Who Made Us*, 154–55; Miller, "Macdonald as Minister of Indian Affairs," 314–15; Smith, "Macdonald's Relationship with Aboriginal Peoples," 64–67, Macdonald quoted on 64.

26. Gwyn, *Man Who Made Us*, 153–54; Miller, "Macdonald as Minister of Indian Affairs," 311–12, 317–18; Smith, "Macdonald's Relationship with Aboriginal Peoples," 67–68.

27. Gwyn, *Man Who Made Us*, 154–55; Smith, "Macdonald's Relationship with Aboriginal Peoples," 67, Benjamin Robinson quoted on 86n52.

28. Curthoys, "Dog That Didn't Bark," 36–40; Great Council quoted in Miller, "Macdonald as Minister of Indian Affairs," 318–19; Smith, "Macdonald's Relationship with Aboriginal Peoples," 68–69; Radforth, *Royal Spectacle*, 230–31.

29. Barman, *West Beyond the West*, 55–64, James Douglas quoted on 60; Morton, *Critical Years*, 25–27, 38–39; Perry, *Colonial Relations*, 177–80.

30. Barman, *West Beyond the West*, 66–67; Marshall, "No Parallel," 41–42, Lucas Edelblute quoted on 42.

31. Barman, *West Beyond the West*, 64–66, miner quoted on 64; Lower, *Western Canada*, 70; Marshall, "No Parallel," 33–34; Perry, *Colonial Relations*, 181–82.

32. Barman, *West Beyond the West*, 66–70, Donald Fraser quoted on 70; Marshall, "No Parallel," 31–33, 39.

33. Barman, *West Beyond the West*, 66–69, James Douglas quoted on 66, Canadian

quoted on 69; Marshall, "No Parallel," 34, 65–66; Perry, *Colonial Relations*, 179–81.

34. Lower, *Western Canada*, 73-74; Marshall, "No Parallel," 65-66.

35. Barman, *West Beyond the West*, 72–73, 77–79, unnamed girl quoted on 83; Bumsted, "Consolidations of British North America," 63; Perry, *Colonial Relations*, 179–81, James Douglas quoted on 180.

36. Barman, *West Beyond the West*, 78–79; Foreman, *World on Fire*, 51–52; Jewell, "Thwarting Southern Schemes," 17–19; Lower, *Western Canada*, 75.

37. Marshall, "No Parallel," 34–38, H. F. Reinhart quoted on 38.

38. Marshall, "No Parallel," 39–50, 54, 65–66, H. W. Reinhart quoted on 39 ("The miners"), Jason O. Allard quoted on 46 ("military formations").

39. Lower, *Western Canada*, 74–76; Marshall, "No Parallel," 49, 62–66; Miller, *Skyscrapers Hide the Heavens*, 145–47; Perry, *Colonial Relations*, 182–86.

40. Fehrenbacher, *Dred Scott Case*, 560n; Simon, *Lincoln and Chief Justice Taney*, 6–12, Taney quoted on 11.

41. Newmyer, *Supreme Court*, 91–117; Simon, *Lincoln and Chief Justice Taney*, 13–37.

42. Fehrenbacher, *Dred Scott Case*, 553–59; Huebner, *Liberty and Union*, 93–94; McPherson, *Battle Cry of Freedom*, 173–74.

43. Fehrenbacher, *Dred Scott Case*, 240–84; Newmyer, *Supreme Court*, 131–33; Simon, *Lincoln and Chief Justice Taney*, 100–103.

44. Fehrenbacher, *Dred Scott Case*, 306–12, Taney quoted on 311; Simon, *Lincoln and Chief Justice Taney*, 113–14, 119–20, Buchanan quoted on 113 (" great object"); Stampp, *America in 1857*, 64–65, 91–92, Buchanan quoted on 65 ("civil and religious").

45. Fehrenbacher, *Dred Scott Case*, 337–64, Taney quoted on 343 ("inferior") and 347 ("had no rights"); Newmyer, *Supreme Court*, 133–34; Simon, *Lincoln and Chief Justice Taney*, 121–24; Stampp, *America in 1857*, 93–95.

46. Fehrenbacher, *Dred Scott Case*, 365–88; Masur, *Until Justice Be Done*, 258–59; Simon, *Lincoln and Chief Justice Taney*, 124–25, 127–30; Stampp, *America in 1857*, 95–100.

47. Egerton, *Year of Meteors*, 38–40; Foner, *Fiery Trial*, 93–98, James Buchanan quoted on 98; Schott, *Alexander H. Stephens*, 229–30, New York *Tribune* quoted on 229; Stampp, *America in 1857*, 101–9.

48. Baumgartner, *South to Freedom*, 215–18; McCurry, *Confederate Reckoning*, 14–16; Roeder, *Juárez*, vol. 1:129–30, Constitution of 1857 quoted on 129; Schwartz, *Across the Rio to Freedom*, 51–54, John Forsyth quoted on 53.

49. Egerton, *Year of Meteors*, 44–45, Stephen A. Douglas quoted on 45 ("I shall have"); Woods, *Arguing Until Doomsday*, 167–68, Douglas quoted on 168 ("the best").

50. Carwardine, *Lincoln*, 71–78; Foner, *Fiery Trial*, 101–2; Woods, *Arguing Until Doomsday*, 168–71.

51. Foner, *Fiery Trial*, 99–101, Lincoln quoted on 99–100 ("I believe"); Lincoln quoted in McPherson, *Battle Cry of Freedom*, 181–82 ("consider" and "modern Democratic").

52. McPherson, *Battle Cry of Freedom*, 182–85, Douglas quoted on 182 ("thinks that"); Woods, *Arguing Until Doomsday*, 172–73, Douglas quoted on 172 ("made by the white man" and "I would not blot").

53. Carwardine, *Lincoln*, 79–80; Foner, *Fiery Trial*, 103–4, 107–9, Lincoln quoted on 104.

54. Carwardine, *Lincoln*, 80–81; Egerton, *Year of Meteors*, 46–47; Foner, *Fiery Trial*, 106–7; Woods, *Arguing Until Doomsday*, 168–72, Stephen A. Douglas quoted on 171.

55. Carwardine, *Lincoln*, 88–90; Egerton, *Year of Meteors*, 46–47; Foner, *Fiery Trial*, 110–11; Woods, *Arguing Until Doomsday*, 174.

56. Egerton, *Year of Meteors*, 53–56; Woods, *Arguing Until Doomsday*, 174–76, 180–85, 192–93, Q. C. Lamar quoted on 174, Jefferson Davis quoted on 175.

57. Egerton, *Year of Meteors*, 62–63; Potter and Fehrenbacher, *Impending Crisis*, 404; Woods, *Arguing Until Doomsday*, 185–88, 194–95, 204–5.

58. Campbell, *Empire for Slavery*, 212–15, C. A. Frazier quoted on 213 ("I have no more"); Potter and Fehrenbacher, *Impending Crisis*, 397–98, southern advocate quoted on 398 ("a sort of spite").

59. Thornton, *Politics and Power in a Slave Society*, 71–72, 211–14; Walther, *Fire-Eaters*, 51–52, Robinson Earle quoted on 52 ("damned"), William L. Yancey quoted on 52.

60. Walther, *Fire-Eaters*, 52–68, W. B. Figures quoted on 67.

61. Freehling, *Road to Disunion*, vol. 2:174–76, William L. Yancey quoted on 176 ("wipe out"); W. Johnson, *River of Dark Dreams*, 395–99; Potter and Fehrenbacher, *Impending Crisis*, 395–397, Yancey quoted on 398 ("If it is right").

62. Freehling, *Road to Disunion*, vol. 2:174–81; McPherson, *Battle Cry of Freedom*, 102–3, unnamed southern proponent quoted on 102 ("With cheap negroes"); Potter and Fehrenbacher, *Impending Crisis*, 398–399; L. White, "South in the 1850s," 36–38.

63. Freehling, *Road to Disunion*, vol. 2:177–83; W. Johnson, *River of Dark Dreams*, 397, 401–2.

64. Fehrenbacher and McAfee, *Slaveholding Republic*, 182; Freehling, *Road to Disunion*, vol. 2:183–84; Grand jurors quoted in McPherson, *Battle Cry of Freedom*, 103.

65. McPherson, *Battle Cry of Freedom*, 202–5, Brown quoted on 203 ("Talk!"); Reynolds, *John Brown*, 248–49, Frank Sanborn quoted on 255 ("the manifest"), Brown quoted on 255 ("If God").

66. Ross, *Recollections and Experiences*, 1–31, quotation on 15.

67. Reynolds, *John Brown*, 257–58; Ross, *Recollections and Experiences*, 20–24, 46–55 quotation from 20–21 ("intelligence"), 24 ("Never before" and "chosen instrument").

68. Dunbar, *She Came to Slay*, 70–74; Horton, *Harriet Tubman*, 42–46; Levine, *Martin Delany*, 181-82; Oertel, *Harriet Tubman*, 45–48; Reynolds, *John Brown*, 249–55, 259–60, Brown quoted on 259 ("the General").

69. Anderson, *Voice from Harpers Ferry*, 9–15; Levine, *Martin Delany*, 181–82; Reynolds, *John Brown*, 259–63; Rhodes, *Mary Ann Shadd Cary*, 129–32; Sterling, *Making of an Afro-American*, 167–75.

70. H. Jackson, *American Radicals*, 211–12; Levine, *Martin Delany*, 182–88; Painter, "Martin R. Delany," 157–61; Sterling, *Making of an Afro-American*, 176–207.

71. Blight, *Frederick Douglass*, 301–3; McPherson, *Battle Cry of Freedom*, 204–5, Douglass quoted on 205; Stauffer, *Black Hearts of Men*, 258–59, Shields Green quoted on 259.

72. Freehling, *Road to Disunion*, vol. 2:213–14; Reynolds, *John Brown*, 335–36, 377–80, *Richmond Enquirer* quoted on 380.

73. Freehling, *Road to Disunion*, vol. 2:209–12; Reynolds, *John Brown*, 309–28, Harriet Newby quoted on 320; Stauffer, *Black Hearts of Men*, 258–59.

74. Guelzo, *Robert E. Lee*, 160–65; McPherson, *Battle Cry of Freedom*, 205–6; Varon, *Disunion*, 328.

75. Freehling, *Road to Disunion*, vol. 2: 213–16, John Brown quoted on 215 ("I can recover"); Reynolds, *John Brown*, 329–31, 370, 377, 386–92, Brown quoted on 331 ("sympathy"), and 387–88 ("In my death"); Stauffer, *Black Hearts of Men*, 259–60, Brown quoted on 260 ("I may be").

76. Link, *Roots of Secession*, 185–87; Reynolds, *John Brown*, 348–57, 392–98, 415, Brown quoted on 354 ("I forfeit"), John Wilkes Booth quoted on 397–98; Stauffer, *Black Hearts of Men*, 259–60, Brown quoted on 260 ("I, John Brown").

77. Link, *Roots of Secession*, 187, 189; Potter and Fehrenbacher, *Impending Crisis*, 375–76; Reynolds, *John Brown*, 332–33, Governor Wise quoted on 332.

78. Horwitz, *Midnight Rising*, 264–66, John Copeland quoted on 265, James Monroe quoted on 266.

79. Blight, *Frederick Douglass*, 305–8; Reynolds, *John Brown*, 340–43, 370–71; Winks, *Blacks in Canada*, 268–69.

80. Stephen A. Douglas quoted in Delbanco, *War Before the War*, 338 ("Abolition party"); Freehling, *Road to Disunion*, vol. 2:216–17; Reynolds, *John Brown*, 339–40, 357–63, 424–29, Douglas quoted on 425 ("Harpers Ferry crime").

81. H. Jackson, *American Radicals*, 220–24; Reynolds, *John Brown*, 344–47, 363–67, 383–84, 432, Ralph Waldo Emerson quoted on 366, Henry David Thoreau quoted on 383.

82. Harrold, *Border War*, 193–94; Link, *Roots of Secession*, 188–90, John Coles Rutherfoord quoted on 188; Walther, *Fire-Eaters*, 184–85.

83. Allmendinger, *Ruffin*, 178–79; Thomas, *Confederate Nation*, 2–4; Edmund Ruffin quoted in Walther, *Fire-Eaters*, 258–59.

84. Allmendinger, *Ruffin*, 8–56; Walther, *Fire-Eaters*, 231–34.

85. Allmendinger, *Ruffin*, 106–25; Walther, *Fire-Eaters*, 234–36, 243–45, James H. Hammond quoted on 245.

86. Allmendinger, *Ruffin*, 113–14, 146–47; Freehling, *Road to Disunion*, vol. 2:219–20; Walther, *Fire-Eaters*, 259–61, Edmund Ruffin quoted on 259–60.

87. Campbell, *Empire for Slavery*, 220–24; Link, *Roots of Secession*, 179–85, 189–90, *New York Evening Post* quoted on 180; Reynolds, *John Brown*, 416–18, *Atlanta Confederacy* quoted on 417.

88. Bordewich, *Congress at War*, 4–5; Stauffer, *Black Hearts of Men*, 256–58; Robert Bunch quoted in L. White, "South in the 1850s," 44–45.

89. Bailey, *Hinton Rowan Helper*, 3–17, 19–40, Helper quoted on 31 ("Nothing"); Frederickson, *Arrogance of Race*, 28–42; Varon, *Disunion*, 311–12, Helper quoted on 311 ("makes us poor").

90. Fredrickson, *Arrogance of Race*, 46–49, Hinton Helper quoted on 46 ("Death to"), and 49 ("gross shame").

91. Bailey, *Hinton Rowan Helper*, 41–45, 50–59, Shelton F. Leake quoted on 66; Freeman, *Field of Blood*, 250–51; Varon, *Disunion*, 312.

92. Fredrickson, *Arrogance of Race*, 29–32; Marten, *Texas Divided*, 7, 16.

93. Campbell, *Empire for Slavery*, 224–26, Benjamin Bowman quoted on 225–26 ("Dallis County"); Reynolds, *John Brown*, 434–36, *Independent South* quoted on 434 ("fair daughters"); Reynolds, *Texas Terror*, 29–53.

94. Campbell, *Empire for Slavery*, 185, 226–28; Keehn, *Knights of the Golden Circle*, 66–67; Reynolds, *Texas Terror*, 54–80, 96–97, William H. Bailey quoted on 156 ("Mystic Red").

95. Reynolds, *Texas Terror*, 80–83, 88–89, David Carey Nance quoted on 83 ("were rounded up").

96. Buenger, *Secession and the Union in Texas*, 56–57; Reynolds, *Texas Terror*, 80–97, Austin *Southern Intelligencer* quoted on 88 ("school boys"), Walter S. South quoted on 96 ("savage deeds").

97. Marten, *Texas Divided*, 6–8; Reynolds, *Texas Terror*, 209–10, anonymous Texan quoted on 210 ("seen perched").

98. Reynolds, *Texas Terror*, 24–28, 32–33, 204–14, A. W. Sparks quoted on 207.

99. Keehn, *Knights of the Golden Circle*, 59–60; Reynolds, *Texas Terror*, 168–96, Sarah Lois Wadley quoted on 174.

100. Friedman, *Field of Blood*, 209–14, 227–30, 233–34, 240–41; Walther, *Fire-Eaters*, 180–81.

101. Freeman, *Field of Blood*, 253–54, knife inscription quoted on 253.

102. Freeman, *Field of Blood*, 251–59; McCardell, *Idea of a Southern Nation*, 326–27, James Henry Hammond quoted on 327 ("general fight" and "No two"); Potter and Fehrenbacher, *Impending Crisis*, 389–90, Hammond quoted on 389 ("only persons"); Hammond quoted in Walther, *Fire-Eaters*, 261 ("come and see").

FIVE: DISUNION

1. H. W. Barclay quoted in Glatthaar, *General Lee's Army*, 17.

2. Buckner, "Creation of the Dominion," 67; Radforth, *Royal Spectacle*, 204, 380–81, Toronto *Leader* quoted on 204; Weintraub, *Edward the Caresser*, 47–56, Prince Albert quoted on 47; Winks, *Canada and the United States*, 5–6.

3. Radforth, *Royal Spectacle*, 48–50, 105–7, 137–40, 377–78, Ottawa *Citizen* quoted on 49, Toronto *Globe* quoted on 377; Weintraub, *Edward the Caresser*, 55–56.

4. Gwyn, *Man Who Made Us*, 114–15; Levine, *Toronto*, 63–66; Radforth, *Royal Spectacle*, 164–69.

5. Levine, *Toronto*, 66–67.

6. Morton, *Critical Years*, 86–87; Radforth, *Royal Spectacle*, 169–77, William Shannon quoted on 170.

7. Gwyn, *Man Who Made Us*, 233–36; Radforth, *Royal Spectacle*, 178–88, Toronto *Globe* quoted on 187; Weintraub, *Edward the Caresser*, 56–58.

8. Levine, *Toronto*, 67–69; Radforth, *Royal Spectacle*, 188–97; Weintraub, *Edward the Caresser*, 58–59.

9. Foreman, *World on Fire*, 54–57; Radforth, *Royal Spectacle*, 316–24, 330–34, *New York Times* quoted on 323 ("socked it"), Duke of Newcastle quoted on 324; Weintraub, *Edward the Caresser*, 62–71.

10. Duke of Newcastle quoted in Foreman, *World on Fire*, 58–59; Stahr, *Seward*, 316–17.

11. Foreman, *World on Fire*, 59–60, Lord Lyons quoted on 60; Radforth, *Royal Spectacle*, 364–65, 374–76; Weintraub, *Edward the Caresser*, 79.

12. Egerton, *Year of Meteors*, 62–74; Walther, *Fire-Eaters*, 73–74, William L. Yancey quoted on 74; Woods, *Arguing Until Doomsday*, 177, 196–98.

13. Egerton, *Year of Meteors*, 74–82, 154–75; Schott, *Alexander H. Stephens*, 295–96; Walther, *Fire-Eaters*, 74–75; L. White, "South in the 1850s," 38–42, Robert Bunch quoted on 40; Woods, *Arguing Until Doomsday*, 198–99.

14. Egerton, *Year of Meteors*, 129–30; Foreman, *World on Fire*, 30–32; Goodwin, *Team of Rivals*, 11–16, 29–31, 69–78, Seward quoted on 70; Potter and Fehrenbacher, *Impending Crisis*, 421–23; Stahr, *Seward*, 5, 182–90.

15. Egerton, *Year of Meteors*, 114–25; Hankinson, *Man of Wars*, 157–58; McPherson, *Battle Cry of Freedom*, 217–20, witness quoted on 220; W. H. Russell, *My Diary*, 22.

16. Carwardine, *Lincoln*, 103–8; Egerton, *Year of Meteors*, 125–30, Lincoln quoted on 128 ("want us"); Foner, *Fiery Trial*, 132–40, Lincoln quoted on 138 ("Let us").

17. Bordewich, *Congress at War*, 8–9, Louis T. Wigfall quoted on 9; Egerton, *Year of Meteors*, 141–42, Stephen A. Douglas quoted on 201–2.

18. Carwardine, *Lincoln*, 118–23; Foner, *Fiery Trial*, 140–41; Fehrenbacher and McAfee, *Slaveholding Republic*. 244–45.

19. Carwardine, *Lincoln*, 111–14, 116–17; Egerton, *Year of Meteors*, 182–83; Foner, *Fiery Trial*, 141–43.

20. Egerton, *Year of Meteors*, 83–101; Foner, *Fiery Trial*, 143–44; McPherson, *Battle Cry of Freedom*, 221–22; Potter and Fehrenbacher, *Impending Crisis*, 417.

21. McPherson, *Battle Cry of Freedom*, 223–25, *New York Herald* quoted on 224; Potter and Fehrenbacher, *Impending Crisis*, 400.

22. Egerton, *Year of Meteors*, 195–98; McPherson, *Battle Cry of Freedom*, 228–31, *Natchez Free Trader* quoted on 229; Jefferson Davis quoted in Quinn, *The Rivals*, 278; Reynolds, *Texas Terror*, 186–87, Louis T. Wigfall quoted on 186.

23. Egerton, *Year of Meteors*, 198–207; Potter and Fehrenbacher, *Impending Crisis*, 440–41; Woods, *Arguing Until Doomsday*, 205–8, Stephen A. Douglas quoted on 207.

24. Bordewich, *Congress at War*, 8–9; Carwardine, *Lincoln*, 129–31; Egerton, *Year of Meteors*, 208–13, Lincoln quoted on 208; Foner, *Fiery Trial*, 143–44.

25. Almendinger, *Ruffin*, 135; Baumgartner, *South to Freedom*, 200–1, banner quoted on 201; Egerton, *Year of Meteors*, 213–14; Walther, *Fire-Eaters*, 262–64, Edmund Ruffin quoted on 263–64; L. White, "South in the 1850s," 45–46.

26. Egerton, *Year of Meteors*, 217–42; McCurry, *Confederate Reckoning,* 40–41, William Grimball quoted on 41 ("Now"); McPherson, *Battle Cry of Freedom*, 234–38, southerner quoted on 237–38 ("People are wild").

27. Bordewich, *Congress at War*, 4–8, 22–23, George Templeton Strong quoted on 23 ("Had this old mollusk"); Potter and Fehrenbacher, *Impending Crisis*, 491–93, 537–38, 548.

28. Fehrenbacher and McAfee, *Slaveholding Republic*, 295–97; Majewski and Wahlstrom, "Geography as Power," 349–50, Matthew Maury quoted on 350; McPherson, *Battle Cry of Freedom*, 241–42; Wigfall quoted in Walther, *Fire-Eaters*, 179.

29. Delbanco, *War Before the War*, 340–41; Manning, *What This Cruel War Was Over*, 23–25; McCurry, *Confederate Reckoning*, 28–29, John Townsend quoted on 29.

30. William L. Yancey quoted in Freeman, *Field of Blood*, 260; Walther, *Fire-Eaters*, 76–78.

31. Crawford, ed., *William Howard Russell's Civil War*, 37; Albert Gallatin Brown quoted in McCardell, *Idea of a Southern Nation*, 323–24 ("The Negro"); McPherson, *Battle Cry of Freedom*, 243–44, Alabaman quoted on 243.

32. Haley, *Sam Houston*, 3–291; Haynes, *Unsettled Land*, 77–78, 101–2, 151–53.

33. Ford, *Rip Ford's Texas*, 17–19; Haley, *Sam Houston*, 348–71, Houston quoted on 347–48 ("Wiggletail") and 350 ("vegetarian").

34. Davis, *Government of our Own*, 327, 342, Charles E. L. Stuart quoted on 327; Russell, *My Diary*, 62–63.

35. Goodheart, *1861*, 71; Walther, *Fire-Eaters*, 175–77.

36. Louis T. Wigfall quoted in Bordewich, *Congress at War*, 132; Freeman, *Field of Blood*, 52, 268–69; King, Louis T. *Wigfall*, 53–64, 77; Walther, *Fire-Eaters*, 162–64, 169–72.

37. Buenger, *Secession and the Union in Texas*, 124–25; Haley, *Sam Houston*, 381–87, Houston quoted on 381 ("the anarchy") and 386 ("War is no").

38. Buenger, *Secession and the Union in Texas*, 125–30, 141–57; Campbell, *Empire of Slavery*, 229–30, state legislators quoted on 229; R. H. Williams quoted in Frazier, *Blood & Treasure*, 17 ("six-shooters" and "Then the shooting"); Marten, *Texas Divided*, 12–13, 22–23, Thomas North quoted on 12 ("a man").

39. Buenger, *Secession and the Union in Texas*, 5–6, 176–77; Sam Houston quoted in Campbell, *Empire for Slavery*, 230 ("Our people"); Haley, *Sam Houston*, 388–97, Hugh McIntyre quoted on 396 ("Now"), and Houston quoted on 397 ("The soil"); Marten, *Texas Divided*, 22–23.

40. Bordewich, *Congress at War*, 10; Walther, *Fire-Eaters*, 187–88; Woodward, ed., *Mary Chesnut's Civil War*, 12.

41. Enslaved woman quoted in Marten, *Texas Divided*, 39.

42. Ayers, *In the Presence of Mine Enemies*, 116–22; Potter and Fehrenbacher, *Impending Crisis*, 475, 494–502; Schott, *Alexander H. Stephens*, 298–307, Stephens quoted on 307; L. White, "South in the 1850s," 46–47.

43. Egerton, *Year of Meteors*, 238–40; Schott, *Alexander H. Stephens*, 309–10, 317–24, Stephens and Lincoln quoted on 310; Manning, *What This Cruel War Was Over*, 22–23.

44. Foreman, *World on Fire*, 82; quotations from Russell, *My Diary*, 87–91.

45. Rable, *Confederate Republic*, 43, 51–53; Schott, *Alexander H. Stephens*, 324–26; Thomas, *Confederate Nation*, 57–65.

46. Cooper, *Jefferson Davis*, 462; Rable, *Confederate Republic*, 39–63, *Richmond Examiner* quoted on 54 ("universal liberty").

47. Crawford, ed., *William Howard Russell's Civil War*, 52; Egerton, *Year of Meteors*, 269–72; Thomas, *Confederate Nation*, 59–60.

48. Sam Houston quoted in Haley, *Sam Houston*, 411; Russell, *My Diary*, 92–94; Schott, *Alexander H. Stephens*, 326–27, 330–32; Rable, *Confederate Republic*, 69–71.

49. Egerton, *Year of Meteors*, 272–73, 281–82; Huebner, *Liberty and Union*, 132–34; Schott, *Alexander H. Stephens*, 334–35, Stephens quoted on 334.

50. Davis, *Government of Our Own*, 241–43.

51. Bordewich, *Congress at War*, 15–16; Guterl, *American Mediterranean*, 60–65; Rable, *Confederate Republic*, 46–47, 121, 123, 180–83; Rubin, *Shattered Nation*, 11–23, the song "Stars and Bars" quoted on 20.

52. Ayers, *In the Presence of Mine Enemies*, 140; Egerton, *Year of Meteors*, 243–44; Potter and Fehrenbacher, *Impending Crisis*, 479–84, 505–13, 548–49.

53. Seward quoted in Delbanco, *War Before the War*, 258; Huebner, *Liberty and Union*, 134–36; Potter and Fehrenbacher, *Impending Crisis*, 479–84, James M. Mason quoted on 483.

54. Bordewich, *Congress at War*, 22–23, John McClernand quoted on 22; Egerton, *Year of Meteors*, 245–46; Potter and Fehrenbacher, *Impending Crisis*, 523–26.

55. Bordewich, *Congress at War*, 21–22; McPherson, *Battle Cry of Freedom*, 250–51.

56. Brettle, *Colossal Ambitions*, 36–39; Egerton, *Year of Meteors*, 294–95; Potter and Fehrenbacher, *Impending Crisis*, 530–32; Woods, *Arguing Until Doomsday*, 218–19.

57. Downs, *Second American Revolution*, 88–89; Egerton, *Year of Meteors*, 246–47, 290–94; Foner, *Fiery Trial*, 152–57; McPherson, *Battle Cry of Freedom*, 251–54, Abraham Lincoln quoted on 253; Morrison, *Slavery and the American West*, 264–65.

58. Barrett and Todd quoted in Bordewich, *Congress at War*, 42 ("We have"); McPherson, *Battle Cry of Freedom*, 254–56, secessionist quoted on 254 ("We spit"); Potter and Fehrenbacher, *Impending Crisis*, 532–35; Walther, *Fire-Eaters*, 187–88.

59. Egerton, *Year of Meteors*, 327–28, Abraham Lincoln quoted on 327; Foner, *Fiery Trial*, 157–60; McPherson, *Battle Cry of Freedom*, 262–63, Stephen A. Douglas quoted on 263; Stahr, *Seward*, 246–47.

60. Bordewich, *Congress at War*, 14–15, Frances Seward quoted on 15; Goodwin, *Team of Rivals*, 317–18, 341; Potter and Fehrenbacher, *Impending Crisis*, 562–64; W. H. Russell, *My Diary*, 42 ("a subtle"); Stahr, *Seward*, 250–62.

61. Foreman, *World on Fire*, 76–77; Goodwin, *Team of Rivals*, 341–42; Jones, *Union in Peril*, 14–15; Stahr, *Seward*, 269–71; Winks, *Canada and the United States*, 35–36.

62. Goodheart, *1861*, 158–59; Goodwin, *Team of Rivals*, 342–43; Jones, *Union in Peril*, 15; Stahr, *Seward*, 272–74, William H. Seward quoted on 291.

63. Bordewich, *Congress at War*, 41–42; Cooper, *Jefferson Davis*, 362–63; Egerton, *Year of Meteors*, 323–26; Potter and Fehrenbacher, *Impending Crisis*, 558–61, 570–80.

64. Mary Boykin Chesnut quoted in Goodheart, *1861*, 323; Potter and Fehrenbacher, *Impending Crisis*, 581–83; Walther, *Fire-Eaters*, 265–66

65. Davis, *Government of Our Own*, 327, 339; Goodheart, *1861*, 174–76, 183–84; King, *Louis T. Wigfall*, 199–22; Russell, *My Diary*, 62–64.

66. Bordewich, *Congress at War*, 49–50; Egerton, *Year of Meteors*, 221, William T. Sherman quoted on 241; Foreman, *World on Fire*, 84–85.

67. Goodheart, *1861*, 176–82, Walt Whitman quoted on 177; McPherson, *Battle Cry of Freedom*, 274–75, George Ticknor quoted on 274 ("The whole"), New York woman quoted on 274 ("It seems").

68. Carwardine, *Lincoln*, 164–66, Stephen A. Douglas quoted on 166, Republican newspaper editor quoted on 166; Egerton, *Year of Meteors*, 321, 328–31.

69. Governor of Tennessee quoted in Bordewich, *Congress at War*, 55; Huebner, *Liberty and Union*, 130–32, John Ellis quoted on 130.

70. Ayers, *In the Presence of Mine Enemies*, 135–36; Crawford, ed., *William Howard Russell's Civil War*, 52 ("excited mob").

71. Link, *Roots of Secession*, 240–47, *Richmond Examiner* quoted on 243; McPherson, *Battle Cry of Freedom*, 278–80, 283–84.

72. Ayers, *In the Presence of Mine Enemies*, 135–36, 139–40; Link, *Roots of Secession*, 251–52; Shade, *Democratizing the Old Dominion*, 289–91.

73. Sam quoted in Link, *Roots of Secession*, 248–50.

74. Ford, *Rip Ford's Texas*, 305 ("He evinced"); Glatthaar, *General Lee's Army*, 123–24; Guelzo, *Robert E. Lee*, 181–97, Lee quoted on 178.

75. Glatthaar, *General Lee's Army*, 124; Guelzo, *Robert E. Lee*, 200–205, Lee quoted on 201; Winfield Scott quoted in McPherson, *Battle Cry of Freedom*, 281.

76. Daniel quoted in Goodheart, *1861*, 364.

77. Ayers, *In the Presence of Mine Enemies*, 141–42; Cooper, *Jefferson Davis*, 368–70; Davis, *Government of Our Own*, 371–400; Thomas, *Confederate Nation*, 98–103.

78. Bordewich, *Congress at War*, 81–82; Carwardine, *Lincoln*, 167–71, 209–10, Lincoln quoted on 209; Donald, *Lincoln*, 368–69; Gallagher, *Union War*, 42–43, 50.

79. Bordewich, *Congress at War*, 81–82, Lincoln quoted on 82 ("If we fail"); Foner, *Fiery Trial*, 171–73; Gallagher, *Union War*, 48–50; Lincoln quoted in Huebner, *Liberty & Union*, 216 ("to elevate").

80. Blight, *Frederick Douglass*, 303–4, 340–42, 350–54, Douglass quoted on 303 ("inconsistent") and 304 ("While the monster"); Foner, *Fiery Trial*, 163–65; Harriet Tubman quoted in Larson, *Bound for the Promised Land*, 206.

81. Gallagher, *Union War*, 1–2, 64–67; Grimsley, *Hard Hand of War*, 220–21, Hugh B. Ewing quoted on 121 ("smoking ruins"); Lang, "Limits of American Exceptionalism," 183–84; Manning, *What This Cruel War Was Over*, 6–7, 39–43; McPherson, *For Cause and Comrades*, 17–19; Varon, *Disunion*, 1–5.

82. Glatthaar, *Forged in Battle*, 11–12; Guelzo, *Fateful Lightning*, 235–36, Samuel McIlvaine quoted on 235; Manning, *What This Cruel War Was Over*, 43–44.

83. Doyle, *Cause of All Nations*, 158–60, 164–66, 169–73, August Horstmann quoted on 166 ("The freedom"); Gallagher, *Union War*, 4–5, 72–73, Peter Welsh quoted on 5 ("the old cry"); Goodheart, *1861*, 256–60.

84. Glatthaar, *General Lee's Army*, 19–22, 29–33; Manning, *What This Cruel War Was Over*, 11–12, 29–30, 38–39; McPherson, *For Cause and Comrades*, 19–21, William M. Thomson quoted on 19; Silber, *Gender and the Sectional Conflict*, 15–16.

85. Guelzo, *Fateful Lightning*, 232–33, Theophilus Perry quoted on 233 ("fighting against"); Manning, *What This Cruel War Was Over*, 30–32, 35–37; Silber, *Gender and the Sectional Conflict*, 15–16; Varon, *Armies of Deliverance*, 27–28.

86. Glatthaar, *General Lee's Army*, 25; Guelzo, *Fateful Lightning*, 233, 240–41, John D. Billings quoted on 241; McPherson, *For Cause and Comrades*, 27–28.

87. Glatthaar, *General Lee's Army*, 34–35, James Langhorne quoted on 35 ("I intend"); Manning, *What This Cruel War Was Over*, 37–38; McPherson, *For Cause and Comrades*, 22–25, Samuel D. Sanders quoted on 24 ("A man who").

88. McCurry, *Masters of Small Worlds*, 208–38; Rubin, *Shattered Nation*, 52; Silber, *Gender and the Sectional Conflict*, xiv–xvi, 19–24.

89. Barr, *All the Days of My Life*, 99 ("In a great many" and "what man"); Glatthaar, *General Lee's Army*, 26–27, 29–30, 37–38, Sam Melton quoted on 26–27 ("It is astonishing"); Goodheart, *1861*, 256–57.

90. McCurry, *Confederate Reckoning*, 92–93; Rubin, *Shattered Nation*, 53–59, Kate Cumming quoted on 55–56.

91. Gallagher and Waugh, *American War*, 148–53; E. D. Leonard, *Yankee Women*, xvii–xxv, 196–201; Silber, *Gender and the Sectional Conflict*, 42–66.

92. Manning, *What This Cruel War Was Over*, 32, 34–35, 41–42, James Williams quoted on 32 ("confound"), Kehukee Association of Primitive Baptists quoted on 34 ("The Kingdome"); Rubin, *Shattered Nation*, 34–42.

93. Glatthaar, *General Lee's Army*, 22–23, 60, 40–41, 154–55, Stephens Smith quoted on 155; Rubin, *Shattered Nation*, 24.

94. James and Charles Steedman quoted in McPherson, *For Cause and Comrade*, 15; Silber, *Gender and the Sectional Conflict*, 12–13, 22–27.

95. James and John Welsh quoted in McPherson, *For Cause and Comrades*, 14–15; Silber, *Gender and the Sectional Conflict*, 12.

96. Ayers, *In the Presence of Mine Enemies*, 273–74; Gallagher, *Union War*, 68–69; Rutherford B. Hayes quoted in Goodheart, *1861*, 438n81 ("superior"); Lang, "Limits of American Exceptionalism," 192–97, Charles H. Smith quoted on 196 ("at least").

97. Keegan, *American Civil War*, 53, 56–57; McPherson, *Battle Cry of Freedom*, 513–14.

98. Bordewich, *Congress at War*, 42–45, 93–94; Foreman, *World on Fire*, 142–43, 168–69; Glatthaar, *General Lee's Army*, 43–45; Huebner, *Liberty and Union*, 140–41; Thomas, *Confederate Nation*, 74-76, 105–6, 134-35.

99. Lowenstein, *Ways and Means*, 31–68; McPherson, *Battle Cry of Freedom*, 442–48.

100. Lowenstein, *Ways and Means*, 68–70; McPherson, *Battle Cry of Freedom*, 442–48; Sainlaude, *France and the American Civil War*, 162–64, Alfred Paul quoted on 163–64; Thomas, *Confederate Nation*, 137–38.

101. Ayers, *In the Presence of Mine Enemies*, 114; Doyle, *Cause of All Nations*, 28–29; Freehling, *South vs. The South*, 3–4; Sainlaude, *France and the American Civil War*, 161–62, Alfred Paul quoted on 162; Thomas, *Confederate Nation*, 104–5.

102. Careless, *Brown of the Globe*, vol. 1:292–93, 300–303, George Brown quoted on 293, vol. 2:37–39, 44; Morton, *Critical Years*, 89–93.

103. Gwyn, *Man Who Made Us*, 244–45; Morton, *Critical Years*, 81–82, 89–93, 103–5, *Minerva* quoted on 93; Winks, *Canada and the United States*, 58–60.

104. Careless, *Brown of the Globe*, vol. 2:44–48, Conservative slogan quoted on 47; Morton, *Critical Years*, 91–95, William McDougall quoted on 92; Winks, *Canada and the United States*, 59–62.

105. Gwyn, *Man Who Made Us*, 241–42, 252–53, 258–59, Macdonald quoted on 241; Morton, *Critical Years*, 92–93.

106. Buckner, "Creation of the Dominion," 66; Morton, "British North America and a Continent," 144–48; Morton, *Critical Years*, 87–93, John A. Macdonald quoted on 93.

107. Morton, *Critical Years*, 99–100; Silverman, *Unwelcome Guests*, 154–55; Winks, *Canada and the United States*, 25–29, 50–51, and 63, *New York Herald* quoted on 29.

108. Hudson, *Mistress of Manifest Destiny*, 153–56, 164–68; Love, *Race Over Empire*, 35–36; Tansill, *United States and Santo Domingo*, 207–15.

109. Bowen, *Spain and the American Civil War*, 2–3, 6, 34–36, 39–40, 44–45, 47, 49–50; Cortada, *Spain and the American Civil War*, 30–33; William H. Seward quoted in Mahoney and Mahoney, *Mexico and the Confederacy*, 48.

110. Bowen, *Spain and the American Civil War*, 84–90; Cortada, *Spain and the American Civil War*, 32–36; Doyle, *Cause of All Nations*, 109–11.

111. Bowen, *Spain and the American Civil War*, 3–8, 69–70, 88, 93–94; Doyle, *Cause of All Nations*, 111–13, Gabriel García Tassara quoted on 111; P. J. Kelly, "Cat's Paw," 62–65; Tansill, *United States and Santo Domingo*, 213–15.

SIX: MISERIES

1. James Harrison quoted in Manning, *What This Cruel War Was Over*, 55.

2. Hildner, "Mexican Envoy," 184–85; P. J. Kelly, "Cat's Paw," 61; R. R. Miller, "Matías Romero," 228–29; Roeder, *Juárez*, vol. 1:365.

3. Hildner, "Mexican Envoy," 185; R. R. Miller, "Matías Romero," 229–30; Romero, dispatches, in Schoonover, ed., *Mexican Lobby*, 2 ("truly fraternal" and "territory") and 18 ("obtain from Mexico").

4. Edward Bates quoted in Mahin, *One War at a Time*, 113; Romero, dispatch, in Schoonover, ed., *Mexican Lobby*, 2–3.

5. Hildner, "Mexican Envoy," 185–87; Ridley, *Maximilian and Juárez*, 70–71; Romero, dispatch, in Schoonover, ed., *Mexican Lobby*, 3 ("simple,"), 4–5, 9–10 9 ("All federal").

6. Ayers, *In the Presence of Mine Enemies*, 256–57, Joseph Waddell quoted on 257; Goodheart, *1861*, 269, 272–74; Glatthaar, *General Lee's Army*, 27; Thomas, *Confederate Nation*, 103–4.

7. Glatthaar, *General Lee's Army*, 17–18, 26–27; McPherson, *Battle Cry of Freedom*, 332–33, Mississippi recruit quoted on 332; Mary Boykin Chesnut quoted on 33; Ulysses S. Grant quoted in Waugh, *U. S. Grant*, 43.

8. Glatthaar, *Forged in Battle*, 20–21; Guelzo, *Fateful Lightning*, 244–45, 248, Robert E. Lee quoted on 244.

9. Guelzo, *Fateful Lightning*, 265–66, Robert E. Lee quoted on 266; McPherson, *Battle Cry of Freedom*, 485–88.

10. Glatthaar, *Forged in Battle*, 20–21, 162–63, George Tate quoted on 21; McPherson, *Battle Cry of Freedom*, 486–87.

11. Bordewich, *Congress at War*, 92–95; Keegan, *American Civil War*, 38–39, 47–48.

12. Glatthaar, *Forged in Battle*, 21–22; Guelzo, *Fateful Lightning*, 246–47, 256–57, 271–72, David L. Thompson quoted on 247 ("Disintegration"), Jacob W. Bartness quoted on 265 ("man-slaughtering"), Alphaeus Williams quoted on 271 ("the crash," "the uproar," and "riderless").

13. Guelzo, *Fateful Lightning*, 271–75, James Madison Williams quoted on 272 ("When I go"), Claiborne Walton quoted on 273–74 ("My hands"); Varon, *Armies of Deliverance*, 145–49, George Henry Gordon quoted on 146 ("too horrible").

14. Walther, *Fire-Eaters*, 192–93, Lawrence Keitt quoted on 192.

15. Guelzo, *Fateful Lightning*, 276–77, Philip Kearny quoted on 276; Varon, *Armies of Deliverance*, 145–49, Rufus Dawes quoted on 145 ("eagerness").

16. Carwardine, *Lincoln*, 171–72; Foner, *Fiery Trial*, 168–69; Guelzo, *Fateful Lightning*, 157–58, 190–91, Lincoln quoted on 190; McPherson, *Battle Cry of Freedom*, 284–85.

17. Brugger, *Maryland*, 273–78, 283, George William Brown quoted on 276 ("there will be"), John A. Dix quoted on 283 ("crack-brained"); Simon, *Lincoln and Chief Justice Taney*, 184–86; Sutherland, *Savage Conflict,* 2–5.

18. Bordewich, *Congress at War*, 57–58, John Merryman quoted on 58; Brugger, *Maryland*, 279–83, War Department quoted on 280; Huebner, *Liberty and Union*, 213–14; Simon, *Lincoln and Chief Justice Taney*, 186–94, Taney quoted on 194.

19. Brugger, *Maryland*, 281; Huebner, *Liberty and Union*, 236.

20. Goodheart, *1861*, 251–55, Claiborne Fox Jackson quoted on 255 ("inhuman"); McPherson, *Battle Cry of Freedom*, 290–91, Jackson quoted on 290 ("to stand").

21. Goodheart, *1861*, 253–58; Oakes, *Freedom National*, 151–52, Nathaniel Lyon quoted on 152; Varon, *Armies of Deliverance*, 38–40.

22. Cutrer, *Theater of a Separate War*, 34–36, 59; Goodheart, *1861*, 258–65, Francis Grierson quoted on 263; Sutherland, *Savage Conflict*, 12–14.

23. Cutrer, *Theater of a Separate War*, 47–51, Nathaniel Lyon quoted on 47; McPherson, *Battle Cry of Freedom*, 350–52.

24. Carwardine, *Lincoln*, 175–77; Einolf, *George Thomas*, 103–5; Rafuse, *McClellan's War*, 98–99, 106–8; Sutherland, *Savage Conflict*, 37–38.

25. Connolly, *Army of the Heartland*, 53–55; Einolf, *George Thomas*,105–6; Hess, *Civil War in the West*, 11–17; Sutherland, *Savage Conflict*, 38–39.

26. Ayers, *In the Presence of Mine Enemies*, 182; Rafuse, *McClellan's War*, 99–100; Sutherland, *Savage Conflict*, 30–31; Varon, *Armies of Deliverance*, 23–24.

27. Ayers, *In the Presence of Mine Enemies*, 181–82; McPherson, *Battle Cry of Freedom*, 299–300, George B. McClellan quoted on 300; Rafuse, *McClellan's War*, 100–13.

28. Ayers, *In the Presence of Mine Enemies*, 182–84, 202–205; Guelzo, *Robert E. Lee*, 209–13, Lee quoted on 213; McPherson, *Battle Cry of Freedom*, 301–3.

29. Gallagher, *Confederate War*, 130–31; Glatthaar, *General Lee's Army*, 125–26; McPherson, *Battle Cry of Freedom*, 301–5, reporter quoted on 301, *Richmond Examiner* quoted on 303.

30. McKenzie, "Contesting Secession," 298–99; Andrew Johnson quoted in McPherson, *Battle Cry of Freedom*, 304; Varon, *Armies of Deliverance*, 56–57.

31. Kelly, "William Gannaway Brownlow, Part 1," 25–34; McKenzie, "Contesting Secession," 297, 309, Knoxville *Daily Register* quoted on 297 ("preached"); Brownlow quoted in McPherson, *Battle Cry of Freedom*, 304 ("fight the Secession").

32. Kelly, "William Gannaway Brownlow, Part 1," 25–35, Brownlow quoted on 29; McKenzie, "Contesting Secession," 297–98; Trefousse, *Andrew Johnson*, 52–53.

33. Kelly, "William Gannaway Brownlow, Part 1," 35–36; McKenzie, "Contesting Secession," 302–4, Brownlow quoted on 303; Trefousse, *Andrew Johnson*, 49–50.

34. Kelly, "William Gannaway Brownlow, Part 1," 39–43, Brownlow quoted on 42; Kelly, "William Gannaway Brownlow, Part 2," 155–56; McKenzie, "Contesting Secession," 299–311.

35. Einolf, *George Thomas*, 108–12, 114–23; Hess, *Civil War in the West*, 22–23, 31–33; Trefousse, *Andrew Johnson*, 145–46.

36. Connolly, *Army of the Heartland*, 42–43; Hess, *Civil War in the West*, 23–25, 56–57; Kelly, "William Gannaway Brownlow, Part 2," 155–56; McCurry, *Confederate Reckoning*, 121–24; Sutherland, *Savage Conflict*, 34–37, 82.

37. Kelly, "William Gannaway Brownlow, Part 2," 156–57, including Brownlow quotation; McKenzie, "Contesting Secession," 294; Trefousse, *Andrew Johnson*, 157; Varon, *Armies of Deliverance*, 122.

38. Ayers, *In the Presence of Mine Enemies*, 186–87; Varon, *Armies of Deliverance*, 2–10.

39. Burke, "Scattered People," 75–78, Lizzie Brannock quoted on 78 ("Our farms"); Sutherland, *Savage Conflict*, 14–15, 31–32, 63–65, 86–90, Lowndes H. Davies quoted on 15 ("Men seem"), Ephraim D. Harris quoted on 63 ("to see").

40. Sutherland, *Savage Conflict*, 132, 204–5.

41. Bordewich, *Congress at War*, 67–68; Goodheart, *1861*, 151–52; Huebner, *Liberty and Union*, 141–42; McPherson, *Battle Cry of Freedom*, 333–34.

42. Bordewich, *Congress at War*, 67–69; Foreman, *World on Fire*, 123–24; Rafuse, *McClellan's War*, 97–101.

43. Ayers, *In the Presence of Mine Enemies*, 196; Bordewich, *Congress at War*, 68–70; Glatthaar, *General Lee's Army*, 2–7, 18; McPherson, *Battle Cry of Freedom*, 335–40.

44. Allmendinger, *Ruffin*, 155–56; Glatthaar, *General Lee's Army*, 3–8; Guelzo, *Fateful Lightning*, 155, Louisiana officer quoted on 276; Walther, *Fire-Eaters*, 266–67.

45. Glatthaar, *General Lee's Army*, 58–61, B. F. White quoted on 58–59 ("weeping" and "This civil war"), G. Campbell Brown quoted on 61 ("I could have sent").

46. Glatthaar, *General Lee's Army*, 61–63; Manning, *What This Cruel War Was Over*, 32–33, T. W. Crowson quoted on 33 ("Run" and "Hurrah"); McPherson, *Battle Cry of Freedom*, 347–50, Thomas Cobb quoted on 347 ("has secured"), Mary Chesnut quoted on 349.

47. Cooper, *Jefferson Davis*, 363–65, 413, 462, 472, Mary Chesnut quoted on 472; Rable, *Confederate Republic*, 82–84, 116–18, Jefferson Davis quoted on 116.

48. John T. Delane quoted in Foreman, *World on Fire*, 150 ("so-called Power"); Gwyn, *Man Who Made Us*, 245; Winks, *Canada and the United States*, 62–64, Susan Sibbald quoted on 63.

49. Ayers, *In the Presence of Mine Enemies*, 198–201; Bordewich, *Congress at War*, 71–72; Glatthaar, *General Lee's Army*, 55–56; McPherson, *Battle Cry of Freedom*, 347–50.

50. Bordewich, *Congress at War*, 95–96; George B. McClellan quoted in McPherson, *Battle Cry of Freedom*, 359–60; Rafuse, *McClellan's War*, 144–46.

51. Bordewich, *Congress at War*, 91–92, George B. McClellan quoted on 91 ("I confess"); Guelzo, *Fateful Lightning*, 158–59, McClellan quoted on 158 ("really sound") and 159 ("I will not fight"); Oakes, *Freedom National*, 104, 112–13, 209–10, McClellan quoted on 112 ("with an iron hand").

52. Carwardine, *Lincoln*, 185, 187; Donald, *Lincoln*, 318–19; McPherson, *Battle Cry of Freedom*, 361–62, 365, George B. McClellan quoted on 365.

53. McPherson, *Battle Cry of Freedom*, 361–62, 423–24, Indiana Republican quoted on 362 ("'Young Napoleon'") and Lyman Trumbull quoted on 362 ("Action"); W. H. Russell, *My Diary*, 318.

54. Carwardine, *Lincoln*, 187–89; McClellan and Lincoln quoted in McPherson, *Battle Cry of Freedom*, 364–65; Rafuse, *McClellan's War*, 157–58.

55. Bordewich, *Congress at War*, 101–2; Rafuse, *McClellan's War*, 176.

56. Bordewich, *Congress at War*, 96–97, Benjamin F. Wade quoted on 96 ("blundering"); Donald, *Lincoln*, 331–33, Wade quoted on 332 ("murdering" and "Are the President"); Foner, *Fiery Trial*, 187–92.

57. Carwardine, *Lincoln*, 221–24, S. W. Oakey quoted on 221 ("Do you"), Noah Brooks quoted on 223 ("sunken").

58. McPherson, *War on the Waters*, 31–32; Sainlaude, *France and the American Civil War*, 24–25.

59. McPherson, *War on the Waters*, 137–38, Samuel F. Du Pont quoted on 137.

60. McPherson, *War on the Waters*, 137–39, Samuel F. DuPont quoted on 139.

61. Foreman, *World on Fire*, 166–68; McPherson, *War on the Waters*, 33–44; Sainlaude, *France and the American Civil War*, 143; Thomas, *Confederate Nation*, 120–23, 125.

62. Bowen, *Spain and the American Civil War*, 123–25; Guterl, *American Mediterranean*, 55; McPherson, *War on the Waters*, 5–9, 47–49, 118–26, 181–83, 224–26.

63. Glatthaar, *General Lee's Army*, 104–5; McPherson, *War on the Waters*, 96–101; Thomas, *Confederate Nation*, 129–31.

64. McPherson, *War on the Waters*, 98–99, 101–9; Thomas, *Confederate Nation*, 131–32.

65. McPherson, *War on the Waters*, 96, 105–7.

66. McPherson, *War on the Waters*, 179.

67. Dashaw, "Story of an Illusion," 333–34; Foreman, *World on Fire*, 281, 369–76; R. F. Jones, "Rebel without a War," 498–508.

68. Foreman, *World on Fire*, 621–24; R. F. Jones, "Rebel without a War," 509–10; McPherson, *War on the Waters*, 112–17, 130–31, 152–53, 201–2, 204–6, Samuel F. DuPont quoted on 116; J. M. Taylor, "Fiery Trail of the *Alabama*," 429–42.

69. Lord Palmerston quoted in Bourne, *Britain and the Balance of Power*, 214 ("men who have"); Doyle, *Cause of all Nations*, 1, 7–8, 41–42, 81; Jones, *Union in Peril*, 19–20; Palmerston quoted in Ridley, *Maximilian and Juárez*, 114 ("Disunited").

70. Doyle, *Cause of all Nations*, 91–98, Lord Palmerston quoted on 41, Achille Fould quoted on 98; Foreman, *World on Fire*, 98–99, 139, Sir John Ramsden quoted on 98–99.

71. Doyle, *Cause of All Mankind*, 100–5; Guelzo, *Fateful Lightning*, 290–91, Empress Eugénie quoted on 290, Leopold quoted on 290; Sainlaude, *France and the American Civil War*, 85–86; Hankinson, *Man of Wars*, 155–56.

72. Doyle, *Cause of All Nations*, 2–3, 15–26, Henry Sanford quoted on 21 ("the fall"); Louis-Antoine Garnier-Pages quoted on 76 ("The future"); Foreman, *World on Fire*, 106–7, Richard Webb quoted on 107 ("Neither Lincoln").

73. William H. Seward quoted in Doyle, *Cause of All Nations*, 51; Foreman, *World on Fire*, 69–70, 80–81, 92–93, 99–105, 160–62, Lord Lyons quoted on 160; Edward Ellice quoted in Winks, *Canada and the United States*, 37.

74. Doyle, *Cause of All Nations*, 2–7, 27–30; Foreman, *World on Fire*, 68, 86, 161–64; Owsley, *King Cotton Diplomacy*, 54–57, 64–66, William Yancey et al. quoted on 65; Sainlaude, *France and the American Civil War*, 84–85.

75. Foreman, *World on Fire*, 78–79, 84–86; Owsley, *King Cotton Diplomacy*, 1–15, *London Economist* quoted on 11; Sainlaude, *France and the American Civil War*, 140–41.

76. Louis T. Wigfall quoted in Foreman, *World on Fire*, 64; Owsley, *King Cotton Diplomacy*, 15–20, De Bow's *Commercial Register* quoted on 16–17.

77. Guterl, *American Mediterranean*, 56–57; May, "Introduction," 7; Owsley, *King Cotton Diplomacy*, 23–48; Sainlaude, *France and the American Civil War*, 146–52, 157–58; William L. Yancey quoted in Walther, *Fire-Eaters*, 79.

78. Doyle, *Cause of All Nations*, 42–46; Foreman, *World on Fire*, 107–8, Lord Russell quoted on 69, William L. Yancey quoted on 108 ("anti-Slavery sentiment"); Owsley, *King Cotton Diplomacy*, 51–52, 64–77; Walther, *Fire-Eaters*, 79–80, Yancey quoted on 80 ("We cannot").

79. Foreman, *World on Fire*, 155, 172–73, 175–80; Jones, *Union in Peril*, 80–81, 83; McPherson, *War on the Waters*, 44–46.

80. Bourne, *Britain and the Balance of Power*, 220–37; Doyle, *Cause of All Nations*, 47–49, Charles Mackay quoted on 48; Foreman, *World on Fire*, 173–74, 180–87, Duke of Newcastle quoted on 180; Winks, *Canada and the United States*, 81–83.

81. Carwardine, *Lincoln*, 182–84; Foreman, *World on Fire*, 122–23, 190–98; Goodwin, *Team of Rivals*, 396–401; Jones, *Union in Peril*, 91–93, 96–97; Winks, *Canada and the United States*, 110–11, British soldier quoted on 111.

82. Morton, *Critical Years*, 102–3, 108, 115–16, J. L. Beaudry quoted on 115 ("land of freedom"), L. T. Drummond quoted on 116 ("Canada's best defence"); Winks, *Canada and the United States*, 81–82, 89–90, 104–5, 113–14.

83. Gwyn, *Man Who Made Us*, 261–63, Lord Monck quoted on 263; Martin, *Britain*

and the Origins of Canadian Confederation, 37–38; Morton, *Critical Years*, 104–8, 112–14; Winks, *Canada and the United States*, 115–19.

84. Mahoney, *Mexico and the Confederacy*, 27–28; Owsley, *King Cotton Diplomacy*, 103–5, Thomas Corwin quoted on 113; Schoonover, *Dollars over Dominion*, 17–24.

85. Doyle, *Cause of all Nations*, 120–21, John T. Pickett quoted on 120 ("natural inheritance" and "gross ignorance"); P. J. Kelly, "Cat's Paw," 61–62, 65–68; May, "Irony of Confederate Diplomacy," 83–85; Owsley, *King Cotton Diplomacy*, 89–103, Pickett quoted on 93 ("for the first time"), and 101 ("out of the reach"); Schoonover, *Dollars over Dominion*, 27–43, Pickett quoted on 38 ("30,000 Confederate").

86. P. J. Kelly, "Cat's Paw," 69–70; Schoonover, *Dollars over Dominion*, 81–82; Sinkin, *Mexican Reform*, 31, 35, 94–96, 105–8; Tyler, *Santiago Vidaurri*, 14–40, 45–46.

87. Hanna and Hanna, *Napoleon III and Mexico*, 155–56, 158–62, 165–66; P. J. Kelly, "Cat's Paw," 71–72; Tyler, *Santiago Vidaurri*, 41–60, 98–108.

88. Brettle, *Colossal Ambitions*, 92–93; P. J. Kelly, "Cat's Paw," 70–71; Owsley, *King Cotton Diplomacy*, 115–16; Tyler, *Santiago Vidaurri*, 57–58.

89. Moneyhon, *Edmund J. Davis*, 48–55; Owsley, *King Cotton Diplomacy*, 123–25, Juan A. Quintero quoted on 124; Tyler, *Santiago Vidaurri*, 83–90.

90. Owsley, *King Cotton Diplomacy*, 126–31; Tyler, *Santiago Vidaurri*, 123–27.

91. Bazant, "From Independence to the Liberal Republic," 31–36; Roeder, *Juárez*, vol. 1:303–15; Scholes, *Mexican Politics*, 71–72, 81–82.

92. Mahoney, *Mexico and the Confederacy*, 44–46; McAllen, *Maximilian and Carlota*, 45–46; Sainlaude, "France's Grand Design," 112–13.

93. Cunningham, *Mexico and the Foreign Policy of Napoleon III*, 28–31; Krauze, *Mexico*, 157; McAllen, *Maximilian and Carlota*, 46–50, Eugénie de Montijo quoted on 50; Sainlaude, *France and the American Civil War*, 80–81.

94. Hanna, "Roles of the South in the French Intervention," 4–8; McAllen, *Maximilian and Carlota*, 48–51, 56–59; Sainlaude, "France's Grand Design," 107–12.

95. Case and Spencer, *United States and France*, 598–99; McAllen, *Maximilian and Carlota*, 51–52, Napoleon III quoted on 52 ("to the Latin race") and 68 ("Never will"); Sainlaude, *France and the American Civil War*, 4–5, 31–32.

96. Hanna and Hanna, *Napoleon III and Mexico*, 100–101, Richard Metternich quoted on 101 ("one of those"); Sainlaude, *France and the American Civil War*, 6–7, 54–55, 58–59, Edouard Drouyn de Lhuys quoted on 7 ("The Emperor"), Lord Palmerston quoted on 68.

97. Cunningham, *Mexico and the Foreign Policy of Napoleon III*, 31–41; Hanna, "Roles of the South in the French Intervention," 6–7; McAllen, *Maximilian and Carlota*, 45–60; Sainlaude, *France and the American Civil War*, 72.

98. Doyle, *Cause of All Nations*, 119–20; Mahoney, *Mexico and the Confederacy*, 46–48; Matías Romero quoted in Ridley, *Maximilian and Juárez*, 70–71; Scholes, *Mexican Politics*, 74–78; Schoonover, ed., *Mexican Lobby*, 1, 11, 14–15.

99. Mahin, *One War at a Time*, 111–21; Roeder, *Juárez*, vol. 1:366–70, Romero quoted on 370; Schoonover, *Dollars over Dominion*, 65–68, 106–7; Schoonover, ed., *Mexican Lobby*, 1, 11, 13–15, Charles Sumner quoted on 15.

100. Bowen, *Spain and the American Civil War*, 63–65; Dabbs, *French Army in Mexico*, 19–20; P. J. Kelly, "Cat's Paw," 62–63; Mahoney, *Mexico and the Confederacy*, 36–37; Owsley, *King Cotton Diplomacy*, 98–99, John T. Pickett quoted on 98.

101. Cortada, *Spain and the American Civil War*, 48–49; Cunningham, *Mexico and the*

Foreign Policy of Napoleon III, 78–116; Dabbs, *French Army in Mexico*, 20–25; McAllen, *Maximilian and Carlotta*, 60–65; Schoonover, "Napoleon is Coming!," 118–19.

102. Cunningham, *Mexico and the Foreign Policy of Napoleon III*, 115–16; Roeder, *Juárez*, vol. 2:440–41, Charles Ferdinand de Lorencez quoted on 441; Sinkin, *Mexican Reform*, 158–59, Manuel Payno quoted on 158.

103. Dabbs, *French Army in Mexico*, 25–30; McAllen, *Maximilian and Carlotta*, 72–75; Roeder, *Juárez*, vol. 2:443–49, Marquis de Saligny quoted on 444; Sainlaude, *France and the American Civil War*, 51–52.

104. Cunningham, *Mexico and the Foreign Policy of Napoleon III*, 119–25, Charles Ferdinand de Lorencez quoted on 121; McAllen, *Maximilian and Carlotta*, 75–77, Napoleon III quoted on 77; Roeder, *Juárez*, vol. 2:448–66, Edgar Quinet quoted on 465 ("senseless enterprises").

105. John Slidell quoted in Case and Spencer, *The United States and France*, 302–3; Hanna and Hanna, *Napoleon III and Mexico*, 117–18; P. J. Kelly, "Cat's Paw," 58–62, 72–74; May, "Irony of Confederate Diplomacy," 69–83, 85–94, 100.

106. Mahin, *One War at a Time*, 104–5, Drouyn de Lhuys quoted on 105 ("He has none"); William Dayton quoted in Owsley, *King Cotton Diplomacy*, 146; Sainlaude, "France's Grand Design," 113–18, Napoleon III quoted on 115 ("intermediate").

107. Hanna, "Roles of the South in the French Intervention," 9–13; William H. Seward quoted in Mahoney, *Mexico and the Confederacy*, 27; Owsley, *King Cotton Diplomacy*, 513–29; Manuel Payno quoted in Sinkin, *Mexican Reform*, 160.

SEVEN: REVOLUTIONS

1. Charles Robinson quoted in Etcheson, *Bleeding Kansas*, 225.

2. Karl Marx quoted in Foner, *Fiery Trial*, 247.

3. Foner, *Fiery Trial*, 184–86; Guyatt, "Future Empire of our Freedmen," 95–100, Thomas Corwin quoted on 96; Oakes, *Freedom National*, 277–81; Schoonover, *Mexican Lobby*, 16–18, Montgomery Blair quoted on 17 and Matías Romero on 19.

4. Guyatt, "Future Empire of our Freedmen," 99–101, Montgomery Blair quoted on 99, Thomas Corwin quoted on 101.

5. Guyatt, "Future Empire of our Freedmen," 99–101; Schoonover, *Mexican Lobby*, 18–19, 104–5, Matías Romero quoted on 18–19.

6. Blight, *Frederick Douglass*, 370–72; Donald, *Lincoln*, 367–68, Lincoln quoted on 367 ("It is better" and "for the good"); Foner, *Fiery Trial*, 223–24, Lincoln quoted on 224 ("Your race," "equality," "But for your race," and "extremely selfish"); Oakes, *Radical and the Republican*, 191–94.

7. Blight, *Frederick Douglass*, 372–75; Foner, *Fiery Trial*, 225–26, A. P. Smith quoted on 225 ("Pray tell us"); Douglass quoted in Hunt, *Haiti's Influence on Antebellum America*, 187 ("awaken"); Oakes, *Radical and the Republican*, 194–95, Douglass quoted on 194 ("pride of race").

8. Foner, *Fiery Trial*, 166–68; Goodheart, *1861*, 300; Oakes, *Radical and the Republican*, 140–41.

9. Foner, *Fiery Trial*, 169–70; Goodheart, *1861*, 296–97, Richmond newspaper and regimental flag quoted on 297; E. D. Leonard, *Benjamin Franklin Butler*, 65–66; Oakes, *Freedom National*, 88–89.

10. Foner, *Fiery Trial*, 169; Goodheart, *1861*, 298–99, 313–15; E. D. Leonard, *Benjamin Franklin Butler*, 66–67; Oakes, *Freedom National*, 95–96.

11. Foner, *Fiery Trial*, 170; Goodheart, *1861*, 300–302; E. D. Leonard, *Benjamin Franklin Butler*, 40–56; Oakes, *Freedom National*, 90–93.

12. Goodheart, *1861*, 314–20, 324–26, 342–43, Edward Pierce quoted on 342; E. D. Leonard, *Benjamin Franklin Butler*, 67–70; Oakes, *Freedom National*, 96–97, 100–2.

13. Goodheart, *1861*, 322–23, 340–41, Mary Chesnut quoted on 323, Edward Pierce quoted on 341.

14. Foner, *Fiery Trial*, 170–71 ("freedom fort"); Goodheart, *1861*, 328–39, 335, newspaper correspondent quoted on 329; Oakes, *Freedom National*, 106–7.

15. Goodheart, *1861*, 335–36, Harry Jarvis quoted on 335; Oakes, *Freedom National*, 102–3.

16. Goodheart, *1861*, 340–44, Harvey Brown quoted on 341 ("poor wretch"); Oakes, *Freedom National*, 100–1, 104, 111–12, Silas Stringham quoted on 101 ("If negroes").

17. Goodheart, *1861*, 332–39, Union soldier quoted on 334 ("There is"); Manning, *What This Cruel War Was Over*, 12–13, 21, 44–45, 49–50, 76–80, Cyrus Boyd quoted on 49 ("By G[o]d"); Oakes, *Freedom National*, 102–3.

18. Oakes, *Freedom National*, 110–44; Abraham Lincoln quoted in Oakes, *Radical and the Republican*, 148; Varon, *Armies of Deliverance*, 33–37.

19. Cutrer, *Theater of a Separate War*, 51–53; Faragher, "The Frémonts," 28–41, Lydia Maria Child quoted on 38; Foner, *Fiery Trial*, 80–82, 176–77; Oakes, *Freedom National*, 103–4, 145–57; Varon, *Armies of Deliverance*, 38, 40.

20. Carwardine, *Lincoln*, 178–81; Swisshelm quoted in Hoffert, *Jane Grey Swisshelm*, 126; Oakes, *Freedom National*, 158–66, Robert Anderson quoted on 162.

21. Carwardine, *Lincoln*, 186–87; Donald, *Lincoln*, 315–17, Lincoln quoted on 315; Faragher, "The Frémonts," 41–43; Foner, *Fiery Trial*, 177–78.

22. Blight, *Frederick Douglass*, 363–64; Foner, *Fiery Trial*, 181–84; Oakes, *Freedom National*, 283–86.

23. Foner, *Fiery Trial*, 181–84, 195–98, Kentucky legislature quoted on 197; Oakes, *Freedom National*, 285–88, Illinois Democrat quoted on 286.

24. Blight, *Frederick Douglass*, 364–65; Foner, *Fiery Trial*, 198–200; Oakes, *Freedom National*, 271–75.

25. Foner, *Fiery Trial*, 200–201, American Colonization Society quoted on 201; Jane Grey Swisshelm quoted in Larsen, ed., *Crusader and Feminist*, 164–65; African Americans quoted in Oakes, *Freedom National*, 275.

26. Foner, *Fiery Trial*, 201–2; Oakes, *Freedom National*, 275–77.

27. Foner, *Fiery Trial*, 212–13, Border State congressmen quoted on 213; McPherson, *Battle Cry of Freedom*, 503–4, Lincoln quoted on 503 ("the institution"); Lincoln quoted in Oakes, *Radical and the Republican*, 148 ("I conceive").

28. Glaze, "His Death," 273–74, Texas officer quoted on 273; McPherson, *Battle Cry of Freedom*, 393–94, Jefferson Davis quoted on 394.

29. Brady, *War Upon the Land*, 25–27; Hess, *Civil War in the West*, 68–69, William T. Sherman quoted on 69; McPherson, *War on the Waters*, 72–73.

30. Connolly, *Army of the Heartland*, 16–22, 71–72, 78–85; Hess, *Civil War in the West*, 9, 19; McPherson, *War on the Waters*, 73–74.

31. Waugh, *U. S. Grant*, 1, 9–35, William T. Sherman quoted on 21.

32. Perret, "Grant's Tennessee Gamble," 106; Waugh, *U. S. Grant*, 35–47.

33. Guelzo, *Fateful Lightning*, 201–202, Ulysses S. Grant quoted on 201; Hess, *Civil War in the West*, 20–21; Waugh, *U. S. Grant*, 52–53.

34. Hess, *Civil War in the West*, 34–37; Perret, "Grant's Tennessee Gamble," 107–20; Varon, *Armies of Deliverance*, 45–47; Waugh, *U. S. Grant*, 54–56.

35. Hess, *Civil War in the West*, 39–43, Andrew H. Foote quoted on 41; McPherson, *Battle Cry of Freedom*, 397, 402–3.

36. Connolly, *Army of the Heartland*, 7–10, 72–74, 133–39; Glaze, "His Death," 274–75; Hess, *Civil War in the West*, 39–40; McPherson, *Battle Cry of Freedom*, 402–6, Jefferson Davis quoted on 405.

37. Hess, *Civil War in the West*, 39–40, 62–63, Andrew Johnson quoted on 63; Trefousse, *Andrew Johnson*, 152–58, 165–66; Varon, *Armies of Deliverance*, 120–22.

38. Cutrer, *Theater of a Separate War*, 82–92, Robert S. Bevier quoted on 83, Earl Van Dorn quoted on 85; Joseph Davis quoted in Hermann, *Joseph E. Davis*, 114.

39. Cutrer, *Theater of a Separate War*, 133–40; Josephy, *Civil War in the American West*, 335–47; Sheehan-Dean, *Struggle for a Vast Future*, 140–41.

40. Connolly, *Army of the Heartland*, 145–68; Hess, *Civil War in the West*, 42–46; Varon, *Armies of Deliverance*, 58–60; Waugh, *U. S. Grant*, 56, 60.

41. Connolly, *Army of the Heartland*, 169–75; Hess, *Civil War in the West*, 47–48; McPherson, *Battle Cry of Freedom*, 410–14, William T. Sherman quoted on 413.

42. McPherson, *Battle Cry of Freedom*, 394–95, 414–15, Abraham Lincoln quoted on 414; Perret, "Grant's Tennessee Gamble," 120–21; Waugh, *U. S. Grant*, 57–58.

43. Connolly, *Army of the Heartland*, 176–77; Hess, *Civil War in the West*, 49–51; McPherson, *Battle Cry of Freedom*, 415–17.

44. Brady, *War Upon the Land*, 31–34; Hess, *Civil War in the West*, 44–45, 57–60; McPherson, *War on the Waters*, 80–89; Varon, *Armies of Deliverance*, 58.

45. Hess, *Civil War in the West*, 75–78, 84; E. D. Leonard, *Benjamin Franklin Butler*, 81–83; McPherson, *Battle Cry of Freedom*, 418–20, George W. Cable quoted on 420.

46. E. D. Leonard, *Benjamin Franklin Butler*, 86–92; McCurry, *Confederate Reckoning*, 108–10, Butler quoted on 109; Varon, *Armies of Deliverance*, 122.

47. E. D. Leonard, *Benjamin Franklin Butler*, 90–94; Manning, *What This Cruel War Was Over*, 62–65; McCurry, *Confederate Reckoning*, 109–13, Butler quoted on 109; Varon, *Armies of Deliverance*, 125–26.

48. McPherson, *Battle Cry of Freedom*, 422–23, Mary Chesnut quoted on 422.

49. McPherson, *Battle Cry of Freedom*, 423–26; Varon, *Armies of Deliverance*, 56, 79.

50. Glatthaar, *General Lee's Army*, 104–9; Grimsley, *Hard Hand of War*, 71–72; McPherson, *Battle Cry of Freedom*, 426–27, Joseph Johnson quoted on 426.

51. Gallagher, *Confederate War*, 128–29; Grimsley, *Hard Hand of War*, 72; Henri Mercier quoted in Sainlaude, *France and the American Civil War*, 132–33.

52. Glatthaar, *General Lee's Army*, 116–18, 127; George B. McClellan quoted in McPherson, *Battle Cry of Freedom*, 426–27.

53. Glatthaar, *General Lee's Army*, 118–22; McPherson, *Battle Cry of Freedom*, 427–28, 461–62; Varon, *Armies of Deliverance*, 80–81.

54. Ayers, *In the Presence of Mine Enemies*, 279–80; Cooper, *Jefferson Davis*, 390–91, 402–4, 421–22; Glatthaar, *General Lee's Army*, 103, 118–19, 123–24, 126–28, George B. McClellan quoted on 126; Varon, *Armies of Deliverance*, 81–83.

55. Glatthaar, *General Lee's Army*, 128–34, Lee quoted on 130, D. H. Hill quoted on 131 ("brothels" and "thousands").

56. Ayers, *In the Presence of Mine Enemies*, 254–55, 258–70; Gallagher, *Lee and His Generals*, 105–17; Glatthaar, *General Lee's Army*, 45, 109–16; McPherson, *Battle Cry of Freedom*, 454–60, soldiers and Thomas Jackson quoted on 455.

57. Ayers, *In the Presence of Mine Enemies*, 279–80; Glatthaar, *General Lee's Army*, 130–31; McPherson, *Battle Cry of Freedom*, 462–65; Varon, *Armies of Deliverance*, 88–89.

58. Gallagher, *Lee and His Generals*, 108–9, 124–26; Glatthaar, *General Lee's Army*, 135–40.

59. Ayers, *In the Presence of Mine Enemies*, 281–83; Gallagher, *Lee and His Generals*, 127–28; McPherson, *Battle Cry of Freedom*, 466–70, George B. McClellan quoted on 468, Philip Kearny quoted on 470; Varon, *Armies of Deliverance*, 89–92.

60. Gallagher, *Lee and His Generals*, 128–29; Glatthaar, *General Lee's Army*, 124–25, 146–47.

61. Glatthaar, *General Lee's Army*, 140–41, Thomas Jackson quoted on 151; McPherson, *Battle Cry of Freedom*, 477–78, Confederate and Yankee witnesses quoted on 477.

62. Ayers, *In the Presence of Mine Enemies*, 283–84, Joseph Waddell quoted on 284; Glatthaar, *General Lee's Army*, 144–45.

63. Cooper, *Jefferson Davis*, 423; Gallagher, *Confederate War*, 10, 63–65, 72, 131; Glatthaar, *General Lee's Army*, 147–49; Guelzo, *Robert E. Lee*, 242–43, Mary Chesnut quoted on 242, Lee quoted on 242; Varon, *Armies of Deliverance*, 92.

64. Carwardine, *Lincoln*, 204; Gallagher, *Antietam*, 2–3; McPherson, *Battle Cry of Freedom*, 502–3, George B. McClellan quoted on 502.

65. Ayers, *In the Presence of Mine Enemies*, 275–76, 308–10; Gallagher, *Union War*, 89–90.

66. Hess, *Civil War in the West*, 27–28, 73–74; Ulysses S. Grant quoted in McPherson, *Battle Cry of Freedom*, 502; Sutherland, *Savage Conflict*, 107–8, Ormsby Mitchel quoted on 107; Varon, *Armies of Deliverance*, 100–103.

67. Carwardine, *Lincoln*, 204–6; Gallagher, *Union War*, 90; Grimsley, *Hard Hand of War*, 67–71, 75–78, 91, 94–95; McPherson, *Battle Cry of Freedom*, 499–500, Militia Act and Confiscation Act quoted on 500; Varon, *Armies of Deliverance*, 103–8.

68. Grimsley, *Hard Hand of War*, 85–88; Guelzo, *Robert E. Lee*, 243–44, John Pope quoted on 243 ("I have come" and "subsist upon"); Hennessy, "Looting and Bombardment of Fredericksburg," 129–31, Pope quoted on 129 ("War means"); Sutherland, *Savage Conflict*, 20–21, 97–98.

69. Hennessy, "Looting and Bombardment of Fredericksburg," 127–29, Fred Burritt quoted on 128 ("little more"); Manning, *What This Cruel War Was Over*, 71–72, Constant Hanks quoted on 72 ("They give"); Sutherland, *Savage Conflict*, 33–34, 59–60, James A. Lancaster quoted on 33–34 ("Our boys").

70. Glatthaar, *General Lee's Army*, 153–54, Robert H. Miller quoted on 153 ("a party of" and "Death to all"); Walther, *Fire-Eaters*, 267–68, graffiti quoted on 267 ("You did fire") and 268 ("You old cuss").

71. Ayers, *In the Presence of Mine Enemies*, 294–95; Glatthaar, *General Lee's Army*, 152–53, Edmund Ruffin quoted on 152, Benjamin Fleet quoted on 152 ("We could do" and "Men went"); Walther, *Fire-Eaters*, 268.

72. Ayers, *In the Presence of Mine Enemies*, 300–7, 313–14, Jed Hotchkiss quoted on

314; Gallagher, *Lee and His Generals*, 152–57; Glatthaar, *General Lee's Army*, 158–63; McPherson, *Battle Cry of Freedom*, 525–33; Varon, *Armies of Deliverance*, 131–32.

73. Grimsley, *Hard Hand of War*, 89; McPherson, *Battle Cry of Freedom*, 527–29, George B. McClellan quoted on 528.

74. Ayers, *In the Presence of Mine Enemies*, 312–13; Greene, "'I Fought the Battle Splendidly,'" 56–58; McPherson, *Battle Cry of Freedom*, 533–34, Lincoln quoted on 533, William H. Powell quoted on 534 ("Men threw").

75. Carwardine, *Lincoln*, 206–10; Donald, *Lincoln*, 362–66, Lincoln quoted on 362; McPherson, *Battle Cry of Freedom*, 503–6, William H. Seward quoted on 505.

76. Ayers, *In the Presence of Mine Enemies*, 313–14; Gallagher, *Antietam*, 8–10; McPherson, *Battle Cry of Freedom*, 534–35, Mary Bedinger Mitchell quoted on 535 ("gaunt starvation"); Varon, *Armies of Deliverance*, 135–37.

77. Gallagher, *Antietam*, 4–7; Glatthaar, *General Lee's Army*, 164; Rubin, *Shattered Nation*, 48–49; Varon, *Armies of Deliverance*, 135.

78. Bowen, *Spain and the American Civil War*, 107–8, 111–13; Gallagher, *Antietam*, 3–4; Lord Palmerston quoted in Jones, "History and Mythology," 37; Sainlaude, *France and the American Civil War*, 34–45, 65–67, 133–34, 141–42.

79. Ayers, *In the Presence of Mine Enemies*, 317–18; Gallagher, *Antietam*, 10–11; Glatthaar, *General Lee's Army*, 165–68, George Templeton Strong quoted on 168.

80. Gallagher, *Antietam*, 12–13; Glatthaar, *General Lee's Army*, 168–71; Greene, "'I Fought the Battle Splendidly,'" 58–65; Varon, *Armies of Deliverance*, 138–40.

81. Ayers, *In the Presence of Mine Enemies*, 316, 319–20; Glatthaar, *General Lee's Army*, 171–72; Guelzo, *Robert E. Lee*, 258–59, John Bell Hood quoted on 258; Varon, *Armies of Deliverance*, 140–42, George Howard quoted on 146 ("We have").

82. Gallagher, *Antietam*, 11–12, 86–90, Lincoln quoted on 12, McClellan quoted on 86 ("defeated"), Edward Porter Alexander quoted on 90 ("commonest" and "backed"); Greene, "'I Fought the Battle Splendidly,'" 56–57, 80–83, McClellan quoted on 56 ("fought"), Union soldier quoted on 81 ("prolongs").

83. Bowen, *Spain and the American Civil War*, 113; Jones, *Union in Peril*, 167–70; Sainlaude, *France and the American Civil War*, 134–35, Henri Mercier quoted on 134.

84. Blight, *Frederick Douglass*, 378–82; Jones, *Union in Peril*, 174–75, Lincoln quoted on 175; Oakes, *Radical and the Republican*, 196–98; Varon, *Armies of Deliverance*, 153–56.

85. Blackett, "Pressure from Without," 69–100; Foreman, *World on Fire*, 318–30; Jones, *Union in Peril*, 174–85, London *Spectator* quoted on 176.

86. Ayers, *In the Presence of Mine Enemies*, 318, 320–21; Cooper, *Jefferson Davis*, 408–9, Davis quoted on 408; Guterl, *American Mediterranean*, 67–68; Manning, *What This Cruel War Was Over*, 81–83, James Harrison quoted on 81.

87. Bordewich, *Congress at War*, 198–99, James F. Robinson quoted on 198 ("fire the whole South"); McPherson, *Battle Cry of Freedom*, 560–61, Ohio newspaper quoted on 560 ("A large majority"); Varon, *Armies of Deliverance*, 157–58, McClellan quoted on 158.

88. Carwardine, *Lincoln*, 212–14; Varon, *Armies of Deliverance*, 160.

89. Grimsley, *Hard Hand of War*, 106; McPherson, *Battle Cry of Freedom*, 562, 569–70; Rafuse, *McClellan's War*, 371–81, Lincoln quoted on 374–75.

90. Gallagher, ed., *Fighting for the Confederacy*, 166–72; Hennessy, "Looting and Bombardment of Fredericksburg," 124–25, 136–51, Minnesota soldier quoted on 139 ("I was reminded"), Union soldier quoted on 145 ("secession families"), Lewis Blackford quoted on 151 ("I hate them"); Varon, *Armies of Deliverance*, 171–72.

91. Gallagher, ed., *Fighting for the Confederacy*, 172–84; Glatthaar, *General Lee's Army*, 174–75, Confederate artillerist quoted on 175 ("looked like"); Varon, *Armies of Deliverance*, 175–78, Georgian hospital steward quoted on 177 ("a complete"), unnamed soldier quoted on 177 ("mashed into").

92. Manning, *What This Cruel War Was Over*, 87–88, Adam Muezenberger quoted on 88 ("the thought"); McPherson, *Battle Cry of Freedom*, 574–75, Union soldier quoted on 574 ("I am sick"), Lincoln quoted on 574-75.

93. Hess, *Civil War in the West*, 52–53, 79–82; McPherson, *War on the Waters*, 89–95.

94. Grimsley, *Hard Hand of War*, 98–99; McPherson, *Battle Cry of Freedom*, 513–15, William T. Sherman quoted on 515; Sutherland, *Savage Conflict*, 77–78.

95. Hess, *Civil War in the West*, 51, 54–55, 62, Ormsby Mitchell quoted on 55; Waugh, *U. S. Grant*, 60–61, William T. Sherman quoted on 61.

96. Grimsley, *Hard Hand of War*, 112; Sutherland, *Savage Conflict*, 51–54, Arkansan quoted on 52 ("I wanted"), John D. Imboden quoted on 94 ("to hunt" and "live & fight").

97. Burke, "Scattered People," 77–78; Cutrer, *Theater of a Separate War*, 250; Sutherland, *Savage Conflict*, 100–1, Joseph Keifer quoted on 101.

98. Sutherland, *Savage Conflict*, 34–35, 58–59, 77–78, 95–96.

99. Grimsley, *Hard Hand of War*, 80–81, John Beatty quoted on 80; McCurry, *Confederate Reckoning*, 120–21; Sutherland, *Savage Conflict*, 80–81, 103–4.

100. Grimsley, *Hard Hand of War*, 96, 99–100, 104–5, 114–18, Sherman quoted on 105 ("Our armies") and 118 ("They cannot"); Hess, *Civil War in the West*, 67–70.

101. Neely, *Civil War and the Limits of Destruction*, 8–19, 37–40, 50, 59, 65.

102. Hess, *Civil War in the West*, 53–54, 60–61, 92–93; McPherson, *Battle Cry of Freedom*, 512–15, Lincoln quoted on 513.

103. Bledsoe, "'The Farce was Complete'," 99–100; Connolly, *Army of the Heartland*, 181–83, 205–6; Hess, *Civil War in the West*, 49, 94, Braxton Bragg quoted on 49.

104. Einolf, *George Thomas*, 129–31, 134–38, 140–42; Grimsley, *Hard Hand of War*, 101–2; Hess, *Civil War in the West*, 94–104; Varon, *Armies of Deliverance*, 164–67.

105. Brady, *War Upon the Land*, 41–42; Hess, *Civil War in the West*, 118–23.

106. Connolly, *Autumn of Glory*, 44–54; Einolf, *George Thomas*, 144–45; Gallagher and Waugh, *American War*, 111; Hess, *Civil War in the West*, 126–29.

107. Connolly, *Autumn of Glory*, 54–68; Einolf, *George Thomas*, 145–53; Hess, *Civil War in the West*, 129–31; Watkins, *Company Aytch*, 57–60, quote on ("whirl-a-gust").

108. Einolf, *George Thomas*, 153; Gallagher and Waugh, *American War*, 111; Hess, *Civil War in the West*, 132–33, Lincoln quoted on 133.

109. Bordewich, *Congress at War*, 197–98; Oakes, *Freedom National*, 340–46, Lincoln quoted on 342; Varon, *Armies of Deliverance*, 184–86.

110. Foner, *Fiery Trial*, 240–45; Horton, *Harriet Tubman*, 61–62, gospel hymn quoted on 62; Oertel, *Harriet Tubman*, 62–63, Thomas W. Higginson quoted on 62.

111. Bordewich, *Congress at War*, 197–98, Frederick Douglass quoted on 198; Foner, *Fiery Trial*, 245–47; Levine, *Fall of the House of Dixie*, 152–53, South Carolina refugee quoted on 153 ("We's"); Oakes, *Freedom National*, 344–45, 398–400.

112. Salmon P. Chase quoted in Jones, *Union in Peril*, 175; Tennessee slaveholder quoted in Varon, *Armies of Deliverance*, 121.

113. Brady, *War Upon the Land*, 69–70; Glatthaar, *Forged in Battle*, 29–30, Henry W. Halleck quoted on 29; Levine, *Fall of the House of Dixie*, 139–40.

EIGHT: WEST

1. Cadete quoted in Masich, *Civil War in the Southwest Borderlands*, 130.

2. Berg, *38 Nooses*, 208–9; Larsen, ed., *Crusader and Feminist*, 26–27, Jane Grey Swisshelm quoted on 26; Hoffert, *Jane Grey Swisshelm*, 150–54.

3. Berg, *38 Nooses*, 209, 235, Swisshelm quoted on 209 ("a Sioux" and "red-jawed"); Hoffert, *Jane Grey Swisshelm*, 126, 152–53, 194; Larsen, ed., *Crusader and Feminist*, 27, 180–84, quotation from 184 ("Our people").

4. Nichols, *Lincoln and the Indians*, 175–77, 186–87, Thomas Galbraith quoted on 176, Lincoln quoted on 187; West, *Essential West*, 102–3.

5. Grant quoted in Hardy, "South of the Border," 68.

6. Kelman, *Misplaced Massacre*, 8–9; Waite, *West of Slavery*, 9–10.

7. Josephy, *Civil War in the American West*, 6–7, Henry David Thoreau quoted on 6.

8. Ball, "Liberty, Empire, and Civil War," 66–67, 70; Josephy, *Civil War in the American West*, 7–9; White, *Republic for Which It Stands*, 114–15.

9. Ball, "Liberty, Empire, and Civil War," 67–68; Josephy, *Civil War in the American West*, 7.

10. Josephy, *Civil War in the American West*, 6; Neely, *Civil War and the Limits of Destruction*, 159–60.

11. Cutrer, *Theater of a Separate War*, 122–24; Josephy, *Civil War in the American West*, 232, 241–42; Paul, *Far West and the Great Plains*, 130–32; West, *Essential West*, 106.

12. Matthews, *Golden State in the Civil War*, 30–31; Paul, *Far West and the Great Plains*, 131–32, Colorado major quoted on 132, Charles A. Huntington quoted on 132.

13. Nichols, *Lincoln and the Indians*, 175–83, Clark Thompson quoted on 180 ("His whole nature"), C. Wood Davis quoted on 182 ("It is"); Paul, *Far West and the Great Plains*, 134–35, quoted on 134 ("tribal relations").

14. Nichols, *Lincoln and the Indians*, 187–88; Paul, *Far West and the Great Plains*, 132–34.

15. Ball, "Liberty, Empire, and Civil War," 68–69, 76; Josephy, *Civil War in the American West*, 231–32, 241–42; Matthews, *Golden State in the Civil War*, 228–29.

16. Scharff, "Empire and Liberty in the Middle of Nowhere," 144–45.

17. Brettle, *Colossal Ambitions*, 2–3, 12–18, 66–67, 86–87; Dawson, "Texas, Jefferson Davis, and Confederate National Strategy," 1–2, 4–6, 9–10; Nelson, "Death in the Distance," 35–37, 40; Waite, *West of Slavery*, 161, 171, Stephens quoted on 164.

18. Majewski and Wahlstrom, "Geography as Power," 346–47; Richards, *California Gold Rush*, 229–30, Grant quoted on 230.

19. Matthews, *Golden State in the Civil War*, 40–41, 89–90; Richards, *California Gold Rush*, 219, 236–37; Stanley, "Senator William Gwin," 250–51.

20. Ellison, "Designs for a Pacific Republic," 334–39, Montgomery quoted on 339 ("I will die"); Matthews, *Golden State in the Civil War*, 84–85; Maxwell, *Civil War Years in Utah*, 39–40, Walter M. Gibson quoted on 40 ("to fascinate").

21. Ellison, "Designs for a Pacific Republic," 335–40; Matthews, *Golden State in the Civil War*, 89–90; St. John, "Unpredictable America of William Gwin," 67–68.

22. Goodheart, *1861*, 228–30, Asbury Harpending quoted on 230 ("reckless"); Josephy, *Civil War in the American West*, 234–39; Harpending quoted in Matthews, *Golden State in the Civil War*, 190 ("I wasn't"); Richards, *California Gold Rush*, 229–32.

23. Ellison, "Designs for a Pacific Republic," 340–41; Matthews, *Golden State in the Civil War*, 85–86, 109–13, 190; Waite, *West of Slavery*, 185, 197.

24. Matthews, *Golden State in the Civil War*, 191–92; Waite, *West of Slavery*, 197–98.

25. Clendenen, "Confederate Spy in California," 221–32; Matthews, *Golden State in the Civil War*, 66–68, 78–81, 93–94, 192–94; Waite, *West of Slavery*, 183–86, 199–203.

26. Brettle, *Colossal Ambitions*, 89–90; Kiser, "'We Must Have Chihuahua and Sonora,'" 196–208; Confederate officer quoted in Waite, *West of Slavery*, 191.

27. Frazier, *Blood & Treasure*, 52–53, Egbert Treadwell quoted on 52; Nelson, "Death in the Distance," 38–40, 48.

28. Blyth, "Kit Carson and the War for the Southwest," 53–54; Dawson, "Texas, Jefferson Davis, and Confederate National Strategy," 7–8.

29. Waite, *West of Slavery*, 167–68.

30. Frazier, *Blood & Treasure*, 18–19, 34, 102; Freeman, *Field of Blood*, 223; Waite, *West of Slavery*, 167–68.

31. Anderson, *Conquest of Texas*, 270, 312–26; Masich, *Civil War in the Southwest Borderlands*, 48–50; Nelson, *Three-Cornered War*, 7–13.

32. Frazier, *Blood & Treasure*, 44–47, 49–50, Henry H. Sibley quoted on 46; Masich, *Civil War in the Southwest Borderlands*, 80–81; Nelson, "Death in the Distance," 37–40.

33. DeLay, *War of a Thousand Deserts*, 144–45; Masich, *Civil War in the Southwest Borderlands*, 40–42, 113–18, 146–51; St. John, *Line in the Sand*, 31–34, 52–54.

34. Jacoby, "'The Broad Platform of Extermination,'" 293–94; John Baylor quoted in Masich, *Civil War in the Southwest Borderland*, 51–52; Waite, *West of Slavery*, 194–95.

35. Frazier, *Blood & Treasure*, 55–56, 64–67, 71–72, Jeff Ake quoted on 65–66; Masich, *Civil War in the Southwest Borderlands*, 52–54.

36. Frazier, *Blood & Treasure*, 54, 70; Masich, *Civil War in the Southwest Borderlands*, 84–85; Lamar, ed., *Reader's Encyclopedia of the American West*, 165–66.

37. Dawson, "Texas, Jefferson Davis, and Confederate National Strategy," 13–14; Masich, *Civil War in the Southwest Borderlands*, 85–96.

38. Frazier, *Blood and Treasure*, 208–67, 280–81; Lamar, *Far Southwest*, 118–22, Henry H. Sibley quoted on 121; Masich, *Civil War in the Southwest Borderlands*, 96–101.

39. Josephy, *Civil War in the American West*, 91–92; Masich, *Civil War in the Southwest Borderlands*, 110–11.

40. Burke, "Scattered People," 74–75; Cutrer, *Theater of a Separate War*, 61–62, Harris Flanagin quoted on 71; Etcheson, *Bleeding Kansas*, 221–22.

41. Cutrer, *Theater of a Separate War*, 63–64, John M. Schofield quoted on 63 ("It is the old"); Etcheson, *Bleeding Kansas*, 223–26, Charles Robinson quoted on 226.

42. Collins, *Jim Lane*, 184–87; Etcheson, *Bleeding Kansas*, 226–27, Charles Robinson quoted on 226; Nichols, *Lincoln and the Indians*, 34–36, Lincoln quoted on 35.

43. Collins, *Jim Lane*, 187–93; Cutrer, *Theater of a Separate War*, 54–55, 63–64 ("Grim Chieftain" and "Bloody Jim" on 63); Etcheson, *Bleeding Kansas*, 227–29, Jayhawk supporter quoted on 227; Sutherland, *Savage Conflict*, 15–18.

44. Cutrer, *Theater of a Separate War*, 63–67, Charles G. Halpine quoted on 63–64, and Henry Halleck quoted on 64; Sutherland, *Savage Conflict*, 58, 60–61.

45. Collins, *Jim Lane*, 194–95, 211–14, Lane quoted on 195 ("This war" and "make it"); Etcheson, *Bleeding Kansas*, 230–31, Lane quoted on 230 ("I would like").

46. Guyatt, "Future Empire of our Freedmen," 101–2, Lane quoted on 102.

47. Collins, *Jim Lane,* 219–21; Etcheson, *Bleeding Kansas,* 232–33; Sutherland, *Savage Conflict,* 64–65.

48. Collins, *Jim Lane,* 221–22; Cutrer, *Theater of a Separate War,* 249–50; Etcheson, *Bleeding Kansas,* 233–34; Sutherland, *Savage Conflict,* 64–65, 201.

49. Collins, *Jim Lane,* 222–25; Etcheson, *Bleeding Kansas,* 235–39, William Quantrill quoted on 235; Sutherland, *Savage Conflict,* 193–94, Kansan quoted on 193; Thomas, *Confederate Nation,* 247–48, raiders quoted on 248; West, *Essential West,* 232–33.

50. Burke, "Scattered People," 71, 83–85; Cutrer, *Theater of a Separate War,* 253–57; Etcheson, *Bleeding Kansas,* 239–42; Sutherland, *Savage Conflict,* 193–96.

51. Cutrer, *Theater of a Separate War,* 324–27, Henry McCulloch quoted on 326; Sutherland, *Savage Conflict,* 198–200, 215, Thomas Reynolds quoted on 200.

52. Neely, *Civil War and the Limits of Destruction,* 61–62; Sutherland, *Savage Conflict,* 199, 203, Frank James quoted on 203; West, *Essential West,* 233–34.

53. Blansett, "When the Stars Fell from the Sky," 89–91; Confer, *Cherokee Nation,* 22–27, 32–41; Cutrer, *Theater of a Separate War,* 69–71, Charles A. Brusle quoted on 71.

54. Confer, *Cherokee Nation,* 42–43; Cutrer, *Theater of a Separate War,* 71–75, 334; Sutherland, *Savage Conflict,* 48–49, M. H. McWillie quoted on 49.

55. Brettle, *Colossal Ambitions,* 65–66, Ben McCulloch quoted on 65; Confer, *Cherokee Nation,* 43–46; Josephy, *Civil War in the American West,* 322–25; Nichols, *Lincoln and the Indians,* 25–27, 30–31, Henry Rector quoted on 26.

56. Blansett, "When the Stars Fell from the Sky," 92–93; Confer, *Cherokee Nation,* 46–47; Nichols, *Lincoln and the Indians,* 28–32.

57. Blansett, "When the Stars Fell from the Sky," 91–94; Confer, *Cherokee Nation,* 47–52; Cutrer, *Theater of a Separate War,* 74–75, Samuel Bell Maxey quoted on 327; Nichols, *Lincoln and the Indians,* 30–32, John Ross quoted on 31.

58. Confer, *Cherokee Nation,* 52–66; Cutrer, *Theater of a Separate War,* 73–80, Allison Sparks quoted on 77; Josephy, *Civil War in the American West,* 330–33.

59. Blansett, "When the Stars Fell from the Sky," 95–100; Confer, *Cherokee Nation,* 85–93; Collins, *Jim Lane,* 197–201; Cutrer, *Theater of a Separate War,* 314–37; Josephy, *Civil War in the American West,* 351–59, 371–77.

60. Bigler, *Forgotten Kingdom,* 221–22; Campbell, *Establishing Zion,* 290–92.

61. Bringhurst, *Brigham Young,* 156–57; Long, *Saints and the Union,* 7–8, 36–37, 43–44, Brigham Young quoted on 37 ("would let") and 50 ("cursed scoundrels"); Maxwell, *Civil War Years in Utah,* 11, 13–16, 39–43, 351–52.

62. Bigler, *Forgotten Kingdom,* 202; Maxwell, *Civil War in Utah,* 96–115, 135–40, 244–45, 351–52, Brigham Young quoted on 244.

63. Bigler, *Forgotten Kingdom,* 201–4; Bringhurst, *Brigham Young,* 160–61; Long, *Saints and the Union,* 36–50; Maxwell, *Civil War Years in Utah,* 47–50, 96–115.

64. Bringhurst, *Brigham Young,* 165–68, Young quoted on 166 ("cow shit"); Long, *Saints and the Union,* 62–70, 73–74; Maxwell, *Civil War Years in Utah,* 116–28, Young quoted on 155 ("that a Government") and 196 ("nigger worshipper").

65. Bigler, *Forgotten Kingdom,* 217–18; Bringhurst, *Brigham Young,* 163–64, Lincoln quoted on 169; Maxwell, *Civil War Years in Utah,* 27, 128–30.

66. Bigler, *Forgotten Kingdom,* 222–25; Bringhurst, *Brigham Young,* 164–65; Long, *Saints*

and the Union, 94–100, Patrick E. Connor quoted on 99; Maxwell, *Civil War Years in Utah*, 11–13, 29, 155–61, John A. Anderson quoted on 166.

67. Bigler, *Forgotten Kingdom*, 224–28; Long, *Saints and the Union*, 100–21; Maxwell, *Civil War Years in Utah*, 161–74, 194–95, Patrick E. Connor quoted on 161.

68. Blackhawk, *Violence over the Land*, 263–66; Josephy, *Civil War in the American West*, 243–44, 254–59; Long, *Saints and the Union*, 128–42; Maxwell, *Civil War Years in Utah*, 185–94.

69. Bigler, *Forgotten Kingdom*, 241–45, *Union Vedette* quoted on 244; Long, *Saints and the Union*, 145–71, 202–21 262–63; Maxwell, *Civil War Years in Utah*, 170, 228, 246–52.

70. Patrick Connor quoted in Josephy, *Civil War in the American West*, 252–53; Long, *Saints and the Union*, 202–3, 220, 222, 224, Brigham Young quoted on 203 ("It behooves") and 224 ("humbugging"); Maxwell, *Civil War Years in Utah*, 235–36.

71. Bigler, *Forgotten Kingdom*, 246–47; Bringhurst, *Brigham Young*, 171–72; Long, *Saints and the Union,* 254–68; Maxwell, *Civil War Years in Utah*, 297–308.

72. Blyth, "Kit Carson and the War for the Southwest," 58–60; Josephy, *Civil War in the American West*, 76, 89–91; Masich, *Civil War in the Southwest Borderlands*, 56–72; Nelson, *Three-Cornered War*, 124–35, 179–80, James Carleton quoted on 207.

73. Josephy, *Civil War in the American West*, 269–81, James Carleton quoted on 269 ("An Indian"); Lamar, *Far Southwest*, 122–24, Carleton quoted on 124 ("reformatory"); Nelson, *Three-Cornered War*, 171–72, 210–13; Reséndez, *Other Slavery*, 277–78, 284–85.

74. Josephy, *Civil War in the American West*, 278–80; Masich, *Civil War in the Southwest Borderlands*, 137–38; Nelson, *Three-Cornered War*, 166–75; West, *Essential West*, 113.

75. Blyth, "Kit Carson and the War for the Southwest," 55–56; Nelson, *Three-Cornered War*, 183–84; Reséndez, *Other Slavery*, 278–84.

76. Lamar, *Far Southwest*, 124–25; Masich, *Civil War in the Southwest Borderlands*, 124–26; Nelson, *Three-Cornered War*, 185–95; Reséndez, *Other Slavery*, 284–89.

77. Blyth, "Kit Carson and the War for the Southwest," 60–64; Masich, *Civil War in the Southwest Borderlands*, 125–30; Reséndez, *Other Slavery*, 290–94.

78. Ball, "Liberty, Empire, and Civil War," 79–81; Nelson, *Three-Cornered War*, 200–13, James Carleton quoted on 201 ("Navajos"); Carleton quoted in Nichols, *Lincoln and the Indians*, 167 ("happiest people").

79. Anderson, *Little Crow*, 4–6, 36–88; Berg, *38 Nooses*, 4–6; Josephy, *Civil War in the American West*, 96, 100, 105, Little Crow quoted on 111.

80. Anderson, *Little Crow*, 89–101; Berg, *38 Nooses*, 10–12, 46–48; Nichols, *Lincoln and the Indians*, 76.

81. Anderson, *Little Crow*, 101–15; Berg, *38 Nooses*, 10–12, 20–24; Josephy, *Civil War in the American West*, 100–105.

82. Anderson, *Little Crow*, 52–64; Berg, *38 Nooses*, 108–10; Josephy, *Civil War in the American West*, 102, 105; Nichols, *Lincoln and the Indians*, 65–75, George F. H. Day quoted on 73 ("robbed"), George A. S. Crooker quoted on 92 ("cohesive power").

83. Anderson, *Little Crow*, 127–28, Andrew Myrick quoted on 128; Berg, *38 Nooses*, 28–29; Josephy, *Civil War in the American West*, 103–10, Big Eagle quoted on 106; Wakefield, *Six Weeks in the Sioux Teepees*, 2–7, quotation on 5–6.

84. Anderson, *Little Crow*, 128–34; Josephy, *Civil War in the American West*, 110–12, Little Crow quoted on 112; Wakefield, *Six Weeks in the Sioux Teepees*, 7.

85. Anderson, *Little Crow*, 135–52; Berg, *38 Nooses*, 32–39, 76–79; Namias, *White Captives*, 216–18; Wakefield, *Six Weeks in the Sioux Teepees*, 8 ("to them").

86. Anderson, *Little Crow*, 152–62; Berg, *38 Nooses*, 155–56; Josephy, *Civil War in the American West*, 122–36; Namias, *White Captives*, 219–20.

87. Berg, *38 Nooses*, 152–53, 162; Josephy, *Civil War in the American West*, 136–37, Henry Hastings Sibley quoted on 137; Namias, *White Captives*, 226–27.

88. Berg, *38 Nooses*, 16–17, 24–26; Namias, *White Captives*, 205–12; Wakefield, *Six Weeks in the Sioux Teepees*, 1 ("and began") and 14 ("Not a day").

89. Berg, *38 Nooses*, 30–31, 35–39, 85–87, 152–53; Namias, *White Captives*, 214–16; Wakefield, *Six Weeks in the Sioux Teepees*, 9–15, 34–36, 59–60, quotation on 12.

90. Berg, *38 Nooses*, 161–62, 164–65, 168–71; Namias, *White Captives*, 220–21; Wakefield, *Six Weeks in the Sioux Teepees*, 70–79, and see 71 ("I was") and 74 ("Captain Grant").

91. Namias, *White Captives*, 221–29; Nichols, *Lincoln and the Indians*, 93, 98–100, 176, Sibley quoted on 98 ("to satisfy") and 112 ("a great example"); Wakefield, *Six Weeks in the Sioux Teepees*, 75.

92. Berg, *38 Nooses*, 220–22, 227–28; Namias, *White Captives*, 230–31; Nichols, *Lincoln and the Indians*, 98–103, 118, 124.

93. Donald, *Lincoln*, 393–95, Morton S. Wilkerson quoted on 394 ("Either") and Lincoln quoted on 395; Nichols, *Lincoln and the Indians*, 108–13, Gideon Welles quoted on 108 ("slightly removed").

94. Berg, *38 Nooses*, 230–40; Namias, *White Captives*, 233–37; Nichols, *Lincoln and the Indians*, 117; Wakefield, *Six Weeks in the Sioux Teepees*, 84–85.

95. Berg, *38 Nooses*, 238–41, 300–1, John F. Meagher quoted on 301.

96. Berg, *38 Nooses*, 252–55, 269–72, Sarah Wakefield quoted on 254 ("I am abased"), 271 ("just cursed me" and "He says"), and 272 ("I can see"); Namias, *White Captives*, 245–49.

97. Donald, *Lincoln*, 394; Nichols, *Lincoln and the Indians*, 96–97, 113–17.

98. Nichols, *Lincoln and the Indians*, 119–27, S. D. Hinman quoted on 126.

99. Anderson, *Little Crow*, 7–8, 171–81; Berg, *38 Nooses*, 266–68, 278–79; Gluek, *Minnesota and the Manifest Destiny*, 172–79.

100. Donald, *Lincoln*, 392–93, John Pope quoted on 393 ("utterly"); Nichols, *Lincoln and the Indians*, 84–85, 87–90, 120, Pope quoted on 89–90 ("It is not").

101. Berg, *38 Nooses*, 277–78, 283–85, Sitting Bull quoted on 284; Cutrer, *Theater of a Separate War*, 125–29; Ostler, *Plains Sioux*, 44–45.

102. Neely, *Civil War and the Limits of Destruction*, 147–49, Robert R. Livingston quoted on 148 ("Universal consternation"), Eugene Ware quoted on 150 ("The fire").

103. Josephy, *Civil War in the American West*, 295–98.

104. Cutrer, *Theater of a Separate War*, 120–21; Josephy, *Civil War in the American West*, 292, 294–95, 300, John P. Slough quoted on 305; Kelman, *Misplaced Massacre*, 9–10.

105. Nichols, *Lincoln and the Indians*, 169–71, John Evans quoted on 171; Kelman, *Misplaced Massacre*, 14–15; West, *Contested Plains*, 299–307.

106. Josephy, *Civil War in the American West*, 308–12; Kelman, *Misplaced Massacre*, 10–12; Utley, *Indian Frontier*, 92–93, *Rocky Mountain News*, quoted on 92.

107. Josephy, *Civil War in the American West*, 312–16, George Bent quoted on 313; Kelman, *Misplaced Massacre*, 12–13, 191–95; Nichols, *Lincoln and the Indians*, 172–74.

108. Josephy, *Civil War in the American West*, 260–61, 267–68, James J. Doty quoted on 261 ("the Americans"); Paul, *Far West and the Great Plains*, 130–34, Francis A. Walker quoted on 133 ("freedom").

109. Thomas Starr King quoted in Matthews, *Golden State in the Civil War*, 229; Nelson, *Three-Cornered War*, 176–79, Lincoln quoted on 177.

110. Lincoln quoted in Long, *Saints and the Union*, 42; Matthews, *Golden State in the Civil War*, 98–99; West, *Essential West*, 78–82, 89–91, 104–7.

111. Bordewich, *Congress at War*, 130–31, 136–37; Richardson, *To Make Men Free*, 33–38; White, *Republic for Which It Stands*, 117–18.

112. Bordewich, *Congress at War*, 131–32, Galusha Grow quoted on 131; McPherson, *Battle Cry of Freedom*, 450–52; Richardson, *To Make Men Free*, 33–34; White, *Republic for Which It Stands*, 120–21.

113. Bordewich, *Congress at War*, 134–36; Richardson, *To Make Men Free*, 34–36.

114. Bordewich, *Congress at War*, 132–34; Matthews, *Golden State in the Civil War*, 100–1; Matthews, *Golden State in the Civil War*, 112–13; White, *Railroaded*, 17–26.

115. Richardson, *Make Men Free*, 36–38, 42–48; West, *Essential West*, 3–6, 53–54; White, *Republic for Which It Stands*, 105, 113–14.

NINE: INVASIONS

1. Harriet Tubman quoted in Oertel, *Harriet Tubman*, 67.

2. Cunningham, *Mexico and the Foreign Policy of Napoleon III*, 132–34; Dabbs, *French Army in Mexico*, 30–32; McAllen, *Maximilian and Carlota*, 61, 76–77.

3. Cunningham, *Mexico and the Foreign Policy of Napoleon III*, 135–43; Dabbs, *French Army in Mexico*, 32–36; Ridley, *Maximilian and Juárez*, 56–57, 134, Napoleon quoted on 134; Roeder, *Juárez*, vol. 2:493–94, Pierre Henri Loizillon quoted on 522.

4. Dabbs, *French Army in Mexico*, 36–50; McAllen, *Maximilian and Carlota*, 81–90; Roeder, *Juárez*, vol. 2:494–510, Pierre Henri Loizillon quoted on 505.

5. Dabbs, *French Army in Mexico*, 51–55; Hanna and Hanna, *Napoleon III and Mexico*, 85–87; Ridley, *Maximilian and Juárez,* 132–34; Roeder, *Juárez*, vol. 2:511–13.

6. Dabbs, *French Army in Mexico*, 56–60, Louis Adrien de Tuce quoted on 60 ("a rascal"); McAllen, *Maximilian and Carlota*, 67–68, 94–96, 101, Pierre Henri Loizillon quoted on 95; Roeder, *Juárez*, vol. 2:519–32, Loizillon quoted on 532.

7. Cunningham, *Mexico and the Foreign Policy of Napoleon III*, 136–37, 145–50, Forey quoted on 137; O'Connor, *Cactus Throne*, 90–91, Charles Wyke quoted on 99 ("places"); Roeder, *Juárez*, vol. 2:523–24, 559–60, Pierre Henri Loizillon quoted on 524.

8. Cunningham, *Mexico and the Foreign Policy of Napoleon III*, 143–44; Dabbs, *French Army in Mexico*, 60–65, Napoleon III quoted on 61; Roeder, *Juárez*, vol. 2:494–97, 528–36, Francois du Barail quoted on 497 ("what he has been").

9. Cunningham, *Mexico and the Foreign Policy of Napoleon III*, 164–66; Dabbs, *French Army in Mexico*, 71–73, 76–81; Hanna and Hanna, *Napoleon III and Mexico*, 105–6; McAllen, *Maximilian and Carlota*, 102–4, François du Barail quoted on 103.

10. Labastida's pamphlet quoted in Hanna and Hanna, *Napoleon III and Mexico*, 106;

McAllen, *Maximilian and Carlota*, 104–6; Roeder, *Juárez*, vol. 2:542, 550–54, François du Barail quoted on 542 ("a little dense").

11. Dabbs, *French Army in Mexico*, 106–8; Duncan, "Political Legitimation," 31–32; Hanna and Hanna, *Napoleon III and Mexico*, 93–95, 111–12.

12. Fowler, *Santa Anna*, 320–25, Juan N. Almonte quoted on 325; Hanna and Hanna, *Napoleon III and Mexico*, 109–10; McAllen, *Maximilian and Carlota*, 115.

13. Reid, *African Canadians in Union Blue*, 30–34, 152–53; Rhodes, *Mary Ann Shadd Cary*, 135–48; Sterling, *Making of an Afro-American*, 176–207.

14. Rhodes, *Mary Ann Shadd Cary*, 147–50, Shadd quoted on 149; Silverman, *Unwelcome Guests*, 127–45, 151–54, 157–58; Winks, *Blacks in Canada*, 215–16, 231–32.

15. Painter, "Martin R. Delany," 162; Reid, *African Canadians in Union Blue*, 47–49, 54–55; Rhodes, *Mary Ann Shadd Cary*, 152–53; Silverman, *Unwelcome Guests*, 156–57, Methodist ministers quoted on 156; Winks, *Blacks in Canada*, 289–90.

16. Painter, "Martin R. Delany," 162–63; Sterling, *Making of an Afro-American*, 233–46, Abraham Lincoln quoted on 243, John E. Bruce quoted on 245–46 ("commanding voice").

17. Bearden and Butler, *Shadd*, 205–6; Rhodes, *Mary Ann Shadd Cary*, 153–60.

18. Dunbar, *She Came to Slay*, 83–90; Horton, *Harriet Tubman*, 56–63, Robert Gould Shaw quoted on 63 ("praying"); Wilson, "In the Shadow of John Brown," 307–10, 317–22, James Montgomery quoted on 322.

19. Dunbar, *She Came to Slay*, 91–94; Horton, *Harriet Tubman*, 63–67; Oertel, *Harriet Tubman*, 53–54, 66–69, 140–41, Tubman quoted on 67, correspondent for the *Wisconsin State Journal* quoted on 141; Sterling, *We Are Your Sisters*, 259–60.

20. Blight, *Frederick Douglass*, 384–85, 391–92, 396–99, Lewis Douglass quoted on 396; Egerton, *Thunder at the Gates*, 70–77, 79, 92–96; Glatthaar, *Forged in Battle*, 135–36; Sterling, *Making of an Afro-American*, 231–32, Longfellow quoted on 232.

21. Egerton, *Thunder at the Gates*, 2–3, 74–77; Black recruit quoted in Freehling, *The South vs The South*, 195 ("I felt"); Glatthaar, *Forged in Battle*, 2–3, 121–22, 153–54, Louisiana soldier quoted on 3 ("fight as long"); Levine, *Fall of the House of Dixie*, 160–61, 166, Prince Rivers quoted on 134.

22. Bordewich, *Congress at War*, 198–99, James F. Robinson quoted on 198 ("fire the whole South"); Egerton, *Thunder at the Gates*, 3–6, *New York Journal of Commerce* quoted on 3–4 ("fanatical idea").

23. Glatthaar, *Forged in Battle*, 9–10, A. E. Berey quoted on 10 ("hate the Negro"); Manning, *What This Cruel War Was Over*, 88–95, Amos Hostetter quoted on 93 ("like the Negro"); Taylor, *Embattled Freedom*, 109–11.

24. Bailey, "USCT in the Confederate Heartland," 227–29; Freehling, *The South vs The South*, 150–53, 165, William Tecumseh Sherman quoted on 153.

25. Blight, *Frederick Douglass*, 402–9; Egerton, *Thunder at the Gates*, 203–9; Glatthaar, *Forged in Battle*, 169–71, James Henry Gooding quoted on 171 ("Now your Excellency"); Reid, *African Canadians in Union Blue*, 89, 97–98, 115–16.

26. Egerton, *Thunder at the Gates*, 65, Robert Gould Shaw quoted on 83; Glatthaar, *Forged in Battle*, 28, 143–45, Thomas W. Higginson quoted on 144; Reid, *African Canadians in Union Blue*, 159–63, 169–70.

27. King, *Louis T. Wigfall*, 132–34, 139–40, Mary Chesnut quoted on 214; Rable, *Confederate Republic*, 85–86, 126, 133–36, 148; Symonds, *Joseph E. Johnston*, 177–81; Walther, *Fire-Eaters*, 80, 190, 192–93, 267, Lawrence Keitt quoted on 192.

28. King, *Louis T. Wigfall*, 141–42; McPherson, *Battle Cry of Freedom*, 428–29, Jefferson Davis quoted on 429; Rable, *Confederate Republic*, 128–29, 173.

29. Levine, *The Fall of the House of Dixie*, 194–95; Janney, *Ends of War*, 73–74, John W. Lewis quoted on 74 ("without"); McCurry, *Confederate Reckoning*, 87–88, 133–37, 153–55, Robert Kean quoted on 163 ("The iron").

30. Rable, *Confederate Republic*, 143–45, 158–59; Thomas, *Confederate Nation*, 150–52.

31. Bynum, *Free State of Jones*, 98–99; Levine, *Fall of the House of Dixie*, 83–86; Rable, *Confederate Republic*, 138–40, 155–56.

32. Levine, *The Fall of the House of Dixie*, 195, 197–98, Warren Aikin quoted on 198 ("Have you ever"), John A. Campbell quoted on 198 ("The sacrosanctity"); McCurry, *Confederate Reckoning*, 266–88.

33. Levine, *Fall of the House of Dixie*, 199–200; Manning, *What This Cruel War Was Over*, 58–62, 102–3, 105, John White quoted on 59.

34. Freehling, *The South vs The South*, 145; Levine, *Fall of the House of Dixie*, 211–12, John A. Campbell quoted on 211.

35. Bynum, *Free State of Jones*, 94–95, Robert S. Hudson quoted on 94 ("rotten hearted"); Levine, *Fall of the House of Dixie*, 209–10, Nancy Mangum quoted on 209 ("we wiimen"), unnamed woman quoted on 210 ("What do I care"); McCurry, *Confederate Reckoning*, 87–89, 124–28.

36. McCurry, *Confederate Reckoning*, 123–24, 128–32, Phoebe Cook quoted on 129.

37. Bynum, *Free State of Jones*, 86–88, 93–100, Newton Knight quoted on 98.

38. Bynum, *Free State of Jones*, 105–28, Newton Knight quoted on 105; Levine, *Fall of the House of Dixie*, 212–13.

39. McCurry, *Confederate Reckoning*, 179–80; Rable, *Confederate Republic*, 184–86; Thomas, *Confederate Nation*, 199–201.

40. McCurry, *Confederate Reckoning*, 140–46, 178–91; McPherson, *Battle Cry of Freedom*, 617–18, bread rioters quoted on 618; Thomas, *Confederate Nation*, 201–5, young woman quoted on 203 ("This is little enough").

41. Rable, *Confederate Republic*, 166–67, 249–51, Alexander H. Stephens quoted on 251; Schott, *Alexander H. Stephens*, 346–47, 357–58, 395–40.

42. McPherson, *Battle Cry of Freedom*, 431–33, Joseph Brown and Jefferson Davis quoted on 433; Rable, *Confederate Republic*, 138–42, 188–93, 199–201.

43. Gallagher, "Disaffection, Persistence, and Nation," 339–41; Manning, *What This Cruel War Was Over*, 55–61, 62–67, 106–7, Edward Brown quoted on 61 ("The Yankees"), Thomas Taylor quoted on 66 ("we are ruined"), *The Vidette* quoted on 107 ("Slavery for").

44. Ayers, *In the Presence of Mine Enemies*, 390–91, 394; Glatthaar, *General Lee's Army*, 150–51, 154–55; Manning, *What This Cruel War Was Over*, 108–9; Rubin, *Shattered Nation*, 23–25, 50–51, 88–89, Emma LeConte and Sarah Morgan quoted on 23–24.

45. John A. Higgins quoted in Sutherland, *Savage Conflict*, 59 ("Our army"); William Thompson Lusk quoted in Varon, *Armies of Deliverance*, 173 ("Were low").

46. Cooper, *Jefferson Davis*, 405–8, 449–50, Jefferson Davis quoted on 407; Hermann, *Pursuit of a Dream*, 39–40; McCurry, *Confederate Reckoning*, 257.

47. Ayers, *In the Presence of Mine Enemies*, 384–85; Glatthaar, *General Lee's Army*, 176–80, Alexander Lawton quoted on 177 ("Our own army"), Cadmus M. Wilcox quoted on 180 ("We have no").

48. Bordewich, *Congress at War*, 186–87; McPherson, *Battle Cry of Freedom*, 584–85,

Charles Francis Adams, Jr., quoted on 585 ("a combination"), Lincoln quoted on 585.

49. Joseph Hooker quoted in Gallagher and Waugh, *American War*, 112–13 ("certain"); McPherson, *Battle Cry of Freedom*, 585–86, 639–40, Hooker quoted on 639 ("May God").

50. Ayers, *In the Presence of Mine Enemies*, 378–84, Jed Hotchkiss quoted on 378; Creighton, *Colors of Courage*, 9–11, 21–24; Glatthaar, *General Lee's Army*, 245–54; Varon, *Armies of Deliverance*, 225–29.

51. Bordewich, *Congress at War*, 181–82, 223–2; Creighton, *Colors of Courage*, 25–28; Horace Greeley quoted in Gallagher and Waugh, *American War*, 113; Lincoln quoted in Levine, *Fall of the House of Dixie*, 144.

52. Gallagher, *Lee and His Generals*, 13–14, 18–19; Glatthaar, *General Lee's Army*, 269–70; E. Thomas, *Robert E. Lee*, 279, 285–89, Lee quoted on 279.

53. McPherson, *Battle Cry of Freedom*, 648–50, James Longstreet quoted on 649; Thomas, *Robert E. Lee*, 292–94.

54. Ayers, *In the Presence of Mine Enemies*, 392–412, Philip Schaff quoted on 397 ("they would burn"); Creighton, *Colors of Courage*, 71–92, 126–35, Black fugitive quoted on 131; Glatthaar, *General Lee's Army*, 270–73, Rachel Carmony quoted on 313.

55. Creighton, *Colors of Courage*, 87–96; Gallagher, *Lee and His Generals*, 64–76, 158–60, 169–81; Glatthaar, *General Lee's Army*, 273–75.

56. Glatthaar, *General Lee's Army*, 275–79; McPherson, *Battle Cry of Freedom*, 656–61, Longstreet quoted on 661; Perry, *Conceived in Liberty*, 209–27.

57. Creighton, *Colors of Courage*, 139–41; Glatthaar, *General Lee's Army*, 279–82, Horatio Dana Chapman quoted on 279–80; Perry, *Conceived in Liberty*, 230–33.

58. Glatthaar, *General Lee's Army*, 283–84, Georgian quoted on 283 ("I have been") and John A. Everett quoted on 284 ("the Armey" and "it Don't"); Perry, *Conceived in Liberty*, 233–35.

59. Glatthaar, *General Lee's Army*, 287–88; King, *Louis T. Wigfall*, 171–72; Rubin, *Shattered Nation*, 82–83, Lee quoted on 82, and Margaret Wight quoted on 83.

60. Lincoln quoted in Bordewich, *Congress at War*, 236; Goodwin, *Team of Rivals*, 535–36.

61. Brady, *War Upon the Land*, 25–26; Levine, *Fall of the House of Dixie*, 144–45, Henry Halleck quoted on 144; Underwood, *Waters of Discord*, 125–27.

62. Brady, *War Upon the Land*, 27–35, 43–48; Symonds, *Joseph E. Johnston*, 204–5.

63. Charles A. Dana quoted in McPherson, *Battle Cry of Freedom*, 589–90; Waugh, *U. S. Grant*, 62–63.

64. Cooper, *Jefferson Davis*, 409–10, Davis quoted on 410; Hess, *Civil War in the West*, 145.

65. Cooper, *Jefferson Davis*, 412–15; Rable, *Confederate Republic*, 171–72; Symonds, *Joseph E. Johnston*, 183–84, 187–92, 198–203.

66. Brady, *War Upon the Land*, 42–43, 52–53; McPherson, *Battle Cry of Freedom*, 626–28, Grant quoted on 628; Waugh, *U. S. Grant*, 63, 71–72.

67. Brady, *War Upon the Land*, 54–59; Hess, *Civil War in the West*, 146–50; Symonds, *Joseph E. Johnston*, 205–7; Varon, *Armies of Deliverance*, 218–20.

68. Hess, *Civil War in the West*, 151–52; McPherson, *Battle Cry of Freedom*, 631–33, Vicksburg woman quoted on 631; Symonds, *Joseph E. Johnston*, 207–10.

69. Brady, *War Upon the Land*, 59–68; Symonds, *Joseph E. Johnston*, 211–14; Thomas, *Confederate Nation*, 218–19, Johnston quoted on 218; Waugh, *U. S. Grant*, 63–64.

70. McPherson, *Battle Cry of Freedom*, 636–37, Vicksburg woman quoted on 637; Symonds, *Joseph E. Johnston*, 214–15; Varon, *Armies of Deliverance*, 264.

71. Hess, *Civil War in the West*, 157–58, 172–74; Symonds, *Joseph E. Johnston*, 216–20; Waugh, *U. S. Grant*, 64–66, Davis quoted on 65, Lincoln quoted on 66.

72. George Templeton Strong quoted in Bordewich, *Congress at War*, 237; Varon, *Armies of Deliverance*, 271.

73. Levine, *Fall of the House of Dixie*, 145–46; Reid, *African Canadians in Union Blue*, 131–32.

74. McPherson, *Battle Cry of Freedom*, 602–3; Varon, *Armies of Deliverance*, 271.

75. Manning, *What This Cruel War Was Over*, 116–17; Sterling, *We are Your Sisters*, 232–33; Varon, *Armies of Deliverance*, 271–72.

76. Bordewich, *Congress at War*, 237–38; Varon, *Armies of Deliverance*, 272–75.

77. Bordewich, *Congress at War*, 238–40; Glatthaar, *Forged in Battle*, 140.

78. Blight, *Frederick Douglass*, 399–402; Egerton, *Thunder at the Gates*, 121–24; Glatthaar, *Forged in Battle*, 136–38, 149–50, Truman Seymour quoted on 137.

79. Egerton, *Thunder at the Gates*, 124–40; Glatthaar, *Forged in Battle*, 138–40, Lewis Douglass quoted on 139; Horton, *Harriet Tubman*, 67–68, Tubman quoted on 68.

80. Wisconsin officer quoted in Freehling, *The South vs The South*, 127 ("I never believed"); Glatthaar, *Forged in Battle*, 126–35, 164–68, John Pierson quoted on 168 ("The truth is"); Manning, *What This Cruel War Was Over*, 95–97, 123–24, Abraham E. Strickle quoted on 124 ("I never more").

81. Glatthaar, *Forged in Battle*, 154–57, Ben F. Stevens quoted on 155; Levine, *Fall of the House of Dixie*, 137–38; Kate Stone quoted in Lowe, "Battle on the Levee," 128.

82. Texan quoted in Bordewich, *Congress at War*, 239 ("We took no"); Levine, *Fall of the House of Dixie*, 168–70; McPherson, *Battle Cry of Freedom*, 566–67, Thomas R. Roulhac quoted on 566 ("either bayoneted"); Taylor, *Embattled Freedom*, 125–26.

83. Cimprich, "Fort Pillow Massacre," 150–65; Glatthaar, *Forged in Battle*, 156–57, Nathan Bedford Forrest quoted on 157; Achilles V. Clark quoted in Levine, *Fall of the House of Dixie*, 169.

84. McPherson, *Battle Cry of Freedom*, 792–96, Confederate official quoted on 792; Reid, *African Canadians in Union Blue*, 92, 120.

85. Gallagher and Waugh, *American War*, 78–79; Varon, *Armies of Deliverance*, 327–31.

86. Bordewich, *Congress at War*, 240–41, Ulysses S. Grant quoted on 241; Freehling, *The South vs The South*, 146–47; Waugh, *U. S. Grant*, 72–73.

87. McCurry, *Confederate Reckoning*, 289–98, 318–20, 326, Kirby Smith quoted on 297, Colcock Jones quoted on 301; Oakes, *Freedom National*, 402–3.

88. Freehling, *The South vs The South*, 127–29; Levine, *Fall of the House of Dixie*, 156–58, 172, Chattanooga editor quoted on 157, Honoria Cannon quoted on 158; McCurry, *Confederate Reckoning*, 242–47; Taylor, *Embattled Freedom*, 108–9.

89. McCurry, *Confederate Reckoning*, 289–95, 299–300; Oakes, *Freedom National*, 402–10, Louisa Alexander quoted on 406–7; Robinson, *Bitter Fruits of Bondage*, 56–57.

90. Glatthaar, *General Lee's Army*, 305–307, Arthur Evans quoted on 306 ("my advice"), Marcy Wade quoted on 307 ("My Slaves"); Levine, *Fall of the House of Dixie*, 156–58.

91. Levine, *Fall of the House of Dixie*, 153–58, 181–82, William J. Minor quoted on 156 ("They are" and "The most of them"); A. M. Taylor, *Embattled Freedom*, 113–21, 124–25, 129–33, John Eaton quoted on 130 ("The ferocity").

92. Hermann, *Pursuit of a Dream*, 54–55; Levine, *Fall of the House of Dixie*, 173–78, Charles Barbour quoted on 173–74 ("I wuz"), chaplain quoted on 178 ("cartridge box").

93. Freehling, *The South vs The South*, 165; Levine, *Fall of the House of Dixie*, 179–81, freedman quoted on 180, James A. Garfield quoted on 182.

94. Hermann, *Pursuit of a Dream*, 38–66, Samuel Thomas quoted on 66; Levine, *Fall of the House of Dixie*, 181, 186; McCurry, *Confederate Reckoning*, 255–57.

95. Downs, *After Appomattox*, 30–32; Freehling, *The South vs The South*, 165–66; William T. Sherman quoted in Levine, *Fall of the House of Dixie*, 181.

96. Levine, *Fall of the House of Dixie*, 184–86, 189–91, freedman quoted on 186, Edward S. Philbrick quoted on 190–91; Taylor, *Embattled Freedom*, 113–14, John P. Hawkins quoted on 123.

97. Levine, *Fall of the House of Dixie*, 186–89, Louisiana planters quoted on 187, Nathaniel P. Banks quoted on 187; Taylor, *Embattled Freedom*, 113, 117.

98. Doyle, *Cause of All Nations*, 158–60, 164–66, 169–73; Foreman, *World on Fire*, 117–18.

99. Doyle, *Cause of All Nations*, 176–79; Foreman, *World on Fire*, 283–84, William H. Seward quoted on 284; Owsley, *King Cotton Diplomacy*, 496–99; Stahr, *Seward*, 393.

100. Doyle, *Cause of All Nations*, 178–80, 260–68, Pius IX quoted on 263; Mahin, *One War at a Time*, 212; Owsley, *King Cotton Diplomacy*, 495–506.

101. Connolly, *Autumn of Glory*, 70–92, 112–34, 137–50, 162–85; Einolf, *George Thomas*, 158–60; Hess, *Braxton Bragg*, 139, 145–57, Bragg quoted on 148; McPherson, *Battle Cry of Freedom*, 668–69; Watkins, *Company Aytch*, 78–79.

102. Connolly, *Autumn of Glory*, 150–53, 159–61; Hess, *Civil War in the West*, 178–87, 190; Watkins, *Company Aytch*, 61–65, quote on 64 ("wanted").

103. Connolly, *Autumn of Glory*, 193–234; Einolf, *George Thomas*, 160–88; Glatthaar, *General Lee's Army*, 349–50; Hess, *Braxton Bragg*, 158–68.

104. Einolf, *George Thomas*, 187, 197–205, Abraham Lincoln quoted on 199; McPherson, *Battle Cry of Freedom*, 674–76, Union officer quoted on 676.

105. Connolly, *Autumn of Glory*, 235–72; Hess, *Braxton Bragg*, 169–97; James Longstreet quoted in McPherson, *Battle Cry of Freedom*, 676; Symonds, *Joseph E. Johnston*, 245–47; Watkins, *Company Aytch*, 89–91.

106. Einolf, *George Thomas*, 209–18; Hess, *Braxton Bragg*, 198–201; Varon, *Armies of Deliverance*, 287–92; Waugh, *U. S. Grant*, 67–68, Charles A. Dana quoted on 68.

107. Einolf, *George Thomas*, 217–21; Hess, *Braxton Bragg*, 201–4, Bragg quoted on 204; Watkins, *Company Aytch*, 94–95 ("I felt sorry").

108. Freehling, *The South vs The South*, 159–60; Levine, *Fall of the House of Dixie*, 151–52; Symonds, *Joseph E. Johnston*, 247–48; Waugh, *U. S. Grant*, 68–71, 73.

109. Gallagher and Waugh, *American War*, 123–25; Glatthaar, *General Lee's Army*, 283–85; Rubin, *Shattered Nation*, 80–81.

110. Bordewich, *Congress at War*, 241; Lincoln quoted in Varon, *Armies of Deliverance*, 280.

111. Bordewich, *Congress at War*, 11–12, Clement Vallandigham quoted on 12.

112. Bordewich, *Congress at War*, 12–13, 60, 63; Donald, *Lincoln*, 416–17.

113. Bordewich, *Congress at War*, 63–66, Clement Vallandigham quoted on 65; Gallman, *Cacophony of Politics*, 91–93, 101; Manning, *What This Cruel War Was Over*, 99–100; Weber, *Copperheads*, 4–7, 89.

114. Gallman, *Cacophony of Politics*, 162–63; Union soldier quoted in Varon, *Armies of Deliverance*, 280; Neely, *Union Divided*, 48–49, 56–57, 61; Weber, *Copperheads*, 2–4.

115. Bordewich, *Congress at War*, 226–32; Gallman, *Cacophony of Politics*, 119–23; McPherson, *Battle Cry of Freedom*, 596–97, Robert Ould quoted on 598; Paludan, *People's Contest*, 240–44; Weber, *Copperheads*, 95–98.

116. Bordewich, *Congress at War*, 232–33, 241–44, Valandigham banner quoted on 242; Gallman, *Cacophony of Politics*, 184–86; McPherson, *Battle Cry of Freedom*, 597–98, 684–86, Ohio Democrats quoted on 685–86; Weber, *Copperheads*, 98–99.

117. Bordewich, *Congress at War*, 244–46; Donald, *Lincoln*, 442–44, 454–58; Gallman, *Cacophony of Politics*, 187–88; Lincoln quoted in Neely, *Union Divided*, 103.

118. Cooper, *Jefferson Davis*, 461–63; Levine, *Fall of the House of Dixie*, 206–10; McPherson, *Battle Cry of Freedom*, 689–92; Rable, *Confederate Republic*, 234–35.

119. Carwardine, *Lincoln*, 231; Foner, *Fiery Trial*, 266–68, includes Lincoln quotations; Donald, *Lincoln*, 460–66; Goodwin, *Team of Rivals*, 583–87.

120. May, "Irony of Confederate Diplomacy," 95–97; Neely, *Civil War and the Limits of Destruction*, 81–82.

TEN: ELECTIONS

1. Macdonald quoted in Gwyn, *Man Who Made Us*, 242.

2. Juárez quoted in Roeder, *Juárez*, vol. 2:567.

3. Glatthaar, *General Lee's Army*, 357–58; Neely, *Union Divided*, 133–35; Nelson, *Bullets, Ballots, and Rhetoric*, 1–17, Benjamin H. Hill quoted on 14.

4. Rubin, *Shattered Nation*, 66–74, Kate Stone quoted on 66 ("People") and 68 ("We cannot bear").

5. Levine, *Fall of the House of Dixie*, 71–73; McCurry, *Confederate Reckoning*, 124–26; Rable, *Confederate Republic*, 150–53, 163–65, Vance quoted on 163.

6. Levine, *Fall of the House of Dixie*, 202–4; McPherson, *Battle Cry of Freedom*, 695–96; Nelson, *Bullets, Ballots, and Rhetoric*, 45–46; Rable, *Confederate Republic*, 200–205.

7. Levine, *Fall of the House of Dixie*, 213–14, 224; McPherson, *Battle Cry of Freedom*, 696–98, Zebulon Vance quoted on 698; Rable, *Confederate Republic*, 246–47, 265–71.

8. Magruder quoted in Casdorph, *Prince John Magruder*, 304 ("dazzling teeth"); Duncan, "Political Legitimation," 28–29; Hanna and Hanna, *Napoleon III and Mexico*, 96–97; McAllen, *Maximilian and Carlota*, 66–68; Roeder, *Juárez*, vol. 2:560–63.

9. Duncan, "Political Legitimation," 51; McAllen, *Maximilian and Carlota*, 98–99, 123, Maximilian quoted on 98; Ridley, *Maximilian and Juárez*, 147–48.

10. Barker, "France, Austria, and the Mexican Venture," 236–37; Blumberg, *Diplomacy of the Mexican Empire*, 10–13; Hanna and Hanna, *Napoleon III and Mexico*, 99–102; McAllen, *Maximilian and Carlota*, 68–69, 97–101, 117.

11. Cunningham, *Mexico and the Foreign Policy of Napoleon III*, 176–79; Hanna and Hanna, *Napoleon III and Mexico*, 126–27, Jesús Teran quoted on 127.

12. Chartrand and Hook, *Mexican Adventure*, 18–24; Dabbs, *French Army in Mexico*, 86–87; McAllen, *Maximilian and Carlota*, 72–73, 80–81, 84.

13. McAllen, *Maximilian and Carlota*, 85; Ridley, *Maximilian and Juárez*, 122–24; *contra-guerrilla* quoted in Roeder, *Juárez*, vol. 2:608.

14. Dabbs, *French Army in Mexico*, 85; McAllen, *Maximilian and Carlota*, 90–92, Charles Du Pin quoted on 92; Ridley, *Maximilian and Juárez*, 122–26.

15. Dabbs, *French Army in Mexico*, 86–94; McAllen, *Maximilian and Carlota*, 106–7, 111–12; Roeder, *Juárez*, vol. 2:543–44, 574–75.

16. Ford, *Rip Ford's Texas*, 403 ("city"); Irby, *Backdoor at Bagdad*, 23, 43–44; Kerby, *Kirby Smith's Confederacy*, 377–78.

17. Hanna and Hanna, *Napoleon III and Mexico*, 162–63, American consul quoted on 163; McAllen, *Maximilian and Carlota*, 109–10; Tyler, *Santiago Vidaurri*, 133–48; Wasserman, *Capitalists, Caciques, and Revolution*, 31–34.

18. Cunningham, *Mexico and the Foreign Policy of Napoleon III*, 152–53, 174–76, du Barail quoted on 153 ("would have acclaimed"); McAllen, *Maximilian and Carlota*, 108–9, Bazaine quoted on 108 ("Indian masses") and 113 ("reasonable people").

19. Duncan, "Political Legitimation," 32; McAllen, *Maximilian and Carlota*, 108–13, Charles Wyke quoted on 108–9.

20. Hanna and Hanna, *Napoleon III and Mexico*, 111–15, 129–30; O'Connor, *Cactus Throne*, 99–112, Marie Amelie quoted on 100; Roeder, *Juárez*, vol. 2:560, 564–68, Charles François du Barail quoted on 567.

21. Duncan, "Political Legitimation," 39–40, 46–48, 54–58, 61–63; Hanna and Hanna, *Napoleon III and Mexico*, 127–28, 131–32, 138–39; McAllen, *Maximilian and Carlota*, 127–28, 130–38; Roeder, *Juárez*, vol. 2:565, 571, 580–81, Carlota quoted on 580–81.

22. Duncan, "Political Legitimation," 42, 46; McAllen, *Maximilian and Carlota*, 164–66, 197.

23. Duncan, "Political Legitimation," 40–42; O'Connor, *Cactus Throne*, 122–28, José Luis Blasio quoted on 123, Maximilian quoted on 140.

24. Cunningham, *Mexico and the Foreign Policy of Napoleon III*, 182–83; Hanna and Hanna, *Napoleon III and Mexico*, 127–28, Charles Wyke quoted on 128 ("with much cleverness"), Emanuel G. Masseras quoted on 137 ("Promises").

25. McAllen, *Maximilian and Carlota*, 136–40, 144, 221–22; O'Connor, *Cactus Throne*, 150–51, 177–80; Maximilian quoted in Roeder, *Juárez*, vol. 2:588.

26. Duncan, "Political Legitimation," 52–54, 64–66; McAllen, *Maximilian and Carlota*, 142–43, 222–23, Maximilian quoted on 182; Pani, "Juárez vs. Maximiliano," 176–79.

27. Duncan, "Political Legitimation," 34, 48–50; McAllen, *Maximilian and Carlota*, 140–42, 152–53; Pani, "Dreaming of a Mexican Empire," 1–32.

28. Duncan, "Political Legitimation," 33–35; Pani, "Dreaming of a Mexican Empire," 1–32; Pani, "Juárez vs. Maximiliano,"175–78.

29. Pani, "Juárez vs. Maximiliano," 179–80; Roeder, *Juárez*, vol. 2:582–83.

30. McAllen, *Maximilian and Carlota*, 150–55, Maximilian quoted on 250; O'Connor, *Cactus Throne*, 142–46, Carlota quoted on 143–44; Roeder, *Juárez*, vol. 2:571, 585–89, Monsignor Pietro Francesco Meglia quoted on 586, Conservatives quoted on 589.

31. Dabbs, *French Army in Mexico*, 124–25, Louis Adrien de Tuce quoted on 125; McAllen, *Maximilian and Carlota*, 153–55; Ridley, *Maximilian & Juárez*, 180–81.

32. Duncan, "Political Legitimation," 34; McAllen, *Maximilian and Carlota*, 115–16; Roeder, *Juárez*, vol. 2:565–67, Juárez quoted on 590.

33. Seward quoted in Hardy, "South of the Border," 71; Lincoln quoted in Mahoney, *Mexico and the Confederacy*, 53; Ridley, *Maximilian and Juárez*, 115–17; Schoonover, *Dollars over Dominion*, 106–7, 114–15, 161–62, Charles Sumner quoted on 162.

34. Brettle, *Colossal Ambitions*, 171–74; Hanna and Hanna, *Napoleon III and Mexico*, 119–20, 123–26; P. J. Kelly, "Cat's Paw," 61–62, 74–76.

35. Downs, "Mexicanization of American Politics," 394–95; Neely, *Civil War and the Limits of Destruction*, 80–83, Amzi Wood quoted on 81; Schoonover, *Dollars over Dominion,* 115, 119–20, 128–30.

36. Case and Spencer, *The United States and France*, 516–25, Cazotte quoted on 523.

37. Schoonover, *Dollars over Dominion*, 107, 115–18, Thaddeus Stevens quoted on 118.

38. Hanna and Hanna, *Napoleon III and Mexico*, 124–25; Schoonover, *Dollars over Dominion*, 120–24, 170–71, Davis resolution quoted on 121; Stahr, *Seward*, 394–95.

39. Careless, *Brown of the Globe*, vol. 2:117–23; Creighton, *John A. Macdonald*, vol. 1:345–53, Macdonald quoted on 345; Moore, *1867*, 17–20.

40. Careless, *Brown of the Globe*, vol. 2:131–36; Gwyn, *Man Who Made Us*, 287–89; Moore, *1867*, 1–5, 13–16, 27–28, 209; Morton, *Critical Years*, 144–47.

41. Gwyn, *Man Who Made Us*, 279–85, 292–93, Macdonald quoted on 307; Moore, *1867*, 206–7; Winks, *Canada and the United States*, 338–39.

42. Beasley, "British Views of Canada," 167–68; Stacey, "Britain's Withdrawal from North America," 187–90; Gladstone quoted in Gwyn, *Man Who Made Us*, 341.

43. Careless, *Brown of the Globe*, vol. 2:139–46, George Brown quoted on 140 ("the power") and 144 ("unanimity"); Gwyn, *Man Who Made Us*, 289–90, 298–99; Martin, *Britain and the Origins of Canadian Confederation*, 20–21.

44. Gwyn, *Man Who Made Us*, 300–302, Arthur Gordon quoted on 302; Moore, *1867*, 45–47; Morton, *Critical Years*, 148–50.

45. Careless, *Brown of the Globe*, vol. 2:153–59; Gwyn, *Man Who Made Us*, 302–8, Macdonald quoted on 308; Moore, *1867*, 49–60; Morton, *Critical Years*, 151–53; P. B. Waite, *Life and Times of Confederation*, 73–84.

46. Creighton, *John A. Macdonald*, vol. 1:370–82; Gwyn, *Man Who Made Us*, 309–15; Moore, *1867*, 101–13, 129–31, 209–10; Phenix, *Private Demons*, 166–67, Feo Monck quoted on 166; P. B. Waite, *Life and Times of Confederation*, 86–103.

47. Careless, *Brown of the Globe*, vol. 2:185–86; Gwyn, *Man Who Made Us*, 345–55; Moore, *1867*, 148–49, 153–55, critic quoted on 148.

48. Careless, *Brown of the Globe*, vol. 2:183–85, Brown quoted on 185; Gwyn, *Man Who Made Us*, 349–54, 430, D'Arcy McGee quoted on 349.

49. Einolf, *George Thomas*, 235–37; Hess, *Civil War in the West*, 221; J. Waugh, *U. S. Grant*, 79–81.

50. Varon, *Armies of Deliverance*, 88–89, Grant quoted on 89.

51. Glatthaar, *General Lee's Army*, 364–68; Trudeau, "Walls of 1864," 414–19; J. Waugh, *U. S. Grant*, 83–85, Longstreet quoted on 85.

52. Hutton, "Paladin of the Republic," 349–54, Lincoln quoted on 349; Union officer quoted in Osborne, *Jubal*, 313–14; J. M. Taylor, "Hawk in the Fowlyard," 318–19.

53. Gallagher et al., *Civil War*, 192–98, witness quoted on 197; Glatthaar, *General Lee's Army*, 368–71; Trudeau, "Walls of 1864," 413–14, 419–22.

54. McPherson, *Battle Cry of Freedom*, 731–34, Captain Oliver Wendell Holmes, Jr., quoted on 734; Waugh, *U. S. Grant*, 85–86, Ulysses S. Grant quoted on 86.

55. Gallagher et al., *Civil War*, 198–200, Evander M. Law quoted on 200; Glatthaar, *General Lee's Army*, 373–77; McPherson, *Battle Cry of Freedom*, 734–35, Meade quoted on 735; E. M. Thomas, *Robert E. Lee*, 329–31, 334.

56. Glatthaar, *General Lee's Army*, 378–79; McPherson, *Battle Cry of Freedom*, 735–41, Union officer quoted on 735; E. M. Thomas, *Robert E. Lee*, 336–42, Lee quoted on 342; Trudeau, "Walls of 1864," 426–28.

57. McPherson, *Battle Cry of Freedom*, 741–43, Gouverneur K. Warren quoted on 742 ("For thirty days"), John H. Martindale quoted on 742 ("great discouragement"); Waugh, *U. S. Grant*, 87.

58. Gallagher, ed., *Fighting for the Confederacy*, 448–59; J. D. Smith, "Let Us All Be Grateful," 58–60; Varon, *Armies of Deliverance*, 345–46.

59. Gallagher et al., *Civil War*, 209–10, John C. C. Sanders quoted on 209 ("mowed down"), Confederate quoted on 210 ("the jubilee"); Glatthaar, *General Lee's Army*, 424–25; McPherson, *Battle Cry of Freedom*, 759–60, Grant quoted on 760.

60. Ayers, *Thin Light of Freedom*, 153–68, 174–83, Yankee soldier quoted on 160; Brady, *War Upon the Land*, 74–79; Gallagher, "Shenandoah Valley in 1864," 1–3; Osborne, *Jubal*, 245–60.

61. Ayers, *Thin Light of Freedom*, 200–4; McPherson, *Battle Cry of Freedom*, 739, 756–57; Osborne, *Jubal*, 261–93; Osborne, "Jubal Early's Raid on Washington," 446–58.

62. Ayers, *Thin Light of Freedom*, 204–17, Joseph Clark quoted on 214; Osborne, *Jubal*, 302–11.

63. Ayers, *Thin Light of Freedom*, 218–21; Democratic newspaper editor quoted in Osborne, "Jubal Early's Raid on Washington," 457 ("Lincoln is"); Weber, *Copperheads*, 142–43, 151–54, Gideon Welles quoted on 143, newspaper editor quoted on 151 ("Lottery").

64. Einolf, *George Thomas*, 239–46; Hess, *Civil War in the West*, 210–15; McPherson, *Battle Cry of Freedom*, 743–45; Symonds, *Joseph E. Johnston*, 261–63, 269–311.

65. Connolly, *Autumn of Glory*, 359–65; Hess, *Civil War in the West*, 215–17; Symonds, *Joseph E. Johnston*, 312–19; Watkins, *Company Aytch*, 130–37, quotation on 133.

66. Hess, *Civil War in the West*, 219–23, John W. Geary quoted on 220; Symonds, *Joseph E. Johnston*, 263–65; Watkins, *Company Aytch*, 117–29.

67. McPherson, *Battle Cry of Freedom*, 752–54, Robert E. Lee quoted on 753; Symonds, *Joseph E. Johnston*, 249–50, 320–32; Watkins, *Company Aytch*, 142–44.

68. Connolly, *Autumn of Glory*, 429–56; Einolf, *George Thomas*, 250–53; Hess, *Civil War in the West*, 223–26; Watkins, *Company Aytch*, 145–56.

69. Bordewich, *Congress at War*, 303–5; Thurlow Weed quoted in McPherson, *Battle Cry of Freedom*, 761; Weber, *Copperheads*, 151–54.

70. Gallman, *Cacophony of Politics*, 237–38; Brick Pomeroy quoted in Paludan, *People's Contest*, 233; Weber, *Copperheads*, 159–60, 167–68.

71. Nelson, *Bullets, Ballots, and Rhetoric*, 114–15, 128–33, 160–61; Schott, *Alexander H. Stephens*, 425–29; Weber, *Copperheads*, 155–56, 170–72.

72. Gallman, *Cacophony of Politics*, 242–44, 247–50; Neely, *Lincoln and the Democrats*, 124–29; J. C. Waugh, *Reelecting Lincoln*, 298–302, McClellan quoted on 301.

73. Levine, *Fall of the House of Dixie*, 189, 191–92, Lincoln's amnesty proclamation quoted on 191; Wendell Phillips quoted in McPherson, *Battle Cry of Freedom*, 716; Varon, *Armies of Deliverance*, 306–12, 339–40, 342–44.

74. Bordewich, *Congress at War*, 318–19, George T. Strong quoted on 319 ("old Roger"); Goodwin, *Team of Rivals*, 603–9; Lowenstein, *Ways and Means*, 217–39; McPherson, *Battle Cry of Freedom*, 714–15, Benjamin Wade quoted on 715.

75. Bordewich, *Congress at War*, 317–18, 322–24; Goodwin, *Team of Rivals*, 658–61, Clark E. Carr quoted on 625; J. C. Waugh, *Reelecting Lincoln*, 145–47, 172–81.

76. Goodwin, *Team of Rivals*, 623–26, *New York Times* quoted on 664; Neely, *Union Divided*, 158–67; Varon, *Armies of Deliverance*, 341–42, 364–65.

77. Nelson, *Bullets, Ballots, and Rhetoric*, 110–11; J. C. Waugh, *Reelecting Lincoln*, 281; Weber, *Copperheads*, 166.

78. Weber, *Copperheads*, 145–46, 165–66, 178–79, T. C. Smithton quoted on 145 ("among neighbors"), Iowa woman quoted on 165.

79. Bordewich, *Congress at War*, 320–22, "miscegenation" quoted on 321; McPherson, *Battle Cry of Freedom*, 788–91, *New York Freeman's Journal* quoted on 790 ("Filthy"); J. C. Waugh, *Reelecting Lincoln*, 314–21.

80. Bordewich, *Congress at War*, 308–10; McPherson, *Battle Cry of Freedom*, 769–71, Abraham Lincoln quoted on 769 ("But no" and "Why should") and 771 ("I am going").

81. Hess, *Civil War in the West*, 282–83; McPherson, *War on the Waters*, 207–12.

82. Connolly, *Autumn of Glory*, 459–69; Hess, *Civil War in the West*, 229–31; McPherson, *Battle Cry of Freedom*, 774–75, Mary Chesnut quoted on 775; Nelson, *Bullets, Ballots, and Rhetoric*, 118–21, Augusta *Chronicle & Sentinel* quoted on 120.

83. Ayers, *Thin Light of Freedom*, 227–28, 232–34, 244–45; Osborne, *Jubal*, 312–48; Varon, *Armies of Deliverance*, 360–61.

84. Brady, *War Upon the Land,* 79–90, Grant quoted on 80, Norval Baker quoted on 81 ("We could always"), Wilbur Fisk quoted on 84 ("teaching"); Sheridan quoted in Hutton, "Paladin of the Republic," 357; Osborne, *Jubal*, 324–25, 349–50, Frank Myers quoted on 350 ("smoky trail").

85. Ayers, *Thin Light of Freedom*, 249–50; Hutton, "Paladin of the Republic," 355–56; Osborne, *Jubal*, 357–84, Confederate officer quoted on 377.

86. Cutrer, *Theater of a Separate War*, 407–10; Etcheson, *Bleeding Kansas*, 242–45; Neely, *Civil War and the Limits of Destruction*, 50–52; Trudeau, "Battle of Westport," 473–79, Confederates quoted on 484.

87. Cutrer, *Theater of a Separate War*, 410–20; Kerby, *Kirby Smith's Confederacy*, 346–52, 356–60; Trudeau, "Battle of Westport," 480–85, Confederate officer quoted on 485.

88. Bordewich, *Congress at War*, 317–18, 324–27, Lincoln quoted on 327; Gallman, *Cacophony of Politics*, 269–71; J. C. Waugh, *Reelecting Lincoln*, 338–50.

89. Bordewitch, *Congress at War*, 330–37; Foner, *Fiery Trial*, 312–13, James S. Rollins quoted on 313; Varon, *Armies of Deliverance*, 392–94.

90. Blight, *Frederick Douglass*, 453–54, Charles Douglass quoted on 454; Foner, *Fiery Trial*, 313–14; Oakes, *Freedom National*, 479–81.

91. Freehling, *The South vs The South*, 189–91; Levine, *Fall of the House of Dixie*, 166–67, Patrick Cleburne quoted on 167 ("our most," and "to face and fight"); McCurry, *Confederate Reckoning*, 325–28, Cleburne quoted on 327 ("The negro").

92. Freehling, *South vs The South*, 190–92; McCurry, *Confederate Reckoning*, 328–29; Confederate general quoted in Rable, *Confederate Republic*, 287.

93. Davis quoted in W. C. Davis, *Jefferson Davis*, 599; Freehling, *South vs The South*, 192–94; McCurry, *Confederate Reckoning*, 330–36; Rubin, *Shattered Nation,* 105–6.

94. Freehling, *South vs The South*, 192–94, Howell Cobb quoted on 194; Rable, *Confederate Republic*, 288–90, Henry Chambers quoted on 288.

95. Manning, *What This Cruel War Was Over*, 207–11; Rable, *Confederate Republic*, 289–90, J. Francis Maides quoted on 290 ("I did not"); Rubin, *Shattered Nation*, 107–10, B. H. Anthony quoted on 109 ("I think").

96. King, *Louis T. Wigfall*, 205–8, 213–14; Levine, *Fall of the House of Dixie*, 250–52; McCurry, *Confederate Reckoning*, 337–40.

97. Doyle, *Cause of All Nations*, 275–79; Foreman, *World on Fire*, 731–32, 742–44; Owsley, *King Cotton Diplomacy*, 531–41.

98. Ayers, *Thin Light of Freedom*, 310–11; McCurry, *Confederate Reckoning*, 340–42, 345–57, Ethelbert Barksdale quoted on 349; Rubin, *Shattered Nation*, 108–9.

99. Freehling, *The South vs The South*, 194–96; Levine, *Fall of the House of Dixie*, 256–58; Rable, *Confederate Republic*, 289–90; Thomas, *Confederate Nation*, 296–97.

100. Sherman quoted in Connelly, *John M. Schofield*, 119–20 ("I can make"); Hess, *Civil War in the West*, 247–52; McPherson, *Battle Cry of Freedom*, 807–9, Sherman quoted on 808 ("smashing things").

101. Hess, *Civil War in the West*, 248; McPherson, *Battle Cry of Freedom*, 808–9, Sherman quoted on 809 ("We are not only"); Paludan, *People's Contest*, 303–4, John Bell Hood and Sherman quoted on 303 ("in studied" and "You who").

102. Brady, *War Upon the Land*, 96–107; Hess, *Civil War in the West*, 258–63; McPherson, *Battle Cry of Freedom*, 809–11, Union officer quoted on 809 ("most gigantic"), soldier quoted on 810 ("destroyed all").

103. Einolf, *George Thomas*, 257–59; McPherson, *Battle Cry of Freedom*, 811–12; Waugh, *U. S. Grant*, 207.

104. Connelly, *John M. Schofield*, 122–30; Einolf, *George Thomas*, 259–60; Hess, *Civil War in the West*, 252–54; Watkins, *Company Aytch*, 196–201.

105. Connelly, *John M. Schofield*, 132–39; Watkins, *Company Aytch*, 201–4, quotation on 203.

106. Connelly, *John M. Schofield*, 139–41; Einolf, *George Thomas*, 260–68, Edwin M. Stanton quoted on 263; Hess, *Civil War in the West*, 255–56.

107. Connelly, *John M. Schofield*, 142–44; Connolly, *Autumn of Glory*, 509–12; Einolf, *George Thomas*, 268–80; Watkins, *Company Aytch*, 205–9, quotation on 206.

108. Bailey, "USCT in the Confederate Heartland," 232–40, Thomas quoted on 239 ("Gentlemen"); Einolf, *George Thomas*, 273–74, 277–78, 287–89, Thomas quoted on 274 ("Well").

109. Connolly, *Autumn of Glory*, 512–14; Watkins, *Company Aytch*, 206–10, quotation on 206 ("feeble"), 209 ("pulling"), and 209–10 ("once proud").

110. Einolf, *George Thomas*, 281–82; McPherson, *Battle Cry of Freedom*, 815–16, Mary Chesnut quoted on 815, Josiah Gorgas quoted on 816.

111. Nelson, *Bullets, Ballots, and Rhetoric*, 165–67, James Holcombe quoted on 166 ("anarchy"); Winks, *Canada and the United States*, 264–65, John B. Jones quoted on 303 ("A war").

112. Brandt, *Man Who Tried to Burn New York*, 155–58; Foreman, *World on Fire*, 678–82, 721; Morton, *Critical Years*, 163; Winks, *Canada and the United States*, 287–91.

113. Brandt, *Man Who Tried to Burn New York*, 93–124, 225–31; Foreman, *World on Fire*, 717–19; Neely, *Civil War and the Limits of Destruction*, 143–44.

114. Foreman, *World on Fire*, 698–99; Stuart, *United States Expansionism*, 180–81; Winks, *Canada and the United States*, 298–300, raider quoted on 299.

115. Careless, *Brown of the Globe*, vol. 2:180–81, Chicago *Tribune* quoted on 181; Stahr, *Seward*, 411, 414–15; Winks, *Canada and the United States*, 301–15.

116. Morton, *Critical Years*, 171–72; Stuart, *United States Expansionism*, 181–82; Winks, *Canada and the United States*, 305–6, 317–22, 326–36.
117. Gwyn, *Man Who Made Us*, 335–36; Morton, *Critical Years*, 186; Stuart, *United States Expansionism*, 196–214; Winks, *Canada and the United States*, 341–47.
118. Buckner, "Creation of the Dominion of Canada," 67–68; Gwyn, *Man Who Made Us*, 349–54, 430, Christopher Dunkin quoted on 353n.
119. William T. Sherman quoted in Paludan, *People's Contest*, 302.

ELEVEN: BORDERS

 1. Sheridan quoted in West, *Essential West*, 108.
 2. Sheridan quoted in R. White, *Republic for Which it Stands*, 112.
 3. H. McPherson, "The Plan of William McKendree Gwin," 379–80; Ulysses S. Grant to Irvin McDowell, Jan. 8, 1865, in Simon., ed., *Papers of Ulysses S. Grant*, vol. 13:250–51; L. Thomas, *Between Two Empires*, 327–31.
 4. Brettle, *Colossal Ambitions*, 169–71, 203–4; St. John, "Unpredictable America of William Gwin," 70; L. Thomas, *Between Two Empires*, 270–79, 284–93.
 5. H. McPherson, "The Plan of William McKendree Gwin," 363–70, Sara Yorke Stevenson quoted on 370n54; St. John, "Unpredictable America of William Gwin," 71–72; L. Thomas, *Between Two Empires*, 293–308, 311–14.
 6. Brettle, *Colossal Ambitions*, 210–11; Cooper, *Jefferson Davis*, 547–49; Doyle, *Cause of All Nations*, 286–87; Matías Romero, Jan. 10, 1865, dispatch, in Schoonover, ed., *Mexican Lobby*, 51–52; Ulysses S. Grant to Francis P. Blair, Jan. 8, 1865, in Simon, ed., *Papers of Ulysses S. Grant*, vol. 13:354–55.
 7. Doyle, *Cause of All Nations*, 287–88.
 8. Hardy, "South of the Border," 69–70; R. R. Miller, "Lew Wallace and the French Intervention," 31–34; Morsberger, *Lew Wallace*, 158–63, Susan Wallace quoted on 163 ("You know"); Lew Wallace to Ulysses S. Grant, in Simon, ed., *Papers of Ulysses S. Grant*, vol. 13:282–83 ("I will wager you").
 9. Hanna and Hanna, *Napoleon III and Mexico*, 147–49, 153–54, 236–38; Hardy, "South of the Border," 69–73, Grant quoted on 70, Seward quoted on 71.
 10. Morsberger, *Lew Wallace*, 159–60; Parks, *Edmund Kirby Smith*, 447–48.
 11. Kerby, *Kirby Smith's Confederacy*, 323–31; Parks, *Edmund Kirby Smith*, 403–19; Settles, *John Bankhead Magruder*, 271–75, Kirby Smith quoted on 272.
 12. Ford, *Rip Ford's Texas*, 388–89; Kerby, *Kirby Smith's Confederacy*, 371–73, John Walker quoted on 372; Morsberger, *Lew Wallace*, 161–65; Wallace to Grant, Mar. 14, 1865, in Simon, ed., *Ulysses S. Grant*, vol. 13:285–87, quote on 286 ("to see his state").
 13. Doyle, *Cause of All Nations*, 274–79; Kerby, *Kirby Smith's Confederacy*, 373–74; Wallace to Grant, Mar. 14 and Apr. 18, 1865, in Simon, ed., *Ulysses S. Grant*, vol. 13: 287–90.
 14. Goodwin, *Team of Rivals*, 690–91, Davis and Lincoln quoted on 691; McPherson, *Battle Cry of Freedom*, 821–22.
 15. Cooper, *Jefferson Davis*, 548–50; Goodwin, *Team of Rivals*, 691–95, Stephens quoted on 693; Schott, *Alexander H. Stephens*, 442–47.
 16. Cooper, *Jefferson Davis*, 551–52, Stephens quoted on 552; Goodwin, *Team of Rivals*, 695–96; Schott, *Alexander H. Stephens*, 447–49.

17. McPherson, *War on the Waters*, 213–19; Quatman, *Young General*, 211–12.

18. Ayers, *Thin Light of Freedom*, 252; Zebulon Vance quoted in Levine, *Fall of the House of Dixie*, 241; Rubin, *Shattered Nation*, 75–77, doctor quoted on 77; Mary Chesnut quoted in Symonds, *Joseph E. Johnston*, 353.

19. Brady, *War Upon the Land*, 108–11, Sherman quoted on 108; Hess, *Civil War in the West*, 268; McPherson, *Battle Cry of Freedom*, 825–27.

20. Brady, *War Upon the Land*, 111–19; Connolly, *Autumn of Glory*, 520–21; Hess, *Civil War in the West*, 268–71; Symonds, *Joseph E. Johnston*, 339–48.

21. Egerton, *Wars of Reconstruction*, 1–2, Sidney Andrews quoted on 1.

22. Brady, *War Upon the Land*, 119–21; Hess, *Civil War in the West*, 274–78, 286–87, Johnston quoted on 287; Symonds, *Joseph E. Johnston*, 339–48.

23. Calkins, "Land Operations in Virginia," 2–7; Glatthaar, *General Lee's Army*, 457–59; Varon, *Armies of Deliverance*, 399–400.

24. Manning, *What This Cruel War Was Over*, 213–15; McFall, "To Danville," 72–74; Varon, *Armies of Deliverance*, 400–1, Confederate captain quoted on 401.

25. Foner, *Fiery Trial*, 328–29, Garland H. White quoted on 328; Manning, *What This Cruel War Was Over*, 213–15; McPherson, *Battle Cry of Freedom*, 846–47, Lincoln quoted on 846; Varon, *Armies of Deliverance*, 401–3.

26. Glatthaar, *General Lee's Army*, 459–61; Janney, *Ends of War*, 7–8; McFall, "To Danville," 71–72; Varon, *Appomattox*, 7–12; Waugh, *U. S. Grant*, 98–99.

27. Glatthaar, *General Lee's Army*, 461–64; Janney, *Ends of War*, 8–13; Varon, *Appomattox*, 12–16, Elisha Hunt Rhodes quoted on 14.

28. Glatthaar, *General Lee's Army*, 462–64, 470; Janney, *Ends of War*, 13–17, 21–23, 26–29, 87, 92–93; Varon, *Appomattox*, 19–25, 33–78; Waugh, *U. S. Grant*, 98–99.

29. Gallagher, "Upon their Success," 100–103, Kate Stone quoted on 100 ("Our only hope"), Henry A. Wise quoted on 101–2, Eliza Andrews quoted on 102; Glatthaar, *General Lee's Army*, 464–65, 470–71; Rubin, *Shattered Nation*, 132–34.

30. Foner, *Fiery Trial*, 330–32, John Wilkes Booth quoted on 332; Goodwin, *Team of Rivals*, 726–28; Stahr, *Seward*, 433–34; Varon, *Appomattox*, 115–17.

31. Carwardine, *Lincoln*, 315–16; Gideon Welles quoted in Foner, *Fiery Trial*, 332; Goodwin, *Team of Rivals*, 731–745; Varon, *Appomattox*, 135–36.

32. Goodwin, *Team of Rivals*, 744–45, Seward quoted on 744; Stahr, *Seward*, 438–40.

33. Carwardine, *Lincoln*, 316–21; Benito Juárez quoted in Roeder, *Juárez*, vol. 2:600–1; Grant quoted in Waugh, *U. S. Grant*, 112.

34. Carwardine, *Lincoln*, 316–17; Foner, *Fiery Trial*, 332–33; Samuel D. Barnes quoted in Hermann, *Pursuit of a Dream*, 64.

35. Blight, *Frederick Douglass*, 460–62, Douglass quoted on 462.

36. Horton, *Harriet Tubman*, 74–75; Oertel, *Harriet Tubman*, 79–84.

37. Allmendinger, *Ruffin*, 152–54, 184–85, Ruffin quoted on 153 ("The End"); Ruffin quoted in P. J. Kelly, "North American Crisis of the 1860s," 349 ("would rather"); Walther, *Fire-Eaters*, 228–30, 268–70, Ruffin quoted on 229 ("I here declare"), Edmund Ruffin, Jr. quoted on 269.

38. Cooper, *Jefferson Davis*, 563–66; W. C. Davis, *Jefferson Davis*, 604–27, Davis quoted on 608 ("impossible"), John Dooley quoted on 627 ("Poor President"); Janney, *Ends of War*, 124–25; Rubin, *Shattered Nation*, 119, 135–38, Davis quoted on 119 ("Nothing").

39. W. C. Davis, *Jefferson Davis*, 626–39, Preston Johnson quoted on 626 ("I fear"),

John Taylor Wood quoted on 626 ("We are"); Janney, *Ends of War*, 70, 85, 100; Levine, *Fall of the House of Dixie*, 281–82.

40. W. C. Davis, *Jefferson Davis*, 622–25; Janney, *Ends of War*, 94–95, 124–28, Joseph E. Johnston quoted on 125 ("It would be" and "complete the devastation"), W. H. Andrews quoted on 125 ("It was nothing"); Levine, *Fall of the House of Dixie*, 278–79, Johnston quoted on 278 ("melting").

41. Hess, *War in the West*, 287–89, Sherman quoted on 288 ("in its last"); Janney, *Ends of War*, 94–95, 125–34, Sherman quoted on 134 ("produce Peace"); Symonds, *Joseph E. Johnston*, 353–57; Varon, *Appomattox*, 151–52.

42. W. C. Davis, *Jefferson Davis*, 625–26; Hess, *Civil War in the West*, 289–91, Johnston quoted on 290; Janney, *Ends of War*, 145–47, 157–59, Edwin Stanton quoted on 146; Symonds, *Joseph E. Johnston*, 357; Varon, *Armies of Deliverance*, 419–20.

43. Cooper, *Jefferson Davis*, 566–75; Hess, *Civil War in the West*, 291–96; Rubin, *Shattered Nation*, 135–38; Varon, *Armies of Deliverance*, 420–21.

44. Gallagher, *Union War*, 12–13; Romero, dispatch, May 30, 1865, in Schoonover, ed., *Mexican Lobby*, 64; Sheridan, *Personal Memoirs*, vol. 2:208–9; Ulysses S. Grant to Philip H. Sheridan, May 17, 1865, in Simon, ed., *Papers of Ulysses S. Grant*, vol. 15:43–44; Varon, *Appomattox*, 154–56.

45. Grant to Edward R. S. Canby, May 18, 1865, Sheridan to John A. Rawlins, June 13, 1865, and Grant to Andrew Johnson, June 19, 1865, in Simon, ed., *Papers of Ulysses S. Grant*, vol. 15:50–51, 148n, and 156–58, quote on 156; Sheridan, *Personal Memoirs*, vol. 2:209–11, quotation on 210.

46. Hardy, "South of the Border," 72–73; R. R. Miller, "Matías Romero," 242–43, Romero quoted on 243 ("Grant could not"); Romero dispatches, Apr. 30, 1865, and May 8, 16, and 20, 1865, in Schoonover, ed., *Mexican Lobby*, 58, 59–60 ("although"), 60–61 and 63.

47. Barr, *All the Days of My Life*, 107 (Amelia Barr quotes); Kerby, *Kirby Smith's Confederacy*, 420–29, private quoted on 421 ("We ar[e] ready"); Rolle, *Lost Cause*, 49–52, J. J. Reynolds quoted on 52 ("The thing").

48. Barr, *All the Days of My Life*, 107–8; R. B. Campbell, *Empire for Slavery*, 249–50.

49. Kerby, *Kirby Smith's Confederacy*, 412–15, 425–26, Smith quoted on 426 ("Soldiers!"); Smith quoted in H. McPherson, "The Plan of William McKendree Gwin," 384 ("vassalage"); Parks, *Edmund Kirby Smith*, 451–52, 469–70, 473–82, Smith quoted on 473 ("to escape").

50. Sutherland, *Confederate Carpetbaggers*, 10–21, Eliza Frances Andrews quoted on 11, John R. Baylor quoted on 20; W. W. Reid, *After the War*, 211–12.

51. Blair, *Why Didn't the North Hang Some Rebels*, 12–13; Gould, *Alexander Watkins Terrell*, 45–48; Parks, *Edmund Kirby Smith*, 481–82, 485–86, Smith quoted on 48; Wahlstrom, *Southern Exodus to Mexico*, 58–60, 74.

52. O'Flaherty, *General Jo Shelby*, 1–8.

53. Jubal Early quoted in Gallagher, *Lee and His Generals*, 202 ("to get out" and "could scalp"); Early to Thomas L. Rosser, May 10, 1866, in Hoyt, ed., "New Light on General Jubal A. Early," 115 ("I went"); Rolle, *Lost Cause*, 122–24.

54. Gould, *Alexander Watkins Terrell*, 48–50; Hanna and Hanna, *Napoleon III and Mexico*, 224–26; Mahoney, *Mexico and the Confederacy*, 125–26; McAllen, *Maximilian and Juárez*, 179–86, 190; Rolle, *Lost Cause*, 75–77.

55. Lewis, *Matthew Fontaine Maury*, 197–98; Parks, *Edmund Kirby Smith*, 482–83, Smith quoted on 482; Mahoney, *Mexico and the Confederacy*, 127–28; Rolle, *Lost Cause*, 114–16; Settles, *John Bankhead Magruder*, 281–83.

56. Casdorph, *Prince John Magruder*, 303; Mahoney, *Mexico and the Confederacy*, 158–60; Rolle, *Lost Cause*, 114–16, Yankee critic quoted on 185–86.

57. Alphonse Dano quoted in Hanna and Hanna, *Napoleon III and Mexico*, 304 ("all at once"); H. McPherson, "Plan of William McKendree Gwin," 375–76; L. Thomas, *Between Two Empires*, 337–42, Gwin quoted on 338.

58. Matías Romero, dispatches, June 18 and 24, and July 8, 1865, in Schoonover, *Mexican Lobby*, 68, 70–71, and 75–76; L. Thomas, *Between Two Empires*, 340–47, William M. Gwin, Jr., quoted on 342.

59. H. McPherson, "Plan of William McKendree Gwin," 371–72, 376–78; Quinn, *The Rivals*, 292–93, Maximilian quoted on 293; Rolle, *Lost Cause*, 63–65; L. Thomas, *Between Two Empires*, 315–26, 333, 348–66, Gwin quoted on 351.

60. Roeder, *Juárez*, vol. 2:598–602, Juárez quoted on 599; Matías Romero dispatch, April 24, 1865, in Schoonover, ed., *Mexican Lobby*, 55–57, quotation on 55.

61. Hanna and Hanna, *Napoleon III and Mexico*, 118–19, 221–23, Maury quoted on 119; Majewski and Wahlstrom, "Geography as Power," 342–46, 348–49.

62. Matthew F. Maury quoted in Hanna and Hanna, *Napoleon III and Mexico*, 230; Majewski and Wahlstrom, "Geography as Power," 350–51, 355–56.

63. A. J. Hanna, "Role of Matthew Fontaine Maury," 109–16; Lewis, *Matthew Fontaine Maury*, 189–91, 194–97; Rolle, *Lost Cause*, 136–40.

64. A. J. Hanna, "Role of Matthew Fontaine Maury," 118–19, Dutch captain quoted on 118; Rolle, *Lost Cause*, 134–40, Maury son-in-law quoted on 136.

65. Majewski and Wahlstrom, "Geography as Power," 354–55; Wahlstrom, *Southern Exodus to Mexico*, 15–17, Maximilian's decree quoted on 16.

66. A. J. Hanna, "Role of Matthew Fontaine Maury," 119–20, Dabney H. Maury quoted on 119 ("They are"); Rolle, *Lost Cause*, 116–17, refugee quoted on 116 ("He blacks"); Worley, ed., "Letter Written by General Thomas C. Hindman," 366–67 ("All our Negroes").

67. Rolle, *Lost Cause*, 89–99, William M. Anderson quoted on 94; Settles, *John Bankhead Magruder*, 288–91; Wahlstrom, *Southern Exodus to Mexico*, 23, 27.

68. A. J. Hanna, "Role of Matthew Fontaine Maury," 119–20, Robert E. Lee quoted on 119, Maury quoted on 120; Rolle, *Lost Cause*, 140–50, Thomas C. Reynolds quoted on 150 ("Maury's"); Sutherland, *Confederate Carpetbaggers*, 21–23.

69. Hanna and Hanna, *Napoleon III and Mexico*, 231–34; McAllen, *Maximilian and Carlota*, 240–41, Sherman quoted on 240; Sheridan to Grant, Nov. 26, 1865, and Feb. 7, 1866, in Simon, ed., *Papers of Ulysses S. Grant*, vol. 15:425n–427n.

70. Schoonover, *Dollars over Dominion*, 195–96, Sheridan quoted on 195 ("We can never"); Sheridan, *Personal Memoirs*, vol. 2:211–13; Sheridan to Grant, June 28, 1865, and Nov. 5, 1865, in Simon, ed., *Papers of Ulysses S. Grant*, vol. 15:163n ("a swindle"), and 364n ("old contest").

71. Sheridan, *Personal Memoirs*, vol. 2:213–28, quotations on 214 ("ample" and "had not"), 215 ("taking care" and "wildfire"), and 222 ("a party"); Sheridan to Grant, July 1, 1865, July 14, and 25, Aug. 1 and 13, and Sept. 22, 1865, in Simon, ed., *Papers of Ulysses S. Grant*, vol. 15:237–38n ("Affairs"), 240n, and 260–61n, 285–86, 298, 366n–367n.

72. Hardy, "South of the Border," 76–78; Romero, dispatch, June 18, 1865, in Schoonover ed., *Mexican Lobby*, 66–68, quotation on 67; Ulysses S. Grant to Edwin M. Stanton, June 20, 1865, in Simon, ed., *Papers of Ulysses S. Grant*, vol. 15:205–6; Gideon Welles quoted in Stahr, *Seward*, 443.

73. Juárez quoted in Schoonover, *Dollars over Dominion*, 209; Matías Romero, dispatches, July 8, Aug. 19, and Oct. 28, 1865, in Schoonover, ed., *Mexican Lobby*, 76–77, 91–92, 102; Seward to Stanton, June 15 and July 5, 1865; Grant to Sheridan, July 30, 1866; and Sheridan to Grant, Oct. n.d., 1866, in Simon, ed., *Papers of Ulysses S. Grant*, vol. 15:147n, 237n, and vol. 16:267 ("Seward is"), and 323.

74. Hanna and Hanna, *Napoleon III and Mexico*, 147–49, 153–54, 263–65.

75. Downs, *After Appomattox*, 89–90; Romero, dispatch, May 20, 1865, in Schoonover, ed., *Mexican Lobby*, 62 ("before"); Sheridan to Grant, Sept. 21, 1865, in Simon, ed., *Papers of Ulysses S. Grant*, vol. 15: 365n–366n.

76. Connelly, *John M. Schofield*, 182–83; Hanna and Hanna, *Napoleon III and Mexico*, 239–43; Hardy, "South of the Border," 78–79; Romero, dispatches, May 30, June 27 and 28, and July 19 and 30, 1865, in Schoonover, ed., *Mexican Lobby*, 64, 71–72, 72–74, 81, and 83–90, quotation on 73; Grant to Andrew Johnson, July 15, 1865, in Simon, ed., *Papers of Ulysses S. Grant*, vol. 15:264–65.

77. Connelly, *John M. Schofield*, 183–86; Hardy, "South of the Border," 79–80; Matías Romero dispatches, July 30, Aug. 4, and Nov. 4, 1865, in Schoonover, ed., *Mexican Lobby*, 89, 90–91, and 103–4; Grant to Philip H. Sheridan, Oct. 22, 1865, in Simon, ed., *Papers of Ulysses S. Grant*, vol. 15:362–63; Seward quoted in Stahr, *Seward*, 444 ("he must" and "squelch[ed]").

78. R. R. Miller, "Lew Wallace and the French Intervention," 41–43; Morsberger, *Lew Wallace*, 196–98, L. Wallace quoted on 196, Susan Wallace quoted on 198.

79. R. R. Miller, "Lew Wallace and the French Intervention," 41–42; Sheridan quoted in Matías Romero, dispatch, Nov. 24, 1865, in Schoonover, ed., *Mexican Lobby*, 106; Sheridan to Grant, Nov. 5, 1865, in Simon, ed., *Papers of Ulysses S. Grant*, vol. 15:363n–364n.

80. McAllen, *Maximilian and Carlota*, 205, 249–50; Miller, "Herman Sturm," 1–15; Morsberger, *Lew Wallace*, 196–97; Schoonover, *Dollars over Dominion*, 137–38.

81. Schoonover, *Dollars over Dominion*, 196–201, Sheridan quoted on 196; Matías Romero, dispatch, Oct. 7, 1865, in Schoonover, ed., *Mexican Lobby*, 96; Sheridan, *Personal Memoirs*, vol. 2:224–28.

82. French soldier quoted in Hanna and Hanna, *Napoleon III and Mexico*, 282 ("We are running"); McAllen, *Maximilian and Carlota*, 197, 205–6, Felix Douay quoted on 197 ("The distances"); Roeder, *Juárez*, vol. 2:599–603, 607–8, Major de Tuce quoted on 572 ("No one sees").

83. Dabbs, *French Army in Mexico*, 144–45; Knapp, *Sebastián Lerdo de Tejada*, 99–104; McAllen, *Maximilian and Carlota*, 183–84; Roeder, *Juárez*, vol. 2:611–16; Matías Romero, dispatch, Aug. 19, 1865, in Schoonover, ed., *Mexican Lobby*, 92–93.

84. Roeder, *Juárez*, vol. 2:599–605; Morsberger, *Lew Wallace*, 207–9, Lew Wallace quoted on 208–9.

85. Hanna and Hanna, *Napoleon III and Mexico*, 261–63; Neely, *Civil War and the Limits of Destruction*, 72–75; Ridley, *Maximilian & Juárez*, 226, 228–29, Black Decree quoted on 228; Roeder, *Juárez*, vol. 2:605–7, Bazaine quoted on 607.

86. Duncan, "Political Legitimation," 59–60; McAllen, *Maximilian and Carlota*, 198–202; Shawcross, *Last Emperor of Mexico*, 164–65.

87. Duncan, "Political Legitimation," 60; McAllen, *Maximilian and Carlota*, 202–3; Ridley, *Maximilian and Juárez*, 219–20; Shawcross, *Last Emperor of Mexico*, 165.

88. McAllen, *Maximilian and Carlota*, 269–70; O'Connor, *Cactus Throne*, 157–58; Roeder, *Juárez*, vol. 2:590, 592; Topik, "When Mexico Had the Blues," 714–19.

89. McAllen, *Maximilian and Carlota*, 158–59, 195–96; Ridley, *Maximilian and Juárez*, 192–94.

90. Hanna and Hanna, *Napoleon III and Mexico*, Emmanuel Domench quoted on 138 ("Mexico is"), Alphonse Dano quoted on 304 ("reasoned"); McAllen, *Maximilian and Carlota*, 155, 194–95, Maximilian quoted on 155 ("The more") and 195 ("incapable"); L. Thomas, *Between Two Empires*, 331–38, William M. Gwin quoted on 333 ("of all men") and 338 ("the emperor").

91. Coffey, *Soldier Princess*, 14–15, 38–44; Ridley, *Maximilian and Juárez*, 242; A. Salm-Salm, *Ten Years of My Life*, 163 ("pugnacious instincts").

92. Coffey, *Soldier Princess*, ix–xiii, 6–7, 14–17; A. Salm-Salm, *Ten Years of My Life*, 19–22, 31–36.

93. Coffey, *Soldier Princess*, 50–54, Sara Yorke quoted on 54; A. Salm-Salm, *Ten Years of My Life*, 118–19.

94. Cunningham, *Mexico and the Foreign Policy of Napoleon III*, 182–85; Dabbs, *French Army in Mexico*, 112, 150–51, 157–59; Hanna and Hanna, *Napoleon III and Mexico*, 139–40, 144–45, 149–50.

95. Cunningham, *Mexico and the Foreign Policy of Napoleon III*, 191–92; Dabbs, *French Army in Mexico*, 158–59; Hanna and Hanna, *Napoleon III and Mexico*, 246–47, 270–72, John Schofield quoted on 246; McAllen, *Maximilian and Carlota*, 232–33.

96. Hanna and Hanna, *Napoleon III and Mexico*, 274–75, Alphonse Dano quoted on 275, Bazaine quoted on 283; McAllen, *Maximilian and Carlota*, 230–31, 233–35, Maximilian quoted on 231.

97. Blumberg, *Diplomacy of the Mexican Empire*, 222–25; McAllen, *Maximilian and Carlota*, 251–53, 260, 304–8, Carlota quoted on 253 ("There is"); Shawcross, *Last Emperor of Mexico*, 188–90, 211–14, 220, Carlota quoted on 189–90 ("only admissible").

98. McAllen, *Maximilian and Carlota*, 215–16, 220, 223–24, 236–37; Ridley, *Maximilian and Juárez*, 241–42; Shawcross, *Last Emperor of Mexico*, 179–80.

99. McAllen, *Maximilian and Carlota*, 254–58, 261–74, Carlota quoted on 270 ("It is all slime"); Ridley, *Maximilian and Juárez*, 247–48, Carlota quoted on 248 ("devil"); Shawcross, *Last Emperor of Mexico*, 190–97, Carlota quoted on 190 ("He has").

100. McAllen, *Maximilian and Carlota*, 283–89, Pius IX quoted on 287; Shawcross, *Last Emperor of Mexico*, 198–202, Carlota quoted on 201 ("Dearly beloved").

101. McAllen, *Maximilian and Carlota*, 290–97, Dr. Samuel Basch quoted on 296, Carlota quoted on 407; Ridley, *Maximilian and Juárez*, 248–49.

102. Blumberg, *Diplomacy of the Mexican Empire*, 219–27; McAllen, *Maximilian and Carlota*, 303–8; Shawcross, *Last Emperor of Mexico*, 216, 222.

103. Dabbs, *French Army in Mexico*, 150–51, 160–62, 166–71, 175–82; McAllen, *Maximilian and Carlota*, 237–38, 259–61, Pierre Loizillon quoted on 259.

104. Hoyt, ed., "New Light on General Jubal A. Early," 116; Rolle, *Lost Cause*, 77, 104–5, 111–20, 121–28, 139–41, 183; Tucker, *Beverley Tucker*, 29, 35–36.

105. Mahoney, *Mexico and the Confederacy*, 128–30, *Mexican Times* quoted on 130; Rolle, *Lost Cause*, 139–42; Wahlstrom, *Southern Exodus to Mexico*, 83–88.

106. W. M. Anderson, *American in Maximilian's Mexico*, 114–17; Mahoney, *Mexico and the Confederacy*, 156–62, *Charleston Courier* quoted on 162; Rolle, *Lost Cause*, 179–82; Wahlstrom, *Southern Exodus to Mexico*, 95–99.

107. Hanna and Hanna, *Napoleon III and Mexico*, 280–83, Bazaine quoted on 283 ("days"); McAllen, *Maximilian and Carlota*, 298–99; and Bazaine quoted in Ridley, *Maximilian and Juárez*, 251 ("moral influence").

108. Hanna and Hanna, *Napoleon III and Mexico*, 285–89, Gideon Welles quoted on 288 ("a miserable"); Ridley, *Maximilian and Juárez*, 251–53, Sherman quoted on 253 ("I have not"); Matías Romero, dispatch, Nov. 3, 1866, in Schoonover, ed., *Mexican Lobby*, 144–46.

109. McAllen, *Maximilian and Carlota*, 243, 258–59; Shawcross, *Last Emperor of Mexico*, 207–8.

110. Hanna and Hanna, *Napoleon III and Mexico*, 299–300; McAllen, *Maximilian and Carlota*, 307, 323–24; Shawcross, *Last Emperor of Mexico*, 237–40.

111. Hanna and Hanna, *Napoleon III and Mexico*, 292–96; Shawcross, *Last Emperor of Mexico*, 181, 235–37, Maximilian quoted on 237.

112. Coffey, *Soldier Princess*, 57–59; A. Salm-Salm, *Ten Years of My Life*, 169–71.

113. Coffey, *Soldier Princess*, 62–63; McAllen, *Maximilian and Carlota*, 325–34, Maximilian quoted on 325; Shawcross, *Last Emperor of Mexico*, 244–48.

114. Coffey, *Soldier Princess*, 63–68; McAllen, *Maximilian and Carlota*, 337–48; Ridley, *Maximilian and Juárez*, 259–61; A. Salm-Salm, *Ten Years of My Life*, 181–82.

115. Coffey, *Soldier Princess*, 66–68; McAllen, *Maximilian and Carlota*, 345–46, 348–51; Shawcross, *Last Emperor of Mexico*, 253–58.

116. Coffey, *Soldier Princess*, 68–69; McAllen, *Maximilian and Carlota*, 351–57, 367; Ridley, *Maximilian and Juárez*, 262–63; Shawcross, *Last Emperor of Mexico*, 258–62.

117. Coffey, *Soldier Princess*, 69–70, 75–77; McAllen, *Maximilian and Carlota*, 368–69, 373–76; A. Salm-Salm, *Ten Years of My Life*, 189–90, 194–218.

118. McAllen, *Maximilian and Carlota*, 364–65, 369–78; Roeder, *Juárez*, vol. 2:666–69, Juárez quoted on 668; A. Salm-Salm, *Ten Years of My Life*, 222–23.

119. Blumberg, *Diplomacy of the Mexican Empire*, 264–66; Coffey, *Soldier Princess*, 80–81; Ridley, *Maximilian and Juárez*, 270–76; Juárez quoted in A. Salm-Salm, *Ten Years of My Life*, 223.

120. Blumberg, *Diplomacy of the Mexican Empire*, 279–80; McAllen, *Maximilian and Carlota*, 396, includes song title; Ridley, *Maximilian and Juárez*, 277–81.

121. Downs, *Second American Revolution*, 99–101; Hanna and Hanna, *Napoleon III and Mexico*, 301–303, Seward quoted on 301, Jules Berthemy quoted on 303; Schoonover, *Dollars over Dominion*, 281–83; Stahr, *Seward*, 535–36.

122. Katz, "Liberal Republic and the Porfiriato," 51; Knapp, *Life of Sebastián Lerdo*, 119; Scholes, *Mexican Politics*, 118, 134, 137–38, 141–42.

123. Doyle, *Cause of All Nations*, 305–6; Katz, "Liberal Republic and the Porfiriato," 51–52; Schoonover, *Dollars over Dominion*, 254–81.

124. Hamnett, *Juárez*, 217–18; Katz, "Liberal Republic and the Porfiriato," 52–56; Scholes, *Mexican Politics*, 140–44, José Bustamante quoted on 141 ("diffusion"); Wasserman, *Everyday Life and Politics*, 131–32.

125. Katz, "Liberal Republic and the Porfiriato," 56–59; Scholes, *Mexican Politics*, 135–36; Voss, *On the Periphery of Nineteenth-Century Mexico*, 236–37.

126. Hale, *Transformation of Liberalism*, 3, 9; Hamnett, *Juárez*, 199–201; Knapp, *Life of Sebastián Lerdo*, 119–21, 125; Scholes, *Mexican Politics*, 137.

127. Hale, *Transformation of Liberalism*, 21, 53, 70–77; Hamnett, *Juárez*, 201–2; Knapp, *Life of Sebastián Lerdo*, 122–23; Roeder, *Juárez*, vol. 2:682–83, Juárez quoted on 682; Scholes, *Mexican Politics*, 118–20; Wasserman, *Everyday Life and Politics*, 129.

128. Hamnett, *Juárez*, 202–7, 221; Knapp, *Life of Sebastián Lerdo*, 123–24, 129; Roeder, *Juárez*, vol. 2:683–86; Scholes, *Mexican Politics*, 120–23, 132.

129. Hamnett, *Juárez*, 207–8, 220–24; A. Salm-Salm, *Ten Years of My Life*, 180 ("man of medium"); Wasserman, *Everyday Life and Politics*, 161–63.

130. Hamnett, *Juárez*, 225–30, Diaz brothers quoted on 226; Knapp, *Life of Sebastián Lerdo*, 150–59; Scholes, *Mexican Politics*, 133, 149–66.

131. Hamnett, *Juárez*, 231–34, 242–43; Roeder, *Juárez*, vol. 2:724–26; Sinkin, *Mexican Reform*, 172–77; Voss, *On the Periphery of Nineteenth-Century Mexico*, 234–35.

132. Dabbs, *French Army in Mexico*, 276–79.

133. Coffey, *Soldier Princess*, 82–92, Pope Pius IX quoted on 87.

134. Krauze, *Mexico* 189; McAllen, *Maximilian and Carlota*, 407–8, Carlota quoted on 408; Shawcross, *Last Emperor of Mexico*, 287–88.

TWELVE: RECONSTRUCTIONS

1. William H. Seward quoted in St. John, "Unpredictable America of William Gwin," 63.

2. Thomas D'Arcy McGee quoted in Gwyn, *Nation Maker*, 57.

3. Martin, *Britain and the Origins of Canadian Confederation*, 240, 244–46, Macdonald quoted on 245; P. B. Waite, *Life and Times of Confederation*, 28–30.

4. Ulysses S. Grant to Edward O. C. Ord, Nov. 26, 1865, in Simon, ed., *Papers of Ulysses S. Grant*, 420–22; D. A. Wilson, *Canadian Spy Story*, 3–21; Winks, *Canada and the United States*, 323–26, 370–71, Fenian song quoted on 323.

5. Errington, "British Migration and British America," 156–57; Morton, *Critical Years*, 183–84, 191–92; D. A. Wilson, *Canadian Spy Story*, 27–31; Winks, *Canada and the United States*, 87, 96, 240–41, 323–24.

6. Careless, *Brown of the Globe*, vol. 2:222–23; Errington, "British Migration and British America," 157; Gwyn, *Man Who Made Us*, 380–81; Morton, *Critical Years*, 195; D. A. Wilson, *Canadian Spy Story*, 145–64, 169–70.

7. Careless, *Brown of the Globe*, vol. 2:224–25; Gwyn, *Man Who Made Us*, 383–84; Morton, *Critical Years*, 195–96; D. A. Wilson, *Canadian Spy Story*, 169–83.

8. Careless, *Brown of the Globe*, vol. 2:223–25; P. B. Waite, *Life and Times of Confederation*, 268–73.

9. Gwyn, *Man Who Made Us*, 363–69, Joseph Howe quoted on 364 ("this crazy"); Martin, *Britain and the Origins of Canadian Confederation*, 291–92.

10. Gwyn, *Man Who Made Us*, 357–61, Charles Tupper quoted on 358 ("impractical"), Joseph Howe quoted on 362 ("wilderness"); Martin, *John A. Macdonald*, 90–91; Moore, *1867*, 176–81, Albert Smith quoted on 176 ("oily brains").

11. Gwyn, *Man Who Made Us*, 370–74, Alexander T. Galt quoted on 373–74 ("games

of all"); Martin, *Britain and the Origins of Canadian Confederation*, 256–58, 262–65, Galt quoted on 265 ("We were treated").

12. Gwyn, *Man Who Made Us*, 370–71, Edward Cardwell quoted on 371 ("to turn"); Martin, *Britain and the Origins of Canadian Confederation*, 274–75, Cardwell quoted on 275 ("great jealousy" and "Imperial influence").

13. Gwyn, *Man Who Made Us*, 379, 381–85; Moore, *1867*, 183–85; Pryke, *Nova Scotia and Confederation*, 33–34; P. B. Waite, "Edward Cardwell and Confederation," 34–35.

14. Creighton, *John A. Macdonald*, vol. 1:436–38; Gwyn, *Man Who Made Us*, 385–88, John A. Macdonald quoted on 387; Martin, *John A. Macdonald*, 96–97.

15. Careless, *Brown of the Globe*, vol. 2:228–29; Gwyn, *Man Who Made Us*, 388–94, Macdonald quoted on 389; Martin, *Britain and the Origins of Canadian Confederation*, 280–82; Moore, *1867*, 186–93, 210–12; Pryke, *Nova Scotia and Confederation*, 34–39.

16. Gwyn, *Man Who Made Us*, 396–98; Martin, *Britain and the Origins of Canadian Confederation*, 282; Morton, *Critical Years*, 212–13.

17. Gwyn, *Man Who Made Us*, 390–91; Martin, *John A. Macdonald*, 97–99; Moore, *1867*, 211–14, Frederic Rogers quote on 214 ("eager dogs"); Morton, *Critical Years*, 203–6, Hector-Louis Langevin quoted on 206 ("Macdonald is").

18. Creighton, *John A. Macdonald*, vol. 1:453–54; Gwyn, *Man Who Made Us*, 391–92, Macdonald quoted on 392; Phenix, *Private Demons*, 176–77.

19. Gwyn, *Man Who Made Us*, 406–13, Edmund Meredith quoted on 421; Martin, *John A. Macdonald*, 102–4; Phenix, *Private Demons*, 158–65, 174–78.

20. Bothwell, *Your Country, My Country*, 122–23; Martin, *Britain and the Origins of Canadian Confederation*, 265, 277–90, 295–96, Edward Cardwell quoted on 265; Moore, *1867*, 41–42, 239; Pryke, *Nova Scotia and Confederation*, 39–41.

21. Gwyn, *Man Who Made Us*, 435–40; Martin, *John A. Macdonald*, 109–10, 112; Morton, *Critical Years*, 219–22; P. B. Waite, *Life and Times of Confederation*, 322–23.

22. Moore, *1867*, 194–95, 216; Morton, *Critical Years*, 229–32; Pryke, *Nova Scotia and Confederation*, 60–66, 69–93; P. B. Waite, *Life and Times of Confederation*, 302–3.

23. Gwyn, *Nation Maker*, 55–60; Phenix, *Private Demons*, 186–93, Thomas D'Arcy McGee quoted on 186 ("If ever"); McGee quoted in P. B. Waite, *Life and Times of Confederation*, 29 ("The days"); D. A. Wilson, *Canadian Spy Story*, 245–65.

24. Gwyn, *Man Who Made Us*, 292–93, 432–34, Macdonald quoted on 293 and 433; Martin, *Britain and the Origins of Canadian Confederation*, 33–34.

25. Zachariah Chandler quoted in Dashaw, "Story of an Illusion," 338 ("This North American"); Gluek, "Riel Rebellion and Canadian-American Relations," 201, Chandler quoted on 209–10 ("standing menace"); [London] *Times* quoted in Gwyn, *Man Who Made Us*, 438.

26. Nugent, *Habits of Empire*, 244–46, 249; Shi, "Seward's Attempt to Annex British Columbia," 218–20, 223; Stahr, *Seward*, 482–91, 495.

27. George T. Strong quoted in Love, *Race over Empire*, 32; Paolino, *Foundations of the American Empire*, 106–18; Stahr, *Seward*, 482–84.

28. Gwyn, *Man Who Made Us*, 431–32, Seward quoted on 431 ("Nature designs"); Krikorian and Cameron, "The 1867 Union of the British North American Colonies," 49–50, Seward quoted on 49 ("help the United States"), *Daily British Colonist* quoted on 49; Shi, "Seward's Attempt to Annex British Columbia," 220–26; Stahr, *Seward*, 484, 489.

29. Barman, *West Beyond the West*, 98–99; Lower, *Western Canada,* 99–100; Shi, "Seward's Attempt to Annex British Columbia," 221–23; P. B. Waite, *Life and Times of Confederation,* 311–18, Frederick Seymour quoted on 312 ("melancholy").

30. Dashaw, "Story of an Illusion," 333–38; McFeely, *Grant,* 333–36; Morton, *Critical Years,* 185, 196–97; Shi, "Seward's Attempt to Annex British Columbia," 221–22.

31. Barman, *West Beyond the West,* 99–102; Morton, *Critical Years,* 246–48; Shi, "Seward's Attempt to Annex British Columbia," 234–37.

32. Dickason, *Canada's First Nations,* 265–68; Gwyn, *Nation Maker,* 88–89; J. R. Miller, *Skyscrapers Hide the Heavens,* 153–54; Owram, *Promise of Eden,* 76–88; P. B. Waite, *Life and Times of Confederation,* 306–10.

33. Gluek, "Riel Rebellion and Canadian American Relations," 199–201; Gwyn, *Nation Maker,* 90–96, John A. Macdonald quoted on 95; Morton, *Critical Years,* 233–35; Winks, *Canada and the United States,* 167–68.

34. Dickason, *Canada's First Nations,* 268–69; Gwyn, *Nation Maker,* 102–4, Oscar Malmros quoted on 103; Lower, *Western Canada,* 89–92.

35. Careless, *Brown of the Globe,* vol. 2:275–76, quote on 275 ("William the Conquered"); Gwyn, *Nation Maker,* 104–5, 109–10, Louis Riel quoted on 105; J. R. Miller, *Skyscrapers Hide the Heavens,* 154–57; Morton, *Critical Years,* 238–42.

36. Dickason, *Canada's First Nations,* 270–71; Gwyn, *Nation Maker,* 125–31; Morton, *Critical Years,* 237; Owram, *Promise of Eden,* 89–94, W. A. Foster quoted on 94.

37. Gluek, "Riel Rebellion and Canadian-American Relations," 203–8; Gwyn, *Nation Maker,* 134–39, 144–52, Oscar Malmros quoted on 120.

38. Careless, *Brown of the Globe,* vol. 2:278–79; Lower, *Western Canada,* 94–97; Martin, *John A. Macdonald,* 122; J. R. Miller, *Skyscrapers Hide the Heavens,* 158–60.

39. Morton, *Critical Years,* 253–54; Owram, *Promise of Eden,* 91–100, *Canadian Monthly and National Review* quoted on 99–100.

40. McNab, "Herman Merivale and Colonial Office Indian Policy," 85–103; J. R. Miller, *Skyscrapers Hide the Heavens,* 152–53, 161–63, Alberini Island Natives quoted on 147 ("We do not want"); Slowey, "Confederation Comes at a Cost," 81–85, Duncan Campbell Scott quoted on 85–85 ("I want").

41. Foner, *Reconstruction,* 124–29; Bragg quoted in Hess, *Braxton Bragg,* 251–52; Sutherland, *Confederate Carpetbaggers,* 9–12, Confederate planter quoted on 12.

42. Downs, *After Appomattox,* 32–33, 39–40; Fellman, Gordon, and Sutherland, *This Terrible War,* 319–22, Georgia woman quoted on 319, Knoxville woman quoted on 322.

43. Barr, *All the Days of My Life,* 108–9; Faust, *Mothers of Invention,* 248–50, Carolina matron quoted on 250 ("being queens"); Rubin, *Shattered Nation,* 145–46, 150–51, Mrs. J. J. Pringle Smith quoted on 145 ("all of us").

44. Woman quoted in Gallagher, *Confederate War,* 79 ("O how"); Rome *Courier* quoted in Schott, *Alexander H. Stephens,* 457 ("When I see"); R. White, *Republic for Which It Stands,* 50–51, Benjamin Perry quoted on 50 ("have learned"); Winik, *April 1865,* 351–53, innkeeper quoted on 351 ("O how").

45. Fellman, Gordon, and Sutherland, *This Terrible War,* 324–26, Virginia freedman quoted on 324 and Florida planter quoted on 325; Foner, *Reconstruction,* 77–84; Hahn, *Nation Under Our Feet,* 119–20.

46. Foner, *Reconstruction,* 84–88; Richardson, *Death of Reconstruction,* 12–13, 32–33, freedman quoted on 33; R. White, *Republic for Which It Stands,* 42–43.

47. Foner, *Reconstruction*, 102–6, Alabama Black convention quoted on 105, Bayley Wyatt quoted on 105.

48. Henry Adams quoted in R. White, *Republic for Which It Stands*, 52.

49. Downs, *After Appomattox*, 19–21, 89–90; R. White, *Republic for Which It Stands*, 31–34.

50. Downs, *Second American Revolution*, 33–34; Foner, *Reconstruction*, 178–79; Hahn, *Nation Without Borders*, 319–21; Summers, *Ordeal of the Reunion*, 90–91.

51. Foner, *Second Founding*, 56–59, Thaddeus Stevens quoted on 87; Richardson, *Death of Reconstruction*, 18–19, Carl Schurz quoted on 18; Summers, *Ordeal of the Reunion*, 82–85, A. J. Hamilton quoted on 98 ("I want").

52. Bergeron, *Andrew Johnson's Civil War and Reconstruction*, 72–74; Foner, *Reconstruction*, 176–78; Summers, *Ordeal of the Reunion*, 62–64.

53. Blight, *Frederick Douglass*, 472–73; Foner, *Reconstruction*, 183–84, 190–91; Richardson, *Death of Reconstruction*, 15–16; Summers, *Ordeal of the Reunion*, 65–67.

54. Blight, *Frederick Douglass*, 474–75, Andrew Johnson quoted on 475 ("I know"); Foner, *Reconstruction*, 178–81, Johnson quoted on 180 ("capacity" and "White men"); Masur, *Until Justice Be Done*, 320–22.

55. Bergeron, *Andrew Johnson's Civil War and Reconstruction*, 76–82; Foner, *Reconstruction*, 182–83, 186–95, Samuel Matthews quoted on 195; Richardson, *Death of Reconstruction*, 16–17; Summers, *Ordeal of the Reunion*, 64–72.

56. Bergeron, *Andrew Johnson's Civil War and Reconstruction*, 84–85, North Carolina freedmen quoted on 85; Blight, *Frederick Douglass*, 470–72, Douglass quoted on 477; Egerton, *Wars of Reconstruction*, 191–92, Martin Delany quoted on 192.

57. Downs, *Declarations of Dependence*, 83–84; Foner, *Reconstruction*, 182–83, 186–92, Christopher G. Memminger quoted on 192 ("held up"); Henry Cleveland quoted in Schott, *Alexander H. Stephens*, 459 ("Our people").

58. Foner, *Reconstruction*, 131–35, 198–201, Natchez newspaper quoted on 133 ("true station"); Masur, *Until Justice Be Done*, 307–10; Summers, *Ordeal of the Reunion*, 72–73; R. White, *Republic for Which It Stands*, 29–30, Carl Schurz quoted on 51 ("elevation").

59. Foner, *Reconstruction*, 131–35, Louisville *Democrat* quoted on 134 ("that he is *free*"); Republican quoted in Richardson, *Death of Reconstruction*, 17 ("lost" and "the blacks").

60. Foner, *Reconstruction*, 196–97, 203–5, 216–27, O. D. Bartlett quoted on 205 ("Murder is"); Hahn, *Nation Without Borders*, 306–8, Georgia militia company quoted on 307; Masur, *Until Justice Be Done*, 310–11.

61. Downs, *Declarations of Dependence*, 85–87; Egerton, *Wars of Reconstruction*, 107–10.

62. Bergeron, *Andrew Johnson's Civil War and Reconstruction*, 104–5, Johnson quoted on 105; Summers, *Ordeal of the Reunion*, 81.

63. Bergeron, *Andrew Johnson's Civil War and Reconstruction*, 89–98, *Chicago Tribune* quoted on 89; Blight, *Frederick Douglass*, 472–73; Foner, *Reconstruction*, 222–27, 243–44; Masur, *Until Justice Be Done*, 308–13.

64. Bergeron, *Andrew Johnson's Civil War and Reconstruction*, 106–8; Downs, *Second American Revolution*, 11–12; Summers, *Ordeal of the Reunion*, 86–89, 100; Varon, *Armies of Deliverance*, 428–29, Ohio newspaper quoted on 428.

65. Foner, *Reconstruction*, 142–47, 244–45; Masur, *Until Justice Be Done*, 314–20, James Wilson quoted on 318; Summers, *Ordeal of the Reunion*, 89–90.

66. Bergeron, *Andrew Johnson's Civil War and Reconstruction*, 110–12; Blight, *Frederick Douglass*, 478–79; Masur, *Until Justice Be Done*, 324–25.

67. Downs, *Second American Revolution*, 46–47; Foner, *Second Founding*, 68–80, 86–92; Masur, *Until Justice Be Done*, 327–40; Summers, *Ordeal of the Reunion*, 90–93.

68. Rosen, *Terror in the Heart of Freedom*, 61–83; Summers, *Ordeal of the Reunion*, 95–96, Clinton B. Fisk quoted on 96.

69. Foner, *Reconstruction*, 261–63; Summers, *Ordeal of the Reunion*, 95–97, New Orleans newspaper quoted on 97; Trefousse, *Andrew Johnson*, 250–51, 258–59, Sheridan quoted on 259; Waugh, *U. S. Grant*, 114–15.

70. Masur, *Until Justice Be Done*, 325–26; Summers, *Ordeal of the Reunion*, 97–99, diarist quoted on 97 ("Andy's adventures"); Trefousse, *Andrew Johnson*, 243–44, 251–54, 255–71, Parson Brownlow quoted on 253, Samuel S. Cox quoted on 271 ("He was"); Waugh, *U. S. Grant*, 114–15, Grant quoted on 115.

71. Bergeron, *Andrew Johnson's Civil War and Reconstruction*, 102–5, Andrew Johnson quoted on 104; Foner, *Reconstruction*, 240, 272; Trefousse, *Andrew Johnson*, 273.

72. Bergeron, *Andrew Johnson's Civil War and Reconstruction*, 116–18, 149–52; Hahn, *Nation Under Our Feet*, 163–65; Summers, *Ordeal of the Reunion*, 101–2, 109–12; Trefousse, *Andrew Johnson*, 274–82; Waugh, *U. S. Grant*, 115–16.

73. Bergeron, *Andrew Johnson's Civil War and Reconstruction*, 145–47, 168–70; Summers, *Ordeal of the Reunion*, 102–6; Trefousse, *Andrew Johnson,* 276–77, 289–91.

74. Bergeron, *Andrew Johnson's Civil War and Reconstruction*, 156–66; Downs, *After Appomattox*, 181–85; Egerton, *Wars of Reconstruction*, 228–29.

75. Bergeron, *Andrew Johnson's Civil War and Reconstruction*, 172–75, 182–97; Simpson, *Let Us Have Peace*, 225–35, 244; Trefousse, *Andrew Johnson*, 300–10, 313–15.

76. Bergeron, *Andrew Johnson's Civil War and Reconstruction*, 198–202; Stahr, *Seward*, 512–15; Simpson, *Let Us Have Peace*, 243–44; Trefousse, *Andrew Johnson*, 316–25.

77. Bergeron, *Andrew Johnson's Civil War and Reconstruction*, 202–8; Summers, *Ordeal of the Reunion*, 138–40; Trefousse, *Andrew Johnson*, 302–3, 325–32.

78. Egerton, *Wars of Reconstruction*, 235; Trefousse, *Andrew Johnson*, 332–34, Thaddeus Stevens quoted on 334, Johnson quoted on 334 ("white man's country").

79. Bergeron, *Andrew Johnson's Civil War and Reconstruction*, 208–11; Trefousse, *Andrew Johnson*, 337, 340–43; Johnson quoted on 299.

80. Bergeron, *Andrew Johnson's Civil War and Reconstruction*, 211–14; Foner, *Reconstruction*, 338–41, Francis Blair, Jr., quoted on 340, Republicans quoted on 341; Simpson, *Let Us Have Peace*, 248–49; Summers, *Ordeal of the Reunion*, 141–42.

81. Simpson, *Let Us Have Peace*, 218–24, 244–46, Grant quoted on 246; Waugh, *U. S. Grant*, 118–20, George T. Strong quoted on 118 ("genius").

82. Egerton, *Wars of Reconstruction*, 240–41; Foner, *Second Founding*, 93–95, 116–17; Georges Clemenceau quoted in Simpson, *Let Us Have Peace*, 250.

83. Downs, *After Appomattox,* 204–8; Egerton, *Wars of Reconstruction*, 236–41, 287–88; Foner, *Reconstruction*, 341–43; Summers, *Ordeal of the Reunion*, 121–22, 146–50.

84. Downs, *Declarations of Dependence*, 116–17, 123–24; Simpson, *Let Us Have Peace*, 249–50; Summers, *Ordeal of the Reunion*, 151–52.

85. Foner, *Second Founding*, 98–105, Oliver P. Morton quoted on 100 ("I assert"); Richardson, *Death of Reconstruction*, 77–80, William Stewart quoted on 79 ("It must").

86. Downs, *Second American Revolution*, 47–48; Foner, *Second Founding*, 105–7; Summers, *Ordeal of the Reunion*, 153–54.

87. Foner, *Second Founding*, 108–11, Jabez Campbell quoted on 111; Richardson, *Death of Reconstruction*, 80–81.

88. Bearden and Butler, *Shadd*, 226–27; Downs, *Declarations of Dependence*, 101–4; Rhodes, *Mary Ann Shadd Cary*, 191; Richardson, *Death of Reconstruction*, 52–63, 68, 81–82; Summers, *Ordeal of the Reunion*, 167–68.

89. Egerton, *Wars of Reconstruction*, 15–16; Richardson, *Death of Reconstruction*, 81–82, 122–23, Albion W. Tourgee quoted on 81.

90. William Allan Blair, "Jubal Early," in Current, ed., *Encyclopedia of the Confederacy*, vol. 2:503; Gallagher, *Lee and His Generals*, 199–212.

91. George H. Thomas quoted in Einolf, *George Thomas*, 324–25.

92. Egerton, *Wars of Reconstruction*, 25–27, 51, 102, Delany quoted on 107 ("We have now"); Painter, "Martin R. Delany," 163–64, Delany quoted on 163 ("had we not").

93. Foner, *Reconstruction*, 546–47; Painter, "Martin R. Delany," 164–67, Delany quoted on 164 ("a union") and 166 ("the wealth").

94. Foner, *Reconstruction*, 571–75, Democrat quoted on 574; Painter, "Martin R. Delany," 167–69, Delany quoted on 169; Richardson, *West from Appomattox*. 14–20, 59, 176–78.

95. Painter, "Martin R. Delany," 169–71.

96. Bynum, *Free State of Jones*, 132–45, 171–72, Ellisville *Progressive* quoted on 172.

97. Doyle, *Cause of All Nations*, 111–13, 300; Hudson, *Mistress of Manifest Destiny*, 180–81; Love, *Race over Empire*, 35–36; May, "Lobbyists for Commercial Empire," 384–406; Tansill, *United States and Santo Domingo*, 220–23, 343–44.

98. Bowen, *Spain and the American Civil War*, 146–48; Hudson, *Mistress of Manifest Destiny*, 181–82; Tansill, *United States and Santo Domingo*, 222–25.

99. Hudson, *Mistress of Manifest Destiny*, 183–84; Tansill, *United States and Santo Domingo*, 225–86.

100. Guyatt, "America's Conservatory," 975–78, 998; Hudson, *Mistress of Manifest Destiny*, 186–89; Love, *Race over Empire*, 33–35, 40–64; McFeely, *Grant*, 333, 337–38.

101. Blight, *Frederick Douglass*, 536–37; Tansill, *United States and Santo Domingo*, 343–420.

102. Blight, *Frederick Douglass*, 538–45; Guyatt, "America's Conservatory," 982, 989–92; Love, *Race over Empire*, 65–66; McFeely, *Grant*, 350–52; Tansill, *United States and Santo Domingo*, 428–36.

103. Blight, *Frederick Douglass*, 544–45, Douglass quoted on 545; Guyatt, "America's Conservatory," 979–81, 994, 997, Charles Sumner quoted on 979; Love, *Race over Empire*, 56–58, 67–68; McFeely, *Grant*, 334, 351–52, Hamilton Fish quoted on 351.

104. Hudson, *Mistress of Manifest Destiny*, 190–200, Jane Cazneau quoted on 195; May, "Lobbyists for Commercial Empire," 410–11.

105. Frederick Douglass quoted in Downs, *Second American Revolution*, 133; Hahn, *Nation Without Borders*, 329–32; Hendrickson, *Union, Nation, or Empire*, 238–40; Summers, *Ordeal of the Reunion*, 3–6.

106. Downs, *Second American Revolution*, 4–6, 46–47, 50–53; Emberton, *Beyond Redemption*, 7–8, 214–16; Foner, *Second Founding*, xix–xxix, 1–7; Summers, *Ordeal of the Reunion*, 398–99.

107. Broeck N. Oder, "Joseph Orville Shelby," in Garraty and Carnes, eds., *American National Biography*, vol. 19:778–79; Rolle, *Lost Cause*, 204–5.

108. Freehling, *Road to Disunion*, vol. 2:218–19, Henry Wise quoted on 219 ("John Brown"); Wise quoted in Horwitz, *Midnight Rising*, 281 ("God knew").

109. Blight, *Frederick Douglass*, 581–753, Douglass quoted on 743 ("Rebel rule"); Roy E. Finkenbine, "Frederick Douglass," in Garraty and Carnes, eds., *American National Biography*, vol. 6:818–19.

110. Hoffert, *Jane Grey Swisshelm*, 155–56, Swisshelm quoted on 155 ("plentifully" and "a matter"); Swisshelm, *Half a Century*, 367 ("Our Government").

111. Hoffert, *Jane Grey Swisshelm*, 126–31, 169–170, 185–87; Larsen, *Crusader and Feminist*, 28–30, St. Paul *Pioneer Press* quoted on 30; Swisshelm, *Half a Century*, 362–63.

112. Bearden and Butler, *Shadd*, 206–8, 210–12, 229–30, Shadd Cary quoted on 36; Green, *Secret City*, 89–100; Lessoff, *Nation and its City*, 40–42; Rhodes, *Mary Ann Shadd Cary*, 163–78.

113. Bearden and Butler, *Shadd*, 226–27; Rhodes, *Mary Ann Shadd Cary*, 178–80, 191, Frederick Douglass quoted on 179; Sterling, *We Are Your Sisters*, 406–7, 465–66.

114. Bearden and Butler, *Shadd*, 212–14; Rhodes, *Mary Ann Shadd Cary*, 185–91, 209–10.

115. Bearden and Butler, *Shadd*, 215–22; Rhodes, *Mary Ann Shadd Cary*, 191–96, 200–202; Sterling, *We Are Your Sisters*, 414.

116. Blight, *Frederick Douglass*, 582–91; Green, *Secret City*, 116–22; Lessoff, *Nation and Its City*, 118–20; Rhodes, *Mary Ann Shadd Cary*, 205–10.

117. Bearden and Butler, *Shadd*, 231–33; Rhodes, *Mary Ann Shadd Cary*, 210–11; Du Bois, *Darkwater*, 85.

EPILOGUE: SLEEPING GIANTS

1. Cora Tappan quoted in West, *Essential West*, 121.

2. Arenson, "John Gast's American Progress," 122–24, spike inscription quoted on 122; Richardson, *West from Appomattox*, 75–76; R. White, *Railroaded*, 37–38, 227–28.

3. Hahn, "Slave Emancipation, Indian Peoples," 309–10; Richardson, *West of Appomattox*, 31–34; S. L. Smith, "Emancipating Peons, Excluding Coolies," 48; West, *Essential West*, 115–16, 118–19.

4. Gleijeses, *America's Road to Empire*, 195–96; Utley, *Indian Frontier*, 99–101, 103–5, 109–12, 118–20; R. White, *Republic for Which It Stands*, 107–8.

5. Neely, *Civil War and the Limits of Destruction*, 145–53; R. White, *Republic for Which It Stands*, 108–11, 128–29; Utley, *Indian Frontier*, 108–9, 112–16, 123–27.

6. Downs and Masur, "Introduction," 10–17; Reséndez, *Other Slavery*, 295–98, 306–7; S. L. Smith, "Emancipating Peons, Excluding Coolies," 48–54.

7. Reséndez, *Other Slavery*, 298–301, 308–14; S. L. Smith, "Emancipating Peons, Excluding Coolies," 50–58, James Harlan quoted on 52.

8. S. L. Smith, "Emancipating Peons, Excluding Coolies," 60–67.

9. Downs and Masur, "Introduction," 9–13; Richardson, *West from Appomattox*, 74–75, 77; Scharff, "Empire and Liberty in the Middle of Nowhere," 150–51; West, *Essential West*, 106-7, 112–17, 120–21, Cora Tappan quoted on 121.

10. Dashaw, "Story of an Illusion," 332–33, 344–45; Glueck, "Riel Rebellion and

Canadian-American Relations," 210–11; Shi, "Seward's Attempt to Annex British Columbia," 218–19, 229; G. Smith, *Treaty of Washington*, 3–6.

11. Messamore, "Diplomacy or Duplicity," 31–36; Shippee, *Canadian-American Relations*, 348–50; G. Smith, *Treaty of Washington*, 46–60; Stacey, "Britain's Withdrawal from North America," 190–93, Lord Clarendon quoted on 193.

12. Gwyn, *Nation Maker*, 163–64, John A. Macdonald quoted on 163; G. Smith, *Treaty of Washington*, 33–34, 60–71.

13. Messamore, "Diplomacy or Duplicity," 40–46, Lord Kimberley quoted on 34; Shippee, *Canadian-American Relations*, 350–62.

14. Gwyn, *Nation Maker*, 171–72; G. Smith, *Treaty of Washington*, 110–21.

15. Messamore, "Diplomacy or Duplicity," 46–47, Macdonald quoted on 46; Pryke, *Nova Scotia and Confederation*, 125, 127–30; Stacey, "Britain's Withdrawal from North America," 193–97.

16. Careless, *Brown of the Globe*, vol. 2:284–85, 299–300; Gwyn, *Nation Maker*, 172–75; Morton, *Critical Years*, 267–71; Shippee, *Canadian-American Relations*, 382–425; G. Smith, *Treaty of Washington*, 114–19.

17. Downs, *Second American Revolution*, 1–2, 38–41, Thaddeus Stevens quoted on 41; Hendrickson, *Union, Nation, or Empire*, 230–33; P. J. Kelly, "North American Crisis of the 1860s," 337–40; Lowenstein, *Ways and Means*, 2–3, 286–315.

18. Morton, "British North America and a Continent," 153–54.

19. Bothwell, *Your Country, My Country*, 119–21; Buckner, "British North America," 534–35; Downs, "Mexicanization of American Politics," 404–5; Sexton, "Civil War and U.S. World Power," 20–21.

20. Downs, "Mexicanization of American Politics," 395–96; Emberton, *Beyond Redemption*, 4–5; Hendrickson, *Union, Nation, or Empire*, 235–38.

21. Downs, *Second American Revolution*, 46–47, 50–51; Emberton, *Beyond Redemption*, 10, 214–16; Foner, *Second Founding*, xix–xxix, 1–7, Charles Sumner quoted on xxviii; Summers, *Ordeal of the Reunion*, 347–71, 398–99.

BIBLIOGRAPHY

Allmendinger, David F., Jr., *Ruffin: Family and Reform in the Old South* (New York: Oxford University Press, 1990).

Anderson, Gary Clayton, *The Conquest of Texas: Ethnic Cleansing in the Promised Land, 1820–1875* (Norman: University of Oklahoma Press, 2005), 18–26.

Anderson, Gary Clayton, *Little Crow: Spokesman for the Sioux* (St. Paul: Minnesota Historical Society, 1986).

Anderson, Osborne P., *A Voice from Harper's Ferry: A Narrative of Events* (Boston: Anderson, 1861).

Anderson, William Marshall, *An American in Maximilian's Mexico, 1865–1866* (San Marino, CA: Huntington Library, 1959).

Arenson, Adam, "John Gast's American Progress: Using Manifest Destiny to Forget the Civil War and Reconstruction," in Scharff, ed., *Empire and Liberty: The Civil War and the West* (Oakland: University of California Press, 2015): 122–39.

Ashworth, John, *Slavery, Capitalism, and Politics in the Antebellum Republic*, 2 vols. (New York: Cambridge University Press, 2007).

Ayers, Edward L., *In the Presence of Mine Enemies: The Civil War in the Heart of America, 1859–1863* (New York: W. W. Norton, 2003).

Ayers, Edward L., *The Thin Light of Freedom: The Civil War and Emancipation in the Heart of America* (New York: W. W. Norton, 2017).

Bailey, Anne J., "The USCT in the Confederate Heartland, 1864," in John David Smith, ed., *Black Soldiers in Blue: African American Troops in the Civil War Era* (Chapel Hill: University of North Carolina Press, 2002): 227–48.

Bailey, Hugh C., *Hinton Rowan Helper: Abolitionist-Racist* (Montgomery: University of Alabama Press, 1965).

Baker, Jean H., *Affairs of Party: The Political Culture of Northern Democrats in the Mid-Nineteenth Century* (New York: Fordham University Press, 1998).

Baker, Jean H., *James Buchanan* (New York: Henry Holt, 2004).

Ball, Durwood, "Liberty, Empire, and Civil War in the American West," in Virginia Scharff, ed., *Empire and Liberty: The Civil War and the West* (Berkeley: University of California Press, 2015): 66–86.

Ballstadt, Carl, "Alexander Milton Ross," in *Dictionary of Canadian Biography*, vol. 12, online at biographi.ca.

Baptist, Edward E., *The Half Has Never Been Told: Slavery and the Making of American Capitalism* (New York: Basic Books, 2014).

Barker, Nancy Nichols, "France, Austria, and the Mexican Venture, 1861–1864," *French Historical Studies*, vol. 3 (Autumn, 1963): 224–45.

Barman, Jean, *The West Beyond the West: A History of British Columbia* (Toronto: University of Toronto Press, 2007).

Barr, Amelia E., *All the Days of My Life* (New York: Okitoka Press, 2018).

Baum, Dale, *The Shattering of Texas Unionism: Politics in the Lone Star State During the Civil War Era* (Baton Rouge: Louisiana State University Press, 1998).

Baumgartner, Alice L., *South to Freedom: Runaway Slaves to Mexico and the Road to the Civil War* (New York: Basic Books, 2020).

Bazant, Jan, "From Independence to the Liberal Republic, 1821–1867," in Leslie Bethell, ed., *Mexico Since Independence* (New York: Cambridge University Press, 1991): 1–48.

Bearden, Jim, and Linda Jean Butler, *Shadd: The Life and Times of Mary Shadd Cary* (Toronto: NC Press, 1977).

Beasley, Edward, "British Views of Canada at the Time of Confederation," in Jacqueline Krikorian, Marcel Martel, and Adrian Shubert, eds., *Globalizing Confederation: Canada and the World in 1867* (Toronto: University of Toronto Press, 2017): 161–77.

Beckert, Sven, *Empire of Cotton: A Global History* (New York: Alfred A. Knopf, 2014).

Beckert, Sven, and Seth Rockman, eds., *Slavery's Capitalism: A New History of American Economic Development* (Philadelphia: University of Pennsylvania Press, 2016).

Berbusse, Edward J., "Two Kentuckians Evaluate the Mexican Scene from Vera Cruz, 1853–1861," *The Americas*, vol. 31 (Apr. 1975): 501–12.

Berg, Scott W., *38 Nooses: Lincoln, Little Crow, and the Beginning of the Frontier's End* (New York: Pantheon, 2012).

Bergeron, Paul H., *Andrew Johnson's Civil War and Reconstruction* (Knoxville: University of Tennessee Press, 2011).

Bigler, David L., *Forgotten Kingdom: The Mormon Theocracy in the American West, 1847–1896* (Spokane: Arthur H. Clark, 1998).

Blackett, R. J. M., "Pressure from Without: African Americans, British Public Opinion, and Civil War Diplomacy," in Robert E. May, ed., *The Union, the Confederacy, and the Atlantic Rim* (West Lafayette: Purdue University Press, 1995): 69–100.

Blackhawk, Ned, *Violence over the Land: Indians and Empires in the Early American West* (Cambridge: Harvard University Press, 2006).

Blair, William, *Why Didn't the North Hang Some Rebels: The Postwar Debate over Punishment for Treason* (Marquette: Marquette University Press, 2004).

Blair, William, "Jubal Early" in Current, *Encyclopedia of the Confederacy*, 4 vols. (New York: Simon & Schuster, 1993).

Blansett, Kent, "When the Stars Fell from the Sky: The Cherokee Nation and Autonomy in the Civil War," in Virginia Scharff, ed., *Empire and Liberty: The Civil War and the West* (Berkeley: University of California Press, 2015): 87–104.

Bledsoe, Andrew S., " 'The Farce was Complete': Braxton Bragg, Field Orders, and the Language of Command at McLemore's Cove," in Andrew S. Bledsoe and Andrew F. Lang, eds., *Upon the Fields of Battle: Essays on the Military History of America's Civil War* (Baton Rouge: Louisiana State University Press, 2018): 92–123.

Blight, David W., *Frederick Douglass: Prophet of Freedom* (New York: Simon & Schuster, 2018).

Blumberg, Arnold, *The Diplomacy of the Mexican Empire, 1863–1867* (Malabar, FL: Robert E. Krieger, 1987).

Blythe, Lance R., "Kit Carson and the War for the Southwest: Separation and Survival along the Rio Grande, 1862–1868," in Adam Arenson and Andrew R. Graybill, eds., *Civil War Wests: Testing the Limits of the United States* (Berkeley: University of California Press, 2015): 53–70.

Boatner, Mark M., III, *The Civil War Dictionary* (New York: Vintage Books, 1991).

Bonner, Robert E., *Mastering America: Southern Slaveholders and the Crisis of American Nationhood* (New York: Cambridge University Press, 2009).

Bordewich, Fergus M., *Congress at War: How Republican Reformers Fought the Civil*

War, Defied Lincoln, Ended Slavery, and Remade America (New York: Alfred M. Knopf, 2020).

Bothwell, Robert, *Your Country, My Country: A Unified History of the United States and Canada* (New York: Oxford University Press, 2015).

Bourne, Kenneth, *British and the Balance of Power in North America, 1815–1908* (Berkeley: University of California Press, 1967).

Bowen, Wayne H., *Spain and the American Civil War* (Columbia: University of Missouri Press, 2011).

Brady, Lisa M., *War Upon the Land: Military Strategy and the Transformation of Southern Landscapes During the American Civil War* (Athens: University of Georgia Press, 2012).

Brandt, Nat, *The Man Who Tried to Burn New York* (Syracuse: Syracuse University Press, 1986).

Brettle, Adrian, *Colossal Ambitions: Confederate Planning for a Post-Civil War World* (Charlottesville: University of Virginia Press, 2020).

Bringhurst, Newell G., *Brigham Young and the Expanding American Frontier* (Boston: Little, Brown, 1986).

Brugger, Robert J., *Maryland, a Middle Temperament, 1634–1980* (Baltimore: Johns Hopkins University Press, 1988).

Buckner, Philip, " 'British North America and a Continent in Dissolution': The American Civil War in the Making of Canadian Confederation," *Journal of the Civil War Era*, vol. 7 (Dec. 2017): 512–40.

Buckner, Philip, "The Creation of the Dominion of Canada, 1860–1901," in Buckner, ed., *Canada and the British Empire* (New York: Oxford University Press, 2008): 66–86.

Buenger, Walter L., *Secession and the Union in Texas* (Austin: University of Texas Press, 1984).

Bumsted, J. M., "The Consolidation of British North America, 1783–1860," in Buckner, ed., *Canada and the British Empire* (New York: Oxford University Press, 2008): 43–65.

Burke, Diane Mutti, "Scattered People: The Long History of Forced Eviction in the Kansas-Missouri Borderlands," in Adam Arenson and Andrew R. Graybill, eds., *Civil War Wests: Testing the Limits of the United States* (Berkeley: University of California Press, 2015): 71–92.

Bynum, Victoria, *The Free State of Jones: Mississippi's Longest Civil War* (Chapel Hill: University of North Carolina Press, 2001).

Calkins, Chris, "Land Operations in Virginia in 1865: Time Catches Up with Lee at Last," in William C. Davis and James I. Robertson, Jr., eds., *Virginia at War, 1865* (Lexington: University Press of Kentucky, 2012): 1–15.

Camp, Stephanie M. H., *Closer to Freedom: Enslaved Women and Everyday Resistance in the Plantation South* (Chapel Hill: University of North Carolina Press, 2004).

Campbell, Eugene E., *Establishing Zion: The Mormon Church in the American West, 1847–1869* (Salt Lake City: Signature Books, 1988).

Campbell, Lyndsay, "The Northern Borderlands: Canada West," in Campbell and Tony Freyer, eds., *Freedom's Conditions in the U. S.—Canadian Borderlands in the Age of Emancipation* (Durham: Carolina Academic Press, 2011): 195–225.

Campbell, Randolph B., *An Empire for Slavery: The Peculiar Institution in Texas, 1821–1865* (Baton Rouge: Louisiana State University Press, 1989).

Careless, J. M. S., *Brown of the Globe*, 2 vols. (Toronto: Macmillan Co., 1959).

Careless, J. M. S., *The Union of the Canadas: The Growth of Canadian Institutions, 1841–1857* (Toronto: McClelland and Stewart, 1967).

Carrigan, William D., and Clive Webb, *Forgotten Dead: Mob Violence Against Mexicans in the United States, 1848–1928* (New York: Oxford University Press, 2013).

Carwardine, Richard, *Lincoln: A Life of Purpose and Power* (New York: Vintage, 2007).

Casdorph, Paul D., *Prince John Magruder: His Life and Campaigns* (New York: John Wiley & Sons, 1996).

Case, Lynn M., and Warren F. Spencer, *The United States and France: Civil War Diplomacy* (Philadelphia: University of Pennsylvania Press, 1970).

[Cazneau, Jane], *Eagle Pass: or Life on the Border* (New York: Putnam, 1852).

Chambers, Stephen M. *No God but Gain: The Untold Story of Cuban Slavery, the Monroe Doctrine, and the Making of the United States* (New York: Verso, 2015).

Chartrand, Rene, and Richard Hook, *The Mexican Adventure, 1861–67* (London: Osprey, 1994).

Cimprich, John, "The Fort Pillow Massacre: Assessing the Evidence," in John David Smith, ed., *Black Soldiers in Blue: African American Troops in the Civil War Era* (Chapel Hill: University of North Carolina Press, 2002): 150–68.

Clark, Christopher, *Social Change in America from the Revolution through the Civil War* (Chicago: Ivan R. Dee, 2006).

Clary, David A., *Eagles and Empire: The United States, Mexico, and the Struggle for a Continent* (New York, Bantam, 2009).

Clendenen, Clarence C., "A Confederate Spy in California: A Curious Incident of the Civil War," *Southern California Quarterly*, vol. 45 (Sept. 1963): 219–34.

Clendenen, Clarence C., "Dan Showalter: California Secessionist," *California Historical Society Quarterly*, vol. 40 (Dec. 1961): 309–25.

Coffey, David, *Soldier Princess: The Life & Legend of Agnes Salm-Salm in North America, 1861–1867* (College Station: Texas A & M University Press, 2002).

Coleman, Willi, "African American Women and Community Development in California, 1848–1900," in Lawrence B. De Graaf and Quintard Taylor, eds., *Seeking El Dorado: African Americans in California* (Seattle: University of Washington Press, 2001): 98–125.

Collins, Robert, *Jim Lane: Scoundrel, Statesman, Kansan* (New Orleans: Pelican Publishing, 2007).

Confer, Clarissa W., *The Cherokee Nation in the Civil War* (Norman: University of Oklahoma Press, 2007).

Connelly, Donald B., *John M. Schofield & the Politics of Generalship* (Chapel Hill: University of North Carolina Press, 2006).

Connolly, Thomas Lawrence, *Army of the Heartland: The Army of Tennessee, 1861–1862* (Baton Rouge: Louisiana State University Press, 1967).

Connolly, Thomas Lawrence, *Autumn of Glory: The Army of Tennessee, 1862–1865* (Baton Rouge: Louisiana State University Press, 1971).

Cooper, William J., *Jefferson Davis, American* (New York: Alfred A. Knopf, 2000).

Cornell, Sarah E., "Citizens of Nowhere: Fugitive Slaves and Free African Americans in Mexico, 1833–1857," *Journal of American History*, vol. 100 (Sept. 2013): 351–74.

Cortada, James W., *Spain and the American Civil War: Relations at Mid-Century, 1855–1868* (Philadelphia: American Philosophical Society, 1980).

Cott, Nancy F., *Bonds of Womanhood: 'Woman's Sphere' in New England, 1780–1835* (New Haven: Yale University Press, 1997).

Crawford, Martin, *William Howard Russell's Civil War: Private Diary and Letters, 1861–1862* (Athens: University of Georgia Press, 1992).

Creighton, Donald, *John A. Macdonald*, 2 vols. (Toronto: Macmillan Co., 1952, 1955).

Creighton, Margaret S., *The Colors of Courage: Gettysburg's Forgotten History, Immigrants, Women, and African Americans in the Civil War's Defining Battle* (New York: Basic Books, 2005).

Cunningham, Michele, *Mexico and the Foreign Policy of Napoleon III* (New York: Palgrave, 2001).

Current, Richard N., ed., *Encyclopedia of the Confederacy*, 4 vols. (New York: Simon & Schuster, 1993).

Curthoys, Ann, "The Dog That Didn't Bark: The Durham Report, Indigenous Dispossession, and Self-Government for Britain's Settler Colonies," in Karen Dubinsky, Adele Perry, and Henry Yu, eds., *Within and Without the Nation: Canadian History as Transnational History* (Toronto: University of Toronto Press, 2015): 25–48.

Cutrer, Thomas W., *Theater of a Separate War: The Civil War West of the Mississippi River, 1861–1865* (Chapel Hill: University of North Carolina Press, 2017).

Dabbs, Jack Autrey, *The French Army in Mexico, 1861–1867: A Study in Military Government* (The Hague: Mouton & Co., 1963).

Dashaw, Doris W., "The Story of an Illusion: The Plan to Trade the *Alabama* Claims for Canada," *Civil War History*, vol. 15 (Dec. 1969): 332–48.

Davis, William C., *"A Government of Our Own": The Making of the Confederacy* (New York: The Free Press, 1994).

Davis, William C., *Jefferson Davis: The Man and His Hour* (New York: Harper Collins, 1991).

Dawson, Joseph G., III, "Texas, Jefferson Davis, and Confederate National Strategy," in Charles D. Grear, ed., *The Fate of Texas: The Civil War and the Lone Star State* (Fayetteville: University of Arkansas Press, 2008): 1–23.

De Graaf, Lawrence B. and Quintard Taylor, "Introduction: African Americans in California History, California in African American History," in De Graaf and Taylor, eds., *Seeking El Dorado: African Americans in California* (Seattle: University of Washington Press, 2001): 3–69.

DeLay, Brian, *War of a Thousand Deserts: Indian Raids and the U.S.—Mexican War* (New Haven: Yale University Press, 2008).

Delbanco, Andrew, *The War Before the War: Fugitive Slaves and the Struggle for America's Soul from the Revolution to the Civil War* (New York: Penguin, 2018).

Deyle, Steven, *Carry Me Back: The Domestic Slave Trade in American Life* (New York: Oxford University Press, 2005).

Dickason, Olive Patricia, *Canada's First Nations: A History of Founding Peoples from Earliest Times* (Toronto: McClelland & Stewart, 1992).

Donald, David Herbert, *Lincoln* (New York: Simon & Schuster, 1995).

Dorsey, Bruce, *Reforming Men & Women: Gender in the Antebellum City* (Ithaca: Cornell University Press, 2002).

Downs, Gregory P., *After Appomattox: Military Occupation and the Ends of War* (Cambridge: Harvard University Press, 2015).

Downs, Gregory P., *Declarations of Dependence: The Long Reconstruction of Popular Politics in the South, 1861–1908* (Chapel Hill: University of North Carolina Press, 2011).

Downs, Gregory P., "The Mexicanization of American Politics: The United States' Transnational Path from Civil War to Stabilization," *American Historical Review*, vol. 117 (Apr. 2012): 387–409.

Downs, Gregory P., *The Second American Revolution: The Civil War–Era Struggle over Cuba and the Rebirth of the American Republic* (Chapel Hill: University of North Carolina Press, 2019).

Downs, Gregory P., and Kate Masur, "Introduction," in Downs and Masur, eds., *The World the Civil War Made* (Chapel Hill: University of North Carolina Press, 2015): 1–21.

Doyle, Don Harrison, *The Cause of All Nations: An International History of the American Civil War* (New York: Basic Books, 2017).

Doyle, Don Harrison, *The Social Order of a Frontier Community: Jacksonville, Illinois, 1825–1870* (Urbana: University of Illinois Press, 1983).

Du Bois, W. E. B., *Darkwater: Voices from Within the Veil* (New York: Oxford University, 2007).

Ducharme, Michel, "Macdonald and the Concept of Liberty," in Patrice Dutil and Roger Hall, eds., *Macdonald at 200: New Reflections and Legacies* (Toronto: Dundurn Press, 2014): 141–69.

Dunbar, Erica Armstrong, *She Came to Slay: The Life and Times of Harriet Tubman* (New York: Simon & Schuster, 2019).

Duncan, Robert H., "Political Legitimation and Maximilian's Second Empire in Mexico, 1864–1867," *Mexican Studies/Estudios Mexicanos*, vol. 12 (Winter 1996): 27–66.

Earle, Jonathan H., "Beecher's Bibles and Broadswords: Paving the Way for the Civil War in the West, 1854–1859," in Virginia Scharff, ed., *Empire and Liberty: The Civil War and the West* (Berkeley: University of California Press, 2015): 50–65.

Earle, Jonathan H., *Jacksonian Antislavery & the Politics of Free Soil, 1824–1854* (Chapel Hill: University of North Carolina Press, 2004).

Edgar, Ann, "Patrick Edward Connor," in John A. Garraty and Mark C. Carnes, eds., *American National Biography*, 24 vols. (New York: Oxford University Press, 1999).

Egerton, Douglas R., *Thunder at the Gates: The Black Civil War Regiments that Redeemed America* (New York: Basic Books, 2016).

Egerton, Douglas R., *The Wars of Reconstruction: The Brief, Violent History of America's Most Progressive Era* (New York: Bloomsbury Press, 2014).

Egerton, Douglas R., *Year of Meteors: Stephen Douglas, Abraham Lincoln, and the Election that Brought on the Civil War* (New York: Bloomsbury Press, 2010).

Einolf, Christopher J., *George Thomas: Virginian for the Union* (Norman: University of Oklahoma Press, 2007).

Ellison, Joseph, "Designs for a Pacific Republic," *Oregon Historical Quarterly*, vol. 31 (Dec. 1930): 330–42.

Ellison, William Henry, ed., "Memoirs of Hon. William M. Gwin," *California Historical Society Quarterly*, vol. 19 (March and June 1940): 1–26, 157–84.

Emberton, Carole, *Beyond Redemption: Race, Violence, and the American South after the Civil War* (Chicago: University of Chicago Press, 2013).

Errington, Elizabeth Jane, "British Migration and British America, 1783–1867," in Philip Buckner, ed., *Canada and the British America* (New York: Oxford University Press, 2008): 140–59.

Etcheson, Nicole, *Bleeding Kansas: Contested Liberty in the Civil War Era* (Lawrence: University Press of Kansas, 2004).

Faragher, John Mack, "The Frémonts: Agents of Empire, Legends of Liberty," in Virginia Scharff, ed., *Empire and Liberty: The Civil War and the West* (Berkeley: University of California Press, 2015): 27–49.

Faust, Drew Gilpin, *James Henry Hammond and the Old South: A Design for Mastery* (Baton Rouge: Louisiana State University Press, 1982).

Faust, Drew Gilpin, *Mothers of Invention: Women of the Slaveholding South in the American Civil War* (Chapel Hill: University of North Carolina Press, 1996).

Fehrenbacher, Don E., *The Dred Scott Case: Its Significance in American Law and Politics* (New York: Oxford University Press, 1978).

Fehrenbacher, Don E., *The Slaveholding Republic: An Account of the United States Government's Relations to Slavery* (New York: Oxford University Press, 2001).

Feldberg, Michael, *The Turbulent Era: Riot & Disorder in Jacksonian America* (New York: Oxford University Press, 1980).

Fellman, Michael, Lesley J. Gordon, and Daniel E. Sutherland, *This Terrible War: The Civil War and Its Aftermath* (New York: Pearson, 2003).

Foner, Eric, *Reconstruction: America's Unfinished Revolution, 1865–1877* (New York: Harper & Row, 1988).

Foner, Eric, *The Fiery Trial: Abraham Lincoln and American Slavery* (New York: W. W. Norton, 2010).

Foner, Eric, *Gateway to Freedom: The Hidden History of the Underground Railroad* (New York: W. W. Norton, 2015).

Foner, Eric, *The Second Founding: How the Civil War and Reconstruction Remade the Constitution* (New York: W. W. Norton, 2019).

Ford, John Salmon, *Rip Ford's Texas*, Stephen B. Oates, ed. (Austin: University of Texas Press, 1987).

Foreman, Amanda, *A World on Fire: Britain's Crucial Role in the American Civil War* (New York: Random House, 2010).

Forster, J. J. Ben, "First Spikes: Railways in Macdonald's Early Political Career," in Patrice Dutil and Roger Hall, eds., *Macdonald at 200: New Reflections and Legacies* (Toronto: Dundurn Press, 2014): 173–92.

Fowler, Will, *Independent Mexico: The Pronunciamiento in the Age of Santa Anna, 1821–1858* (Lincoln: University of Nebraska Press, 2016).

Fowler, Will, *Santa Anna of Mexico* (Lincoln: University of Nebraska Press, 2007).

Franklin, John Hope, and Loren Schweninger, *Runaway Slaves: Rebels on the Plantation* (New York: Oxford University Press, 1999).

Frazier, Donald S., *Blood & Treasure: Confederate Empire in the Southwest* (College Station: Texas A&M University Press, 1995).

Fredrickson, George M., *The Arrogance of Race: Historical Perspectives on Slavery, Racism, and Social Inequality* (Middletown: Wesleyan University Press, 1988).

Freehling, William W., *The Road to Disunion*, 2 vols. (New York: Oxford University Press, 1990, 2007).

Freehling, William W., *The South vs. The South: How Anti-Confederate Southerners Shaped the Course of the Civil War* (New York: Oxford University Press, 2001).

Freeman, Joanne B., *The Field of Blood: Violence in Congress and the Road to Civil War* (New York: Farrar, Straus and Giroux, 2018).

Gallagher, Gary W., *Antietam: Essays on the 1862 Maryland Campaign* (Kent: Kent State University Press, 1989).

Gallagher, Gary W., *The Confederate War* (Cambridge: Harvard University Press, 1997).

Gallagher, Gary W., "Disaffection, Persistence, and Nation: Some Directions in Recent Scholarship on the Confederacy," *Civil War History*, vol. 55 (Sept. 2009): 329–53.

Gallagher, Gary W., ed., *Fighting for the Confederacy: The Personal Recollections of General Edward Porter Alexander* (Chapel Hill: University of North Carolina Press, 1989).

Gallagher, Gary W., *Lee and His Generals in War and Memory* (Baton Rouge: Louisiana State University Press, 1998).

Gallagher, Gary W., "The Shenandoah Valley in 1864," in Gallagher, ed., *Struggle for the Shenandoah: Essays on the 1864 Valley Campaign* (Kent: Kent State University Press, 1991): 1–18.

Gallagher, Gary W., *The Union War* (Cambridge: Harvard University Press, 2011).

Gallagher, Gary W., "'Upon Their Success Hang Momentous Interests': Generals," in Gabor S. Boritt, *Why the Confederacy Lost* (New York: Oxford University Press, 1992): 79–108.

Gallagher, Gary W., and Joan Waugh, *The American War: A History of the Civil War Era* (State College: Flip Learning, 2016).

Gallagher, Gary W., Stephen Engle, Robert Krick, and Joseph Glatthaar, *Civil War: Fort Sumter to Appomattox* (New York: Osprey, 2003).

Gallman, J. Matthew, *The Cacophony of Politics: Northern Democrats and the American Civil War* (Charlottesville: University of Virginia Press, 2021).

Garraty, John A., and Mark C. Carnes, eds., *American National Biography*, 24 vols. (New York: Oxford University Press, 1999).

Glatthaar, Joseph T., *Forged in Battle: The Civil War Alliance of Black Soldiers and White Officers* (Baton Rouge: Louisiana State University Press, 1990).

Glatthaar, Joseph T., *General Lee's Army: From Victory to Collapse* (New York: Free Press, 2008).

Glaze, Robert L., "'His Death May have Lost the South her Independence: Albert Sidney Johnston and Civil War Memory," in Andrew S. Bledsoe and Andrew F. Lang, eds., *Upon the Fields of Battle: Essays on the Military History of America's Civil War* (Baton Rouge: Louisiana State University Press, 2018): 271–90.

Gleijeses, Piero, *America's Road to Empire: Foreign Policy from Independence to World War One* (New York: Bloomsbury Academic, 2022).

Gluek, Alvin C., Jr., *Minnesota and the Manifest Destiny of the Canadian Northwest: A Study in Canadian-American Relations* (Toronto: University of Toronto Press, 1965).

Gluek, Alvin C., Jr., "The Riel Rebellion and Canadian-American Relations," *Canadian Historical Review*, vol. 36 (Sept. 1955): 199–221.

Glymph, Thavolia, *Out of the House of Bondage: The Transformation of the Plantation Household* (New York: Cambridge University Press, 2008).

Goodheart, Adam, *1861: The Civil War Awakening* (New York: Random House, 2011).

Goodwin, Doris Kearns, *Team of Rivals: The Political Genius of Abraham Lincoln* (New York: Simon & Schuster, 2005).

Gould, Lewis L., *Alexander Watkins Terrell: Civil War Soldier, Texas Lawmaker, American Diplomat* (Austin: University of Texas Press, 2004).

Green, Constance McLaughlin, *The Secret City: A History of Race Relations in the Nation's Capital* (Princeton: Princeton University Press, 1967).

Greenberg, Amy S., *Manifest Manhood and the Antebellum American Empire* (New York: Cambridge University Press, 2005).

Greenberg, Amy S., *A Wicked War: Polk, Clay, Lincoln, and the 1846 U.S. Invasion of Mexico* (New York: Alfred A. Knopf, 2012).

Greene, A. Wilson, "'I Fought the Battle Splendidly': George B. McClellan and the Maryland Campaign," in Gary W. Gallagher, *The Union War* (Cambridge: Harvard University Press, 2011): 56–83.

Grimsley, Mark, *The Hard Hand of War: Union Military Policy toward Southern Civilians, 1861–1865* (New York: Cambridge University Press, 1995).

Guardino, Peter, *The Dead March: A History of the Mexican-American War* (Cambridge: Harvard University Press, 2017).

Guelzo, Allen C., *Fateful Lightning: A New History of the Civil War and Reconstruction* (New York: Oxford University Press, 2012).

Guelzo, Allen C., *Lincoln and Douglas: The Debates that Defined America* (New York: Simon & Schuster, 2008).

Guelzo, Allen C., *Robert E. Lee: A Life* (New York: Alfred A. Knopf, 2021).

Guterl, Matthew Pratt, *American Mediterranean: Southern Slaveholders in the Age of Emancipation* (Cambridge: Harvard University Press, 2008).

Guyatt, Nicholas, "America's Conservatory: Race, Reconstruction, and the Santo Domingo Debate," *Journal of American History*, vol. 97 (March 2011): 974–1000.

Guyatt, Nicholas, "'The Future Empire of Our Freedmen': Republican Colonization Schemes in Texas and Mexico, 1861–1865," in Adam Arenson and Andrew R. Graybill, eds., *Civil War Wests: Testing the Limits of the United States* (Berkeley: University of California Press, 2015): 95–117.

Gwyn, Richard, *The Man Who Made Us: The Life and Times of John A. Macdonald, 1815–1867* (Toronto: Vintage Canada, 2007).

Gwyn, Richard, *Nation Maker: Sir John A. Macdonald, 1867–1891* (Toronto: Vintage Canada, 2012).

Hahn, Steven, "Afterword: What Sort of World Did the Civil War Make?," in Gregory P. Downs and Kate Masur, eds., *The World the Civil War Made* (Chapel Hill: University of North Carolina Press, 2015): 337–56.

Hahn, Steven, *A Nation Under Our Feet: Black Political Struggles in the Rural South from Slavery to the Great Migration* (Cambridge: Harvard University Press, 2003).

Hahn, Steven, *Political Worlds of Slavery and Freedom* (Cambridge: Harvard University Press, 2009).

Hahn, Steven, "Slave Emancipation, Indian Peoples, and the Projects of a New American Nation-State," *Journal of the Civil War*, vol. 3 (Sept. 2013): 307–30.

Hahn, Steven, *A Nation Without Borders: The United States and Its World in an Age of Civil Wars, 1830–1910* (New York: Viking Penguin, 2016).

Hale, Charles A., *The Transformation of Liberalism in Late Nineteenth-Century Mexico* (Princeton: Princeton University Press, 1989).

Haley, James L., *Sam Houston* (Norman: University of Oklahoma Press, 2002).

Hamnett, Brian, *Juárez* (New York: Longman, 1994).

Hankinson, Alan, *Man of Wars: William Howard Russell of The Times* (London: Heinemann, 1982).

Hanna, Alfred J., and Kathryn A. Hanna, *Napoleon III and Mexico: American Triumph over Monarchy* (Chapel Hill: University of North Carolina Press, 1971).

Hanna, Alfred J., "The Role of Matthew Fontaine Maury in the Mexican Empire," *Virginia Magazine of History and Biography*, vol. 55 (April 1947): 105–25.

Hanna, Kathryn Abbey, "The Roles of the South in the French Intervention in Mexico," *Journal of Southern History*, vol. 20 (Feb. 1954): 3–21.

Hardy, William E., "South of the Border: Ulysses S. Grant and the French Intervention," *Civil War History*, vol. 54 (March 2008): 63–86.

Harrold, Stanley, *Border War: Fighting over Slavery before the Civil War* (Chapel Hill: University of North Carolina Press, 2010).

Haynes, Sam W., *Unfinished Revolution: The Early American Republic in a British World* (Charlottesville: University of Virginia Press, 2010).

Haynes, Sam W., *Unsettled Land: From Revolution to Republic, the Struggle for Texas* (New York: Basic Books, 2022).

Hendrickson, David C., "Escaping Insecurity: The American Founding and the Control of Violence," in Patrick Griffin, Robert G. Ingram, Peter S. Onuf, and Brian Schoen, eds., *Between Sovereignty and Anarchy: The Politics of Violence in the American Revolutionary Era* (Charlottesville: University of Virginia Press, 2015): 216–42.

Hendrickson, David C., "The First Union: Nationalism versus Internationalism in the American Revolution," in Eliga H. Gould and Peter S. Onuf, eds., *Empire and Nation: The American Revolution in the Atlantic World* (Baltimore: Johns Hopkins University Press, 2005): 35–53.

Hendrickson, David C., *Union, Nation, or Empire: The American Debate over International Relations, 1789–1941* (Lawrence: University Press of Kansas, 2009).

Hennessy, John J., "The Looting and Bombardment of Fredericksburg: 'Vile Spirits' or War Transformed?," in Andrew S. Bledsoe and Andrew F. Lang, eds., *Upon the Fields of Battle: Essays on the Military History of America's Civil War* (Baton Rouge: Louisiana State University Press, 2018): 124–63.

Hermann, Janet Sharp, *Joseph E. Davis: Pioneer Patriarch* (Jackson: University Press of Mississippi, 1990).

Hermann, Janet Sharp, *The Pursuit of a Dream* (Jackson: University Press of Mississippi, 1999).

Hess, Earl J., *The Civil War in the West: Victory and Defeat from the Appalachians to the Mississippi* (Chapel Hill: University of North Carolina Press, 2012).

Hess, Earl J., *Braxton Bragg: The Most Hated Man of the Confederacy* (Chapel Hill: University of North Carolina Press, 2016).

Hietala, Thomas R., *Manifest Design: Anxious Aggrandizement in Late Jacksonian America* (Ithaca: Cornell University Press, 1985).

Hildner, Ernest G., Jr., "The Mexican Envoy Visits Lincoln," *Abraham Lincoln Quarterly*, vol. 6 (Sept. 1950): 184–88.

Hoffert, Sylvia, D., *Jane Grey Swisshelm: An Unconventional Life, 1815–1884* (Chapel Hill: University of North Carolina Press, 2004).

Holt, Michael F., *Franklin Pierce* (New York: Henry Holt, 2010).

Holt, Michael F., *The Rise and Fall of the American Whig Party: Jacksonian Politics and the Onset of the Civil War* (New York: Oxford University Press, 1999).

Horton, James Oliver, and Lois E. Horton, *Slavery and the Making of America* (New York: Oxford University Press, 2005).

Horton, Lois E., *Harriet Tubman and the Fight for Freedom: A Brief History with Documents* (Boston: Bedford/St. Martin's, 2013).

Horwitz, Tony, *Midnight Rising: John Brown and the Raid that Sparked the Civil War* (New York: Henry Holt and Co., 2011).

Howe, Daniel Walker, *What Hath God Wrought: The Transformation of America, 1815–1848* (New York: Oxford University Press, 2007).

Hoyt, William D., Jr., ed., "New Light on General Jubal A. Early After Appomattox," *Journal of Southern History,* vol. 9 (Feb. 1943): 113–17.

Hudson, Linda S., *Mistress of Manifest Destiny: A Biography of Jane McManus Storm Cazneau, 1807–1878* (Austin: Texas State Historical Association, 2001).

Huebner, Timothy S., *Liberty & Union: The Civil War Era and American Constitutionalism* (Lawrence: University of Kansas Press, 2016).

Hunt, Alfred N., *Haiti's Influence on Antebellum America: Slumbering Volcano in the Caribbean* (Baton Rouge: Louisiana State University, 1988).

Hutton, Paul Andrew, "Paladin of the Republic: Philip H. Sheridan," in Robert Cowley, ed., *With My Face to the Enemy: Perspectives on the Civil War* (New York: G. P. Putnam's Sons, 2001): 348–63.

Ignatiev, Noel, *How the Irish Became White* (New York: Routledge, 1995).

Irby, James A., *Backdoor at Bagdad: The Civil War on the Rio Grande* (El Paso: Texas Western Press, 1977).

Jackson, Holly, *American Radicals: How Nineteenth-Century Protest Shaped the Nation* (New York: Crown, 2019).

Jackson, Kellie Carter, *Force and Freedom: Black Abolitionists and the Politics of Violence* (Philadelphia: University of Pennsylvania Press, 2019).

Jacoby, Karl, " 'The Broad Platform of Extermination': Arizona Territory, 1860–1870," in Brian DeLay, ed., *North American Borderlands* (New York: Routledge, 2013): 284–304.

Janney, Caroline E., *The Ends of War: The Unfinished Fight of Lee's Army after Appomattox* (Chapel Hill: University of North Carolina Press, 2021).

Jewell, James Robbins, "Thwarting Southern Schemes and British Bluster in the Pacific Northwest," in Adam Arenson and Andrew R. Graybill, eds., *Civil War Wests: Testing the Limits of the United States* (Berkeley: University of California Press, 2015): 15–32.

Johnson, J. K., "John A. Macdonald and the Kingston Business Community," in Gerald Tulchinsky, ed., *To Preserve & Defend: Essays on Kingston in the Nineteenth Century* (Montreal: McGill-Queen's University Press, 1976): 141–56.

Johnson, Walter, *Soul by Soul: Life Inside the Antebellum Slave Market* (Cambridge: Harvard University Press, 1999).

Johnson, Walter, *River of Dark Dreams: Slavery and Empire in the Cotton Kingdom* (Cambridge: Harvard University Press, 2013).

Jones, Howard, *Union in Peril: The Crisis over British Intervention in the Civil War* (Chapel Hill: University of North Carolina Press, 1992).

Jones, Howard, *Abraham Lincoln and a New Birth of Freedom: The Union and Slavery in the Diplomacy of the Civil War* (Lincoln: University of Nebraska Press, 1999).

Jones, Jacqueline, *A Dreadful Deceit: The Myth of Race from the Colonial Era to Obama's America* (New York: Basic Books, 2013).

Jones, Robert F., "Rebel Without a War: The *Shenandoah*," in Robert Cowley, ed., *With My Face to the Enemy: Perspectives on the Civil War* (New York: G. P. Putnam's Sons, 2001): 498–510.

Josephy, Alvin M., Jr., *The Civil War in the American West* (New York: Alfred A. Knopf, 1991).

Karp, Matthew, *This Vast Southern Empire: Slaveholders at the Helm of American Foreign Policy* (Cambridge: Harvard University Press, 2016).

Katz, Friedrich, "The Liberal Republic and the Porfiriato, 1867–1910," in Leslie Bethell, ed., *Mexico Since Independence* (New York: Cambridge University Press, 1991): 49–124.

Keegan, John, *The American Civil War: A Military History* (New York: Vintage, 2009).

Keehn, David C., *Knights of the Golden Circle: Secret Empire, Southern Secession, Civil War* (Baton Rouge: Louisiana State University Press, 2013).

Kelley, Sean M., "'Mexico in His Head': Slavery and the Texas-Mexico Border, 1810–1860," *Journal of Social History*, vol. 37 (Spring 2004): 709–23.

Kelley, Sean M., *Los Brazos de Dios: A Plantation Society in the Texas Borderlands, 1821–1865* (Baton Rouge: Louisiana State University Press, 2010).

Kelly, James C., "William Gannaway Brownlow, Part 1," *Tennessee Historical Quarterly*, vol. 43 (Spring 1984): 25–43.

Kelly, James C., "William Gannaway Brownlow, Part 2," *Tennessee Historical Quarterly*, vol. 43 (Summer, 1984): 155–72.

Kelly, Patrick J., "The Cats-Paw: Confederate Ambitions in Latin America," in Don H. Doyle, ed., *American Civil Wars: The United States, Latin America, Europe, and the Crisis of the 1860s* (Chapel Hill: University of North Carolina Press, 2017): 58–81.

Kelly, Patrick J., "The North American Crisis of the 1860s," *Journal of the Civil War Era*, vol. 2 (Sept. 2012): 337–68.

Kelman, Ari, *A Misplaced Massacre: Struggling Over the Memory of Sand Creek* (Cambridge: Harvard University Press, 2012).

Kerby, Robert L., *Kirby Smith's Confederacy: The Trans-Mississippi South, 1863–1865* (New York: Columbia University Press, 1972).

Kersh, Rogan, *Dreams of a More Perfect Union* (Ithaca: Cornell University Press, 2001).

King, Alvy L., *Louis T. Wigfall: Southern Fire-Eater* (Baton Rouge: Louisiana State University, 1970).

Kiser, William S., "'We Must Have Chihuahua and Sonora': Civil War Diplomacy in the U.S.-Mexico Borderlands," *Journal of the Civil War Era*, vol. 9 (June 2019): 196–222.

Knapp, Frank Averill, Jr., *The Life of Sebastián Lerdo de Tejada, 1823–1889: A Study of Influence and Obscurity* (New York: Greenwood Press, 1968).

Kolchin, Peter, *American Slavery, 1619–1877* (New York: Hill & Wang, 2003).

Krauthamer, Barbara, "Indian Territory and the Treaties of 1866: A Long History of Emancipation," in Gregory P. Downs and Kate Masur, eds., *The World the Civil War Made* (Chapel Hill: University of North Carolina Press, 2015): 226–48.

Krauze, Enrique, *Mexico Biography of Power: A History of Modern Mexico, 1810–1996* (New York: Harper Collins, 1997).

Krikorian, Jacqueline, and David R. Cameron, "The 1867 Union of the British North American Colonies: A View from the United States," in Marcel Martel Krikorian and Adrian Shubert, eds., *Globalizing Confederation: Canada and the World in 1867* (Toronto: University of Toronto Press, 2017): 47–60.

Kushner, Howard I., "Visions of the Northwest Coast: Gwin and Seward in the 1850s," *Western Historical Quarterly*, vol. 4 (July 1973): 295–306.

Lamar, Howard R., *The Far Southwest, 1846–1912: A Territorial History* (New Haven: Yale University Press, 1966).

Lamar, Howard R., ed., *The New Encyclopedia of the American West* (New Haven: Yale University Press, 1998).

Lamar, Howard R., ed., *The Reader's Encyclopedia of the American West* (New York: Thomas Y. Crowell, 1977).

Lang, Andrew F., "The Limits of American Exceptionalism: Military Occupation, Emancipation, and the Preservation of Union," in Andrew S. Bledsoe and Andrew F. Lang, eds., *Upon the Fields of Battle: Essays on the Military History of America's Civil War* (Baton Rouge: Louisiana State University Press, 2018): 183–204.

Larsen, Arthur J., ed., *Crusader and Feminist: Letters of Jane Grey Swisshelm, 1858-1865* Saint Paul: Minnesota Historical Society, 1934).

Larsen, John Lauritz, *The Market Revolution in America: Liberty, Ambition, and the Eclipse of the Common Good* (New York: Cambridge University Press, 2009).

Larson, Kate Clifford, *Bound for the Promised Land: Harriet Tubman, Portrait of an American Hero* (New York: One World, 2004).

Lehman, Christopher P., *Slavery's Reach: Southern Slaveholders in the North Star State* (St. Paul: Minnesota Historical Society, 2019).

Leonard, Elijah, *The Honorable Elijah Leonard: A Memoir* (London, Ontario: Advertiser Print. Co., 1894).

Leonard, Elizabeth D., *Benjamin Franklin Butler: A Noisy, Fearless Life* (Chapel Hill: University of North Carolina, 2022).

Leonard, Elizabeth D., *Yankee Women: Gender Battles in the Civil War* (New York: W. W. Norton, 1994).

Lepore, Jill, *These Truths: A History of the United States* (New York: W. W. Norton, 2018).

Lessoff, Alan, *The Nation and Its City: Politics, "Corruption," and Progress in Washington, D. C., 1861–1902* (Baltimore: Johns Hopkins Press, 1994).

Levine, Allan, *Toronto: Biography of a City* (Toronto: Douglas & McIntyre, 2014).

Levine, Bruce, *Half Slave and Half Free: The Roots of Civil War* (New York: Hill and Wang, 2005).

Levine, Bruce, *The Fall of the House of Dixie: The Civil War and the Social Revolution that Transformed the South* (New York: Random House, 2014).

Levine, Robert S., *Martin Delany, Frederick Douglass and the Politics of Representative Identity* (Chapel Hill: University of North Carolina Press, 1997).

Levy, Leonard W., "Sims' Case: The Fugitive Slave Law in Boston in 1851," *Journal of Negro History*, vol. 35 (Jan. 1950): 39–74.

Lewis, Charles Lee, *Matthew Fontaine Maury* (New York: Arno Press, 1980).

Libby, David J., *Slavery and Frontier Mississippi, 1720–1835* (Jackson: University Press of Mississippi, 2004).

Link, William A., *Roots of Secession: Slavery and Politics in Antebellum Virginia* (Chapel Hill: University of North Carolina Press, 2003).

Long, E. B., *The Saints and the Union: Utah Territory during the Civil War* (Urbana: University of Illinois Press, 1981).

Love, Eric T. L., *Race Over Empire: Racism and U. S. Imperialism, 1865–1900* (Chapel Hill: University of North Carolina Press, 2004).

Lowe, Richard, "Battle on the Levee: The Fight at Milliken's Bend," in John David Smith, ed., *Black Soldiers in Blue: African American Troops in the Civil War Era* (Chapel Hill: University of North Carolina Press, 2002): 107–35.

Lowenstein, Roger, *Ways and Means: Lincoln and His Cabinet and the Financing of the Civil War* (New York: Penguin Press, 2022).

Lower, Arthur R. M., "The Character of Kingston," in Gerald Tulchinsky, ed., *To Preserve & Defend: Essays on Kingston in the Nineteenth Century* (Montreal: McGill-Queen's University Press, 1976): 17–35.

Lower, J. Arthur, *Western Canada: An Outline History* (Vancouver: Douglas & McIntyre, 1983).

Lynch, John, *The Spanish American Revolutions, 1808–1826* (New York: W. W. Norton, 1986).

Mahin, Dean B., *One War at a Time: The International Dimensions of the American Civil War* (Washington, DC: Brassey's, 1999).

Mahoney, Harry Thayer, and Marjorie Locke Mahoney, *Mexico and the Confederacy, 1860–1867* (San Francisco: Austin & Winfield, 1998).

Majewski, John, and Todd W. Wahlstrom, "Geography as Power: The Political Economy of Matthew Fontaine Maury," *Virginia Magazine of History and Biography*, vol. 120 (Dec. 2012): 340–71.

Manning, Chandra, *What This Cruel War Was Over: Soldiers, Slavery, and the Civil War* (New York: Vintage, 2007).

Manning, William R., ed., *Diplomatic Correspondence of the United States, Inter-American Affairs, 1831–1860*, vol. 9: *Mexico, 1848–1860* (Washington: Carnegie Endowment for International Peace, 1937).

Marshall, Daniel P., "No Parallel: American Miner-Soldiers at War with the Nlakpamux of the Canadian West," in John M. Findlay and Ken S. Coates, eds., *Parallel Destinies: Canadian-American Relations West of the Rockies* (Seattle: University of Washington Press, 2002): 31–79.

Marten, James, *Texas Divided: Loyalty and Dissent in the Lone Star State, 1856–1874* (University Press of Kentucky, 1990).

Martin, Ged, *Britain and the Origins of Canadian Confederation, 1837–1867* (London: Macmillan, 1995).

Martin, Ged, *John A. Macdonald: Canada's First Prime Minister* (Toronto: Dundurn, 2013).

Masich, Andrew E., *Civil War in the Southwest Borderlands, 1861–1867* (Norman: University of Oklahoma Press, 2017).

Masur, Kate, *Until Justice be Done: America's First Civil Rights Movement, from the Revolution to Reconstruction* (New York: W. W. Norton, 2021).

Matthews, Glenna, *The Golden State in the Civil War: Thomas Starr King, the Republican Party, and the Birth of Modern California* (New York: Cambridge University Press, 2012).

Maxwell, John Gary, *The Civil War Years in Utah: The Kingdom of God and the Territory That Did Not Fight* (Norman: University of Oklahoma Press, 2016).

May, Robert E., "Introduction," in Robert E. May, ed., *The Union, the Confederacy, and the Atlantic Rim* (West Lafayette: Purdue University Press, 1995): 1–27.

May, Robert E., "The Irony of Confederate Diplomacy: Visions of Empire, the Monroe Doctrine, and the Quest for Nationhood," *Journal of Southern History*, vol. 83 (Feb. 2017): 69–106.

May, Robert E., "Lobbyists for Commercial Empire: Jane Cazneau, William Cazneau, and U.S. Caribbean Policy, 1846–1878," *Pacific Historical Review*, vol. 48 (Aug. 1979): 383–412.

May, Robert E., *Manifest Destiny's Underworld: Filibustering in America* (Chapel Hill: University of North Carolina Press, 2002).

May, Robert E., *Slavery, Race, and Conquest in the Tropics: Lincoln, Douglas, and the Future of Latin America* (New York: Cambridge University Press, 2013).

May, Robert E., *The Southern Dream of a Caribbean Empire: 1854–1861* (Baton Rouge: Louisiana State University Press, 1973).

McAllen, M. M., *Maximilian and Carlota: Europe's Last Empire in Mexico* (San Antonio: Trinity University Press, 2014).

McCardell, John, *The Idea of a Southern Nation: Southern Nationalists and Southern Nationalism, 1830–1860* (New York: W. W. Norton, 1979).

McCurdy, Charles W., "Prelude to Civil War: A Snapshot of the California Supreme Court at Work in 1858," *California Supreme Court Historical Society Yearbook*, vol. 1 (1994): 3–32.

McCurry, Stephanie, *Confederate Reckoning: Power and Politics in the Civil War South* (Cambridge: Harvard University Press, 2010).

McCurry, Stephanie, *Masters of Small Worlds: Yeoman Households, Gender Relations, and the Political Culture of the Antebellum South Carolina Low Country* (New York: Oxford University Press, 1995).

McDaniel, W. Caleb, *The Problem of Democracy in the Age of Slavery: Garrisonian Abolitionists & Transatlantic Reform* (Baton Rouge: Louisiana State University Press, 2013).

McFall, F. Lawrence, Jr., "To Danville: 'A Government on Wheels,'" in William C. Davis and James I. Robertson, Jr., eds., *Virginia at War, 1865* (Lexington: University Press of Kentucky, 2012): 71–84.

McFeely, William S., *Grant: A Biography* (New York: W. W. Norton, 1981).

McKenzie, Robert Tracy, "Contesting Secession: Parson Brownlow and the Rhetoric of Proslavery Unionism, 1860–1861," *Civil War History*, vol. 48 (Dec. 2002): 294–312.

McNab, David T., "Herman Merivale and Colonial Office Indian Policy in the Mid-Nineteenth Century," in Ian A. L. Getty and Antoine S. Lussier, eds., *As Long as the Sun Shines and Water Flows: A Reader in Canadian Native Studies* (Vancouver: University of British Columbia Press, 2016): 85–103.

McPherson, Hallie M., "The Plan of William McKendree Gwin for a Colony in North Mexico, 1863–1865," *Pacific Historical Review*, vol. 2 (Dec. 1933): 357–86.

McPherson, James M., *Battle Cry of Freedom: The Civil War Era* (New York: Oxford University Press, 1988).

McPherson, James M., *For Cause and Comrades: Why Men Fought in the Civil War* (New York: Oxford University Press, 1997).

McPherson, James M., *War on the Waters: The Union and Confederate Navies, 1861–1865* (Chapel Hill: University of North Carolina Press, 2012).

Messamore, Barbara J., "Diplomacy or Duplicity?: Lord Lisgar, John A. Macdonald, and the Treaty of Washington, 1871," *Journal of Imperial and Commonwealth History*, vol. 32 (May 2004): 29–53.

Messamore, Barbara J., "Macdonald and the Governors General: The Prime Minister's Use and Abuse of the Crown," in Patrice Dutil and Roger Hall, eds., *Macdonald at 200: New Reflections and Legacies* (Toronto: Dundurn Press, 2014): 253–81.

Miller, J. R., "Macdonald as Minister of Indian Affairs: The Shaping of Canadian Indian Policy," in Patrice Dutil and Roger Hall, eds., *Macdonald at 200: New Reflections and Legacies* (Toronto: Dundurn Press, 2014): 311–40.

Miller, J. R., *Skyscrapers Hide the Heavens: A History of Indian-White Relations in Canada* (Toronto: University of Toronto Press, 1989).

Miller, Robert Ryal, "Herman Sturm: Hoosier Secret Agent for Mexico," *Indiana Magazine of History*, 58 (March 1962): 1–15.

Miller, Robert Ryal, "Lew Wallace and the French Intervention," *Indiana Magazine of History*, vol. 59 (March 1963): 31–50.

Miller, Robert Ryal, "Matías Romero: Mexican Minister to the United States during the Juárez-Maximilian Era," *Hispanic American Historical Review*, vol. 45 (May 1965): 228–45.

Monehon, Carl H., *Edmund J. Davis: Civil War General, Republican Leader, Reconstruction Governor* (Fort Worth: Texas Christian University Press, 2010).

Montejano, David, *Anglos and Mexicans in the Making of Texas, 1836–1986* (Austin: University of Texas Press, 1987).

Montgomery, Cora [Jane Cazneau], *Eagle Pass; Or, Life on the Border* (New York: George P. Putnam, 1852).

Moore, Christopher, *1867: How the Fathers Made a Deal* (Toronto: McClelland & Stewart, 1997).

Morrison, Michael A., *Slavery and the American West: The Eclipse of Manifest Destiny and the Coming of the Civil War* (Chapel Hill: University of North Carolina Press, 1997).

Morsberger, Katharine M., and Robert E. Morsberger, *Lew Wallace: Militant Romantic* (New York: McGraw-Hill, 1980).

Morton, W. L., "British North America and a Continent in Dissolution, 1861–1871," *History*, vol. 47 (1962): 139–56.

Morton, W. L., *The Critical Years: The Union of British North America, 1857–1873* (Toronto: McClelland and Stewart, 1964).

Namias, June, *White Captives: Gender and Ethnicity on the American Frontier* (Chapel Hill: University of North Carolina Press, 1993).

Neely, Mark E., Jr., *The Civil War and the Limits of Destruction* (Cambridge: Harvard University Press, 2007).

Neely, Mark E., Jr., *The Fate of Liberty: Abraham Lincoln and Civil Liberties* (New York: Oxford University Press, 1991).

Neely, Mark E., Jr., *Lincoln and the Democrats: The Politics of Opposition in the Civil War* (New York: Cambridge University Press, 2017).

Neely, Mark E., Jr., *The Union Divided: Party Conflict in the Civil War North* (Cambridge: Harvard University Press, 2002).

Nelson, Larry E., *Bullets, Ballots, and Rhetoric: Confederate Policy for the United States Presidential Contest of 1864* (Tuscaloosa: University of Alabama Press, 1980).

Nelson, Megan Kate, "Death in the Distance: Confederate Manifest Destiny and the Campaign for New Mexico, 1861–1862," in Adam Arenson and Andrew R. Graybill, eds., *Civil War Wests: Testing the Limits of the United States* (Berkeley: University of California Press, 2015): 33–52.

Nelson, Megan Kate, *The Three-Cornered War: The Union, the Confederacy, and Native Peoples in the Fight for the West* (New York: Scribner, 2020).

Newmyer, R. Kent, *The Supreme Court under Marshall and Taney* (Wheeling, IL: Harland Davidson, 2006).

Nichols, David A., *Lincoln and the Indians: Civil War Policy and Politics* (Columbia: University of Missouri Press, 1978).

Nichols, James David, "The Line of Liberty: Runaway Slaves and Fugitive Peons in the Texas-Mexico Borderlands," *Western Historical Quarterly*, vol. 44 (Winter 2013): 413–33.

Nugent, Walter, *Habits of Empire: A History of American Expansion* (New York: Random House, 2008).

Oakes, James, *Freedom National: The Destruction of Slavery in the United States, 1861–1865* (New York: W. W. Norton, 2013).

Oakes, James, *The Radical and the Republican: Frederick Douglass, Abraham Lincoln, and the Triumph of Antislavery Politics* (New York: W. W. Norton, 2007).

Oakes, James, *The Ruling Race: A History of American Slaveholders* (New York: Alfred A. Knopf, 1982).

Oakes, James, *The Scorpion's Sting: Antislavery and the Coming of the Civil War* (New York: W. W. Norton, 2013).

Oakes, James, *Slavery and Freedom: An Interpretation of the Old South* (New York: Alfred A. Knopf, 1990).

O'Connor, Richard, *The Cactus Throne: The Tragedy of Maximilian and Carlotta* (New York: G. P. Putnam's Sons, 1971).

Oertel, Kristen T., *Harriet Tubman: Slavery, the Civil War, and Civil Rights in the Nineteenth Century* (New York: Routledge, 2016).

O'Flaherty, Daniel, *General Jo Shelby: Undefeated Rebel* (Chapel Hill: University of North Carolina Press, 1954).

Olliff, Donathan C., *Reforma Mexico and the United States: A Search for Alternatives to Annexation, 1854–1861* (Tuscaloosa: University of Alabama Press, 1981).

Osborne, Charles C., *Jubal: The Life and Times of General Jubal A. Early, C.S.A., Defender of the Lost Cause* (Chapel Hill: Algonquin Books, 1992).

Osborne, Charles C., "Jubal Early's Raid on Washington," in Robert Cowley, ed., *With My Face to the Enemy: Perspectives on the Civil War* (New York: G. P. Putnam's Sons, 2001): 443–58.

Ostler, Jeffrey, *The Plains Sioux and U.S. Colonialism from Lewis and Clark to Wounded Knee* (New York: Cambridge University Press, 2004).

Owsley, Frank Lawrence, and Harriet Chappel Owsley, *King Cotton Diplomacy: Foreign Relations of the Confederate States of America* (Chicago: University of Chicago Press, 1959).

Owram, Doug, *Promise of Eden: The Canadian Expansionist Movement and the Idea of the West, 1856–1900* (Toronto: University of Toronto Press, 1980).

Painter, Nell Irvin, "Martin R. Delany: Elitism and Black Nationalism," in Leon
    Litwack and August Meier, eds., *Black Leaders of the Nineteenth Century* (Urbana:
    University of Illinois Press, 1988): 148–171.

Paludan, Phillip Shaw, *"A People's Contest": The Union and Civil War, 1861–1865* (Law-
    rence: University Press of Kansas, 1996).

Pani, Erika, "Dreaming of a Mexican Empire: The Political Projects of the 'Imperi-
    alistas,'" *Hispanic American Historical Review*, vol. 82, no. 1 (2002): 1–32.

Pani, Erika, "Juárez vs. Maximiliano: Mexico's Experiment with Monarchy," in Don
    H. Doyle, ed., *American Civil Wars: The United States, Latin America, Europe, and
    the Crisis of the 1860s* (Chapel Hill: University of North Carolina Press, 2017):
    167–84.

Paolino, Ernest N., *The Foundations of the American Empire: William Henry Seward and
    U.S. Foreign Policy* (Ithaca: Cornell University Press, 1973).

Parks, Joseph Howard, *General Edmund Kirby Smith, C.S.A.* (Baton Rouge: Louisiana
    State University Press, 1962).

Paul, Rodman W., *The Far West and the Great Plains in Transition, 1859–1900* (New
    York: Harper & Row, 1988).

Perret, Geoffrey, "Grant's Tennessee Gamble," in Robert Cowley, ed., *With My Face to the
    Enemy: Perspectives on the Civil War* (New York: G. P. Putnam's Sons, 2001): 105–21.

Perry, Adele, *Colonial Relations: The Douglas-Connolly Family and the Nineteenth-Century
    Imperial World* (New York: Cambridge University Press, 2015).

Perry, Mark, *Conceived in Liberty: Joshua Chamberlain, William Oates, and the American
    Civil War* (New York: Viking, 1997).

Phenix, Patricia, *Private Demons: The Tragic Personal Life of John A. Macdonald* (Toronto:
    McClelland & Stewart, 2006).

Ponce, Pearl T., "'As Dead as Julius Caesar': The Rejection of the McLane-Ocampo
    Treaty," *Civil War History*, vol. 53 (Dec. 2007): 342–78.

Potter, David M., and Don E. Fehrenbacher, *The Impending Crisis: America Before the
    Civil War: 1848–1861* (New York: Harper Perennial, 2011).

Pryke, Kenneth G., *Nova Scotia and Confederation, 1864–74* (Toronto: University of
    Toronto Press, 1979).

Quarles, Benjamin, "Harriet Tubman's Unlikely Leadership," in Leon Litwack and
    August Meier, eds., *Black Leaders of the Nineteenth Century* (Urbana: University of
    Illinois Press, 1988): 43–57.

Quatman, G. William, *A Young General and the Fall of Richmond: The Life and Career
    of Godfrey Weitzel* (Athens: Ohio University Press, 2015).

Quinn, Arthur, *The Rivals: William Gin, David Broderick, and the Birth of California*
    (Lincoln: University of Nebraska Press, 1994).

Rable, George C., *The Confederate Republic: A Revolution Against Politics* (Chapel Hill:
    University of North Carolina Press, 1994).

Radforth, Ian, *Royal Spectacle: The 1860 Visit of the Prince of Wales to Canada and the
    United States* (Toronto: University of Toronto Press, 2004).

Rafuse, Ethan S., *McClellan's War: The Failure of Moderation in the Struggle for the Union*
    (Bloomington: Indiana University Press, 2005).

Reid, Richard M., *African Canadians in Union Blue: Volunteering for the Cause in the Civil
    War* (Vancouver: UBC Press, 2014).

Reid, Whitelaw W., *After the War: A Southern Tour, May 1, 1865 to May 1, 1866* (New York: Moore, Wilstach, & Baldwin, 1866).

Reséndez, Andrés, *The Other Slavery: The Uncovered Story of Indian Enslavement in America* (Boston: Houghton Mifflin Harcourt, 2016).

Reynolds, David S., *John Brown, Abolitionist: The Man Who Killed Slavery, Sparked the Civil War, and Seeded Civil Rights* (New York: Vintage Books, 2005).

Reynolds, David S., *Mightier Than the Sword: Uncle Tom's Cabin and the Battle for America* (New York: W. W. Norton, 2011).

Reynolds, Donald E., *Texas Terror: The Slave Insurrection Panic of 1860 and the Secession of the Lower South* (Baton Rouge: Louisiana State University Press, 2007).

Rhodes, Jane, *Mary Ann Shadd Cary: The Black Press and Protest in the Nineteenth Century* (Bloomington: Indiana University Press, 1998).

Richards, Leonard L., *The California Gold Rush and the Coming of the Civil War* (New York: Random House, 2008).

Richards, Leonard L. *The Slave Power: The Free North and Southern Domination, 1780–1860* (Baton Rouge: Louisiana State University, 2000).

Richardson, Heather Cox, *The Death of Reconstruction: Race, Labor, and Politics in the Post–Civil War North, 1865–1901* (Cambridge: Harvard University Press, 2001).

Richardson, Heather Cox, *To Make Men Free: A History of the Republican Party* (New York: Basic Books, 2014).

Richardson, Heather Cox, *West from Appomattox: The Reconstruction of America after the Civil War* (New Haven: Yale University Press, 2007).

Ridley, Jasper, *Maximilian and Juárez* (London: Phoenix Press, 1992).

Robinson, Armstead L., *Bitter Fruits of Bondage: The Demise of Slavery and the Collapse of the Confederacy, 1861–1865* (Charlottesville: University of Virginia Press, 2005).

Roeder, Ralph, *Juárez and His Mexico*, 2 vols. (New York: Viking Press, 1947).

Rolle, Andrew, *The Lost Cause: The Confederate Exodus to Mexico* (Norman: University of Oklahoma Press, 1965).

Rosen, Hannah, *Terror in the Heart of Freedom: Citizenship, Sexual Violence, and the Meaning of Race in the Postemancipation South* (Chapel Hill, University of North Carolina, 2009).

Ross, Alexander Milton, *Recollections and Experiences of an Abolitionist, from 1855 to 1865* (Toronto: Rowsell and Hutchison, 1875).

Rothman, Joshua D., *Flush Times and Fever Dreams: A Story of Capitalism and Slavery in the Age of Jackson* (Athens: University of Georgia Press, 2012).

Rubin, Anne Sarah, *A Shattered Nation: The Rise and Fall of the Confederacy, 1861–1868* (Chapel Hill: University of North Carolina Press, 2005).

Russell, Philip L., *The History of Mexico from Pre-Conquest to Present* (New York: Routledge, 2010).

Russell, William Howard, *My Diary North and South*, ed. Fletcher Pratt (New York: Harper & Bros., 1954).

Ryan, Mary P., *Womanhood in America: From Colonial Times to the Present* (New York: Franklin Watts, 1983).

Sainlaude, Stève, *France and the American Civil War: A Diplomatic History* (Chapel Hill: University of North Carolina Press, 2019).

Sainlaude, Stève, "France's Grand Design and the Confederacy," in Don H. Doyle, ed., *American Civil Wars: The United States, Latin America, Europe, and the Crisis of the 1860s* (Chapel Hill: University of North Carolina Press, 2017): 107–24.

Salm-Salm, Agnes zu, *Ten Years of My Life* (New York: R. Worthington, 1877).

Scharff, Virginia, "Empire and Liberty in the Middle of Nowhere," in Scharff, ed., *Empire and Liberty: The Civil War and the West* (Oakland: University of California Press, 2015): 140–58.

Schermerhorn, Calvin, *The Business of Slavery and the Rise of American Capitalism* (New Haven: Yale University Press, 2015).

Schmalz, Peter S., *The Ojibwa of Southern Ontario* (Toronto: University of Toronto Press, 1991).

Schoen, Brian, "Calculating the Price of Union: Republican Economic Nationalism and the Origins of Southern Sectionalism, 1790–1828," *Journal of the Early Republic*, vol. 23 (Summer 2003): 173–206.

Schoen, Brian, *The Fragile Fabric of Union: Cotton, Federal Politics, and the Global Origins of the Civil War* (Baltimore: Johns Hopkins University Press, 2009).

Scholes, Walter V., *Mexican Politics During the Juárez Regime, 1855–1872* (Columbia: University of Missouri, 1957).

Schott, Thomas, *Alexander H. Stephens of Georgia: A Biography* (Baton Rouge: Louisiana State University Press, 1988).

Schoonover, Thomas D., *Dollars over Dominion: The Triumph of Liberalism in Mexican–United States Relations, 1861–1867* (Baton Rouge: Louisiana State University Press, 1978).

Schoonover, Thomas D., *Mexican Lobby: Matías Romero in Washington, 1861–1867* (Lexington: University Press of Kentucky, 1986).

Schoonover, Thomas, "Napoleon is Coming! Maximilian is Coming?: The International History of the Civil War in the Caribbean Basin," in Robert E. May, ed., *The Union, the Confederacy, and the Atlantic Rim* (West Lafayette: Purdue University Press, 1995): 101–30.

Schwartz, Rosalie, *Across the Rio to Freedom: U.S. Negroes in Mexico* (El Paso: Texas Western Press, 1975).

Sernett, Milton C., *Harriet Tubman Myth, Memory, and History* (Durham: Duke University Press, 2007).

Settles, Thomas M., *John Bankhead Magruder: A Military Reappraisal* (Baton Rouge: Louisiana State University Press, 2009).

Sexton, Jay, "The Civil War and U.S. World Power," in Don H. Doyle, ed., *American Civil Wars: The United States, Latin America, Europe, and the Crisis of the 1860s* (Chapel Hill: University of North Carolina Press, 2017): 15–33.

Shadd, Mary A., *A Plea for Emigration: or, Notes of Canada West, in its Moral, Social, and Political Aspect* (Detroit: George W. Pattison, 1852).

Shade, William G., *Democratizing the Old Dominion: Virginia and the Second Party System, 1824–1861* (Charlottesville: University Press of Virginia, 1996).

Shawcross, Edward, *The Last Emperor of Mexico: The Dramatic Story of the Habsburg Archduke Who Created a Kingdom in the New World* (New York: Basic Books, 2021).

Shearer, Ernest C., "The Callahan Expedition, 1855," *Southwestern Historical Quarterly*, vol. 54 (Apr. 1951): 430–51.

Shearer, Ernest C., "The Carvajal Disturbances," *Southwestern Historical Quarterly*, vol. 55 (Oct. 1951): 201–30.

Sheehan-Dean, Aaron, ed., *Struggle for a Vast Future: The American Civil War* (Oxford: Osprey, 2006).

Sheridan, Philip, *Personal Memoirs of P. H. Sheridan, General United States Army*, 2 vols. (New York: C. L. Webster, 1888).

Shi, David E., "Seward's Attempt to Annex British Columbia, 1865–1869," *Pacific Historical Review*, vol. 47 (May 1978): 217–38.

Shippee, Lester Burrell, *Canadian-American Relations, 1849–1874* (New Haven: Yale University Press, 1939).

Silber, Nina, *Gender and the Sectional Conflict* (Chapel Hill: University of North Carolina Press, 2008).

Silverman, Jason H., *Unwelcome Guests: Canada West's Response to American Fugitive Slaves, 1800–1865* (New York City: Associated Faculty Press, 1985).

Silverman, Jason H., "Mary Ann Shadd and the Search for Equality," in Leon Litwack and August Meier, eds., *Black Leaders of the Nineteenth Century* (Urbana: University of Illinois Press, 1988): 86–100.

Simon, James F., *Lincoln and Chief Justice Taney: Slavery, Secession, and the President's War Powers* (New York: Simon & Schuster, 2006).

Simon, John F., ed., *The Papers of Ulysses S. Grant*, 31 vols. (Carbondale: Southern Illinois University Press, 1967–2009).

Simpson, Brooks D., *Let Us Have Peace: Ulysses S. Grant and the Politics of War and Reconstruction, 1861–1868* (Chapel Hill: University of North Carolina Press, 1991).

Sinha, Manisha, *The Slave's Cause: A History of Abolition* (New Haven: Yale University Press, 2016).

Sinkin, Richard N., *The Mexican Reform, 1855–1876: A Study in Liberal Nation-Building* (Austin: University of Texas Press, 1979).

Slowey, Gabrielle, "Confederation Comes at a Cost: Indigenous Peoples and the Ongoing Reality of Colonialism in Canada," in Jacqueline Krikorian, Marcel Martel, and Adrian Shubert, eds., *Globalizing Confederation: Canada and the World in 1867* (Toronto: University of Toronto Press, 2017): 79–93.

Smith, Donald B., "Macdonald's Relationship with Aboriginal People," in Patrice Dutil and Roger Hall, eds., *Macdonald at 200: New Reflections and Legacies* (Toronto: Dundurn Press, 2014): 58–93.

Smith, Goldwin, *The Treaty of Washington, 1871: A Study in Imperial History* (Ithaca: Cornell University Press, 1941).

Smith, John David, "Let Us All Be Grateful," in Smith, ed., *Black Soldiers in Blue: African American Troops in the Civil War Era* (Chapel Hill: University of North Carolina Press, 2002): 1–77.

Smith, Stacey L., "Emancipating Peons, Excluding Coolies: Reconstructing Coercion in the American West," in Gregory P. Downs and Kate Masur, eds., *The World the Civil War Made* (Chapel Hill: University of North Carolina Press, 2015): 46–74.

Smith, Stacey L., *Freedom's Frontier: California and the Struggle over Unfree Labor, Emancipation, and Reconstruction* (Chapel Hill: University of North Carolina Press, 2013).

Stacey, C. P., "Britain's Withdrawal from North America, 1864–1871," *Canadian Historical Review*, vol. 36 (Sept. 1955): 185–98.

Stahr, Walter, *Seward: Lincoln's Indispensable Man* (New York: Simon & Schuster, 2012).

Stampp, Kenneth M., *America in 1857: A Nation on the Brink* (New York: Oxford University Press, 1990).

Stanley, Gerald, "Senator William Gwin: Moderate or Racist?" *California Historical Quarterly* (Sept. 1971): 243–55.

Stauffer, John, *The Black Hearts of Men: Radical Abolitionists and the Transformation of Race* (Cambridge: Harvard University Press, 2001).

Sterling, Dorothy, *The Making of an Afro-American: Martin Robison Delany, 1812–1885* (New York: Da Capo Press, 1996).

St. John, Rachel, *Line in the Sand: A History of the Western U.S.—Mexico Border* (Princeton: Princeton University Press, 2011).

St. John, Rachel, "The Unpredictable America of William Gwin: Expansion, Secession, and the Unstable Borders of Nineteenth-Century North America," *Journal of the Civil War Era*, vol. 6 (Mar. 2016): 56–84.

Sterling, Dorothy, ed., *We Are Your Sisters: Black Women in the Nineteenth Century* (New York: W. W. Norton, 1997).

Stuart, Reginald C., *United States Expansionism and British North America, 1775–1871* (Chapel Hill: University of North Carolina Press, 1988).

Summers, Mark Wahlgren, *The Ordeal of the Reunion: A New History of Reconstruction* (Chapel Hill: University of North Carolina Press, 2014).

Surtees, Robert J., *Canadian Indian Policy: A Critical Bibliography* (Bloomington: Indiana University Press, 1982).

Sutherland, Daniel E., *The Confederate Carpetbaggers* (Baton Rouge: Louisiana State University Press, 1988).

Sutherland, Daniel E., *A Savage Conflict: The Decisive Role of Guerrillas in the American Civil War* (Chapel Hill: University of North Carolina Press, 2009).

Swisshelm, Jane Grey, *Half a Century* (Chicago: Jansen, McClung & Co., 1880).

Symonds, Craig L., *A Battlefield Atlas of the Civil War* (Baltimore: Nautical and Aviation Publishing, 1983).

Symonds, Craig L., *Joseph E. Johnston: A Civil War Biography* (New York: W. W. Norton, 1992).

Tansill, Charles Callan, *The United States and Santo Domingo, 1798–1873* (Gloucester: Peter Smith, 1967).

Taylor, Amy Murell, *Embattled Freedom: Journeys through the Civil War's Slave Refugee Camps* (Chapel Hill: University of North Carolina Press, 2018).

Taylor, John M., "The Fiery Trail of the *Alabama*," in Robert Cowley, ed., *With My Face to the Enemy: Perspectives on the Civil War* (New York: G. P. Putnam's Sons, 2001): 429–42.

Taylor, John M., "Hawk in the Fowlyard: Jeb Stuart," in Robert Cowley, ed., *With My Face to the Enemy: Perspectives on the Civil War* (New York: G. P. Putnam's Sons, 2001): 307–19.

Thomas, Emory M., *The Confederate Nation, 1861–1865* (New York: Harper & Row, 1979).

Thomas, Emory M., *Robert E. Lee: A Biography* (New York: W. W. Norton, 1995).

Thomas, Lately, *Between Two Empires: The Life Story of California's First Senator, William McKendree Gwin* (Boston: Houghton Mifflin, 1969).

Thornton, J. Mills, *Politics and Power in a Slave Society: Alabama, 1800–1860* (Baton Rouge: Louisiana State University Press, 1978).

Topik, Steven C., "When Mexico Had the Blues: A Transatlantic Tale of Bonds, Bankers, and Nationalists, 1862–1910," *American Historical Review*, vol. 105 (June 2000): 714–38.

Trefousse, Hans L., *Andrew Johnson: A Biography* (New York: W. W. Norton, 1989).

Trudeau, Noah Andre, "The Battle of Westport," in Robert Cowley, ed., *With My Face to the Enemy: Perspectives on the Civil War* (New York: G. P. Putnam's Sons, 2001): 472–85.

Trudeau, Noah Andre, "The Walls of 1864," in Robert Cowley, ed., *With My Face to the Enemy: Perspectives on the Civil War* (New York: G. P. Putnam's Sons, 2001): 412–28.

Tucker, Jane Ellis, *Beverley Tucker, a Memoir by His Wife* (Richmond: Frank Baptist Printing Co., n.d.).

Tyler, Ronnie C., "Fugitive Slaves in Mexico," *Journal of Negro History*, vol. 57 (Jan. 1972): 1–12.

Tyler, Ronnie C., *Santiago Vidaurri and the Southern Confederacy* (Austin: Texas State Historical Association, 1973).

Underwood, Rodman L., *Waters of Discord: The Union Blockade of Texas During the Civil War* (Jefferson, NC: McFarland & Co., 2003).

Utley, Robert M., *The Indian Frontier of the American West, 1846–1890* (Albuquerque: University of New Mexico Press, 1984).

Vanderwood, Paul J., *Disorder and Progress: Bandits, Police, and Mexican Development* (Wilmington, DE: Scholarly Resources, 1992).

Varon, Elizabeth R., *Appomattox: Victory, Defeat, and Freedom at the End of the Civil War* (New York: Oxford University Press, 2014).

Varon, Elizabeth R., *Armies of Deliverance: A New History of the Civil War* (New York: Oxford University Press, 2019).

Varon, Elizabeth R., *Disunion!: The Coming of the American Civil War, 1789–1859* (Chapel Hill: University of North Carolina Press, 2008).

Voss, Stuart F., *On the Periphery of Nineteenth-Century Mexico: Sonora and Sinaloa, 1810–1877* (Tucson: University of Arizona Press, 1982).

Wahlstrom, Todd W., *The Southern Exodus to Mexico: Migration across the Borderlands after the American Civil War* (Lincoln: University of Nebraska Press, 2015).

Waite, Kevin, *West of Slavery: The Southern Dream of a Transcontinental Empire* (Chapel Hill: University of North Carolina Press, 2021).

Waite, P. B., "Edward Cardwell and Confederation," *Canadian Historical Review*, vol. 43 (March 1962): 17–41.

Waite, P. B., *The Life and Times of Confederation, 1864–1867: Politics, Newspapers, and the Union of British North America* (Toronto: University of Toronto Press, 1962).

Wakefield, Sarah F., *Six Weeks in the Sioux Tepees* (New York: Rowman & Littlefield, 2016).

Walters, Ronald G., *American Reformers, 1815–1860* (New York: Hill & Wang, 1978).

Walther, Eric H., *The Fire-Eaters* (Baton Rouge: Louisiana State University Press, 1992).

Wasserman, Mark, *Capitalists, Caciques, and Revolution: The Native Elite and Foreign Enterprise in Chihuahua, Mexico, 1854–1911* (Chapel Hill: University of North Carolina Press, 1984).

Wasserman, Mark, *Everyday Life and Politics in Nineteenth-Century Mexico: Men, Women, and War* (Albuquerque: University of New Mexico Press, 2000).

Watkins, Sam, *Company Aytch: Or, a Side Show of the Big Show* (New York: Penguin, 1999).

Watson, Harry L., *Liberty and Power: The Politics of Jacksonian America* (New York: Noonday Press, 1990).

Waugh, Joan, *U. S. Grant: American Hero, American Myth* (Chapel Hill: University of North Carolina Press, 2009).

Waugh, John C., *Reelecting Lincoln: The Battle for the 1864 Presidency* (New York: Crown, 1997).

Weber, Jennifer L., *Copperheads: The Rise and Fall of Lincoln's Opponents in the North* (New York: Oxford University Press, 2006).

Weintraub, *Edward the Caresser: The Playboy Prince Who Became Edward VII* (New York: Free Press, 2001).

West, Elliott, *The Contested Plains: Indians, Goldseekers, and the Rush to Colorado* (Lawrence: University Press of Kansas, 1998).

West, Elliott, *The Essential West: Collected Essays* (Norman: University of Oklahoma Press, 2012).

White, Deborah Gray, *Ar'n't I a Woman?: Female Slaves in the Plantation South* (New York: W. W. Norton, 1999).

White, Jonathan W., *Emancipation, the Union Army, and the Reelection of Abraham Lincoln* (Baton Rouge: Louisiana State University Press, 2014).

White, Laura A., "The South in the 1850s as Seen by British Consuls," *Journal of Southern History*, vol. 1 (Feb. 1935): 29–48.

White, Richard, *Railroaded: The Transcontinentals and the Making of Modern America* (New York: W. W. Norton, 2011).

White, Richard, *The Republic for Which It Stands: The United States during Reconstruction and the Gilded Age, 1865–1896* (New York: Oxford University Press, 2017).

Wilentz, Sean, *The Rise of American Democracy: Jefferson to Lincoln* (New York: W. W. Norton, 2005).

Wilson, David A., *Canadian Spy Story: Irish Revolutionaries and the Secret Police* (Montreal: McGill-Queen's University Press, 2022).

Wilson, Keith, "In the Shadow of John Brown: The Military Service of Colonels Thomas Higginson, James Montgomery, and Robert Shaw in the Department of the South," in John David Smith, ed., *Black Soldiers in Blue: African American Troops in the Civil War Era* (Chapel Hill: University of North Carolina Press, 2002): 306–35.

Wilton, Carol, *Popular Politics and Political Culture in Upper Canada, 1800–1850* (Montreal: McGill-Queen's University Press, 2000).

Winik, Jay, *April 1865: The Month That Saved America* (New York: Harper Collins, 2001).

Winks, Robin W., *Canada and the United States: The Civil War Years* (Baltimore: Johns Hopkins Press, 1960).

Winks, Robin W., *The Blacks in Canada: A History* (New Haven: Yale University Press, 1971).

Wise, S. F., and Robert Craig Brown, *Canada Views the United States: Nineteenth-Century Political Attitudes* (Seattle: University of Washington Press, 1967).

Woods, Michael E., *Arguing Until Doomsday: Stephen Douglas, Jefferson Davis, and the Struggle for American Democracy* (Chapel Hill: University of North Carolina Press, 2020).

Woodward, C. Vann, ed., *Mary Chesnut's Civil War* (New Haven: Yale University Press, 1981).

Worley, Ted R., ed., "A Letter Written by General Thomas C. Hindman in Mexico," *Arkansas Historical Quarterly*, vol. 15 (Dec. 1956): 366–67.

ILLUSTRATIONS AND CREDITS

iv   Library of Congress pga.08518
I   Library of Congress USZ62-52105
16   Library of Congress ppmsca.33122
47   Library of Congress pga.04268
56   National Portrait Gallery 76.101
69   Left: Library of Congress cph.3c1003;
     Right: Library of Congress cwpbh.02513
103 Left: Library of Congress pga.12565;
     Right: Library of Congress cwpbh.00486
130 Library of Congress USZ62–14827
161 Library of Congress cph.3c07095
193 Library of Congress USZ62-31165
228 Library of Congress pga.07671
241 Library of Congress LC-DIG-ppmsca-35363
263 Library of Congress ds.05099
299 Library of Congress USZ62-7333
336 Library of Congress USZ-62-19759
375 Library of Congress USZ62-19549
410 Library of Congress USZ62-29247

Illustration Inserts

Abraham Lincoln (1809–1865). *Library of Congress USP6-2415-A.*
Jefferson Davis (1808–1889). *Library of Congress DIG-ppmsca-23852.*
Benito Juárez (1806–1872). *Library of Congress USZ62-7875.*
John A. Macdonald (1815–1891). *Library of Congress DIG-cwpbh-00412.*
Mary Ann Shadd Cary (1823–1893). *Library of Congress C29977.*
Jane Grey Cannon Swisshelm (1815–1884). *Library of Congress DIG-ppmsca-58123.*
Harriet Tubman (1822–1913). *Library of Congress DIG-ppmsca-54230.*
Harriet Beecher Stowe (1811–1896). *Library of Congress USZ62-19301.*
Stephen A. Douglas (1813–1861). *Library of Congress DIG-cwpbh-00880.*
Alexander H. Stephens (1812–1883). *Library of Congress DIG-cwpb-04947.*
John A. Quitman (1798–1858). *Library of Congress DIG-cwpbh-02323.*
William Walker (1824–1860). *Library of Congress DIG-cwpbh-01279.*
Roger B. Taney (1777–1864). *Library of Congress DIG-cwpbh-00788.*
William H. Seward (1801–1872). *Library of Congress DIG-bellcm-01069.*
Louis T. Wigfall (1816–1874). *Library of Congress USZ62-15904.*
Samuel Houston (1793–1863). *Library of Congress USZ62-75930.*
Robert E. Lee (1807–1870). *Library of Congress B8172-0001.*
Parson William G. Brownlow (1805–1877). *Library of Congress DIG-cwpbh-00157.*
Frederick Douglass (1818–1895). *Library of Congress USZ62-15887.*
George B. McClellan (1826–1885). *Library of Congress DIG-pga-00378.*
Albert Sidney Johnson (1803–1862). *Library of Congress DIG-cwpb-07469.*

Ulysses S. Grant (1822–1885). *Library of Congress USZ62-91985.*

Thomas "Stonewall" Jackson (1824–1863). *Library of Congress DIG-ds-03251.*

William Tecumseh Sherman (1820–1891). *Library of Congress DIG-cwpb-06583.*

James Longstreet (1821–1904). *Library of Congress USZ62-55424.*

Henry Hopkins Sibley, CSA (1816–1886). *Library of Congress DIG-cwpb-05992.*

William Quantrill (1837–1865). *Library of Congress DIG-ppmsca-56450.*

James Henry Lane (1814–1866). *Library of Congress DIG-ppmsca-11516.*

John Ross (1790–1866). *Library of Congress DIG-pga-07513.*

Stand Watie (1806–1871). *Library of Congress USZ62-14735.*

Patrick Edward Connor (1820–1891). *Library of Congress DIG-cwpb-06318.*

Brigham Young (1801–1877). *Library of Congress USZ62-76684.*

Little Crow (1810–1863). *Library of Congress USZ61-83.*

Gen. Henry Hastings Sibley, USA (1811–1891). *Library of Congress USZ62-14964.*

Red Cloud (1822–1909). *Library of Congress USZ62-91032.*

James H. Carleton (1814–1873). *Library of Congress DIG-cwpb-07383.*

Matías Romero (1837–1898). *Library of Congress USZ62-9838.*

Thomas Corwin (1794–1865). *Library of Congress USZ62-132117.*

Leonardo Márquez (1820–1913). *Library of Congress USZ62-22168.*

Miguel Miramón (1831–1867). *Library of Congress USZ62-40078.*

Napoleon III (1808–1873). *Library of Congress USZ62-131393.*

François Achille Bazaine (1811–1888). *Library of Congress cph 3a20797.*

Empress Carlota of Mexico (1840–1927). *Library of Congress USZ62-131391.*

Emperor Maximilian of Mexico (1832–1867). *Library of Congress USZ62-17159.*

Joshua L. Chamberlain (1828–1914). *Library of Congress DIG-cwpbh-03163.*

Clement Vallandigham (1820–1871). *Library of Congress DIG-cwpbh-01194.*

Joseph E. Johnston (1807–1891). *Library of Congress DIG-pga-08242.*

Braxton Bragg (1817–1876). *Library of Congress USZ62-4888.*

Jubal A. Early (1816–1894). *Library of Congress DIG-cwpb-07033.*

Philip H. Sheridan (1831–1888). *Library of Congress USZ62-131934.*

Sterling Price (1809–1867). *Library of Congress USZ62-14975.*

John Bell Hood (1831–1879). *Library of Congress USZ62-116391.*

Patrick Cleburne (1828–1864). *Library of Congress USZ62-107446.*

George H. Thomas (1816–1870). *Library of Congress DIG-cwpbh-03123.*

Lew Wallace (1827–1905). *Library of Congress DIG-cwpb-06442.*

Francis Preston Blair, Sr. (1791–1876). *Library of Congress USZ62-38438.*

E. Kirby Smith (1824–1893). *Library of Congress DIG-cwpb-06080.*

Matthew F. Maury (1806–1873). *Library of Congress DIG-cwpb-04808.*

Felix Constantin Alexander Johann Nepomuk zu Salm-Salm (1828–1870). *Library of Congress, USZ62-55275.*

Agnes Elizabeth Winona Leclerq Joy Salm-Salm (1844–1912). *Library of Congress USZ62-22178.*

Santiago Vidaurri (1809–1867). *Library of Congress USZ62-22170.*

Porfirio Díaz (1830–1915). *Library of Congress USZ62-22174.*

George Brown (1818–1880). *Library Archives Canada 3213212.*

Thomas D'Arcy McGee (1825–1868). *Library Archives Canada 410433.*

INDEX

abolition and antislavery, 5, 12, 21, 32–33, 51–58, 102, 120–25, 177, 183, 196–98, 241–42, 409

Acapulco, Mex., 99

Adams, Henry, 389

Adams, John Quincy, 2

Africa and Africans, 118–19, 121, 402

African Americans, 11–12, 47–68, 102, 113–16, 123, 193–94, 200
  during and after Reconstruction, 349–50, 355, 388–90, 391–94, 395, 398–99, 400, 401, 405–6, 408–9
  as Union troops and sailors, 241–42, 268–72, 285–88, 297, 317, 323, 331, 341, 342, 359

Alabama, 68, 118–19, 137, 138, 212, 221, 274, 332, 347, 389

Alabama, CSS, and the *Alabama* claims, 180, 384, 414

Alamán, Lucas, 98

Alaska, 383

Albany, N.Y., 74, 133

Albert, Prince, 130

Albuquerque, N.M., 239

Almonte, Juan Nepomuceno, 265–68

American Colonization Society, 27, 113–14, 200

American Revolution, 143, 157, 298

Anderson, Osborne P., 123

Anderson, Robert, 147

Anderson, William "Bloody Bill," 242–43

Andersonville, Ga., prison at, 287

Andrews, Eliza, 343

Antietam, Battle of, 216–17

Apaches, 44, 92, 96, 238, 250–51

Appomattox Courthouse, Va., surrender at, 343, 347

Arapahos, 258–59

Arizona, 9, 96, 230, 231, 236–38, 337, 349

Arkansas, 101, 150, 167, 240, 244–45, 284, 398

Arkansas River, 258, 325

Arlington, Va., 122, 150

Army of the Cumberland, 293

Army of the Potomac, 173–76, 207–11, 215–17, 219–20, 278–81, 314–18

Arriaga, Ponciano, 105

Assiniboia, 254, 257, 382, 384–85

Atchison, David R., 76, 78

Atlanta, Ga., 74, 125, 314, 323–24, 328
  campaign against, 318–20

Austin, Tex., 349

Austrian Empire, 188, 189

Ayutla, Mex., 99

Bagdad, Mex., 359

Baja California, Mex., 84–85, 96, 189, 367

Baker, Frank, 196

Ball's Bluff, Va., Battle of, 176

Baltimore, Md., 134, 166

Banks, Nathaniel, 291

Barbour, Charles, 289

Barclay, H. W., 130

Barr, Amelia, ix, 153, 349

Bates, Edward, 62

Baxter Springs, massacre at, 243

Baylor, John, 237, 349–50

Bazaine, François Achille, 265–67, 303–5, 359, 360, 361, 362, 364, 365, 366, 367, 368, 373

Beall, John Yates, 332–33

Bear River, Utah, 249

Beauregard, Pierre G.T., 173–74, 205–6

Beecher, Henry Ward, 77, 405

Bell, John, 130–31, 135–36, 137

Belleville, Can., 132

Berthemy, Jules, 370

Bewley, Anthony, 128

Bibb, Henry, 63–64

Bickley, George, 100–101

Bigelow, John, 358

Black Codes, Southern, 392–93, 394

Black Kettle, 258–59, 412

Blair, Francis, Jr., 398

Blair, Francis, Sr., 337–38, 339–40

Blair, Mongomery, 194, 322

Blake, or the Huts of America, 57, 64

blockade, Union naval, 177–79, 180,
  186–87, 323, 341

Blunt, James, 246

Booth, John Wilkes, 101, 123, 344, 391

borders and borderlands, 44, 65, 82–83,
  97–101, 186–87, 304, 338

Border States, U.S., 165–69, 198–201,
  218, 326

Bosque Redondo, N.M., 250–52

Boston, 51, 54–55, 147, 270

Bowdoin College, 52

Bozeman Trail, 411

Bragg, Braxton, 224, 225, 282, 284,
  292–94, 387

Brazil, 350, 366

Brazos de Santiago, Tex., 338

Breckenridge, John C., 134, 136, 168,
  196, 225

Brenham, Tex., 140

Brent, Joseph Lancaster, 235

Britain and British Empire, 5–6, 34–42,
  60, 85, 86–87, 91, 109–11, 130–33,
  146, 159, 182–85, 189–90, 215–16,
  302, 311–13, 353, 366, 376–81, 384
  antislavery influence in, 5, 183, 218, 328

British Columbia, 94–95, 111–13, 312,
  382, 383–84, 387, 414

British North American Act, 381

Broderick, David C., 69, 95

Brooks, Preston, 76, 78–79, 139

Brough, John, 297

Brown, Albert Gallatin, 70

Brown, George, 35–36, 40, 41, 157, 158,
  311–13, 377, 378

Brown, John, 79–80, 83, 103–4, 120–
  24, 226, 269, 406

Brown, Joseph, 276, 297

Brownlow, Parson William G., 170–71,
  204, 292

Brownsville, Tex., 66–67, 187, 338, 339,
  359

Buchanan, James, 80–82, 89, 107–9,
  114–15, 137, 159, 195

Buchanan, Tex., 127

Buck, Eliza, 52

Buckner, Simon Bolivar, 203

Buell, Don Carlos, 205, 223–24

Bunch, Robert, 125, 134

Burns, Anthony 47–48, 55

Burnside, Ambrose E., 219–20, 278,
  296, 317

Burr, Aaron, 18

Butler, Andrew P., 78

Butler, Benjamin F., 195–97, 206–7,
  314

Butterfield Overland Stage Company,
  93

Cadete, 228

Calhoun, John C., 34, 42, 69

California, 9, 33–34, 69, 81, 84, 91–96,
  99, 111, 201, 231, 232, 336–37, 354,
  384
  during the Civil War, 233–36, 353

Callahan, James Hughes, 66

Camels, 92–93

Campobello, N.B., 377

Canada, 5–7, 34–42, 109–11, 115, 120, 130–32, 366
confederation, 310–14, 375–82
Dominion of, 380–82, 384–87, 413–16
during the U.S. Civil War, 157–59, 174, 184–85, 268–69, 296–97, 310–14, 332–34
and First Nations, 109–11, 115

Canada East, 6, 38, 157–58, 311–13
see also Quebec, province of

Canada West, 6, 38, 59–60, 109–11, 130–32, 157–58, 311–13
see also Ontario, Can.

Canby, Edward R. S., 238–39

Cannon, Honoria, 288

capitalism and capitalists, 44, 85, 156, 261–62, 290, 371

Cardwell, Edward, 379

Carleton, James, 250–51

Carlota, Empress, 302, 305–7, 308–9, 364–66, 373–74

Carlota, Mex., 355, 367

Carson, Christopher "Kit," 238, 251

Cartier, George-Etienne, 39–40, 311–13

Carvajal, José Maria Jesús, 97

Catholicism and Catholics, 10–11, 40, 43, 104, 106–7, 188, 265–67, 308–9, 376, 385–86

caudillos, 99, 186, 304, 371

Cazneau, Jane McManus, 19–20, 23, 46, 65, 85–86, 87–88, 91, 159, 403, 405
see also McManus, Jane Maria Eliza

Cazneau, William Leslie, 19, 91, 159, 403–4, 405

Cedar Creek, Va., Battle of, 324–25

Central Pacific Railroad Co., 262

Centralia, Mo., massacre at, 243

Chamberlain, Joshua L., 280

Chambers, Henry, 327

Chambersburg, Pa., 280, 318, 351

Chancellorsville, Va., Battle of, 278–79

Chandler, Zachariah, 382

Chapultepec, Mex., 306

Charleston, S.C., 133, 134, 137, 177–78, 263, 285–86, 341

Charleston, Va., 57, 122–23

Charlottetown, P.E.I., 312–13

Chase, Salmon P., 156, 227, 321

Chaska, 254–56

Chatham, Can., 64, 121, 123

Chattahoochee River, 319

Chattanooga, Tenn., 223, 224, 264, 279, 288, 292–93, 314
Battle of, 293–94

Cherbourg, Fr., 180

Cherokees, 139, 244–46

Chesapeake Bay, 197, 207

Chesnut, James, 147

Chesnut, Mary Boykin, 141, 147, 163, 174, 207, 211, 272, 293, 324, 332, 341

Chester, Pa., 62

Cheyennes, 258–59, 412

Chiapas, Mex., 367

Chicago, 4, 134–35

Chickahominy River, 209–10

Chickamauga, Ga., Battle of, 293, 294

Chickasaws, 244–45

Chihuahua, Mex., 96, 189, 304, 360, 367

Child, Lydia Maria, 198

China, immigrants from, 94, 95, 399, 412–13

Chivington, John, 239, 258–59

Choctaws, 29, 244–45

Christiana, Pa., 51

Churchwell, William, 107

Cincinnati, Ohio, 52

Cinco de Mayo, 191

citizenship, 115–16, 394–95

civil rights and liberties, 166, 273–76,
    296, 393–95, 399–400, 405–6,
    408–9, 412–13

Civil War:
    American, 140–41, 145–57, 163–84,
        201–17, 219–26, 229–30, 237–39,
        242–46, 263–64, 268–94, 314–20,
        323–25, 340–46
    Mexican, 99, 106–9, 264–68, 301–5,
        336–37, 348, 359–71

Clarke, Lewis Garrard, 50

Clay, Henry, 1, 2, 3, 27, 67

Cleburne, Patrick, 294, 326–27, 331

Clemenceau, Georges, 398–99

Coahuilla, Mex., 186, 304

Cobb, Howell, 327

Cobourg, Can., 132

Cold Harbor, Va., Battle of, 316

Colorado, 231, 239, 258–59

Columbia, S.C., 125, 341

Columbus, Ky., 168, 202

Comanches, 44, 65, 251

Combahee, S.C., 263–64, 269–70

Comonfort, Ignacio, 106, 304

Compromise of 1850, 33–34, 69

Cone, Francis H., 74

Confederate States of America, or
    Confederacy, 141–43, 145, 146–50,
    152, 154, 156–57
  collapse of, 340–50, 387
  congress of, 174, 297
  constitution of, 142–43
  debates emancipation, 326–29
  diplomacy of, 181–84, 186–87, 191–92,
    215–16, 298, 309–10, 328, 339
  dissent within, 168, 169–71, 272–76,
    297, 301

economic distress in, 275–76
  soldiers of, 215, 216, 221–23
  support for, 277–78, 295, 301
  western expansion by, 233–39,
    244–46

Congress, U.S., 10, 69, 78–79, 82, 108–9,
    129, 139–40, 141, 144–45, 212
  after the Civil War, 353, 356, 393,
    394–400, 412
  during the Civil War, 166, 175–76,
    190, 198–200, 219, 325, 326

Connecticut, 393

Connor, Patrick Edward, 248–50

conscription, and resistance to, 273,
    276, 284–85, 318, 320

Conservatives, of Mexico, 43, 97–98,
    104, 108, 188, 265–67, 304–5,
    308–9
  see also Imperialistas, Mexican

Constitution, U. S. Federal, 27–28, 50,
    51, 114–16, 135, 166, 199, 398
  amendments to, 326, 392, 395,
    399–400, 405–6, 408, 412, 416

contrabands, *see* fugitive slaves and
    fugitive slave laws

Copeland, John, 123

Copperheads, 295–97, 322–23

Corinth, Miss., 205, 206, 221, 224

Cormany, Rachel, 280

Cortina, Juan Nepomuceno, 66–67

Corwin, Thomas, 185–86, 189–90,
    194

cotton, 29–30, 92, 183, 186–87, 304

Coursol, Charles J., 333–34

Cozumel, Mex., 194

Crabb, Henry, 99–100, 352

Craig, Fort, 239

Crater, Battle of the, 316–17

Creeks, 138, 244–46

Crittenden, John J., 144–45

Cuba, 70, 83, 87–90, 102, 145, 159, 160, 186, 350, 366
Cumberland River, 202, 203, 293
Cumming, Kate, 153
Curtis, Samuel R., 204
Custer, George Armstrong, 411–12

Dakota Territory, 256–57
Dakotas, 229, 252–57
Dallas, Tex., 127
Dana, Charles A., 282
Dano, Alphonse, 364
Danville, Va., 342–43
Davis Bend, Miss., 31, 277–78, 289–90, 393, 400
Davis, Edmund J., 187
Davis, Henry Winter, 311
Davis, Jefferson, 29–32, 33, 46, 48, 89, 91–94, 96, 118, 119, 136, 196, 289–90
    after the Civil War, 391, 393, 400
    as Confederate president, 142–43, 148, 169, 174, 183, 186, 201, 204, 207, 211, 215, 224, 227, 237, 272–73, 276, 277–78, 279, 281, 282, 283–84, 292, 293–94, 297, 319, 327, 328, 332, 337–38, 339–40, 342, 345, 346, 347
Davis, Joseph, 31, 289–90, 393
Davis, Samuel, 29–30
Davis, Varina Banks, 31, 32
Dawn, Can., 59
Dawson, John W., 247
Dayton, William, 192
Delany, Martin, 55–58, 59, 64, 121, 268–69, 270, 341, 401–2
Delany, Toussaint L'Ouverture, 270
Delaware, 61–62, 165, 325
Demarest, Sylvanus, 64
Democratic Review, 18–19

Democrats, political party of, 9–11, 18–19, 22, 26, 32, 46, 49–50, 74–75, 93, 94, 108–9, 114, 116–18, 123
    after the Civil War, 390, 394, 397, 398–400, 402, 405
    during the Civil War, 133–34, 170, 218–19, 270–71, 285, 295–97, 316, 318, 320–21, 322–23, 325–26, 333
Deseret, 246–50
    see also Utah Territory
desertion, military, 274–75, 300–1, 320, 341, 349
Detroit, Mich., 132, 297
Díaz, Felix, 372
Díaz, Porfirio, 265, 368–69, 372
diplomacy, 107–9, 160, 180–84, 189–90, 191–92, 217, 309–11, 328, 333–34, 339
disunion, 136–50
Dominican Republic, see Santo Domingo
Donelson, Fort, 202–3
Dostie, Anthony P., 395
Douglas, James, 112–13
Douglas, Stephen A., 26, 34, 71–75, 78, 82–83, 85, 92, 115, 116–18, 123, 133–34, 136, 145, 148, 295
Douglass, Charles, 326
Douglass, Frederick, 12, 51, 55–57, 58, 60, 63, 72, 79, 95, 121, 151, 195, 226, 270, 345, 391–92, 404, 405, 407, 408
Douglass, Lewis, 270, 286
Dred Scott decision, 113–16, 120
Du Bois, W. E. B., 409
duels and dueling, 94, 95
Dunkin, Christopher, 334
Du Pin, Charles, 303, 360
DuPont, Samuel F., 177–78
Durham, Lord, 38

Eagle Pass, Tx., 19, 65

Early, Jubal, 317–18, 320, 324–25,
    350–51, 401

Eastport, Me., 377

education, 17, 21, 25, 30, 35, 60, 62,
    98

Edward, Prince, 130–33

elections:
    in Canada, 36, 38, 414
    in the Confederacy, 297, 300–1
    in Mexico, 299, 304–5, 372
    in the U.S., 9–10, 25–26, 48, 75,
        80–81, 299–300, 398–99
    of 1860, 133–38
    of 1862 and 1863, 215, 218–19,
        296–97
    of 1864, 299–300, 314, 318, 320–23

Elgin, Lord, 60

Ellis, John, 148

El Paso, Tex., 65, 236, 237

El Paso del Norte, Mex., 360

emancipation and the Emancipation
    Proclamation, 214–15, 217–19,
    226–27, 247, 323, 347, 349

Emerson, John, 114

Emerson, Ralph Waldo, 54, 61, 124

Escobedo, Mariano, 368, 369

Estrada, José María Gutiérrez, 188

Eugénie de Montijo, Empress, 181, 188

Evans, John, 258–59

Evans, Lemuel D., 70–71

Ewing, Thomas, Jr., 243

expansion, American, 3, 7–8, 18–20,
    39, 69–102, 145, 158–59, 383–86,
    403–4

Farragut, David G., 207, 221, 323

Fayetteville, N.C., 148

Fenians, 376–78, 379, 381, 382, 414

Fetterman, William J., 411

Filibusters, 83–90, 96–101, 186, 352

Fillmore, Millard, 34, 51, 55

finance, 156, 187–90, 239, 302–3,
    362

Fish, Hamilton, 413

Fisher, Fort, N.C., Battle of, 340–41

fisheries, Canadian, 413–14

Fisher's Hill, Va., Battle of, 324

Five Forks, Va., Battle of, 342

Florida, 137, 197, 388

Florida, CSS, 180

Floyd, John B., 67, 137, 203

Ford, John Salmon, 65–66, 67, 97, 149,
    339, 359

Forey, Louis Elie Frederic, 191, 264,
    265–67

Forrest, Nathan Bedford, 287, 399

Forsyth, John, 106, 107, 116

Fort Erie, Can., 377

Fort Wise Treaty, 258

Fort Worth, Tex., 128

France and the French Empire, 91,
    92–93, 98, 146, 159, 188–92,
    215–16, 264–68, 301–5, 309–11,
    328, 337, 338–39, 356–57, 359–60,
    362–66, 368

Francophone Canadians, 6, 38–39,
    40–42, 157–58, 185, 311, 385–86

Franklin, Tenn., Battle of, 330–31

Franz Josef, Emperor, 188, 301–2, 374

Fraser River, 111–12

Fredericksburg, Va., Battle of, 219–20

Freedmen's Bureau, 393, 394, 395,
    401–2

Freeport Doctrine, 117–18

Free Soilers, and Free Staters, 32–33,
    75, 76–78, 79–83, 242

Frémont, Jessie Anne Benton, 198–99

Frémont, John C., 80–81, 198–99,
    321–22

fugitive slaves and fugitive slave laws, 3, 12, 15, 34, 47–68, 94, 116, 120, 135, 144, 145, 184, 195, 196, 200, 280, 287–88
    wartime assistance to the Union, 179, 195–98, 212, 213, 226–27

Gadsden, James, and the Gadsden Purchase, 92, 98–99
Galt, Alexander T., 378
Galveston, Tex., 349
Garfield, James A., 289
Garry, Fort, Can., 385
Geary, John W., 80, 81
gender and gender relations, 16–17, 20–23, 53, 152–54, 207, 274–75
Georgia, and Georgians, 55, 73–74, 137, 141–42, 274, 290, 292–93, 318–20, 329–30, 343, 347, 350
    after the Civil War, 387, 388, 392, 393
Germans, 167, 291
Gettysburg, Pa., Battle of, 280–81, 301, 319
Gettysburg Address, 298
Giddings, Joshua R., 53
Gladstone, William, 312
Glorietta Pass, N.M., Battle of, 239, 259
Glover, Joshua, 54
gold rushes, 111–13, 232–33, 249, 258, 337, 411
Gooding, James, 285
Gorgas, Josiah, 332
Gosport, Va., 149
Gradual Civilization Act, 110–11, 115
Grant, Julia Dent, 202
Grant, Ulysses S., 163, 202–3, 205–6, 212, 224–25, 227, 229–30, 263–4, 281–84, 293–94, 314–18, 324, 330, 331, 336–38, 340, 342–43, 347–48

after the Civil War, 356–59, 366, 397, 398, 399, 403
Great Basin, 229–30, 231, 261–62
Great Plains, 249–50, 257–59, 261
Great Salt Lake, 231
Greeley, Horace, 279
Green, Samuel, 53
Green, Shields, 121, 123
Grey, Earl, 7
Grow, Galusha, 261
Guadalajara, Mex., 303
Guanajuato, Mex., 303, 368
Guayamas, Mex., 367
Guerrero, Mex., 65, 367
guerrilla warfare, 172, 213, 221–23, 240–44, 303, 324, 343, 350, 360, 366–67
Gwin, William McKendree, 69, 93–96, 233–34, 235, 336–37, 352–53, 363

Haiti, and Haitians, 87, 90, 91, 159–60, 403, 404
Hale, John P., 71
Halifax, N.S., 312
Halleck, Henry, 205–6, 221, 223, 224, 227, 241, 281
Hamilton, Alexander, 18
Hamilton, Alexander, Jr., 18
Hamlin, Hannibal, 135, 322
Hammond, James Henry, 28–29, 124, 129
Hampton, Wade, III, 402
Hampton Roads, Va., 178, 340
hard-war, strategy of, 212–14, 222–23, 257–58, 277–78, 317–18, 319, 324, 329–30
Harlan, James, 412
Harpending, Asbury, 234–35
Harper, Frances, 60

Harpers Ferry, Va., 121–22, 123, 149,
    168, 216, 226
Harrison, James, 161
Harrison's Landing, Va., 210, 211
Harvard University, 58, 186
Havana, Cuba, 88, 370
Hawthorne, Nathaniel, 48
Haywood, Felix, 65
Helper, Hinton, 125–27
Henry, Fort, 202–3
Henson, Josiah, 58–59, 64
Herbert, Philemon T., 237
Higginson, Thomas Wentworth, 226,
    271–72
Hill, Benjamin H., 300
Hill, John H., 61
Hispanics and Hispanos, 66–67, 92, 94,
    96, 231, 236, 238, 239, 412–13
Holden, William W., 301
Holly, James Theodore, 63
Holly Springs, Miss., Battle of, 224
Holmes, Oliver Wendell, Jr., 315
Homestead Act, 135, 140, 260–61, 291
Honduras, 86–87
Honey Springs, Indian Territory, Battle
    of, 246
Hood, John Bell, 217, 319–20, 323–24,
    329–32, 335
Hooker, Joseph, 278–79, 293, 294
Housatonic, USS, 180
Houston, Sam, 138–40, 143
Howard University, 408
Howe, Joseph, 378, 381
Hudson Bay Company, 111–13,
    384–85
Hunley, CSS, 179–80
Hunter, David, 317
Hutchinson Family Singers, 175
Hyns, Walter, 141

Idaho Territory, 259
Illinois, 24–27, 71–72, 77, 81, 116–17,
    135, 137, 154–55, 171, 219, 248
immigrants and immigration, 4,
    10–11, 34–35, 94, 151–52, 154, 167,
    291–92, 387
impeachment of Andrew Johnson, 397
Imperialistas, Mexican, 304–5, 356,
    359–71
Indiana, 24, 75, 77, 81, 135, 137, 151,
    171, 219, 338
Indians, *see* Natives
Indian Territory, 231–33, 240, 244–46
industries and industrialization, 4–5,
    29, 156
Iowa, 171, 231, 322
Irish immigrants, 11, 151–52,
    237, 284–85, 291–92, 376–78
ironclad warships, 179, 224, 323
Island No. 10, Battle of, 206
Iturbide, Agustín de, 303, 361–62,
    366
Iturbide, Alice Green de, 361–62, 366

Jackson, Alexander, 96
Jackson, Andrew, 114
Jackson, Claiborne, 73, 166–67
Jackson, Thomas "Stonewall," 173,
    209–10, 211, 216, 279
Jackson, Miss., Battle of, 283
Jamaica, 403, 405
James, Frank and Jesse, 243
James River, 207, 210, 314, 316
Japan, 366
Jarvis, Harry, 197
Jayhawkers, 82–83, 240–42
Jecker, Jean-Baptiste, and his loan, 188,
    190, 302, 362
Jefferson City, Mo., 167

Johnson, Andrew, 170, 171, 204, 322
  impeachment of, 397
  presidency of, 347, 353, 357, 367,
    390–99, 407
Johnston, Albert Sidney, 201–2, 203,
  204, 205, 206, 235
Johnston, Joseph E., 173–74, 208–9,
  272, 282–84, 294, 318–19, 327, 330,
  341–42, 343, 346–47
Jones County, Miss., 275, 402
Juárez, Benito, 16, 42–45, 98, 104, 106,
  107, 108–9, 162, 185, 186, 187–90,
  191, 194, 264, 265, 299, 303–4,
  308, 309, 311, 337, 338, 344–45,
  348, 353, 359, 360–61, 362, 367–68,
  369–73
Jumel, Eliza, 18

Kansas, 72–83, 86, 116–17, 120, 231,
  246, 269, 350, 386, 406
  during the Civil War, 240–43
Kansas City, Mo., 242–43, 406
Kansas-Nebraska Act, 73–75, 90, 94
Kearny, Philip, 165
Keitt, Lawrence, 165, 272
Kenner, Duncan F., 328
Kennesaw Mountain, Ga., Battle of,
  319
Kentucky, 20–21, 24, 29, 48, 63, 95, 97,
  134, 136, 144
  after the Civil War, 393
  in the Civil War, 165, 168, 224, 238,
    244, 271, 297, 325
King, Sarah "Kate," 242
King, Thomas Butler, 94
Kingston, Can., 35–36, 40, 131–32
Knight, Newton and Rachel, 275, 402
Knights of the Golden Circle, 100–101
Know-Nothings, 11

Knoxville, Tenn., 170–71, 292, 293,
  294, 330, 387–88
Ku Klux Klan, 399

Labastida, Pelagio Antonio de, 266–67
Lakotas, 257–58, 411
Lamar, Charles Augustus, 119
Lamar, Q. C., 117–18
Land-Grant Act, 260, 261
Lane, James, 77, 78, 240–42, 243
Langevin, Hector, 380
La Paz, Mex., 84–85
La Reforma, 105–6
Larwill, Edwin, 60–61
Latin America, 146, 189, 192, 302, 370
Lawrence, Amos A., 55
Lawrence, Kans., 78, 82, 242–43, 350
lawyers and the law, 26, 35–36
Lecompton, Kans., 77
Lecompton Constitution, 80–83
Lee, Archy, 94–95
Lee, Robert E., 30, 66, 122, 123,
  149–50
  after the Civil War, 355, 401
  during the Civil War, 163, 169, 201,
    208–12, 214–17, 219–20, 263, 264,
    278–81, 292, 294, 314–18, 328, 338,
    340–41, 342–43
Leopold I, King of Belgium, 302, 365
Lerdo, Miguel, 104
Lerdo, Sebastian, 372
liberalism and liberals, 44–46, 103–7,
  108–9, 191, 192, 260–62, 264,
  307–8, 371–72, 411–13
Lincoln, Abraham, 47, 67, 74
  and African Americans, 194–95,
    198–201, 214–15, 217–19, 226, 342,
    344, 345
  assassination of, 344–45, 391

Lincoln, Abraham (*continued*)
  early life of, 23–28
  in Lincoln-Douglas debates, 116–18
  and Native Americans, 229, 245–46,
    255–56
  as a presidential candidate, 134–37,
    299–300, 314, 318, 320–23,
    325–26
  as wartime president, 141–42, 143,
    145–46, 150–51, 162, 165, 166, 171,
    173, 175, 176–77, 185, 191, 192,
    203, 205, 208, 211–12, 214, 219,
    220, 224, 225, 240, 247–48, 269,
    278, 279, 282, 293, 295, 309, 333–
    34, 338, 339–40, 363, 373
Lincoln, Mary Todd, 26, 136, 176,
  344
Lincoln, Thomas, 24–25
literature, 25, 52–54
Little Crow, 252–54, 256, 257
Loizillon, Pierre Henri, 266
Longfellow, Henry Wadsworth, 270
Longstreet, James, 202, 280–81, 292–
  94, 314–15
López, Miguel, 369
López, Narciso, 87–88
Lorencez, Comte de, 190–91
Lost Cause mythology, 401
Louisiana, 59, 137, 221, 270, 277, 290,
  291, 387, 389, 399
Louisville, Ky., 20–21
Lowry, Robert, 402
Lowry, Sylvanus B., 22
Lynchburg, Va., 401
Lyon, Nathaniel, 167–68
Lyons, Lord, 133, 184

Macdonald, Helen Shaw, 35
Macdonald, Isabella Clark, 36–38

Macdonald, John A., 34–42, 45, 110,
  158, 174, 185, 299, 311–13, 333–34,
  375–76, 377, 378–82, 385–86,
  413–14
Macdonald, John Sandfield, 311
Macdonald, Susan Agnes Bernard, 380
Magoffin, Beriah, 168
Magruder, John B., 208, 339, 354
Mallory, Charles K., 195–96
Mallory, Shepard, 196
Malmros, Oscar, 386
Manassas, Va., Battles of, 173–74, 214
Mangas Coloradas, 250–51
Manitoba, Can., 385–86, 414
Mankato, Minn., 255
Marcy, William, 89–90, 91
Maritime Provinces of Canada, 312–13,
  378–80
Márquez, Leonardo, 106, 187, 265, 304,
  365, 368, 370
Marshall, John (chief justice), 114
Marshall, John (of Texas), 139
Martin, Martha, 72
Marx, Karl, 193
Maryland, 49, 53, 59, 81, 113, 114
  in the Civil War, 165–66, 215–17,
    318
masculinity, 9, 83–84, 152–53, 270
Mason, James M., 144, 183–84
Mason, John Y., 89
Massachusetts, 151
Matamoros, Mex., 65, 97, 186–87, 304,
  310, 359, 368
Maury, Mathew F., 137–38, 353–56,
  366–67
Maximilian, Archduke and Emperor,
  188, 266–67, 301–3, 305–9, 310,
  311, 345, 348, 351–56, 361–70, 373,
  374

Mayo, William W., and the Mayo Clinic, 255–56

Maza, Margarita, 42

Mazatlan, Mex., 108, 368

McCausland, John, 318, 351

McClellan, George B., 91, 169, 174–76, 197, 203, 207–10, 211–17, 219, 281, 331

as a presidential candidate, 320–21

McDougall, William, 158, 385

McDowell, Irvin, 173, 174, 336–37

McGee, Thomas D'Arcy, 312, 313, 375, 376–77, 379, 381–82

McIlvaine, Samuel, 151

McLane, Robert, 107–8

McLane-Ocampo Treaty, 108–9

McManus, Jane Maria Eliza, 16–19

See also Cazeneau, Jane McManus

McPherson, James B., 318, 319

Meade, George, 279–81, 314, 316

Mechanicsville, Va., Battle of, 210

Mecklenburg Co., Va., 149

medicine and medical practice, 154, 163–65, 210–11

Medicine Bottle, 257

Meglia, Pietro Francesco, 308

Mejía, Tomás, 356, 359, 369–70

Memphis, Tenn., 206, 221, 330, 395

Mercier, Henri, 208, 217

Merryman, John, 166

Mesilla Valley, 92, 96, 98, 236

Metis, 384–86

Mexico, 8–9, 14–15, 42–45, 64–66, 83, 84–85, 89, 96–101, 103–9, 115–16, 162, 335

Confederate migration to, 349–51, 353–56, 366–67, 406

post-war reconstruction of, 369–73, 415

war with France and the *Imperialistas*, 185–92, 230, 264–68, 298, 301–5, 308, 336–37, 348, 351–53, 356, 358–71

war with the United States, 8–9, 19, 32, 44

Mexico City, 9, 43, 98, 106, 186, 190, 191, 264, 265–67, 303, 306, 308, 351, 352, 355, 368, 369

Michoacán, 103, 187

military:

means and organization, 155–57, 163–65

strategy, 172–73, 203, 207–8, 212–13, 215, 263–64, 314, 329–30

Milliken's Bend, Battle of, 286

Mill Springs, Battle of, 171

Milwaukee, Wis., 54

Minnesota, territory and state, 22–23, 229, 231, 252–57, 385, 393

Minnesota Historical Society, 256, 257

Minnesota River, 252, 254

Miramón, Miguel, 106, 108, 109, 188, 365, 368–70

Missouri Compromise, 73, 74, 75, 115, 171

Mississippi, territory and state, 29–32, 72, 88, 93, 137, 138, 221, 274–75, 337, 345, 392

Mississippi River and Valley, 201–2, 206, 220–21, 224–25, 264, 281–84, 286

Missouri, state of, 73, 75–76, 80, 81–83, 93, 136–37, 202

in the American Civil War, 165, 166–68, 198–99, 204, 240–43, 244–45, 325, 326

Missouri River and Valley, 325

Mitchell, Ormsby, 212

Mobile Bay, Ala., 314, 323

mobility, geographic and social, 19,
    23–26, 28–30, 34–36, 135, 170

Monitor, USS, 179

Monroe Doctrine, 146

Monroe, Fort, 178, 195–97, 226–27

Monterrey, Mex., 304, 350

Montgomery, Ala., 142, 147, 150

Montgomery, James, 269–70

Montgomery, William W., 187

Montreal, 6, 40, 184, 185, 385

Morgan, Sarah, 277

Mormonism and Mormons, 76,
    229–30, 246–50

Morny, Duc de, 188, 337, 339

Morrill Act, 248

Morrill, Justin, 248, 261

Mosby, John S., 359

Myrick, Andrew, 253

Napoleon I, 188

Napoleon III, 188–92, 218, 264–67, 298,
    309–10, 311, 339, 345, 352, 357, 358,
    362, 364, 365, 373

Nashville, Tenn., 203–4, 221, 330
    Battle of, 331–32

Natchez, Miss., 289

Natives:
    of Canada, 89–91, 109–11, 384–85, 387
    of Mexico, 42, 44, 107, 304–5, 307
    of the United States, 228–29, 231–33,
        236, 237, 238, 244–46, 249–60, 262,
        411–12

nativism, 10

Navajos, 251–52

naval power, 160, 177–80, 184, 189

Nebraska Territory, 258

Nevada, 399

New Brunswick, Can., 6, 312, 377, 378,
    379

Newby, Dangerfield and Harriet, 122

Newcastle, Duke of, 132–33, 184

New England, 49

Newfoundland, 6, 130

New Jersey, 81, 219, 325, 358

New Mexico, 9, 34, 92, 96, 230, 231,
    249–52, 412–13
    during the Civil War, 236–39

New Orleans, La., 87–88, 98, 108, 150,
    206–7, 353, 356, 367, 395

New Salem, Ill., 25–26

newspapers, 20–23, 63–64, 170, 292,
    301, 351, 407

New York, N.Y., 62, 95, 148, 179, 333,
    372
    draft riots in, 284–85

New York, state of, 219

Niagara River, 377

Nicaragua, 85–86, 186

Nlaka'pamux, 111–12

Norfolk, Va., 179

North Carolina, 126–27, 148, 150, 154,
    274, 275, 300–301, 340–41, 341–42,
    346–47, 392

Northwest Ordinance of 1787, 115

Nova Scotia, 6, 312, 378, 378, 381

Nuevo Leon, Mex., 186, 304, 350

Oaxaca, Mex., 42–43, 98, 162, 372

Ocampo, Melchor, 103–6, 107, 108,
    109, 187

Ohio River and Valley, 24, 27, 59

Ohio, state of, 120, 202, 295–96, 394,
    395

Okanogan Lake, 113

Oklahoma, *see* Indian Territory

Olmsted, Frederick Law, 65

Omaha, Neb., 262

Ontario, Can., 386
    see also Canada West

Orange Order and Orangemen,
131–32, 376
Oregon, 231, 234
Orizaba, Mex., 191
Ortega, Jesús González, 265, 360–61
Osawatomie, Kans, 79–80
Ostend Manifesto, 89–90
O'Sullivan, John L., 18
Ottawa, Can., 41, 131, 381, 384

Pacific Railway Act, 260–61
Palmerston, Lord, 7, 84, 180, 189
Paris, France, 337, 339, 352, 358, 364,
365
Parker, William, 50
Parsons, Mosby M., 350
Paul, Alfred, 156–57
Pea Ridge, Battle of, 204
Pemberton, John C., 282–84
Pennsylvania, 51, 62, 81, 279–81, 297,
317, 318
Perrysville, Ky, Battle of, 224
Pesquiera, Ignacio, 99–100
Petersburg, Va., siege of, 316–17, 318,
320, 328, 340–41, 342
Pezuela, Juan de la, 89
Philadelphia, Pa., 345
Philbrick, Edward S., 290
Phillips, Wendell, 71, 321
Pickens, Fort, 197
Pickett, George, 112, 281, 342
Pickett, John T., 186
Piedras Negras, Mex., 65, 66
Pierce, Franklin, 48–49, 55, 74, 77, 80,
85, 89, 90, 91
Pig War, 112–13, 414
Pike, Albert, 245
Pillow, Fort, 287, 399
Pilot Knob, Mo., Battle of, 325
Pittsburgh, Pa., 20, 21, 22, 57, 407

Pius IX, Pope, 267, 291–92
Platte River, 259, 411
Polignac, Camille de, 339
Polk, James K, 8, 74
polygamy, 229–30, 246, 248
Pope, John, 206, 212–14, 257–58
popular sovereignty, 73, 83, 115, 117–18
Porter, David, 340–41
Port Hudson, La., Battle of, 284
Port Royal, S.C., 178
Potomac River, 317
Potter, John 129
Price, Sterling, 325, 351, 355
Prince Edward Island, Can., 6, 312–13
prisoners-of-war, 287
proslavery ideology, 12, 19, 28–29, 31,
327–28
Protestant Christianity, 10–11, 20,
21–23, 25, 97, 154
Prussia, 312, 373
Pryor, Roger, 129
Puebla, Mex., 191, 264, 265, 303, 368
Puerto Rico, 159
Puros, 103–5

Quantrill, William, 242–44
Quebec, city of, 312, 313
Quebec, province of, 363, 386
see also Canada East
Queretaro, Mex., 303, 368–70
Quintero, Juan A., 186, 187
Quitman, John, 32, 88–90

race and racism, 9–11, 19–22, 24,
49–50, 57–58, 60–62, 72, 75, 77,
88, 91, 94–95, 108, 113–17, 136,
143, 145, 155, 162, 170, 175, 219,
270–72, 284–85, 295, 297, 323, 344,
391–92, 400, 404, 412–13
see also slavery and enslaved people

railroads, 4, 72, 92, 93, 96, 108, 135, 156, 168–69, 221, 223, 292–93, 315, 329, 330
  transcontinental, 260–62, 384, 410–11, 414
Ramsden, Sir John, 181
Ramsey, Alexander, 252–53, 255
Rapidan River, 314
Rappahannock River, 219–20
Reciprocity Treaty, 334, 413–14
Reconstruction of the Southern states, 321, 387–402, 407
Rector, Henry, 244
Red Cloud, 411
Redpath, James, 102
Red River (of Canada), 254, 257, 382, 384–85
Reeder, Andrew, 77, 81
Reform Party, Canadian, 157–58
reform societies and reformers, 153
republic and republicanism, 2, 180–81
Republicans, political party of, 75, 77, 81, 108–9, 116–18, 123–24, 129, 134–36, 138, 144, 154–55, 202, 228
  after the Civil War, 390, 394, 395–98, 400, 402, 405–6
  during the Civil War, 175–76, 193–94, 198, 199–201, 219, 260–62, 264, 285, 286, 291, 296, 310–11, 321–23, 325–26
Reynolds, Thomas, 243, 351
Rhett, Robert Barnwell, 67, 69, 147
Rhode Island, 254
Richmond, Va., 133, 134, 149, 150, 163, 169, 196, 201, 207, 208, 209, 211, 227, 276, 314, 315, 328, 339, 341, 342
Ridgeway, Can., Battle of, 377
Riel, Louis, 385–86
Riley, Isaac, 59

Rio Grande River and Valley, 19, 65, 97–101, 108, 186–87, 231, 237, 338, 350, 356, 359
Rivers, Prince, 270
Robinson, Charles, 193, 240
Rochester, N.Y., 270, 345
Rocky Mountains, 231, 261–62, 384
Rollins, James S., 326
Romero, Matías, 162, 185, 190, 194, 310–11, 352, 353, 357, 358, 359, 370
Rosecrans, William S., 169, 224, 225, 292–93, 331
Ross, Alexander Milton, 61, 120
Ross, John, 245–46
Ruffin, Edmund, 124–25, 129, 137, 147, 213, 345–46
Russell, Lord, 183
Russell, William Howard, 134, 139, 142, 146, 148, 176
Russia and Russians, 312, 383

Sacramento, Calif., 262
sailors, 91, 177–80
Sailor's Creek, Va., Battle of, 343
St. Albans, Vt., raid on, 333–34
St. Catherines, Can., 120, 269
St. Cloud, Minn., 22, 229, 407
St. Lawrence River, 35, 313
St. Louis, Mo., 167, 201, 202, 325
St. Paul, Minn., 256
Salas, José Mariano, 266, 267
Saligny, Duc de, 188, 191, 265–67
Salm-Salm, Agnes Le Clerq Joy, 42, 363–64, 368–69, 372, 373
Salm-Salm, Felix zu, 363–64, 368–69, 373
Salt Lake City, Utah, 248
Samana Bay, Dominican Republic, 91, 159, 403
San Antonio, Tex., 64–65, 140

Sand Creek, Colo., massacre at, 257–59

San Francisco, Calif., 80, 81, 85, 93, 95, 235, 310

Sanitary Commission, U.S., 154

San Jacinto, USS, 184

San Juan Island, Wash., 112, 414

San Luis Potosí, 265, 303, 304, 368

Santa Anna, Antonio López de, 9, 43, 97–99, 103, 105, 268

Santa Fe, N.M., 239

Santana, Pedro, 159–60

Santo Domingo, 90–91, 146, 159–60, 403–5

Savannah, Ga., 55, 119, 143, 329, 330, 341

Schurz, Carl, 390

Schofield, John, 330–31, 358, 364, 397

Scotland and Scots, 34–36

Scott, Dred and Harriet, 114–15

Scott, Thomas, 385–86

Scott, Winfield, 48, 149–50, 172–73, 175

Sea Islands, 226, 269–70, 290

secession, *see* disunion

Seminoles, 244–45

Semmes, Raphael, 180

Senior, Nassau W., 54

settlers and settlement, 24, 73, 76, 110, 252–53, 260–61

Seven Days' Battles, 209–11

Seven Pines, Battle of, 208–9

Seymour, Horatio, 398, 399

Seymour, Truman, 285

Seward, Frances, 146

Seward, William H., 54, 76, 101, 123
    in retirement, 370, 375
    as secretary of state, 133, 134, 144, 146, 158–59, 184, 192, 291, 310–11, 333–34, 338–39, 340, 344, 357–58, 367, 383, 384, 403

Shadd, Abraham, 62

Shadd, Isaac, 64, 400

Shadd, Mary Ann, 61–64, 123, 268–69, 400, 408–9

Shakopee, 257

Shannon, Wilson, 80

Shaw, Robert Gould, 272

Shelby, Joseph, 350, 355, 406

Shenandoah, CSS, 180

Shenandoah Valley, Va., 209, 314, 317, 324–25

Sheridan, Philip H., 315, 324–25, 336, 342, 343, 348, 349, 351, 355–59, 395, 397

Sherman, William T., 147, 201, 202, 205, 221, 222–23, 224–25, 271, 283, 290, 294, 314, 318–20, 323–24, 329–30, 332, 335, 338, 341–42, 346–47, 367

Shiloh, Battle of, 205–6

Shoshones, 249

Sibley, Henry Hastings, 252–55, 257

Sibley, Henry Hopkins, 237–39

Simmons, Robert J., 285

Sims, Thomas 54

Sinaloa, Mex., 96, 189

Sioux, *see* Dakotas

Sitting Bull, 258

Slaughter, James, 339

slaveholders, 72, 74, 88, 93, 113–14, 273–74

slave revolts (and fear of), 120–22, 125–29, 138, 218, 286

slavery and enslaved people, 5, 11–15, 27–31, 59, 113–17, 177
    as a cause of the U.S. Civil War, 137–38, 140, 142, 143, 145, 150, 152, 155, 174, 240, 277, 327–28
    erosion of, 212–14, 288–91, 319, 326–27, 349–50
    see also fugitive slaves and fugitive slave laws

slave trade, Atlantic, 118–19

Slidell, John, 70, 183–84, 191

Smalls, Robert, 177–78

Smith, A. P., 195

Smith, E. Kirby, 288, 339, 348–50, 351, 356, 366

soldiers:

in combat, 163–65, 205, 220, 280–81

motives of, 151–55, 222, 270, 325–26

Sonora, Mex., 85, 96, 189, 336–37, 352–53, 362, 367

Soulé, Pierre, 86, 89–90

South, American, 5, 28–32, 33–34, 42, 53–54, 86, 117–19, 124–29, 218

postwar reconstruction of, 387–402, 405–7

secession by, 136–50

South Carolina, 76, 78–79, 137, 139, 145–47, 226, 269–70, 274, 341, 388, 392, 398, 401–2

Spain and Spanish Empire, 87–91, 146, 159–60, 189–90, 302, 373, 403

Sparks, A. W., 128

Spotsylvania Courthouse, Va., Battle of, 315

Springfield, Ill., 26, 345

Stanford, Leland, 235

Stanton, Edwin M., 208, 269, 331, 347, 397

Staunton, Va., 211

Steedman, Charles and James, 154

Stephens, Alexander H., 28, 48, 73–74, 141, 233, 276, 340

Stevens, Thaddeus, 310, 397, 415

Stockton, Calif., 99

Stone, Charles P., 176

Stones River, Tenn., Battle of, 225

Storm, Allen, B., 17

Stowe, Calvin, 51

Stowe, Harriet Beecher, 51–54, 56–57, 58–59, 64, 77, 170, 183, 405

Stuart, J. E. B., 209, 315

submarine warfare, 179–80

Sumner, Charles, 78–79, 139, 190, 309, 384, 404, 416

Sumner, Edwin V., 235

Sumter, Fort, 145–48

Supreme Court, U.S., 114–16, 321, 395

Swisshelm, James, 20–21

Swisshelm, Jane Grey, 9, 20–23, 46, 64, 199, 200, 228–29, 252, 407

Tabasco, Mex., 367

Tacubaya, Mex., 106

Tahlequah, Indian Territory, 246

Tamaulipas, Mex., 96, 97, 186, 304

Tampico, Mex., 360, 368

Taney, Roger B., 113–16, 120, 166, 268, 321

Tassara, Gabriel García, 160

taxes and taxation, 156

Taylor, Zachary, 30, 33–34

Tehuantepec, Isthmus of, 97, 107, 108

telegraph, 260

Tennessee, 48, 84, 93, 136, 138–39, 150, 201–4, 221, 223–25, 227, 264, 279, 330–32

eastern, 169–71

Tenure of Office Act, 397

terrorism, 332–34, 398–401

Terry, Alfred, 340–41

Terry, David S., 95, 235, 351

Texas and Texans, 8, 9, 34, 64–67, 95, 96, 97–101, 118, 127–29, 356

after the Civil War, 353

during the Civil War, 137, 138–41, 186–87, 236–37, 243, 284, 300, 304, 338–39, 347, 348–50

Texas Rangers, 65–67

Thayer, Sylvanus, 30

Thomas, George H., 171, 293–94, 330–32, 401

Thomas, Richard, 166

Thompson River, 111–12

Thoreau, Henry David, 124, 230

three-fifths clause, 390

Tilley, Leonard, 378, 379

Tocqueville, Alexis de, 5

Toombs, Robert, 81, 102

Topeka, Kans., 77

Toppan, Cora, 410, 413

Toronto, Can., 64, 130–31, 132, 333

Townshend, James, 196

transportation revolution, 4

Transylvania University, 30, 93

Tredegar Iron Works, 149

Trent, 183–84

Tubac, Ariz., 236

Tubman, Harriet, 49, 53, 120–21, 151, 263, 269–70, 286, 345

Tucson, Ariz., 236

Tupper, Charles, 378, 379

Uncle Tom's Cabin, 52–54, 56–59, 104, 170, 183

Underground Railroad, 49, 151

Union, Fort, 239

Unionists, American Civil War, 144, 150–52, 154–55, 165–72, 196, 204, 222, 227, 234, 335

Union Pacific Railroad Co., 262

Union, the American, 1–3, 7–8, 19–20, 27–28, 67–68, 69–71, 72–73, 88, 96–97, 114–15, 117–18, 135–38, 410–11, 415–16

  Indian policy of, 231–33, 250–60, 262, 411

United States, *see* Congress, U.S.; Union, the American

Uraga, José López, 304

Utah Territory, 230, 246–50, 260

Vallandigham, Clement, 295–97, 320, 325–26

Valverde, N.M., Battle of, 239

Vance, Zebulon, 300–1, 341

Vancouver, Can., 111

Vanderbilt, Cornelius, 85, 86

Van Dorn, Earl, 204–5

Veracruz, Mex., 106, 107, 108, 190, 191, 266, 303, 350, 355, 361, 362, 367, 368, 370

Vermont, 71, 131, 363

Vicksburg, Miss., 99, 128, 263–64, 301

  battles for, 220–21, 224–25, 279, 281–84

Victoria, Fort, 111

Victoria, Queen, 41, 111, 131, 183, 378, 381

Vidaurri, Santiago, 186–87, 304, 368–70

vigilantes, 125, 127–28, 138

Virginia and Virginians, 55, 67, 101, 120–25, 137, 144, 149–50, 207–14, 278–79, 281, 353, 354, 388

  western, 168–69, 209

Virginia, CSS, 149, 179

Waddell, Joseph, 211

Wade, Benjamin F., 176, 321

Wadley, Sarah Lois, 128–29

Wagner, Fort, 285–86

Wakefield, Sarah F., 253, 254–56

Walker, John, 339

Walker, Robert J., 81–82, 99

Walker, William, 83–87, 234

Wallace, Lew, 338–39, 358–59, 361

Wallace, Susan, 358

Warren, Gouverneur, 316

war with Mexico, 8–9, 19, 26, 97, 201, 202

Washington, D.C., 34, 90, 122, 125, 133, 135, 145, 150, 199–200, 208, 214, 215, 237, 263, 317–18, 339, 343–44, 347–48, 407–9

Washington, George, 123, 143

Washington Territory, 231, 234, 383

Washington, Treaty of, 413–14

Washita River, 412

Watie, Stand, 245–46

Watkins, Sam, 225, 330–32

Webster, Daniel, 2, 50–51, 54–55

Weed, Thurlow, 320

Welles, Gideon, 177, 318, 344

Welsh, James and John, 154–55

West, American, 71, 144, 228–62, 410–13

West Point, American military academy at, 30, 169, 201, 202, 204

Wheelan, Patrick James, 382

Wheeler, Joseph, 329

Whigs, political party of, 9–11, 25–26, 31, 33–34, 48, 55, 74, 75, 135, 170

White House, 148, 199, 200, 229, 326, 344, 353, 391, 404

Whitman, Walt, 147

Wide-Awakes, 135, 136

Wigfall, Louis T., 108, 135, 136, 138, 139–41, 147, 183, 272

Wilberforce, Ohio, 402

Wilderness, Battle of the (Va.), 314–15

Wilkes, Charles, 184

Williamson, Elizabeth, 61

Wilmington, N.C., 340–41

Wilmot, David, and the Wilmot Proviso, 32–33, 74

Wilson's Creek, Battle of, 167–68, 245

Winchester, Va., Battle of, 324

Windsor, Can., 63–64, 296–97

Winnebagos, 256, 259

Winnipeg, Can., 384–86

Wisconsin, 129, 393

Wise, Henry A., 122, 123, 149, 343, 406

women, 16–23, 25, 36–37, 51–54, 152–54, 207, 213, 274–75, 350, 387–89

movement for their rights, 20–23, 56–57, 408–9

World War I, 374

Wyatt, Bayley, 389

Wyke, Charles, 305

Yancey, William Lowndes, 118–19, 133, 138, 183

Yellow Tavern, Va., Battle of, 315

York River and Yorktown, Va., 207, 208

Young, Bennett, 333

Young, Brigham, 246–50

Yucatan, Mex., 194

Zacatecas, Mex., 368

Zaragoza, Ignacio, 191

Zuloaga, Félix, 106, 108